Historic Documents
of 2017

Sara Miller McCune founded SAGE Publishing in 1965 to support the dissemination of usable knowledge and educate a global community. SAGE publishes more than 1000 journals and over 800 new books each year, spanning a wide range of subject areas. Our growing selection of library products includes archives, data, case studies and video. SAGE remains majority owned by our founder and after her lifetime will become owned by a charitable trust that secures the company's continued independence.

Los Angeles | London | New Delhi | Singapore | Washington DC | Melbourne

Historic Documents
of 2017

Heather Kerrigan, Editor

Contents

JANUARY

A statement by Turkish president Recep Tayyip Erdoğan on January 1, 2017, following an attack in Istanbul; a June 4, 2017, statement by British Prime Minister Theresa May after twin attacks in London; a June 7, 2017, statement by Iranian President Rouhani following a suicide bombing in Tehran; and an August 18, 2017, statement by Spanish President Mariano Rajoy after a terrorist attack struck Barcelona.

The excerpted text of the Director of National Intelligence report, declassified on January 6, 2017, outlining the attempt by Russia to influence the outcome of the 2016 U.S. presidential election.

A decision adopted by the African Union Peace and Security Council in response to the post-election situation in the Gambia, announced on January 13, 2017; the resolution from the United Nations Security Council endorsing the African Union's recognition of Adama Barrow as president, on January 19, 2017; and a joint declaration by the Economic Community of West African States (ECOWAS), the African Union, and the United Nations on the Gambia's political situation from January 21, 2017.

The text of the address delivered by Donald Trump on January 20, 2017, after his inauguration as President of the United States.

FEBRUARY

corruption allegations; and a press release from the office of
the attorney general from June 26, 2017, announcing corruption
charges against the president.

A press release from the United Nations News Centre on
February 20, 2017, detailing the declaration of famine in
South Sudan; a summary from the Integrated Food Security Phase
Classification issued on May 31, 2017, indicating that South Sudan
was no longer classified in famine; and a statement by the president
of the United Nations Security Council on August 9, 2017, urging a
global response to the ongoing food crisis.

A press release from NASA from February 22, 2017, announcing the
largest discovery of habitable-zone planets around a single star outside
the solar system; a press release from SpaceX from February 27, 2017,
announcing the company's plans to fly private citizens beyond the moon
in 2018; a press release issued by Sen. Ted Cruz, R-Texas, on March 7, 2017,
announcing congressional passage of the NASA Transition Authorization
Act; remarks by President Donald Trump at the signing of the NASA
Transition Authorization Act on March 21, 2017; and an executive order
signed by Trump on June 30, 2017, reviving the National Space Council.

The text of the address delivered by President Donald Trump before
a joint session of Congress on February 28, 2017, and the
Democratic response delivered by former Kentucky governor
Steve Beshear, also on February 28, 2017.

MARCH

A statement from Organization of American States (OAS)
Secretary General Luis Almagro from March 20, 2017, responding
to the Venezuela Supreme Court of Justice's decision to strip power
from the National Assembly; a press release issued by the U.S. Treasury
Department on July 31, 2017, announcing sanctions against President
Nicolás Maduro; a message from Almagro from July 31, 2017,
denouncing the National Constituent Assembly election; an Office of
the UN High Commissioner for Human Rights report from
August 8, 2017, about human rights violations during mass protests in

APRIL

MAY

JUNE

SEPTEMBER

OCTOBER

the public during the election runoff and eventual transition of power; and a December 28, 2017, tweet from President-elect George Weah after his runoff election victory.

NOVEMBER

DECEMBER

Thematic Table of Contents

HEALTH AND SOCIAL SERVICES

INTERNATIONAL AFFAIRS

AFRICA

INTERNATIONAL AFFAIRS

ASIA

INTERNATIONAL AFFAIRS

AUSTRALIA

INTERNATIONAL AFFAIRS

EUROPE

INTERNATIONAL AFFAIRS

LATIN AMERICA AND THE CARIBBEAN

INTERNATIONAL AFFAIRS

MIDDLE EAST

INTERNATIONAL AFFAIRS

RUSSIA AND THE FORMER SOVIET REPUBLIC

INTERNATIONAL AFFAIRS

GLOBAL ISSUES

NATIONAL SECURITY AND TERRORISM

RIGHTS, RESPONSIBILITIES, AND JUSTICE

List of Document Sources

CONGRESS

EXECUTIVE DEPARTMENTS, AGENCIES, FEDERAL OFFICES, AND COMMISSIONS

INTERNATIONAL GOVERNMENTAL ORGANIZATIONS

INTERNATIONAL NONGOVERNMENTAL ORGANIZATIONS

JUDICIARY

NONGOVERNMENTAL ORGANIZATIONS

NON-U.S. GOVERNMENTS

U.S. STATE AND LOCAL GOVERNMENTS

WHITE HOUSE AND THE PRESIDENT

Preface

The first year of Donald Trump's presidency, accusations of collusion between the Trump campaign and the Russian government, elections and transitions of power throughout Africa and Europe, the beginnings of the Brexit process, major milestones in space exploration, ISIL-affiliated attacks across Europe and the Middle East, the installment of a newly appointed justice to the U.S. Supreme Court, and Supreme Court decisions on immigration law, political districting and gerrymandering, same-sex marriage parental rights, and grant money and religious institutions are just a few of the topics of national and international significance chosen for discussion in *Historic Documents of 2017*. This edition marks the forty-fifth volume of a CQ Press project that began with *Historic Documents of 1972*. This series allows students, librarians, journalists, scholars, and others to research and understand the most important domestic and foreign issues and events of the year through primary source documents. To aid research, many of the lengthy documents written for specialized audiences have been excerpted to highlight the most important sections. The official statements, news conferences, speeches, special studies, and court decisions presented here should be of lasting public and academic interest.

Historic Documents of 2017 opens with an "Overview of 2017," a sweeping narrative of the key events and issues of the year, which provides context for the documents that follow. The balance of the book is organized chronologically, with each article comprising an introduction titled "Document in Context" and one or more related documents on a specific event, issue, or topic. Often an event is not limited to a particular day. Consequently, readers will find that some events include multiple documents that may span several months. Their placement in the book corresponds to the date of the first document included for that event. The event introductions provide context and an account of further developments during the year. A thematic table of contents (page xvii) and a list of documents organized by source (page xxi) follow the standard table of contents and assist readers in locating events and documents.

As events, issues, and consequences become more complex and far-reaching, these introductions and documents yield important information and deepen understanding about the world's increasing interconnectedness. As memories of current events fade, these selections will continue to further understanding of the events and issues that have shaped the lives of people around the world.

How to Use This Book

Each of the entries in this edition consists of two parts: a comprehensive introduction followed by one or more primary source documents. The articles are arranged in chronological order by month. Articles with multiple documents are placed according to the date of the first document. There are several ways to find events and documents of interest:

By date: If the approximate date of an event or document is known, browse through the titles for that month in the table of contents. Alternatively, browse the tables of contents that appear at the beginning of each month's articles.

By theme: To find a particular topic or subject area, browse the thematic table of contents.

By document type or source: To find a particular type of document or document source, such as the White House or Congress, review the list of document sources.

By index: The index allows researchers to locate references to specific events or documents as well as entries on the same or related subjects.

An online edition of this volume, as well as an archive going back to 1972, is available and offers advance search and browse functionality.

Each article begins with an introduction. This feature provides historical and intellectual contexts for the documents that follow. Documents are reproduced with the original spelling, capitalization, and punctuation of the original or official copy. Ellipsis points indicate textual omissions (unless they were present in the documents themselves indicating pauses in speech), and brackets are used for editorial insertions within documents for text clarification. The excerpting of Supreme Court opinions has been done somewhat differently from other documents. In-text references and citations to laws and other cases have been removed when not part of a sentence to improve the readability of opinions. In those documents, readers will find ellipses used only when sections of narrative text have been removed.

Full citations appear at the end of each document. If a document is not available on the Internet, this too is noted. For further reading on a particular topic, consult the "Other Historic Documents of Interest" section at the end of each article. These sections provide cross-references for related articles in this edition of *Historic Documents* as well as in previous editions. References to articles from past volumes include the year and page number for easy retrieval.

Overview of 2017

In the United States, 2017 was characterized by the activities and actions surrounding President Donald Trump's first year in office. Trump quickly made headway dismantling the policies of his predecessor, Barack Obama, including ending U.S. participation in the Paris climate agreement, decertifying the Iranian nuclear deal, and seeking to revoke the temporary protected status of so-called Dreamers, immigrants who were brought into the country illegally as children. The Trump administration took a hard line on immigration, attempting on multiple occasions to implement a travel ban on individuals coming to the United States from specific Middle Eastern and African nations. The ban was struck down by various federal courts, but the U.S. Supreme Court, with the backing of a new Trump-appointed justice, did allow the ban to go into effect, at least temporarily, while they reviewed the case. Trump's success in implementing key items of his agenda was clouded, however, by the investigation into potential links between his presidential campaign and the Russian government. In May, a special counsel was appointed to oversee the investigation, and by year's end, it had handed down a number of indictments against members of Trump's inner circle. With control of both the House and Senate, along with the White House, congressional Republicans quickly set to work on their legislative agenda, foremost of which was ending the Affordable Care Act (ACA), or Obamacare. After spending seven months drafting, debating, and passing various iterations of the legislation, the House and Senate ultimately could not reach a compromise on how to repeal or replace the law. Republicans found greater success in passing the first U.S. tax system overhaul in three decades. The new law was expected to bring relief to all taxpayers—although the greatest benefits went to corporations and the highest income earners—at least through 2026, at which time Congress will either need to pass an extension or millions could see their taxes increase.

Internationally, instability in Africa, South America, and the Middle East dominated headlines, while a potential shift toward more nationalist governments raised concern in Europe. The Netherlands, Germany, and France all held elections in 2017, and each featured far-right parties that some observers speculated could end up leading the government. Ultimately, that prediction did not come to fruition, but in Germany the populist Alternative for Germany gained seats in the nation's parliament for the first time. Although elections were not due in the United Kingdom, Prime Minister Theresa May called an early vote that was seen as a referendum on the ongoing British exit, or Brexit, from the European Union (EU). Despite early projections that the prime minister and her party would be comfortably victorious, they lost seats in parliament and May was nearly unseated by Labour candidate Jeremy Corbyn. In Africa, The Gambia, Kenya, and Liberia held presidential elections. A bloodless takeover by Zimbabwe's military resulted in the end of the nearly four-decade-long rule of Robert Mugabe, and the installation of a government that promised to hold democratic elections, while in the Democratic Republic of the Congo, Joseph Kabila continued to refuse to hold elections or relinquish his power. In the Middle East, Syria's civil war raged on and President Bashar al-Assad reportedly utilized sarin gas in a chemical attack against the rebels, resulting in outcry from Western governments and increased airstrikes. Turkey's leader continued to maintain his grip on power by reinstating a state of emergency and overseeing the passage of a constitutional referendum that would consolidate power in the executive. And in the Gulf, Saudi Arabia, United Arab Emirates, Bahrain, and Egypt set off a diplomatic crisis when they imposed a blockade on trade with Qatar that remained unresolved by year end.

DOMESTIC ISSUES

President Trump's First Year in Office

After taking office, Trump moved quickly to act on promises made during his campaign, with an early focus on immigration. A central theme of Trump's campaign had been strengthening security along the United States' southern border with Mexico, including by building a "beautiful wall," to stem the flow of illegal immigrants. A series of executive orders signed by Trump early in his presidency included one calling on the Department of Homeland Security to begin the process for wall construction. Despite claiming that he would make the Mexican government pay for the wall, Trump followed his executive order with a request to Congress for initial funding, which was approved by the House of Representatives but was not taken up by the Senate. Trump also issued an executive order making sanctuary cities (those that provide limited assistance in enforcing national immigration law) ineligible for federal grants; this order was permanently blocked by a federal judge after two California counties and the City of San Francisco filed suit. A subsequent effort by the Trump administration to require sanctuary cities to meet certain immigration-related requirements before they could receive grant money was also blocked following legal challenges.

Yet another executive order introduced highly controversial restrictions on people arriving in the United States from Iran, Iraq, Libya, Somalia, Sudan, Syria, and Yemen. In addition to instituting a ninety-day ban on entry from these countries, Trump's order reduced the total number of refugees who would be admitted to the United States in 2017, suspended the entry of any Syrian refugees indefinitely, suspended entry for other refugees for 120 days, and called for preference to be given to religious minorities when refugees were once again allowed to enter. Trump argued that such measures were vital to the United States' national security interests, particularly the need to reduce terrorism threats from the Islamic State of Iraq and the Levant (ISIL). The order's immediate implementation caused chaos at U.S. airports, with travelers being detained or put on flights out of the United States. Thousands of protestors descended on the airports, as did immigration lawyers who quickly filed suits against the order. A series of rapid judicial decisions resulted in a nationwide injunction that prompted the administration to issue a revised order in hopes of avoiding further legal challenges. However, the second order was also immediately challenged, with two courts issuing nationwide injunctions. The federal government appealed these rulings to the U.S. Supreme Court, which, prior to hearing oral arguments, issued an unsigned opinion allowing the government to begin implementing the ban with an exception for people who had a credible relationship with a person or entity, such as a university, in the United States. Before the Court could hear the case, the Trump administration issued a third iteration of its order. Lower courts once again issued injunctions, but the Court granted an emergency stay that allowed the order to take full effect while legal challenges work their way through the court system.

Trump's immigration push continued into the fall when his administration announced that the Deferred Action for Childhood Arrivals (DACA) program implemented by Obama would be rescinded. DACA had extended temporary status to roughly 800,000 undocumented immigrants who were brought to the United State as children—also known as Dreamers. Trump said the program would be wound down over a six-month period to give Congress an opportunity to pass legislation that would address illegal immigration and provide a permanent solution for the Dreamers. Congress failed to make progress on this issue, despite broad bipartisan support for the Dreamers and attempts to attach immigration measures to two federal budget deals in early 2018.

Trump's concerted effort to reverse Obama-era policies extended to the international arena and included the United States' withdrawal from the Paris Climate Agreement. Adopted in 2015, the agreement set a global goal for carbon emissions reduction, with each of the 195 signing countries establishing their own voluntary emissions reduction targets. In announcing his decision, Trump claimed the Paris Agreement threatened U.S. sovereignty and would cost millions of American jobs. World leaders reproached Trump and reaffirmed their commitment to the agreement, while hundreds of state and local officials and business leaders declared they would work together to follow the agreement's guidelines, without the president's support. Scientists and environmental activists repeatedly expressed concern over Trump's rejection of established climate science, with some later citing a devastating Atlantic hurricane season and flash flooding caused by historic monsoon rains in Asia as proof of climate change and the need for urgent action.

Trump drew a further rebuke from the United States' European allies when he announced he would not recertify the Iranian nuclear agreement, under which Iran has significantly scaled back its nuclear activities in exchange for sanctions relief. Despite the International Atomic Energy Agency's repeated confirmation that Iran was complying with the agreement's terms, Trump claimed Iran had violated the accord and threatened that the United States would withdraw from the deal if it was not amended so that Iran was permanently barred from developing nuclear weapons.

Back home, the Trump administration struggled to address ongoing racial tensions within the United States. Amid a national debate about whether to preserve or take down Confederate statues, monuments, and other memorials, white supremacists and white nationalists organized a rally in Charlottesville, Virginia, that turned violent as counter protestors clashed with rally goers. One counter protestor was killed by a white supremacist, prompting a major public outcry and swift condemnations from local, state, and federal officials. While Trump ultimately denounced white supremacist and white nationalist groups for causing violence in the name of racism, he faced widespread criticism for his initial response and other remarks in which he seemed to blame those groups and counter protestors equally.

Congressional Action and Inaction

The Republican legislative agenda for 2017 revolved around ending the landmark ACA. After years of trying to take down the law through the courts, Republicans, who held a majority in the House and Senate, as well as control of the White House, had their best shot at legislative action. President Trump had campaigned on ending the law and promised to sign any legislation that crossed his desk. Drafting and debate began in earnest in the spring, but negotiations quickly broke down and compromise between the House and Senate waned. Congressional Democrats and Republicans sparred over whether they should repeal and replace the law in one piece of legislation, simply pass fixes to unpopular provisions, or repeal the law without a replacement. Despite a massive show of support from the White House and cajoling by House and Senate Republican leadership, Republicans narrowly passed their version in the House, but it failed to get a vote in the Senate. With Senate Republicans unable to whip their caucus on their own version of a repeal bill, in late July Congress agreed to put the issue on the backburner to move on to other items.

The ACA repeal debate was reprised in conjunction with another key Republican legislative agenda item, tax reform. Both Democrats and Republicans have long promised to fix the antiquated U.S. tax system, but over the course of thirty years, no proposal garnered enough support to be signed into law. That changed in late 2017, when Republicans put forth a revision to the tax code that would lower the personal income tax in all seven tax brackets and would permanently cut the corporate tax rate from 35 percent to 21 percent. Notably, the bill also ended the ACA's individual mandate that penalized any American who did not have health insurance. Democrats argued that the provisions of the bill were a clear handout to businesses and the wealthy, while Republicans noted that not only would all taxpayers see a reduction in their tax bills, but lower- and middle-income earners would also benefit from economic growth and job creation. The tax reform package easily passed the House and Senate, and the president signed it into law. Republicans experienced some early wins, with a handful of major corporations announcing one-time bonuses for employees, repatriation of funds held overseas, and thousands of new hires. However, many more companies announced that they would use the windfall tax savings to increase dividends for shareholders or to buy back shares.

There also appeared to be some appetite among both Democrats and Republicans to introduce new gun regulations in the weeks after the mass shooting in Las Vegas, Nevada, that left fifty-seven dead and more than 500 injured. Specifically, talk began about the regulation of bump stocks, devices that allow semi-automatic weapons to fire like automatic weapons. Bills were introduced in the House and Senate to ban their sale, and the National Rifle Association (NRA), an organization that has long worked to prevent regulations on gun ownership, signaled its support of a ban. However, both the House and Senate Judiciary Committees refused to consider the bills, effectively ending any further action on gun control in Congress for the year.

Elections across the Country

Despite a poor showing in the 2016 House, Senate, and presidential elections, Democrats began to turn the tide in their favor in special elections held across the country in 2017. Virginia was one of the most closely watched, where candidates were vying to replace Gov. Terry McAuliffe. Despite polls showing the two candidates running neck and neck, the lieutenant governor, Democrat Ralph Northam, was the victor with 54 percent of the vote. Virginia also elected a Democratic lieutenant governor and attorney general, and the party secured a number of upset victories in the House of Delegates, where Democrats came just one seat shy of winning a majority after losing a random name draw in a tied contest for one state house seat.

Democrats also had a significant victory in Alabama, where former U.S. attorney Doug Jones, a Democrat, squared off against Republican Roy Moore, a former Alabama Supreme Court justice. The two were seeking to fill the seat left vacant by Jeff Sessions after his appointment to the position of U.S. Attorney General in February. The race received national attention not only because it could narrow the margin of Republican control in the Senate, but also because eight women came forward in the months leading up to the election to accuse Moore of unwanted sexual advances or sexual abuse when they were teenagers and Moore was in his thirties. Moore vehemently denied the allegations, which came at a time when a number of high-profile men across the country—including two members of Congress—were resigning or forced out of their jobs over similar accusations. On December 12, Jones was declared the winner, but Moore refused to concede and filed a lawsuit alleging voter fraud. On December 28, Moore's case was rejected and the results were certified.

Possible Link between Trump Campaign and Russian Government

The waning months of the Trump presidential campaign were consumed by allegations that the president and members of his campaign team may have colluded with the Russian government to secure Trump's victory. Those claims followed the president into his first year in office. In January, the Director of National Intelligence declassified a report confirming that the Russian government had attempted to influence the U.S. presidential election through the use of Internet trolls and social media campaigns to spread fake news about Democratic challenger Hillary Clinton. The report concluded that, although multiple efforts were made to influence the outcome of the 2016 election, there was no evidence that the Russians had successfully hacked into tallying systems and rigged the vote. The report further noted that it was not directed to make a determination about whether the influence campaign ordered by the Kremlin impacted the opinion of U.S. voters in support of or opposition to either candidate. President Trump remained skeptical of the findings of the report, and the Russian government denied that it had ordered any such campaign. Congressional Democrats and Republicans, however, called for additional sanctions to be levied against Russia.

In July 2016, the Federal Bureau of Investigation (FBI), under Director James Comey, opened an investigation into a possible link between the Trump campaign and the Russian government. That investigation began, it was later learned, because a Trump campaign adviser told an Australian diplomat that the Russians had potentially damaging information on Clinton. This diplomat subsequently gave that information to the U.S. government. President Trump had been highly critical of Comey throughout the summer and fall of 2016 for Comey's management of the investigation into Clinton's handling of classified information during her time as Secretary of State. Once in the White House, however, Trump publicly assured the FBI director that he had the president's full support. But that came to an end on May 9 when Trump fired Comey. In his notification to Comey, Trump outlined his belief that Comey could not effectively lead the FBI and cited a recommendation from Attorney General Sessions and Deputy Attorney General Rod Rosenstein supporting his decision.

The move quickly drew criticism from Democrats and Republicans alike, some of whom alleged that the decision appeared to be an attempt to cover up or end the investigation into any link between the Trump campaign and the Russian government. Comey would go on to testify on Capitol Hill that he felt he was fired because of the Russia investigation. Dozens of members of Congress called for an independent investigation into any Trump–Russia connection, and on May 17, Rosenstein announced the appointment of former FBI director Robert Mueller as special counsel to oversee the Russia investigation.

The work of Mueller's team was largely kept secret until October 30, when the first indictments were released against Trump's former campaign manager, Paul Manafort, and Manafort's former business partner, Richard Gates, on charges ranging from money laundering to failure to register as a foreign agent to conspiracy against the United States. Both pleaded not guilty after surrendering to the FBI. On the day Manafort and Gates surrendered, a charging document was unsealed, listing the charges against George Papadopoulos, the Trump campaign adviser who had leaked information to the Australian diplomat. Papadopoulos agreed to plead guilty to one charge of lying to the FBI in exchange for his cooperation with Mueller's ongoing investigation. Less than one month later, Michael Flynn, a member of the Trump campaign and transition teams, and the former national security advisor under Trump, pleaded guilty to lying to the FBI, also in exchange for his cooperation. By the end of 2017, the Mueller investigation was ongoing and President Trump continued to allege that there was no collusion.

Supreme Court Decisions

More than a year after the death of Antonin Scalia left the Supreme Court with only eight justices and an even division of liberals and conservatives, Neil Gorsuch was sworn in as an associate justice. Nominated by Trump days after his inauguration, Gorsuch was the second judge put forward to fill Scalia's seat. Obama had nominated centrist Appellate Court Judge Merrick Garland a month after Scalia's passing, but Senate Republicans refused to consider his nomination, arguing that—since it was an election year—the next president should fill the seat. Facing the threat of a Democratic filibuster of Gorsuch's nomination, Republican leadership eliminated filibusters for Supreme Court selections, invoking what became known as "the nuclear option" and effectively securing Gorsuch's confirmation.

Despite not having a full complement of justices until April 2017, the Supreme Court issued several major rulings during its 2016–2017 term. This included *Cooper v. Harris*, in which the Court struck down two North Carolina congressional districts as unconstitutionally drawn based on racial considerations. The Court found that North Carolina's Republican-dominated legislature had, after the 2010 Census, redrawn and gerrymandered the two reliably Democratic districts to include tens of thousands of additional black voters to limit the total number of districts that could be won by Democrats. Legal scholars noted the wording of the Court's opinion may blur the distinction between racial and partisan gerrymandering, which could make future legal challenges to redistricting easier.

On June 26, the Court released a short, unsigned opinion in the case of *Pavan v. Smith*, which concerned an Arkansas state law requiring birth certificates to include the name of the mother's male spouse, regardless of his biological relationship to the child. Two same-sex couples challenged this law after the state refused to list both mothers as parents on their children's birth certificates. The Court ruled that Arkansas was treating same-sex and opposite-sex couples differently. Such disparate treatment, the Court said, was at odds with its historic ruling in *Obergefell v. Hodges*, which found that same-sex couples have the same constitutionally protected right to marry as opposite-sex couples, because the state was essentially using its birth certificates to give legal recognition to married parents.

Also on June 26, the Court ruled in *Trinity Lutheran Church of Columbia, Inc. v. Comer* that it was unconstitutional for Missouri to categorically disqualify religious institutions from competing for state grant money, finding that this denial violated the church's First Amendment rights. While the majority limited the application of its opinion to playground resurfacing grant—the specific type of grant at issue in the case—it is likely that lower courts will use the opinion for broader guidance on future cases involving public funding for religious institutions.

Foreign Affairs

Elections and Instability in Africa

A number of African nations held presidential elections in 2017, including The Gambia, Liberia, and Kenya. In its first ever democratic transition of power, The Gambia's authoritarian ruler, Yahya Jammeh, was defeated by coalition candidate Adama Barrow. In response to the unexpected upset, Jammeh insisted he had won and refused to leave office. As the new president was sworn in, Jammeh reportedly stole tens of millions of dollars in public funds before finally relinquishing his office, leaving the country in even deeper financial distress.

In Liberia, soccer star George Weah succeeded Nobel Peace Prize winner and first female African leader, Ellen Johnson Sirleaf. The election marked the first democratic transition of power since 1944, and the new president promised to begin his term by ending corruption that was rampant in his predecessor's government and improving the long-suffering economy.

Kenyans went to the polls twice in 2017 after the results of the first round of voting were thrown out by the country's Supreme Court for alleged irregularities. President Uhuru Kenyatta would be victorious in the second round, after his opponent, former prime minister Raila Odinga, withdrew from the race. Odinga promised to develop a parallel government, and in early 2018, he held a counter swearing in and a number of his supporters, including members of parliament, were arrested by Kenyatta's government for political insurgency.

In Zimbabwe, the nation's military forced long-time President Robert Mugabe's resignation, in what was referred to as a "bloodless takeover" rather than a coup. The interim president promised to hold elections in 2018.

South African President Jacob Zuma was also forced out. Despite surviving a vote of no confidence in the nation's National Assembly, brought by the opposition party over alleged mismanagement and corruption, Zuma resigned amid significant pressure from both the public and his own party, the African National Congress.

Political turmoil continued to roil the Democratic Republic of the Congo (DRC), where President Joseph Kabila failed for the second year in a row to hold elections to select his successor, instead maintaining power and disregarding a peace agreement struck with the opposition. Kabila's ongoing refusal to leave office, and the ensuing unrest, emboldened armed rebels operating in the country, resulting in an attack by the Allied Democratic Forces against United Nations (UN) peacekeepers, the deadliest in more than two decades.

The ongoing political vacuum in South Sudan, coupled with extensive drought and ethnic violence, led to a severe famine that forced a growing number of South Sudanese from their homes. According to the UN, South Sudan was the fastest growing source of displaced people.

Elections and Controversial Reforms in Europe

With terrorist attacks and the global refugee crisis giving rise to growing anti-immigrant sentiment in Europe, speculation was widespread that far-right parties and candidates would win a significant share of the votes in national elections in France and Germany in 2017. In France, the second round of the presidential election pitted Marine Le Pen—the anti-immigrant, anti-Muslim, anti-EU leader of the National Front—against centrist and relative political newcomer Emmanuel Macron. While Le Pen was able to capitalize on terrorism fears to drive support for the National Front to new heights, Macron secured a decisive victory, winning 66 percent of the vote.

In Germany, Chancellor Angela Merkel appeared poised to win a fourth term in the run up to parliamentary elections. The country's acceptance of one million Syrian refugees since the last national election proved to have an important influence on the vote, creating an opportunity for the far-right, anti-Muslim Alternative for Germany party to win seats in parliament for the first time. Although Merkel's Christian Democratic Union and sister party Christian Social Union still won the largest portion of the vote, their flagging support resulted in a more fragmented parliament and created challenges to forming a coalition government.

In the United Kingdom, Prime Minister Theresa May called parliamentary elections three years early, betting that her Conservative Party could capitalize on turmoil within the main opposition party, the Labour Party, to increase its majority ahead of Brexit negotiations with the EU. However, May miscalculated, and the Conservatives lost their majority as Labour gained seats. Conservatives formed a partnership with Northern Ireland's Democratic Unionist Party, enabling them to remain in control of the government with May at the helm. Roughly two months prior to the election, May, with Parliament's approval, invoked Article 50 of the EU Treaty, thereby formally initiating the United Kingdom's departure from the EU. Negotiations around the separation began in June.

Spanish politics were also impacted by a vote: An independence referendum held by the northeastern region of Catalonia. The federal government declared the vote illegal, as did Spain's Constitutional Court, and mobilized national police to disrupt the referendum vote. While less than half of registered Catalans voted, 90 percent of those who did supported independence. The Catalan parliament formally declared the region's independence from Spain on October 27, prompting Prime Minister Mariano Rajoy to invoke an article of the Spanish Constitution that enables him to suspend Catalonia's autonomy. The Catalan government was subsequently dismissed. Snap elections were held in December, with pro-independence parties winning a narrow majority.

In Poland, President Andrzej Duda collaborated with lawmakers to pass a series of judicial reforms that appeared to politicize the country's court system. Changes included shifting the power to select members of the National Judicial Council from the judicial community to parliament and establishing a judicial oversight group within the Supreme Court whose staff would be selected by lawmakers. The European Union denounced the measures, claiming they violated the rule of law, and initiated legal proceedings that could result in sanctions against Poland if the country does not bring its judicial system back in line with EU values.

North Korea Defies Sanctions

With no sign of North Korea ending its nuclear program, the United Nations and the United States extended existing and imposed new sanctions against the country. Some of the strongest measures limited North Korea's ability to import crude oil and refined petroleum products, banned its textile exports, and prohibited North Koreans from working in foreign countries. In addition, China, which accounts for nearly all North Korea's external trade, announced that it would close all joint business ventures with and ban all imports of coal from North Korea. Despite these efforts, North Korea continued to test nuclear weapons, including a warhead that it claimed could reach the mainland United States. Indeed, Trump and North Korean leader Kim Jong Un engaged in a heated war of words throughout the fall, which left many wondering if either country would attack the other. Amid these rising tensions, the 2017 Nobel Peace Prize was awarded to the International Campaign to Abolish Nuclear Weapons, a coalition of nongovernmental organizations dedicated to stopping the development of nuclear weapons.

Rohingya Flee Myanmar

Developments in Southeast Asia also made global headlines, particularly a mass exodus of more than half a million Rohingya from Myanmar. Long-simmering tensions between the country's Buddhist majority and the Rohingya, an ethnic Muslim minority, came to a head in August when armed Rohingya attacked police and army outposts, prompting a brutal military crackdown that destroyed entire Rohingya villages and caused them to flee. UN officials described the crisis as ethnic cleansing and called for the government to end the crackdown. At the request of Aung Suu Kyi, Myanmar's de facto leader, an advisory commission was formed to recommend solutions to the internal conflict; however, none of the commission's recommendations were implemented during the year, and the government largely denied that any violence was taking place.

Unrest in the Middle East

Six years into the conflict, the Syrian Civil War took a nasty turn in April 2017, as President Bashar al-Assad's government launched a chemical attack against rebels in Khan Shaykhun. Reports from those on the ground suggested that rather than the often-used chemical chlorine the deadly nerve agent sarin had been released during the attack, which killed more than eighty people, including civilians. World leaders denounced the attack and called for Iran and Russia, key Syrian allies, to remove their support for the Assad regime. The Syrian government denied involvement and claimed rebels had initiated the attack, while Russia contended that government planes had accidentally hit a chemical weapons cache during a routine bombing run. The United States launched retaliatory airstrikes against a Syrian military base and threatened further action if Syria continued to use chemical weapons.

In Turkey, the state of emergency declared following an attempted coup against President Recep Tayyip Erdoğan in 2016 was extended through 2017. Lawmakers also resumed an effort to amend Turkey's constitution to transition from a parliamentary to a presidential system of government. Approved by 51 percent of voters in an April referendum, the amendments also consolidated more power in the office of the president, including the authority to unilaterally declare a state of emergency or dismiss parliament. Opponents challenged the results, citing voting irregularities, which led to speculation that the EU may drop consideration of Turkey's bid to join the bloc. The EU had previously announced a suspension of membership negotiations amid the government's arrest or firing of tens of thousands of people allegedly connected to the coup.

Regional tensions in the Middle East led to a diplomatic crisis in June 2017 because Saudi Arabia, United Arab Emirates, Bahrain, and Egypt severed ties with Qatar and imposed a blockade on trade with the country. Led by the Saudis, the quartet initially claimed their actions were in response to Qatar's support for terrorist groups but later indicated that Qatar's perceived interference in the affairs of other states—including through its television network Al Jazeera—was a greater threat to regional stability. In July, the quartet issued conditions that Qatar was expected to meet before the blockade was lifted; however, Qatar's government refused to make concessions and largely circumvented the blockade with relief shipments from Turkey, Iran, and the United States.

—Heather Kerrigan and Linda Grimm

January

ISIL Carries Out Attacks across the Globe

JANUARY 1, JUNE 4 AND 7, AND AUGUST 18, 2017

The Islamic State of Iraq and the Levant (ISIL), alternately referred to as the Islamic State of Iraq and Syria (ISIS) or the Islamic State (IS), carried out deadly attacks in Turkey, the United Kingdom, Iran, and Spain in 2017. Two of the incidents—one in Iran and one in Spain—were the first ISIL-perpetrated attacks carried out in those countries. United in their response to the violence, the leaders of these nations said they would do anything within in their power to defeat radical ideology, both within and outside their borders, that threatens the freedoms their citizens enjoy. This resolve resulted in both extensive raids seeking terrorist-affiliated individuals and additional airstrikes in Iraq and Syria aimed at ISIL targets.

JANUARY ATTACK IN ISTANBUL

On New Year's Day, a gunman opened fire at a popular nightclub in Turkey's capital city, Istanbul, killing thirty-nine and wounding dozens more. An estimated 600 were in the club at the time of the attack, and some reportedly jumped into the Bosporus River for safety. "A terrorist . . . brutally and savagely carried out this incident by firing bullets on innocent people who were there solely to celebrate the New Year and have fun," Istanbul Governor Vasip Sahin said immediately following the attack. Police quickly arrived on the scene, but the gunman escaped in the chaos. News outlets in Turkey had initially reported that police killed the lone attacker, but as the victims were identified, it was discovered that he was not among the dead.

While offering condolences to the families of the victims, Turkish President Recep Tayyip Erdoğan strongly condemned the attack and said his nation remained "determined to eradicate threats and attacks against our country," adding, "Every single life we lose in this process makes our hearts bleed, but at the same time, further sharpens our perseverance and determination to struggle." Turkey had been the target of an increasing number of attacks during the years preceding the incident at the Istanbul nightclub. According to a *New York Times* analysis updated on January 5, since June 2015, more than 400 had been killed in major attacks.

Immediately following the attack, the Turkish government called for a media blackout that it claimed was necessary to ensure public safety and help police locate those responsible. The manhunt to find the individual who perpetrated the attack lasted more than two weeks before Abdulgadir Masharipov, an Uzbek national, was arrested by Turkish security forces. ISIL said on Twitter that it was responsible for the attack. "In continuation of the blessed operations which ISIS carries out against Turkey, a soldier of the brave caliphate attacked one of the most popular nightclubs while Christians were celebrating their holiday," the terrorist group said. Masharipov reportedly told police that he had carried out the attack on behalf of ISIL. With the suspected gunman in custody, from January 30 to February 6, Turkish security forces, under the order of the president, conducted nation-wide raids targeting ISIL members and arrested more than 800.

Multiple Attacks Strike the United Kingdom

The United Kingdom was the site of three ISIL-perpetrated attacks in 2017. The first, in March, took place in London near the British parliament building. The attacker, Khalid Masood, drove a car into pedestrians, killing five and wounding nearly fifty. The attacker, who reportedly sent a text indicating that he intended to wage jihad, was killed at the scene by police. This was the first multiple-casualty terrorist attack in the United Kingdom since a number of bombings on the Underground in 2005. On May 22, a suicide bomber stood near the exit of an Ariana Grande concert at the Manchester Arena, where he detonated himself as crowds were leaving the building, killing twenty-two and wounding more than 100. British police named Salman Abedi the attacker; ISIL claimed responsibility, stating the bombing was carried out against "infidels . . . in response to their transgressions against the lands of the Muslims." One month later, on June 3, a van struck pedestrians on the London Bridge, before proceeding to Borough Market, where three attackers got out of the vehicle and stabbed their victims before being shot and killed by police. Seven civilians were killed and nearly fifty were wounded. It was initially reported that each of the terrorists was wearing an explosive vest, but upon further investigation, police determined that the vests were fake. ISIL's media organization claimed responsibility for the attack.

The day after the June attack, Prime Minister Theresa May responded, noting that attacks of this type were becoming the new normal in the United Kingdom. "We believe we are experiencing a new trend in the threat we face, as terrorism breeds terrorism, and perpetrators are inspired to attack not only on the basis of carefully-constructed plots after years of planning and training—and not even as lone attackers radicalised online—but by copying one another and often using the crudest of means of attack." As such, May outlined four necessary steps for the nation to take to combat violent extremism, which included solidifying British values as superior to extremism and hate; working with governments around the globe to prevent the spread of terrorism; taking military action against ISIL in Iraq and Syria, as well as identifying extremism within the United Kingdom; and providing British security forces the support they need to enforce an effective counterterrorism strategy.

ISIL Attack Targets Iran

Four days after the June attack in London, on June 7, ISIL struck Tehran with suicide bombings at the nation's parliament building and Ayatollah Khomeini's mausoleum. Iranian President Hassan Rouhani called the attacks "insensitive" and "cowardly." The suicide bombings were the first major attacks to hit the nation's capital since the early 1980s. It was also the first time Iran, which has been fighting ISIL in Syria and Iraq, was attacked by the terrorist organization on its own soil. Six attackers were killed in the explosions, along with eighteen civilians. More than forty were wounded. According to Iranian government officials, police thwarted a third attack that had been planned for the same day.

ISIL quickly claimed responsibility for the attack, stating in a video, "Do you think we will leave? We will remain, God willing." Despite the claim of responsibility, some in Iran, including the Minister of Foreign Affairs, claimed Saudi Arabia was complicit in the attack, an accusation it denied. The Islamic Revolutionary Guard Corps (IRGC) went a step further to indicate it was an attack coordinated by Saudi Arabia with the assistance of the United States and Israel. "This terrorist action, coming one week after the meeting of the president of the United States with the leader of one of the region's reactionary government [Saudi Arabia] . . . shows they are involved in this savage action," IRGC said in a statement.

Rouhani, who laid blame solely on extremist terrorist groups, said the "attacks in Tehran will further strengthen the Islamic Iran's resolve in its combat against regional terrorism, extremism and violence more than before." He added that "terrorism is a universal problem and unity in fighting extremism, violence and terrorism with regional and international cooperation is the most important need of today's global community." Under Rouhani's guidance, the IRGC launched attacks in the Syrian city of Dayr al-Zawr against ISIL. The government claimed that the strikes resulted in the destruction of military equipment and the deaths of many terrorists in the region. The IRGC said ISIL should view the strikes as a warning. "IRGC warns the Takfiri terrorists and their regional and trans-regional supporters that they would be engulfed by its revolutionary wrath and flames of the fire of its revenge in case they repeat any such devilish and dirty move in the future," a statement from IRGC read.

THIRTEEN KILLED IN SPAIN'S CAPITAL

In the early evening of August 18, a van plowed into the crowded tourist area of Las Ramblas, in Spain's capital city of Barcelona. Thirteen were killed and more than 100 were injured. It was the first time ISIL had carried out an attack on Spanish soil. In his response to the event, Spanish President Mariano Rajoy said the nation was "above all, united in our firm will to defeat those who wish to tear down our values and our way of life." Noting that the Spanish government and security forces would work to protect citizens, Rajoy called on nations around the globe to band together to defeat terrorism. "This is a global threat and the response must be global. All of those who share the same passion for liberty, for the dignity of human beings and for a society based on justice and not on fear and hatred, are allied in this same cause," he said.

ISIL quickly claimed responsibility for the attack in Barcelona, stating, "The executors of the Barcelona attack were soldiers of the Islamic State," an ISIL-linked news outlet reported, adding that the attack was conducted in response to Spain's involvement in the coalition working to defeat ISIL in Iraq and Syria. Initially, police believed that seventeen-year-old Moussa Oukabir had driven the van, following allegations that he had rented the vehicle using his brother's identification. Oukabir was killed in Cambrils, south of Barcelona, when he and four others targeted pedestrians with another vehicle; no one was injured. Police later announced their suspect as Moroccan-born Younes Abouyaaqoub, who fled the scene of the van attack on foot before hijacking a car. Abouyaaqoub spent a handful of days on the run before being shot by police. In total, Spanish authorities reported that twelve member ISIL cells made up of radicalized Moroccan natives had planned and carried out the van attack as well as a subsequent attempt in Cambrils and that all twelve had been arrested or killed.

—Heather Kerrigan

Following is a statement by Turkish President Recep Tayyip Erdoğan on January 1, 2017, following an attack in Istanbul; a June 4, 2017, statement by British Prime Minister

Theresa May after twin attacks in London; a June 7, 2017, statement by Iranian president Hassan Rouhani following a suicide bombing in Tehran; and an August 18, 2017, statement by Spanish President Mariano Rajoy after a terrorist attack struck Barcelona.

DOCUMENT

President Erdogan Issues Statement on Istanbul Terror Attack

January 1, 2017

President Recep Tayyip Erdoğan made a written statement on the terror attack carried out in the Ortaköy district of Istanbul:

I strongly condemn the terror attack that took place in the early hours of 2017 in the Ortaköy district of Istanbul.

I wish Allah's mercy upon our security personnel and citizens who lost their lives in the attack, and pay homage to our foreign guests killed in this deplorable incident.

I offer my condolences to victims' relatives, and wish a speedy recovery to the wounded.

Those aiming at the peace of our nation, and their pawns, are working to destabilize our country and trigger chaos by demoralizing our people through their heinous attacks that also target civilians.

However, we, as the nation, will never give passage to these dirty games, further uniting together and preserving our calmness.

Turkey, continuing its fight against terror, is extremely determined to do whatever it takes in the region, too, to ensure the security and peace of its citizens.

We are aware that these attacks, carried out by various terror organizations against our country, are not independent from incidents happening in our region. We are determined to eradicate threats and attacks against our country at their source.

Every single life we lose in this process makes our hearts bleed, but at the same time, further sharpens our perseverance and determination to struggle.

As the country and nation, we will fight against not only armed attacks of terror organizations and the powers behind them, but also against their economic, political and social attacks, to the end.

The brutal attack in Istanbul has clearly showed that terror aims to shed blood, claim lives, and hurt people without any discrimination.

I once again wish Allah's mercy and grace upon our security personnel and citizens who lost their lives in this heinous attack, and a quick recovery to the wounded.

SOURCE: Presidency of the Republic of Turkey. "Statement by President Erdogan on Terror Attack in Istanbul." January 1, 2017. https://www.tccb.gov.tr/en/speeches-statements/558/69626/statement-by-president-erdogan-on-terror-attack-in-istanbul.html.

Prime Minister May Addresses UK Terrorist Attack

June 4, 2017

Last night, our country fell victim to a brutal terrorist attack once again. As a result I have just chaired a meeting of the government's emergency committee and I want to update you with the latest information about the attack.

Shortly before 10:10 yesterday evening, the Metropolitan Police received reports that a white van had struck pedestrians on London Bridge. It continued to drive from London Bridge to Borough Market, where 3 terrorists left the van and attacked innocent and unarmed civilians with blades and knives.

All 3 were wearing what appeared to be explosive vests, but the police have established that this clothing was fake and worn only to spread panic and fear.

As so often in such serious situations, the police responded with great courage and great speed. Armed officers from the Metropolitan Police and the City of London Police arrived at Borough Market within moments, and shot and killed the 3 suspects. The terrorists were confronted and shot by armed officers within 8 minutes of the police receiving the first emergency call.

Seven people have died as a result of the attack, in addition to the 3 suspects shot dead by the police. Forty-eight people are being treated in several hospitals across London. Many have life-threatening conditions.

On behalf of the people of London, and on behalf of the whole country, I want to thank and pay tribute to the professionalism and bravery of the police and the emergency services—and the courage of members of the public who defended themselves and others from the attackers. And our thoughts and prayers are with the victims and with their friends, families and loved ones.

This is, as we all know, the third terrorist attack Britain has experienced in the last 3 months. In March, a similar attack took place, just around the corner on Westminster Bridge. Two weeks ago, the Manchester Arena was attacked by a suicide bomber. And now London has been struck once more.

And at the same time, the security and intelligence agencies and police have disrupted 5 credible plots since the Westminster attack in March.

In terms of their planning and execution, the recent attacks are not connected. But we believe we are experiencing a new trend in the threat we face, as terrorism breeds terrorism, and perpetrators are inspired to attack not only on the basis of carefully-constructed plots after years of planning and training—and not even as lone attackers radicalised online—but by copying one another and often using the crudest of means of attack.

We cannot and must not pretend that things can continue as they are. Things need to change, and they need to change in 4 important ways.

First, while the recent attacks are not connected by common networks, they are connected in one important sense. They are bound together by the single, evil ideology of

Islamist extremism that preaches hatred, sows division, and promotes sectarianism. It is an ideology that claims our Western values of freedom, democracy and human rights are incompatible with the religion of Islam. It is an ideology that is a perversion of Islam and a perversion of the truth.

Defeating this ideology is one of the great challenges of our time. But it cannot be defeated through military intervention alone. It will not be defeated through the maintenance of a permanent, defensive counter-terrorism operation, however skilful its leaders and practitioners. It will only be defeated when we turn people's minds away from this violence—and make them understand that our values—pluralistic, British values—are superior to anything offered by the preachers and supporters of hate.

Second, we cannot allow this ideology the safe space it needs to breed. Yet that is precisely what the internet—and the big companies that provide internet-based services—provide. We need to work with allied, democratic governments to reach international agreements that regulate cyberspace to prevent the spread of extremism and terrorist planning. And we need to do everything we can at home to reduce the risks of extremism online.

Third, while we need to deprive the extremists of their safe spaces online, we must not forget about the safe spaces that continue to exist in the real world. Yes, that means taking military action to destroy ISIS in Iraq and Syria. But it also means taking action here at home. While we have made significant progress in recent years, there is—to be frank—far too much tolerance of extremism in our country.

So we need to become far more robust in identifying it and stamping it out—across the public sector and across society. That will require some difficult and often embarrassing conversations, but the whole of our country needs to come together to take on this extremism—and we need to live our lives not in a series of separated, segregated communities but as one truly United Kingdom.

Fourth, we have a robust counter-terrorism strategy that has proved successful over many years. But as the nature of the threat we face becomes more complex, more fragmented, more hidden, especially online, the strategy needs to keep up. So in light of what we are learning about the changing threat, we need to review Britain's counter-terrorism strategy to make sure the police and security services have all the powers they need.

And if we need to increase the length of custodial sentences for terrorism-related offences, even apparently less serious offences, that is what we will do.

Since the emergence of the threat from Islamist-inspired terrorism, our country has made significant progress in disrupting plots and protecting the public. But it is time to say enough is enough. Everybody needs to go about their lives as they normally would. Our society should continue to function in accordance with our values. But when it comes to taking on extremism and terrorism, things need to change.

As a mark of respect the 2 political parties have suspended our national campaigns for today. But violence can never be allowed to disrupt the democratic process. So those campaigns will resume in full tomorrow. And the general election will go ahead as planned on Thursday.

As a country, our response must be as it has always been when we have been confronted by violence. We must come together, we must pull together, and united we will take on and defeat our enemies.

SOURCE: United Kingdom Prime Minister's Office. 10 Downing Street. "PM Statement following London Terror Attack: 4 June 2017." June 4, 2017. https://www.gov.uk/government/speeches/pm-statement-following-london-terror-attack-4-june-2017.

Iranian President Issues Statement on Attack in Tehran

June 7, 2017

In the Name of Allah, the Most Beneficent, the Most Merciful

Great Iranian nation and brave men and women of this land; you have paid the price of your dignity, independence, and freedom alongside great conspiracies from savage terrors to the imposed war with sacrifice and martyrdom of your children. The insensitive, cowardly actions today by terrorist mercenaries in killing a number of innocent, fasting people near the tomb of the founder of the Islamic Republic of Iran and "House of People" is not an unexpected incident.

About four decades after the formation of the Islamic Revolution and the crystallisation of "religious democracy", today's Iran has realised all elements of national power. Today, Iran is the most secure country at the heart of a turbulent region thanks to the brilliant leadership of the Supreme Leader and also the authority and integrity of the security, defense, intelligence and law enforcement forces. On the other hand, people's unparalleled attendance in the elections once again proved national integrity and peoples support.

It is natural that the enemies of the Islamic Iran do not tolerate the honours and unity between the government, administration and nation, hiring and supporting retrogressive and takfiri elements in an attempt to hide the collapse of Islamic values and dissatisfactions in their own societies, unaware of the fact that we have passed this test and the Iranian nation, which is acts based on the culture of Ashura, will prove again this time that it will shatter any conspiracy and plots by the enemies with more unity and integrity and its powerful security system.

Without a doubt, today's terrorist attacks in Tehran will further strengthen the Islamic Iran's resolve in its combat against regional terrorism, extremism and violence more than before. Iran's message, like always, has been that terrorism is a universal problem and unity in fighting extremism, violence and terrorism with regional and international cooperation is the most important need of today's global community.

I hereby express my condolences to the bereaved families who lost their loved ones in these terrorist attacks during the month of God's feast, asking the Almighty the highest places for the martyrs, patience and reward for the bereaved families and swift recovery for the injured.

It is obvious that the powers, organs and security organisations will not abandon attempt until all aspects of the insensitive action and their overt and covert supporters are identified.

SOURCE: Office of the President of Iran. "Iranian Nation to Shatter Any Conspiracy by Enemies with More Unity, Integrity/Stressing following the Issue until All Aspects of the Insensitive Actions, Their Supporters/ Condoling Bereaved Families." June 7, 2017. http://www.president.ir/en/99324.

Spanish President Expresses Condolences in Barcelona

August 18, 2017

The President of the Government, Mariano Rajoy, travelled to Barcelona to closely follow the events unfolding as a result of the terrorist attack in the city. Mariano Rajoy expressed his support for the victims and their families, and met with the State law enforcement agencies at the Government Representation Office in Catalonia, to make the following institutional declaration:

"Ladies and gentlemen, a very good evening to you. Thank you very much for attending at this late hour.

I would like my opening words tonight in Barcelona to be ones of grief, of remembrance and of solidarity with the victims of this attack and for their families and friends. These are our top priorities at this time.

I also want to express the solidarity of the whole of Spain with the city of Barcelona, hit hard today by Jihadi terrorism, as other cities around the world have been before. The people of such places as Madrid, Paris, Nice, Brussels, Berlin and London have all experienced the same pain and the same apprehension as the people of Barcelona are suffering today, and I want these opening words to be for them, to convey to them the affection, solidarity and empathy from the whole of Spain and from the rest of the world.

As testimony of the pain of the Spanish nation to this criminal attack, the government decrees a period of official mourning from 00:00 hours on 18 August 2017 until 24:00 hours on 20 August, during which time the national flag will be flown at half mast on all public buildings and Navy vessels.

Today Spain, and more specifically Barcelona, receives the affection and solidarity that we have shared at other times with other cities and other countries that have been hard hit by the barbarity of terrorism. I also want to say that not only are we united in grief; we are, above all, united in our firm will to defeat those who wish to tear down our values and our way of life. That is why I wanted to come here to Barcelona as soon as possible to meet up with the State law enforcement agencies, and express my support to them in their close and effective collaboration with the Mossos d'Esquadra [Regional Police Force of Catalonia] and Guardia Urbana [Barcelona City Police Force] in tackling this savage terrorist attack.

It is also important that on such a harsh and sad day as today, all of the security forces and our intelligence services, civil protection and emergency authorities and, in short, all of those who oversee our security, know that they can count on the unconditional support of the people and Government of Spain. It is true that today we are suffering from the pain of a terrible blow, but it is no less true that the selfless work of these men and women over so many years has managed to protect us for a very long time and frustrate a multitude of criminal plans, which they will assuredly continue to do in the future.

Regrettably, the people of Spain are all too familiar with the absurd and irrational pain caused by terrorism. We have suffered from the scourge of terrorism in our most recent history, but we also know that terrorism can be defeated. It can be defeated through institutional unity, police cooperation, prevention, international support and the firm determination to defend the values of our civilisation: democracy, liberty and the rights of individuals. And terrorism can also be defeated through broad agreements between political parties, as indeed happens in Spain. We will shortly call the Counter-Terrorism Pact to reaffirm our unity and all work together in the future, as we have been doing to date.

Ladies and gentlemen,

This terrible tragedy we have suffered today in Barcelona unites us in the pain suffered by so many other countries around the world. Tonight I also want to express my gratitude, here and now, to all the international leaders who have passed on to me their messages of support and solidarity. I have been unable to speak to them as it was more urgent to get up to speed with events, but I will personally thank them for their messages over the coming days.

Lastly, I would like to reiterate what I have already expressed to Regional President Puigdemont in private—that he has the full and unconditional support of the government and the Spanish State in providing aid to the victims and comforting the families affected, re-establishing normality in the streets as soon as possible and bringing to justice those responsible for this act of barbarity. You should also be aware that the whole of Spain shares the same sentiments as those felt today by the people who live here in Barcelona.

Today, the fight against terrorism is the main priority of free and open societies such as ours. This is a global threat and the response must be global. All of those who share the same passion for liberty, for the dignity of human beings and for a society based on justice and not on fear and hatred, are allied in this same cause.

As I said just a moment ago, it is true that we are united in our pain, but above all, we are all united in our desire to do away with this senselessness and this barbarity. Let us never forget that Spain is united by certain values that we are proud of: democracy, liberty and human rights. We have fought many battles against terrorism over the course of our history, and we have always come out on top, and on this occasion the Spanish people will once again triumph.

Thank you very much."

SOURCE: Government of Spain. "Mariano Rajoy Expresses Solidarity with Victims of Attack in Barcelona." August 18, 2017. http://www.lamoncloa.gob.es/lang/en/presidente/news/Paginas/2017/20170818_barce lona.aspx.

OTHER HISTORIC DOCUMENTS OF INTEREST

FROM PREVIOUS HISTORIC DOCUMENTS

Director of National Intelligence Declassifies Report on Russian Interference in 2016 U.S. Election

JANUARY 6, 2017

On January 6, 2017, the Office of the Director of National Intelligence (DNI) declassified a report confirming what many had already suspected: that Russian President Vladimir Putin ordered a campaign aimed at influencing the outcome of the 2016 U.S. presidential election. The report, requested by then-President Barack Obama, determined that the effort had specifically sought to discredit Democratic candidate Hillary Clinton while supporting the chances of Republican Donald Trump. However, the report concluded, while multiple efforts were made to influence the election outcome, there was no evidence of successful hacking into tallying systems that would have resulted in the victory of one candidate over the other. The report was notable in that it was the first time in history that U.S. intelligence agencies reached a conclusion that a foreign government had worked to influence a U.S. election.

DNI RELEASES DECLASSIFIED REPORT

On December 9, 2016, Obama directed the intelligence community to review the 2016 election process, and, more specifically, potential Russian hacking activity and whether it was done in an attempt to influence the election outcome. Throughout the 2016 presidential election process, the U.S. government frequently blamed Russia for cyberattacks against organizations including the Democratic National Committee (DNC), allegations Russia repeatedly denied. The report that was declassified on January 6, 2017, was the culmination of information collected in response to the president's request by the Central Intelligence Agency (CIA), Federal Bureau of Investigation (FBI), and National Security Agency (NSA).

The report cautioned readers that, while it did not include complete evidence related to the investigation, the findings were the same as those in the full, classified version. Noting that the intelligence agencies involved had "high confidence" in the findings, the overall conclusion of the report was that "Russian President Vladimir Putin ordered an influence campaign in 2016 aimed at the US presidential election. Russia's goals were to undermine public faith in the US democratic process, denigrate Secretary Clinton, and harm her electability and potential presidency. We further assess Putin and the Russian Government developed a clear preference for President-elect Trump." This campaign was most likely led by the Main Intelligence Directorate (GRU), Russia's foreign military intelligence unit, under the online persona Guccifer 2.0. Notably, the report did not make a finding related to whether the Russian influence campaign had any impact on the opinion of voters that would have affected the outcome of the election.

In the report, U.S. intelligence agencies indicate that the Russian influence campaign sought to support Trump because it preferred "Western political leaders whose business interests made them more disposed to deal with Russia." However, the attempt to influence the election began in 2015, when the Russian operation infiltrated the DNC and Clinton campaign. This timeline makes clear that the effort was first and foremost focused on discrediting Clinton. Russian distaste for the former senator began in 2011, according to the report, when Putin believed Clinton utilized her position as secretary of state to incite protests across Russia against his government. Once the Russian operation realized that Clinton was the more likely victor in the 2016 election, it released information that painted a negative view of her potential presidency, which included the use of e-mail gathered during the DNC cyberattack.

The Russian operation relied heavily on social media trolls to spread its message, along with various third-party organizations such as WikiLeaks and Russian state-run media including RT, the nation's English-language news outlet. Together, the intelligence community viewed Russian efforts as its boldest attempt to infiltrate and influence a U.S. election, calling it "a significant escalation in directness, level of activity and scope of effort" that may become the "new normal." The report concluded that the information gathered and lessons learned through the Russian operation will likely be utilized by Putin's government in future attempts to influence elections in the United States and abroad.

RESPONSE TO THE REPORT

The report was shared separately with both then-President Obama and president-elect Trump. Ahead of the report's release, Trump called the investigation a "political witch hunt" and encouraged the country to "move on." The president elect had previously questioned allegations that the Russians were behind the infiltration of the DNC's servers and postulated that China may have been the source of the cyberattack. Following his intelligence briefing, Trump released a statement noting the Russian campaign had "no effect on the outcome of the election" and that there was no evidence that the Russians preferred his candidacy over that of Clinton. Rep. Adam Schiff, D-Calif., ranking member of the House Select Intelligence Committee said Trump's opinion was "not supported by the briefing, report, or common sense."

Some Congressional Republicans, including Sens. Lindsey Graham of South Carolina and John McCain of Arizona, called for levying more sanctions against the Russian government for their interference in the election. In December 2016, the Obama administration issued new sanctions against Russian intelligence officials and contractors and seized some Russian-owned U.S. property. On January 10, a bipartisan group of senators unveiled a bill to go beyond the Obama sanctions by imposing visa bans, making it more difficult for U.S. banks to do business with certain Russian agencies, and freezing the assets of "those who undermine the cybersecurity of public or private infrastructure and democratic institutions." The bill also called for federal funds to be dedicated to countering fake news like that spread by Russia through social media and news outlets ahead of the 2016 presidential election. The bill was referred to the Senate Committee on Banking, Housing, and Urban Affairs, but had not left committee by the end of 2017.

The Russian government vehemently denied the allegations in the report. "These are baseless allegations substantiated with nothing, done on a rather amateurish, emotional level," Putin spokesperson Dmitry Peskov said. "We are growing rather tired of these accusations. It is becoming a full-on witch hunt," he added. Putin said his government had not "been involved in this. We aren't planning to be involved in it. Quite the opposite. We are trying to combat it inside our country." He went on to allege that modern technology allows those involved in cyberattacks to make it appear as though Russia had undertaken the effort. Commentators in Russia—and some in the United States—criticized the report for leaving out classified technical details that would have provided the evidence necessary to give more weight to the report. Susan Hennessey, a former NSA attorney, called the report "underwhelming at best. There is essentially no new information for those who have been paying attention."

ALLEGATIONS OF A LINK TO TRUMP'S CAMPAIGN

Questions surrounding the Trump campaign's links to members of the Russian government had been swirling prior to the DNI report being made public, but its release heightened calls for an investigation into whether the campaign colluded with the Russian government to secure Trump's victory. Three investigations got underway in Congress— one in the House and two in the Senate—although by the close of 2017, they had produced little of substance and some were still struggling to define the scope of their efforts. On May 17, the Justice Department announced that it would appoint former FBI director Robert Mueller as special counsel to oversee an investigation into Russian efforts to influence the 2016 election. Trump responded that "a thorough investigation will confirm what we already know—there was no collusion between my campaign and any foreign entity."

The Trump White House quickly felt the effect of heightened public concern about possible Russian influence. On February 13, National Security Advisor Michael Flynn, who had been in his position less than one month, resigned after it was revealed that he misled Vice President Mike Pence regarding his contact with the Russian ambassador to the United States in December 2016. Flynn had initially denied having any substantive conversation with the ambassador, an assertion Pence then went on to share in television interviews. In reality, however, Flynn had discussed with the ambassador the sanctions imposed against Russia by the Obama administration, a conversation some U.S. officials believe could have signaled a potential softening of the sanctions under Trump. In his resignation letter, Flynn characterized the information he provided to Pence as "incomplete" and expressed his deep apologies. Lt. Gen. Joseph Kellogg Jr. replaced Flynn in the interim, and Flynn would become a key subject in both Congressional investigations and that led by Mueller.

A few weeks after Flynn's departure, Trump's attorney general, Jeff Sessions, announced that he would recuse himself from any investigation related to the 2016 Trump campaign, following direction from the Justice Department's ethics division. "They said that since I had involvement with the campaign, I should not be involved in any campaign investigation," he said. The recusal, which was allegedly met with anger inside the White House, came after it was revealed that Sessions also had contact with the Russian ambassador, something he failed to disclose during his confirmation hearings.

Trump would continue to state throughout 2017 that there was no collusion between his presidential election campaign and the Russian government, an assertion frequently called into question as more evidence came to light that members of the Trump campaign team had, at times, frequent contact with individuals with deep ties to the Russian government. Although such contact itself is not illegal, the larger question surrounds the rationale or motivation behind any potential coordination, what information the Trump campaign may or may not have gained, and how that information was obtained or ultimately used.

—Linda Grimm

Following is the excerpted text of the Director of National Intelligence report, declassified on January 6, 2017, outlining the attempt by Russia to influence the outcome of the 2016 U.S. presidential election.

DNI Releases Declassified Report on Russian Interference in U.S. Election

January 6, 2017

[The background on the classification of the document, scope of the investigation, and sourcing has been omitted.]

Assessing Russian Activities and Intentions in Recent US Elections
ICA 2017-01D
6 January 2017

Key Judgements

Russian efforts to influence the 2016 US presidential election represent the most recent expression of Moscow's longstanding desire to undermine the US-led liberal democratic order, but these activities demonstrated a significant escalation in directness, level of activity, and scope of effort compared to previous operations.

We assess Russian President Vladimir Putin ordered an influence campaign in 2016 aimed at the US presidential election. Russia's goals were to undermine public faith in the US democratic process, denigrate Secretary Clinton, and harm her electability and potential presidency. We further assess Putin and the Russian Government developed a clear preference for President-elect Trump. We have high confidence in these judgments.

- **We also assess Putin and the Russian Government aspired to help President-elect Trump's election chances when possible by discrediting Secretary Clinton and publicly contrasting her unfavorably to him.** All three agencies agree with this judgment. CIA and FBI have high confidence in this judgment; NSA has moderate confidence.

- Moscow's approach evolved over the course of the campaign based on Russia's understanding of the electoral prospects of the two main candidates. When it appeared to Moscow that Secretary Clinton was likely to win the election, the

Russian influence campaign began to focus more on undermining her future presidency.

- Further information has come to light since Election Day that, when combined with Russian behavior since early November 2016, increases our confidence in our assessments of Russian motivations and goals.

Moscow's influence campaign followed a Russian messaging strategy that blends covert intelligence operations—such as cyber activity—with overt efforts by Russian Government agencies, state-funded media, third-party intermediaries, and paid social media users or "trolls." Russia, like its Soviet predecessor, has a history of conducting covert influence campaigns focused on US presidential elections that have used intelligence officers and agents and press placements to disparage candidates perceived as hostile to the Kremlin.

- Russia's intelligence services conducted cyber operations against targets associated with the 2016 US presidential election, including targets associated with both major US political parties.

- We assess with high confidence that Russian military intelligence (General Staff Main Intelligence Directorate or GRU) used the Guccifer 2.0 persona and DCLeaks.com to release US victim data obtained in cyber operations publicly and in exclusives to media outlets and relayed material to WikiLeaks.

- Russian intelligence obtained and maintained access to elements of multiple US state or local electoral boards. DHS assesses that the types of systems Russian actors targeted or compromised were not involved in vote tallying.

- Russia's state-run propaganda machine contributed to the influence campaign by serving as a platform for Kremlin messaging to Russian and international audiences.

We assess Moscow will apply lessons learned from its Putin-ordered campaign aimed at the US presidential election to future influence efforts worldwide, including against US allies and their election processes.

[The table of contents has been omitted.]

Russia's Influence Campaign Targeting the 2016 US Presidential Election

Putin Ordered Campaign To Influence US Election

We assess with high confidence that Russian President Vladimir Putin ordered an influence campaign in 2016 aimed at the US presidential election, the consistent goals of which were to undermine public faith in the US democratic process, denigrate Secretary Clinton, and harm her electability and potential presidency. We further assess Putin and the Russian Government developed a clear preference for President-elect Trump. When it appeared to Moscow that Secretary Clinton was likely to win the election, the Russian influence campaign then focused on undermining her expected presidency.

- We also assess Putin and the Russian Government aspired to help President-elect Trump's election chances when possible by discrediting Secretary Clinton and publicly contrasting her unfavorably to him. All three agencies agree with this judgment. CIA and FBI have high confidence in this judgment; NSA has moderate confidence.

- In trying to influence the US election, we assess the Kremlin sought to advance its longstanding desire to undermine the US-led liberal democratic order, the promotion of which Putin and other senior Russian leaders view as a threat to Russia and Putin's regime.

- Putin publicly pointed to the Panama Papers disclosure and the Olympic doping scandal as US-directed efforts to defame Russia, suggesting he sought to use disclosures to discredit the image of the United States and cast it as hypocritical.

- Putin most likely wanted to discredit Secretary Clinton because he has publicly blamed her since 2011 for inciting mass protests against his regime in late 2011 and early 2012, and because he holds a grudge for comments he almost certainly saw as disparaging him.

We assess Putin, his advisers, and the Russian Government developed a clear preference for President-elect Trump over Secretary Clinton.

- Beginning in June, Putin's public comments about the US presidential race avoided directly praising President-elect Trump, probably because Kremlin officials thought that any praise from Putin personally would backfire in the United States. Nonetheless, Putin publicly indicated a preference for President-elect Trump's stated policy to work with Russia, and pro-Kremlin figures spoke highly about what they saw as his Russia-friendly positions on Syria and Ukraine. Putin publicly contrasted the President-elect's approach to Russia with Secretary Clinton's "aggressive rhetoric."

- Moscow also saw the election of President-elect Trump as a way to achieve an international counterterrorism coalition against the Islamic State in Iraq and the Levant (ISIL).

- Putin has had many positive experiences working with Western political leaders whose business interests made them more disposed to deal with Russia, such as former Italian Prime Minister Silvio Berlusconi and former German Chancellor Gerhard Schroeder.

- Putin, Russian officials, and other pro-Kremlin pundits stopped publicly criticizing the US election process as unfair almost immediately after the election because Moscow probably assessed it would be counterproductive to building positive relations.

We assess the influence campaign aspired to help President-elect Trump's chances of victory when possible by discrediting Secretary Clinton and publicly contrasting her unfavorably to the President-elect. When it appeared to Moscow that Secretary Clinton was likely to win the presidency the Russian influence campaign focused more on undercutting Secretary Clinton's legitimacy and crippling her presidency from its start, including by impugning the fairness of the election.

- Before the election, Russian diplomats had publicly denounced the US electoral process and were prepared to publicly call into question the validity of the results. Pro-Kremlin bloggers had prepared a Twitter campaign, #DemocracyRIP, on election night in anticipation of Secretary Clinton's victory, judging from their social media activity.

Russian Campaign Was Multifaceted

Moscow's use of disclosures during the US election was unprecedented, but its influence campaign otherwise followed a longstanding Russian messaging strategy that blends covert intelligence operations—such as cyber activity—with overt efforts by Russian Government agencies, state-funded media, third-party intermediaries, and paid social media users or "trolls."

- We assess that influence campaigns are approved at the highest levels of the Russian Government—particularly those that would be politically sensitive.

- Moscow's campaign aimed at the US election reflected years of investment in its capabilities, which Moscow has honed in the former Soviet states.

- By their nature, Russian influence campaigns are multifaceted and designed to be deniable because they use a mix of agents of influence, cutouts, front organizations, and false-flag operations. Moscow demonstrated this during the Ukraine crisis in 2014, when Russia deployed forces and advisers to eastern Ukraine and denied it publicly.

The Kremlin's campaign aimed at the US election featured disclosures of data obtained through Russian cyber operations; intrusions into US state and local electoral boards; and overt propaganda. Russian intelligence collection both informed and enabled the influence campaign.

Cyber Espionage Against US Political Organizations. Russia's intelligence services conducted cyber operations against targets associated with the 2016 US presidential election, including targets associated with both major US political parties.

We assess Russian intelligence services collected against the US primary campaigns, think tanks, and lobbying groups they viewed as likely to shape future US policies. In July 2015, Russian intelligence gained access to Democratic National Committee (DNC) networks and maintained that access until at least June 2016.

- The General Staff Main Intelligence Directorate (GRU) probably began cyber operations aimed at the US election by March 2016. We assess that the GRU operations resulted in the compromise of the personal e-mail accounts of Democratic Party officials and political figures. By May, the GRU had exfiltrated large volumes of data from the DNC.

Public Disclosures of Russian-Collected Data. We assess with high confidence that the GRU used the Guccifer 2.0 persona, DCLeaks.com, and WikiLeaks to release US victim data obtained in cyber operations publicly and in exclusives to media outlets.

- Guccifer 2.0, who claimed to be an independent Romanian hacker, made multiple contradictory statements and false claims about his likely Russian identity throughout the election. Press reporting suggests more than one person claiming to be Guccifer 2.0 interacted with journalists.

- Content that we assess was taken from e-mail accounts targeted by the GRU in March 2016 appeared on DCLeaks.com starting in June.

We assess with high confidence that the GRU relayed material it acquired from the DNC and senior Democratic officials to WikiLeaks. Moscow most likely chose WikiLeaks because of its self-proclaimed reputation for authenticity. Disclosures through WikiLeaks did not contain any evident forgeries.

- In early September, Putin said publicly it was important the DNC data was exposed to WikiLeaks, calling the search for the source of the leaks a distraction and denying Russian "state-level" involvement.

- The Kremlin's principal international propaganda outlet RT (formerly Russia Today) has actively collaborated with WikiLeaks. RT's editor-in-chief visited WikiLeaks founder Julian Assange at the Ecuadorian Embassy in London in August 2013, where they discussed renewing his broadcast contract with RT, according to Russian and Western media. Russian media subsequently announced that RT had become "the only Russian media company" to partner with WikiLeaks and had received access to "new leaks of secret information." RT routinely gives Assange sympathetic coverage and provides him a platform to denounce the United States

These election-related disclosures reflect a pattern of Russian intelligence using hacked information in targeted influence efforts against targets such as Olympic athletes and other foreign governments. Such efforts have included releasing or altering personal data, defacing websites, or releasing emails.

- A prominent target since the 2016 Summer Olympics has been the World Anti-Doping Agency (WADA), with leaks that we assess to have originated with the GRU and that have involved data on US athletes.

Russia collected on some Republican-affiliated targets but did not conduct a comparable disclosure campaign.

Russian Cyber Intrusions Into State and Local Electoral Boards. Russian intelligence accessed elements of multiple state or local electoral boards. Since early 2014, Russian intelligence has researched US electoral processes and related technology and equipment.

- DHS assesses that the types of systems we observed Russian actors targeting or compromising are not involved in vote tallying.

Russian Propaganda Efforts. Russia's state-run propaganda machine—comprised of its domestic media apparatus, outlets targeting global audiences such as RT and Sputnik, and a network of quasi-government trolls—contributed to the influence campaign by serving as a platform for Kremlin messaging to Russian and international audiences. State-owned Russian media made increasingly favorable comments about President-elect Trump as the 2016 US general and primary election campaigns progressed while consistently offering negative coverage of Secretary Clinton.

- Starting in March 2016, Russian Government-linked actors began openly supporting President-elect Trump's candidacy in media aimed at English-speaking audiences. RT and Sputnik—another government-funded outlet producing pro-Kremlin radio and online content in a variety of languages for international audiences—consistently cast President-elect Trump as the target of unfair coverage from traditional US media outlets that they claimed were subservient to a corrupt political establishment.

- Russian media hailed President-elect Trump's victory as a vindication of Putin's advocacy of global populist movements—the theme of Putin's annual conference for Western academics in October 2016—and the latest example of Western liberalism's collapse.

- Putin's chief propagandist Dmitriy Kiselev used his flagship weekly newsmagazine program this fall to cast President-elect Trump as an outsider victimized by a corrupt political establishment and faulty democratic election process that aimed to prevent his election because of his desire to work with Moscow.

- Pro-Kremlin proxy Vladimir Zhirinovskiy, leader of the nationalist Liberal Democratic Party of Russia, proclaimed just before the election that if President-elect Trump won, Russia would "drink champagne" in anticipation of being able to advance its positions on Syria and Ukraine.

RT's coverage of Secretary Clinton throughout the US presidential campaign was consistently negative and focused on her leaked e-mails and accused her of corruption, poor physical and mental health, and ties to Islamic extremism. Some Russian officials echoed Russian lines for the influence campaign that Secretary Clinton's election could lead to a war between the United States and Russia.

- In August, Kremlin-linked political analysts suggested avenging negative Western reports on Putin by airing segments devoted to Secretary Clinton's alleged health problems.

- On 6 August, RT published an English-language video called "Julian Assange Special: Do WikiLeaks Have the E-mail That'll Put Clinton in Prison?" and an exclusive interview with Assange entitled "Clinton and ISIS Funded by the Same Money." RT's most popular video on Secretary Clinton, "How 100% of the Clintons' 'Charity' Went to . . . Themselves," had more than 9 million views on social media platforms. RT's most popular English language video about the President-elect, called "Trump Will Not Be Permitted To Win," featured Assange and had 2.2 million views.

- For more on Russia's past media efforts—including portraying the 2012 US electoral process as undemocratic—please see Annex A: Russia—Kremlin's TV Seeks To Influence Politics, Fuel Discontent in US.

Russia used trolls as well as RT as part of its influence efforts to denigrate Secretary Clinton. This effort amplified stories on scandals about Secretary Clinton and the role of WikiLeaks in the election campaign.

- The likely financier of the so-called Internet Research Agency of professional trolls located in Saint Petersburg is a close Putin ally with ties to Russian intelligence.

- A journalist who is a leading expert on the Internet Research Agency claimed that some social media accounts that appear to be tied to Russia's professional trolls—because they previously were devoted to supporting Russian actions in Ukraine—started to advocate for President-elect Trump as early as December 2015.

Influence Effort Was Boldest Yet in the US

Russia's effort to influence the 2016 US presidential election represented a significant escalation in directness, level of activity, and scope of effort compared to previous operations aimed at US elections. We assess the 2016 influence campaign reflected the Kremlin's recognition of the worldwide effects that mass disclosures of US Government and other private data—such as those conducted by WikiLeaks and others—have achieved in recent years, and their understanding of the value of orchestrating such disclosures to maximize the impact of compromising information.

- During the Cold War, the Soviet Union used intelligence officers, influence agents, forgeries, and press placements to disparage candidates perceived as hostile to the Kremlin, according to a former KGB archivist.

Since the Cold War, Russian intelligence efforts related to US elections have primarily focused on foreign intelligence collection. For decades, Russian and Soviet intelligence services have sought to collect insider information from US political parties that could help Russian leaders understand a new US administration's plans and priorities.

- The Russian Foreign Intelligence Service (SVR) Directorate S (Illegals) officers arrested in the United States in 2010 reported to Moscow about the 2008 election.

- In the 1970s, the KGB recruited a Democratic Party activist who reported information about then-presidential hopeful Jimmy Carter's campaign and foreign policy plans, according to a former KGB archivist.

Election Operation Signals "New Normal" in Russian Influence Efforts

We assess Moscow will apply lessons learned from its campaign aimed at the US presidential election to future influence efforts in the United States and worldwide, including against US allies and their election processes. We assess the Russian intelligence services would have seen their election influence campaign as at least a qualified success because of their perceived ability to impact public discussion.

- Putin's public views of the disclosures suggest the Kremlin and the intelligence services will continue to consider using cyber-enabled disclosure operations because of their belief that these can accomplish Russian goals relatively easily without significant damage to Russian interests.

- Russia has sought to influence elections across Europe.

We assess Russian intelligence services will continue to develop capabilities to provide Putin with options to use against the United States, judging from past practice and current efforts. Immediately after Election Day, we assess Russian intelligence began a spearphishing campaign targeting US Government employees and individuals associated with US think tanks and NGOs in national security, defense, and foreign policy fields. This campaign could provide material for future influence efforts as well as foreign intelligence collection on the incoming administration's goals and plans.

[Annex A, outlining Russian strategies to influence the U.S. presidential election, and Annex B, containing information on federal estimative language, have been omitted.]

SOURCE: Office of the Director of National Intelligence. "Assessing Russian Activities and Intentions in Recent US Elections." January 6, 2017. https://www.dni.gov/files/documents/ICA_2017_01.pdf.

OTHER HISTORIC DOCUMENTS OF INTEREST

FROM THIS VOLUME

FROM PREVIOUS *HISTORIC DOCUMENTS*

Gambian Election Throws
Nation into Political Crisis

JANUARY 13, 19, AND 21, 2017

Former president of the Republic of The Gambia, Yahya Jammeh, was defeated in a stunning and contentious election that ultimately led to the country's first democratic transition of power. Jammeh seized control from the former British Colony's first president in 1994, and had relied on force to maintain his position since that time. As his authoritarian reign was ending, an attempt to strong-arm his way into another term threw the tiny country into political crisis. The emphasis that regional intergovernmental organizations placed on diplomacy in navigating the standoff, as well as his ultimate exile, was a historically atypical turn for a continent of so-called leaders for life and was heralded as a sign of hope for the progression of democracy in Africa.

A DICTATORSHIP OVERTURNED BY AN
UNLIKELY PRESIDENTIAL CANDIDATE

Although he led one of the world's smallest countries, Jammeh cultivated an outsized reputation for irrational behavior (such as claiming an ability to cure AIDS with little more than prayer and a banana). He had long received and ignored international condemnation for widespread human rights abuses and ruthless repression of dissent. He relied heavily on force and intimidation to maintain power for 22 years, and as he told the BBC in 2011, he planned to "rule this country for one billion years . . . if Allah says so." With no presidential term limits, he had been expected to sweep the 2016 election as he had the past four.

While amassing vast wealth, Jammeh did little to help the many Gambians who were mired in abject poverty. Such severely limited economic opportunity compounded by extensive human rights violations made The Gambia, despite its population of about 2 million, the fifth largest source of African refugees. Making Islam a focal point of his presidency, he used religion to justify homophobia, as well as brutal prosecution of journalists, opposition activists, and political opponents. He declared The Gambia an Islamic Republic in 2015 to strengthen ties with Arab states, and in response, the European Union revoked a sizeable amount of funding and threatened to impose sanctions in an effort to push humanitarian reform. Jammeh further isolated his nation by withdrawing from the International Criminal Court (ICC) and the British Commonwealth, which had been applying similar pressures.

Detention of a major opposition leader and other prominent activists prompted a shift in the political landscape that made the necessary level of cooperation among opposition groups possible. With the country's median age of 21, many Gambians have known no other leader. Their disaffection engendered large opposition rallies that quickly became protests with crowds chanting, "We are tired; we need change." This change was personified by Adama Barrow, an accidental presidential candidate who represented a coalition of eight opposition parties. A former real estate agent, then treasurer of the United Democratic Party, Barrow was not widely known even among supporters of the opposition and had never held political office. As a candidate, he was perceived as industrious but unassuming and was particularly well-liked among young voters. Describing Jammeh as a "soulless dictator," Barrow campaigned on promises of increased freedoms for media and civil society.

An Election Brings Political Turmoil

Observers in the United States praised high voter turnout and generally peaceful conditions in the December 1, 2016, election, but along with various human rights organizations, cited areas of concern such as sudden disruption of Internet and telephone service. Intimidation and fear of reprisal was evident because many voters were reluctant to comment on which candidate they supported. The Economic Community of Western African States (ECOWAS) had refused to participate in the electoral process, claiming that The Gambia lacks a friendly environment for free and fair elections. Jammeh banned the European Union from participating, but observers from the African Union monitored polling stations, and the vote and subsequent tallying were largely transparent.

When Jammeh lost the election on December 2, he surprised the world by quickly and calmly conceding defeat in a speech broadcast on state television. One week later, citing fabricated irregularities in the electoral process, he made an abrupt reversal insisting that "nobody can deprive me of that victory" and sent soldiers to take control of the electoral commission office. The electoral commission acknowledged that there may have been some minor errors, but none that would have affected the final outcome. Among wide international condemnation, the U.S. State Department called it "an egregious attempt to undermine a credible election process and remain in power illegitimately." Barrow appealed to the United Nations to enforce the constitutional legitimacy of his electoral win, and the Security Council unanimously lent its support. Similarly, ECOWAS pledged to "take all necessary actions" to defend Barrow's victory.

The country braced for a period of tense uncertainty: Food prices skyrocketed as civilians stocked up on supplies. The capital city, Banjul, was deserted while the military patrolled downtown. With a mounting security and humanitarian crisis, heads of state from Ghana, Liberia, Nigeria, and Sierra Leone, all ECOWAS members, met with Jammeh at the State House on December 13 but were unable after the initial meeting to convince him to accept that his two decades of rule were ending. President Ellen Johnson Sirleaf of Liberia stated, "We come to help Gambians find a way through a transition. That's not something that can happen in one day." Because repeated attempts at diplomacy failed, preparations were made for a possible military intervention. Although ECOWAS does not have a standing army, it can assemble troops from member nations. The bloc secured approval from the UN Security Council to oust Jammeh by force if needed, but reaffirmed that use of military force should remain a last resort.

A Presidential Standoff

During this period of political turmoil and deepening civil unrest, according to the UN Refugee Agency, approximately 45,000 people fled to Senegal. With tensions rising, president-elect Barrow was relocated to The Gambian embassy in Dakar, Senegal, as a security measure, while Jammeh threatened that his own forces were prepared to defend what he perceived to be The Gambia's sovereignty under threat. However, the unlikelihood of a sustained military conflict between Gambian and other West African troops became apparent after Jammeh's Chief of Defense refused to defend him. His administration began showing cracks when many prominent cabinet members, and even security forces, who had staunchly defended him for years resigned in protest, or were otherwise fired for disloyalty. Dealing a further blow, the Islamic Supreme Council, once a strong ally of Jammeh, sided in favor of president-elect Barrow.

Despite the African Union's warning that he would not be recognized as president after his term expired, Jammeh refused to relinquish power. On January 17, 2017, two days before he was due to leave office, Jammeh declared a state of emergency citing foreign interference in the 2016 election. The National Assembly, controlled by his own party, passed a motion condemning "unlawful and malicious interference" by the African Union and Senegal. One day later, the body adopted a resolution granting Jammeh a ninety-day extension of his term, hours before he was required to leave to allow for the seating of his successor. ECOWAS held that the extension was inconsequential, and maintained that his term would end at midnight on January 18.

Still in Dakar, Barrow was sworn in as scheduled on the morning of January 19, and his legitimacy as president was universally recognized. After taking the oath of office, he told a small crowd of government officials, "This is a day no Gambian will ever forget. This is the first time . . . that The Gambia has changed the government from the ballot box." Still refusing to stand down, ECOWAS gave Jammeh an ultimatum to leave by 16:00 on January 20, or be forcibly removed from the State House. Anticipating his refusal, troops from Ghana, Mali, Nigeria, and Senegal arrived at the Gambian border and were prepared to force him out. The deadline passed, and troops crossed the border en route to Banjul, but the operation was paused to allow for a final attempt at a diplomatic resolution as heads of state from Guinea, Liberia, and Mauritania met with Jammeh again, offering him one last chance to leave peacefully.

His motivation in trying to maintain power was likely to avoid trial and prosecution in the ICC for crimes committed while in office. Trying to ease his way out, he had unsuccessfully attempted to negotiate amnesty. On January 20, as the regional force was poised to remove him, he was left with little choice but to step down. In brief remarks on state television, Jammeh stated, "I have decided today in good conscience to relinquish the mantle of this great nation." The night of the January 21, he departed to Equatorial Guinea. His final destination was unclear, but the fact that Guinea is not a member of the ICC significantly lowers the likelihood that he will be held accountable for his crimes.

Regional troops encountered no resistance from Gambian forces while they were deployed throughout the country on January 22 to allow President Barrow to take office. With broad international support, the new president set out immediately to assemble a cabinet and work with the National Assembly to address the state of emergency Jammeh had left in place. Upon arrival, Barrow's administration found the country in financial distress, as Jammeh had apparently siphoned off tens of millions of dollars in public funds before departing. Citizens demanded that it be returned, and the new government began an investigation into the alleged financial crimes with assistance from the United States and the World Bank.

EMBARKING ON A DEMOCRATIC FUTURE

The Gambia celebrated its first democratic transition of power as the world watched with cautious optimism. Upon taking office, Barrow established a Truth and Reconciliation Commission, to offer reparations to victims of Jammeh's regime. A broad and ambitious social agenda was also announced to reverse many controversial policies, along with development of free basic education, affordable health care, and youth empowerment programs. Barrow also suggested reinstating presidential term limits and indicated a plan to step down within three years.

The legislative election in April to fill National Assembly seats presented a key test for the former opposition parties that had united to oust Jammeh: Fault lines among these groups still remain, and making progress on promised reforms required cooperation. Some Gambians had expressed frustration that the coalition parties had not been able to present a united front, but Barrow defended the discord, saying, "There is no (cabinet) split. This is about democracy and this is the new Gambia." Nonetheless, the country's ability to organize free and fair elections was hailed as a success. The regional support Barrow received is remarkable, but the same backing will be paramount as he leads The Gambia's democratic political and economic way forward.

—Megan Howes

Following is a decision adopted by the African Union Peace and Security Council in response to the post-election situation in The Gambia, announced on January 13, 2017; the resolution from the United Nations Security Council endorsing the African Union's recognition of Adama Barrow as president, on January 19, 2017; and a joint declaration by the Economic Community of West African States (ECOWAS), the African Union, and the United Nations on The Gambia's political situation from January 21, 2017.

African Union Meets to Discuss Election in The Gambia

January 13, 2017

The Peace and Security Council of the African Union (AU), at its 647th meeting held on 13 January 2017, adopted the following decision on the post-election situation in The Islamic Republic of The Gambia:

Council:

1. Takes note of the briefing made by the Chairperson of the Commission, Dr. Nkosazana Dlamini-Zuma, as well as the presentation made by the Commissioner for Political Affairs, Dr. Aisha Laraba Abdullahi, on the latest developments in the post-electoral situation in The Gambia, following the presidential election held in that country on 1 December 2016. Council also takes note of the statements made by the representatives of The Gambia, as well as of Liberia, in its capacity as Chair of the Authority of the Economic Community of West African States (ECOWAS), Egypt, Ethiopia and Senegal, as African Members of the UN Security Council and the United Nations (UN);

2. Recalls Article 23 (4) of the African Charter on Democracy, Elections and Governance. Council further recalls communiqué PSC/PR/COMM. (DCXLIV)

adopted at its 644th meeting held on 12 December 2016, in which Council strongly rejected any attempt to circumvent or reverse the outcome of the presidential election held in The Gambia on 1 December 2016, which is a clear expression of the popular will and choice of the Gambian people, and called upon outgoing President Yahya Jammeh to keep to the letter and spirit of the speech he delivered on 2 December 2016, in which he welcomed the maturity of democracy in The Gambia and congratulated the president-elect, Adama Barrow;

3. Commends ECOWAS for its principled stand with regard to the situation in The Gambia, and reaffirms its full support to the decisions adopted by the 50th Ordinary Summit of the ECOWAS Authority held in Abuja, on 17 December 2016, including the consideration to use all necessary means to ensure the respect of the will of the people of The Gambia. In this respect, Council pays tribute to the leadership and commitment demonstrated by Her Excellency President Ellen Johnson-Sirleaf, of Liberia, Chairperson of the ECOWAS Authority, as well as to His Excellency President Muhammadu Buhari of Nigeria, ECOWAS Mediator, and to Former President John Dramani Mahama, of Ghana, co-Mediator, for their continued efforts aimed at ensuring a peaceful and smooth transfer of power in The Gambia;

4. Calls upon, once again, the outgoing President, Yahya Jammeh, to respect the Constitution of the Gambia, the ECOWAS and AU instruments, in particular the AU Constitutive Act and the African Charter on Democracy, Elections and Governance, by handing over power, on 19 January 2017, as stated in the Constitution, to the newly-elected President of The Gambia, Adama Barrow, as decided by the people of the country;

5. Decides, in line with Articles 24 and 25 of the AU Charter on Democracy, Elections and Governance, as well as Article 7 (m) of the Protocol Relating to the Establishment of the Peace and Security Council, to take the following steps with a view to ensuring respect for the will of the Gambian people:

   i) Solemnly declares the inviolable nature of the outcome of the presidential elections held on 1 December 2016 in The Gambia. In this respect, Council strongly reaffirms the AU's zero tolerance policy with regard to coup d'état and unconstitutional changes of government in Africa;

   ii) Further Declares that, as of 19 January 2017, outgoing President Yahya Jammeh will cease to be recognized by the AU as legitimate President of the Republic of The Gambia;

   iii) Warns outgoing President Yahya Jammeh of serious consequences in the event that his action causes any crisis that could lead to political disorder, humanitarian and human rights disaster, including loss of innocent lives and destruction of properties;

6. Stresses the need for the outgoing President Yahya Jammeh and his Government to refrain from any action that could undermine the process leading up to the swearing in of the president-elect, on 19 January 2017. Reiterates its call to the Gambian stakeholders, including the defense and security forces, to exercise utmost restraint and to strictly abide by the Constitution and uphold the rule of law, including the respect for the freedom of speech. Council stresses the duty

and obligation of the defense and security forces to place themselves at the disposal of the democratically elected authorities of their country;

7. Further stresses the importance of a common and unequivocal message and continued coordination of efforts within the international community, in support to ECOWAS endeavours in The Gambia;

8. Expresses its appreciation to the Chairperson of the Union, as well as to the Chairperson of the Commission, for their initiatives and efforts aimed at supporting those of ECOWAS and countries of the region to urgently find a way for a speedy and peaceful transfer of power in The Gambia;

9. Looks forward with keen interest to the outcome of the visit to The Gambia, today, 13 January 2017, by the ECOWAS Mediation, with the participation of the AU and the UN;

10. Agrees to meet, as soon as possible, to assess the post-electoral situation in The Gambia and take appropriate decisions as may be deemed necessary;

11. Decides to remain actively seized of the matter.

SOURCE: African Union. "The 647th Meeting of the AU Peace and Security Council on the Post-election Situation in The Islamic Republic of The Gambia." January 13, 2017. http://www.peaceau.org/en/article/the-647th-meeting-of-the-au-peace-and-security-council-on-the-post-election-situation-in-the-islamic-republic-of-the-gambia.

DOCUMENT

UN Security Council Recognizes Election of Gambian Challenger Barrow

January 19, 2017

The full text of resolution 2337 (2017) reads as follows:

"*The Security Council*,

"*Reaffirming* its strong commitment to the sovereignty, independence, territorial integrity and unity of The Islamic Republic of the Gambia, and recalling the importance of the principles of good-neighbourliness, non-interference and regional cooperation,

"*Recalling* the Statement of its President on 21 December 2016 on Peace consolidation in West Africa and the Press Statement of its Members on 10 December 2016 on the Gambia elections,

"*Recalling* the relevant provisions of Article 23 (4) of the African Union (AU) Charter on Democracy, Elections and Governance and the provisions of the Supplementary Protocol of the Economic Community of West African States (ECOWAS) on Democracy and Good Governance,

"*Congratulating* the Gambian people for the holding of the peaceful and transparent Presidential election on 1 December 2016,

"*Noting* the official results of the elections of 1 December 2016 issued by the Gambian Independent Electoral Commission which proclaimed the election of Mr. Adama Barrow as President, and which the former President of The Islamic Republic of the Gambia, Mr. Yahya Jammeh, himself publicly recognized and accepted on 2 December,

"*Strongly condemning* the statement by former President Jammeh, on 9 December rejecting the December 1 official election results and the takeover of the Independent Electoral Commission by the Gambian Armed Forces on 13 December 2016, and the attempt by the Parliament on 18 January 2017 to extend President Jammeh's term for three months beyond his current mandate,

"*Condemning in the strongest possible terms* the attempts to usurp the will of the people and undermine the integrity of the electoral process in the Gambia,

"*Condemning* the attempt to prevent a peaceful and orderly transfer of power to President Barrow by declaring a state of emergency,

"*Expressing* grave concern at the risk of deterioration of the situation in the Gambia, *recalling* that the Gambian government bears primary responsibility for protecting human rights and protecting the civilian population in the Gambia and *demanding* that all stakeholders and parties act with maximum restraint, refrain from violence and remain calm,

"*Commending* the declaration of the Peace and Security Council of the African Union (AU) at its 647th meeting held on 13 January 2017 that as of 19 January 2017, outgoing President, Yahya Jammeh, will cease to be recognized by the AU as legitimate President of the Republic of the Gambia,

"*Taking note* of the communiqué of the Chairman of the African Union on 10 December 2016 and the joint Communique of The ECOWAS Commission, the African Union Commission and the United Nations Office for West Africa and the Sahel (UNOWAS) on 10 December 2016,

"*Commending* the initiatives of ECOWAS, including the visit of a ECOWAS/UN high level delegation in Banjul on 13 December 2016, led by Her Excellency Ellen Johnson Sirleaf, President of the Republic of Liberia and Chairperson of the ECOWAS authority, aimed at ensuring a peaceful and orderly transition of process in the Gambia, as well as the ECOWAS high level delegation in Banjul on 13 January 2017,

"*Further welcoming* the efforts of His Excellency, Muhammadu Buhari, President and Commander in chief of the Federal Republic of Nigeria as the ECOWAS Mediator in the Gambia and His Excellency, John Dramani Mahama, former President of the Republic of Ghana as the Co-chair,

"*Recognizing* the important mediation role of Mr. Mohammed Ibn Chambas, Special Representative of the Secretary General and Head of the United Nations Office for West Africa and the Sahel (UNOWAS),

"*Commending* and strongly supporting the continued efforts of the African Union and ECOWAS to promote peace, stability and good governance in the Region,

"1.   *Urges* all Gambian parties and stakeholders to respect the will of the people and the outcome of the election which recognized Adama Barrow as President-elect of the Gambia and representative of the freely expressed voice of the Gambian people as proclaimed by the Independent Electoral Commission;

"2.   *Endorses* the decisions of ECOWAS and the African Union to recognize Mr. Adama Barrow as President of the Gambia;

"3.   *Calls upon* the countries in the region and the relevant regional organisation to cooperate with President Barrow in his efforts to realize the transition of power;

"4.   *Welcomes* the decisions on the Gambia of the Fiftieth Ordinary Session of the ECOWAS Authority held in Abuja on 17 December 2016 and the decisions of The Peace and Security Council of the African Union (AU), at its 644th meeting held on 12 December 2016 and its 647th meeting held on 13 January 2017;

"5.   *Welcomes further* the decisions of the Peace and Security Council of the African Union (AU), declaring the inviolable nature of the outcome of the presidential elections held on 1 December 2016 in the Gambia, calling upon former President Yahya Jammeh to keep to the letter and spirit of the speech he delivered on 2 December 2016, in which he welcomed the maturity of democracy in the Gambia and congratulated the President, Adama Barrow, and declaring further that, as of 19 January 2017, outgoing President Yahya Jammeh will cease to be recognized as legitimate President of the Republic of the Gambia;

"6.   *Expresses* its full support to the ECOWAS in its commitment to ensure, by political means first, the respect of the will of the people of the Gambia as expressed in the results of 1st December elections;

"7.   *Requests* former President Jammeh to carry out a peaceful and orderly transition process, and to transfer power to President Adama Barrow by 19 January 2017 in accordance with the Gambian constitution;

"8.   *Emphasizes* the importance that the safety of President Adama Barrow, and that of all Gambian citizens be fully ensured, and noted the decision of ECOWAS Fiftieth Session in this regard;

"9.   *Requests* all stakeholders, within and outside the Gambia, to exercise restraint, respect the rule of law and ensure the peaceful transfer of power;

"10. *Further requests* the Gambian defence and security forces to demonstrate maximum restraint to maintain an atmosphere of calm in the Gambia and stresses their duty and obligation to place themselves at the disposal of the democratically elected authorities;

"11. *Requests* the Secretary General to update the Security Council on the implementation of this resolution within ten (10) days after its adoption;

"12. *Requests* the Secretary-General, including through his Special Representative, to facilitate, as appropriate, political dialogue between the Gambian stakeholders in order to ensure peace in the Gambia and respecting the outcome of the Presidential election as recognized by ECOWAS and African Union, and to provide technical assistance to the ECOWAS mediation where required;

"13. *Decides* to remain seized of the matter."

SOURCE: United Nations Security Council. "Security Endorses Recognition by African Union, Regional States, of Adama Barrow as President-elect of Gambia, Unanimously Adopting 2337 (2017)." Reprinted with the permission of the United Nations. January 19, 2017. https://www.un.org/press/en/2017/sc12688.doc.htm.

ECOWAS, AU, UN *Jointly Respond to Political Situation in The Gambia*

January 21, 2017

1. Following the Decision of the Summit of the ECOWAS Authority taken on 17th December 2016 in Abuja, Nigeria, Mediation efforts, including visits to Banjul, were undertaken by the Chair of the Authority of ECOWAS Heads of State and Government, HE President Ellen Johnson Sirleaf, the Mediator, HE President Muhammadu Buhari and Co-Mediator on The Gambia, HE former President John Dramani Mahama, along with HE President Ernest Bai Koroma to mediate on the political impasse with Sheikh Professor Alhaji Dr. Yahya A. J. J. Jammeh.

2. Following further mediation efforts by HE President Mohamed Ould Abdel Aziz of the Islamic Republic of Mauritania and HE President Alpha Conde of the Republic of Guinea Conakry with HE Sheikh Professor Alhaji Dr. Yahya A. J. J. Jammeh, the former President of the Republic of The Gambia, and in consultation with the Chairperson of the ECOWAS Authority of Heads of State and Government, the Chairperson of the African Union and the Secretary-General of the United Nations, this declaration is made with the purpose of reaching a peaceful resolution to the political situation in The Gambia.

3. ECOWAS, the AU and the UN commend the goodwill and statesmanship of His Excellency former President Jammeh, who with the greater interest of the Gambian people in mind, and in order to preserve the peace, stability and security of The Gambia and maintain its sovereignty, territorial integrity and the dignity of the Gambian people, has decided to facilitate an immediate peaceful and orderly transition process and transfer of power to President Adama Barrow in accordance with the Gambian constitution.

4. In furtherance of this, ECOWAS, the AU and the UN commit to work with the Government of The Gambia to ensure that it assures and ensures the dignity, respect, security and rights of HE former President Jammeh, as a citizen, a party leader and a former Head of State as provided for and guaranteed by the 1997 Gambian Constitution and other Laws of The Gambia.

5. Further, ECOWAS, the AU and the UN commit to work with the Government of The Gambia to ensure that it fully guarantees, assures and ensures the dignity, security, safety and rights of former President Jammeh's immediate family, cabinet members, government officials, Security Officials and party supporters and loyalists.

6. ECOWAS, the AU and the UN commit to work with the Government of The Gambia to ensure that no legislative measures are taken by it that would be inconsistent with the previous two paragraphs.

7. ECOWAS, the AU and the UN urge the Government of The Gambia to take all necessary measures to assure and ensure that there is no intimidation, harassment of former regime members and supporters, in conformity with the Constitution and other laws of The Gambia.

8. ECOWAS, the AU and the UN commit to work with the Government of The Gambia to prevent the seizure of assets and properties lawfully belonging to former President Jammeh or his family and those of his Cabinet members, government officials and Party supporters, as guaranteed under the Constitution and other Laws of The Gambia.

9. In order to avoid any recriminations, ECOWAS, the AU and the UN commit to work with the Government of The Gambia on national reconciliation to cement social, cultural and national cohesion.

10. ECOWAS, the AU and the UN underscore strongly the important role of the Gambian Defence and Security Forces in the maintenance of peace and stability of The Gambia and commit to work with the Government of The Gambia to ensure that it takes all appropriate measures to support the maintenance of the integrity of the [Defence and] Security Forces and guard against all measures that can create division and a breakdown of order.

11. ECOWAS, the AU and the UN will work to ensure that host countries that offer "African hospitality" to former President Jammeh and his family do not become undue targets of harassment, intimidation and all other pressures and sanctions.

12. In order to assist a peaceful and orderly transition and transfer of power and the establishment of a new government, HE former President Jammeh will temporarily leave The Gambia on 21 January 2017, without any prejudice to his rights as a citizen, a former President and a Political Party Leader.

13. ECOWAS, the AU and the UN will work with the Government of The Gambia to ensure that former President Jammeh is at liberty to return to The Gambia at any time of his choosing in accordance with international human rights law and his rights as a citizen of the Gambia and a former head of state.

14. Pursuant to this declaration, ECOWAS will halt any military operations in The Gambia and will continue to pursue peaceful and political resolution of the crisis.

Done this 21st day of January, 2017 in Banjul, The Gambia

SOURCE: United Nations. "Joint Declaration by the Economic Community of West African States, the African Union and the United Nations on the Political Situation of the Islamic Republic of The Gambia." Reprinted with the permission of the United Nations. January 21, 2017. https://www.un.org/sg/en/content/note-correspondents/2017-01-21/note-correspondents-joint-declaration-political-situation.

OTHER HISTORIC DOCUMENTS OF INTEREST

FROM PREVIOUS *HISTORIC DOCUMENTS*

■ Russia and African States Revoke Support for International Criminal Court, *2016*, p. 578

Donald J. Trump Sworn In as 45th President of the United States

JANUARY 20, 2017

On November 8, 2016, businessman and reality television star Donald J. Trump defeated former senator and Secretary of State Hillary Clinton to become the 45th President of the United States. After a nearly two-year primary process that began with more than twenty Democratic and Republican candidates, Trump took 304 electoral votes to Clinton's 227, despite losing the popular vote by nearly 2.9 million. In his inaugural address, the new president briefly outlined some of the priorities for his administration including creating jobs for the middle class, renegotiating foreign trade deals, and curbing immigration, both legal and illegal. Inauguration Day was followed by pro- and anti-Trump gatherings around the country, the most sizable of which was the Women's March on January 21, 2017, that drew an estimated half million individuals to Washington, D.C., to protest the positions of the president.

TRUMP DELIVERS INAUGURAL ADDRESS

Standing next to his wife, Melania, before hundreds of thousands of flag-waving attendees on the National Mall, Trump took the Oath of Office at exactly 12:00 p.m. Trump delivered a speech that differed from his predecessors in both length and tone. During the sixteen-minute address, which echoed the populist rhetoric of the speeches delivered during his campaign, Trump promised to stop the "carnage" in America by giving the power back to the people and putting the country first. "What truly matters is not which party controls our Government, but whether our Government is controlled by the people. January 20, 2017, will be remembered as the day the people became the rulers of this Nation again. The forgotten men and women of our country will be forgotten no longer. Everyone is listening to you now," Trump said.

The new president was highly critical of past U.S. policies that he said had put other nations ahead of America. Trump promised that every decision made by his administration would "be made to benefit American workers and American families." He went on, "America will start winning again, winning like never before. We will bring back our jobs. We will bring back our borders. We will bring back our wealth. And we will bring back our dreams." Throughout the brief speech, the new president promised to improve infrastructure across the country, put people back to work, build new foreign alliances, and unite the world against "radical Islamic terrorism," a phrase his predecessors have shied away from using. But, he said, these foreign concerns would all be dealt with through the lens of putting America, its citizens, and its security first.

Trump ended his speech on a hopeful note, promising, "Your voice, your hopes, and your dreams will define our American destiny. And your courage and goodness and love will forever guide us along the way. Together, we will make America strong again. We will make America wealthy again. We will make America proud again. We will make America safe again. And, yes, together we will make America great again."

Protesters quickly took to the streets following the address. Some clashed with police, who responded with tear gas and stun grenades. Scenes depicted across news outlets showed shattered store windows, burning vehicles, and black clad activists tossing rocks at riot police near Pennsylvania Avenue. Six were injured and dozens arrested during the protests. The anti-Trump groups who protested the inauguration were met by a number of organized efforts aimed at supporting the new president, the largest of which was Bikers for Trump, a collection of motorcycle riders who promised to secure the parade route by blocking Trump protesters. "In the event we are needed, we certainly will form a wall of meat," said Chris Cox, the group's founder, adding, "We'll be shoulder-to-shoulder with our brothers and we'll be toe-to-toe with anyone that is going to break through police barriers . . . we are anticipating a peaceful transition of power."

INAUGURATION CROWDS

The Trump administration came under fire just one day after the inauguration for its claims about the size of the crowd that attended the swearing in. According to then White House Press Secretary Sean Spicer, "That was the largest audience to witness an inauguration, period." Photos released by media outlets and the National Park Service of the National Mall at the time of the event showed a sparse crowd, and one that paled in comparison to the 1.8 million who attended President Barack Obama's first inauguration in 2009. Media estimates put Trump's crowd size somewhere between 250,000 and 600,000, whereas Spicer claimed it was closer to 720,000 and Trump himself said it was approximately 1.5 million.

Spicer criticized the media for "deliberately false reporting" and noted that no one could know the true crowd size because "[n]o one had numbers, because the National Park Service, which controls the National Mall, does not put any out." (Because it can be difficult to estimate crowd size, the National Park Service stopped providing such calculations in 1995 after it faced significant criticism following the Million Man March.) He continued, "Photographs of the inaugural proceedings were intentionally framed in a way, in one particular Tweet, to minimize the enormous support that had gathered on the National Mall." Spicer blamed the inaccurate calculations of crowd size on the coverings used to protect the grass, which highlight areas where there are no attendees, as well as the use of fencing and magnetometers that prevented "hundreds of thousands of people being able to access the Mall as quickly as they had in inaugurations past."

The White House continued to double down on its claim about the president's inauguration crowd size in the days following Spicer's initial press conference. On January 23, the press secretary said, "If you add up the network streaming numbers, Facebook, YouTube, all of the various live streamings that we have information on so far, I don't think there's any question that it was the largest watched inauguration ever." Indeed, Nielsen data indicates that 30.6 million viewers watched across twelve networks, while CNN had 16.9 million livestreams. However, in 2009, Obama drew a television crowd of 37.8 million and 27 million livestreams.

PUBLIC REACTION

Reaction in the mainstream media—a group Trump frequently derided as "totally dishonest"—focused primarily on the dark view the president took of the current state of the country and his isolationist rhetoric. "America First" is a term first used by isolationists before World War II that some believe contributed to the strength of the Nazi regime and its spread across Europe. Throughout his campaign, Trump frequently reaffirmed this platform with promises popular among his supporters such as building a wall along the Mexican border to slow illegal immigration, banning Muslims from traveling to the United States, and withdrawing from or renegotiating international pacts and foreign trade agreements. The media also took issue with some of the characterizations of the United States that the president has repeated throughout campaign appearances. For example, Trump frequently speaks of American cities ravaged by increasing crime. However, while crime increased slightly in 2015, it remains at the lowest levels since the 1970s. And while Trump spoke about American industry being left behind because of trade deals, in fact corporate profits continue to grow in tandem with expanded globalization. Workers are sometimes the losers in these deals, something on which the new president and the media agreed.

In the lead up to the inauguration, there was some expectation among Trump supporters, opponents, and the media alike that he would use his first address as president to begin healing the nation and closing divisions that had been widened during the long primary and election process. Instead, Trump seemed to speak primarily to his supporters, with whom the speech resonated most. House Majority Leader Kevin McCarthy, R-Calif., said of the speech that America can now "look to the future with confidence that President Trump will lead America to greatness again." Wisconsin Gov. Scott Walker, who was defeated by Trump in the Republican primary, congratulated the president after his speech, noting that he was confident the president would "make America great again."

A Gallup poll conducted shortly after Trump's address found that Americans had a less favorable reaction to the Trump speech than that given at Obama's first inauguration. Nearly 40 percent of those polled said they were more hopeful about the next four years, while 30 percent reported being less hopeful. These figures are similar to the polls taken after former president George W. Bush's and Obama's second inaugurations. As expected, the favorability ratings were split largely along party lines. Of those who identified as Republican or Republican-leaning independents, 78 percent reported being more hopeful about the next four years, while 56 percent of Democrats and Democratic-leaning independents were less hopeful. Another 36 percent said the speech did not make a difference in their opinion.

Worldwide, Trump's inauguration was met with mixed response. In many Western cities, including London and Mexico City, protesters gathered at the U.S. embassies to speak out against Trump and his isolationist policies. So, too, did their leaders voice concern. "We can't sit around & hope for US support & cooperation," tweeted Belgium's Prime Minister Guy Verhofstadt, who characterized the speech as "hostile." But in Israel and Russia, and among anti-European Union nationalists, the dawn of a new American presidency was celebrated. "Congrats to my friend President Trump. Look fwd to working closely with you to make the alliance between Israel&USA stronger than ever," tweeted Israeli Prime Minister Benjamin Netanyahu. Similarly, Nigel Farage, a key backer of the effort for Britain to leave the European Union, said, "The old order wasn't working. I think it's going to be great." In Russia, the spokesperson for the Foreign Ministry wrote on Facebook that "President Obama can't say anything anymore about Russia," while Alexei Pushkov, a Russian senator, said a meeting between Trump and President Vladimir Putin would "be the most important event in world politics" and that cooperation between the two nations would be instrumental to defeating the Islamic State of Iraq and the Levant (ISIL).

WOMEN'S MARCH

In the early morning of November 9, Americans learned that Trump would be victorious over Clinton, who for many months held a significant lead in the polls and who many expected would become the first female president of the United States. Some, including Teresa Shook, Evvie Harmon, and Fontaine Pearson, three private citizens from Hawaii, South Carolina, and Tennessee, respectively, responded to the outcome by taking action to ensure that their voices would still be heard in a Trump presidency and that issues that they were passionate about, particularly women's rights, would remain at the forefront of public policy discussions. Through a Facebook event, Shook, Harmon, and Pearson invited their friends to join them to march on Washington, D.C., following Trump's inauguration. The three would eventually band together to develop what would become The Women's March on Washington, an event, according to the organizers, intended to "send a bold message to our new administration on their first day in office, and to the world that women's rights are human rights."

The event quickly grew in popularity, and on January 21, 2017, an estimated 500,000 men, women, and children gathered in Washington, D.C., in support of the march. Although organizers said the purpose of the march was not to directly oppose the election of President Trump, many of the group's key platforms appeared in direct conflict with Trump's past statements, and it was characterized by some media outlets as an anti-Trump event. During the course of the five-hour event, those gathered marched along the National Mall to the Ellipse near the White House, where they heard from speakers ranging from celebrated feminist Gloria Steinem to Planned Parenthood President Cecile Richards, actress Ashley Judd, and Sen. Tammy Duckworth, D-Ill. Steinem called the event "the upside of the downside. This is an outpouring of energy and true democracy like I have never seen in my very long life," and called on the group to keep pushing forward "and decide what we're going to do tomorrow, and tomorrow and tomorrow . . . we're never turning back." Scarlett Johansson, another actress who spoke at the event, noted that she did not vote for Trump but that she wants to be able to support him. "But first," she said, "I ask that you support me. Support my sister. Support my mother. Support my best friend and all of our girlfriends."

The Women's March on Washington movement gained traction across the United States and around the world, with "sister marches" hosted on all seven continents and in all fifty states. It was estimated that more than 2.5 million people took part in 673 marches around the world on January 21. In some cities, the crowds were so large that the march itself had to be called off and the event turned into a stationary rally. Clinton, who did not join a march in person, showed her support for the movement on Twitter, saying, "Thanks for standing, speaking & marching for our values @womensmarch. Important as ever. I truly believe we're always Stronger Together." President Trump tweeted twice about the march. The first reaction, early on the morning of January 22, read "Watched protests yesterday but was under the impression that we just had an election! Why didn't these people vote? Celebs hurt cause badly." Two hours later, the president tweeted a more conciliatory message: "Peaceful protests are a hallmark of our democracy. Even if I don't always agree, I recognize the rights of people to express their views."

After its inaugural event, the organizers of the march issued one call to action every ten days for the first 100 days of the Trump presidency. Activities ranged from writing postcards to senators, organizing meetings to talk about how to move forward, and the March 8 Day Without a Woman, where supporters were encouraged to take the day off from paid and unpaid work, avoid shopping, and wear red. Following the first 100 days, the group has continued to issue action items for its members, speak out about legislation in Congress, and in October 2017 held a convention in Detroit to strategize and discuss preparation for the 2018 midterm elections.

TRUMP CABINET

Shortly before taking office, President Trump began announcing the names of those he intended to appoint to cabinet-level positions. As anticipated, he appointed primarily conservative individuals, many of who had more experience in the private than public sector. According to *The Washington Post*, the cabinet would be the wealthiest in American history and would include at least two billionaires. What was notable throughout 2017 was the lack of speed at which Trump appointed individuals to upper-level posts in a number of departments. By the close of the year, many posts remained unfilled, specifically at the Department of State, which some in the administration feared would cripple the president's agenda by leaving department leadership spread too thin.

Appointments to key positions included former ExxonMobil CEO Rex Tillerson as Secretary of State, Alabama Sen. Jeff Sessions as Attorney General, Ret. Gen. James Mattis as Secretary of Defense, and Steve Mnuchin, a former CEO of OneWest Bank, as Treasury Secretary. Two of Trump's opponents in the Republican presidential primary—Ben Carson and Rick Perry—were appointed and confirmed as Secretary of Housing and Urban Development and Secretary of Energy, respectively. One of Trump's more controversial nominees was Betsy DeVos as Secretary of Education. DeVos was roundly criticized during her confirmation hearings as having a general lack of knowledge about the public education system in America, never having attended a public school herself. Support for DeVos was so divided that Vice President Mike Pence had to break a tie in the Senate to secure her nomination.

There were other missteps for both Cabinet-level posts and positions within the White House. For example, Michael Flynn, who was appointed National Security Advisor, was in the position for just twenty-four days before resigning when it became known that he had misled Pence about the circumstances of his communications with the Russian ambassador. Flynn had informed the vice president that the conversations were inconsequential, when in fact Flynn had spoken with the ambassador about sanctions put in place by outgoing President Barack Obama against Russia. Flynn would be replaced by Lt. Gen. H. R. McMaster, and would become a key focus of the investigation into the Trump campaign's potential involvement with the Russian government prior to the 2016 election. Within the White House, Trump's beleaguered chief of staff and former head of the RNC, Reince Priebus, resigned in July and was replaced by then-Homeland Security Secretary John Kelly. Shortly thereafter, the president's chief strategist, Steve Bannon, resigned. Bannon proved to be a significantly controversial figure in the Trump White House due to his overtly nationalist plans for the administration. His departure was reportedly due to a disagreement with Kelly over the direction of the White House. Bannon returned to far right *Brietbart News* as executive chairman, where he promised to use his platform to uphold Trump's ideals.

The president also went through multiple press secretaries and communications directors. Spicer was the first press secretary and was replaced in late July by Sarah Huckabee Sanders, the daughter of former Arkansas governor Mike Huckabee. Spicer had temporarily acted as communications director for the White House and was replaced by Anthony Scaramucci, a former Goldman Sachs investment banker, who lasted ten days in the position before being replaced by Hope Hicks after an expletive-ridden interview with *The New Yorker* that referred to key members of the Trump administration in derogatory fashion.

—Heather Kerrigan

Following is the text of the address delivered by Donald Trump on January 20, 2017, upon his inauguration as President of the United States.

President Trump Delivers Remarks upon His Inauguration

January 20, 2017

Chief Justice Roberts, President Carter, President Clinton, President Bush, President Obama, fellow Americans, and people of the world: Thank you.

We, the citizens of America, are now joined in a great national effort to rebuild our country and restore its promise for all of our people. Together, we will determine the course of America and the world for many, many years to come. We will face challenges, we will confront hardships, but we will get the job done.

Every 4 years, we gather on these steps to carry out the orderly and peaceful transfer of power, and we are grateful to President Obama and First Lady Michelle Obama for their gracious aid throughout this transition. They have been magnificent. Thank you.

Today's ceremony, however, has very special meaning. Because today we are not merely transferring power from one administration to another or from one party to another, but we are transferring power from Washington, DC, and giving it back to you, the people.

For too long, a small group in our Nation's Capital has reaped the rewards of Government while the people have borne the cost. Washington flourished, but the people did not share in its wealth. Politicians prospered, but the jobs left, and the factories closed. The establishment protected itself, but not the citizens of our country. Their victories have not been your victories; their triumphs have not been your triumphs; and while they celebrated in our Nation's Capital, there was little to celebrate for struggling families all across our land.

That all changes, starting right here and right now, because this moment is your moment: It belongs to you. It belongs to everyone gathered here today and everyone watching all across America. This is your day. This is your celebration. And this, the United States of America, is your country.

What truly matters is not which party controls our Government, but whether our Government is controlled by the people. January 20, 2017, will be remembered as the day the people became the rulers of this Nation again. The forgotten men and women of our country will be forgotten no longer. Everyone is listening to you now.

You came by the tens of millions to become part of a historic movement the likes of which the world has never seen before. At the center of this movement is a crucial conviction: that a nation exists to serve its citizens. Americans want great schools for their children, safe neighborhoods for their families, and good jobs for themselves. These are just and reasonable demands of righteous people and a righteous public.

But for too many of our citizens, a different reality exists: Mothers and children trapped in poverty in our inner cities; rusted-out factories scattered like tombstones across the landscape of our Nation; an education system, flush with cash, but which leaves our young and beautiful students deprived of all knowledge; and the crime and the gangs and the drugs that have stolen too many lives and robbed our country of so much unrealized potential.

This American carnage stops right here and stops right now. We are one Nation, and their pain is our pain, their dreams are our dreams, and their success will be our success. We share one heart, one home, and one glorious destiny.

The oath of office I take today is an oath of allegiance to all Americans.

For many decades, we've enriched foreign industry at the expense of American industry, subsidized the armies of other countries while allowing for the very sad depletion of our military. We've defended other nations' borders while refusing to defend our own and spent trillions and trillions of dollars overseas while America's infrastructure has fallen into disrepair and decay. We've made other countries rich while the wealth, strength, and confidence of our country has dissipated over the horizon.

One by one, the factories shuttered and left our shores, with not even a thought about the millions and millions of American workers that were left behind. The wealth of our middle class has been ripped from their homes and then redistributed all across the world.

But that is the past. And now we are looking only to the future.

We, assembled here today, are issuing a new decree to be heard in every city, in every foreign capital, and in every hall of power. From this day forward, a new vision will govern our land. From this day forward, it's going to be only America first. America first.

Every decision on trade, on taxes, on immigration, on foreign affairs, will be made to benefit American workers and American families.

We must protect our borders from the ravages of other countries making our products, stealing our companies, and destroying our jobs. Protection will lead to great prosperity and strength. I will fight for you with every breath in my body, and I will never, ever let you down.

America will start winning again, winning like never before. We will bring back our jobs. We will bring back our borders. We will bring back our wealth. And we will bring back our dreams.

We will build new roads and highways and bridges and airports and tunnels and railways all across our wonderful Nation.

We will get our people off of welfare and back to work, rebuilding our country with American hands and American labor. We will follow two simple rules: Buy American and hire American.

We will seek friendship and good will with the nations of the world, but we do so with the understanding that it is the right of all nations to put their own interests first. We do not seek to impose our way of life on anyone, but rather to let it shine as an example—we will shine—for everyone to follow.

We will reinforce old alliances and form new ones and unite the civilized world against radical Islamic terrorism, which we will eradicate completely from the face of the Earth.

At the bedrock of our politics will be a total allegiance to the United States of America, and through our loyalty to our country, we will rediscover our loyalty to each other. When you open your heart to patriotism, there is no room for prejudice. The Bible tells us, "How good and pleasant it is when God's people live together in unity." We must speak our minds openly, debate our disagreements honestly, but always pursue solidarity. When America is united, America is totally unstoppable. There should be no fear: We are protected, and we will always be protected. We will be protected by the great men and women of our military and law enforcement, and most importantly, we will be protected by God.

Finally, we must think big and dream even bigger. In America, we understand that a nation is only living as long as it is striving.

We will no longer accept politicians who are all talk and no action, constantly complaining, but never doing anything about it. The time for empty talk is over. Now arrives the hour of action.

Do not allow anyone to tell you that it cannot be done. No challenge can match the heart and fight and spirit of America. We will not fail. Our country will thrive and prosper again.

We stand at the birth of a new millennium, ready to unlock the mysteries of space, to free the Earth from the miseries of disease, and to harness the energies, industries, and technologies of tomorrow. A new national pride will stir our souls, lift our sights, and heal our divisions.

It's time to remember that old wisdom our soldiers will never forget: that whether we are Black or Brown or White, we all bleed the same red blood of patriots, we all enjoy the same glorious freedoms, and we all salute the same great American flag.

And whether a child is born in the urban sprawl of Detroit or the windswept plains of Nebraska, they look up at the same night sky, they fill their heart with the same dreams, and they are infused with the breath of life by the same almighty Creator.

So to all Americans in every city near and far, small and large, from mountain to mountain, from ocean to ocean, hear these words: You will never be ignored again. Your voice, your hopes, and your dreams will define our American destiny. And your courage and goodness and love will forever guide us along the way.

Together, we will make America strong again. We will make America wealthy again. We will make America proud again. We will make America safe again.

And, yes, together, we will make America great again. Thank you. God bless you, and God bless America. Thank you. God bless America.

SOURCE: Executive Office of the President. "Inaugural Address." January 20, 2017. *Compilation of Presidential Documents* 2017, no. 00058 (January 20, 2017). https://www.gpo.gov/fdsys/pkg/DCPD-201700058/pdf/DCPD-201700058.pdf.

OTHER HISTORIC DOCUMENTS OF INTEREST

FROM THIS VOLUME

FROM PREVIOUS *HISTORIC DOCUMENTS*

President Trump Issues Immigration Orders

JANUARY 25 AND 27, MARCH 6, APRIL 25, JUNE 12
AND 26, SEPTEMBER 24, AND DECEMBER 4, 2017

Donald Trump launched his presidential campaign in 2016 with a speech that described Mexican immigrants: "They're bringing drugs. They're bringing crime. They're rapists. And some, I assume, are good people." His subsequent campaign promises included mass deportations of undocumented immigrants and the building of "a great wall" along the southern border with Mexico. He consistently warned at rallies and during media interviews of crimes committed by undocumented immigrants, threatened to withhold all federal funds from so-called "sanctuary cities" that declined to help enforce federal immigration law, and promised "a total and complete shutdown of Muslims entering the United States."

Just days after his inauguration, President Trump, seeking to move quickly to fulfill these campaign promises, signed multiple executive orders addressing immigration issues, including orders relating to the building of a wall on the Mexican border, cutting off federal funds to sanctuary cities, and immediately suspending entry into the United States for travelers from seven predominantly Muslim countries. While progress on the border wall would require the president to convince Congress (or Mexico) to provide funding, and the sanctuary order was little more than a vague statement of policy, the travel ban went into effect immediately causing widespread chaos and triggering massive litigation in courts across the country. By the end of the year, the president's original executive order had resulted in three differing iterations of the ban itself, dozens of district court challenges, multiple nationwide injunctions, and several federal appellate court opinions. The Supreme Court weighed in to modify the injunctions preventing the ban from taking effect and was days away from hearing argument on the second version of the law in October when the administration released a third version of the ban, rendering the previous legal issues moot and restarting the cycle of litigation.

TRAVEL BAN EXECUTIVE ORDERS

First Travel Ban

Late in the day, on Friday, January 27, 2017, President Trump, in a public ceremony at the Pentagon, signed Executive Order Number 13739, titled "Protecting the Nation From Foreign Terrorist Entry Into the United States." At its core, the order was a ninety-day complete ban on entry into the United States for anyone from the seven countries the administration identified as presenting heightened terrorism risks, namely Iran, Iraq, Libya, Somalia, Sudan, Syria, and Yemen. This was a historic and unprecedented use of presidential authority because, according to the Congressional Research Report, no president before Trump has ever sought to ban entry based on national citizenship. During that ninety-day period, executive officials were to review the adequacy of the current immigration rules. The order also drastically reduced the total number of refugees to be admitted during the 2017 fiscal year and suspended the entry of all refugees under the U.S. Refugee Admissions Program for 120 days with new instructions that when the refugee program is resumed, the Secretary of State is to prioritize the claims of religious minorities from the listed countries, in effect giving preference to Christians. The order indefinitely suspended all Syrian refugees, declaring their entry to be detrimental to national interest. The order took effect immediately. News outlets reported that it had not been circulated to the State Department, the Defense Department, Homeland Security, or the Justice Department before being announced. The agency most responsible for its enforcement, Customs and Border Protection (CBP), were, according to officials, only briefed by telephone as it was being signed.

The immediate result of this travel ban was chaos and confusion at airports both in the United States and around the world. Many travelers left their countries with valid paperwork, only to arrive and discover it had been invalidated while they were in the air. Some who had boarded flights for the United States were removed before takeoff and those who arrived were subject to lengthy detentions or put back on flights leaving the United States. Further contributing to the confusion were conflicting interpretations given by officials about whether the new rule barred the return of legal permanent residents of the United States with valid green cards.

Word of what was happening at the airports spread quickly and large crowds of protesters poured into international airports around the country. Immigration lawyers flooded the airports as well, offering services and advice to those who had been detained. The first lawsuits were filed on Saturday morning. A federal judge in Brooklyn heard the case of Hameed Khalid Darweesh, traveling on a special immigrant visa that had been granted in recognition of his decade of vital interpretation services for U.S. forces in Iraq, and entered a nationwide order blocking the deportation of all people who had been detained in U.S. airports due to the executive order. Minutes later, another ruling, this time by a judge in Alexandria, Virginia, ordered the release of green card holders detained at Dulles Airport.

A week later, Judge James Robart of the United States District Court for the Western District of Washington, issued the first nationwide injunction, barring the federal government from enforcing key provisions of the order. This led the president to tweet that "the opinion of this so-called judge, which essentially takes law-enforcement away from our country, is ridiculous and will be overturned!" The government filed an emergency motion with the Ninth Circuit Court of Appeals to stay this injunction and allow the travel ban to operate pending the appeal. The Ninth Circuit, in a unanimous decision, declined to do so, expressing dismay at the government's position "that the President's decisions about immigration policy, particularly when motivated by national-security concerns, are *unreviewable*, even if those actions potentially contravene constitutional rights and protections." Not only is there no precedent to support this, the court wrote, but also it "runs contrary to the fundamental structure of our constitutional democracy." The president responded to this rejection in capital letters on Twitter, "SEE YOU IN COURT, THE SECURITY OF OUR NATION IS AT STAKE!" The government, however, did not file an appeal, opting instead to revoke the travel ban, rendering moot the legal cases against it, and then issue a new, revised executive order.

Second Travel Ban

President Trump's second travel ban order came on March 6, replacing the one that had been repeatedly rejected by the courts. Drafted over several weeks and with input from departments of State, Justice, and Homeland Security, it differed from the first in several ways and was designed to avoid further legal challenge and protests. First, it blocked citizens of six, rather than seven, predominately Muslim countries from entering the country. According to the administration, Defense Secretary James Mattis, Secretary of State Rex Tillerson, and national security adviser H. R. McMaster requested dropping Iraq from the list to foster its ongoing cooperation in the conflict with the Islamic State of Iraq and the Levant (ISIL). The new version of the order explicitly exempted permanent residents (green card holders) and current visa holders from the ban. It also eliminated language about persecuted religious minorities in the countries originally listed, language that was cited as evidence of a bias in favor of Christian over Muslim citizens. Finally, the effective start date of the order was set ten days away, to avoid the turmoil at the airports that followed the first order.

In most respects, the orders were very similar. Both suspended entry of nationals from the now six countries for ninety days to prevent dangerous individuals from entering while the government worked to establish "adequate standards . . . to prevent infiltration by foreign terrorists." The new order still suspended the entry of refugees from Syria, but, while the first ban did so indefinitely, this one included a 120-day suspension. Both bans decreased the number of refugees admitted to the United States each year from 110,000 to 50,000. Just like the first executive order, this new travel ban was challenged immediately in court; federal district courts in Maryland and Hawaii granted nationwide injunctions barring the Trump administration from implementing the new order before it took effect. The government appealed both to their respective circuits.

On May 25, 2017, the United States Court of Appeals for the Fourth Circuit, upholding the Maryland court, ruled that the travel order violated the Establishment Clause of the Constitution, which, among other things, prohibits the government from favoring one religion over another. The government had argued that the courts lack the authority to second-guess the president on matters of national security and immigration, but Chief Judge Roger Gregory, writing for the court, denied that this had ever been true. Courts have a duty to intervene, he wrote, "where constitutional rights, values, and principles are at stake." The opinion relied on extensive campaign statements advocating a "Muslim ban" to find that the stated rationale for the order, national security, was a pretext for its true purpose, discrimination against Muslims. Trump's executive order, the opinion found, "speaks with vague words of national security, but in context drips with religious intolerance, animus, and discrimination."

In June, the United States Court of Appeals for the Ninth Circuit unanimously upheld the Hawaii district court's injunction. This time the court did not rely on the Establishment Clause and so avoided the need to find the order's true purpose through campaign statements and tweets. Instead, the court based its ruling on the Immigration and Nationality Act, holding that, by seeking to suspend the U.S. refugee program and bar people from six majority-Muslim nations from entering the United States, Trump had "exceeded the scope of authority delegated to him by Congress." The order, the court wrote, "does not offer a sufficient justification to suspend the entry of more than 180 million people on the basis of nationality. National security is not a 'talismanic incantation' that, once invoked, can support any and all exercise of executive power."

The Supreme Court Agrees to Hear the Appeals

The Trump administration appealed both rulings to the Supreme Court and asked it to lift the injunctions to allow the provisions of the executive order to take effect pending a final ruling in the case, arguing that doing so was necessary to prevent potentially dangerous individuals from entering the United States while a review of the current policies is underway.

The Court set a date in October for oral argument and, in the meantime, issued an unsigned opinion that crafted a compromise on the issue of the preliminary injunctions. The opinion allowed the government to start implementing the travel ban, but with an exception. The Court prohibited the government from applying the ban to foreign nationals who have a "credible claim of a bona fide relationship with a person or entity in the United States." Individuals from the banned countries or those seeking admission as refugees may enter if they have a "close familial relationship," or if the relationship is "formal, documented, and formed in the ordinary course" with a U.S. entity, such as a student who has been admitted to an American university. In the face of the Court's use of vague language, the government issued guidelines to define who has a "close" relationship with people or institutions in the United States, under which parents, spouses, children, and siblings are "close" relatives and grandparents, grandchildren, nieces, nephews, aunts, and uncles are not.

Third Travel Ban

On September 24, 2017, the expiration day of the second travel ban's temporary ninety-day freeze on travel to the United States by citizens of six countries, President Trump signed a proclamation to replace that ban with a new one set to go into effect on October 18. The previous two orders were temporary, but this one imposed an indefinite ban on travel to the United States from five of the six countries listed in the previous ban (Iran, Libya, Somalia, Syria, and Yemen, dropping Sudan). It also imposed new restrictions on citizens of three more countries: Chad, North Korea, and certain government officials from Venezuela. People who currently hold valid visas would not lose them under this new order, and it allowed for, but did not guarantee, case-by-case waivers for those who meet certain criteria such as previous experience or "significant contacts" in the United States.

The Supreme Court responded by taking the travel ban cases off its October argument calendar, and then, declaring the issues moot, it dismissed the appeal, effectively resetting litigation to the starting line. Immediately, multiple challengers returned to district courts bringing cases against the newest iteration of the travel ban. Just the day before it was set to go into effect, two district courts issued nationwide orders halting the third travel ban. In the first order, arising out of a case in Hawaii, on October 17, Judge Derrick K. Watson found it likely that the government had violated federal immigration statutes. Writing that the third travel ban "suffers from precisely the same maladies as its predecessor," he issued a nationwide order blocking the Trump administration from banning almost all travel from Chad, Iran, Libya, Somalia, Syria, and Yemen. On October 18, Maryland federal court Judge Theodore Chuang relied on both statutory and constitutional arguments to block the nationwide implementation of a law he described as "an unprecedented eight-country travel ban," but only as it applied to travelers with a "bona fide" tie to a person or business in the United States, the standard used by the Supreme Court in regard to the second version of the ban. Judge Chuang's opinion relied on presidential tweets and statements to undercut the government's arguments that the law was motivated by security concerns and to show that this version of the ban was unconstitutionally designed to target Muslims. In addition to Hawaii and Maryland, other challenges to the ban were filed in courts in Seattle and Washington, D.C.

Attorney General Jeff Sessions, speaking before the Senate Judiciary Committee on October 18, promised that the Justice Department would appeal both the decisions, and, describing the order as both lawful and necessary, he expressed confidence that they would ultimately prevail. Becca Heller, director of the International Refugee Assistance Project and one of the plaintiffs in the Maryland case, said, "We've cleared our schedules." On November 13, the Court of Appeals for the Ninth Circuit issued a two-paragraph ruling on the government's challenge to the Hawaii decision that blocked nationwide implementation of the president's September proclamation. The ruling partially upheld the lower court's ruling, agreeing that those with a "bona fide relationship" to a person or institution within the United States could be allowed entry. However, the court overturned a portion of the lower court's ruling that would have allowed entry into the United States from Chad, Iran, Libya, Somalia, Syria, and Yemen for those individuals without such a relationship, meaning the government could deny entry to those individuals. The Justice Department announced that it would begin enforcing the travel ban in line with the Ninth Circuit Court's ruling.

On December 4, the Supreme Court responded to a request from the Trump administration and granted an emergency stay of the Fourth and Ninth Circuit Courts' rulings that would allow the travel ban to fully go into effect while the remaining cases against the September 24 proclamation work their way through the court system. Justices Ruth Bader Ginsburg and Sonia Sotomayor were the only dissenters to both orders. While the ban was allowed to go into effect, there was no guarantee that it would not later be overturned.

SANCTUARY CITY EXECUTIVE ORDER

On January 25, President Trump signed Executive Order 13768, titled "Enhancing Public Safety in the Interior of the United States," which, among other things, instructs the Attorney General and the Secretary of Homeland Security to ensure that sanctuary jurisdictions, that is "jurisdictions that willfully refuse to comply" with applicable federal immigration laws, "are not eligible to receive Federal grants." Two California counties and the City of San Francisco brought a federal lawsuit challenging this sweeping order and arguing that, although they had not yet lost any funding, the budget uncertainty stemming from a potential loss of $1.7 billion in federal grants gave them standing to sue. Judge William H. Orrick agreed and on April 25 granted a nationwide injunction halting the enforcement of the president's order. The Constitution, his opinion explained, gives spending authority to Congress but not the president. Therefore, when the president places new conditions on federal funds, as he did with this order, it violates separation of powers. Judge Orrick also found that the order violated the Tenth Amendment, which requires that any conditions put on federal funds that go to the states must bear some relation to the funds at issue and must not be coercive. "Federal funding that bears no meaningful relationship to immigration enforcement cannot be threatened merely because a jurisdiction chooses an immigration enforcement strategy of which the President disapproves," he ruled. Judge Orrick then reaffirmed his nationwide injunction on July 20, and on November 20 permanently blocked implementation of the president's order. Similar lawsuits were filed in other cities.

On July 26, Attorney General Sessions escalated his conflict with sanctuary cities by announcing new conditions on states and localities applying for funds from the millions of dollars available in federal public safety grants. Localities must certify that they are not sanctuary cities, he announced, agree to allow federal immigration officers access to their local detention facilities, and provide forty-eight hours' notice before they release an undocumented immigrant wanted by federal authorities. Sanctuary cities generally will not continue to hold someone for immigration agents when a warrant is not in place. Sessions stated that "these long overdue requirements will help us take down MS-13 and other violent transnational gangs and make our cities safer." Mayors of major cities expressed hostility to the announcement, pointing out that it would undermine public safety because cities are safer when immigrants feel they can come forward to report a crime or serve as a witness without fear of deportation. Chicago Mayor Rahm Emanuel responded that his city will not "be blackmailed" into changing its values as a welcoming city, and he filed a lawsuit on August 7 seeking to remove the immigration-related conditions for federal grants. Within weeks the cities of Philadelphia and San Francisco, and the state of California followed suit, arguing that the rule both undermines public safety and violates the Constitution. On September 15, the federal judge hearing the case in Chicago, Judge Harry Leinenweber, held that making public safety grants contingent on cooperation with federal immigration authorities likely exceeded the Attorney General's constitutional authority, and he granted a nationwide injunction blocking its application.

BORDER WALL EXECUTIVE ORDER

On January 25, 2017, President Trump signed an executive order, "Border Security and Immigration Enforcement Improvements," directing the Department of Homeland Security (DHS) to take immediate steps to "plan, design, and construct a physical wall along the southern border" to "prevent further illegal immigration." Although he promised on the campaign trail that Mexico would pay for this wall, President Trump asked Congress for an initial $1.6 billion in startup funding to build sixty miles of new wall in Texas and fourteen miles near San Diego. In July, the House approved the funding as part of a broad national security spending bill that primarily funded the departments of Defense and Veterans Affairs. The Senate is unlikely to take up the measure before December when a temporary spending bill to keep the government running will expire. Passing funding measures for the wall will be challenging, particularly because apprehensions of illegal crossers at the border have reached their lowest level in decades. Three Republican senators from border states have publicly opposed the bill, including Will Hurd of Texas who voted against including the border wall funding into the recent appropriations package. Expressing a preference for "a border security solution based on improved technology and manpower," Senator Hurd stated, "[b]uilding a physical wall from sea to shining sea is the most expensive and least effective way to secure the border."

In the meantime, CBP solicited requests for proposals and selected six companies to build eight prototypes for the border wall. They would be built near San Diego, each thirty feet long and costing up to $500,000. The schedule required that they be completed in late October 2017, after which CBP plans to test their ability to withstand assault from sledge-hammers, pickaxes, torches, and chisels. Whether any of the prototypes become part of Trump's "big, beautiful" wall stretching the 1,950-mile southern border will, however, depend on action from Congress, which is unlikely to occur within a year of being mandated by the presidential executive order.

—Melissa Feinberg

Following is the text of four executive orders and a proclamation issued by President Donald Trump on January 25, January 27, March 6, and September 24, regarding the building of a wall along the U.S.–Mexico border, prohibiting federal funding for sanctuary cities, and banning travelers from certain Muslim-majority nations from entering the United States; the April 25, 2017, District Court injunction against the sanctuary city order; a June 12, 2017, ruling by the Ninth Circuit Court of Appeals on Trump's January 27 travel ban; the Supreme Court's June 26, 2017, initial ruling on the president's travel ban; and the text of two December 4, 2017, Supreme Court orders allowing the September 24 travel ban proclamation to go fully into effect.

President Trump Issues Executive Order on a U.S.–Mexico Border Wall

January 25, 2017

By the authority vested in me as President by the Constitution and the laws of the United States of America, including the Immigration and Nationality Act (8 U.S.C. 1101 et seq.) (INA), the Secure Fence Act of 2006 (Public Law 109–367) (Secure Fence Act), and the Illegal Immigration Reform and Immigrant Responsibility Act of 1996 (Public Law 104–208 Div. C) (IIRIRA), and in order to ensure the safety and territorial integrity of the United States as well as to ensure that the Nation's immigration laws are faithfully executed, I hereby order as follows:

Section 1. Purpose. Border security is critically important to the national security of the United States. Aliens who illegally enter the United States without inspection or admission present a significant threat to national security and public safety. Such aliens have not been identified or inspected by Federal immigration officers to determine their admissibility to the United States. The recent surge of illegal immigration at the southern border with Mexico has placed a significant strain on Federal resources and overwhelmed agencies charged with border security and immigration enforcement, as well as the local communities into which many of the aliens are placed.

Transnational criminal organizations operate sophisticated drug- and human-trafficking networks and smuggling operations on both sides of the southern border, contributing to a significant increase in violent crime and United States deaths from dangerous drugs. Among those who illegally enter are those who seek to harm Americans through acts of terror or criminal conduct. Continued illegal immigration presents a clear and present danger to the interests of the United States.

Federal immigration law both imposes the responsibility and provides the means for the Federal Government, in cooperation with border States, to secure the Nation's southern border. Although Federal immigration law provides a robust framework for Federal-State partnership in enforcing our immigration laws—and the Congress has authorized and provided appropriations to secure our borders—the Federal Government has failed to discharge this basic sovereign responsibility. The purpose of this order is to direct executive departments and agencies (agencies) to deploy all lawful means to secure the Nation's southern border, to prevent further illegal immigration into the United States, and to repatriate illegal aliens swiftly, consistently, and humanely.

Sec. 2. Policy. It is the policy of the executive branch to:

(a) secure the southern border of the United States through the immediate construction of a physical wall on the southern border, monitored and supported by adequate personnel so as to prevent illegal immigration, drug and human trafficking, and acts of terrorism;

(b) detain individuals apprehended on suspicion of violating Federal or State law, including Federal immigration law, pending further proceedings regarding those violations;

(c) expedite determinations of apprehended individuals' claims of eligibility to remain in the United States;

(d) remove promptly those individuals whose legal claims to remain in the United States have been lawfully rejected, after any appropriate civil or criminal sanctions have been imposed; and

(e) cooperate fully with States and local law enforcement in enacting Federal-State partnerships to enforce Federal immigration priorities, as well as State monitoring and detention programs that are consistent with Federal law and do not undermine Federal immigration priorities.

Sec. 3. Definitions. (a) "Asylum officer" has the meaning given the term in section 235(b)(1)(E) of the INA (8 U.S.C. 1225(b)(1)).

(b) "Southern border" shall mean the contiguous land border between the United States and Mexico, including all points of entry.

(c) "Border States" shall mean the States of the United States immediately adjacent to the contiguous land border between the United States and Mexico.

(d) Except as otherwise noted, "the Secretary" shall refer to the Secretary of Homeland Security.

(e) "Wall" shall mean a contiguous, physical wall or other similarly secure, contiguous, and impassable physical barrier.

(f) "Executive department" shall have the meaning given in section 101 of title 5, United States Code.

(g) "Regulations" shall mean any and all Federal rules, regulations, and directives lawfully promulgated by agencies.

(h) "Operational control" shall mean the prevention of all unlawful entries into the United States, including entries by terrorists, other unlawful aliens, instruments of terrorism, narcotics, and other contraband.

Sec. 4. Physical Security of the Southern Border of the United States. The Secretary shall immediately take the following steps to obtain complete operational control, as determined by the Secretary, of the southern border:

(a) In accordance with existing law, including the Secure Fence Act and IIRIRA, take all appropriate steps to immediately plan, design, and construct a physical wall along the southern border, using appropriate materials and technology to most effectively achieve complete operational control of the southern border;

(b) Identify and, to the extent permitted by law, allocate all sources of Federal funds for the planning, designing, and constructing of a physical wall along the southern border;

(c) Project and develop long-term funding requirements for the wall, including preparing Congressional budget requests for the current and upcoming fiscal years; and

(d) Produce a comprehensive study of the security of the southern border, to be completed within 180 days of this order, that shall include the current state of southern border security, all geophysical and topographical aspects of the southern border, the availability of Federal and State resources necessary to achieve complete operational control of the southern border, and a strategy to obtain and maintain complete operational control of the southern border.

Sec. 5. Detention Facilities. (a) The Secretary shall take all appropriate action and allocate all legally available resources to immediately construct, operate, control, or establish contracts to construct, operate, or control facilities to detain aliens at or near the land border with Mexico.

(b) The Secretary shall take all appropriate action and allocate all legally available resources to immediately assign asylum officers to immigration detention facilities for the purpose of accepting asylum referrals and conducting credible fear determinations pursuant to section 235(b)(1) of the INA (8 U.S.C. 1225(b)(1)) and applicable regulations and reasonable fear determinations pursuant to applicable regulations.

(c) The Attorney General shall take all appropriate action and allocate all legally available resources to immediately assign immigration judges to immigration detention facilities operated or controlled by the Secretary, or operated or controlled pursuant to contract by the Secretary, for the purpose of conducting proceedings authorized under title 8, chapter 12, subchapter II, United States Code.

Sec. 6. Detention for Illegal Entry. The Secretary shall immediately take all appropriate actions to ensure the detention of aliens apprehended for violations of immigration law pending the outcome of their removal proceedings or their removal from the country to the extent permitted by law. The Secretary shall issue new policy guidance to all Department of Homeland Security personnel regarding the appropriate and consistent use of lawful detention authority under the INA, including the termination of the practice commonly known as "catch and release," whereby aliens are routinely released in the United States shortly after their apprehension for violations of immigration law.

Sec. 7. Return to Territory. The Secretary shall take appropriate action, consistent with the requirements of section 1232 of title 8, United States Code, to ensure that aliens described in section 235(b)(2)(C) of the INA (8 U.S.C. 1225(b)(2)(C)) are returned to the territory from which they came pending a formal removal proceeding.

Sec. 8. Additional Border Patrol Agents. Subject to available appropriations, the Secretary, through the Commissioner of U.S. Customs and Border Protection, shall take all appropriate action to hire 5,000 additional Border Patrol agents, and all appropriate action to ensure that such agents enter on duty and are assigned to duty stations as soon as is practicable.

Sec. 9. Foreign Aid Reporting Requirements. The head of each executive department and agency shall identify and quantify all sources of direct and indirect Federal aid or assistance to the Government of Mexico on an annual basis over the past five years, including all bilateral and multilateral development aid, economic assistance, humanitarian aid, and military aid. Within 30 days of the date of this order, the head of each executive department and agency shall submit this information to the Secretary of State. Within 60 days of the date of this order, the Secretary shall submit to the President a consolidated report reflecting the levels of such aid and assistance that has been provided annually, over each of the past five years.

Sec. 10. Federal-State Agreements. It is the policy of the executive branch to empower State and local law enforcement agencies across the country to perform the functions of an immigration officer in the interior of the United States to the maximum extent permitted by law.

(a) In furtherance of this policy, the Secretary shall immediately take appropriate action to engage with the Governors of the States, as well as local officials, for the purpose of preparing to enter into agreements under section 287(g) of the INA (8 U.S.C. 1357(g)).

(b) To the extent permitted by law, and with the consent of State or local officials, as appropriate, the Secretary shall take appropriate action, through agreements under section 287(g) of the INA, or otherwise, to authorize State and local law enforcement officials, as the Secretary determines are qualified and appropriate, to perform the functions of immigration officers in relation to the investigation, apprehension, or detention of aliens in the United States under the direction and the supervision of the Secretary. Such authorization shall be in addition to, rather than in place of, Federal performance of these duties.

(c) To the extent permitted by law, the Secretary may structure each agreement under section 287(g) of the INA in the manner that provides the most effective model for enforcing Federal immigration laws and obtaining operational control over the border for that jurisdiction.

Sec. 11. Parole, Asylum, and Removal. It is the policy of the executive branch to end the abuse of parole and asylum provisions currently used to prevent the lawful removal of removable aliens.

(a) The Secretary shall immediately take all appropriate action to ensure that the parole and asylum provisions of Federal immigration law are not illegally exploited to prevent the removal of otherwise removable aliens.

(b) The Secretary shall take all appropriate action, including by promulgating any appropriate regulations, to ensure that asylum referrals and credible fear determinations pursuant to section 235(b)(1) of the INA (8 U.S.C. 1125(b)(1)) and

8 CFR 208.30, and reasonable fear determinations pursuant to 8 CFR 208.31, are conducted in a manner consistent with the plain language of those provisions.

(c) Pursuant to section 235(b)(1)(A)(iii)(I) of the INA, the Secretary shall take appropriate action to apply, in his sole and unreviewable discretion, the provisions of section 235(b)(1)(A)(i) and (ii) of the INA to the aliens designated under section 235(b)(1)(A)(iii)(II).

(d) The Secretary shall take appropriate action to ensure that parole authority under section 212(d)(5) of the INA (8 U.S.C. 1182(d)(5)) is exercised only on a case-by-case basis in accordance with the plain language of the statute, and in all circumstances only when an individual demonstrates urgent humanitarian reasons or a significant public benefit derived from such parole.

(e) The Secretary shall take appropriate action to require that all Department of Homeland Security personnel are properly trained on the proper application of section 235 of the William Wilberforce Trafficking Victims Protection Reauthorization Act of 2008 (8 U.S.C. 1232) and section 462(g)(2) of the Homeland Security Act of 2002 (6 U.S.C. 279(g)(2)), to ensure that unaccompanied alien children are properly processed, receive appropriate care and placement while in the custody of the Department of Homeland Security, and, when appropriate, are safely repatriated in accordance with law.

Sec. 12. Authorization to Enter Federal Lands. The Secretary, in conjunction with the Secretary of the Interior and any other heads of agencies as necessary, shall take all appropriate action to:

(a) permit all officers and employees of the United States, as well as all State and local officers as authorized by the Secretary, to have access to all Federal lands as necessary and appropriate to implement this order; and

(b) enable those officers and employees of the United States, as well as all State and local officers as authorized by the Secretary, to perform such actions on Federal lands as the Secretary deems necessary and appropriate to implement this order.

Sec. 13. Priority Enforcement. The Attorney General shall take all appropriate steps to establish prosecution guidelines and allocate appropriate resources to ensure that Federal prosecutors accord a high priority to prosecutions of offenses having a nexus to the southern border.

Sec. 14. Government Transparency. The Secretary shall, on a monthly basis and in a publicly available way, report statistical data on aliens apprehended at or near the southern border using a uniform method of reporting by all Department of Homeland Security components, in a format that is easily understandable by the public.

Sec. 15. Reporting. Except as otherwise provided in this order, the Secretary, within 90 days of the date of this order, and the Attorney General, within 180 days, shall each submit to the President a report on the progress of the directives contained in this order.

Sec. 16. Hiring. The Office of Personnel Management shall take appropriate action as may be necessary to facilitate hiring personnel to implement this order.

Sec. 17. General Provisions. (a) Nothing in this order shall be construed to impair or otherwise affect:

(i)   the authority granted by law to an executive department or agency, or the head thereof; or

(ii) the functions of the Director of the Office of Management and Budget relating to budgetary, administrative, or legislative proposals.

(b) This order shall be implemented consistent with applicable law and subject to the availability of appropriations.

(c) This order is not intended to, and does not, create any right or benefit, substantive or procedural, enforceable at law or in equity by any party against the United States, its departments, agencies, or entities, its officers, employees, or agents, or any other person.

DONALD J. TRUMP
The White House,
January 25, 2017.

SOURCE: Executive Office of the President. "Executive Order 13767—Border Security and Immigration Enforcement Improvements." January 25, 2017. *Compilation of Presidential Documents* 2017, no. 00071 (January 25, 2017). https://www.gpo.gov/fdsys/pkg/DCPD-201700071/pdf/DCPD-201700071.pdf.

President Trump Issues Executive Order on Sanctuary Cities

January 25, 2017

By the authority vested in me as President by the Constitution and the laws of the United States of America, including the Immigration and Nationality Act (INA) (8 U.S.C. 1101 *et seq.*), and in order to ensure the public safety of the American people in communities across the United States as well as to ensure that our Nation's immigration laws are faithfully executed, I hereby declare the policy of the executive branch to be, and order, as follows:

Section 1. Purpose. Interior enforcement of our Nation's immigration laws is critically important to the national security and public safety of the United States. Many aliens who illegally enter the United States and those who overstay or otherwise violate the terms of their visas present a significant threat to national security and public safety. This is particularly so for aliens who engage in criminal conduct in the United States.

Sanctuary jurisdictions across the United States willfully violate Federal law in an attempt to shield aliens from removal from the United States. These jurisdictions have caused immeasurable harm to the American people and to the very fabric of our Republic.

Tens of thousands of removable aliens have been released into communities across the country, solely because their home countries refuse to accept their repatriation. Many of these aliens are criminals who have served time in our Federal, State, and local jails. The presence of such individuals in the United States, and the practices of foreign nations that refuse the repatriation of their nationals, are contrary to the national interest.

Although Federal immigration law provides a framework for Federal-State partnerships in enforcing our immigration laws to ensure the removal of aliens who have no right to be in the United States, the Federal Government has failed to discharge this basic sovereign responsibility. We cannot faithfully execute the immigration laws of the United States if we exempt classes or categories of removable aliens from potential enforcement. The purpose of this order is to direct executive departments and agencies (agencies) to employ all lawful means to enforce the immigration laws of the United States.

Sec. 2. Policy. It is the policy of the executive branch to:

(a) Ensure the faithful execution of the immigration laws of the United States, including the INA, against all removable aliens, consistent with Article II, Section 3 of the United States Constitution and section 3331 of title 5, United States Code;

(b) Make use of all available systems and resources to ensure the efficient and faithful execution of the immigration laws of the United States;

(c) Ensure that jurisdictions that fail to comply with applicable Federal law do not receive Federal funds, except as mandated by law;

(d) Ensure that aliens ordered removed from the United States are promptly removed; and

(e) Support victims, and the families of victims, of crimes committed by removable aliens.

Sec. 3. Definitions. The terms of this order, where applicable, shall have the meaning provided by section 1101 of title 8, United States Code.

Sec. 4. Enforcement of the Immigration Laws in the Interior of the United States. In furtherance of the policy described in section 2 of this order, I hereby direct agencies to employ all lawful means to ensure the faithful execution of the immigration laws of the United States against all removable aliens.

Sec. 5. Enforcement Priorities. In executing faithfully the immigration laws of the United States, the Secretary of Homeland Security (Secretary) shall prioritize for removal those aliens described by the Congress in sections 212(a)(2), (a)(3), and (a)(6)(C), 235, and 237(a)(2) and (4) of the INA (8 U.S.C. 1182(a)(2), (a)(3), and (a)(6)(C), 1225, and 1227(a)(2) and (4)), as well as removable aliens who:

(a) Have been convicted of any criminal offense;

(b) Have been charged with any criminal offense, where such charge has not been resolved;

(c) Have committed acts that constitute a chargeable criminal offense;

(d) Have engaged in fraud or willful misrepresentation in connection with any official matter or application before a governmental agency;

(e) Have abused any program related to receipt of public benefits;

(f) Are subject to a final order of removal, but who have not complied with their legal obligation to depart the United States; or

(g) In the judgment of an immigration officer, otherwise pose a risk to public safety or national security.

Sec. 6. Civil Fines and Penalties. As soon as practicable, and by no later than one year after the date of this order, the Secretary shall issue guidance and promulgate regulations, where required by law, to ensure the assessment and collection of all fines and penalties that the Secretary is authorized under the law to assess and collect from aliens unlawfully present in the United States and from those who facilitate their presence in the United States.

Sec. 7. Additional Enforcement and Removal Officers. The Secretary, through the Director of U.S. Immigration and Customs Enforcement, shall, to the extent permitted by law and subject to the availability of appropriations, take all appropriate action to hire 10,000 additional immigration officers, who shall complete relevant training and be authorized to perform the law enforcement functions described in section 287 of the INA (8 U.S.C. 1357).

Sec. 8. Federal-State Agreements. It is the policy of the executive branch to empower State and local law enforcement agencies across the country to perform the functions of an immigration officer in the interior of the United States to the maximum extent permitted by law.

(a) In furtherance of this policy, the Secretary shall immediately take appropriate action to engage with the Governors of the States, as well as local officials, for the purpose of preparing to enter into agreements under section 287(g) of the INA (8 U.S.C. 1357(g)).

(b) To the extent permitted by law and with the consent of State or local officials, as appropriate, the Secretary shall take appropriate action, through agreements under section 287(g) of the INA, or otherwise, to authorize State and local law enforcement officials, as the Secretary determines are qualified and appropriate, to perform the functions of immigration officers in relation to the investigation, apprehension, or detention of aliens in the United States under the direction and the supervision of the Secretary. Such authorization shall be in addition to, rather than in place of, Federal performance of these duties.

(c) To the extent permitted by law, the Secretary may structure each agreement under section 287(g) of the INA in a manner that provides the most effective model for enforcing Federal immigration laws for that jurisdiction.

Sec. 9. Sanctuary Jurisdictions. It is the policy of the executive branch to ensure, to the fullest extent of the law, that a State, or a political subdivision of a State, shall comply with 8 U.S.C. 1373.

(a) In furtherance of this policy, the Attorney General and the Secretary, in their discretion and to the extent consistent with law, shall ensure that jurisdictions that willfully refuse to comply with 8 U.S.C. 1373 (sanctuary jurisdictions) are not eligible to receive Federal grants, except as deemed necessary for law enforcement purposes by the Attorney General or the Secretary. The Secretary has the authority to designate, in his discretion and to the extent consistent with law, a jurisdiction as a sanctuary jurisdiction. The Attorney General shall take appropriate enforcement action against any entity that violates 8 U.S.C. 1373, or which has in effect a statute, policy, or practice that prevents or hinders the enforcement of Federal law.

(b) To better inform the public regarding the public safety threats associated with sanctuary jurisdictions, the Secretary shall utilize the Declined Detainer Outcome

Report or its equivalent and, on a weekly basis, make public a comprehensive list of criminal actions committed by aliens and any jurisdiction that ignored or otherwise failed to honor any detainers with respect to such aliens.

(c) The Director of the Office of Management and Budget is directed to obtain and provide relevant and responsive information on all Federal grant money that currently is received by any sanctuary jurisdiction.

Sec. 10. Review of Previous Immigration Actions and Policies. (a) The Secretary shall immediately take all appropriate action to terminate the Priority Enforcement Program (PEP) described in the memorandum issued by the Secretary on November 20, 2014, and to reinstitute the immigration program known as "Secure Communities" referenced in that memorandum.

(b) The Secretary shall review agency regulations, policies, and procedures for consistency with this order and, if required, publish for notice and comment proposed regulations rescinding or revising any regulations inconsistent with this order and shall consider whether to withdraw or modify any inconsistent policies and procedures, as appropriate and consistent with the law.

(c) To protect our communities and better facilitate the identification, detention, and removal of criminal aliens within constitutional and statutory parameters, the Secretary shall consolidate and revise any applicable forms to more effectively communicate with recipient law enforcement agencies.

Sec. 11. Department of Justice Prosecutions of Immigration Violators. The Attorney General and the Secretary shall work together to develop and implement a program that ensures that adequate resources are devoted to the prosecution of criminal immigration offenses in the United States, and to develop cooperative strategies to reduce violent crime and the reach of transnational criminal organizations into the United States.

Sec. 12. Recalcitrant Countries. The Secretary of Homeland Security and the Secretary of State shall cooperate to effectively implement the sanctions provided by section 243(d) of the INA (8 U.S.C. 1253(d)), as appropriate. The Secretary of State shall, to the maximum extent permitted by law, ensure that diplomatic efforts and negotiations with foreign states include as a condition precedent the acceptance by those foreign states of their nationals who are subject to removal from the United States.

Sec. 13. Office for Victims of Crimes Committed by Removable Aliens. The Secretary shall direct the Director of U.S. Immigration and Customs Enforcement to take all appropriate and lawful action to establish within U.S. Immigration and Customs Enforcement an office to provide proactive, timely, adequate, and professional services to victims of crimes committed by removable aliens and the family members of such victims. This office shall provide quarterly reports studying the effects of the victimization by criminal aliens present in the United States.

Sec. 14. Privacy Act. Agencies shall, to the extent consistent with applicable law, ensure that their privacy policies exclude persons who are not United States citizens or lawful permanent residents from the protections of the Privacy Act regarding personally identifiable information.

Sec. 15. Reporting. Except as otherwise provided in this order, the Secretary and the Attorney General shall each submit to the President a report on the progress of the directives contained in this order within 90 days of the date of this order and again within 180 days of the date of this order.

Sec. 16. Transparency. To promote the transparency and situational awareness of criminal aliens in the United States, the Secretary and the Attorney General are hereby directed to collect relevant data and provide quarterly reports on the following:

(a) the immigration status of all aliens incarcerated under the supervision of the Federal Bureau of Prisons;

(b) the immigration status of all aliens incarcerated as Federal pretrial detainees under the supervision of the United States Marshals Service; and

(c) the immigration status of all convicted aliens incarcerated in State prisons and local detention centers throughout the United States.

Sec. 17. Personnel Actions. The Office of Personnel Management shall take appropriate and lawful action to facilitate hiring personnel to implement this order.

Sec. 18. General Provisions. (a) Nothing in this order shall be construed to impair or otherwise affect:

(i) the authority granted by law to an executive department or agency, or the head thereof; or

(ii) the functions of the Director of the Office of Management and Budget relating to budgetary, administrative, or legislative proposals.

(b) This order shall be implemented consistent with applicable law and subject to the availability of appropriations. (c) This order is not intended to, and does not, create any right or benefit, substantive or procedural, enforceable at law or in equity by any party against the United States, its departments, agencies, or entities, its officers, employees, or agents, or any other person.

DONALD J. TRUMP
The White House,
January 25, 2017.

SOURCE: Executive Office of the President. "Executive Order 13768—Enhancing Public Safety in the Interior of the United States." January 25, 2017. *Compilation of Presidential Documents* 2017, no. 00072 (January 25, 2017). https://www.gpo.gov/fdsys/pkg/DCPD-201700072/pdf/DCPD-201700072.pdf.

President Trump Issues Executive Order Banning Travel from Seven Muslim-Majority Countries

January 27, 2017

By the authority vested in me as President by the Constitution and laws of the United States of America, including the Immigration and Nationality Act (INA), 8 U.S.C. 1101 et seq., and section 301 of title 3, United States Code, and to protect the American people from terrorist attacks by foreign nationals admitted to the United States, it is hereby ordered as follows:

Section 1. Purpose. In order to protect Americans, the United States must ensure that those admitted to this country do not bear hostile attitudes toward it and its founding principles. The United States cannot, and should not, admit those who do not support the Constitution, or those who would place violent ideologies over American law. In addition, the United States should not admit those who engage in acts of bigotry or hatred (including "honor" killings, other forms of violence against women, or the persecution of those who practice religions different from their own) or those who would oppress Americans of any race, gender, or sexual orientation.

Sec. 2. Policy. It is the policy of the United States to protect its citizens from foreign nationals who intend to commit terrorist attacks in the United States; and to prevent the admission of foreign nationals who intend to exploit United States immigration laws for malevolent purposes.

Sec. 3. Suspension of Issuance of Visas and Other Immigration Benefits to Nationals of Countries of Particular Concern. (a) The Secretary of Homeland Security, in consultation with the Secretary of State and the Director of National Intelligence, shall immediately conduct a review to determine the information needed from any country to adjudicate any visa, admission, or other benefit under the INA (adjudications) in order to determine that the individual seeking the benefit is who the individual claims to be and is not a security or public safety threat.

(b) The Secretary of Homeland Security, in consultation with the Secretary of State and the Director of National Intelligence, shall submit to the President a report on the results of the review described in subsection (a) of this section, including the Secretary of Homeland Security's determination of the information needed for adjudications and a list of countries that do not provide adequate information, within 30 days of the date of this order. The Secretary of Homeland Security shall provide a copy of the report to the Secretary of State and the Director of National Intelligence.

(c) To temporarily reduce investigative burdens on relevant agencies during the review period described in subsection (a) of this section, to ensure the proper review and maximum utilization of available resources for the screening of foreign nationals, and to ensure that adequate standards are established to prevent infiltration by foreign terrorists or criminals, pursuant to section 212(f) of the INA, 8 U.S.C. 1182(f), I hereby proclaim that the immigrant and nonimmigrant entry into the United States of aliens from countries referred to in section 217(a)(12) of the INA, 8 U.S.C. 1187(a)(12), would be detrimental to the interests of the United States, and I hereby suspend entry into the United States, as immigrants and nonimmigrants, of such persons for 90 days from the date of this order (excluding those foreign nationals traveling on diplomatic visas, North Atlantic Treaty Organization visas, C–2 visas for travel to the United Nations, and G–1, G–2, G–3, and G–4 visas).

(d) Immediately upon receipt of the report described in subsection (b) of this section regarding the information needed for adjudications, the Secretary of State shall request all foreign governments that do not supply such information to start providing such information regarding their nationals within 60 days of notification.

(e) After the 60-day period described in subsection (d) of this section expires, the Secretary of Homeland Security, in consultation with the Secretary of State, shall submit to the President a list of countries recommended for inclusion on a Presidential proclamation that would prohibit the entry of foreign nationals (excluding those foreign nationals traveling on diplomatic visas, North Atlantic Treaty Organization visas, C–2 visas for travel to the United Nations, and G–1, G–2, G–3, and G–4 visas) from countries that do not provide the information requested pursuant to subsection (d) of this section until compliance occurs.

(f) At any point after submitting the list described in subsection (e) of this section, the Secretary of State or the Secretary of Homeland Security may submit to the President the names of any additional countries recommended for similar treatment.

(g) Notwithstanding a suspension pursuant to subsection (c) of this section or pursuant to a Presidential proclamation described in subsection (e) of this section, the Secretaries of State and Homeland Security may, on a case-by-case basis, and when in the national interest, issue visas or other immigration benefits to nationals of countries for which visas and benefits are otherwise blocked.

Sec. 4. Implementing Uniform Screening Standards for All Immigration Programs.
(a) The Secretary of State, the Secretary of Homeland Security, the Director of National Intelligence, and the Director of the Federal Bureau of Investigation shall implement a program, as part of the adjudication process for immigration benefits, to identify individuals seeking to enter the United States on a fraudulent basis with the intent to cause harm, or who are at risk of causing harm subsequent to their admission. This program will include the development of a uniform screening standard and procedure, such as in-person interviews; a database of identity documents proffered by applicants to ensure that duplicate documents are not used by multiple applicants; amended application forms that include questions aimed at identifying fraudulent answers and malicious intent; a mechanism to ensure that the applicant is who the applicant claims to be; a process to evaluate the applicant's likelihood of becoming a positively contributing member of society and the applicant's ability to make contributions to the national interest; and a mechanism to assess whether or not the applicant has the intent to commit criminal or terrorist acts after entering the United States.

(b) The Secretary of Homeland Security, in conjunction with the Secretary of State, the Director of National Intelligence, and the Director of the Federal Bureau of Investigation, shall submit to the President an initial report on the progress of this directive within 60 days of the date of this order, a second report within 100 days of the date of this order, and a third report within 200 days of the date of this order.

Sec. 5. Realignment of the U.S. Refugee Admissions Program for Fiscal Year 2017.
(a) The Secretary of State shall suspend the U.S. Refugee Admissions Program (USRAP) for 120 days. During the 120-day period, the Secretary of State, in conjunction with the Secretary of Homeland Security and in consultation with the Director of National Intelligence, shall review the USRAP application and adjudication process to determine what additional procedures should be taken to ensure that those approved

for refugee admission do not pose a threat to the security and welfare of the United States, and shall implement such additional procedures. Refugee applicants who are already in the USRAP process may be admitted upon the initiation and completion of these revised procedures. Upon the date that is 120 days after the date of this order, the Secretary of State shall resume USRAP admissions only for nationals of countries for which the Secretary of State, the Secretary of Homeland Security, and the Director of National Intelligence have jointly determined that such additional procedures are adequate to ensure the security and welfare of the United States.

(b) Upon the resumption of USRAP admissions, the Secretary of State, in consultation with the Secretary of Homeland Security, is further directed to make changes, to the extent permitted by law, to prioritize refugee claims made by individuals on the basis of religious-based persecution, provided that the religion of the individual is a minority religion in the individual's country of nationality. Where necessary and appropriate, the Secretaries of State and Homeland Security shall recommend legislation to the President that would assist with such prioritization.

(c) Pursuant to section 212(f) of the INA, 8 U.S.C. 1182(f), I hereby proclaim that the entry of nationals of Syria as refugees is detrimental to the interests of the United States and thus suspend any such entry until such time as I have determined that sufficient changes have been made to the USRAP to ensure that admission of Syrian refugees is consistent with the national interest.

(d) Pursuant to section 212(f) of the INA, 8 U.S.C. 1182(f), I hereby proclaim that the entry of more than 50,000 refugees in fiscal year 2017 would be detrimental to the interests of the United States, and thus suspend any such entry until such time as I determine that additional admissions would be in the national interest.

(e) Notwithstanding the temporary suspension imposed pursuant to subsection (a) of this section, the Secretaries of State and Homeland Security may jointly determine to admit individuals to the United States as refugees on a case-by-case basis, in their discretion, but only so long as they determine that the admission of such individuals as refugees is in the national interest—including when the person is a religious minority in his country of nationality facing religious persecution, when admitting the person would enable the United States to conform its conduct to a preexisting international agreement, or when the person is already in transit and denying admission would cause undue hardship—and it would not pose a risk to the security or welfare of the United States.

(f) The Secretary of State shall submit to the President an initial report on the progress of the directive in subsection (b) of this section regarding prioritization of claims made by individuals on the basis of religious-based persecution within 100 days of the date of this order and shall submit a second report within 200 days of the date of this order.

DONALD J. TRUMP
The White House,
January 27, 2017.

Source: Executive Office of the President. "Executive Order 13769—Protecting the Nation from Foreign Terrorist Entry into the United States." January 27, 2017. *Compilation of Presidential Documents* 2017, no. 00076 (January 27, 2017). https://www.gpo.gov/fdsys/pkg/DCPD-201700076/pdf/DCPD-201700076.pdf.

President Trump Issues
Amended Travel Ban

March 6, 2017

By the authority vested in me as President by the Constitution and the laws of the United States of America, including the Immigration and Nationality Act (INA), 8 U.S.C. 1101 et seq., and section 301 of title 3, United States Code, and to protect the Nation from terrorist activities by foreign nationals admitted to the United States, it is hereby ordered as follows:

Section 1. Policy and Purpose. (a) It is the policy of the United States to protect its citizens from terrorist attacks, including those committed by foreign nationals. The screening and vetting protocols and procedures associated with the visa-issuance process and the United States Refugee Admissions Program (USRAP) play a crucial role in detecting foreign nationals who may commit, aid, or support acts of terrorism and in preventing those individuals from entering the United States. It is therefore the policy of the United States to improve the screening and vetting protocols and procedures associated with the visa-issuance process and the USRAP.

(b) On January 27, 2017, to implement this policy, I issued Executive Order 13769 (Protecting the Nation from Foreign Terrorist Entry into the United States).

   (i) Among other actions, Executive Order 13769 suspended for 90 days the entry of certain aliens from seven countries: Iran, Iraq, Libya, Somalia, Sudan, Syria, and Yemen. These are countries that had already been identified as presenting heightened concerns about terrorism and travel to the United States. Specifically, the suspension applied to countries referred to in, or designated under, section 217(a)(12) of the INA, 8 U.S.C. 1187(a)(12), in which Congress restricted use of the Visa Waiver Program for nationals of, and aliens recently present in, (A) Iraq or Syria, (B) any country designated by the Secretary of State as a state sponsor of terrorism (currently Iran, Syria, and Sudan), and (C) any other country designated as a country of concern by the Secretary of Homeland Security, in consultation with the Secretary of State and the Director of National Intelligence. In 2016, the Secretary of Homeland Security designated Libya, Somalia, and Yemen as additional countries of concern for travel purposes, based on consideration of three statutory factors related to terrorism and national security: "(I) whether the presence of an alien in the country or area increases the likelihood that the alien is a credible threat to the national security of the United States; (II) whether a foreign terrorist organization has a significant presence in the country or area; and (III) whether the country or area is a safe haven for terrorists." 8 U.S.C. 1187(a)(12)(D)(ii). Additionally, Members of Congress have expressed concerns about screening and vetting procedures following recent terrorist attacks in this country and in Europe.

   (ii) In ordering the temporary suspension of entry described in subsection (b)(i) of this section, I exercised my authority under Article II of the Constitution and under section 212(f) of the INA, which provides in relevant part: "Whenever the President finds that the entry of any aliens or of any class of aliens into the United States would be detrimental to the interests of the United States, he may by proclamation, and for such period as he shall deem necessary, suspend the entry of all aliens or any class of aliens as immigrants or nonimmigrants, or impose on the entry of aliens any restrictions he may deem to be appropriate." 8 U.S.C. 1182(f). Under these authorities, I determined that, for a brief period of 90 days, while existing screening and vetting procedures were under review, the entry into the United States of certain aliens from the seven identified countries—each afflicted by terrorism in a manner that compromised the ability of the United States to rely on normal decision-making procedures about travel to the United States—would be detrimental to the interests of the United States. Nonetheless, I permitted the Secretary of State and the Secretary of Homeland Security to grant case-by-case waivers when they determined that it was in the national interest to do so.

(iii)   Executive Order 13769 also suspended the USRAP for 120 days. Terrorist groups have sought to infiltrate several nations through refugee programs. Accordingly, I temporarily suspended the USRAP pending a review of our procedures for screening and vetting refugees. Nonetheless, I permitted the Secretary of State and the Secretary of Homeland Security to jointly grant case-by-case waivers when they determined that it was in the national interest to do so.

(iv)   Executive Order 13769 did not provide a basis for discriminating for or against members of any particular religion. While that order allowed for prioritization of refugee claims from members of persecuted religious minority groups, that priority applied to refugees from every nation, including those in which Islam is a minority religion, and it applied to minority sects within a religion. That order was not motivated by animus toward any religion, but was instead intended to protect the ability of religious minorities—whoever they are and wherever they reside—to avail themselves of the USRAP in light of their particular challenges and circumstances.

(c)   The implementation of Executive Order 13769 has been delayed by litigation. Most significantly, enforcement of critical provisions of that order has been temporarily halted by court orders that apply nationwide and extend even to foreign nationals with no prior or substantial connection to the United States. On February 9, 2017, the United States Court of Appeals for the Ninth Circuit declined to stay or narrow one such order pending the outcome of further judicial proceedings, while noting that the "political branches are far better equipped to make appropriate distinctions" about who should be covered by a suspension of entry or of refugee admissions.

(d)   Nationals from the countries previously identified under section 217(a)(12) of the INA warrant additional scrutiny in connection with our immigration policies because the conditions in these countries present heightened threats. Each of these countries is a state sponsor of terrorism, has been significantly compromised by terrorist organizations, or contains active conflict zones. Any of these circumstances diminishes the foreign government's willingness or ability to share or validate important information about individuals seeking to travel to the United States. Moreover, the significant presence in each of these countries of terrorist organizations, their members, and others exposed to those organizations increases the chance that conditions will be exploited to enable terrorist operatives or sympathizers to travel to the United States. Finally, once foreign nationals from these countries are admitted to the United States, it is often difficult to remove them, because many of these countries typically delay issuing, or refuse to issue, travel documents.

(e)   The following are brief descriptions, taken in part from the Department of State's Country Reports on Terrorism 2015 (June 2016), of some of the conditions in six of the previously designated countries that demonstrate why their nationals continue to present heightened risks to the security of the United States:

   (i)   *Iran.* Iran has been designated as a state sponsor of terrorism since 1984 and continues to support various terrorist groups, including Hizballah, Hamas, and terrorist groups in Iraq. Iran has also been linked to support for al-Qa'ida and has permitted al-Qa'ida to transport funds and fighters through Iran to Syria and South Asia. Iran does not cooperate with the United States in counterterrorism efforts.

   (ii)   *Libya.* Libya is an active combat zone, with hostilities between the internationally recognized government and its rivals. In many parts of the country, security and law enforcement functions are provided by armed militias rather than state institutions. Violent extremist groups, including the Islamic State of Iraq and Syria (ISIS), have exploited these conditions to expand their presence in the country. The Libyan government provides some cooperation with the United States' counterterrorism efforts, but it is unable to secure thousands of miles of its land and maritime borders, enabling the illicit flow of weapons, migrants, and foreign terrorist fighters. The United States Embassy in Libya suspended its operations in 2014.

   (iii)   *Somalia.* Portions of Somalia have been terrorist safe havens. Al-Shabaab, an al-Qa'ida-affiliated terrorist group, has operated in the country for years and continues to plan and mount operations within Somalia and in neighboring countries. Somalia has porous borders, and most countries do not recognize Somali identity documents. The Somali government cooperates with the United States in some counterterrorism operations but does not have the capacity to sustain military pressure on or to investigate suspected terrorists.

   (iv)   *Sudan.* Sudan has been designated as a state sponsor of terrorism since 1993 because of its support for international terrorist groups, including Hizballah and Hamas. Historically, Sudan provided safe havens for al-Qa'ida and other terrorist groups to meet and train. Although Sudan's support to al-Qa'ida has ceased and it provides some cooperation with the United States' counterterrorism efforts, elements of core al-Qa'ida and ISIS-linked terrorist groups remain active in the country.

   (v)   *Syria.* Syria has been designated as a state sponsor of terrorism since 1979. The Syrian government is engaged in an ongoing military conflict against ISIS and others for control of portions of the country. At the same time, Syria continues to support other terrorist groups. It has allowed or encouraged extremists to pass through its territory to enter Iraq. ISIS continues to attract foreign fighters to Syria and to use its base in Syria to plot or encourage attacks around the globe, including in the United States. The United States Embassy in Syria suspended its operations in 2012. Syria does not cooperate with the United States' counterterrorism efforts.

(vi) *Yemen.* Yemen is the site of an ongoing conflict between the incumbent government and the Houthi-led opposition. Both ISIS and a second group, al-Qa'ida in the Arabian Peninsula (AQAP), have exploited this conflict to expand their presence in Yemen and to carry out hundreds of attacks. Weapons and other materials smuggled across Yemen's porous borders are used to finance AQAP and other terrorist activities. In 2015, the United States Embassy in Yemen suspended its operations, and embassy staff were relocated out of the country. Yemen has been supportive of, but has not been able to cooperate fully with, the United States in counterterrorism efforts.

(f) In light of the conditions in these six countries, until the assessment of current screening and vetting procedures required by section 2 of this order is completed, the risk of erroneously permitting entry of a national of one of these countries who intends to commit terrorist acts or otherwise harm the national security of the United States is unacceptably high. Accordingly, while that assessment is ongoing, I am imposing a temporary pause on the entry of nationals from Iran, Libya, Somalia, Sudan, Syria, and Yemen, subject to categorical exceptions and case-by-case waivers, as described in section 3 of this order.

(g) Iraq presents a special case. Portions of Iraq remain active combat zones. Since 2014, ISIS has had dominant influence over significant territory in northern and central Iraq. Although that influence has been significantly reduced due to the efforts and sacrifices of the Iraqi government and armed forces, working along with a United States-led coalition, the ongoing conflict has impacted the Iraqi government's capacity to secure its borders and to identify fraudulent travel documents. Nevertheless, the close cooperative relationship between the United States and the democratically elected Iraqi government, the strong United States diplomatic presence in Iraq, the significant presence of United States forces in Iraq, and Iraq's commitment to combat ISIS justify different treatment for Iraq. In particular, those Iraqi government forces that have fought to regain more than half of the territory previously dominated by ISIS have shown steadfast determination and earned enduring respect as they battle an armed group that is the common enemy of Iraq and the United States. In addition, since Executive Order 13769 was issued, the Iraqi government has expressly undertaken steps to enhance travel documentation, information sharing, and the return of Iraqi nationals subject to final orders of removal. Decisions about issuance of visas or granting admission to Iraqi nationals should be subjected to additional scrutiny to determine if applicants have connections with ISIS or other terrorist organizations, or otherwise pose a risk to either national security or public safety.

(h) Recent history shows that some of those who have entered the United States through our immigration system have proved to be threats to our national security. Since 2001, hundreds of persons born abroad have been convicted of terrorism-related crimes in the United States. They have included not just persons who came here legally on visas but also individuals who first entered the country as refugees. For example, in January 2013, two Iraqi nationals admitted to the United States as refugees in 2009 were sentenced to 40 years and to life in prison, respectively, for multiple terrorism-related offenses. And in October 2014, a native of Somalia who had been brought to the United States as a child refugee and later became a naturalized United States citizen was sentenced to 30 years in prison for attempting to use a weapon of mass destruction as part of a plot to detonate a bomb at a crowded Christmas-tree-lighting ceremony in Portland, Oregon. The Attorney General has reported to me that more than 300 persons who entered the United States as refugees are currently the subjects of counterterrorism investigations by the Federal Bureau of Investigation.

(i) Given the foregoing, the entry into the United States of foreign nationals who may commit, aid, or support acts of terrorism remains a matter of grave concern. In light of the Ninth Circuit's observation that the political branches are better suited to determine the appropriate scope of any suspensions than are the courts, and in order to avoid spending additional time pursuing litigation, I am revoking Executive Order 13769 and replacing it with this order, which expressly excludes from the suspensions categories of aliens that have prompted judicial concerns and which clarifies or refines the approach to certain other issues or categories of affected aliens.

Sec. 2. Temporary Suspension of Entry for Nationals of Countries of Particular Concern During Review Period. (a) The Secretary of Homeland Security, in consultation with the Secretary of State and the Director of National Intelligence, shall conduct a worldwide review to identify whether, and if so what, additional information will be needed from each foreign country to adjudicate an application by a national of that country for a visa, admission, or other benefit under the INA (adjudications) in order to determine that the individual is not a security or public-safety threat. The Secretary of Homeland Security may conclude that certain information is needed from particular countries even if it is not needed from every country.

(b) The Secretary of Homeland Security, in consultation with the Secretary of State and the Director of National Intelligence, shall submit to the President a report on the results of the worldwide review described in subsection (a) of this section, including the Secretary of Homeland Security's determination of the information needed from each country for adjudications and a list of countries that do not provide adequate information, within 20 days of the effective date of this order. The Secretary of Homeland Security shall provide a copy of the report to the Secretary of State, the Attorney General, and the Director of National Intelligence.

(c) To temporarily reduce investigative burdens on relevant agencies during the review period described in subsection (a) of this section, to ensure the proper review and maximum utilization of available resources for the screening and vetting of foreign nationals, to ensure that adequate standards are established to prevent infiltration by foreign terrorists, and in light of the national security concerns referenced in section 1 of this order, I hereby proclaim, pursuant to sections 212(f) and 215(a) of the INA, 8 U.S.C. 1182(f) and 1185(a), that the unrestricted entry into the United States of nationals of Iran, Libya, Somalia, Sudan, Syria, and Yemen would be detrimental to the interests of the United States. I therefore direct that the entry into the United States of nationals of those six countries be suspended for 90 days from the effective date of this order, subject to the limitations, waivers, and exceptions set forth in sections 3 and 12 of this order.

(d) Upon submission of the report described in subsection (b) of this section regarding the information needed from each country for adjudications, the Secretary of State shall request that all foreign governments that do not supply such information regarding their nationals begin providing it within 50 days of notification.

(e) After the period described in subsection (d) of this section expires, the Secretary of Homeland Security, in consultation with the Secretary of State and the Attorney General, shall submit to the President a list of countries recommended for inclusion in a Presidential proclamation that would prohibit the entry of appropriate categories of foreign nationals of countries that have not provided the information requested until they do so or until the Secretary of Homeland Security certifies that the country has an adequate plan to do so, or has adequately shared information through other means. The Secretary of State, the Attorney General, or the Secretary of Homeland Security may also submit to the President the names of additional countries for which any of them recommends other lawful restrictions or limitations deemed necessary for the security or welfare of the United States.

(f) At any point after the submission of the list described in subsection (e) of this section, the Secretary of Homeland Security, in consultation with the Secretary of State and the Attorney General, may submit to the President the names of any additional countries recommended for similar treatment, as well as the names of any countries that they recommend should be removed from the scope of a proclamation described in subsection (e) of this section.

(g) The Secretary of State and the Secretary of Homeland Security shall submit to the President a joint report on the progress in implementing this order within 60 days of the effective date of this order, a second report within 90 days of the effective date of this order, a third report within 120 days of the effective date of this order, and a fourth report within 150 days of the effective date of this order.

Sec. 3. Scope and Implementation of Suspension.

(a) *Scope.* Subject to the exceptions set forth in subsection (b) of this section and any waiver under subsection (c) of this section, the suspension of entry pursuant to section 2 of this order shall apply only to foreign nationals of the designated countries who:

   (i) are outside the United States on the effective date of this order;

   (ii) did not have a valid visa at 5:00 p.m., eastern standard time on January 27, 2017; and

   (iii) do not have a valid visa on the effective date of this order.

(b) *Exceptions.* The suspension of entry pursuant to section 2 of this order shall not apply to:

   (i) any lawful permanent resident of the United States;

   (ii) any foreign national who is admitted to or paroled into the United States on or after the effective date of this order;

   (iii) any foreign national who has a document other than a visa, valid on the effective date of this order or issued on any date thereafter, that permits him or her to travel to the United States and seek entry or admission, such as an advance parole document;

(iv)　any dual national of a country designated under section 2 of this order when the individual is traveling on a passport issued by a non-designated country;

(v)　any foreign national traveling on a diplomatic or diplomatic-type visa, North Atlantic Treaty Organization visa, C–2 visa for travel to the United Nations, or G–1, G–2, G–3, or G–4 visa; or

(vi)　any foreign national who has been granted asylum; any refugee who has already been admitted to the United States; or any individual who has been granted withholding of removal, advance parole, or protection under the Convention Against Torture.

(c)　*Waivers.* Notwithstanding the suspension of entry pursuant to section 2 of this order, a consular officer, or, as appropriate, the Commissioner, U.S. Customs and Border Protection (CBP), or the Commissioner's delegee, may, in the consular officer's or the CBP official's discretion, decide on a case-by-case basis to authorize the issuance of a visa to, or to permit the entry of, a foreign national for whom entry is otherwise suspended if the foreign national has demonstrated to the officer's satisfaction that denying entry during the suspension period would cause undue hardship, and that his or her entry would not pose a threat to national security and would be in the national interest. Unless otherwise specified by the Secretary of Homeland Security, any waiver issued by a consular officer as part of the visa issuance process will be effective both for the issuance of a visa and any subsequent entry on that visa, but will leave all other requirements for admission or entry unchanged. Case-by-case waivers could be appropriate in circumstances such as the following:

(i)　the foreign national has previously been admitted to the United States for a continuous period of work, study, or other long-term activity, is outside the United States on the effective date of this order, seeks to reenter the United States to resume that activity, and the denial of reentry during the suspension period would impair that activity;

(ii)　the foreign national has previously established significant contacts with the United States but is outside the United States on the effective date of this order for work, study, or other lawful activity;

(iii)　the foreign national seeks to enter the United States for significant business or professional obligations and the denial of entry during the suspension period would impair those obligations;

(iv)　the foreign national seeks to enter the United States to visit or reside with a close family member (e.g., a spouse, child, or parent) who is a United States citizen, lawful permanent resident, or alien lawfully admitted on a valid nonimmigrant visa, and the denial of entry during the suspension period would cause undue hardship;

(v)　the foreign national is an infant, a young child or adoptee, an individual needing urgent medical care, or someone whose entry is otherwise justified by the special circumstances of the case;

    (vi) the foreign national has been employed by, or on behalf of, the United States Government (or is an eligible dependent of such an employee) and the employee can document that he or she has provided faithful and valuable service to the United States Government;

  (vii) the foreign national is traveling for purposes related to an international organization designated under the International Organizations Immunities Act (IOIA), 22 U.S.C. 288 et seq., traveling for purposes of conducting meetings or business with the United States Government, or traveling to conduct business on behalf of an international organization not designated under the IOIA;

 (viii) the foreign national is a landed Canadian immigrant who applies for a visa at a location within Canada; or

  (ix) the foreign national is traveling as a United States Government-sponsored exchange visitor.

Sec. 4. Additional Inquiries Related to Nationals of Iraq. An application by any Iraqi national for a visa, admission, or other immigration benefit should be subjected to thorough review, including, as appropriate, consultation with a designee of the Secretary of Defense and use of the additional information that has been obtained in the context of the close U.S.-Iraqi security partnership, since Executive Order 13769 was issued, concerning individuals suspected of ties to ISIS or other terrorist organizations and individuals coming from territories controlled or formerly controlled by ISIS. Such review shall include consideration of whether the applicant has connections with ISIS or other terrorist organizations or with territory that is or has been under the dominant influence of ISIS, as well as any other information bearing on whether the applicant may be a threat to commit acts of terrorism or otherwise threaten the national security or public safety of the United States.

Sec. 5. Implementing Uniform Screening and Vetting Standards for All Immigration Programs. (a) The Secretary of State, the Attorney General, the Secretary of Homeland Security, and the Director of National Intelligence shall implement a program, as part of the process for adjudications, to identify individuals who seek to enter the United States on a fraudulent basis, who support terrorism, violent extremism, acts of violence toward any group or class of people within the United States, or who present a risk of causing harm subsequent to their entry. This program shall include the development of a uniform baseline for screening and vetting standards and procedures, such as in-person interviews; a database of identity documents proffered by applicants to ensure that duplicate documents are not used by multiple applicants; amended application forms that include questions aimed at identifying fraudulent answers and malicious intent; a mechanism to ensure that applicants are who they claim to be; a mechanism to assess whether applicants may commit, aid, or support any kind of violent, criminal, or terrorist acts after entering the United States; and any other appropriate means for ensuring the proper collection of all information necessary for a rigorous evaluation of all grounds of inadmissibility or grounds for the denial of other immigration benefits.

(b) The Secretary of Homeland Security, in conjunction with the Secretary of State, the Attorney General, and the Director of National Intelligence, shall submit to the President an initial report on the progress of the program described in subsection (a) of this section within 60 days of the effective date of this order, a second report within 100 days of the effective date of this order, and a third report within 200 days of the effective date of this order.

Sec. 6. Realignment of the U.S. Refugee Admissions Program for Fiscal Year 2017. (a) The Secretary of State shall suspend travel of refugees into the United States under the USRAP, and the Secretary of Homeland Security shall suspend decisions on applications for refugee status, for 120 days after the effective date of this order, subject to waivers pursuant to subsection (c) of this section. During the 120-day period, the Secretary of State, in conjunction with the Secretary of Homeland Security and in consultation with the Director of National Intelligence, shall review the USRAP application and adjudication processes to determine what additional procedures should be used to ensure that individuals seeking admission as refugees do not pose a threat to the security and welfare of the United States, and shall implement such additional procedures. The suspension described in this subsection shall not apply to refugee applicants who, before the effective date of this order, have been formally scheduled for transit by the Department of State. The Secretary of State shall resume travel of refugees into the United States under the USRAP 120 days after the effective date of this order, and the Secretary of Homeland Security shall resume making decisions on applications for refugee status only for stateless persons and nationals of countries for which the Secretary of State, the Secretary of Homeland Security, and the Director of National Intelligence have jointly determined that the additional procedures implemented pursuant to this subsection are adequate to ensure the security and welfare of the United States.

(b) Pursuant to section 212(f) of the INA, I hereby proclaim that the entry of more than 50,000 refugees in fiscal year 2017 would be detrimental to the interests of the United States, and thus suspend any entries in excess of that number until such time as I determine that additional entries would be in the national interest.

(c) Notwithstanding the temporary suspension imposed pursuant to subsection (a) of this section, the Secretary of State and the Secretary of Homeland Security may jointly determine to admit individuals to the United States as refugees on a case-by-case basis, in their discretion, but only so long as they determine that the entry of such individuals as refugees is in the national interest and does not pose a threat to the security or welfare of the United States, including in circumstances such as the following: the individual's entry would enable the United States to conform its conduct to a preexisting international agreement or arrangement, or the denial of entry would cause undue hardship.

(d) It is the policy of the executive branch that, to the extent permitted by law and as practicable, State and local jurisdictions be granted a role in the process of determining the placement or settlement in their jurisdictions of aliens eligible to be admitted to the United States as refugees. To that end, the Secretary of State shall examine existing law to determine the extent to which, consistent with applicable law, State and local jurisdictions may have greater involvement in the process of determining the placement or resettlement of refugees in their jurisdictions, and shall devise a proposal to lawfully promote such involvement.

Sec. 7. Rescission of Exercise of Authority Relating to the Terrorism Grounds of Inadmissibility. The Secretary of State and the Secretary of Homeland Security shall, in consultation with the Attorney General, consider rescinding the exercises of authority permitted by section 212(d)(3)(B) of the INA, 8 U.S.C. 1182(d)(3)(B), relating to the terrorism grounds of inadmissibility, as well as any related implementing directives or guidance.

Sec. 8. Expedited Completion of the Biometric Entry-Exit Tracking System. (a) The Secretary of Homeland Security shall expedite the completion and implementation of a biometric entry-exit tracking system for in-scope travelers to the United States, as recommended by the National Commission on Terrorist Attacks Upon the United States.

(b)   The Secretary of Homeland Security shall submit to the President periodic reports on the progress of the directive set forth in subsection (a) of this section. The initial report shall be submitted within 100 days of the effective date of this order, a second report shall be submitted within 200 days of the effective date of this order, and a third report shall be submitted within 365 days of the effective date of this order. The Secretary of Homeland Security shall submit further reports every 180 days thereafter until the system is fully deployed and operational.

Sec. 9. Visa Interview Security. (a) The Secretary of State shall immediately suspend the Visa Interview Waiver Program and ensure compliance with section 222 of the INA, 8 U.S.C. 1202, which requires that all individuals seeking a nonimmigrant visa undergo an in-person interview, subject to specific statutory exceptions. This suspension shall not apply to any foreign national traveling on a diplomatic or diplomatic-type visa, North Atlantic Treaty Organization visa, C–2 visa for travel to the United Nations, or G–1, G–2, G–3, or G–4 visa; traveling for purposes related to an international organization designated under the IOIA; or traveling for purposes of conducting meetings or business with the United States Government.

(b)   To the extent permitted by law and subject to the availability of appropriations, the Secretary of State shall immediately expand the Consular Fellows Program, including by substantially increasing the number of Fellows, lengthening or making permanent the period of service, and making language training at the Foreign Service Institute available to Fellows for assignment to posts outside of their area of core linguistic ability, to ensure that nonimmigrant visa-interview wait times are not unduly affected.

Sec. 10. Visa Validity Reciprocity. The Secretary of State shall review all nonimmigrant visa reciprocity agreements and arrangements to ensure that they are, with respect to each visa classification, truly reciprocal insofar as practicable with respect to validity period and fees, as required by sections 221(c) and 281 of the INA, 8 U.S.C. 1201(c) and 1351, and other treatment. If another country does not treat United States nationals seeking nonimmigrant visas in a truly reciprocal manner, the Secretary of State shall adjust the visa validity period, fee schedule, or other treatment to match the treatment of United States nationals by that foreign country, to the extent practicable.

Sec. 11. Transparency and Data Collection. (a) To be more transparent with the American people and to implement more effectively policies and practices that serve the national interest, the Secretary of Homeland Security, in consultation with the Attorney General, shall, consistent with applicable law and national security, collect and make publicly available the following information:

(i)   information regarding the number of foreign nationals in the United States who have been charged with terrorism-related offenses while in the United States; convicted of terrorism-related offenses while in the United States; or removed from the United States based on terrorism-related activity, affiliation with or provision of material support to a terrorism-related organization, or any other national-security-related reasons;

(ii) information regarding the number of foreign nationals in the United States who have been radicalized after entry into the United States and who have engaged in terrorism-related acts, or who have provided material support to terrorism-related organizations in countries that pose a threat to the United States;

(iii) information regarding the number and types of acts of gender-based violence against women, including so-called "honor killings," in the United States by foreign nationals; and

(iv) any other information relevant to public safety and security as determined by the Secretary of Homeland Security or the Attorney General, including information on the immigration status of foreign nationals charged with major offenses.

(b) The Secretary of Homeland Security shall release the initial report under subsection (a) of this section within 180 days of the effective date of this order and shall include information for the period from September 11, 2001, until the date of the initial report. Subsequent reports shall be issued every 180 days thereafter and reflect the period since the previous report.

Sec. 12. Enforcement. (a) The Secretary of State and the Secretary of Homeland Security shall consult with appropriate domestic and international partners, including countries and organizations, to ensure efficient, effective, and appropriate implementation of the actions directed in this order.

(b) In implementing this order, the Secretary of State and the Secretary of Homeland Security shall comply with all applicable laws and regulations, including, as appropriate, those providing an opportunity for individuals to claim a fear of persecution or torture, such as the credible fear determination for aliens covered by section 235(b)(1)(A) of the INA, 8 U.S.C. 1225(b)(1)(A).

(c) No immigrant or nonimmigrant visa issued before the effective date of this order shall be revoked pursuant to this order.

(d) Any individual whose visa was marked revoked or marked canceled as a result of Executive Order 13769 shall be entitled to a travel document confirming that the individual is permitted to travel to the United States and seek entry. Any prior cancellation or revocation of a visa that was solely pursuant to Executive Order 13769 shall not be the basis of inadmissibility for any future determination about entry or admissibility.

(e) This order shall not apply to an individual who has been granted asylum, to a refugee who has already been admitted to the United States, or to an individual granted withholding of removal or protection under the Convention Against Torture. Nothing in this order shall be construed to limit the ability of an individual to seek asylum, withholding of removal, or protection under the Convention Against Torture, consistent with the laws of the United States.

Sec. 13. Revocation. Executive Order 13769 of January 27, 2017, is revoked as of the effective date of this order.

Sec. 14. Effective Date. This order is effective at 12:01 a.m., eastern daylight time on March 16, 2017.

Sec. 15. Severability. (a) If any provision of this order, or the application of any provision to any person or circumstance, is held to be invalid, the remainder of this order and the application of its other provisions to any other persons or circumstances shall not be affected thereby.

(b) If any provision of this order, or the application of any provision to any person or circumstance, is held to be invalid because of the lack of certain procedural requirements, the relevant executive branch officials shall implement those procedural requirements.

Sec. 16. General Provisions. (a) Nothing in this order shall be construed to impair or otherwise affect:

(i) the authority granted by law to an executive department or agency, or the head thereof; or

(ii) the functions of the Director of the Office of Management and Budget relating to budgetary, administrative, or legislative proposals.

(b) This order shall be implemented consistent with applicable law and subject to the availability of appropriations.

(c) This order is not intended to, and does not, create any right or benefit, substantive or procedural, enforceable at law or in equity by any party against the United States, its departments, agencies, or entities, its officers, employees, or agents, or any other person.

DONALD J. TRUMP
The White House,
March 6, 2017.

SOURCE: Executive Office of the President. "Executive Order 13780—Protecting the Nation from Foreign Terrorist Entry into the United States." March 6, 2017. *Compilation of Presidential Documents* 2017, no. 00158 (March 6, 2017). https://www.gpo.gov/fdsys/pkg/DCPD-201700158/pdf/DCPD-201700158.pdf.

DOCUMENT

District Court Issues Injunction against Sanctuary City Executive Order

April 25, 2017

United States District Court

Northern District of California

County of Santa Clara, Plaintiff,

v.

Donald J. Trump, et al., Defendants.

Case No. 17-cv-00574-WHO

City and County of San Francisco, Plaintiff,

v.

Donald J. Trump, et al., Defendants.

Case No. 17-cv-00485-WHO

ORDER GRANTING THE COUNTY OF SANTA CLARA'S AND CITY AND COUNTY OF SAN FRANCISCO'S MOTIONS TO ENJOIN SECTION 9(a) OF EXECUTIVE ORDER 13768

INTRODUCTION

This case involves Executive Order 13768, "Enhancing Public Safety in the Interior of the United States," which, in addition to outlining a number of immigration enforcement policies, purports to "[e]nsure that jurisdictions that fail to comply with applicable Federal law do not receive Federal funds, except as mandated by law" and to establish a procedure whereby "sanctuary jurisdictions" shall be ineligible to receive federal grants. Executive Order 13768, 82 Fed. Reg. 8799 (Jan. 25, 2017) (the "Executive Order"). In two related actions, the County of Santa Clara and the City and County of San Francisco have challenged Section 9 of the Executive Order as facially unconstitutional and have brought motions for preliminary injunction seeking to enjoin its enforcement . . . .

[The remainder of the Introduction, the Background section, the Legal Standard section, and discussion of the standing in the case, have been omitted.]

II. LIKELIHOOD OF SUCCESS ON THE MERITS

The Counties challenge the Executive Order on several constitutional grounds and bear the burden of demonstrating a likelihood of success on the merits. The Government presents no defense to these constitutional arguments; it focused on standing and ripeness. I conclude that the Counties have demonstrated likely success on the merits in several ways.

A. Separation of Powers

The Counties argue that the Executive Order is unconstitutional because it seeks to wield powers that belong exclusively to Congress, the spending powers. Article I of the Constitution grants Congress the federal spending powers. See U.S. Const. art. I, § 8, cl. 1 . . . .

After a bill becomes law, the President is required to "take Care that the Law be faithfully executed." See U.S. Const. art. II, § 3, cl. 5. Where Congress has failed to give the President discretion in allocating funds, the President has no constitutional authority to withhold such funds and violates his obligation to faithfully execute the laws duly enacted by Congress if he does so. See City of New York, 524 U.S. at 439; U.S. Const. art. I, § 8, cl. 1. Further, "[w]hen the President takes measures incompatible with the expressed or implied will of Congress, his power is at its lowest ebb . . ." Youngstown Sheet & Tube Co. v. Sawyer, 343 U.S. 579, 637 (1952) (Jackson, J., concurring). Congress has intentionally limited the ability of the President to withhold or "impound" appropriated funds and has provided that the President may only do so after following particular procedures and after receiving Congress's express permission. See Impoundment Control Act of 1974, 2 U.S.C. §§ 683 et seq . . . .

Section 9 is particularly problematic as Congress has repeatedly, and frequently, declined to broadly condition federal funds or grants on compliance with Section 1373 or other federal immigration laws as the Executive Order purports to do . . . This puts the President's power "at its lowest ebb." Youngstown, 343 U.S. at 637. The Order's attempt to place new conditions on federal funds is an improper attempt to wield Congress's exclusive spending power and is a violation of the Constitution's separation of powers principles.

B. Spending Clause Violations

The Counties also argue that, even if the President had the spending power, the Executive Order would be unconstitutional under the Tenth Amendment as it exceeds those powers. The Counties are likely to succeed on this claim as well.

While Congress has significant authority to encourage policy through its spending power, the Supreme Court has articulated a number of limitations to the conditions Congress can place on federal funds. The Executive Order likely violates at least three of these restrictions: (1) conditions must be unambiguous and cannot be imposed after funds have already been accepted; (2) there must be a nexus between the federal funds at issue and the federal program's purpose; and (3) the financial inducement cannot be coercive . . . .

C. Tenth Amendment Violations

The Counties argue that Section 9(a) violates the Tenth Amendment because it attempts to conscript states and local jurisdictions into carrying out federal immigration law. The Counties are likely to succeed on this claim as well.

"The Federal Government may not compel the States to enact or administer a federal regulatory program." New York, 505 U.S. at 188. "The Federal Government may neither issue directives requiring the States to address particular problems, nor command the States' officers, or those of their political subdivisions, to administer or enforce a federal regulatory program." Printz v. United States, 521 U.S. 898, 935 (1997). "That is true whether Congress directly commands a State to regulate or indirectly coerces a State to adopt a federal regulatory system as its own." . . .

[Information and discussion on Fifth Amendment violations, the county assertions that the Executive Order would cause irreparable harm, and a balance of the harms in light of public interest, has been omitted.]

V. NATIONWIDE INJUNCTION

The Government argues that, if an injunction is issued, it should be issued only with regards to the plaintiffs and should not apply nationwide. But where a law is unconstitutional on its face, and not simply in its application to certain plaintiffs, a nationwide injunction is appropriate. See Califano v. Yamasaki, 442 U.S. 682, 702 (1979) ("[T]he scope of injunctive relief is dictated by the extent of the violation established, not by the geographical extent of the plaintiff."); Washington, 847 F.3d at 1166-67 (affirming nationwide injunction against executive travel ban order). The Counties have demonstrated that they are likely to succeed on their claims that the Executive Order purports to wield powers exclusive to Congress, and violates the Tenth and Fifth Amendments. These constitutional violations are not limited to San Francisco or Santa Clara, but apply equally to all states and local jurisdictions. Given the nationwide scope of the Order, and its apparent constitutional flaws, a nationwide injunction is appropriate.

VI. INJUNCTION AGAINST THE PRESIDENT

The Government also argues that, if an injunction is issued, it should not issue against the President. An injunction against the President personally is an "extraordinary measure not lightly to be undertaken." Swan v. Clinton, 100 F.3d 973, 978 (D.C. Cir. 1996); see Newdow v. Bush, 391 F. Supp. 2d 95, 106 (D.D.C. 2005) ("[T]he Supreme Court has sent a clear message that an injunction should not be issued against the President for official acts."). The Counties assert that the court "has discretion to determine whether the constitutional violations in the Executive Order may be remedied by an injunction against the named inferior officers, or whether this is an extraordinary circumstance where injunctive relief against the President himself is warranted."

I conclude that an injunction against the President is not appropriate. The Counties seek to enjoin the Executive Order which directs the Attorney General and the Secretary to carry out the provisions of Section 9. The President has no role in implementing Section 9. It is not clear how an injunction against the President would remedy the constitutional violations the Counties have alleged. On these facts, the extraordinary remedy of enjoining the President himself is not appropriate.

CONCLUSION

The Counties have demonstrated that they are likely to succeed on the merits of their challenge to Section 9(a) of the Executive Order, that they will suffer irreparable harm absent an injunction, and that the balance of harms and public interest weigh in their favor. The Counties' motions for a nationwide preliminary injunction, enjoining enforcement of Section 9(a), are GRANTED. The defendants (other than the President) are enjoined from enforcing Section 9(a) of the Executive Order against jurisdictions they deem as sanctuary jurisdictions. This injunction does not impact the Government's ability to use lawful means to enforce existing conditions of federal grants or 8 U.S.C. 1373, nor does it restrict the Secretary from developing regulations or preparing guidance on designating a jurisdiction as a "sanctuary jurisdiction."

IT IS SO ORDERED.

Dated: April 25, 2017
William H. Orrick
United States District

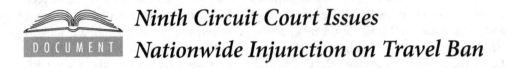

Ninth Circuit Court Issues
Nationwide Injunction on Travel Ban

June 12, 2017

[All footnotes have been omitted.]

United States Court of Appeals for the Ninth Circuit
State of Hawai'i; Ismail Elshikh, Plaintiffs-Appellees,

v.

Donald J. Trump, in his official capacity as President of the United States; U.S. Department of Homeland Security; John F. Kelly, in his official capacity as Secretary of Homeland Security; U.S. Department of State; Rex W. Tillerson, in his official capacity as Secretary of State; United States of America, Defendants-Appellants.

No. 17-15589
D.C. No. 1:17-cv-00050-DKW-KSC

Appeal from the United States District Court for the District of Hawai'i

Derrick Kahala Watson, District Judge, Presiding

Argued and Submitted May 15, 2017

Seattle, Washington

Filed June 12, 2017

Before: Michael Daly Hawkins, Ronald M. Gould,
and Richard A. Paez, Circuit Judges.

Per Curiam Opinion

[The list of counsel has been omitted.]

OPINION

PER CURIAM:

We are asked to delineate the statutory and constitutional limits to the President's power to control immigration in this appeal of the district court's order preliminarily enjoining two sections of Executive Order 13780 ("EO2" or "the Order"), "Protecting the Nation

From Foreign Terrorist Entry Into the United States." The Immigration and Nationality Act ("INA") gives the President broad powers to control the entry of aliens, and to take actions to protect the American public. But immigration, even for the President, is not a one-person show. The President's authority is subject to certain statutory and constitutional restraints. We conclude that the President, in issuing the Executive Order, exceeded the scope of the authority delegated to him by Congress. In suspending the entry of more than 180 million nationals from six countries, suspending the entry of all refugees, and reducing the cap on the admission of refugees from 110,000 to 50,000 for the 2017 fiscal year, the President did not meet the essential precondition to exercising his delegated authority: The President must make a sufficient finding that the entry of these classes of people would be "detrimental to the interests of the United States." Further, the Order runs afoul of other provisions of the INA that prohibit nationality-based discrimination and require the President to follow a specific process when setting the annual cap on the admission of refugees. On these statutory bases, we affirm in large part the district court's order preliminarily enjoining Sections 2 and 6 of the Executive Order.

[The background of the case and the Executive Order has been omitted.]

1

Under Article I of the Constitution, the power to make immigration laws "is entrusted exclusively to Congress." . . .

In the INA of 1952, Congress delegated some of its power to the President through Section 212(f), which provides:

> Whenever the President *finds* that the entry of any aliens or of any class of aliens into the United States would be detrimental to the interests of the United States, he may by proclamation, and for such period as he shall deem necessary, suspend the entry of all aliens or any class of aliens as immigrants or nonimmigrants, or impose on the entry of aliens any restrictions he may deem to be appropriate.

8 U.S.C. § 1182(f) . . .

To be sure, § 1182(f) gives the President broad authority to suspend the entry of aliens or classes of aliens. However, this authority is not unlimited. Section 1182(f) requires that the President *find* that the entry of a class of aliens into the United States *would be detrimental* to the interests of the United States. This section requires that the President's findings support the conclusion that entry of all nationals from the six designated countries, all refugees, and refugees in excess of 50,000 would be harmful to the national interest . . . .

The Order does not tie these nationals in any way to terrorist organizations within the six designated countries. It does not identify these nationals as contributors to active conflict or as those responsible for insecure country conditions. It does not provide any link between an individual's nationality and their propensity to commit terrorism or their inherent dangerousness. In short, the Order does not provide a rationale explaining why permitting entry of nationals from the six designated countries under current protocols would be detrimental to the interests of the United States . . . .

In conclusion, the Order does not offer a sufficient justification to suspend the entry of more than 180 million people on the basis of nationality. National security is not a "talismanic incantation" that, once invoked, can support any and all exercise of executive power under § 1182(f). *United States v. Robel,* 389 U.S. 258, 263–64 (1967); *see also Korematsu v. United States,* 323 U.S. 214, 235 (1944) (Murphy, J., dissenting) ("[T]he exclusion order necessarily must rely for its reasonableness upon the assumption that all persons of Japanese ancestry may have a dangerous tendency to commit sabotage and espionage and to aid our Japanese enemy in other ways. It is difficult to believe that reason, logic or experience could be marshalled in support of such an assumption."). Section 1182(f) requires that the President exercise his authority only after meeting the precondition of finding that entry of an alien or class of aliens *would be* detrimental to the interests of the United States. Here, the President has not done so.

[The remainder of the opinion, further detailing the court's findings, has been omitted.]

Source: United States Court of Appeals for the Ninth Circuit. *Hawai'i v. Trump.* June 12, 2017. https://cdn.ca9.uscourts.gov/datastore/opinions/2017/06/12/17-15589.pdf.

Supreme Court Issues
Initial Ruling on Travel Ban

June 26, 2017

SUPREME COURT OF THE UNITED STATES

DONALD J. TRUMP, PRESIDENT OF THE UNITED STATES, ET AL.

v.

INTERNATIONAL REFUGEE ASSISTANCE PROJECT, ET AL.

ON APPLICATION FOR STAY AND PETITION FOR WRIT OF CERTIORARI TO THE UNITED STATES COURT OF APPEALS FOR THE FOURTH CIRCUIT

DONALD J. TRUMP, PRESIDENT OF THE UNITED STATES, ET AL.

v.

HAWAII, ET AL.

ON APPLICATION FOR STAY AND PETITION FOR WRIT OF CERTIORARI TO THE UNITED STATES COURT OF APPEALS FOR THE NINTH CIRCUIT

[June 26, 2017]

PER CURIAM.

These cases involve challenges to Executive Order No. 13780, Protecting the Nation From Foreign Terrorist Entry Into the United States. The order alters practices concerning the entry of foreign nationals into the United States by, among other things, suspending entry of nationals from six designated countries for 90 days. Respondents challenged the order in two separate lawsuits. They obtained preliminary injunctions barring enforcement of several of its provisions, including the 90-day suspension of entry. The injunctions were upheld in large measure by the Courts of Appeals.

The Government filed separate petitions for certiorari, as well as applications to stay the preliminary injunctions entered by the lower courts. We grant the petitions for certiorari and grant the stay applications in part.

[Section I, which outlines the background of President Trump's executive order and the various lawsuits filed against it, has been omitted.]

II.

[The introduction to Section II and Section II part A, detailing the government's request for Supreme Court review, have been omitted.]

B

We now turn to the preliminary injunctions barring enforcement of the §2(c) entry suspension. We grant the Government's applications to stay the injunctions, to the extent the injunctions prevent enforcement of §2(c) with respect to foreign nationals who lack any bona fide relationship with a person or entity in the United States. We leave the injunctions entered by the lower courts in place with respect to respondents and those similarly situated, as specified in this opinion.

Crafting a preliminary injunction is an exercise of discretion and judgment, often dependent as much on the equities of a given case as the substance of the legal issues it presents. The purpose of such interim equitable relief is not to conclusively determine the rights of the parties, University of Tex. v. Camenisch, 451 U. S. 390, 395 (1981), but to balance the equities as the litigation moves forward. In awarding a preliminary injunction a court must also "conside[r] . . . the overall public interest." Winter, supra, at 26. In the course of doing so, a court "need not grant the total relief sought by the applicant but may mold its decree to meet the exigencies of the particular case."

Here, of course, we are not asked to grant a preliminary injunction, but to stay one. In assessing the lower courts' exercise of equitable discretion, we bring to bear an equitable judgment of our own. Nken v. Holder, 556 U. S. 418, 433 (2009). Before issuing a stay, "[i]t is ultimately necessary . . . to balance the equities—to explore the relative harms to applicant and respondent, as well as the interests of the public at large." This Court may, in its discretion, tailor a stay so that it operates with respect to only "some portion of the proceeding."

The courts below took account of the equities in fashioning interim relief, focusing specifically on the concrete burdens that would fall on Doe, Dr. Elshikh, and Hawaii if §2(c) were enforced. They reasoned that §2(c) would "directly affec[t]" Doe and Dr. Elshikh by delaying entry of their family members to the United States. The Ninth Circuit concluded that §2(c) would harm the State by preventing students from the designated nations who had been admitted to the University of Hawaii from entering this country. These hardships, the courts reasoned, were sufficiently weighty and immediate to outweigh the Government's interest in enforcing §2(c). Having adopted this view of the equities, the courts approved injunctions that covered not just respondents, but parties similarly situated to them—that is, people or entities in the United States who have relationships with foreign nationals abroad, and whose rights might be affected if those foreign nationals were excluded.

But the injunctions reach much further than that: They also bar enforcement of §2(c) against foreign nationals abroad who have no connection to the United States at all. The equities relied on by the lower courts do not balance the same way in that context. Denying entry to such a foreign national does not burden any American party by reason of that party's relationship with the foreign national. And the courts below did not conclude that exclusion in such circumstances would impose any legally relevant hardship on the foreign national himself. See id., at 762 ("[A]n unadmitted and nonresident alien . . . ha[s] no constitutional right of entry to this country"). So whatever burdens may result from enforcement of §2(c) against a foreign national who lacks any connection to this country, they are, at a minimum, a good deal less concrete than the hardships identified by the courts below.

At the same time, the Government's interest in enforcing §2(c), and the Executive's authority to do so, are undoubtedly at their peak when there is no tie between the foreign national and the United States. Indeed, EO–2 itself distinguishes between foreign nationals who have some connection to this country, and foreign nationals who do not, by establishing a case-by-case waiver system primarily for the benefit of individuals in the former category. The interest in preserving national security is "an urgent objective of the highest order." Holder v. Humanitarian Law Project, 561 U. S. 1, 28 (2010). To prevent the Government from pursuing that objective by enforcing §2(c) against foreign nationals unconnected to the United States would appreciably injure its interests, without alleviating obvious hardship to anyone else.

We accordingly grant the Government's stay applications in part and narrow the scope of the injunctions as to §2(c). The injunctions remain in place only with respect to parties similarly situated to Doe, Dr. Elshikh, and Hawaii. In practical terms, this means that §2(c) may not be enforced against foreign nationals who have a credible claim of a bona fide relationship with a person or entity in the United States. All other foreign nationals are subject to the provisions of EO–2.

The facts of these cases illustrate the sort of relationship that qualifies. For individuals, a close familial relationship is required. A foreign national who wishes to enter the United States to live with or visit a family member, like Doe's wife or Dr. Elshikh's mother-in-law, clearly has such a relationship. As for entities, the relationship must be formal, documented, and formed in the ordinary course, rather than for the purpose of evading EO–2. The students from the designated countries who have been admitted to the University of Hawaii have such a relationship with an American entity. So too would a worker who accepted an offer of employment from an American company or a lecturer invited to address an American audience. Not so someone who enters into a relationship simply to avoid §2(c): For example, a nonprofit group devoted to immigration issues may not contact foreign nationals from the designated countries, add them to client lists, and then secure their entry by claiming injury from their exclusion . . . .

C

The Hawaii injunction extends beyond §2(c) to bar enforcement of the §6(a) suspension of refugee admissions and the §6(b) refugee cap. In our view, the equitable balance struck above applies in this context as well. An American individual or entity that has a bona fide relationship with a particular person seeking to enter the country as a refugee can legitimately claim concrete hardship if that person is excluded. As to these individuals and entities, we do not disturb the injunction. But when it comes to refugees who lack any such connection to the United States, for the reasons we have set out, the balance tips in favor of the Government's compelling need to provide for the Nation's security. See supra, at 9–11; Haig v. Agee, 453 U. S. 280, 307 (1981).

The Government's application to stay the injunction with respect to §§6(a) and (b) is accordingly granted in part. Section 6(a) may not be enforced against an individual seeking admission as a refugee who can credibly claim a bona fide relationship with a person or entity in the United States. Nor may §6(b); that is, such a person may not be excluded pursuant to §6(b), even if the 50,000-person cap has been reached or exceeded. As applied to all other individuals, the provisions may take effect.

* * *

Accordingly, the petitions for certiorari are granted, and the stay applications are granted in part.

It is so ordered.

[The opinion of Justice Thomas, concurring in part and dissenting in part with the majority ruling, has been omitted.]

Source: Supreme Court of the United States. *Trump v. International Refugee Assistance Project.* 582 U.S.__(2017). https://www.supremecourt.gov/opinions/16pdf/16-1436_l6hc.pdf.

President Trump Issues Proclamation Regarding Travel into the United States

DOCUMENT

September 24, 2017

In Executive Order 13780 of March 6, 2017 (Protecting the Nation from Foreign Terrorist Entry into the United States), on the recommendations of the Secretary of Homeland Security and the Attorney General, I ordered a worldwide review of whether, and if so what, additional information would be needed from each foreign country to assess adequately whether their nationals seeking to enter the United States pose a security or safety threat. This was the first such review of its kind in United States history. As part of the review, the Secretary of Homeland Security established global requirements for information sharing in support of immigration screening and vetting. The Secretary of Homeland Security developed a comprehensive set of criteria and applied it to the information-sharing practices, policies, and capabilities of foreign governments. The Secretary of State thereafter engaged with the countries reviewed in an effort to address deficiencies and achieve improvements. In many instances, those efforts produced positive results. By obtaining additional information and formal commitments from foreign governments, the United States Government has improved its capacity and ability to assess whether foreign nationals attempting to enter the United States pose a security or safety threat. Our Nation is safer as a result of this work.

Despite those efforts, the Secretary of Homeland Security, in consultation with the Secretary of State and the Attorney General, has determined that a small number of countries—out of nearly 200 evaluated—remain deficient at this time with respect to their identity-management and information-sharing capabilities, protocols, and practices. In some cases, these countries also have a significant terrorist presence within their territory.

As President, I must act to protect the security and interests of the United States and its people. I am committed to our ongoing efforts to engage those countries willing to cooperate, improve information-sharing and identity-management protocols and procedures, and address both terrorism-related and public-safety risks. Some of the countries with remaining inadequacies face significant challenges. Others have made strides to improve their protocols and procedures, and I commend them for these efforts. But until they satisfactorily address the identified inadequacies, I have determined, on the basis of recommendations from the Secretary of Homeland Security and other members of my Cabinet, to impose certain conditional restrictions and limitations, as set forth more fully below, on entry into the United States of nationals of the countries identified in section 2 of this proclamation.

NOW, THEREFORE, I, DONALD J. TRUMP, by the authority vested in me by the Constitution and the laws of the United States of America, including sections 212(f) and 215(a) of the Immigration and Nationality Act (INA), 8 U.S.C. 1182(f) and 1185(a), and section 301 of title 3, United States Code, hereby find that, absent the measures set forth in this proclamation, the immigrant and nonimmigrant entry into the United States of persons described in section 2 of this proclamation would be detrimental to the interests of the United States, and that their entry should be subject to certain restrictions, limitations, and exceptions. I therefore hereby proclaim the following:

[Section 1, outlining the purpose of the proclamation and associated policy, has been omitted.]

Sec. 2. Suspension of Entry for Nationals of Countries of Identified Concern. The entry into the United States of nationals of the following countries is hereby suspended and limited, as follows, subject to categorical exceptions and case by-case waivers, as described in sections 3 and 6 of this proclamation:

(a) *Chad.*

    (i) The government of Chad is an important and valuable counterterrorism partner of the United States, and the United States Government looks forward to expanding that cooperation, including in the areas of immigration and border management. Chad has shown a clear willingness to improve in these areas. Nonetheless, Chad does not adequately share public-safety and terrorism-related information and fails to satisfy at least one key risk criterion. Additionally, several terrorist groups are active within Chad or in the surrounding region, including elements of Boko Haram, ISIS-West Africa, and al-Qa'ida in the Islamic Maghreb. At this time, additional information sharing to identify those foreign nationals applying for visas or seeking entry into the United States who represent national security and public-safety threats is necessary given the significant terrorism-related risk from this country.

    (ii) The entry into the United States of nationals of Chad, as immigrants, and as nonimmigrants on business (B-1), tourist (B-2), and business/tourist (B-1/B-2) visas, is hereby suspended.

(b) *Iran.*

    (i) Iran regularly fails to cooperate with the United States Government in identifying security risks, fails to satisfy at least one key risk criterion, is the source of significant terrorist threats, and fails to receive its nationals subject to final orders of removal from the United States. The Department of State has also designated Iran as a state sponsor of terrorism.

    (ii) The entry into the United States of nationals of Iran as immigrants and as nonimmigrants is hereby suspended, except that entry by such nationals under valid student (F and M) and exchange visitor (J) visas is not suspended, although such individuals should be subject to enhanced screening and vetting requirements.

(c) *Libya.*

    (i) The government of Libya is an important and valuable counterterrorism partner of the United States, and the United States Government looks forward to expanding on that cooperation, including in the areas of immigration and border management. Libya, nonetheless, faces significant challenges in sharing several types of information, including public-safety and terrorism-related information necessary for the protection of the national security and public safety of the United States. Libya also has significant inadequacies in its identity-management protocols. Further, Libya fails to satisfy at least one key risk criterion and has been assessed to be not fully cooperative with respect to receiving its nationals subject to final orders of removal from the United States. The substantial terrorist presence within Libya's territory amplifies the risks posed by the entry into the United States of its nationals.

    (ii) The entry into the United States of nationals of Libya, as immigrants, and as nonimmigrants on business (B-1), tourist (B-2), and business/tourist (B-1/B-2) visas, is hereby suspended.

(d) *North Korea.*

    (i) North Korea does not cooperate with the United States Government in any respect and fails to satisfy all information-sharing requirements.

    (ii) The entry into the United States of nationals of North Korea as immigrants and nonimmigrants is hereby suspended.

(e) *Syria.*

    (i) Syria regularly fails to cooperate with the United States Government in identifying security risks, is the source of significant terrorist threats, and has been designated by the Department of State as a state sponsor of terrorism. Syria has significant inadequacies in identity-management protocols, fails to share public-safety and terrorism information, and fails to satisfy at least one key risk criterion.

    (ii) The entry into the United States of nationals of Syria as immigrants and nonimmigrants is hereby suspended.

(f) *Venezuela.*

    (i) Venezuela has adopted many of the baseline standards identified by the Secretary of Homeland Security and in section 1 of this proclamation, but its government is uncooperative in verifying whether its citizens pose national security or public-safety threats. Venezuela's government fails to share public-safety and terrorism-related information adequately, fails to satisfy at least one key risk criterion, and has been assessed to be not fully cooperative with respect to receiving its nationals subject to final orders of removal from the United States. There are, however, alternative sources for obtaining information to verify the citizenship and identity of nationals from Venezuela. As a result, the restrictions imposed by this proclamation focus on government officials of Venezuela who are responsible for the identified inadequacies.

(ii) Notwithstanding section 3(b)(v) of this proclamation, the entry into the United States of officials of government agencies of Venezuela involved in screening and vetting procedures—including the Ministry of the Popular Power for Interior, Justice and Peace; the Administrative Service of Identification, Migration and Immigration; the Scientific, Penal and Criminal Investigation Service Corps; the Bolivarian National Intelligence Service; and the Ministry of the Popular Power for Foreign Relations—and their immediate family members, as nonimmigrants on business (B-1), tourist (B-2), and business/tourist (B-1/B-2) visas, is hereby suspended. Further, nationals of Venezuela who are visa holders should be subject to appropriate additional measures to ensure traveler information remains current.

(g) *Yemen.*

(i) The government of Yemen is an important and valuable counterterrorism partner, and the United States Government looks forward to expanding that cooperation, including in the areas of immigration and border management. Yemen, nonetheless, faces significant identity-management challenges, which are amplified by the notable terrorist presence within its territory. The government of Yemen fails to satisfy critical identity-management requirements, does not share public-safety and terrorism-related information adequately, and fails to satisfy at least one key risk criterion.

(ii) The entry into the United States of nationals of Yemen as immigrants, and as nonimmigrants on business (B-1), tourist (B-2), and business/tourist (B-1/B-2) visas, is hereby suspended.

(h) *Somalia.*

(i) The Secretary of Homeland Security's report of September 15, 2017, determined that Somalia satisfies the information-sharing requirements of the baseline described in section 1(c) of this proclamation. But several other considerations support imposing entry restrictions and limitations on Somalia. Somalia has significant identity-management deficiencies. For example, while Somalia issues an electronic passport, the United States and many other countries do not recognize it. A persistent terrorist threat also emanates from Somalia's territory. The United States Government has identified Somalia as a terrorist safe haven. Somalia stands apart from other countries in the degree to which its government lacks command and control of its territory, which greatly limits the effectiveness of its national capabilities in a variety of respects. Terrorists use under-governed areas in northern, central, and southern Somalia as safe havens from which to plan, facilitate, and conduct their operations. Somalia also remains a destination for individuals attempting to join terrorist groups that threaten the national security of the United States. The State Department's 2016 Country Reports on Terrorism observed that Somalia has not sufficiently degraded the ability of terrorist groups to plan and mount attacks from its territory. Further, despite having made significant progress toward formally federating its member states, and its willingness to fight terrorism, Somalia continues to struggle to provide the governance needed to limit terrorists' freedom of movement, access to resources, and capacity to operate. The government of Somalia's lack of territorial control also compromises Somalia's ability, already limited because of poor recordkeeping, to share information about its nationals who pose criminal or terrorist risks. As a result of these and other factors, Somalia presents special concerns that distinguish it from other countries.

(ii) The entry into the United States of nationals of Somalia as immigrants is hereby suspended. Additionally, visa adjudications for nationals of Somalia and decisions regarding their entry as nonimmigrants should be subject to additional scrutiny to determine if applicants are connected to terrorist organizations or otherwise pose a threat to the national security or public safety of the United States.

Sec. 3. Scope and Implementation of Suspensions and Limitations. (a) Scope. Subject to the exceptions set forth in subsection (b) of this section and any waiver under subsection (c) of this section, the suspensions of and limitations on entry pursuant to section 2 of this proclamation shall apply only to foreign nationals of the designated countries who:

(i) are outside the United States on the applicable effective date under section 7 of this proclamation;

(ii) do not have a valid visa on the applicable effective date under section 7 of this proclamation; and

(iii) do not qualify for a visa or other valid travel document under section 6(d) of this proclamation.

(b) *Exceptions.* The suspension of entry pursuant to section 2 of this proclamation shall not apply to:

(i) any lawful permanent resident of the United States;

(ii) any foreign national who is admitted to or paroled into the United States on or after the applicable effective date under section 7 of this proclamation;

(iii) any foreign national who has a document other than a visa—such as a transportation letter, an appropriate boarding foil, or an advance parole document—valid on the applicable effective date under section 7 of this proclamation or issued on any date thereafter, that permits him or her to travel to the United States and seek entry or admission;

(iv) any dual national of a country designated under section 2 of this proclamation when the individual is traveling on a passport issued by a non-designated country;

(v) any foreign national traveling on a diplomatic or diplomatic-type visa, North Atlantic Treaty Organization visa, C-2 visa for travel to the United Nations, or G-1, G-2, G-3, or G-4 visa; or

(vi) any foreign national who has been granted asylum by the United States; any refugee who has already been admitted to the United States; or any individual who has been granted withholding of removal, advance parole, or protection under the Convention Against Torture.

(c) *Waivers.* Notwithstanding the suspensions of and limitations on entry set forth in section 2 of this proclamation, a consular officer, or the Commissioner, United States Customs and Border Protection (CBP), or the Commissioner's designee, as appropriate, may, in their discretion, grant waivers on a case-by-case basis to permit the entry of foreign nationals for whom entry is otherwise suspended or limited if such foreign nationals demonstrate that waivers would be appropriate and consistent with subsections (i) through (iv) of this subsection. The Secretary of State and the Secretary of Homeland Security shall coordinate to adopt guidance addressing the circumstances in which waivers may be appropriate for foreign nationals seeking entry as immigrants or nonimmigrants.

[The remainder of the proclamation, outlining its enforcement, has been omitted.]

IN WITNESS WHEREOF, I have hereunto set my hand this twenty-fourth day of September, in the year of our Lord two thousand seventeen, and of the Independence of the United States of America the two hundred and forty-second.

DONALD J. TRUMP

SOURCE: Executive Office of the President. "Proclamation 9645—Enhancing Vetting Capabilities and Processes for Detecting Attempted Entry into the United States by Terrorists or Other Public-Safety Threats." September 24, 2017. *Compilation of Presidential Documents* 2017, no. 00685 (September 24, 2017). https://www.gpo.gov/fdsys/pkg/DCPD-201700685/pdf/DCPD-201700685.pdf.

Supreme Court Issues Emergency Stay on Travel Ban Case in Fourth Circuit

DOCUMENT

December 4, 2017

17A560 TRUMP, PRESIDENT OF U.S., ET AL. V.
INT'L REFUGEE ASSISTANCE, ET AL.

The application for a stay presented to The Chief Justice and by him referred to the Court is granted, and the District Court's October 17, 2017 order granting a preliminary injunction is stayed pending disposition of the Government's appeal in the United States Court of Appeals for the Fourth Circuit and disposition of the Government's petition for a writ of certiorari, if such writ is sought. If a writ of certiorari is sought and the Court denies the petition, this order shall terminate automatically. If the Court grants the petition for a writ of certiorari, this order shall terminate when the Court enters its judgment.

In light of its decision to consider the case on an expedited basis, we expect that the Court of Appeals will render its decision with appropriate dispatch.

Justice Ginsburg and Justice Sotomayor would deny the application.

SOURCE: Supreme Court of the United States. Order in Pending Case. 17A560 *Trump, President of U.S., et al. v. Int'l Refugee Assistance, et al.* December 4, 2017. https://www.supremecourt.gov/orders/courtorders/120417zr1_j4ek.pdf.

Supreme Court Issues Emergency Stay on Travel Ban Case in Ninth Circuit

December 4, 2017

17A550 TRUMP, PRESIDENT OF U.S., ET AL. V. HAWAII, ET AL.

The application for a stay presented to Justice Kennedy and by him referred to the Court is granted, and the District Court's October 20, 2017 order granting a preliminary injunction is stayed pending disposition of the Government's appeal in the United States Court of Appeals for the Ninth Circuit and disposition of the Government's petition for a writ of certiorari, if such writ is sought. If a writ of certiorari is sought and the Court denies the petition, this order shall terminate automatically. If the Court grants the petition for a writ of certiorari, this order shall terminate when the Court enters its judgment.

In light of its decision to consider the case on an expedited basis, we expect that the Court of Appeals will render its decision with appropriate dispatch.

Justice Ginsburg and Justice Sotomayor would deny the application.

SOURCE: Supreme Court of the United States. Order in Pending Case. 17A550 *Trump, President of U.S., et al. v. Hawaii, et al.* December 4, 2017. https://www.supremecourt.gov/orders/courtorders/120417zr_4gd5.pdf.

OTHER HISTORIC DOCUMENTS OF INTEREST

FROM THIS VOLUME

FROM PREVIOUS *HISTORIC DOCUMENTS*

Neil Gorsuch Confirmed and Sworn In as Supreme Court Justice

JANUARY 31, MARCH 20, AND APRIL 7 AND 10, 2017

On April 10, 2017, Neil M. Gorsuch was sworn in as an Associate Justice for the United States Supreme Court, ending a more than year-long battle over the vacant seat that tested constitutional norms and for the first time in decades determined the ideological split of the court. The seat to which Gorsuch was nominated by President Donald Trump in January 2017 had been subject to a fierce and heated debate since the death of Antonin Scalia in early 2016 that left an even division of liberals and conservatives on the nine-member court. Complicating matters, Scalia's death came during a presidential election year, elevating control of the nation's highest court for the first time in decades to a daily campaign issue in a contentious election. Democrats contended that Merrick Garland, President Obama's nomination, should fill the seat, while Republicans argued that the seat should be held open for the next president; the Senate ultimately never considered Garland's nomination. Gorsuch faced more than twenty hours of questioning at his Senate confirmation, after which Senate Republicans chose to implement what is known as the nuclear option—a rule allowing the Senate to break a Democratic filibuster with fifty-one votes instead of the typical sixty—to confirm Gorsuch as the fifth conservative member of the court.

THE DEATH OF JUSTICE ANTONIN SCALIA

On February 13, 2016, United States Supreme Court Justice Antonin Scalia passed away in his sleep at the age of seventy-nine. Despite a history of heart trouble, including high blood pressure, Justice Scalia's death was unexpected and came as a shock to the nation. His passing set off a contentious battle over control of the nine-member Supreme Court that would take more than a year to settle and would test and fray democratic norms in the nation's legislative chambers.

Justice Scalia was appointed to the Supreme Court by then-president Ronald Reagan on September 26, 1986. He quickly cemented himself as one of the most conservative members of the body and was known for his caustic dissents that alienated his allies nearly as often as his critics. A constitutional originalist, Scalia staunchly believed that the constitution should be interpreted as written. After Justice John Paul Stevens retired in 2010, Justice Scalia became the longest-serving member of the court and the chief writer on a number of historic opinions ranging from handgun ownership and gay marriage to the Affordable Care Act. Despite welcoming Justice Steven's replacement, Elena Kagan, a liberal, the contours of the modern court remained how they had been for more than six decades: a five conservative–four liberal division, with Chief Justice John Roberts acting as both a conservative and a swing vote in divided cases.

Supreme Court Seat Remains
Unfilled Ahead of 2016 Election

Scalia's death left then-president Barack Obama and Senate Republicans in an unusual position: The last time a Senate Republican majority oversaw a Democratic president's Supreme Court nominee was more than a century earlier. A contentious presidential election and a hyper-partisan political climate vastly complicated matters. Republicans remained unwilling to give a Democratic president the chance to reshape the court for decades to come, while Democrats remained eager to fulfill their constitutional duty to appoint a replacement.

In an address to the nation commemorating Scalia's life, President Obama laid down a marker to Senate Republicans. "I plan to fulfill my constitutional responsibilities to nominate a successor in due time," President Obama said. A month later, President Obama nominated centrist Appellate Judge Merrick Garland, saying in his formal announcement ceremony, "Presidents do not stop working in the final year of their term; neither should a senator."

Senate Republicans dug in their heels. Senate Majority Leader Mitch McConnell, R-Ky., vowed to block consideration of any nominee until after the next president was chosen. "The American people may well elect a president who decides to nominate Judge Garland for Senate consideration," Mr. McConnell said. "The next president may also nominate someone very different. Either way, our view is this: Give the people a voice in the filling of this vacancy," he added. McConnell followed his speech by calling Garland to explain he would not meet with him nor would he take any action on his nomination.

The standoff quickly seeped into the 2016 presidential election. Republican nominee Donald Trump announced over the course of the campaign two short lists of nominees he would consider should he win the presidency. More traditional nominees such as legal scholars and judges, including Tenth Circuit Appellate Judge Neil Gorsuch, dotted the list, while Trump's inclusion of those outside legal and political structures, such as a Tea Party senator and an antiabortion activist, raised eyebrows.

Gorsuch Confirmation Hearings
Flame Political Frustrations

Days after his inauguration, President Trump formally nominated Gorsuch for Supreme Court justice at a ceremony at the White House. "Judge Gorsuch has a superb intellect, an unparalleled legal education, and a commitment to interpreting the Constitution according to its text," President Trump said. Gorsuch began his law career serving as a judicial clerk for Justice Anthony Kennedy, another Reagan appointee, in the early 1990s. Following his judicial clerkship, Gorsuch left for private practice and then served as Principal Deputy Associate Attorney General at the U.S. Department of Justice before being appointed by then-President George W. Bush to the United States Court of Appeals for the Tenth Circuit.

Gorsuch's Supreme Court nomination was first considered by the Senate Judiciary Committee. Confirmation hearings began on the morning of March 20, 2017. Over the next four days, Senate Democrats and Republicans, and Judge Gorsuch himself, outlined the contours of the debate around his nomination. Senate Democrats dissected Judge Gorsuch's legal record and opinions, focusing in particular on his rulings around workers' rights while also sharply criticizing their Republican colleagues for, what Sen. Dianne Feinstein, D-Calif., called, the "unprecedented treatment" of President Obama's nominee.

Senate Republicans took a more congenial tone, seeking to insulate a traditionally conservative and qualified candidate. Judge Gorsuch attempted to sit above the party politics, positioning himself as a creature of consensus. Judge Gorsuch's appeal for comity was evident from his opening remarks. He insisted that he put no one above the law including corporations, an attempt to preempt attacks on his legal record and his apparent deference to corporate interests. "I have ruled for disabled students, prisoners, and workers alleging civil rights violations," Gorsuch said. "Sometimes, I have ruled against such persons too. But my decisions have never reflected a judgment about the people before me—only my best judgment about the law and facts at issue in each particular case," Gorsuch noted.

On the second day of questioning, Judge Gorsuch sought to assert himself as independent from politics and the White House. With questions around the president's campaign and Russia swirling outside the confirmation room, several Democratic Senators, including Patrick J. Leahy, D-Vt., pressed Judge Gorsuch on whether he could hold President Trump accountable. "No man is above the law," Judge Gorsuch responded. Later, Judge Gorsuch again asserted his independence, stating that the White House had not asked him to make any commitments on legal issues prior to his nomination. "I have offered no promises on how I'd rule to anyone on any case," he said.

Senate Democrats also probed Judge Gorsuch on several hot-button issues. The nominee refused to be pinned down, declining to answer questions on abortion, gun rights, and President Trump's travel ban. Senate Democrats, including the top Democrat on the committee, did find traction with Judge Gorsuch on torture. Sen. Feinstein pressed Judge Gorsuch on his involvement as a Justice Department official in several war-on-terror disputes, including torture, warrantless surveillance, and the scope of the president's power as commander-in-chief. In response, Judge Gorsuch downplayed his role in the Bush-era disputes, describing his role as merely a speechwriter. "I was the scribe," the nominee said. Sen. Leahy picked up Sen. Feinstein's line of questioning, pressing Judge Gorsuch on the legality of torture. The nominee answered by rattling off legal precedents that ban torture, seemingly distancing himself from the President's past comments calling for the reinstatement of torture.

Senate Republicans lobbed less pointed questions—even "softballs." Judiciary Chairman Sen. Chuck Grassley, R-Iowa, opened his questioning asking if Judge Gorsuch would have "any trouble" ruling against the president who appointed him. "That's a softball, Mr. Chairman," Judge Gorsuch replied in a scripted response, saying that he would have no difficulty ruling for or against any party. Sen. Ted Cruz, R-Texas, asked the nominee, "What is the answer to the ultimate question of life, the universe and everything?" Judge Gorsuch responded, "Forty-two," a joke from the book "The Hitchhiker's Guide to the Galaxy."

Other Republicans, however, sought clarifications on the nominee's overarching legal principles. Sen. Orrin Hatch, R-Utah, questioned Judge Gorsuch on how to apply new technologies to constitutional principles written two centuries ago. The nominee affirmed his stance as a constitutional originalist, saying, "Technology changes, but the principles don't." Judge Gorsuch noted that he believed "it can't be the case the U.S. Constitution is any less protective" of people's privacy than when it was written.

The most pointed questioning and criticisms addressed his case history on corporations and employees' rights. Senate Democrats repeatedly highlighted Judge Gorsuch's dissent arguing in favor of a trucking company that fired a driver for abandoning his truck and cargo in subzero temperatures for his own safety. Critics contended that his decision was reflective of his bias toward corporate interests over their workers and became the backbone for Democratic objection to his nomination. The subzero weather was frigid, Sen. Dick Durbin, D-Ill., said, but "not as cold as your dissent, Judge Gorsuch."

Even after questioning ended, Judge Gorsuch remained cagey. In a seventy-six-page response to written questions from senators, the nominee refused to elaborate on his personal views, relying on boilerplate phrases contending it would be "improper" and "risk violating my ethical obligations as a judge" to discuss matters that could come before the court. Despite dodging pointed questions and over the repeated criticisms of Senate Democrats, Judge Gorsuch was confirmed by the Senate Judiciary Committee on a party-line vote.

THE NUCLEAR OPTION

The Republican Party made several advances during the 2016 elections, most notably electing a Republican president with the power to fill Scalia's vacant seat with a conservative voice. However, Republicans fell short of winning sixty Senate seats, a crucial threshold that would have allowed the majority party to break any Democratic filibuster of judicial nominees.

With Judge Gorsuch's confirmation before the Senate floor, he needed a simple fifty-one vote majority to assume his seat. Democrats, however, signaled a willingness to filibuster the vote. Eight votes shy of the necessary sixty to break a filibuster, McConnell, with the urging of President Trump and the backing of his caucus, signaled that he would eliminate filibusters for Supreme Court selections by invoking what became known as "the nuclear option." Invoking the nuclear option would allow Republicans to break a filibuster with only fifty-one votes—the same number of members in their caucus—and push though Gorsuch's confirmation. Judge Gorsuch was confirmed by a vote of 54–45 on April 7, 2017. Three Democrats—Joe Manchin, D-W.V., Heidi Heitkamp, D-N.D., and Joe Donnelly, D-Ind.—who represent states that voted heavily for Trump, joined the Republicans in voting yes. Speaking from the Senate floor, McConnell praised Gorsuch. "He's an exceptional choice, and I'm very much looking forward to confirming him today," McConnell said, adding, "Of course, I wish that important aspects of this process had played out differently."

Three days after his confirmation, Gorsuch was sworn in as the newest Associate Justice at a ceremony in the Rose Garden. President Trump celebrated the justice, saying, "Americans are blessed to have in Neil Gorsuch a man who will, likewise, be a devoted servant of the law." Justice Kennedy, his former boss and now colleague, administered the oath of office. Justice Gorsuch offered his appreciation to friends, family, colleagues, Senate leaders, and the public at the ceremony. "To the American people, I am humbled by the trust placed in me today," Justice Gorsuch said. "I will never forget that to whom much is given, much will be expected. And I promise you that I will do all my powers permit to be a faithful servant of the Constitution and laws of this great nation."

—Robert Howard

Following is a press release issued by the White House after the nomination of Judge Neil Gorsuch to the U.S. Supreme Court on January 31, 2017; excerpted remarks delivered by Judge Gorsuch to the Senate Judiciary Committee on March 20, 2017, during his confirmation process; a statement by President Trump on April 7, 2017, after Judge Gorsuch's confirmation; and the edited remarks delivered by President Trump and Judge Gorsuch at his swearing-in ceremony on April 10, 2017.

Trump Nominates Judge Gorsuch to Supreme Court

January 31, 2017

Today, President Donald J. Trump nominated Judge Neil Gorsuch of the U.S. Court of Appeals for the Tenth Circuit to fill the Supreme Court vacancy created by the passing of Justice Antonin Scalia. The nomination of Judge Gorsuch comes after a selection process marked by an unprecedented level of transparency and involvement by the American voters.

"I am proud to announce the nomination of Judge Neil Gorsuch for Justice of the Supreme Court," President Trump said. "This has been the most transparent and most important Supreme Court selection process in the history of our country and I wanted the American people to have a voice in this nomination. Judge Gorsuch has a superb intellect, an unparalleled legal education, and a commitment to interpreting the Constitution according to its text. He will make an incredible Justice as soon as the Senate confirms him."

Judge Gorsuch was born and raised in Colorado. He attended Columbia University and Harvard Law School. After graduating with honors, he received his doctorate from Oxford University as a Marshall Scholar. Judge Gorsuch clerked for Judge David Sentelle of the D.C. Circuit and both Justices Byron White and Anthony Kennedy on the Supreme Court. Following a successful career in private practice, Judge Gorsuch joined the Department of Justice as the Principal Deputy Associate Attorney General. In 2006, President George W. Bush nominated him for the U.S. Court of Appeals for the Tenth Circuit, and he was confirmed by voice vote without objection. He has served with distinction, earning a reputation as a brilliant jurist with an outstanding intellect and a clear, incisive writing style, and he is universally respected for his integrity and fairness to all parties.

"I am honored and humbled to receive this nomination," said Judge Gorsuch. "I look forward to meeting with Senators over the coming weeks as we begin this process."

SOURCE: The White House. "President Donald J. Trump Nominates Judge Neil Gorsuch to the United States Supreme Court." January 31, 2017. https://www.whitehouse.gov/presidential-actions/president-donald-j-trump-nominates-judge-neil-gorsuch-united-states-supreme-court/.

Judge Gorsuch Delivers Remarks before the Senate Judiciary Committee

March 20, 2017

Mr. Chairman, Sen. Feinstein, Members of the Committee:

I am honored and I am humbled to be here. Since coming to Washington, I have met with over 70 senators. You have offered a warm welcome and wise advice. Thank you. I also want to thank the President and Vice President. They and their teams have been very gracious to me and I thank them for this honor. I want to thank Senators Bennet and Gardner and General Katyal for their introductions. Reminding us that—long before we are Republicans or Democrats—we are Americans. Sitting here I am acutely aware of my own imperfections. But I pledge to each of you and to the American people that, if confirmed, I will do all my powers permit to be a faithful servant of the Constitution and laws of our great nation. . . .

Mr. Chairman, these days we sometimes hear judges cynically described as politicians in robes. Seeking to enforce their own politics rather than striving to apply the law impartially. But I just don't think that's what a life in the law is about.

As a lawyer working for many years in the trial court trenches, I saw judges and juries—while human and imperfect—trying hard every day to decide fairly the cases I presented.

As a judge now for more than a decade, I have watched my colleagues spend long days worrying over cases. Sometimes the answers we reach aren't ones we would personally prefer.

Sometimes the answers follow us home and keep us up at night. But the answers we reach are always the ones we believe the law requires. For all its imperfections, the rule of law in this nation truly is a wonder—and it is no wonder that it is the envy of the world.

Once in a while, of course, we judges do disagree. But our disagreements are never about politics—only the law's demands. Let me offer an example. The first case I wrote as a judge to reach the Supreme Court divided 5 to 4. The Court affirmed my judgment with the support of Justices Thomas and Sotomayor—while Justices Stevens and Scalia dissented. Now that's a lineup some might think unusual. But actually it's exactly the sort of thing that happens—quietly, day in and day out—in the supreme court and in courts across our country. I wonder if people realize that Justices Thomas and Sotomayor agree about 60% of the time, or that Justices Scalia and Breyer agreed even more often than that. All in the toughest cases in our whole legal system.

Here's another example. Over the last decade, I've participated in over 2,700 appeals. Often these cases are hard too: only about 5% of all federal lawsuits make their way to decision in a court of appeals. I've served with judges appointed by President Obama all the way back to President Johnson. And in the Tenth Circuit we hear cases from 6 states—in two time zones—covering 20% of the continental United States. But in the West we listen to one another respectfully, we tolerate and cherish different points of view, and we seek consensus whenever we can. My law clerks tell me that 97% of the 2,700 cases I've decided were decided unanimously. And that I have been in the majority 99% of the time.

Of course, I make my share of mistakes. As my daughters never tire of reminding me, putting on a robe doesn't make me any smarter. I'll never forget my first day on the job. Carrying a pile of papers up steps to the bench, I tripped on my robe and everything just about went flying. But troublesome as it can be, the robe does mean something—and not just that I can hide coffee stains on my shirt. Putting on a robe reminds us that it's time to lose our egos and open our minds. It serves, too, as a reminder of the modest station we judges are meant to occupy in a democracy. In other countries, judges wear scarlet, silk, and ermine. Here, we judges buy our own plain black robes. And I can report that the standard choir outfit at the local uniform supply store is a pretty good deal. Ours is a judiciary of honest black polyester.

When I put on the robe, I am also reminded that under our Constitution, it is for this body, the people's representatives, to make new laws. For the executive to ensure those laws are faithfully enforced. And for neutral and independent judges to apply the law in the people's disputes. If judges were just secret legislators, declaring not what the law is but what they would like it to be, the very idea of a government by the people and for the people would be at risk. And those who came to court would live in fear, never sure exactly what governs them except the judge's will. As Alexander Hamilton explained, "liberty can have nothing to fear from" judges who apply the law, but liberty "ha[s] every thing to fear" if judges try to legislate too.

In my decade on the bench, I have tried to treat all who come to court fairly and with respect. I have decided cases for Native Americans seeking to protect tribal lands, for class actions like one that ensured compensation for victims of nuclear waste pollution by corporations in Colorado. I have ruled for disabled students, prisoners, and workers alleging civil rights violations. Sometimes, I have ruled against such persons too. But my decisions have never reflected a judgment about the people before me—only my best judgment about the law and facts at issue in each particular case. For the truth is, a judge who likes every outcome he reaches is probably a pretty bad judge, stretching for the policy results he prefers rather than those the law compels. . . .

SOURCE: Senate Judiciary Committee. "Gorsuch Testimony." March 20, 2017. https://www.judiciary.sen ate.gov/imo/media/doc/03-20-17%20Gorsuch%20Testimony.pdf.

President Trump Responds to Judge Gorsuch's Confirmation

April 7, 2017

It is a great honor to announce the historic confirmation of Judge Neil M. Gorsuch as Associate Justice to the Supreme Court of the United States. Judge Gorsuch's confirmation process was one of the most transparent and accessible in history, and his judicial temperament, exceptional intellect, unparalleled integrity, and record of independence makes him the perfect choice to serve on the Nation's highest court. As a deep believer in the rule of law, Judge Gorsuch will serve the American people with distinction as he continues to faithfully and vigorously defend our Constitution.

I would also like to thank Justice Scalia and his wife Maureen for their immeasurable service to this country. Justice Scalia's legacy of fidelity to our laws and our Constitution will never be forgotten.

SOURCE: Executive Office of the President. "Statement on Senate Confirmation of Neil M. Gorsuch as Supreme Court Associate Justice." April 7, 2017. *Compilation of Presidential Documents* 2017, no. 00241 (April 7, 2017). https://www.gpo.gov/fdsys/pkg/DCPD-201700241/pdf/DCPD-201700241.pdf.

President Trump, Judge Gorsuch Deliver Remarks at the Swearing-In Ceremony

April 10, 2017

The President. Thank you very much. Friends and distinguished guests, welcome to the White House. We are gathered here today for a truly momentous occasion in our democracy: the swearing-in of a United States Supreme Court justice. . . .

Americans are blessed to have in Neil Gorsuch a man who will, likewise, be a devoted servant of the law. Over the past 2 months, the American people have gotten to know, respect and truly admire our newest member of the United States Supreme Court. In Justice Gorsuch, they see a man of great and unquestioned integrity. They see a man of unmatched qualifications. And most of all—and most importantly—they see a man who is deeply faithful to the Constitution of the United States. He will decide cases based not on his personal preferences, but based on a fair and objective reading of the law.

Today we have all three branches of Government represented at this event. It is a very special thing and a very special happening. And it's worth taking just a minute to remember what it all means.

In our Founders' incredible wisdom, they gave each branch of Government a different role in our great Republic. We have a Congress to write the laws on behalf of the people. We have a President to enforce those laws and defend our Nation. And we have a Supreme Court to apply and interpret the law in a fair and impartial manner when disagreements arise. The Founders separated power because they knew it was the best way to protect our citizens and keep our Constitution secure.

Justice Gorsuch, you are now entrusted with the sacred duty of defending our Constitution. Our country is counting on you to be wise, impartial, and fair; to serve under our laws, not over them; and to safeguard the right of the people to govern their own affairs. I have no doubt you will rise to the occasion and that the decisions you will make will not only protect our Constitution today, but for many generations of Americans to come.

In just a moment, Justice Gorsuch will be sworn in by Justice Kennedy, a great man of outstanding accomplishment. Throughout his nearly 30 years on the Supreme Court, Justice Kennedy has been praised by all for his dedicated and dignified service. We owe him an enormous debt of gratitude, and I am honored that he is with us today.

This is a very, very special moment, because many years ago, a young Neil Gorsuch started his legal career as a law clerk to Justice Kennedy. You remember that, right? [Laughter] It is a fitting testament to Justice Kennedy's impact that, upon giving the oath to Justice Gorsuch, he will become the first-ever Supreme Court justice to serve with one of his former law clerks.

That's sort of a big deal, isn't it? I sort of like that. That's sort of good. It has never happened before. That's pretty good. It also shows you have a lot of respect for this man. That's very good.

We're thrilled to share this historic moment with Justice Kennedy, with all of you here today, and with all Americans watching us at home.

Justice Gorsuch, I again congratulate you and your entire family, and I wish God's blessings on your amazing journey ahead. I have no doubt you will go down as one of the truly great justices in the history of the United States Supreme Court.

I now invite Justice Kennedy to say a few words. Thank you very much. . . .

[At this point, Associate Justice Kennedy administered the oath of office. Following the administration of the oath, Associate Justice Gorsuch made remarks, as follows.]

Associate Justice Gorsuch. I see before me so many to whom I owe so much. I know I would not be here today without your friendship and support. Thank you all from the bottom of my heart.

I want to thank the President for nominating me and for the great confidence and trust he's reposed in me. I want to thank the Vice President for his constant encouragement and friendship throughout this process. . . .

And to the American people, I am humbled by the trust placed in me today. I will never forget that to whom much is given, much will be expected. And I promise you that I will do all my powers permit to be a faithful servant of the Constitution and laws of this great nation. Thank you.

SOURCE: Executive Office of the President. "Remarks at a Swearing-In Ceremony for Neil M. Gorsuch as a Supreme Court Associate Justice." April 10, 2017. *Compilation of Presidential Documents* 2017, no. 00245 (April 10, 2017). https://www.gpo.gov/fdsys/pkg/DCPD-201700245/pdf/DCPD-201700245.pdf.

OTHER HISTORIC DOCUMENTS OF INTEREST

FROM PREVIOUS *HISTORIC DOCUMENTS*

- Senate Leadership Refuses to Consider Supreme Court Nominee, *2016*, p. 87

February

United Nations and Myanmar Leaders Respond to Rohingya Crisis

FEBRUARY 3, AUGUST 24, AND SEPTEMBER 6,
11, AND 19, 2017

The Rohingya, an ethnic Muslim minority in Myanmar, is considered by the United Nations one of the most persecuted minorities on Earth in modern history. They are barred from claiming citizenship in the nation in which they reside, and since 2012 have faced a brutal campaign perpetrated by citizens, the army, and, many believe, the government of Myanmar, that has driven them from their homes into nations such as Bangladesh, Indonesia, Malaysia, and Thailand where many reside in squalid refugee camps. Half a million Rohingya are thought to have fled Myanmar in the latter half of 2017 due to increasing violence. The nation's government, which had its first democratic power transfer in a generation in 2016, was slow to respond to the crisis and denied both its involvement and that any ethnic cleansing was being carried out. The country's de facto leader, Aung San Suu Kyi, who won the Nobel Peace Prize for her effort to instill democratic norms within Myanmar, faced significant criticism from around the world for her inaction and seeming disinterest in helping the fleeing Rohingya.

ROHINGYA IN MYANMAR

The Rohingya trace their roots in Myanmar back to the fifteenth century when Muslims moved into what was then known as the Arakan Kingdom, now Rakhine, the westernmost state of Myanmar; they were joined by additional Sunni Muslims, along with Buddhists, in the eighteenth and nineteenth centuries. Since then, the Myanmar government has denied recognition and citizenship of the Rohingya (a self-identifying term used by the minority Muslims in Rakhine State), for decades arguing that the Rohingya were illegal immigrants from Bangladesh. Until 2015, the Rohingya were permitted to register for identification cards that afforded them some rights, including the ability to vote. However, that privilege was stripped by then-President Thein Sein who was under pressure from the nation's Buddhist majority that feared granting such rights to Muslims. Today, there are an estimated 1 million Rohingya in Rakhine state—approximately one-third of the area's population—and because they are essentially stateless, they enjoy few rights and have limited access to resources such as employment, schools, food, and health care. According to the Council on Foreign Relations, the Rohingya also have limited freedoms in Myanmar and are required to ask permission of the government to travel, move, and marry and—in some parts of Rakhine State—are only permitted to have two children.

The Buddhist majority and Muslim minority in Rakhine State have frequently clashed with one another, increasingly so because employment opportunities have decreased and poverty has risen to 78 percent. Recently, in 2012, the Rohingya reportedly faced ethnic cleansing at the hands of the Buddhist inhabitants of Rakhine spurred by the murder of a

Buddhist Rakhine woman by three Muslim men. The outbreak of violence killed many and forced an estimated 140,000 into refugee and internally displaced person (IDP) camps. International organizations claimed that the attack on the Rohingya was organized, potentially by the government or politicians who saw it as important to secure the nation's Buddhist majority against any Muslim incursion. Although the government denied any such involvement, those responsible for the 2012 events were never prosecuted.

More recently, in October 2016, armed Rohingya attacked three police border posts, resulting in the death of nine officers. Following the incident, the Myanmar army reportedly began targeting the Rohingya community. According to human rights organizations including Amnesty International, the crackdown on the minority group included killings, arrests, and destruction of property. Following the election in 2015, the government and army reached a power-sharing agreement that has given the army relative autonomy from the central government and the power of the army's commander-in-chief can outweigh that of the nation's president. Still, some international observers argued that the army had not been operating alone, but that the government was playing a part in allowing the violence to continue.

MASSIVE EXODUS OF ROHINGYA FROM MYANMAR

Tensions between the Buddhist and Muslim populations in Rakhine State continued to simmer into 2017. On August 25, the situation reached a fever pitch when the Arakan Rohingya Salvation Army (ARSA) carried out a second attack on police and army outposts. Twelve members of the government security force were killed. In response, ARSA was declared a terrorist organization by the Myanmar government, and the army began a targeted campaign against the Rohingya. Entire villages were destroyed, and an estimated 582,000 Rohingya fled the country, half the group's population in Rakhine State. Of those left in Myanmar, many are thought to be unable to pass safely out of remote locations near Buddhist-majority villages. According to eyewitness accounts, as the Rohingya tried to leave the country, the military fired on them.

Those Rohingya who escaped Myanmar faced multiple challenges, including finding a safe place to live that could provide basic necessities. A vast majority of the Rohingya crossed the border into Bangladesh. The nation is home to hundreds of thousands of refugees, some registered and others not, who often live in tightly packed refugee camps that give rise to unsanitary conditions and the threat of outbreaks of deadly diseases such as cholera. In September, due to the overwhelming influx of refugees from Myanmar, aid groups operating in Bangladesh issued a plea to the international community for $77 million to help support those crossing its borders. An estimated 61,000 Rohingya refugees had landed in Malaysia, while some arrived by boat in Thailand or Indonesia. The growing number of refugees fleeing Myanmar gave rise to an increased volume of human smuggling and trafficking across the region.

Representatives of the United Nations have stated on multiple occasions that the Rohingya are the targets of crimes against humanity and ethnic cleansing. U.S. Ambassador to the United Nations Nikki Haley called the situation in Myanmar a "brutal, sustained campaign to cleanse the country of an ethnic minority." In October, Zeid Ra'ad al-Hussein, the UN High Commissioner for Human Rights, called the crisis "a textbook example of ethnic cleansing." Hussein suggested that reports from the country—which can be difficult to obtain because the government has blocked access for many international organizations—indicate that landmines are being laid by the government along the border with Bangladesh and that the government has insinuated that it is the Rohingya who are burning their own villages. "This complete denial of reality is doing great damage to the international standing of a Government which, until recently, benefited from immense good will," Hussein said. He called on the government to "end its current cruel military operation, with accountability for all violations that have occurred and to reverse the pattern of severe and widespread discrimination against the Rohingya population."

MYANMAR GOVERNMENT RESPONDS TO ROHINGYA CRISIS

Suu Kyi became the de facto ruler of Myanmar after her party, the National League for Democracy (NLD), won 348 seats in the country's parliament in 2015. Officially, she holds the title of State Counsellor; the nation's constitution prohibits her from becoming president because her children are foreign nationals. However, the nation's president, Htin Kyaw, is a close confidante. Suu Kyi notably led the campaign to bring democracy to Myanmar and because of her actions spent more than twenty years in detention, including two long stints under house arrest. Suu Kyi used her time to continue speaking out against the military-led government and working with the NLD to encourage reform. She was released from house arrest in November 2010, six days after the nation's first election in twenty years, and won a seat in parliament two years later. Seeking to put an end to the simmering tensions between the Buddhist population and the Muslim minority in Rakhine, in August 2016, Suu Kyi called on former UN secretary general Kofi Annan to form an advisory commission on the Rakhine State that would propose solutions to the challenges in the area. The commission released its final report to the Myanmar government on August 24, 2017, shortly before the attack on police outposts in Rakhine State. After the report's release, Annan noted, "Rakhine State faces complex political, economic and social challenges; they can only be surmounted through a sustained and coordinated effort by the civilian and military authorities—at the Union, State and the local levels." The report called for the Myanmar government, Rakhine residents, and the international community to come together to support reforms that would include greater socioeconomic development in Rakhine State, citizenship and enhanced freedom of movement for the Rohingya, greater political representation for minority groups, the closure of IDP camps and the reintegration of refugees into their communities, enhanced security in Rakhine, and improved dialogue between all parties involved, including a strengthening of the relationship with Bangladesh. The commission called on the government to appoint a minister who would be responsible for overseeing the implementation of the recommendations, but noted that Myanmar's government would ultimately decide whether it would move forward with any of the suggestions. By the close of 2017, none of the commission's recommendations had been implemented.

Following the mass exodus of Rohingya in August and September 2017, Suu Kyi faced increasing pressure from around the world to respond to the crisis and was heavily criticized for her failure to do so swiftly. It was not until September 19 when Suu Kyi publicly addressed the situation in Rakhine in a thirty-minute speech during which she reached out to the international community to help the nation with the litany of issues it faces, not just the Rohingya crisis. Despite claims ahead of her speech by the government and state run media that the August attacks were led by "extreme terrorists," Suu Kyi said in her speech that "it is not the intention of the Myanmar government to apportion blame or to abnegate responsibility. We condemn all human rights violations and unlawful violence." Suu Kyi denied that any ethnic cleansing had taken place and stated that there had been no ongoing violence in Rakhine State since early September, despite evidence to the contrary obtained by human rights organizations through eyewitness reports of clashes between the Myanmar military and Rohingya and satellite images showing burning Rohingya villages. And to her critics Suu Kyi said her government had "already started defending all the people in Rakhine in the best way possible." Amnesty International expressed disappointment that Suu Kyi failed to speak directly about the Myanmar army's involvement in the violence perpetrated against the Rohingya, calling her speech a "mix of untruths and victim blaming." NLD spokesperson Nyan Win, however, said the speech struck a conciliatory tone that "did not blame . . . any other person" and "tried to do the best things for the Rakhine state situation."

Regional response to the Rohingya crisis was similarly slow. Three of the nations that had accepted refugees—Indonesia, Malaysia, and Thailand—had not yet ratified the UN's 1951 Refugee Convention and related protocol that outlines who qualifies as a refugee, the rights afforded to those individuals, and the responsibility of the countries accepting refugees. The ten-nation regional body, the Association of Southeast Asian Nations (ASEAN), was also unable by the close of 2017 to develop a coordinated response, largely because its member states had committed to remaining uninvolved in the domestic affairs of other members. Although the United Nations used some of the strongest rhetoric to respond to the situation in Myanmar, its ability to help end the crisis would be dependent on the desire of member states—and specifically neighboring countries—to act.

—Heather Kerrigan

Following is a press release from the United Nations issued on February 3, 2017, announcing the release of a report detailing the crisis for the Rohingya in Myanmar; an August 24, 2017, press release from an advisory committee looking into the crisis in Myanmar; a September 6, 2017, press release detailing the Myanmar president's response to the August attack on police outposts; a September 11, 2017, UN Human Rights Commission press release calling the situation in Myanmar against the Rohingya "ethnic cleansing"; and a press release from the government of Myanmar detailing Aung San Suu Kyi's address about the Rohingya on September 19, 2017.

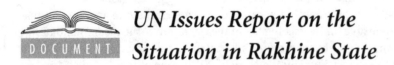

UN Issues Report on the Situation in Rakhine State

DOCUMENT

February 3, 2017

Mass gang-rape, killings—including of babies and young children, brutal beatings, disappearances and other serious human rights violations by Myanmar's security forces in a sealed-off area north of Maungdaw in northern Rakhine State have been detailed in a new UN report issued Friday based on interviews with victims across the border in Bangladesh.

Of the 204 people individually interviewed by a team of UN human rights investigators, the vast majority reported witnessing killings, and almost half reported having a family member who was killed as well as family members who were missing. Of the

101 women interviewed, more than half reported having suffered rape or other forms of sexual violence.

Especially revolting were the accounts of children—including an eight-month old, a five-year-old and a six-year-old—who were slaughtered with knives. One mother recounted how her five-year-old daughter was trying to protect her from rape when a man "took out a long knife and killed her by slitting her throat." In another case, an eight-month-old baby was reportedly killed while his mother was gang-raped by five security officers.

"The devastating cruelty to which these Rohingya children have been subjected is unbearable—what kind of hatred could make a man stab a baby crying out for his mother's milk. And for the mother to witness this murder while she is being gang-raped by the very security forces who should be protecting her—what kind of 'clearance operation' is this? What national security goals could possibly be served by this?" High Commissioner Zeid said, noting the report suggests the recent level of violence to be unprecedented.

"I call on the international community, with all its strength, to join me in urging the leadership in Myanmar to bring such military operations to an end. The gravity and scale of these allegations begs the robust reaction of the international community."

After the repeated failure of the Government of Myanmar to grant the UN Human Rights Office unfettered access to the worst-affected areas of northern Rakhine State, High Commissioner Zeid deployed a team of human rights officers to the Bangladeshi border with Myanmar, where an estimated 66,000 Rohingya have fled since 9 October 2016.

All the individuals interviewed by the team had fled Myanmar after the 9 October attacks against three border guard posts, which had prompted intense military operations and a lockdown in north Maungdaw. The military indicated that it was conducting "area clearance operations" in the region.

The report cites consistent testimony indicating that hundreds of Rohingya houses, schools, markets, shops, madrasas and mosques were burned by the army, police and sometimes civilian mobs. Witnesses also described the destruction of food and food sources, including paddy fields, and the confiscation of livestock.

"Numerous testimonies collected from people from different village tracts . . . confirmed that the army deliberately set fire to houses with families inside, and in other cases pushed Rohingyas into already burning houses," the report states. "Testimonies were collected of several cases where the army or Rakhine villagers locked an entire family, including elderly and disabled people, inside a house and set it on fire, killing them all."

Several people were killed in indiscriminate and random shooting, many while fleeing for safety. Those who suffered serious physical injuries had almost no access to emergency medical care, and many of the people interviewed remained visibly traumatized by the human rights violations they survived or witnessed. People who did not know the fate of loved ones who had been rounded up by the army or separated while fleeing were particularly distressed.

Many witnesses and victims also described being taunted while they were being beaten, raped or rounded up, such as being told "you are Bangladeshis and you should go back" or "What can your Allah do for you? See what we can do?" The violence since 9 October follows a long-standing pattern of violations and abuses; systematic and systemic discrimination; and policies of exclusion and marginalization against the Rohingya that have been in place for decades in northern Rakhine State, the report notes.*

Reports suggest that operations by security forces in the area have continued into January 2017, although their intensity and frequency may have reduced.

"The killing of people as they prayed, fished to feed their families or slept in their homes, the brutal beating of children as young as two and an elderly woman aged 80—the perpetrators of these violations, and those who ordered them, must be held accountable," High Commissioner Zeid said. "The Government of Myanmar must immediately halt these grave human rights violations against its own people, instead of continuing to deny they have occurred, and accepts the responsibility to ensure that victims have access to justice, reparations and safety."

The report concludes that the widespread violations against the Rohingya population indicate the very likely commission of crimes against humanity.

*To read the full report, visit: http://www.ohchr.org/Documents/Countries/MM/FlashReport3Feb2017.pdf

SOURCE: United Nations Office of the High Commissioner for Human Rights. "Devastating Cruelty against Rohingya Children, Women and Men Detailed in UN Human Rights Report." February 3, 2017. http://www.ohchr.org/EN/NewsEvents/Pages/DisplayNews.aspx?NewsID=21142.

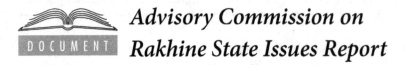

Advisory Commission on Rakhine State Issues Report

August 24, 2017

OVERVIEW OF KEY POINTS AND RECOMMENDATIONS

FINAL REPORT OF THE ADVISORY COMMISSION ON RAKHINE STATE

Recurring conflict in Rakhine State is a major impediment to national peace and reconciliation in Myanmar, as well as a significant obstacle to the development of the State, which is among the poorest in the Union of Myanmar.

The challenges facing communities across the State are dangerous and demand urgent action. This includes—but is not limited to—the unresolved status of the large number of currently stateless Muslims, which exacerbates numerous socio-economic challenges facing the State.

The final report of the Advisory Commission on Rakhine State: Towards a Peaceful, Fair and Prosperous Future for the People of Rakhine builds on the Commission's interim report to provide a comprehensive set of recommendations to achieve lasting peace and prosperity in Rakhine. Below is an outline of some of the report's main points and recommendations.

Socio-Economic Development

The Commission notes that local communities would benefit more from investment in Rakhine and calls for their increased participation in decision-making on issues related to development. Recognising that the question of resource sharing between the Union and State Governments is a consideration in the broader peace process, the Commission nonetheless calls on the Government to ensure that local communities benefit from natural resource extractions in Rakhine State.

It recommends that the government ensure adequate compensation for appropriated land, and to invest heavily in infrastructure including roads, jetties, electricity, drinking water and internet access. The planned airport at Mrauk-U should be constructed.

It also calls for the provision of vocational training which prioritises women and is based on labour-market assessments, and urges the government to reduce red tape to promote business, and to address regulatory issues that currently constrain small businesses, including access to lending and agricultural credit.

In light of the state's vulnerability to the effects of climate change, the Commission recommends that the government urgently step-up efforts to strength the capabilities of communities to adopt climate resilient options, and to improve the state's irrigation systems.

Citizenship

While Myanmar's cultural diversity and pluralism deserve to be celebrated, identity and ethnicity are sensitive issues in Myanmar and have a direct impact on the determination of citizenship. Identity and ethnicity are sensitive issues. Citizenship rights and deficiencies in national legislation remain a broad concern, as does the unresolved status of many Muslims. In the short-run, the Commission calls for an acceleration of the citizenship verification process in line with the 1982 Citizenship Law. The Government should develop a clear strategy and timeline for the process, communicated through a broad outreach campaign. Those who have already been verified should immediately be allowed to enjoy all benefits, rights and freedoms associated with citizenship.

The Commission recommends that complaints regarding the verification process be addressed swiftly by a government authority independent of the institutions responsible for the process. It also calls for the rights of those whose citizenship application is not accepted to be clarified.

The Commission also notes the need to revisit the law itself and calls on the government to set in motion a process to review the law. Such a review should consider—amongst other issues—aligning the law with international standards, re-examining the current linkage between citizenship and ethnicity, and considering provisions to allow for the possibility of acquiring citizenship by naturalisation, particularly for those who are stateless. The Commission calls for the rights of non-citizens who live in Myanmar to be regulated, and for the clarification of residency rights.

Pending such a review, the Commission calls on the Government to ensure that existing legislation is interpreted and applied in a manner that is non-discriminatory.

Freedom of Movement

Both Rakhines and Muslims face movement restrictions, although Muslims—and in particular IDPs—are particularly affected. In general, the Commission calls on the Government to ensure freedom of movement for all people irrespective of religion, ethnicity, or citizenship status, and to that end reiterates its earlier call for a mapping exercise to identify all existing restrictions on freedom of movement, and calls for the introduction of measures to prohibit informal restrictions including unofficial payments and arbitrary roadblocks.

Communal Participation and Representation

Urgent steps are needed to promote communal representation and participation for underrepresented groups, including ethnic minority groups, stateless and displaced communities. This affects Muslims disproportionally. Women should be included in political decision-making.

Household leaders, Village Administrators and Village Tract Administrators should be directly elected by the residents of each village/village tract. Registration processes for CSOs should be greatly simplified.

Internally displaced people (IDPs)

The Commission commends the government for acting swiftly on the recommendation in the interim report on camp closures, but noted that the outcome of the return/relocation process was mixed. It reiterates the need for a comprehensive strategy towards closing all IDP camps in Rakhine State.

It calls for the government to cooperate with international partners to ensure that return/relocation is carried out in accordance with international standards, is voluntary, safe, and takes place in a dignified manner.

In the interim, and without affecting the closure of IDP camps—the Commission calls on the government to ensure dignified living conditions in camps, including improved shelter, water and sanitation, education, and access to livelihood opportunities.

Cultural Developments

In its final report, the Commission reiterates its recommendation that the Government of Myanmar should declare Mrauk U as a candidate for UNESCO world heritage status, and continue its positive engagement with UNESCO and other international partners to move this process forward.

The Commission also urges the Government of Myanmar to list and protect historic, religious and cultural sites of all communities in Rakhine.

Inter-communal Cohesion

Inter-communal dialogue must be fostered at all levels; township, state and Union. Activities that help to create an environment conducive for dialogue should be initiated by the government, including joint vocational training, infrastructure projects and cultural events, and the establishment of communal youth centres.

Security of all communities

The Commission recognises the threat posed from potential radicalisation, but advises against a purely security response in Rakhine. Commission members have instead called for a calibrated response that combines political, developmental, security and human rights approaches that address the root causes of violence and reduce inter-communal tensions.

To strengthen and professionalise policing in Rakhine, the Commission recommends simplifying the security infrastructure in Rakhine by creating a unified agency for all policing in the state, with a single chain of command reporting directly to the chief of

Myanmar's Police Force. This could be done, for instance, by folding the Border Guard Police into the national police. Improved training—including in human rights, community policing, civilian protection and languages—should be provided to all members of the security forces in order to improve intelligence gathering and relations with local communities. In general, and as recommended in the interim report, the police force should reflect the population in all components, including women and minorities.

Bilateral relations with Bangladesh

Given the importance of strong bilateral cooperation to secure the border and address shared challenges—including drug trafficking—the Commission welcomes steps taken to improve cooperation with Bangladesh over the past year, which are in line with the recommendations of its interim report. The Commission recommends that Myanmar and Bangladesh further strengthen their bilateral cooperation in various areas.

Implementation of the Commission's recommendations

With the submission of its final report, the Advisory Commission on Rakhine has completed its mandate. However the Commission has proposed a mechanism by which the Government can ensure effective implementation of its recommendations.

It calls for a ministerial level appointment to be made with the sole function of coordinating policy on Rakhine State and ensuring the effective implementation of the Rakhine Advisory Commission's recommendations. The appointee should be supported by a permanent and well-staffed secretariat, which will be an integral part of the Central Committee on Implementation of Peace and Development in Rakhine State and support its work.

SOURCE: Advisory Commission on Rakhine State. "Overview of Key Points and Recommendations." August 24, 2017. http://www.rakhinecommission.org/app/uploads/2017/08/final_report-20170822-Overview-of-key-points-and-recommendations_For-Web.pdf.

Myanmar Government Responds to August ARSA Attack

September 6, 2017

The President of the Republic of the Union of Myanmar was debriefed at the Presidential Palace today by the Union Ministers who visited Maungtaw and Buthidaung regions in Rakhine State following the terrorist attacks which took place there in August 2017.

The Union Ministers debriefed the President on the latest situation in the Rakhine State.

The government's plans to restore peace and stability to the region was discussed by the participants at the briefing.

On 5th September 2017, the Office of the State Counsellor issued a statement to prevent unwarranted tension and unrest due to news of possible ARSA terrorist group's attacks in the country.

The Office of the State Counsellor has urged the people to remain vigilant against possible incitements.

Necessary measures are being put in place by security forces to safeguard against possible terrorist attacks. At the same time, taking into account that people with extreme ideology can use the climate of fear to incite unrest, instructions were issued to the security forces to deter such attempts and to take legal action against perpetrators.

Peace, stability and rule of law are of the utmost importance to the State. Therefore, the people are urged to render their cooperation to the Government by respecting the rule of law.

SOURCE: Republic of the Union of Myanmar. President Office. "Statement on Peace, Stability and Rule of Law." September 6, 2017. http://www.president-office.gov.mm/en/?q=briefing-room/statements-and-releases/2017/09/07/id-7662.

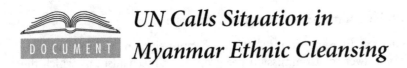

UN Calls Situation in Myanmar Ethnic Cleansing

September 11, 2017

The United Nations human rights chief today lashed out at the treatment of the Rohingya in Myanmar which has led to more than 300,000 people fleeing to Bangladesh in the past three weeks, as security forces and local militia reportedly burn villages and shoot civilians.

"The situation seems a textbook example of ethnic cleansing," Zeid Ra'ad al-Hussein told the UN Human Rights Council in Geneva, noting that the current situation cannot yet be fully assessed since Myanmar has refused access to human rights investigators.

He cited reports of Myanmar authorities laying landmines along the border with Bangladesh and requiring returnees to provide "proof of nationality," an impossibility given that successive Myanmar governments have since 1962 progressively stripped the Rohingya population of their political and civil rights, including citizenship rights.

The latest security operation in Rakhine state follows attacks by militants on 25 August against 30 police posts.

The High Commissioner called the response "clearly disproportionate" and "without regard for basic principles of international law," and said the Government should "stop claiming that the Rohingyas are setting fire to their own homes and laying waste to their own villages."

"This complete denial of reality is doing great damage to the international standing of a Government which, until recently, benefited from immense good will," he said.

"I call on the Government to end its current cruel military operation, with accountability for all violations that have occurred and to reverse the pattern of severe and widespread discrimination against the Rohingya population," he added, calling for his Office (OHCHR) to obtain unfettered access to the country.

Last year, Mr. Zeid issued a report warning that the pattern of gross violations of the human rights of the Rohingya suggested a widespread or systematic attack against the community, possibly amounting to crimes against humanity.

In today's statement, he also addressed Bangladeshi authorities, encouraging them to maintain open borders for the refugees, and the international community to help support the refugees. Humanitarian agencies in Bangladesh today appealed for $77 million to aid an estimated 300,000 refugees through the end of the year.

At the same time, he deplored measures taken by India, which has said it is not a signatory to the Refugee Convention and can deport Rohingyas . . . .

[The remainder of the article, detailing ongoing violence in Venezuela and Yemen, has been omitted.]

SOURCE: United Nations. "UN Human Rights Chief Points to 'Textbook Example of Ethnic Cleansing' in Myanmar." September 11, 2017. https://refugeesmigrants.un.org/un-human-rights-chief-points-%E2%80%98textbook-example-ethnic-cleansing%E2%80%99-myanmar.

Aung San Suu Kyi Delivers Address on Rakhine

DOCUMENT

September 19, 2017

State Counsellor Daw Aung San Suu Kyi yesterday condemned human rights violations in Rakhine State and said violators would be brought to justice, and addressed international concerns.

The State Counsellor made the remarks in a speech delivered from Nay Pyi Taw, in her first address to the nation since the 25 August attacks by ARSA extremist terrorists, which sparked a military response that has forced thousands of refugees into neighbouring Bangladesh and thousands of others to temporary camps in southern Rakhine.

"There has been much concern around the world with regard to the situation in Rakhine. It is not the intention of the Myanmar government to apportion blame or abnegate responsibility. We condemn all human rights violations and unlawful violence. We are committed to the restoration of peace, stability and the rule of law throughout the state", Daw Aung San Suu Kyi said.

"The security forces have been instructed to adhere strictly to the code of conduct in carrying out security operations, to exercise all due restraint and to take full measures to avoid collateral damage and the harming of innocent civilians. Human rights violations and all other acts that affect stability and harmony and undermine the rule of law will be addressed in accordance with the strict norms of justice.

"We feel deeply for the suffering of all the people who have been caught up in the conflict. Those who have had to flee their homes are many. Not just Muslims and Rakhines but also small minority groups such as Daing-net, Mro, Thet, Magyi and Hindus, of whose presence most of the world is totally unaware.

The State Counsellor addressed international concerns on the situation in western Myanmar.

"I am aware of the fact that the world's attention is focused on the situation in Rakhine State and, as I said at the General Assembly last year, as a responsible member of the community of nations, Myanmar does not fear international scrutiny and we are committed to a sustainable solution that would lead to peace, stability and development for all communities.

"After several months of seeming peace and quiet, on the twenty-fifth of August, 30 police outposts, the regimental headquarters in Taungala Village were attacked by armed groups.

Consequent to these attacks the government declared the Arakan Rohingya Salvation Army and its supporters responsible for acts of terrorism as a terrorist group in accordance with the Counter-Terrorism Law Section 6, Subsection 5".

The State Counsellor also said she wanted to explore the reasons why there was an exodus of Muslims to Bangladesh, but also why most of the Muslim community in north Rakhine State did not choose to leave.

"The government is working to restore the situation to normalcy. Since the 5th of September, there have been no armed clashes and there have been no clearance operations. Nevertheless, we are concerned to hear that numbers of Muslims are fleeing across the border to Bangladesh. We want to find out why this exodus is happening. We would like to talk to those who have fled, as well as those who have stayed. I think it is very little known that the great majority of Muslims in the Rakhine State have not joined the exodus. More than 50 per cent of the villagers of Muslims are intact. They are as they were before the attacks took place. And we would like to know why.

This is what I think we have to work towards. Not just looking at the problems but also looking at these areas where there are no problems. Why have we been able to avoid these problems in certain areas? And for this reason, we would like to invite members of the diplomatic community to join us in our endeavour to learn more from the Muslims who have integrated successfully into the Rakhine State", she said.

SOURCE: Republic of the Union of Myanmar. State Counsellor Office. "State Counsellor: 'Myanmar Does Not Fear World Scrutiny.'" September 19, 2017. http://www.statecounsellor.gov.mm/en/node/1054.

OTHER HISTORIC DOCUMENTS OF INTEREST

FROM PREVIOUS HISTORIC DOCUMENTS

Officials Respond to Strikes in Brazil; Temer Refutes Corruption Charges

FEBRUARY 8 AND 25, APRIL 28, MAY 17, AND JUNE 26, 2017

Brazil's crippling economic recession continued into 2017, leaving state governments struggling to pay civil servants. The federal government's push for strict austerity measures led to strikes and protests across the country. At the same time, President Michel Temer and members of his administration faced new corruption charges in an ever-broadening investigation into a national scandal.

Record-Setting Recession

As 2017 began, Brazil's latest economic recession became the longest in its history, after two consecutive years of negative growth. The country's Gross Domestic Product shrank by 3.6 percent in 2016 as the overall budget deficit rose to 562.8 billion reals (roughly $180 billion). Unemployment also rose to 13.7 percent in the first quarter of 2017. Many civil servants went unpaid while others were underpaid, with some state governments slashing services to cut down on deficits.

Facing a bleak economic outlook, the Temer government proposed a series of austerity measures intended to slow the country's tailspin. These proposals included implementing a twenty-year cap on federal spending that would limit the growth in spending to the rate of inflation and setting a minimum retirement age of sixty-five, which would reduce the costs associated with Brazil's pension system. Lawmakers also approved a labor reform package in July 2017 that relaxed restrictions on outsourcing, provided more flexibility for part-time work and temporary contracts, reduced the scope of possible legal action in labor disputes, and made labor union dues voluntary instead of mandatory.

Espírito Santo Police Strike

Dissatisfaction with their government pay led police in the state of Espírito Santo and their families to initiate a strike on February 4. The police union claimed that the officers had not received a pay raise in four years and were among the lowest paid in the country. The state's governor, Paulo Hartung, countered that the government was paying employees on time and close to the ceiling established by Brazil's Fiscal Responsibility Law. He characterized the strike as "open blackmailing" of the state and claimed it was "the same thing as hijacking the freedom and rights of the citizens and collecting ransom."

Although state police are forbidden from striking because they provide an essential service, Espírito Santo officers were able to circumvent this restriction by reporting to work and having their family and friends blockade police stations to prevent anyone from going out on patrol. The strike's impact was felt almost immediately, with increased reports of robberies and looting as well as a spike in homicides. The state government reported that 143 people were killed between February 4 and February 13; by comparison, only four people were killed in January. Public transportation came to a halt, and schools, health clinics, and businesses were closed. The state retail association estimated that business lost about ninety million reals ($28.87 million) in the first week of the strike. Approximately 3,000 federal soldiers and police were sent to Espírito Santo to patrol the streets and maintain order.

Negotiations between the police union, officers' wives, and state officials began on February 8. Two days later, officials announced that they had agreed to look for opportunities to promote officers who were eligible and to address concerns about police workload, but did not agree to a pay raise. Roughly 600 officers returned to work on February 11, even though family members rejected the agreement and continued their blockade. State officials met again with officers' relatives on February 24 and announced a new agreement the following day. The state agreed to suspend in-process disciplinary procedures for fifteen days and not initiate new disciplinary actions, withdraw lawsuits against officers' relatives and associations, and to return any police who had been transferred to their original posts within forty-five days. Both sides agreed to participate in future negotiations about police benefits, to be mediated by the state's Public Labor Ministry. Following the agreement's announcement, the families withdrew from police stations and all officers returned to duty on February 25. Military Police Commander-in-Chief Colonel Nylton Rodrigues apologized to Espírito Santo's citizens "for this tragic moment that you all lived" and assured them they could count on the police.

AUSTERITY STRIKE

A similar dissatisfaction with the austerity measures proposed by Temer's government led to a national general strike on April 28 that was organized by various labor unions and underscored Temer's growing unpopularity. According to an Ipsos poll released in April, 92 percent of Brazilians believed the country was on the wrong path and Temer's approval rating was only 4 percent. Commentators speculated that public opinion of Temer's government was influenced in part by perceptions that officials were trying to protect their own wealth while they were pushing austerity measures. The day before the strike began, for example, the Supreme Court ruled that elite public servants could receive salaries higher than $140,000, a limit that had been established by Brazil's constitution. By contrast, a Brazilian making minimum wage earns about $4,000 per year. In response to the strike, Temer issued a statement reaffirming the federal government's "commitment to democracy and to Brazilian institutions," adding that "work towards the modernization of national legislation will continue, with broad and frank debate, held in the appropriate arena for such discussion, which is the National Congress."

CORRUPTION CHARGES BROUGHT AGAINST TEMER

Temer assumed the presidency in 2016 following the impeachment of former president Dilma Rousseff. While Rousseff's impeachment centered on charges that she violated Brazil's fiscal responsibility law by using funds from state banks to cover budget shortfalls, she also faced allegations that her presidential campaigns were funded with money from Operation Car Wash, a wide-reaching scandal involving state-owned oil company Petrobras. Brazil's largest construction companies had allegedly overcharged Petrobras for building contracts and then gave portions of the overpayments to Petrobras executives and politicians who were in on the deal.

While Temer was not directly implicated in Operation Car Wash, by the end of 2017 approximately one-third of his cabinet were the subject of Operation Car War–related investigations. In May 2017, Brazilian newspaper *O Globo* reported that Joesly Batista, the chief executive of J&F Investments (which controls major meatpacking company JBS), had secretly taped a conversation with Temer during a visit to the president's official residence on March 7. The recording was made as part of a plea bargain arranged between Batista and his brother and federal prosecutors. Batista told Temer that he had been paying bribes to Eduardo Cunha, the former speaker of the Chamber of Deputies who had been removed from office due to his connections to Operation Car Wash, to keep him from talking about the Petrobras scandal. Temer reportedly endorsed Batista's payments and told him they may need to continue. Temer allegedly also directed Batista to bribe a lawmaker to help resolve an issue at a company-owned power plant. Temer denied all allegations, with his office issuing a statement declaring that he "never asked for payments to gain the silence" of Cunha and "did not authorize any action with the goal of avoiding bargaining or collaboration" between Cunha and prosecutors.

On June 26, Brazil's Prosecutor General Rodrigo Janot announced the filing of corruption charges against Temer. Janot accused Temer and former deputy Rodrigo Rocha Loures of accepting a $154,000 bribe from Batista in exchange for help in resolving the power plant issue. According to Janot, JBS executives also testified that Temer accepted bribes for resolving tax disputes and making loans available from state-run banks, among other favors. The filing alleged that JBS promised to pay an additional $12 million in bribes to Temer and Loures. Janot's filing sought more than $3.5 million in damages "resulting from corruption."

Under Brazil's laws, the president can only face trial while in office if two-thirds of the Chamber of Deputies (172 members) votes to accept charges against the president and send them to the Supreme Court. On August 2, 263 members of the Chamber of Deputies voted to reject Janot's corruption charges, protecting Temer from prosecution. Less than a week later, Temer's lawyers requested that the Supreme Court remove Janot from the investigation into Temer, claiming that Janot's "motivation is personal." The court rejected Temer's appeal.

Janot had promised that additional charges against Temer are imminent. These charges would need to be voted on separately by the Chamber of Deputies.

—Linda Grimm

Following is a statement by Espírito Santo Governor Paulo Hartung on February 8, 2017, in response to the police strike; a press release from the Military Police of Espírito Santo from February 25, 2017, announcing the resumption of police operations; a statement by President Michel Temer on April 28, 2017, in response to the general strike; a statement by President Temer on May 17, 2017, denying corruption allegations; and a press release from the office of the attorney general from June 26, 2017, announcing corruption charges against the president.

Espírito Santo Governor Comments on Police Strike

February 8, 2017

At a press conference held on Wednesday (8th) morning, state governor Paulo Hartung stated that the strike held by the Military Police (PM-ES) is illegal, unconstitutional and is making the population of Espírito Santo hostage to such a movement. The conference was held at the Official Government Residence (Resof), at Praia da Costa, in Vila Velha, and was attended by the governor-in-office, Cesar Colnago, and the Secretary of State for Public Security and Social Defense (Sesp) André Garcia.

"What is happening in Espírito Santo is blackmailing and if the population of Espírito Santo and Brazil in general does not face this situation, it might happen again tomorrow in the rest of the country. This is open blackmailing. It's the same thing as hijacking the freedom and rights of the citizens and collecting ransom. We cannot pay the ransom. Both for ethical and tax liability reasons," stated state governor Paulo Hartung.

During the press conference, Paulo Hartung explained that the Government is paying employees on time and close to the ceiling established by Fiscal Responsibility Law (LRF). He stressed that the attitude of a few military members is harming the whole military force. "I ask that they respect the institution [they work for], as the State of Espírito Santo is the one that pays taxes and keeps the public machine running. This movement is illegal, unconstitutional, and our leaders should be ashamed because what they're doing is black-mailing," said the governor.

The governor-in-office, César Colnago, also stressed the need for the military to return to the streets. "We are asking for rationality and common sense from our police officers to return to their jobs and comply with the law. All this must come to an end. The Government is open to dialogue and awaits the commitment of the police to return to work," said the governor-in-office, stressing that dialog has been open since the beginning of the demonstrations.

Colnago added that it is important to emphasize that we are experiencing an economic crisis in the country, where millions of people are unemployed, and our revenue has been falling since 2013. "We want and are willing to hold talks with the movement and present what path we can take in light of such a serious financial situation. But we must resume policing," he said.

The Secretary of State for Public Security and Social Defense, André Garcia, stressed that the Government remains open for dialogue and calls for the return of the Military Police to the streets. Garcia thanked the Civil Police, the Brazilian Federal Highway Police, the Municipal Guards and the military police who are working to protect the citizens of Espírito Santo during this crisis. "We are working to get everything under control so that everyone can return to their normal routines," he said.

REINFORCED SUPPORT

During this period, the Government of Espírito Santo counted on the reinforcement of the Armed Forces, which, since Monday (6th), have begun to patrol in the municipalities of the State.

We are immediately counting on the help of troops from the National Public Security Force, the Army and the Navy, who are already on the streets, totaling 1,200 men, with more military officers expected to arrive in the State in the coming days.

"More support is on the way. We will take every measure provided for by law to guarantee order and peace for our population," said Colnago . . .

SOURCE: Government of the State of Espírito Santo. "Hartung Says Population Cannot Be Hostage to the Military Police Strike." February 8, 2017. Translated by SAGE Publishing. https://www.es.gov.br/Noticia/hartung-afirma-que-populacao-nao-pode-ser-refem-de-greve-da-pm.

Espírito Santo Military Police Commander-in-Chief Announces End of Police Strike

DOCUMENT

February 25, 2017

After 22 days of strike, the 17 municipalities of Espírito Santo that were still obstructed in Military Police units return to their normal routine this Saturday morning (25th). Now, all 78 municipalities in the State have complete policing and the military is ready to serve the citizens of Espírito Santo.

According to the commander-in-chief of the Military Police of Espírito Santo (PMES), Colonel Nylton Rodrigues, during the standstill period, operational calls were made where the military gradually assumed service outside the Battalions. Now, with the complete resumption of work, the police usually respond to their shifts, thus returning to the normal operational routine of the corporation.

The commander also apologized to the citizens of Espírito Santo for the last three weeks. "On behalf of the police officers who are no longer here, on behalf of the reserve military and pensioners, and also on behalf of those who are still to enter the PMES, I hereby apologize for this tragic moment that you all lived, but I want to stress that we are back and that the citizens of Espírito Santo can count on us, because we are always here to help them. After this episode, the Military Police comes out much more strengthened and valued. I trust, respect and admire this troop that will regain the image of our corporation."

CARNIVAL

Under the coordination of the Task Force, commanded by Army General Adilson Carlos Katibe, a special scheme was set up to ensure the safety of the revelers during the Carnival period. The Military Police will be placed from North to South, acting on the beaches, in the parades and where there is any agglomeration of people enjoying the revelry. However, it is important for the population to take certain precautions to prevent crimes, such as taking care of personal belongings, being careful and not neglecting their belongings in the sand.

As for roads, drivers passing through state highways must be aware of the direction and also any road signs, as this minimizes the risk of accidents.

Ciodes

The Integrated Center for Operations and Social Defense (Ciodes) will continue to answer calls uninterruptedly, and after the stoppage period, any calls made through number 190 will be passed on to the Military Police.

Source: Government of the State of Espírito Santo. "PMES Battalions Are Unobstructed and Operational Routine Is Resumed." February 25, 2017. Translated by SAGE Publishing. https://www.es.gov.br/Noticia/batalhoes-da-pmes-sao-desobstruidos-e-rotina-operacional-e-retomada.

President Temer Statement on General Strike

April 28, 2017

The political demonstrations called for this Friday occurred freely in the entire country. There was the broadest guarantee of the right of expression, even in the smallest clusters. Unfortunately, small groups blocked roads and avenues to prevent the citizen's right to come and go, which ended up keeping him from reaching his workplace or move freely. Isolated events of violence were also recorded, such as the unfortunate and serious incidents in Rio de Janeiro.

The federal government reaffirms its commitment to democracy and to Brazilian institutions. Work towards the modernization of national legislation will continue, with broad and frank debate, held in the appropriate arena for such discussion, which is the National Congress. In an orderly and obstinate manner, the Brazilian worker fights intensively in recent months to overcome the greatest economic recession the country has faced in its history. To this effort are added all the actions of the government, which believes in the strength of our country's unity to overcome the crisis we inherited and bring Brazil back to the path of social development and economic growth.

Source: Presidency of the Republic of Brazil. "Official Note." April 28, 2017. Translated by SAGE Publishing. http://www2.planalto.gov.br/acompanhe-planalto/notas-oficiais/notas-oficiais-do-presidente/nota-oficial-14.

President Temer Statement on Corruption Allegations

May 17, 2017

President Michel Temer never asked for payments to gain the silence of former deputy Eduardo Cunha. He did not participate and did not authorize any action with the goal of avoiding bargaining or collaboration with the Justice by the ex-parliamentarian.

The meeting with businessman Joesley Batista took place in early March at the official residence of the Vice-President, Palácio do Jaburu, but there was nothing in the dialogue that would jeopardize the conduct of the President of the Republic.

The president defends a wide and deep investigation to determine all the claims published by the press, with the responsibility of those involved in any illegal acts that may be proven.

SOURCE: Presidency of the Republic of Brazil. "Press Release." May 17, 2017. Translated by SAGE Publishing. http://www2.planalto.gov.br/acompanhe-planalto/notas-oficiais/notas-oficiais-do-presidente/nota-a-imprensa-28.

Federal Public Prosecutor Files Corruption Charges against President Temer

DOCUMENT

June 26, 2017

The attorney general, Rodrigo Janot, referred to the Federal Supreme Court (STF) a complaint against the President of the Republic, Michel Temer, and former federal deputy Rodrigo Rocha Loures (PMDB-PR). The two are accused of passive corruption (article 317 of the Criminal Code), for receiving an unfair advantage in the amount of a thousand 500 R$, offered by Joesley Batista and delivered by the executive of J&F, Ricardo Saud. According to the attorney general, the payments could reach R$ 38 million over 9 months.

The claim was based on criminal investigation that proved the materiality and the authorship of the crime of passive corruption. According to the narrative presented in the brief, the various episodes narrated point to the criminal unfolding that began at the meeting between Michel Temer and Joesley Batista at Palácio do Jaburu on March 7th, 2017, around 10:40 pm, and culminated in the delivery of R$ 500 thousand, made by Ricardo Saud to Rodrigo Loures on April 28th of this year.

In addition to the conviction for passive corruption, the attorney general seeks compensation for the transindividual damages caused, in a minimum amount equivalent to R$ 10 million for Michel Temer and R$ 2 million for Rodrigo Loures, since the damages resulting from corruption are diffuse, being difficult to quantify. It also calls for the loss of the civil service for holders of public office, public employment or elective office, for having violated their duties towards the State and society.

Non-Republican talks—According to the claim, the meeting between the businessman and the president was scheduled by Loures to deal with non-Republican issues, but to initiate criminal negotiations. There was a report of Joesley about payment of unfair advantage to Eduardo Cunha, imprisoned in Curitiba/PR; information that the businessman corrupted a judge and a procurator of the Republic; and request of an interlocutor because the usual contacts were not possible. That is when President Temer indicates Rodrigo Loures, a person of his "strictest confidence".

"The circumstances of this meeting—at night and without any record in the official agenda of the President of the Republic—reveal the purpose of not leaving traces of the criminal acts practiced there," says Janot. Although the president affirms in official statements that he listens to many entrepreneurs, politicians, workers, intellectuals and people from various sectors of the Brazilian society at night, there is no record of commitments after 10 pm on his official agenda.

"Therefore, the version given by Michel Temer in his public declarations it is not sustained, according to which he indicated Rodrigo Loures to 'get rid of' Joesley," says the attorney general. The accusation highlights the fragile versions presented by the president on the conversation and the use of a businessman's jet. For the PGR, the president confessed the conversation extrajudicially; the monitoring confirms the payment of bribes by the businessman received by the president in a night meeting and outside the official agenda; the interlocutor even returns the received value.

Secret meetings—According to the accusation, later dialogues and meetings show that a second meeting was planned between the president and the businessman in New York. Still, it is settled in the Palácio de Jaburu to keep secret meetings without official records, like the occurred, when it was necessary. "The conversation at the Palácio de Jaburu was only the starting point for the requests and receipts of unfair advantages that would follow," he says.

After the conversation at the palace, Joesley meets with Loures—authorized by Michel Temer—to initiate criminal negotiations, basically the major political and commercial interests of Joesley Batista before the federal government, and matters related to crimes that the businessman had been practicing to ensure the combination of versions with some defendants of "Lava Jato" Operation, such as buying their silence through monthly payments. In a meeting on March 13th, Loures shows interest and availability to defend the interests of the company.

The investigations show Rodrigo Loures' actions for the Administrative Council for Economic Defense (Cade) to grant a favorable decision to the Energy Producing Company of Cuiabá, of the J&F Group, in Petrobras' alleged anticompetitive practice related to the acquisition of natural gas from Bolivia. In the dialogue with Gilvandro Araújo, acting president of Cade, Loures makes it clear that he speaks on behalf of Michel Temer.

From then on, a bribe is defined as 5% of the value of the estimated profit from the operation. The bribe could vary from R$ 19 million to R$ 38 million, depending on the value of the gas during the term of the contract—04/17/2017 to 12/31/2017. By the magnitude of the values, Rodrigo Loures would not have the power and autonomy to act without the support of Michel Temer.

"Rodrigo Loures, during the whole criminal undertaking, makes clear and verbalizes that he is acting on behalf of President Temer, with his science, including bringing up-to-date information about Michel Temer's positions on the issues dealt with, which makes it clear that Rodrigo Loures reported permanently to Temer about the progress of the crimes perpetrated," says the PGR. For Ricardo Saud, Loures said that he checked every Thursday with the president, after undertaking the mandate of federal deputy. Through Loures, Temer operates the receipt of unfair advantages in exchange for favors for the use of the structure and bodies of the State.

Details—On April 24th, Saud details the weekly bribe payment: R$ 500 thousand per week, when the PLD (Differences Settlement Price) was set with the price between

R$ 300 and R$ 400, and R$ 1 million, when the PLD exceeded R$ 400. The amount is set by the Electric Energy Trading Chamber, in R$/MWh, for energy commercialization. Loures agrees with the payment and defines how this would be made possible, since the "traditional channels are all obstructed", in the words of the former deputy.

Janot emphasizes in the accusation that the facts narrated in the brief "are part of a spurious scheme involving Michel Temer and his cronies for some years. On this occasion, Rodrigo Loures figured as Michel Temer's representative, replacing others who served as intermediaries for past bribe receipts."

The accusation points out that Rodrigo Loures, a man of the "strictest confidence" of Michel Temer: scheduled the meeting between Temer and Joesley Batista, in the Palácio do Jaburu; he met three times with Joesley to hear their pleadings and make an effort to attend to them, always speaking in the name of Temer; met with Ricardo Saud to discuss details of the payment of the bribe, making it clear that he would submit questions regarding the form of payment to the president; he received, on Temer's behalf, a suitcase containing R$ 500,000 as payment for resolving a J&F's pending issue with Cade and to Petrobras; exchanged cell phone messages with Joesley to set up a meeting in New York in which Michel Temer would be present in order to outline strategies for J&F to continue to benefit from the gas maneuver.

For the PGR, the evidence brought in the process reinforce the employees' narrative that at no time was Loures the final recipient of the bribe. "The unfair advantage, in fact, was intended for Michel Temer, whom the collaborators and Rodrigo Loures himself refer to as 'chief' or 'President,'" he says.

The accusation also emphasizes that he, in his official declarations as President of the Republic, recognized the dialogue with Joesley Baptist, as well as the content of the conversations. He adds that, according to the report produced by the Federal Police, the audio of the conversation between them is authentic and leaves no room for doubt regarding the trustworthiness of the dialogues. In addition, Rodrigo Loures also did not deny the receipt of the illicit values, having even refunded the amount received as a bribe, without any explanation.

And for me? What do you have?—Joesley Batista and Ricardo Saud described the spurious relationship between the J&F Group and President Michel Temer in recent years. He details that, in 2015, Temer intervened with the president of Companhia Docas do Estado de São Paulo (Codesp), when it embargoed Eldorado's construction of a cargo terminal in the Port of Santos.

He also said he had watched a World Cup match at the president's home in São Paulo, where he took Joesley's note with the values discussed with senators (Eduardo Braga, Vital do Rego, Eunício Oliveira, Jader Barbalho, Renan Calheiros and Katia Abreu) to support the PT in the 2014 presidential campaign. According to Saud, Temer was indignant with the situation, stating that the PMDB had to go through him and questioning "and for me? What do you have?".

On August 18th, 2014, Michel Temer again met with Ricardo Saud, stating that he had been allocated the amount of R$ 15 million, which was the result of the BNDES contract and pension funds.

Collaboration—Joesley Batista, a former president of the J&F Group, volunteered to narrate illicit facts, present documents relating to various crimes committed under "Lava Jato" Operation, and others involving persons holding a jurisdiction under the function prerogative, as well as other evidence of the recent past. Among the evidence submitted to the Federal Public Prosecutor's Office, the recording of the president and the former deputy stands out.

"The seriousness of the recording, however, was in the fact that, unlike previous episodes in which criminal facts revealed by the applicant were limited to past criminal acts, the present settlement negotiation has brought into question crimes whose practice or termination was occurring or to occur, on expected or expectable dates. This made it mandatory, with respect to the constitutional mission of the Public Prosecution Office, to intervene immediately to provide for the monitoring of conduct and its undoubted and rigorous investigation," explains the attorney general.

In order to do so, a pre-agreement of collaboration with testimony was made, in order to allow for precautionary measures and controlled actions to prove the facts narrated by the employees. After implementing every measure and confirming the accuracy of the information provided, on May 3rd, a collaboration agreement was signed with seven group executives.

SOURCE: Federal Public Prosecutor's Office. "PGR Denounces Michel Temer and Rodrigo Loures for Passive Corruption." June 26, 2017. Translated by SAGE Publishing. http://www.mpf.mp.br/sp/sala-de-imprensa/noticias-sp/pgr-denuncia-michel-temer-versao-pr-sp.

OTHER HISTORIC DOCUMENTS OF INTEREST

FROM PREVIOUS *HISTORIC DOCUMENTS*

United Nations Agencies Respond to Worsening Famine in South Sudan

FEBRUARY 20, MAY 31, AND AUGUST 9, 2017

South Sudan, the world's newest country, which has been in an almost constant state of conflict since declaring independence in 2011, was hit by another crisis in 2017 as famine swept across the nation. This was the first famine declared in any part of the world in nearly six years and was brought on by a confluence of factors including drought, ethnic violence, and a political vacuum. Global monetary response to the famine was slow, and aid workers struggled to reach those in need, but by mid-year, the United Nations (UN) lifted its declaration of famine while subsequently offering a warning that the citizens of South Sudan were still in dire need of assistance with many remaining on the brink of starvation.

Ongoing Civil War, Drought Lead to Famine

Unlike many other famines brought on by drought or natural disaster, South Sudan's crisis was largely manmade. Since the country devolved into civil war in 2013, its warring factions pushed citizens from their homes, blocked outside organizations from accessing the country, and attacked humanitarian aid workers. Drought heightened the crisis, and when they could find food, citizens faced inflation nearing 900 percent. The political instability in the country was driven by a dispute between President Salva Kiir and the former vice president, Riek Machar, who at the end of 2017 continued to live in exile. The two represent different ethnic groups—Kiir the larger Dinka ethic group and Machar the minority Nuer. Many Somalians, particularly those in Unity State, the portion of the country hardest hit by the famine, are farmers. The warring ethnic groups have raided and claimed these farms, leaving families without an income source or food. The lack of rain in 2016 produced hostile, arid conditions that further impacted those still able to work their land.

This collection of factors forced the United Nations to declare a famine in parts of South Sudan on February 20, 2017. According to the body, at that time 100,000 people faced starvation with another million "on the brink of famine." "Many families have exhausted every means they have to survive," said Serge Tissot, the United Nations Food and Agriculture Organization's representative in South Sudan, noting that many families in the north central part of the country are farmers who have lost access to their livelihood. The United Nations Children's Fund (UNICEF) estimated that more than one million children were acutely malnourished and another 250,000 were severely malnourished. Jeremy Hopkins, the UNICEF representative in South Sudan, summarized the dire situation, noting, "If we do not reach these children with urgent aid many of them will die." Reaching the children—and all those in need across the country—in a way that would provide long-term relief remained a challenge. "There is only so much that humanitarian assistance can achieve in the absence of meaningful peace and security, both for relief workers and the crisis-affected people they serve," said World Food Programme (WFP) Country Director Joyce Luma.

South Sudan was only one of a handful of nations facing dire food shortages in 2017. According to the United Nations, the situation in Nigeria, Somalia, South Sudan, and Yemen in 2017 marked the worst humanitarian crisis since the end of World War II, with twenty million facing famine. And in many of these nations, it was not just a food shortage, but also a lack of clean drinking water, which can lead to a host of diseases, and ongoing violence and political instability that heightens the humanitarian crisis. In many of these nations, thousands were forced into displaced person camps where, despite access to food and water, diseases including cholera spread rapidly. And similar to the situation in South Sudan, aid organizations struggled to deliver vital assistance due to ongoing civil conflict or the threat imposed by terrorist organizations. The United Nations Security Council called on all affected nations "to allow the safe, timely and unhindered access for humanitarian assistance to all areas" and "compliance with international humanitarian law" to allow aid workers to reach those in need.

GLOBAL RESPONSE

Response to the crisis in South Sudan was slow. According to the International Rescue Committee, a nongovernmental organization that provides humanitarian assistance, by early March 2017, only 0.9 percent of the need in the nation had been funded. Since December 2013, the United States had been the largest provider of aid to South Sudan, giving $2.1 billion through early 2017. The United Kingdom and European Union each stepped up their offer of aid after the declaration of famine, announcing that they would provide 100 million pounds and 82 million euro, respectively.

Further hampering the response, aid organizations struggled to reach those in need because many had been forced into hiding in remote areas. The World Food Programme was able to drop grain from airplanes over some portions of South Sudan, but in other areas, aid workers were kidnapped and held for ransom. Shortly after the famine was declared, South Sudan's President Kiir announced that the price of permits for aid workers would increase from $100 to $10,000, which he said was a means to help the government increase revenue. Many aid organizations accused the government of trying to block aid workers from reaching civilians. "The government and the army have largely contributed to the humanitarian situation. And now, they want to create profit from the crisis they have created," said Amnesty International's Elizabeth Deng.

By the end of May 2017, a UN-backed Integrated Food Security Phase Classification (IPC) report determined that the nation was no longer in famine, but noted that 1.7 million South Sudanese were still at risk of food insecurity, with another six million at risk of starvation. Stephen O'Brien, the UN's Emergency Relief Coordinator, urged caution with regard to the end of the famine declaration noting, "Across South Sudan, more people are on the brink of famine today than were in February." Echoing his remarks, the United Nations Food and Agriculture Organization Director of Emergencies, Dominique Burgeon, said, "The crisis is not over. We are merely keeping people alive . . . the only way to stop this desperate situation is to stop the conflict, ensure unimpeded access and enable people to resume their livelihoods." Despite worldwide calls for an end to the conflict in South Sudan, by the close of 2017, a political solution appeared unlikely and aid organizations worked to keep pace with the humanitarian need they anticipated in the coming year.

—Heather Kerrigan

Following is a press release from the United Nations News Centre on February 20, 2017, detailing the declaration of famine in South Sudan; a summary from the Integrated Food Security Phase Classification issued on May 31, 2017, indicating that South Sudan was no longer classified in famine; and a statement by the president of the United Nations Security Council on August 9, 2017, urging a global response to the ongoing food crisis.

United Nations on the Declaration of Famine in South Sudan

February 20, 2017

Famine has been formally declared in parts of South Sudan, the United Nations said today, warning that war and a collapsing economy have left some 100,000 people facing starvation there and a further one million people are classified as being on the brink of famine.

"Famine has become a tragic reality in parts of South Sudan and our worst fears have been realised," said Serge Tissot, the Food and Agriculture Organization (FAO) Representative in South Sudan, in a news release issued jointly with the United Nations Children's Fund (UNICEF) and the World Food Programme (WFP).

"Many families have exhausted every means they have to survive," he stated, explaining that these people are predominantly farmers who have lost their livestock, even their farming tools.

Famine is currently affecting parts of Unity state in the northern-central part of the country. A formal famine declaration means people have already started dying of hunger.

The situation is the worst hunger catastrophe since fighting erupted more than three years ago between rival forces—the Sudan People's Liberation Army (SPLA) loyal to President Salva Kiir and the SPLA in Opposition backing First Vice-President Riek Machar.

The three UN agencies warned that urgent action is needed to prevent more people from dying of hunger.

According to the Integrated Food Security Phase Classification (IPC) update released today by the government, the three agencies and other humanitarian partners, 4.9 million people—more than 40 percent of South Sudan's population—are in need of urgent food, agriculture and nutrition assistance.

The total number of food insecure people is expected to rise to 5.5 million at the height of the lean season in July if nothing is done to curb the severity and spread of the food crisis.

"More than one million children are currently estimated to be acutely malnourished across South Sudan; over a quarter of a million children are already severely malnourished. If we do not reach these children with urgent aid many of them will die," said Jeremy Hopkins, UNICEF Representative a.i in South Sudan.

"We have also warned that there is only so much that humanitarian assistance can achieve in the absence of meaningful peace and security, both for relief workers and the crisis-affected people they serve," said WFP Country Director Joyce Luma.

Source: United Nations News Centre. "Famine Declared in Region of South Sudan – UN." February 20, 2017. http://www.un.org/apps/news/story.asp?NewsID=56205#.WacJrZOGMRF.

IPC Removes Famine
Classification from South Sudan

DOCUMENT

May 31, 2017

Current Period Classified: May 2017

Projection Period for Most Likely Scenarios: June-July 2017

- Food security in South Sudan has further deteriorated due to armed conflict, economic crisis, and below average harvests that were exhausted well before the ongoing lean season. **An estimated 6.01 million (50% of the population) people are expected to be severely food insecure in June-July 2017, compared to 5.5 million (45% of the population) people in May 2017.** This is the greatest number of people ever to experience severe food insecurity (IPC Phases 3, 4 and 5) in South Sudan.

- **Famine is no longer occurring in Leer and Mayendit counties, and further deterioration was prevented in Koch and Panyijiar counties of former Southern Unity State as a result of immediate and sustained multi-sector humanitarian assistance delivered to the affected population since March 2017.** The early detection of the deterioration of the food security situation into famine followed by the subsequent large-scale immediate response averted further loss of life, thus underscoring the importance of evidence based analysis and response. However, in June-July 2017, approximately 45,000 people will still be facing Humanitarian Catastrophe in Leer, Koch, Mayendit in former Unity State and Ayod County in former Jonglei state based on most likely assumptions of continued armed conflict, food shortages associated with seasonality, and humanitarian assistance delivery constraints.

- **Even though no county has been classified under famine (Phase 5) in this IPC update, the situation continues to be very critical.** In June-July 2017, in addition to approximately 45,000 people estimated to be facing Humanitarian Catastrophe2, an estimated 1.7 million people are likely to be facing food security emergency (IPC Phase 4)—one-step below Famine on the IPC scale. This is based on most likely assumptions of continued armed conflict, food shortages associated with seasonality, and humanitarian assistance delivery constraints. This projected number in June-July 2017 is up from 1.0 million projected for February-April 2017 period in the last IPC report.

- While effective response was provided in the famine affected areas, thus avoiding what would have most likely been significant loss of life due to the interaction of starvation and disease, the situation in central former Unity remains extremely vulnerable with some populations in Humanitarian Catastrophe (IPC Phase 5) in June-July 2017. **Gains made in previously Famine-affected and Famine-risk counties must not be jeopardized through the reallocation of humanitarian assistance** to ongoing and developing acute food insecurity hotspots because the affected populations' livelihoods are effectively eroded thus leaving them heavily reliant on humanitarian assistance. Should humanitarian assistance be compromised, the areas could easily slip into Famine again.

- Of great concern is former Greater Jonglei State, where food security is rapidly deteriorating, predominantly in the counties of Ayod, Canal/Pigi, Duk, Nyirol and Uror, which are facing Emergency (IPC Phase 4) acute food insecurity, **with Ayod having an estimated 20,000 people experiencing Humanitarian Catastrophe (IPC Phase 5) at least through July 2017.** The conflict-related displacement of over 200,000 people from northern, central, and eastern former Jonglei has severely disrupted livelihoods and access to social services, thus severely undermining food security in the State. The situation has been further exacerbated by last year's poor harvests as well as the economic crisis that has eroded households' purchasing power. The classification for Nyirol and Urol is based on professional judgement of the IPC ERC and the South Sudan IPC Technical Working Group (TWG) but not in accordance with the minimal evidence requirements of the IPC Protocols.

- **Greater Equatoria, and particularly some of the country's most productive Greenbelt counties from Yei, Lainya, Morobo, Kajo Keji and Magwi, are facing Crisis (IPC Phase 3) and Emergency (IPC Phase 4) levels of acute food insecurity, driven largely by armed conflict that has had severe effects on agricultural activities and markets.** Large farming populations have been driven across the border into Uganda and the Democratic Republic of the Congo, severely inhibiting the 2016 harvest and causing large portions of the population to miss the first planting season of 2017. There is a high likelihood that this population will also miss the second planting season—a situation that will most likely result in a record high national cereal deficit in 2018.

- **The Western Bank of former Upper Nile state is experiencing Emergency (IPC Phase 4) food insecurity, mainly in Manyo, Panyikang, and Fashoda where large displacements have occurred due to ongoing armed conflict.** This has resulted in disruptions to livelihoods, markets, and access to humanitarian assistance.

- **Former Northern Bahr el Ghazal state is facing severe food insecurity caused by high food prices and diminished household purchasing power.** All counties except Aweil Center are experiencing Emergency (IPC Phase 4) acute food insecurity through July 2017. In former Western Bahr el Ghazal, a spike in armed conflict in the counties of Wau and Raga has disrupted trade, displaced populations, and destroyed livelihoods.

- **Acute malnutrition remains a major public health emergency in several parts of South Sudan.** A total of 12 SMART surveys were conducted between March-May 2017, and 10 showed Global Acute Malnutrition Weight-for-Height (GAM (WHZ)) prevalence above the WHO emergency threshold of 15%, with a peak of 26.1% in Duk, bordering Extremely Critical classification. Alarming proxy GAM (MUAC) prevalence above 20% was observed in Ayod, (Karmoun, Normanyang, and Kandak payams) between January-April 2017. Widespread fighting, displacement and poor access to services, disease outbreaks, extremely poor diet (in terms of both quality and quantity), low coverage of sanitation facilities and poor hygiene practices are the key drivers of the high levels of acute malnutrition across South

Sudan. Levels of acute malnutrition are expected to deteriorate even further as the peak lean season approaches in July 2017, with Mayendit, Aweil North, and Ayod projected to be at Extreme Critical nutrition levels.

[All maps, graphs, and footnotes have been omitted.]

SOURCE: Integrated Food Security Phase Classification. "The Republic of South Sudan – May 2017 – Communication Summary." May 31, 2017. http://www.ipcinfo.org/fileadmin/user_upload/ipcinfo/docs/IPC_South_Sudan_AcuteFI_May2017_June-July2017.pdf.

DOCUMENT

Security Council President Calls for Global Aid for Famine

August 9, 2017

"The Security Council expresses its grave concern about the unprecedented level of global humanitarian needs and the threat of famine presently facing more than 20 million people in Yemen, Somalia, South Sudan and north-east Nigeria, and notes with appreciation the Secretary-General's leadership in the efforts to respond.

"The Security Council notes the devastating impact on civilians of ongoing armed conflict and violence. The Security Council also emphasizes with deep concern that ongoing conflicts and violence have devastating humanitarian consequences and hinder an effective humanitarian response in the short, medium and long term and are therefore a major cause of famine in the situations above. In this regard, the Security Council also notes the links between food scarcity and increased vulnerability of women, children and persons with disabilities.

"The Security Council reiterates its commitment to work with the Secretary-General to pursue all possible avenues to end conflicts, including through addressing their underlying root causes in an inclusive and sustainable manner.

"The Security Council stresses that responding effectively to these crises requires respect for international humanitarian law by all parties.

"The Security Council underlines the obligations of all parties to armed conflict to respect and protect civilians. The Security Council encourages those with influence over parties to armed conflict to remind the latter of their obligation to comply with international humanitarian law.

"The Security Council further underlines the need to ensure the security of humanitarian operations and personnel in conflict-affected countries. The Security Council calls on all parties to respect and protect medical facilities and personnel and their means of transport and equipment.

"The Security Council deplores that in the conflict-affected Yemen, South Sudan, Somalia and north-east Nigeria, certain parties have failed to ensure unfettered and sustained access for deliveries of vital food assistance, as well as other forms of humanitarian aid. The Security Council reiterates its calls on all parties to allow the safe, timely and unhindered access for humanitarian assistance to all areas and to facilitate access for essential imports of food, fuel and medical supplies into each country, and their distribution throughout. The Security Council further urges all parties to protect civilian infrastructure which is critical to the delivery of humanitarian aid in the affected countries.

"The Security Council calls upon all parties in Yemen, South Sudan, Somalia and north-east Nigeria to urgently take steps that would enable a more effective humanitarian response.

"The Security Council commends efforts by international donors to provide humanitarian assistance in response to these four crises. The Security Council calls for the immediate disbursement of the funds already pledged to Yemen, Somalia, South Sudan and north-east Nigeria at successive international conferences, including those held in Oslo, Geneva and London, if possible in the form of multi-year and unearmarked funding. The Security Council calls on Member States to provide additional resources and funding to pull people back from the brink of famine.

"The Security Council stresses the need to enhance longer-term recovery and resilience of conflict-affected countries.

"The Security Council requests the Secretary-General to continue to provide information on the humanitarian situation and response, including on the risk of famine, in the conflict-affected Yemen, Somalia, South Sudan and north-east Nigeria, as part of his regular comprehensive reporting.

"In light of the unprecedented threat of famine in conflict-affected Yemen, Somalia, South Sudan and north-east Nigeria, the Security Council further requests the Secretary-General to provide an oral briefing, during the month of October 2017, on country-specific impediments to an effective response to the risk of famine in Yemen, South Sudan, Somalia and north-east Nigeria and make specific recommendations on how to address these impediments, in order to enable a more robust short- and long-term response in the four countries. The Security Council welcomes the Secretary-General's letters on the risk of famine in Yemen, South Sudan, Somalia and north-east Nigeria of 21 February and 27 June 2017 and in this regard requests the Secretary-General to provide early warning when a conflict having devastating humanitarian consequences and hindering an effective humanitarian response risks leading to an outbreak of famine.

"The Security Council expresses its readiness to continue to support the Secretary-General's call to action to avert famine in conflict-affected countries and commits to engage constructively on the Secretary-General's specific recommendations."

SOURCE: United Nations. "Security Council Presidential Statement Urges Greater Humanitarian Access to Famine-Threatened Yemen, South Sudan, Somalia, Nigeria." August 9, 2017. https://www.un.org/press/en/2017/sc12946.doc.htm.

OTHER HISTORIC DOCUMENTS OF INTEREST

FROM PREVIOUS HISTORIC DOCUMENTS

- Renewed Fighting in South Sudan; Continuation of Border Negotiations, *2016*, p. 309
- President of South Sudan on Nation's Independence, *2011*, p. 447

NASA and SpaceX Announce
Milestones in Space Exploration;
Congress Sets Timeline for
Mission to Mars

FEBRUARY 22 AND 27, MARCH 7 AND 21, AND JUNE 30, 2017

New milestones in public space exploration and private spaceflight were announced in 2017, including the National Aeronautics and Space Administration's (NASA) record discovery of habitable-zone planets orbiting a single star and SpaceX's plan to transport private citizens around the moon. Meanwhile, Congress passed the first NASA authorization bill since 2010, directing the agency to conduct a manned mission to Mars by the 2030s and outlining other space program priorities. Additionally, President Donald Trump reestablished the National Space Council to help guide and coordinate his administration's space policy.

NASA FINDS RECORD NUMBER OF HABITABLE-ZONE PLANETS

On February 22, 2017, NASA announced that its Spitzer Space Telescope found "the first known system of seven Earth-size planets around a single star." Located approximately forty light years, or 235 trillion miles, from Earth in the constellation Aquarius, the Transiting Planets and Planetesimals Small Telescope (TRAPPIST)-1 system was confirmed to have three planets in the habitable zone—the area around a star in which a planet is most likely to have liquid water and, therefore, the possibility of life. The discovery set a record for the number of habitable-zone planets found orbiting a single star outside our solar system.

Launched in August 2003, the Spitzer Space Telescope mission is the last of NASA's Great Observatories Program, which consists of four space-based telescopes, including the Hubble Space Telescope. Spitzer is an infrared telescope designed to capture images of the early universe that optical telescopes are unable to capture and was the first telescope to see light from a planet outside our solar system. Spitzer observed the TRAPPIST-1 system for 500 hours in 2016, following the system's initial discovery by researchers using the Belgian TRAPPIST. The TRAPPIST researchers identified three planets in the system in 2016; Spitzer and observations from several ground-based telescopes confirmed the existence of two of the three planets and found another five.

"This discovery could be a significant piece in the puzzle of finding habitable environments, places that are conducive to life," said Thomas Zurbuchen, associate administrator of NASA's Science Mission Directorate. "Answering the question 'are we alone' is a top science priority and finding so many planets like these for the first time in the habitable zone is a remarkable step forward toward that goal."

In August, NASA released a study from TRAPPIST-1 researchers that estimated the system's star was between 5.4 and 9.8 billion years old. By comparison, researchers estimate our solar system to have formed roughly 4.5 billion years ago. The star's age has important implications for the planets' habitability and the likelihood of liquid water being present. Because it is an older star and the planets orbit it closely, they may have been exposed to many more years of high radiation, which could have boiled their atmospheres and water away. However, it is possible that the planets have thicker atmospheres than does Earth, in which case liquid water and any life forms may have been protected from the star's radiation.

NASA planned to use Spitzer to collect additional observations of the system through fall 2017. This information will be used to plan studies to be conducted by the more sensitive James Webb Space Telescope—scheduled to launch in 2018—to detect water, methane, and other components of the planets' atmospheres. NASA is also using Hubble to screen four of the TRAPPIST-1 planets, including those in the habitable zone, to assess whether they have atmospheres and, if so, whether they are like that of Earth. Additionally, NASA's Kepler telescope is studying the system with a focus on the star and changes in its brightness as the planets orbit. The Kepler mission generated its own news in June 2017, following the discovery of 219 possible exoplanets, ten of which were rocky bodies in their stars' habitable zones. These planets will also require further study to confirm their existence and composition.

SpaceX Plans First Private Flight beyond Earth Orbit

On February 27, 2017, SpaceX announced plans to fly two private citizens around the moon in 2018, along with the possibility of flying additional passengers expressing interest in future flights. "These individuals will travel into space carrying the hopes and dreams of all humankind, driven by the universal human spirit of exploration," read a release issued by the company. If the flight proceeds as planned, SpaceX would become the first private company to take passengers beyond Earth's orbit. Other commercial aerospace companies, such as Virgin Galactic and XCOR Aerospace, offer suborbital flights only, and Space Adventures has been offering rides to the International Space Station (ISS) on Russian Soyuz spacecraft since 2001. (Flight availability is dependent on the Russian ships having empty seats.)

The commercial spaceflight industry has grown significantly following implementation of NASA's Commercial Orbital Transportation Services and Commercial Crew Programs. The Commercial Orbital Transportation Services Program started in 2006 with the goal of developing commercially operated, automated cargo spacecraft that could conduct supply missions to the ISS; SpaceX and Orbital Sciences Corporation received contracts through this program. Then in 2010, NASA initiated the Commercial Crew Program, through which it is working with SpaceX and Boeing to develop launch systems and spacecraft capable of carrying astronaut crews to the ISS. One of the program's goals is to "return human spaceflight launches to U.S. soil, providing reliable and cost-effective access to low-Earth orbit on systems that meet [NASA's] safety and mission requirements." (Since the space shuttle program ended in July 2011, NASA has relied on Russia to transport astronauts to and from the ISS.) Leveraging commercial technology to support the ISS will also allow NASA to focus its budget and resources on developing the rockets and spacecraft needed for deep space missions, including those to Mars.

SpaceX's selection for both NASA programs provided the company with the funding it needed to accelerate its development of spaceflight technology, including the Dragon 2 spacecraft that would be used to transport astronauts to the ISS and take private passengers around the moon. SpaceX is scheduled to test launch the Dragon 2 in February 2018, when the spacecraft will fly in automatic mode, without passengers, to the ISS. A crewed Dragon 2 mission to the ISS is planned for June 2018. Once crewed missions are underway for NASA, SpaceX will launch its private passengers on their circumnavigation of the moon.

In addition to its ISS missions, SpaceX partnered with various public and private entities to launch various satellites into orbit and continues working to develop other spaceflight technology. In March 2017, for example, SpaceX reused the first stage of a Falcon 9 rocket that had previously launched an ISS resupply mission, a step forward in the company's efforts to develop a rocket that can be quickly and fully reused for multiple missions. Rockets are generally designed to burn up upon reentry into Earth's atmosphere; developing a reusable rocket could significantly reduce costs associated with spaceflight. SpaceX is also planning its own mission to Mars, with the goal of testing the technology needed to land heavy equipment on the planet's surface. Speaking at the International Astronautical Congress in Adelaide, Australia, SpaceX CEO Elon Musk said the company plans to send its first cargo mission to Mars in 2022 and its first crewed spacecraft to the red planet in 2024. If the company makes the journey, it will once again make history for conducting the first private mission to Mars.

Congress Calls for Manned Mars Mission in 2030s

Early in 2017, members of Congress began considering the NASA Transition Authorization Act of 2017. Sponsored by Sen. Ted Cruz, R-Texas, and Rep. Lamar Smith, R-Texas, the bill authorized approximately $19.5 billion in FY2017 funding for NASA, an increase over the $19.3 billion the agency received in FY2016. The bill also amended current law to add the expansion of "permanent human presence beyond low-Earth orbit" and the "capability to extend human presence, including potential habitation on another celestial body and a thriving space economy in the 21st Century" to NASA's long-term goals. Perhaps most notably, the bill added "human exploration of Mars and beyond" to the agency's key objectives and required NASA to develop and submit a plan to Congress for achieving "the long-term goal of human missions near or on the surface of Mars in the 2030s." The bill went on to direct NASA to continue developing its Space Launch System and Orion spacecraft to facilitate the mission to Mars and other deep space missions, calling for an uncrewed launch of both in 2018.

Other key provisions of the bill expressed Congress's support for continued collaboration between NASA and the private sector, including crew and supply transportation to the ISS. The bill called for NASA to develop and submit a plan to Congress for facilitating the "commercialization and economic development" of low-Earth orbit activities and asked NASA to explore transferring the ISS to the private sector. The bill also established the TREAT Astronauts Act, which allows the government to provide medical coverage to astronauts who spend extended periods in space and provides for long-term medical monitoring of those astronauts once they have returned to Earth and after they retire.

The bill easily progressed through Congress, passing the Senate on February 17 and the House on March 7. "With the passage of this bipartisan legislation, the future of the U.S. space program is now more secure and stable," said Sen. Cruz. "We are also making a serious commitment to the manned exploration of space, laying the groundwork for the mission to Mars, and enabling commercial space ventures to flourish."

While the bill passed unanimously in the Senate and no one spoke against it in the House, some lawmakers raised concerns about what the bill did not cover. For example, the bill did not include language about Earth sciences programs or NASA's collaboration with the National Oceanic and Atmospheric Administration, both of which had been included in the NASA Authorization Act of 2010. "Those programs provide the space-based measurements to help scientists understand the Earth's systems and changing climate to predict space weather events, which can have devastating impacts on our terrestrial infrastructure," said Rep. Eddie Bernice Johnson, D-Texas. Some observers also commented that the bill was not particularly groundbreaking because it largely instructed NASA to continue the work it had already been doing and did not provide a strong sense of President Donald Trump's space policy priorities.

Trump signed the bill on March 21, saying that it reaffirmed the United States' "national commitment to the core mission of NASA: human space exploration, space science, and technology." He added, "This bill will make sure that NASA's most important and effective programs are sustained. It orders NASA to continue . . . transitioning activities to the commercial sector where we have seen great progress."

The authorization bill must now go through the congressional appropriations process before a final NASA budget is set.

TRUMP RESURRECTS NATIONAL SPACE COUNCIL

After the NASA Transition Authorization Act signing, Vice President Mike Pence indicated that Trump soon planned to reestablish the National Space Council—a promise kept on June 30, when the president signed Executive Order 13803.

NASA initially formed the council in 1958. Called the National Aeronautics and Space Council, the group coordinated U.S. space priorities among the various government entities with a stake in space until it was abolished by President Richard Nixon in 1973. The group was reformed as the National Space Council under President George H. W. Bush, but was disbanded in 1993.

Per Trump's Executive Order, the revived council "shall advise and assist the President regarding national space policy and strategy, and perform such other duties as the President may, from time to time, prescribe." Pence will chair the group, which will also include the secretaries of state, defense, commerce, transportation, and homeland security; the director of national intelligence; the director of the Office of Management and Budget; the chairman of the Joint Chiefs of Staff; the NASA administrator, who has not yet been confirmed; and the director of the White House Office of Science and Technology Policy, who has not yet been appointed by Trump. Scott Pace, director of the Space Policy Institute and professor of the Practice of International Affairs at the George Washington University's Elliott School of International Affairs, will serve as the council's executive secretary. A Users' Advisory Group composed of "non-Federal representatives of industries and other persons involved in aeronautical and space activities" (generally interpreted to mean representatives of the states and from the private sector) will also be established to work with and provide guidance to the council.

—Linda Grimm

Following is a press release from NASA from February 22, 2017, announcing the largest discovery of habitable-zone planets around a single star outside the solar system; a press release from SpaceX from February 27, 2017, announcing the company's plans to fly private citizens beyond the moon in 2018; a press release issued by Sen. Ted Cruz, R-Texas, on March 7, 2017, announcing congressional passage of the NASA Transition Authorization Act; remarks by President Donald Trump at the signing of the NASA Transition Authorization Act on March 21, 2017; and an executive order signed by Trump on June 30, 2017, reviving the National Space Council.

NASA Announces Largest Discovery of Earth-size, Habitable-Zone Planets around Single Star

DOCUMENT

February 22, 2017

NASA's Spitzer Space Telescope has revealed the first known system of seven Earth-size planets around a single star. Three of these planets are firmly located in the habitable zone, the area around the parent star where a rocky planet is most likely to have liquid water.

The discovery sets a new record for greatest number of habitable-zone planets found around a single star outside our solar system. All of these seven planets could have liquid water—key to life as we know it—under the right atmospheric conditions, but the chances are highest with the three in the habitable zone.

"This discovery could be a significant piece in the puzzle of finding habitable environments, places that are conducive to life," said Thomas Zurbuchen, associate administrator of the agency's Science Mission Directorate in Washington. "Answering the question 'are we alone' is a top science priority and finding so many planets like these for the first time in the habitable zone is a remarkable step forward toward that goal."

At about 40 light-years (235 trillion miles) from Earth, the system of planets is relatively close to us, in the constellation Aquarius. Because they are located outside of our solar system, these planets are scientifically known as exoplanets.

This exoplanet system is called TRAPPIST-1, named for The Transiting Planets and Planetesimals Small Telescope (TRAPPIST) in Chile. In May 2016, researchers using TRAPPIST announced they had discovered three planets in the system. Assisted by several ground-based telescopes, including the European Southern Observatory's Very Large Telescope, Spitzer confirmed the existence of two of these planets and discovered five additional ones, increasing the number of known planets in the system to seven.

The new results were published Wednesday in the journal Nature, and announced at a news briefing at NASA Headquarters in Washington.

Using Spitzer data, the team precisely measured the sizes of the seven planets and developed first estimates of the masses of six of them, allowing their density to be estimated.

Based on their densities, all of the TRAPPIST-1 planets are likely to be rocky. Further observations will not only help determine whether they are rich in water, but also possibly reveal whether any could have liquid water on their surfaces. The mass of the seventh and farthest exoplanet has not yet been estimated—scientists believe it could be an icy, "snowball-like" world, but further observations are needed.

"The seven wonders of TRAPPIST-1 are the first Earth-size planets that have been found orbiting this kind of star," said Michael Gillon, lead author of the paper and the principal investigator of the TRAPPIST exoplanet survey at the University of Liege, Belgium. "It is also the best target yet for studying the atmospheres of potentially habitable, Earth-size worlds." . . .

Spitzer, an infrared telescope that trails Earth as it orbits the sun, was well-suited for studying TRAPPIST-1 because the star glows brightest in infrared light, whose wavelengths are longer than the eye can see. In the fall of 2016, Spitzer observed TRAPPIST-1 nearly continuously for 500 hours . . .

"This is the most exciting result I have seen in the 14 years of Spitzer operations," said Sean Carey, manager of NASA's Spitzer Science Center at Caltech/IPAC in Pasadena, California. "Spitzer will follow up in the fall to further refine our understanding of these planets so that the James Webb Space Telescope can follow up. More observations of the system are sure to reveal more secrets."

Following up on the Spitzer discovery, NASA's Hubble Space Telescope has initiated the screening of four of the planets, including the three inside the habitable zone. These observations aim at assessing the presence of puffy, hydrogen-dominated atmospheres, typical for gaseous worlds like Neptune, around these planets . . .

"The TRAPPIST-1 system provides one of the best opportunities in the next decade to study the atmospheres around Earth-size planets," said Nikole Lewis, co-leader of the Hubble study and astronomer at the Space Telescope Science Institute in Baltimore, Maryland. NASA's planet-hunting Kepler space telescope also is studying the TRAPPIST-1 system, making measurements of the star's minuscule changes in brightness due to transiting planets. Operating as the K2 mission, the spacecraft's observations will allow astronomers to refine the properties of the known planets, as well as search for additional planets in the system. The K2 observations conclude in early March and will be made available on the public archive.

Spitzer, Hubble, and Kepler will help astronomers plan for follow-up studies using NASA's upcoming James Webb Space Telescope, launching in 2018. With much greater sensitivity, Webb will be able to detect the chemical fingerprints of water, methane, oxygen, ozone, and other components of a planet's atmosphere. Webb also will analyze planets' temperatures and surface pressures—key factors in assessing their habitability . . .

SOURCE: National Aeronautics and Space Administration. "NASA Telescope Reveals Largest Batch of Earth-size, Habitable-Zone Planets around Single Star." February 22, 2017. https://www.nasa.gov/press-release/nasa-telescope-reveals-largest-batch-of-earth-size-habitable-zone-planets-around.

SpaceX Announces Plan to Send Private Spacecraft beyond the Moon

February 27, 2017

We are excited to announce that SpaceX has been approached to fly two private citizens on a trip around the Moon late next year. They have already paid a significant deposit to do a Moon mission. Like the Apollo astronauts before them, these individuals will travel into space carrying the hopes and dreams of all humankind, driven by the universal human spirit of exploration. We expect to conduct health and fitness tests, as well as begin initial training later this year. Other flight teams have also expressed strong interest and we expect more to follow. Additional information will be released about the flight teams, contingent upon their approval and confirmation of the health and fitness test results.

Most importantly, we would like to thank NASA, without whom this would not be possible. NASA's Commercial Crew Program, which provided most of the funding for Dragon 2 development, is a key enabler for this mission . . .

Later this year, as part of NASA's Commercial Crew Program, we will launch our Crew Dragon (Dragon Version 2) spacecraft to the International Space Station. This first demonstration mission will be in automatic mode, without people on board. A subsequent mission with crew is expected to fly in the second quarter of 2018. SpaceX is currently contracted to perform an average of four Dragon 2 missions to the ISS per year, three carrying cargo and one carrying crew. By also flying privately crewed missions, which NASA has encouraged, long-term costs to the government decline and more flight reliability history is gained, benefiting both government and private missions.

Once operational Crew Dragon missions are underway for NASA, SpaceX will launch the private mission on a journey to circumnavigate the Moon and return to Earth. Lift-off will be from Kennedy Space Center's historic Pad 39A near Cape Canaveral—the same launch pad used by the Apollo program for its lunar missions. This presents an opportunity for humans to return to deep space for the first time in 45 years and they will travel faster and further into the Solar System than any before them.

Designed from the beginning to carry humans, the Dragon spacecraft already has a long flight heritage. These missions will build upon that heritage, extending it to deep space mission operations, an important milestone as we work towards our ultimate goal of transporting humans to Mars.

SOURCE: SpaceX. "SpaceX to Send Privately Crewed Dragon Spacecraft beyond the Moon Next Year." February 27, 2017. http://www.spacex.com/news/2017/02/27/spacex-send-privately-crewed-dragon-spacecraft-beyond-moon-next-year.

Senator Ted Cruz Announces Passage of the NASA Transition Authorization Act

DOCUMENT

March 7, 2017

The U.S. House of Representatives today passed S. 442, The National Aeronautics and Space Administration (NASA) Transition Authorization Act of 2017 . . . The legislation provides stability for NASA to sustain and build upon existing national space investments designed to advance space exploration and science with an overall authorization level of $19.508 billion for fiscal year 2017. With the House's passage of the bill today, the legislation now heads to the White House to await President Donald Trump's signature.

"The importance of NASA and space exploration to Houston and the state of Texas cannot be underestimated," said Sen. Cruz. "With the passage of this bipartisan legislation, the future of the U.S. space program is now more secure and stable, and we have provided much-needed certainty to the missions of the International Space Station and Johnson Space Center. We are also making a serious commitment to the manned exploration of space, laying the groundwork for the mission to Mars, and enabling commercial space ventures to flourish, all of which will foster extraordinary economic growth and job creation throughout Texas. I'm grateful for the hard work and collaboration of Senators Bill Nelson, John Thune, and Gary Peters, Congressmen Lamar Smith and Brian Babin, and organizations like the Bay Area Houston Economic Partnership, all of whom all helped forge this legislation to help ensure America continues to lead the way in space exploration."

Highlights of S. 442, The NASA Transition Authorization Act of 2017:

Sustaining National Space Commitments and Utilizing the International Space Station

- Support for Continuity—Affirms Congress' support for sustained space investments across presidential administrations to advance recent achievements in space exploration and space science. This includes the development of the Space Launch System heavy-lift rocket and the Orion crew vehicle for deep space exploration, maximizing utilization of the International Space Station (ISS), the James Webb Space Telescope, and continued commitment to a national, government-led space program.

- International Space Station—Supports full and complete utilization of the ISS through at least 2024, and the use of private sector companies partnering with NASA to deliver cargo and experiments. Also facilitates the development of vehicles to transport astronauts from U.S. soil to end our reliance on Russian launches for crew transport.

- Facilitating Commercialization and Economic Development of Low-Earth Orbit—Requires NASA to submit a report to Congress outlining a plan to facilitate a transformation of operations in low-earth orbit from a model largely reliant on government support to one reflecting a more commercially viable future.

Advancing Human Deep Space Exploration

- Journey to Mars—Amends current law by adding human exploration of Mars as one of the goals and objectives of NASA and directs NASA to manage human space flight programs to enable humans to explore Mars and other destinations. Requires NASA to develop and submit a plan to Congress on a strategic framework and critical decision plan based on current technologies to achieve the exploration goals and objectives.

- Development of Deep Space Capabilities—Directs NASA to continue the development of the Space Launch System and Orion for a broad deep space mission set, with specific milestones for an uncrewed exploration mission by 2018 and a crewed exploration mission by 2021.

Medical Monitoring of Astronauts

- Medical Effects of Space—Authorizes NASA to provide for the medical monitoring, diagnosis, and treatment of astronauts, including scientific and medical tests for psychological and medical conditions deemed by NASA to be associated with human space flight . . .

SOURCE: Office of Senator Ted Cruz. "Congress Sends Bipartisan Cruz-Nelson NASA Transition Authorization Act to the President's Desk." March 7, 2017. https://www.cruz.senate.gov/?id=3026&p=press_release.

Remarks by President Trump on Signing the NASA Transition Authorization Act of 2017

March 21, 2017

. . . For almost six decades, NASA's work has inspired millions and millions of Americans to imagine distant worlds and a better future right here on Earth. I'm delighted to sign this bill—it's been a long time since a bill like this has been signed—reaffirming our national commitment to the core mission of NASA: human space exploration, space science, and technology.

With this legislation, we support NASA's scientists, engineers, astronauts, and their pursuit of discovery. We support jobs; it's about jobs also. This bill calls for ongoing medical monitoring and treatment of our heroic astronauts for health conditions that result from their service . . .

This bill will make sure that NASA's most important and effective programs are sustained. It orders NASA to continue—and it does, it orders just that—to continue transitioning activities to the commercial sector where we have seen great progress. It's amazing what's going on; so many people and so many companies are so into exactly what NASA stands for. So the commercial and the private sector will get to use these facilities . . .

It continues support for the commercial crew program, which will carry American astronauts into space from American soil once again—been a long time. It supports NASA's deep space exploration, including the Space Launch System and the ORION spacecraft. It advances space science by maintaining a balanced set of mission and activities to explore our solar system and the entire universe. And it ensures that through NASA's astronauts and aeronautics research, the United States will remain a total leader in aviation.

Now, these astronauts are amazing—I've met some of them—they are very brave people, and their right at the forefront. So we salute them with this legislation. And we salute the ones that have lost their lives doing what they love to do.

America's space program has been a blessing to our people and to the entire world. Almost half a century ago, our brave astronauts first planted the American flag on the Moon. That was a big moment in our history. Now this Nation is ready to be the first in space once again. Today we're taking the initial steps toward a bold and bright new future for American spaceflight . . .

So I just want to thank all of the people standing behind me. They've done a great service for the country and for their communities. It's a lot of jobs, and these are great jobs. So thank you very much. And we'll sign this . . .

[The following two pages have been omitted and contain brief remarks by members of Congress and administration officials present at the bill signing.]

Source: Executive Office of the President. "Remarks on Signing the National Aeronautics and Space Administration Authorization Act of 2017." March 21, 2017. *Compilation of Presidential Documents* 2017, no. 00183 (March 21, 2017). https://www.gpo.gov/fdsys/pkg/DCPD-201700183/pdf/DCPD-201700183.pdf.

Executive Order 13803 Reviving the National Space Council

June 30, 2017

By the authority vested in me as President by the Constitution and the laws of the United States of America, and in order to provide a coordinated process for developing and monitoring the implementation of national space policy and strategy, it is hereby ordered as follows:

Section 1. Purpose. The National Space Council (Council) was established by Title V of Public Law 100-685 and Executive Order 12675 of April 20, 1989 (Establishing the National Space Council). The Council was tasked with advising and assisting the President regarding national space policy and strategy. The Council was never formally disestablished, but it effectively ceased operation in 1993. This order revives the Council and provides additional details regarding its duties and responsibilities.

Sec. 2. Revival and Composition of the National Space Council. (a) The Council is hereby revived and shall resume operations.

(b) The Council shall be composed of the following members:

    (i) The Vice President, who shall be Chair of the Council;

    (ii) The Secretary of State;

    (iii) The Secretary of Defense;

    (iv) The Secretary of Commerce;

    (v) The Secretary of Transportation;

    (vi) The Secretary of Homeland Security;

    (vii) The Director of National Intelligence;

    (viii) The Director of the Office of Management and Budget;

    (ix) The Assistant to the President for National Security Affairs;

    (x) The Administrator of the National Aeronautics and Space Administration;

    (xi) The Director of the Office of Science and Technology Policy;

    (xii) The Assistant to the President for Homeland Security and Counterterrorism;

(xiii) The Chairman of the Joint Chiefs of Staff; and

(xiv) The heads of other executive departments and agencies (agencies) and other senior officials within the Executive Office of the President, as determined by the Chair.

Sec. 3. Functions of the Council. (a) The Council shall advise and assist the President regarding national space policy and strategy, and perform such other duties as the President may, from time to time, prescribe.

(b) In particular, the Council is directed to:

(i) review United States Government space policy, including long-range goals, and develop a strategy for national space activities;

(ii) develop recommendations for the President on space policy and space-related issues;

(iii) monitor and coordinate implementation of the objectives of the President's national space policy and strategy;

(iv) foster close coordination, cooperation, and technology and information exchange among the civil, national security, and commercial space sectors;

(v) advise on participation in international space activities conducted by the United States Government; and

(vi) facilitate the resolution of differences concerning major space and space related policy matters.

(c) The Council shall meet at least annually.

(d) The revival and operation of the Council shall not interfere with the existing lines of authority in or responsibilities of any agencies.

(e) The Council shall have a staff, headed by a civilian Executive Secretary appointed by the President . . .

Sec. 5. National Space Policy and Strategy Planning Process. (a) Each agency represented on the Council shall provide such information to the Chair regarding its current and planned space activities as the Chair shall request.

(b) The head of each agency that conducts space-related activities shall, to the extent permitted by law, conform such activities to the President's national space policy and strategy.

(c) On space policy and strategy matters relating primarily to national security, the Council shall coordinate with the National Security Council (NSC) to create policies and procedures for the Council that respect the responsibilities and authorities of the NSC under existing law.

Sec. 6. Users' Advisory Group. (a) The Council shall convene a Users' Advisory Group (Group) pursuant to Public Law 101–611, section 121, composed of non-Federal representatives of industries and other persons involved in aeronautical and space activities . . .

Sec. 8. Report. Within 1 year of the date of this order, and annually thereafter, the Council shall submit a report to the President setting forth its assessment of, and recommendations for, the space policy and strategy of the United States Government . . .

DONALD J. TRUMP
The White House,
June 30, 2017.

SOURCE: Executive Office of the President. "Executive Order 13803—Reviving the National Space Council." June 30, 2017. *Compilation of Presidential Documents* 2017, no. 00449 (June 30, 2017). https://www.gpo.gov/fdsys/pkg/DCPD-201700449/pdf/DCPD-201700449.pdf.

OTHER HISTORIC DOCUMENTS OF INTEREST

FROM PREVIOUS *HISTORIC DOCUMENTS*

President Trump Addresses
a Joint Session of Congress;
Democratic Response

FEBRUARY 28, 2017

In his first address before a joint session of Congress, President Donald Trump outlined his priorities for the next year of his presidency without offering much detail on how any of them would be accomplished. "Dying industries will come roaring back to life, heroic veterans will get the care they so desperately need. Our military will be given the resources its brave warriors so richly deserve. Crumbling infrastructure will be replaced with new roads, bridges, tunnels, airports, and railways, gleaming across our very, very beautiful land. Our terrible drug epidemic will slow down and ultimately stop, and our neglected inner cities will see a rebirth of hope," the president said. "Above all else," he added, "we will keep our promises to the American people." Trump's February speech diverged from his inaugural address in tone, offering a more optimistic view of the future of the country and noting that at the nation's 250th anniversary, "we will look back on tonight as when this new chapter of American Greatness began." The hour-long speech was focused primarily on domestic priorities and was littered with encouragement to members of both parties to come together to achieve his agenda.

DOMESTIC PRIORITIES

Trump's speech included multiple references to priorities he had addressed on the campaign trail, including bringing manufacturing jobs back to America to shore up the middle class, rebuilding the nation's infrastructure, repealing the Affordable Care Act (ACA), and reforming the country's immigration system. He framed these issues by first explaining the way in which he viewed the nation he inherited. Trump explained that he had taken over at a time when there were 43 million Americans who rely on the Supplemental Nutrition Assistance Program (SNAP), commonly referred to as food stamps, as well as the 94 million outside the labor market. Notably, at the time of his speech, the nation's unemployment rate was 4.7 percent, below the historical norm and more than half of what it was following the 2007 to 2009 recession. Politicians tend to disagree over which figure more accurately depicts the strength of the U.S. labor market—the unemployment rate or the number of those outside the labor market. The latter is impacted by those who simply do not want to enter the job force at present, like students, stay at home parents, or retirees, and the metric has continued to climb as more Baby Boomers retire.

In presenting his vision for rebuilding the middle class, the president focused specifically on bringing manufacturing back to America, and pointed to his success thus far in convincing companies like General Motors, Walmart, and Lockheed Martin to invest more in America and create new jobs. Although many of these companies had announced their intent to do so ahead of Trump's election, Ford, in particular, canceled a plan to build a new factory in Mexico and said it would instead invest more in a facility in Michigan, reportedly at the president's urging. The president claimed that the manufacturing industry had largely been impacted by trade deals like the North American Free Trade Agreement (NAFTA) and international bodies like the World Trade Organization (WTO), which he credited with the loss of tens of thousands of jobs. "For too long," the president said, "we have watched our middle-class shrink as we have exported our jobs and wealth to foreign countries." Trump noted many times on the campaign trail that he planned to renegotiate or leave trade deals he saw as a detriment to American workers.

The president spoke many times during his campaign about the necessity of reforming the U.S. immigration system in a way that would limit the number of individuals legally entering the country each year and would also significantly crack down on those entering the nation—or who had already entered—illegally. "By finally enforcing our immigration laws, we will raise wages, help the unemployed, and save billions and billions of dollars, and make our communities safer for everyone." Despite Trump's repeated arguments that immigration hurts American workers, economists generally agree that immigration is an overall benefit to the nation's economy, although there are some pockets of the nation that suffer more than others, including individuals without high school diplomas. To enforce current immigration law, the president promised to seek out and deport those already in the country illegally, who the president said were responsible for rising crime rates. To emphasize this point, Trump invited the families of victims of crimes allegedly perpetrated by illegal immigrants as his guests at the joint session address. He further stated that he would direct his administration to review current law to ensure those entering the United States did so without ill intent against the country. "We cannot allow our nation to become a sanctuary for extremists. That is why my administration has been working on improved vetting procedures, and we will shortly take new steps to keep our nation safe and to keep those out who will do us harm." That effort began on January 27, ahead of the address to Congress, when Trump signed an executive order banning citizens from seven Muslim-majority countries—Iran, Iraq, Libya, Somalia, Sudan, Syria, and Yemen—from entering the United States for ninety days. The measure also placed an indefinite ban on Syrian refugees entering the country. (The United States had promised under President Barack Obama's administration to accept 85,000 Syrian refugees in 2016 and 100,000 in 2017.) The ban was temporarily halted by federal judges and a revised executive order was issued in early February that reduced the number of nations subject to the ban to six by removing Iraq and allowed green card holders from those countries to enter the United States as they had before. This second ban was blocked, and the Trump administration appealed the decision to the U.S. Supreme Court, which agreed to allow the ban to be enacted in part, awaiting its review that was scheduled for October. However, on September 24, the president issued a proclamation that again revised the travel ban. This ban was also blocked by federal courts, and the Supreme Court scrapped its plan to hear arguments because this proclamation rendered the challenges to the second ban moot.

Turning to a long-running promise of the Republican Party, Trump called on Congress "to repeal and replace Obamacare—with reforms that expand choice, increase access, lower costs, and at the same time, provide better healthcare." Calling the ACA a "disaster," the president asked Congress to develop more affordable care that is available to everyone. He spoke about increasing premiums—including the 116 percent increase in Arizona—as well as the lack of insurance options in many states. He asked that the plan produced by Congress give those with preexisting conditions access to coverage, help Americans purchase coverage through health savings accounts and tax credits, provide governors more flexibility in expanding Medicaid, allow for the purchase of insurance across state lines, and bring down the cost of prescription drugs. At the time of the president's speech, Republicans in Congress had already begun work on repealing Obamacare, but had been unable to develop a replacement that was palatable enough for both the moderate and far-right members of the caucus to secure the votes needed for passage. Despite multiple attempts, by the end of 2017, the House and Senate were unable to reach a compromise and pass health care reform. On October 13, the Trump administration halted all cost-sharing subsidy payments that insurance companies receive through the ACA for offering federally mandated discounted deductibles and copayments to low-income individuals. The president called on Congress to develop a plan to address Obamacare subsidies, and, on October 17, a bipartisan group of senators announced that they had reached an agreement in principle to allow the subsidies to remain in place for two years. By the end of 2017, Congress had not yet passed a fix for subsidies; however, the tax plan passed by Congress in December did repeal Obamacare's individual mandate, perhaps doing more to upend the landmark health care legislation to date than any other legislative, executive, or judicial attempt.

FOREIGN AFFAIRS

The president spoke only briefly about foreign policy, and when he did, addressed it through an "America First" lens. At the start of his speech, Trump promised, "Our allies will find that America is once again ready to lead" and later said that the nation's foreign policy, under his presidency, "calls for a direct, robust and meaningful engagement with the world. It is American leadership based on vital security interests that we share with our allies across the globe." However, he noted, the alliances forged would require that every nation put forth effort—monetarily or otherwise—to support international organizations and coalitions around the globe. The president spoke on the campaign trail about the need for North Atlantic Treaty Organization (NATO) members to pay their full share to support the organization, or risk a U.S. exit. The president noted during his address that NATO members were beginning to pay due to "very strong and frank discussions."

The president spoke about sanctions he had issued via executive order against those who support Iran's nuclear program. Trump had promised multiple times during his campaign and following his election to withdraw the United States from the 2015 Iranian nuclear deal, but it was not until October 2017 when he took his first official action on the issue by refusing to make a required certification to Congress affirming that Iran was adhering to the terms of the nuclear agreement and punting the issue to Congress to weigh in.

The president did address the Islamic State of Iraq and the Levant (ISIL), alternately known as the Islamic State of Iraq and Syria (ISIS), during his speech, specifically as it related to immigration into the United States. He did, however, promise to work with U.S. allies to root out "radical Islamic terrorism"—a term his predecessors had shied away from using—abroad. "I directed the Department of Defense to develop a plan to demolish and destroy ISIS, a network of lawless savages that have slaughtered Muslims and Christians, and men and women and children of all faiths and beliefs. We will work with our allies, including our friends in the Muslim world, to extinguish this vile enemy from our planet," the president said.

BESHEAR DELIVERS DEMOCRATIC RESPONSE

Democrats chose former Kentucky governor Steve Beshear to deliver the response to the president's address. Not only was Beshear a Democratic governor in a red state, he was also chosen for his state's success in developing an insurance marketplace following the implementation of the ACA that allowed Kentucky to reduce its uninsured population more than any other state.

Beshear was regarded as a personification of the segment of America that Democrats did poorly with in the 2016 election: older, white, middle class voters. Kentucky itself voted overwhelmingly for Trump 62.5 percent to Hillary Clinton's 32.7 percent. Seeking to work toward reshaping the image of the party as the one that best represents the working class, Beshear began his rebuttal noting, "We Democrats are committed to creating the opportunity for every American to succeed by growing our economy with good paying jobs, educating and training our people to fill those jobs, giving our businesses the freedom to innovate, keeping our country safe and providing health care that families can afford and rely on." But, the former governor added, "as a candidate, [Trump] promised to be a champion for people struggling to make ends meet . . . but one of your first executive orders makes it harder for those families to even afford a mortgage." Beshear referred to Trump's first order, which stopped a reduction in federally backed mortgage insurance that would have lowered the cost for many Americans.

Beshear spent a majority of his speech focused on the president's promise to repeal Obamacare. "Does the Affordable Care Act need some repairs? Sure it does. But so far, every Republican idea to replace the Affordable Care Act would reduce the number of Americans covered, despite promises to the contrary," Beshear said. He went on to explain that the Republican plans would allow access to care, but that it would be unaffordable for many Americans because it would remove cost-sharing subsidies that offset copayments. "Behind these ideas is the belief that folks at the lower end of the economic ladder just don't deserve health care," Beshear said, before adding that Democrats would make every effort to uphold that the commitment made to Americans in 2010 through the ACA.

Beshear issued a call to all Americans, on both sides of the political spectrum, to come together to make progress and help American families, and in closing asked the president to understand that while some might disagree with him, that does not give him the privilege to attack and vilify. "Real leaders don't spread derision and division. Real leaders strengthen, unify, partner, and offer real solutions instead of ultimatums and blame. I may be old fashioned, but I still believe that dignity, compassion, honesty and accountability are basic American values," Beshear said.

—Heather Kerrigan

Following is the text of the address delivered by President Donald Trump before a joint session of Congress on February 28, 2017; and the Democratic response delivered by former Kentucky governor Steve Beshear, also on February 28, 2017.

President Trump Addresses a Joint Session of Congress

DOCUMENT

February 28, 2017

Thank you very much. Mr. Speaker, Mr. Vice President, Members of Congress, the First Lady of the United States, and citizens of America: Tonight, as we mark the conclusion of our celebration of Black History Month, we are reminded of our Nation's path towards civil rights and the work that still remains to be done. Recent threats targeting Jewish community centers and vandalism of Jewish cemeteries, as well as last week's shooting in Kansas City, remind us that while we may be a nation divided on policies, we are a country that stands united in condemning hate and evil in all of its very ugly forms.

Each American generation passes the torch of truth, liberty, and justice in an unbroken chain, all the way down to the present. That torch is now in our hands, and we will use it to light up the world. I am here tonight to deliver a message of unity and strength, and it is a message deeply delivered from my heart. A new chapter of American greatness is now beginning. A new national pride is sweeping across our Nation. And a new surge of optimism is placing impossible dreams firmly within our grasp.

What we are witnessing today is the renewal of the American spirit. Our allies will find that America is once again ready to lead. All the nations of the world—friend or foe—will find that America is strong, America is proud, and America is free.

In 9 years, the United States will celebrate the 250th anniversary of our founding: 250 years since the day we declared our independence. It will be one of the great milestones in the history of the world. But what will America look like as we reach our 250th year? What kind of country will we leave for our children?

I will not allow the mistakes of recent decades past to define the course of our future. For too long, we've watched our middle class shrink as we've exported our jobs and wealth to foreign countries. We've financed and built one global project after another, but ignored the fates of our children in the inner cities of Chicago, Baltimore, Detroit, and so many other places throughout our land.

We've defended the borders of other nations, while leaving our own borders wide open for anyone to cross and for drugs to pour in at a now unprecedented rate. And we've spent trillions and trillions of dollars overseas, while our infrastructure at home has so badly crumbled.

Then, in 2016, the Earth shifted beneath our feet. The rebellion started as a quiet protest, spoken by families of all colors and creeds, families who just wanted a fair shot for their children and a fair hearing for their concerns.

But then the quiet voices became a loud chorus, as thousands of citizens now spoke out together, from cities small and large, all across our country. Finally, the chorus became an earthquake, and the people turned out by the tens of millions, and they were all united by one very simple, but crucial demand: that America must put its own citizens first. Because only then can we truly make America great again.

Dying industries will come roaring back to life. Heroic veterans will get the care they so desperately need. Our military will be given the resources its brave warriors so richly deserve. Crumbling infrastructure will be replaced with new roads, bridges, tunnels, airports, and railways gleaming across our very, very beautiful land. Our terrible drug epidemic will slow down and, ultimately, stop. And our neglected inner cities will see a rebirth of hope, safety, and opportunity. Above all else, we will keep our promises to the American people. [Applause] Thank you.

It's been a little over a month since my Inauguration, and I want to take this moment to update the Nation on the progress I've made in keeping those promises.

Since my election, Ford, Fiat Chrysler, General Motors, Sprint, Softbank, Lockheed, Intel, Walmart, and many others have announced that they will invest billions and billions of dollars in the United States and will create tens of thousands of new American jobs.

The stock market has gained almost $3 trillion in value since the election on November 8—a record. We've saved taxpayers hundreds of millions of dollars by bringing down the price of fantastic—and it is a fantastic—new F–35 jet fighter, and we'll be saving billions more on contracts all across our Government. We have placed a hiring freeze on non-military and nonessential Federal workers.

We have begun to drain the swamp of government corruption by imposing a 5-year ban on lobbying by executive branch officials and a lifetime ban—*[applause]*—thank you. Thank you. And a lifetime ban on becoming lobbyists for a foreign government.

We have undertaken a historic effort to massively reduce job-crushing regulations, creating a deregulation Task Force inside of every Government agency. And we're imposing a new rule which mandates that for every one new regulation, two old regulations must be eliminated. We're going to stop the regulations that threaten the future and livelihood of our great coal miners.

We have cleared the way for the construction of the Keystone and Dakota Access pipelines, thereby creating tens of thousands of jobs. And I've issued a new directive that new American pipelines be made with American steel.

We have withdrawn the United States from the job-killing Trans-Pacific Partnership. And with the help of Prime Minister Justin Trudeau, we have formed a council with our neighbors in Canada to help ensure that women entrepreneurs have access to the networks, markets, and capital they need to start a business and live out their financial dreams.

To protect our citizens, I have directed the Department of Justice to form a Task Force on Reducing Violent Crime. I have further ordered the Departments of Homeland Security and Justice, along with the Department of State and the Director of National Intelligence, to coordinate an aggressive strategy to dismantle the criminal cartels that have spread all across our Nation. We will stop the drugs from pouring into our country and poisoning our youth, and we will expand treatment for those who have become so badly addicted.

At the same time, my administration has answered the pleas of the American people for immigration enforcement and border security. By finally enforcing our immigration laws, we will raise wages, help the unemployed, save billions and billions of dollars, and make our communities safer for everyone. We want all Americans to succeed, but that can't happen in an environment of lawless chaos. We must restore integrity and the rule of law at our borders.

For that reason, we will soon begin the construction of a great, great wall along our southern border. As we speak tonight, we are removing gang members, drug dealers, and criminals that threaten our communities and prey on our very innocent citizens. Bad ones are going out as I speak, and as I've promised throughout the campaign.

To any in Congress who do not believe we should enforce our laws, I would ask you this one question: What would you say to the American family that loses their jobs, their income, or their loved one because America refused to uphold its laws and defend its borders?

Our obligation is to serve, protect, and defend the citizens of the United States. We are also taking strong measures to protect our Nation from radical Islamic terrorism. According to data provided by the Department of Justice, the vast majority of individuals convicted of terrorism and terrorism-related offenses since 9/11 came here from outside of our country. We have seen the attacks at home, from Boston to San Bernardino to the Pentagon, and, yes, even the World Trade Center.

We have seen the attacks in France, in Belgium, in Germany, and all over the world. It is not compassionate, but reckless to allow uncontrolled entry from places where proper vetting cannot occur. Those given the high honor of admission to the United States should support this country and love its people and its values. We cannot allow a beachhead of terrorism to form inside America. We cannot allow our Nation to become a sanctuary for extremists.

That is why my administration has been working on improved vetting procedures, and we will shortly take new steps to keep our Nation safe and to keep those out who will do us harm.

As promised, I directed the Department of Defense to develop a plan to demolish and destroy ISIS, a network of lawless savages that have slaughtered Muslims and Christians, and men and women and children of all faiths and all beliefs. We will work with our allies, including our friends and allies in the Muslim world, to extinguish this vile enemy from our planet.

I have also imposed new sanctions on entities and individuals who support Iran's ballistic missile program and reaffirmed our unbreakable alliance with the State of Israel.

Finally, I have kept my promise to appoint a Justice to the United States Supreme Court, from my list of 20 judges, who will defend our Constitution.

I am greatly honored to have Maureen Scalia with us in the gallery tonight. Thank you, Maureen. Her late, great husband, Antonin Scalia, will forever be a symbol of American justice. To fill his seat, we have chosen Judge Neil Gorsuch, a man of incredible skill and deep devotion to the law. He was confirmed unanimously by the Court of Appeals, and I am asking the Senate to swiftly approve his nomination.

Tonight, as I outline the next steps we must take as a country, we must honestly acknowledge the circumstances we inherited. Ninety-four million Americans are out of the labor force. Over 43 million people are now living in poverty, and over 43 million Americans are on food stamps. More than 1 in 5 people in their prime working years are not working. We have the worst financial recovery in 65 years. In the last 8 years, the past administration has put on more new debt than nearly all of the other Presidents combined.

We've lost more than one-fourth of our manufacturing jobs since NAFTA was approved, and we've lost 60,000 factories since China joined the World Trade Organization in 2001. Our trade deficit in goods with the world last year was nearly $800 billion dollars. And overseas we have inherited a series of tragic foreign policy disasters. Solving these and so many other pressing problems will require us to work past the differences of party. It will require us to tap into the American spirit that has overcome every challenge throughout our long and storied history. But to accomplish our goals at home and abroad, we must restart the engine of the American economy, making it easier for companies to do business in the United States, and much, much harder for companies to leave our country.

Right now American companies are taxed at one of the highest rates anywhere in the world. My economic team is developing historic tax reform that will reduce the tax rate on our companies so they can compete and thrive anywhere and with anyone. It will be a big, big cut.

At the same time, we will provide massive tax relief for the middle class. We must create a level playing field for American companies and our workers—have to do it. Currently, when we ship products out of America, many other countries make us pay very high tariffs and taxes. But when foreign companies ship their products into America, we charge them nothing, or almost nothing.

I just met with officials and workers from a great American company, Harley-Davidson. In fact, they proudly displayed five of their magnificent motorcycles, made in the U.S.A., on the front lawn of the White House. *[Laughter]* And they wanted me to ride one, and I said, "No, thank you." *[Laughter]*

At our meeting, I asked them, how are you doing, how is business? They said that it's good. I asked them further, how are you doing with other countries, mainly international sales? They told me—without even complaining, because they have been so mistreated for so long that they've become used to it—that it's very hard to do business with other countries because they tax our goods at such a high rate. They said that in the case of another country, they taxed their motorcycles at 100 percent. They weren't even asking for a change. But I am.

I believe strongly in free trade, but it also has to be fair trade. It's been a long time since we had fair trade. The first Republican President, Abraham Lincoln, warned that the "abandonment of the protective policy by the American Government will produce want and ruin among our people." Lincoln was right, and it's time we heeded his advice and his words. I am not going to let America and its great companies and workers be taken advantage of us any longer. They have taken advantage of our country. No longer.

I am going to bring back millions of jobs. Protecting our workers also means reforming our system of legal immigration. The current, outdated system depresses wages for our poorest workers and puts great pressure on taxpayers. Nations around the world like Canada, Australia, and many others, have a merit-based immigration system. It's a basic principle that those seeking to enter a country ought to be able to support themselves financially. Yet, in America, we do not enforce this rule, straining the very public resources that our poorest citizens rely upon. According to the National Academy of Sciences, our current immigration system costs American taxpayers many billions of dollars a year.

Switching away from this current system of lower skilled immigration, and instead adopting a merit-based system, we will have so many more benefits. It will save countless dollars, raise workers' wages, and help struggling families—including immigrant families—enter the middle class. And they will do it quickly, and they will be very, very happy, indeed.

I believe that real and positive immigration reform is possible, as long as we focus on the following goals: to improve jobs and wages for Americans, to strengthen our Nation's security, and to restore respect for our laws. If we are guided by the wellbeing of American citizens, then I believe Republicans and Democrats can work together to achieve an outcome that has eluded our country for decades.

Another Republican President, Dwight D. Eisenhower, initiated the last truly great national infrastructure program—the building of the Interstate Highway System. The time has come for a new program of national rebuilding. America has spent approximately $6 trillion in the Middle East; all the while, our infrastructure at home is crumbling. With this $6 trillion, we could have rebuilt our country twice, and maybe even three times if we had people who had the ability to negotiate. *[Laughter]*

To launch our national rebuilding, I will be asking Congress to approve legislation that produces a $1 trillion investment in infrastructure of the United States—financed through both public and private capital—creating millions of new jobs. This effort will be guided by two core principles: buy American and hire American.

Tonight I am also calling on this Congress to repeal and replace Obamacare with reforms that expand choice, increase access, lower costs, and at the same time, provide better health care.

Mandating every American to buy Government-approved health insurance was never the right solution for our country. The way to make health insurance available to everyone is to lower the cost of health insurance, and that is what we are going do.

Obamacare premiums nationwide have increased by double and triple digits. As an example, Arizona went up 116 percent last year alone. Governor Matt Bevin of Kentucky just said Obamacare is failing in his State—the State of Kentucky—and it's unsustainable and collapsing.

One-third of the counties have only one insurer, and they are losing them fast. They are losing them so fast. They are leaving, and many Americans have no choice at all. There's no choice left. Remember when you were told that you could keep your doctor and keep your plan? We now know that all of those promises have been totally broken. Obamacare is collapsing, and we must act decisively to protect all Americans.

Action is not a choice, it is a necessity. So I am calling on all Democrats and Republicans in Congress to work with us to save Americans from this imploding Obamacare disaster.

Here are the principles that should guide the Congress as we move to create a better health care system for all Americans:

First, we should ensure that Americans with preexisting conditions have access to coverage, and that we have a stable transition for Americans currently enrolled in the health care exchanges.

Secondly, we should help Americans purchase their own coverage through the use of tax credits and expanded health savings accounts, but it must be the plan they want, not the plan forced on them by our Government.

Thirdly, we should give our State Governors the resources and flexibility they need with Medicaid to make sure no one is left out.

Fourth, we should implement legal reforms that protect patients and doctors from unnecessary costs that drive up the price of insurance and work to bring down the artificially high price of drugs and bring them down immediately. And finally, the time has come to give Americans the freedom to purchase health insurance across State lines, which will create a truly competitive national marketplace that will bring costs way down and provide far better care. So important.

Everything that is broken in our country can be fixed. Every problem can be solved. And every hurting family can find healing and hope.

Our citizens deserve this and so much more, so why not join forces and finally get the job done, and get it done right? On this and so many other things, Democrats and Republicans should get together and unite for the good of our country and for the good of the American people.

My administration wants to work with members of both parties to make childcare accessible and affordable; to help ensure new parents that they have paid family leave; to invest in women's health; and to promote clean air and clean water; and to rebuild our military and our infrastructure.

True love for our people requires us to find common ground, to advance the common good, and to cooperate on behalf of every American child who deserves a much brighter future.

An incredible young woman is with us this evening, who should serve as an inspiration to us all. Today is Rare Disease Day, and joining us in the gallery is a rare disease survivor, Megan Crowley.

Megan was diagnosed with Pompe disease, a rare and serious illness, when she was 15 months old. She was not expected to live past 5. On receiving this news, Megan's dad

John fought with everything he had to save the life of his precious child. He founded a company to look for a cure and helped develop the drug that saved Megan's life. Today she is 20 years old and a sophomore at Notre Dame.

Megan's story is about the unbounded power of a father's love for a daughter. But our slow and burdensome approval process at the Food and Drug Administration keeps too many advances, like the one that saved Megan's life, from reaching those in need. If we slash the restraints, not just at the FDA, but across our Government, then we will be blessed with far more miracles just like Megan. In fact, our children will grow up in a nation of miracles.

But to achieve this future, we must enrich the mind and the souls of every American child. Education is the civil rights issue of our time. I am calling upon members of both parties to pass an education bill that funds school choice for disadvantaged youth, including millions of African American and Latino children. These families should be free to choose the public, private, charter, magnet, religious, or home school that is right for them.

Joining us tonight in the gallery is a remarkable woman, Denisha Merriweather. As a young girl, Denisha struggled in school and failed third grade twice. But then, she was able to enroll in a private center for learning—great learning center—with the help of a tax credit and a scholarship program.

Today, she is the first in her family to graduate, not just from high school, but from college. Later this year she will get her master's degree in social work. We want all children to be able to break the cycle of poverty just like Denisha.

But to break the cycle of poverty, we must also break the cycle of violence. The murder rate in 2015 experienced its largest single-year increase in nearly half a century. In Chicago, more than 4,000 people were shot last year alone, and the murder rate so far this year has been even higher. This is not acceptable in our society.

Every American child should be able to grow up in a safe community, to attend a great school, and to have access to a high-paying job. But to create this future, we must work with, not against—not against—the men and women of law enforcement. We must build bridges of cooperation and trust, not drive the wedge of disunity, and really, it's what it is—division. It's pure, unadulterated division. We have to unify.

Police and sheriffs are members of our community. They're friends and neighbors, they're mothers and fathers, sons and daughters, and they leave behind loved ones every day who worry about whether or not they'll come home safe and sound. We must support the incredible men and women of law enforcement.

And we must support the victims of crime. I have ordered the Department of Homeland Security to create an office to serve American victims. The office is called VOICE: Victims of Immigration Crime Engagement. We are providing a voice to those who have been ignored by our media and silenced by special interests. Joining us in the audience tonight are four very brave Americans whose Government failed them. Their names are Jamiel Shaw, Susan Oliver, Jenna Oliver, and Jessica Davis.

Jamiel's 17-year-old son was viciously murdered by an illegal immigrant gang member who had just been released from prison. Jamiel Shaw, Jr. was an incredible young man, with unlimited potential, who was getting ready to go to college where he would have excelled as a great college quarterback. But he never got the chance. His father, who is in the audience tonight, has become a very good friend of mine. Jamiel, thank you. Thank you.

Also with us are Susan Oliver and Jessica Davis. Their husbands, Deputy Sheriff Danny Oliver and Detective Michael Davis, were slain in the line of duty in California. They were pillars of their community. These brave men were viciously gunned down by an illegal immigrant with a criminal record and two prior deportations. Should have never been in our country.

Sitting with Susan is her daughter, Jenna. Jenna, I want you to know that your father was a hero, and that tonight you have the love of an entire country supporting you and praying for you.

To Jamiel, Jenna, Susan, and Jessica: I want you to know that we will never stop fighting for justice. Your loved ones will never, ever be forgotten. We will always honor their memory.

Finally, to keep America safe, we must provide the men and women of the United States military with the tools they need to prevent war. If they must, they have to fight and they only have to win.

I am sending Congress a budget that rebuilds the military, eliminates the defense sequester, and calls for one of the largest increases in national defense spending in American history. My budget will also increase funding for our veterans. Our veterans have delivered for this Nation, and now we must deliver for them.

The challenges we face as a nation are great, but our people are even greater. And none are greater or are braver than those who fight for America in uniform.

We are blessed to be joined tonight by Carryn Owens, the widow of U.S. Navy Special Operator, Senior Chief William "Ryan" Owens. Ryan died as he lived: a warrior and a hero, battling against terrorism and securing our Nation. I just spoke to our great General Mattis, just now, who reconfirmed that—and I quote—"Ryan was a part of a highly successful raid that generated large amounts of vital intelligence that will lead to many more victories in the future against our enemy." Ryan's legacy is etched into eternity. Thank you. *[Applause]* And Ryan is looking down, right now—you know that—and he is very happy because I think he just broke a record. *[Laughter]*

For as the Bible teaches us, there is no greater act of love than to lay down one's life for one's friends. Ryan laid down his life for his friends, for his country, and for our freedom. And we will never forget Ryan.

To those allies who wonder what kind of a friend America will be, look no further than the heroes who wear our uniform. Our foreign policy calls for a direct, robust, and meaningful engagement with the world. It is American leadership based on vital security interests that we share with our allies all across the globe.

We strongly support NATO, an alliance forged through the bonds of two world wars that dethroned fascism, and a cold war, and defeated communism.

But our partners must meet their financial obligations. And now, based on our very strong and frank discussions, they are beginning to do just that. In fact, I can tell you, the money is pouring in. Very nice. We expect our partners—whether in NATO, the Middle East, or in the Pacific—to take a direct and meaningful role in both strategic and military operations, and pay their fair share of the cost. Have to do that.

We will respect historic institutions, but we will respect the foreign rights of all nations, and they have to respect our rights as a nation also. Free nations are the best vehicle for expressing the will of the people, and America respects the right of all nations to chart their own path. My job is not to represent the world. My job is to represent the United States of America.

But we know that America is better off when there is less conflict, not more. We must learn from the mistakes of the past. We have seen the war and the destruction that have ravaged and raged throughout the world—all across the world. The only long-term solution for these humanitarian disasters, in many cases, is to create the conditions where displaced persons can safely return home and begin the long, long process of rebuilding.

America is willing to find new friends and to forge new partnerships where shared interests align. We want harmony and stability, not war and conflict. We want peace, wherever peace can be found.

America is friends today with former enemies. Some of our closest allies, decades ago, fought on the opposite side of these terrible, terrible wars. This history should give us all faith in the possibilities for a better world. Hopefully, the 250th year for America will see a world that is more peaceful, more just, and more free.

On our 100th anniversary, in 1876, citizens from across our Nation came to Philadelphia to celebrate America's centennial. At that celebration, the country's builders and artists and inventors showed off their wonderful creations. Alexander Graham Bell displayed his telephone for the first time. Remington unveiled the first typewriter. An early attempt was made at electric light. Thomas Edison showed an automatic telegraph and an electric pen. Imagine the wonders our country could know in America's 250th year. Think of the marvels we can achieve if we simply set free the dreams of our people. Cures to the illnesses that have always plagued us are not too much to hope. American footprints on distant worlds are not too big a dream. Millions lifted from welfare to work is not too much to expect. And streets where mothers are safe from fear, schools where children learn in peace, and jobs where Americans prosper and grow are not too much to ask.

When we have all of this, we will have made America greater than ever before—for all Americans. This is our vision. This is our mission. But we can only get there together. We are one people with one destiny. We all bleed the same blood. We all salute the same great American flag. And we all are made by the same God.

When we fulfill this vision, when we celebrate our 250 years of glorious freedom, we will look back on tonight as when this new chapter of American greatness began. The time for small thinking is over. The time for trivial fights is behind us. We just need the courage to share the dreams that fill our hearts, the bravery to express the hopes that stir our souls, and the confidence to turn those hopes and those dreams into action.

From now on, America will be empowered by our aspirations, not burdened by our fears; inspired by the future, not bound by failures of the past; and guided by our vision, not blinded by our doubts.

I am asking all citizens to embrace this renewal of the American spirit. I am asking all Members of Congress to join me in dreaming big and bold, and daring things for our country. I am asking everyone watching tonight to seize this moment. Believe in yourselves, believe in your future, and believe, once more, in America.

Thank you, God bless you, and God bless the United States.

SOURCE: Executive Office of the President. "Address before a Joint Session of the Congress." February 28, 2017. *Compilation of Presidential Documents* 2017, no. 00150 (February 28, 2017). https://www.gpo.gov/fdsys/pkg/DCPD-201700150/pdf/DCPD-201700150.pdf.

Former Governor Beshear Delivers Democratic Response

February 28, 2017

I'm Steve Beshear. I was governor of Kentucky from 2007 to 2015. Now, I'm a private citizen.

I'm here in Lexington, Kentucky—some 400 miles from Washington—at a diner with some neighbors—Democrats and Republicans—where we just watched the president's address.

I'm a proud Democrat, but first and foremost, I'm a proud American.

And like many of you, I'm worried about the future of our nation.

I grew up in Kentucky in a small town called Dawson Springs. My Dad and Granddad were Baptist preachers. My family owned a funeral home.

And my wife, Jane, and I have been married for almost 50 years.

I became governor at the start of the global recession, and after eight years we left things a lot better than we found them.

By being fiscally responsible—I even cut my own pay—we balanced our budget and turned deficits into surpluses without raising taxes.

We cut our unemployment rate in half.

We made huge gains in high school graduation rates.

And we found health coverage for over half a million Kentuckians.

We did that through trust and mutual respect.

I listened.

And I built partnerships with business leaders and with Republicans in our legislature.

We put people first and politics second.

The America I love allowed a small-town preacher's kid to get elected governor, and it taught me to embrace people who are different from me, not vilify them.

The America I love has always been about looking forward, not backward.

... about working together to find solutions, regardless of party, instead of allowing our differences to divide us and hold us back.

And we Democrats are committed to creating the opportunity for every American to succeed by growing our economy with good-paying jobs, educating and training our young people to fill those jobs, giving our businesses the freedom to innovate, keeping our country safe and providing health care that families can afford and rely on.

***

Mr. President, as a candidate, you promised to be a champion for people struggling to make ends meet . . . and I hope you live up to that promise.

But one of your first executive orders makes it harder for those families to afford a mortgage.

Then you started rolling back rules that provide oversight of the financial industry and safeguard us against another national economic meltdown.

And you picked a Cabinet of billionaires and Wall Street insiders who want to eviscerate the protections that most Americans count on and that help level the playing field.

That's not being our champion.

That's being Wall Street's champion.

***

And even more troubling is that you and your Republican allies in Congress seem determined to rip affordable health insurance away from millions of Americans who most need it.

Does the Affordable Care Act need some repairs?

Sure it does.

But so far, every Republican idea to "replace" the Affordable Care Act would reduce the number of Americans covered, despite promises to the contrary.

Mr. President, folks here in Kentucky expect you to keep your word. Because this isn't a game—it's life and death for people.

These ideas promise "access" to care but deny the importance of making care affordable and effective. They would charge families more for fewer benefits and put insurance companies back in control.

Behind these ideas is the belief that folks at the lower end of the economic ladder just don't deserve health care—that it's somehow their fault that their employer doesn't offer insurance or that they can't afford to buy expensive health plans.

But who are these 22 million Americans, including 500,000 people here in Kentucky, who now have health care that didn't have it before?

They aren't aliens from a distant planet.

They're our friends and neighbors.

We sit in the bleachers with them on Friday night and pray in the pews with them on Sunday morning.

They're farmers, restaurant workers, part-time teachers, nurses' aides, construction workers and entrepreneurs working at high-tech start-ups.

And before the Affordable Care Act, they woke up every morning and went to work, praying they wouldn't get sick; knowing they were just one bad diagnosis away from bankruptcy.

In 2010, this country made a commitment: that every American deserved health care they could afford and rely on.

And we Democrats are going to do everything in our power to keep President Trump and the Republican Congress from reneging on that commitment.

But we're going to need your help . . . by speaking out.

***

Another commitment now being tested is to our national security.

Make no mistake, I'm a military veteran myself and I know that protecting America is a president's highest duty.

Yet, President Trump is ignoring serious threats to our national security from Russia, who's not our friend—while alienating our allies, who've fought with us side by side and are our friends in a dangerous world.

His approach makes us less safe and should worry every freedom-loving American.

Instead, President Trump has all but declared war on refugees and immigrants.

The president can and should enforce our immigration laws.

But we can protect America without abandoning our principles and our moral obligation to help those fleeing war and terror.

. . . without tearing families apart.

. . . and without needlessly jeopardizing our military men and women fighting overseas.

Another Republican president, Ronald Reagan, once said, "In America, our origins matter less than our destination, and that is what democracy is all about."

***

President Trump also needs to understand that people may disagree with him—but that doesn't make them his enemies.

When the president attacks the loyalty and credibility of our intelligence agencies, the court system, the military, the free press and individual Americans—simply because he doesn't like what they say—he is eroding our democracy.

And that's reckless.

***

Real leaders don't spread derision and division.

Real leaders strengthen, unify, partner—and offer real solutions instead of ultimatums and blame.

I may be old-fashioned but I still believe that dignity, compassion, honesty and accountability are basic American values.

As a Democrat, I believe that if you work hard, you deserve the opportunity to realize the American Dream—regardless of whether you're a coal miner here in Kentucky, a teacher in Rhode Island, an autoworker in Detroit or a software engineer in San Antonio.

Our political system is broken because too many of our leaders think it's all about them.

They need to remember that they work for us and helping us is their work.

Kentucky made real progress while I was governor because we were motivated by one thing: Helping families.

Democrats are trying to bring that same focus back to Washington.

Americans are a diverse people. We may disagree on some things . . . but we've always come together when we remember that we are one nation, under God, indivisible, with liberty and justice for all.

Thank you.

SOURCE: Office of Congresswoman Nancy Pelosi. "Former Kentucky Governor Steve Beshear's Democratic Response to President Trump's Address to a Joint Session of Congress." February 28, 2017.

OTHER HISTORIC DOCUMENTS OF INTEREST

FROM THIS VOLUME

- President Trump Issues Immigration Orders, p. 42
- House and Senate Vote on Affordable Care Act Repeal, p. 187
- U.S. Government Seeks to Impose New Immigration Limits, p. 417

FROM PREVIOUS HISTORIC DOCUMENTS

- Donald Trump Elected U.S. President, *2016*, p. 612

March

International Community Responds to Political Upheaval in Venezuela

MARCH 20, JULY 31, AND AUGUST 8 AND 24, 2017

With political tensions rising amid a severe economic crisis, Venezuelan President Nicolás Maduro faced allegations in 2017 that he and his government were attempting to consolidate power in Socialist Party–controlled institutions following controversial decisions by the Supreme Court that stripped the National Assembly of its legislative authority and the election of a National Constituent Assembly charged with rewriting the constitution. Through economic sanctions, denunciations, and investigations into human rights offenses against opposition members, the international community sought to pressure the Maduro government to abandon what were widely viewed as undemocratic actions.

VENEZUELA'S NATIONAL CRISIS

Venezuela's economic crisis deepened in 2017, with the International Monetary Fund reporting in its October 2017 World Economic Outlook that the country's inflation rate stood at 652.7 percent—a dramatic increase from 275 percent at the end of 2015. Chronic shortages of food, medicine, and basic items such as toilet paper had left many Venezuelans without access to or unable to afford necessary goods and services. The crisis was widely attributed to mismanagement by and corruption within the Socialist Party government that had been in place since the late President Hugo Chavez was elected in 1998.

The ongoing crisis fueled political tensions in the country and strengthened opposition to Maduro's government and the Socialist Party. The Democratic Unity Roundtable (MUD), a coalition of political parties that serves as the primary opposition, won a supermajority in Venezuela's National Assembly during the December 2015 election. MUD pursued a recall referendum against Maduro in 2016, but the effort was suspended by the National Electoral Council on grounds that several thousand signatures collected in MUD's preliminary petition for the referendum were fraudulent, following challenges filed by pro-Maduro governors in several states. The National Assembly pursued several legislative measures aimed at ousting Maduro and his allies as well, including a vote to open an impeachment trial against the president; however, these measures never gained traction due to the Socialist Party's control of much of the government, including the Supreme Court. Shortly before the new National Assembly took office, the outgoing National Assembly (in which the Socialist Party had a majority) named thirteen Supreme Court justices in what the opposition described as an effort to pack the court with government sympathizers.

SUPREME COURT STRIPS NATIONAL
ASSEMBLY OF LEGISLATIVE POWERS

In March 2017, the Supreme Court issued two rulings that collectively stripped the National Assembly of its legislating power. A March 27 ruling declared all legislation passed by the National Assembly to be unconstitutional and eliminated members' parliamentary immunity from prosecution. A March 29 ruling declared the National Assembly "to be in contempt" and nullified its actions, shifting "parliamentary functions" to the Constitutional Chamber of the Supreme Court "in order to guarantee the rule of law." The court had considered the National Assembly to be in contempt since August 2016, following the Assembly's swearing in of three lawmakers who won seats in the 2015 election but had been blocked by the court from taking office while it considered vote-buying allegations filed by the Socialist Party. Preventing these lawmakers from taking their seats had temporarily deprived MUD of its supermajority.

The rulings generated immediate blowback from the opposition and from some who previously supported Maduro's government and were viewed as a continuation of the government's ongoing efforts to consolidate power. Maduro and the Supreme Court had been working together to slowly limit the National Assembly's powers, including through a March 2016 law that removed National Assembly oversight of judicial, electoral, and civil authorities and an October 2016 ruling that stripped the National Assembly of its ability to review the annual budget, giving Maduro all power over budgetary decision making. "They have kidnapped the Constitution, they have kidnapped our rights, they have kidnapped our liberty," said National Assembly President Julio Borges. Attorney General Luisa Ortega characterized the rulings as "a rupture in the constitutional order," and the neighboring governments of Chile, Columbia, and Peru withdrew their ambassadors. The Organization of American States (OAS) issued a sharply worded statement from Secretary General Luis Almagro who denounced the "self-inflicted coup d'état perpetrated by the Venezuelan regime against the National Assembly, the last branch of government to be legitimized by the will of the people of Venezuela." He added that the rulings "are the latest actions taken by the authoritarian regime to subvert the constitutional order in Venezuela and eliminate all semblance of democracy." Several thousand Venezuelans demonstrated in the capital in support of the National Assembly.

Facing mounting criticism at home and abroad, Maduro asked the court to review its decisions on March 31. The following day, the court moved to restore the National Assembly's powers. Chief Justice Maikel Moreno said that the court is "only an arbiter" and should not be in conflict with other branches of government.

MADURO CALLS FOR CONSTITUTIONAL
REWRITE, NATIONAL CONSTITUENT ASSEMBLY

One month later, Maduro called for the election of a National Constituent Assembly to rewrite Venezuela's constitution. Maduro said the new assembly would bring reconciliation and peace to the country, but the opposition decried it as another presidential power grab. In addition to rewriting the constitution, the constituent assembly was expected to have authority to legislate and dissolve state institutions and to eventually replace the National Assembly. Maduro also said the constituent assembly would strengthen "the communal state," which was interpreted to mean that more power would be given to communal councils in poor neighborhoods, which are generally led by government loyalists.

Some also expressed concerns that the constituent assembly would cancel the already-postponed 2017 gubernatorial elections and the 2018 presidential election.

In a symbolic gesture, the opposition organized a nonbinding referendum on July 16, in which roughly 7.2 million Venezuelans voted. More than 98 percent of voters opposed the constituent assembly's formation, supported asking the military to defend the country's existing constitution, and favored holding new elections before the end of Maduro's term. The government claimed the referendum was illegal and pressed forward with preparations for the constituent assembly election, scheduled for July 30.

On July 26, the opposition initiated a forty-eight-hour strike to protest the upcoming vote. The strike shut down portions of the capitol, with most businesses in the western half of Caracas and the city's main highways shut down. The following day, the government announced a ban on public gatherings and protests, effective July 29 through August 3, and threatened those who disobeyed with up to ten years of jail time. Despite the warnings, the opposition persisted in calling for nationwide protests ahead of the vote.

Various international groups and foreign governments, including the United States, urged Maduro to forgo the election. On July 26, the United States announced sanctions against thirteen current and former officials in the Venezuelan government, security services, and oil industry, including the heads of the National Electoral Council and the Presidential Commission for the Constituent Assembly. The sanctions froze the individuals' assets under U.S. jurisdiction and prohibited U.S. citizens and financial institutions from dealing with them. Further sanctions were threatened if Maduro did not cancel the vote.

The election proceeded as planned on July 30, though protests took place across the country. The National Electoral Council claimed that roughly eight million Venezuelans—about forty-one percent of eligible voters—voted, while the opposition claimed turnout amounted to less than seven percent of registered voters. The opposition also claimed the vote could not be verified because certain electoral procedures had not been followed, such as marking voters' little fingers with indelible ink or having independent observers at polling stations. In interviews with various media outlets, state workers indicated that their jobs had been threatened if they did not vote in the election, and Maduro publicly acknowledged earlier in the month that the government was pressuring its employees to vote. Similar threats were reportedly made against families who relied on government food distribution services and patients needing certain medications.

Opposition parties boycotted the election and did not field any candidates, meaning the 545 winning candidates—who included Maduro's wife—were all supporters of the Maduro government. The president hailed the election as a victory, calling it a "vote for the revolution," but the poll was quickly condemned by others, with countries including Argentina, Brazil, Chile, Colombia, Costa Rica, Mexico, Panama, Peru, and Spain rejecting the results. OAS Secretary General Almagro denounced "the entire fraudulent process," declaring, "The election of the Constituent Assembly was carried out by massacring the basic principles of transparency, neutrality and universality that should characterize free and fair elections." Almagro also commented on the deaths of sixteen Venezuelans who were killed during protests against the vote. "This crisis has led the Dictatorship to murder its citizens in a dirty war of repression against the people," he said.

On July 31, the U.S. Treasury Department sanctioned Maduro for "undermining democracy in Venezuela," stating that the National Constituent Assembly "aspires illegitimately to usurp the constitutional role of the democratically elected National Assembly, rewrite the constitution, and impose an authoritarian regime on the people of Venezuela." The agency urged those elected to the assembly to decline to take office. More sanctions followed on August 24, this time prohibiting U.S. financial institutions from providing new loans or credit to or dealing in new bonds and stocks issued by the Venezuelan government and the state oil company Petróleos de Venezuela. The sanctions were intended to prevent U.S. financial institutions from helping fund or support Maduro's push to gain more power.

Maduro accused National Assembly President Borges of being directly involved in the sanctions effort and called for the Supreme Court and National Constituent Assembly to conduct a judgement of "betrayal of the homeland" for anyone who had encouraged the sanctions. Delcy Rodríguez, president of the National Constituent Assembly, criticized the United States. "They think that with economic sanctions, they'll be able to suffocate the Venezuelan people," she said. "But we've pledged and will keep pledging to defend Venezuela no matter the type of imperial threat." The government conducted national military exercises on August 26 in response to the U.S. sanctions and President Donald Trump's earlier comments that he was "not going to rule out a military option" for ending Venezuela's crisis.

The National Constituent Assembly held its first session on August 5, during which it unanimously voted to remove the attorney general from office, barred her from seeking public office in Venezuela again, prohibited her from leaving the country, and froze her assets. Prior to the session, the attorney general had pledged to investigate fraud allegations stemming from the July 30 election. Maduro ally Tarek William Saab was nominated as the new attorney general and sworn in the same day. The assembly also unanimously approved extending the amount of time it would be in power from six months to two years.

UN REPORT FINDS PATTERNS OF HUMAN RIGHTS VIOLATIONS

Mass antigovernment demonstrations took place across Venezuela in 2016 and continued in 2017, particularly following the Supreme Court's efforts to strip the National Assembly of its powers and in the run up to the National Constituent Assembly election. In one high-profile incident in June, a former Venezuelan intelligence officer fired on the Interior Ministry building and threw grenades at the Supreme Court from a police helicopter. The government has increasingly cracked down on protestors, with security forces reportedly using tear gas, rubber bullets, water cannons, and other methods to break up the crowds. Maduro also created an "Anti-Coup Commando" unit that has been arresting activists and political opponents and charging them with treason since January 2017. Human rights group Penal Forum says the government is holding at least 114 political prisoners. Government supporters have also pushed back on the opposition. On July 5, several dozen government supporters stormed the National Assembly, violently attacking lawmakers and injuring seven in the process. Reportedly, several journalists were also assaulted.

On August 8, the Office of the UN High Commissioner for Human Rights reported that a team of its officers had found "widespread and systematic use of excessive force and arbitrary detentions against demonstrators in Venezuela," as well as "patterns of other human rights violations." Based on interviews conducted with victims, witnesses, civil society organizations and others, the team concluded that Venezuelan security forces used tear gas and fired buckshot at protestors without warning, with some using deadly force. Interviewees also described house raids that were conducted without warrants to find demonstrators and armed progovernment groups called *colectivos* who reportedly drove into protests on motorcycles to harass and sometimes shoot protestors. The team estimated that between April 1 and July 31, more than 5,000 people had been "arbitrarily detained" and stated there were "credible reports of cruel, inhuman or degrading treatment by security forces of such detainees, amounting in several cases to torture." The Venezuelan attorney general's office was reportedly investigating 124 deaths related to the demonstrations; the UN team's analysis of those deaths indicated that security forces were responsible for at least forty-six of them and that armed progovernment groups were responsible for another twenty-seven. "The responsibility for the human rights violations we are recording lies at the highest levels of Government," said Zeid Ra'ad Al Hussein, the UN High Commissioner for Human Rights.

—Linda Grimm

Following is a statement from Organization of American States (OAS) Secretary General Luis Almagro from March 20, 2017, responding to the Venezuela Supreme Court of Justice's decision to strip power from the National Assembly; a press release issued by the U.S. Treasury Department on July 31, 2017, announcing sanctions against President Nicolás Maduro; a message from Almagro from July 31, 2017, denouncing the National Constituent Assembly election; an Office of the UN High Commissioner for Human Rights report from August 8, 2017, about human rights violations during mass protests in Venezuela; and an executive order issued by President Donald Trump on August 24, 2017, imposing additional sanctions on Venezuela.

OAS Secretary General on Supreme Court of Justice Decisions

March 20, 2017

The Secretary General of the OAS denounces the self-inflicted coup d'état perpetrated by the Venezuelan regime against the National Assembly, the last branch of government to be legitimized by the will of the people of Venezuela.

"Unfortunately, what we had warned has now come to pass" said the Secretary General of the OAS, Luis Almagro.

The Supreme Court of Justice (TSJ) has issued two decisions which strip parliamentary immunity from members of the National Assembly and which, contrary to all constitutional norms, provide for the TSJ to assume the legislative function. This was done in a manner which ignores even the most basic guarantees of due process . . .

[The following paragraphs summarizing the court's decisions have been omitted.]

Universal norms as well as regional and international agreements, to which Venezuela is a Party and therefore obligated to enforce, define the separation of powers as a necessary guarantee to protect the rights of citizens and defend democracy and the rule of law.

The unconstitutional decisions by the TSJ to strip parliamentary immunity from the members of the National Assembly and assume the legislative function are the latest actions taken by the authoritarian regime to subvert the constitutional order in Venezuela and eliminate all semblance of democracy.

Section 4.4 of the TSJ decision states: "So long as the National Assembly remains in contempt and its actions nullified, the Constitutional Chamber of the Supreme Court will ensure that parliamentary functions are exercised directly by the Chamber or by the organ that it designates, in order to guarantee the rule of law."

This decision violates Article 187 of the Constitution which outlines the legislative powers of the National Assembly. Sub-section 24 guarantees those powers in accordance with the Constitution and the law.

The restoration of democracy is an obligation we all share. It is time for the hemisphere to work together to help restore democracy in Venezuela. We have an obligation to the people of Venezuela to act without further delay. To be silent in the face of a dictatorship is the lowest indignity in politics.

"The question is between liberty or despotism." Our oppressors are our oppressors because they threaten the very basis of our liberty and therefore must be the object of our struggle.

The Secretary General calls for the urgent convocation of the Permanent Council under Article 20 of the Democratic Charter. He stated that the situation has reached this point despite the warnings outlined in the reports of May 30, 2016 and March 14, 2017.

The head of the OAS recalled the preventive nature of the Inter-American Democratic Charter, which should have been rigorously followed to prevent another coup d'état in the hemisphere.

SOURCES: Organization of American States. "Venezuela: OAS SG Denounces Self-inflicted Coup d'Etat." March 30, 2017. http://www.oas.org/en/media_center/press_release.asp?sCodigo=E-019/17; The General Secretariat of the Organization of American States (GS/OAS), through its Press and Communications Department, at [http://www.oas.org/en/media_center/press_release.asp?sCodigo=E-019/17], is the official source of this document.

U.S. Treasury Department
Sanctions Nicolás Maduro

DOCUMENT

July 31, 2017

Today, the U.S. Department of the Treasury's Office of Foreign Assets Control (OFAC) designated the President of Venezuela, Nicolas Maduro Moros, pursuant to Executive Order (E.O.) 13692, which authorizes sanctions against current or former officials of the Government of Venezuela and others undermining democracy in Venezuela. These sanctions come a day after the Maduro government held elections for a National Constituent Assembly (Asamblea Nacional Constituyente, or ANC) that aspires illegitimately to usurp the constitutional role of the democratically elected National Assembly, rewrite the constitution, and impose an authoritarian regime on the people of Venezuela. As such, it represents a rupture in Venezuela's constitutional and democratic order. The Maduro administration has proceeded with the ANC even though Venezuelans and democratic governments worldwide have overwhelmingly opposed it as a fundamental assault on the freedoms of the Venezuelan people. The creation of the ANC follows years of Maduro's efforts to undermine Venezuela's democracy and the rule of law.

As a result of today's actions, all assets of Nicolas Maduro subject to U.S. jurisdiction are frozen, and U.S. persons are prohibited from dealing with him.

"Yesterday's illegitimate elections confirm that Maduro is a dictator who disregards the will of the Venezuelan people. By sanctioning Maduro, the United States makes clear our opposition to the policies of his regime and our support for the people of Venezuela who seek to return their country to a full and prosperous democracy," said Secretary of the Treasury Steven T. Mnuchin. "Anyone who participates in this illegitimate ANC could be exposed to future U.S. sanctions for their role in undermining democratic processes and institutions in Venezuela." . . .

Treasury undertook the action, in consultation with the State Department, pursuant to Executive Order 13692. The U.S. government and democratic governments worldwide continue to call on the Venezuelan government to halt the ANC process and allow Venezuela's democratic processes and institutions to function as intended. We urge those who were elected to the Constituent Assembly to decline to take office.

SOURCE: U.S. Treasury Department. "Treasury Sanctions the President of Venezuela." July 31, 2017. https://www.treasury.gov/press-center/press-releases/Pages/sm0137.aspx.

OAS Secretary General on Venezuela's National Constituent Assembly Election

July 31, 2017

Yesterday is a day that Venezuelans will mourn. It was a day of violence and death perpetrated by the cowardly dictatorship, against the people. Yesterday the repressive forces massacred the Venezuelan people.

Sixteen people, including minors, were murdered in the numerous protests that took place during the vote for the fraudulent National Constituent Assembly.

The repression against the people was extreme, surpassing even the violent standard that has be enforced since the demonstrations began last April . . .

The process carried out yesterday is absolutely void. The election of the Constituent Assembly was carried out by massacring the basic principles of transparency, neutrality and universality that should characterize free and fair elections.

The processes of technical verification of the voters list, the electronic machinery, and the system of verification of results did not take place. Therefore, it is impossible for the electoral authority to provide reliable results.

A legitimate election cannot be held in an environment of repression and violence. Coercion and vote buying was evident. The principle of universal suffrage was blatantly violated.

Finally the results announced by the National Electoral Council lack veracity. They were produced in a climate of secrecy that is aggravated by the lack of national and international observation.

It was an election that reflects what the dictatorship wants for Venezuela, a one-party system, an automatic mechanism to execute the will of those in power and to serve its interests. A mechanism that represses and muzzles any contrary opinion through fear, imposition and repression.

Meanwhile, various South American countries, the European Union, the United States and Canada, do not recognize the legitimacy of the National Constituent Assembly.

The OAS General Secretariat denounces the entire fraudulent process that took place yesterday. From the outset, we have denounced the illegitimacy of its origin, its unconstitutionality and the forced and selective manipulation of parochial constituencies to force results favoring the perpetuation of the Regime.

In this sense—and with even greater conviction—we do not recognize the results announced yesterday by an electoral tribunal that has lost all vestiges of legitimacy and that, far from respecting the expression of popular will, has given repeated evidence of its service to the Dictatorship.

We can no longer delay the return of democracy to Venezuela.

Today we saw once again that the Venezuelan people are not afraid. Tyrants are afraid. They live in fear, because no one can win against the people. This crisis has led the Dictatorship to murder its citizens in a dirty war of repression against the people . . .

We cannot allow more time to escape us. Venezuela's return to democracy cannot wait.

Allowing it to reach this point is unjust. Venezuelans should not bear the cost of the annihilation of the Rule of Law. There is no greater injustice than for a people to be subjected to the humiliation at the hands of repressive forces.

And as a result, it is the people who have been the first to take to the streets to fight for justice. It is the people who are demanding justice for a dictator responsible for the murders that took place yesterday, and for those of the last four months. The people will never surrender to a justice that is not just.

But fundamentally, and first and foremost, the people must return to power.

Repressive forces must return to their barracks. The will of the people is in the streets and it must be respected. Yesterday, the people showed that only they are the true sovereign.

Venezuela is great and the fight will be very difficult; but the end of that fight will be a future of liberty.

You have to be strong and have convictions to negotiate. As Uruguayan leader Wilson Ferreira said during the struggle against the dictatorship in my country, "we know what the people want, we know what they think and we know that the people will do what is necessary to achieve it."

Sources: Organization of American States. "Message from the Secretary General on Venezuela." July 31, 2017. http://www.oas.org/en/media_center/press_release.asp?sCodigo=S-025/17; The General Secretariat of the Organization of American States (GS/OAS), through its Press and Communications Department, at [http://www.oas.org/en/media_center/press_release.asp?sCodigo=S-025/17], is the official source of this document.

UN Report on Human Rights Violations during Venezuela Protests

DOCUMENT

August 8, 2017

Interviews conducted remotely by a UN human rights team paint a picture of widespread and systematic use of excessive force and arbitrary detentions against demonstrators in

Venezuela. The team's findings also indicate patterns of other human rights violations, including violent house raids, torture and ill-treatment of those detained in connection with the protests.

In the absence of responses from the Venezuelan authorities to requests for access, UN High Commissioner for Human Rights Zeid Ra'ad Al Hussein deployed a team of human rights officers to conduct remote monitoring of the human rights situation in the country from 6 June to 31 July, including from Panama. The team conducted some 135 interviews with victims and their families, witnesses, civil society organisations, journalists, lawyers, doctors, first responders and the Attorney-General's Office, and also received information in writing from the Ombudsperson's Office.

Witnesses spoke of security forces firing tear gas and buckshot at anti-Government protestors without warning. Several of the individuals interviewed said tear gas canisters were used at short range, and marbles, buckshot and nuts and bolts were used as ammunition. Security forces have reportedly also resorted to the use of deadly force against demonstrators.

Witness accounts suggest that security forces, mainly the National Guard, the National Police and local police forces, have systematically used disproportionate force to instil [sic] fear, crush dissent, and to prevent demonstrators from assembling, rallying and reaching public institutions to present petitions. Government authorities have rarely condemned such incidents.

As of 31 July, the Attorney General's Office was investigating 124 deaths in the context of the demonstrations. According to the UN Human Rights team's analysis, security forces are allegedly responsible for at least 46 of those deaths, while pro-Government armed groups, referred to as "armed colectivos" are reportedly responsible for 27 of the deaths. It is unclear who the perpetrators in the remaining deaths may be. The Attorney-General's Office was also investigating at least 1,958 reported cases of injuries, although the actual number of people injured may be considerably higher. Information collected by the team suggests that armed colectivos routinely break into protests on motorcycles, wielding firearms and harassing or in some cases shooting at people.

While no official data is available on the number of detentions, reliable estimates suggest that between April 1, when the mass demonstrations began, and 31 July, more than 5,051 people have been arbitrarily detained. More than 1,000 reportedly remain in detention. In several of the cases reviewed by the UN Human Rights Office, there were credible reports of cruel, inhuman or degrading treatment by security forces of such detainees, amounting in several cases to torture. Tactics used included electric shocks, beatings, including with helmets and sticks while handcuffed, hanging detainees by the wrists for long periods, suffocation with gas, and threats of killings—and in some cases threats of sexual violence—against the detainees or their families.

"Since the wave of demonstrations began in April, there has been a clear pattern of excessive force used against protesters. Several thousand people have been arbitrarily detained, many reportedly subjected to ill-treatment and even torture, while several hundred have been brought before military rather than civilian courts," said Zeid. "And these patterns show no signs of abating."

"These violations have occurred amid the breakdown of the rule of law in Venezuela, with constant attacks by the Government against the National Assembly and the Attorney-General's Office," Zeid added. "The responsibility for the human rights violations we are recording lies at the highest levels of Government."

The High Commissioner said the decision by the Constituent Assembly on 5 August to dismiss the Attorney-General was deeply worrying, and he urged the authorities to guarantee independent and effective investigations of human rights violations involving security forces and armed colectivos. He called on the authorities to heed the call of the Inter-American Commission for Human Rights, which has requested the State to take measures to ensure the protection of the former Attorney-General.

High Commissioner Zeid also expressed serious concern about the many cases of violent and illegal house raids reported to the team. Victims and witnesses told the team that the raids were conducted without warrants, allegedly to weed out demonstrators. Reports also suggest that private property was destroyed during such raids.

Journalists and media workers have indicated that security forces targeted them to prevent them from covering demonstrators. Journalists reported being shot at with tear gas canisters and buckshot, despite being clearly identified. They have been detained, threatened and have had their equipment stolen on several occasions.

Some groups of demonstrators have also resorted to violence, with attacks reported against security officers. Eight officers have been killed in the context of the demonstrations.

High Commissioner Zeid urged the authorities to immediately end the excessive use of force against demonstrators, to halt arbitrary detentions and to release all those arbitrarily detained. Zeid reminded the authorities that there is an absolute prohibition on the use of torture, under international human rights law. He also called for an end to the use of military justice to try civilians.

"I call on all parties to work towards a solution to the rapidly worsening tensions in the country, to renounce the use of violence and to take steps towards meaningful political dialogue," Zeid said.

Source: United Nations Office of the High Commissioner for Human Rights. "UN Human Rights Team's Findings Indicate Patterns of Rights Violations amid Mass Protests in Venezuela." August 8, 2017. http://www.ohchr.org/EN/NewsEvents/Pages/DisplayNews.aspx?NewsID=21948&LangID=E.

DOCUMENT

U.S. Executive Order Imposing Additional Sanctions in Venezuela

August 24, 2017

... I, DONALD J. TRUMP, President of the United States of America, in order to take additional steps with respect to the national emergency declared in Executive Order 13692 of March 8, 2015, and particularly in light of recent actions and policies of the Government of Venezuela, including serious abuses of human rights and fundamental freedoms; responsibility for the deepening humanitarian crisis in Venezuela; establishment of an illegitimate Constituent Assembly, which has usurped the power of the democratically elected National Assembly and other branches of the Government of Venezuela; rampant public corruption; and ongoing repression and persecution of, and violence toward, the political opposition, hereby order as follows:

Section 1. (a) All transactions related to, provision of financing for, and other dealings in the following by a United States person or within the United States are prohibited:

    (i)   new debt with a maturity of greater than 90 days of Petroleos de Venezuela, S.A. (PdVSA);

    (ii) new debt with a maturity of greater than 30 days, or new equity, of the Government of Venezuela, other than debt of PdVSA covered by subsection (a)(i) of this section;

    (iii) bonds issued by the Government of Venezuela prior to the effective date of this order; or

    (iv) dividend payments or other distributions of profits to the Government of Venezuela from any entity owned or controlled, directly or indirectly, by the Government of Venezuela.

(b) The purchase, directly or indirectly, by a United States person or within the United States, of securities from the Government of Venezuela, other than securities qualifying as new debt with a maturity of less than or equal to 90 or 30 days as covered by subsections (a)(i) or (a)(ii) of this section, respectively, is prohibited.

(c) The prohibitions in subsections (a) and (b) of this section apply except to the extent provided by statutes, or in regulations, orders, directives, or licenses that may be issued pursuant to this order, and notwithstanding any contract entered into or any license or permit granted before the effective date of this order . . . .

[Sec. 3, which defines terms used in the Executive Order, has been omitted.]

Sec. 4. The Secretary of the Treasury, in consultation with the Secretary of State, is hereby authorized to take such actions, including promulgating rules and regulations, and to employ all powers granted to the President by IEEPA as may be necessary to implement this order . . .

Sec. 5. For those persons whose property or interests in property are affected by this order who might have a constitutional presence in the United States, I find that because of the ability to transfer funds or other assets instantaneously, prior notice to such persons of measures to be taken pursuant to this order would render those measures ineffectual. I therefore determine that for these measures to be effective in addressing the national emergency declared in Executive Order 13692, there need be no prior notice of a listing or determination made pursuant to this order.

Sec. 6. This order is not intended to, and does not, create any right or benefit, substantive or procedural, enforceable at law or in equity by any party against the United States, its departments, agencies, or entities, its officers, employees, or agents, or any other person.

Sec. 7. This order is effective at 12:01 a.m. eastern daylight time on August 25, 2017.

DONALD J. TRUMP
The White House,
August 24, 2017

Source: Executive Office of the President. "Executive Order 13808—Imposing Additional Sanctions with Respect to the Situation in Venezuela." August 24, 2017. *Compilation of Presidential Documents* 2017, no. 00583 (August 24, 2017). https://www.gpo.gov/fdsys/pkg/DCPD-201700583/pdf/DCPD-201700583.pdf.

OTHER HISTORIC DOCUMENTS OF INTEREST

FROM PREVIOUS *HISTORIC DOCUMENTS*

- Presidential Recall Referendum Suspended in Venezuela, *2016*, p. 588
- Venezuelan Government Cracks Down on Protests amid U.S. Concern, *2014*, p. 64
- OPEC Fails to Respond to Falling Oil Prices, *2014*, p. 571
- International Leaders Respond to Death of Venezuelan Leader Hugo Chavez, *2013*, p. 84

United Nations and United States Issue Sanctions against North Korea

MARCH 23, JUNE 2, AUGUST 5, AND
SEPTEMBER 11 AND 21, 2017

The United Nations first began issuing sanctions against the reclusive North Korean state over the development of a nuclear weapons program more than two decades ago. The international body continued to pass resolutions that sanction the government in Pyongyang that are often met with additional measures put in place by the country's neighbors and Western states. The government of North Korea continued to defy the sanctions, ramping up its nuclear program and testing long-range ballistic missiles that threatened its neighbors and the United States alike. In 2017, the situation appeared to reach a fever pitch as China, North Korea's primary trading partner, put an end to some imports and exports and reportedly ordered its central bank to cease any financial dealings with North Korea. The situation on the Korean peninsula became tenser following heated rhetoric lobbed between U.S. President Donald Trump and North Korean leader Kim Jong Un, which at times appeared to indicate either an imminent nuclear strike on the United States or a U.S. invasion in North Korea.

UNITED NATIONS SANCTIONS AGAINST NORTH KOREA

The first sanctions issued by the United Nations against North Korea came in 1993 when the nation announced its intent to withdraw from the Nuclear Non-Proliferation Treaty and refused to allow inspectors from the International Atomic Energy Agency to enter the country. The next sanction came in 2006—and dozens more followed—calling on North Korea to end its nuclear weapons development program. In November 2016, the United Nations issued what were considered the toughest sanctions against North Korea to date. These sanctions strengthened earlier measures put in place, while imposing additional restrictions on revenue generation and cargo inspection, while also creating new mechanisms to enforce the sanctions.

In March 2017, the United Nations issued Resolution 2345, which expanded to March 24, 2018, the mandate of the Panel of Experts, a group first established in 2009 that was tasked with ensuring UN member states comply with sanctions issued against North Korea. It also requested that the Panel provide a midterm report on its work by September 6, 2017, asked for a program of work to address any noncompliance issues, and urged all states to cooperate with the work of the panel. Three months later, on June 2, the UN Security Council issued another round of sanctions and condemned "in the strongest terms the nuclear weapons and ballistic missile development activities" conducted by North Korea since September 9, 2016. It further reaffirmed its opinion that the nation should "abandon all nuclear weapons and existing nuclear programs." Because North Korea had not yet complied with UN requests to dismantle its nuclear program, the United

Nations expanded its list of individuals and businesses subject to travel or asset freezes under Resolution 1718, issued in 2006. Those added to the revised list included the president of the Korea Kumsan Trading Corporation, the group responsible for supplying North Korea's General Bureau of Atomic Energy, an individual accused of overseeing espionage operations for the government, and various directors and vice directors of North Korean agencies.

Following ballistic missile tests by North Korea on July 4 and July 28, on August 5 the United Nations issued Resolution 2371, which banned the export of coal, iron, iron ore, lead, lead ore, and seafood from North Korea, prohibited North Korean citizens from working in foreign countries, and banned UN member states from forming new joint ventures with organizations operating inside North Korea. The new sanctions again expanded the list of those subject to a travel ban or asset freezes. One month later, the United Nations issued a fourth round of sanctions for the year, this time limiting North Korea's ability to import crude oil, refined petroleum products, and natural gas condensate and liquid, banning textile exports, and banning North Korean nationals from working abroad. This resolution, penned by the United States, was the toughest of the year, and sought to cripple North Korea's ability to finance and supply its nuclear program. Chinese Ambassador to the UN Liu Jieyi said of the new sanctions, "The resolution adopted by the security council today . . . demonstrates the unanimous position of the international community of opposing DPRK's development of its nuclear and ballistic missile capabilities."

In recent years, China had become a key player in mitigating the growing threat of North Korea's nuclear power. The nation accounted for more than 90 percent of North Korea's external trade, and leaders at the United Nations, and within the United States and other countries, had been frank that Chinese involvement in the enforcement of sanctions was critical to encouraging North Korea to come to the negotiating table in an effort to end its nuclear program. The Chinese government consistently asserted that it sought to end the North Korean nuclear program, specifically through diplomatic means. "China is . . . committed to the denuclearization of the Korean peninsula, to the peace and stability of the peninsula and to the solution of the issue through dialogue and consultation," UN Ambassador Liu said. In February 2017, China made its first indication that it intended to be party to the international actions against North Korea by banning all imports of coal for the remainder of the year. By September, China announced that it would begin closing all joint business ventures set up between China and North Korea.

U.S. IMPLEMENTS EXECUTIVE ORDERS, LAWS AIMED AT NORTH KOREA

The United States put in place four measures targeting North Korea in 2017. The first, on August 2, banned Americans from visiting North Korea beginning on September 1. This order followed the death of Otto Warmbier, an American tourist who was held in a North Korean prison before being released to the United States in a coma. That same day, the Countering America's Adversaries Through Sanctions Act became law. The law targets acts of aggression carried out by the government or North Korea, as well as those by Russia and Iran. The provisions against North Korea gave the president additional discretion to impose sanctions on those found in violation of UN resolutions against North Korea; banned U.S. financial bodies from providing indirect financial services to North Korea; disallowed any government from receiving U.S. foreign assistance if it was found to have accepted items or services for defense from North Korea; called on the State Department to decide whether North Korea is a state sponsor of terrorism (North Korea was removed from the list in 2008 under the direction of then-President George W. Bush); and issued sanctions against those who employ North Korean forced laborers, goods produced by forced laborers, and North Korean cargo and shipping. President Trump issued two statements against the act, saying the White House would review the measures and put in place those it deemed appropriate, based on presidential authority. "The bill remains seriously flawed—particularly because it encroaches on the executive branch's authority to negotiate," Trump said, adding, "By limiting the Executive's flexibility, this bill makes it harder for the United States to strike good deals for the American people, and will drive China, Russia, and North Korea much closer together." It was widely believed that Trump's objection to the new law had less to do with North Korea and more to do with Russia given allegations that those involved with his presidential campaign had discussed with members of the Russian government eliminating some sanctions.

In September, President Trump issued two executive orders against North Korea. One, issued on September 25, banned entry of North Korean nationals into the United States while the other, issued on September 21, would allow the United States to freeze the assets of and cut off access to U.S. financial institutions for any individual or business found to be trading goods, services, or technology with North Korea. It further banned any aircraft or ship that had entered North Korean waters from entering the United States for 180 days. Treasury Secretary Steve Mnuchin said the order made clear that "foreign financial institutions are now on notice that going forward they can choose to do business with the United States or North Korea, but not both." Trump stated that China had quickly begun to adhere to the U.S. order, noting, "China, their central bank has told their other banks—that's a massive banking system—to immediately stop doing business with North Korea." Reuters published an article citing unnamed sources that appeared to confirm the president's statement. China, however, made no public announcement either confirming or denying such action.

Trump's comments about North Korea were met with both celebration and caution around the world. On August 8, Trump promised "fire and fury" against North Korea, warning that the United States was "locked and loaded" to respond to ongoing provocations from Kim. At the United Nations, Trump referred to Kim as "Little Rocket Man" and promised to "thoroughly destroy" North Korea if its missile tests continued. Those who supported the president's tactics said it was a departure from the diplomatic efforts of former administrations where the result did not end North Korea's nuclear program. Detractors, including Rep. Eliot Engle, D-N.Y., the ranking Democrat on the House Foreign Affairs Committee, called such remarks "unhinged," while Sen. Ben Cardin, D-Md., said the statements "were not helpful and once again show that [Trump] lacks the temperament and judgement to deal with the serious crisis the United States confronts." Globally, Russian officials indicated that the comments could encourage further instability in the region that could have dire consequences for U.S. allies Japan and South Korea.

NORTH KOREA CONTINUES TO DEVELOP NUCLEAR WEAPONS

North Korea continued to defy the sanctions, at one point insinuating that it planned to develop a weapon that could strike Guam. In July, the nation conducted two weapons tests, one of which was thought to have intercontinental range. One month later, on August 28, North Korea launched a ballistic missile that passed through Japanese airspace before landing in the sea. The launch prompted air raid sirens across Japan and was followed just a few days later by the country's sixth nuclear test of 2017, which the United Nations estimated at "more than five times more powerful than the atomic bomb detonated over Hiroshima in 1945." The test was hailed by North Korean state-run media as a "perfect success" and the last step in developing a "state nuclear force" that the government believes is an essential tool to protect the state from outside incursion. An additional missile test would follow in late November, equipped with a warhead that North Korea claimed had the capability of reaching the mainland of the United States.

In September, North Korea announced that it had established a Sanctions Damage Investigation Committee tasked with determining the impact of sanctions issued by the United Nations, United States, and other nations. A spokesperson for the committee called the combined sanctions "a brutal criminal act," adding, "The colossal amount of damage caused by these sanctions to the development of our state and the people's livelihood is beyond anyone's calculation." However, the unnamed spokesperson went on to state that the world should not believe that such sanctions would lead to the end of its nuclear weapons program, which it views as essential to the security of North Korea.

—Heather Kerrigan

Following are the text of sanctions issued by the United Nations against North Korea on March 23, June 2, August 5, and September 11, 2017; and the text of a sanction against North Korea issued by the United States on September 21, 2017.

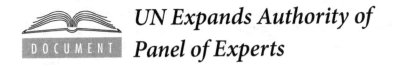

UN Expands Authority of Panel of Experts

DOCUMENT

March 23, 2017

Resolution 2345 (2017)

Adopted by the Security Council at its 7904th meeting, on 23 March 2017

The Security Council,

Recalling its previous relevant resolutions . . .

Recalling the creation, pursuant to paragraph 26 of resolution 1874 (2009), of a Panel of Experts, under the direction of the Committee, to carry out the tasks provided for by that paragraph,

Recalling the interim report by the Panel of Experts appointed by the Secretary-General pursuant to paragraph 26 of resolution 1874 (2009) and the 27 February 2017 final report (S/2017/150) by the Panel,

Recalling the methodological standards for reports of sanctions monitoring mechanisms contained in the Report of the Informal Working Group of the Security Council on General Issues of Sanctions (S/2006/997),

Welcoming the efforts made by the Secretariat to expand and improve the roster of experts for the Security Council Subsidiary Organs Branch, bearing in mind the guidance provided by the Note of the President (S/2006/997),

Emphasizing, in that regard, the importance of credible, fact-based, independent assessments, analysis, and recommendations, in accordance with the mandate of the Panel of Experts, as specified in paragraph 26 of resolution 1874 (2009),

Determining that proliferation of nuclear, chemical, and biological weapons, as well as their means of delivery, continues to constitute a threat to international peace and security,

Acting under Article 41 of Chapter VII of the Charter of the United Nations,

1. *Decides* to extend until 24 April 2018 the mandate of the Panel of Experts, as specified in paragraph 26 of resolution 1874 (2009) and modified in paragraph 29 of resolution 2094 (2013), *decides* that this mandate shall apply also with respect to the measures imposed in resolution 2321 (2016), *expresses* its intent to review the mandate and take appropriate action regarding further extension no later than 24 March 2018, and *requests* the Secretary-General to take the necessary administrative measures to this effect;

2. *Requests* the Panel of Experts to provide to the Committee no later than 5 August 2017 a midterm report on its work, as requested in paragraph 43 of resolution 2321 (2016), and *further requests* that, after a discussion with the Committee, the Panel of Experts submit to the Council its midterm report by 6 September 2017, and *requests* also a final report to the Committee no later than 1 February 2018 with its findings and recommendations, and *further requests* that, after a discussion with the Committee, the Panel of Experts submit to the Council its final report no later than 14 March 2018;

3. *Requests* the Panel of Experts to provide to the Committee a planned program of work no later than thirty days after the Panel's reappointment, *encourages* the Committee to engage in regular discussions about this program of work and to engage regularly with the Panel about its work, and further *requests* the Panel of Experts to provide to the Committee any updates to this program of work;

4. *Expresses* its intent to continue to follow the work of the Panel;

5. *Urges* all States, relevant United Nations bodies and other interested parties, to cooperate fully with the Committee established pursuant to resolution 1718 (2006) and the Panel of Experts, in particular by supplying any information at their disposal on the implementation of the measures imposed by resolution 1718 (2006), resolution 1874 (2009), resolution 2087 (2013), resolution 2094 (2013), resolution 2270 (2016), and resolution 2321 (2016);

6. *Decides* to remain actively seized of the matter.

SOURCE: United Nations Security Council. "Resolution 2345 (2017)." March 23, 2017. http://www.un.org/en/ga/search/view_doc.asp?symbol=S/RES/2345%282017%29.

UN Security Council Expands List of Individuals and Businesses Targeted for Sanctions

DOCUMENT

June 2, 2017

Resolution 2356 (2017)

Adopted by the Security Council at its 7958th meeting, on 2 June 2017

The Security Council,

Recalling its previous relevant resolutions . . .

Reaffirming that proliferation of nuclear, chemical and biological weapons, as well as their means of delivery, constitutes a threat to international peace and security,

Expressing serious concern that the DPRK has continued to violate relevant Security Council resolutions through repeated launches and attempted launches of ballistic missiles, and *noting* that all such ballistic missile activities contribute to the DPRK's development of nuclear weapons delivery systems and increase tension in the region and beyond,

Expressing great concern that the DPRK's prohibited arms sales have generated revenues that are diverted to the pursuit of nuclear weapons and ballistic missiles while DPRK citizens have unmet needs,

Expressing its gravest concern that the DPRK's ongoing nuclear- and ballistic missile-related activities have further generated increased tension in the region and beyond, and *determining* that there continues to exist a clear threat to international peace and security,

Acting under Chapter VII of the Charter of the United Nations, and taking measures under its Article 41,

1. *Condemns* in the strongest terms the nuclear weapons and ballistic missile development activities including a series of ballistic missile launches and other activities conducted by the DPRK since 9 September 2016 in violation and flagrant disregard of the Security Council's resolutions;

2. *Reaffirms* its decisions that the DPRK shall abandon all nuclear weapons and existing nuclear programmes in a complete, verifiable and irreversible manner, and immediately cease all related activities; shall not conduct any further launches that use ballistic missile technology, nuclear tests, or any other provocation; shall suspend all activities related to its ballistic missile programme and in this context re-establish its pre-existing commitments to a moratorium on missile launches; and shall abandon any other existing weapons of mass destruction and ballistic missile programmes in a complete, verifiable and irreversible manner;

3. *Recalls* the measures imposed by paragraph 8 of resolution 1718 (2006), as modified by subsequent resolutions, and *decides* that the measures specified in

paragraph 8 (d) of resolution 1718 (2006) shall apply to the individuals and entities listed in Annex I and II of this resolution and to any individuals or entities acting on their behalf or at their direction, and to entities owned or controlled by them, including through illicit means, and that the measures specified in paragraph 8 (e) of resolution 1718 (2006) shall apply to the individuals listed in Annex I of this resolution and to individuals acting on their behalf or at their direction . . .

[Annexes I and II, containing the names of individuals and businesses added to the list of those targeted for sanctions, have been omitted.]

SOURCE: United Nations Security Council. "Resolution 2356 (2017)." June 2, 2017. https://undocs.org/S/RES/2356(2017).

UN Sanctions Export of North Korean Oil

August 5, 2017

Resolution 2371 (2017)

Adopted by the Security Council at its 8019th meeting, on 5 August 2017

The Security Council,

Recalling its previous relevant resolutions . . .

Reaffirming that proliferation of nuclear, chemical and biological weapons, as well as their means of delivery, constitutes a threat to international peace and security,

Expressing its gravest concern at the July 3 and July 28 of 2017 ballistic missile tests by the Democratic People's Republic of Korea ("the DPRK"), which the DPRK has stated were tests of intercontinental ballistic missiles . . .

Underlining once again the importance that the DPRK respond to other security and humanitarian concerns of the international community,

Underlining also that measures imposed by this resolution are not intended to have adverse humanitarian consequences for the civilian population of the DPRK,

Expressing serious concern that the DPRK has continued to violate relevant Security Council resolutions through repeated launches and attempted launches of ballistic missiles, and *noting* that all such ballistic missile activities contribute to the DPRK's development of nuclear weapons delivery systems and increase tension in the region and beyond,

Expressing continued concern that the DPRK is abusing the privileges and immunities accorded under the Vienna Conventions on Diplomatic and Consular Relations,

Expressing great concern that the DPRK's prohibited arms sales have generated revenues that are diverted to the pursuit of nuclear weapons and ballistic missiles while DPRK citizens have unmet needs,

Expressing its gravest concern that the DPRK's ongoing nuclear- and ballistic missile-related activities have further generated increased tension in the region and beyond, and *determining* that there continues to exist a clear threat to international peace and security,

Acting under Chapter VII of the Charter of the United Nations, and taking measures under its Article 41,

1. *Condemns* in the strongest terms the ballistic missile launches conducted by the DPRK on 3 July and 28 July of 2017, which the DPRK has stated were launches of intercontinental ballistic missiles, and which used ballistic missile technology in violation and flagrant disregard of the Security Council's resolutions;

2. *Reaffirms* its decisions that the DPRK shall not conduct any further launches that use ballistic missile technology, nuclear tests, or any other provocation; shall suspend all activities related to its ballistic missile program and in this context re-establish its pre-existing commitments to a moratorium on missile launches; shall abandon all nuclear weapons and existing nuclear programs in a complete, verifiable and irreversible manner, and immediately cease all related activities; and shall abandon any other existing weapons of mass destruction and ballistic missile programs in a complete, verifiable and irreversible manner;

Designations

3. *Decides* that the measures specified in paragraph 8 (d) of resolution 1718 (2006) shall apply also to the individuals and entities listed in Annex I and II of this resolution and to any individuals or entities acting on their behalf or at their direction, and to entities owned or controlled by them, including through illicit means, and *decides* further that the measures specified in paragraph 8 (e) of resolution 1718 (2006) shall also apply to the individuals listed in Annex I of this resolution and to individuals acting on their behalf or at their direction;

4. *Decides* to adjust the measures imposed by paragraph 8 of resolution 1718 (2006) and this resolution through the designation of additional goods, *directs* the Committee to undertake its tasks to this effect and to report to the Security Council within fifteen days of adoption of this resolution, and *further decides* that, if the Committee has not acted, then the Security Council will complete action to adjust the measures within seven days of receiving that report;

5. *Decides* to adjust the measures imposed by paragraph 7 of resolution 2321 (2016) through the designation of additional conventional arms-related items, materials, equipment, goods, and technology, *directs* the Committee to undertake its tasks to this effect and to report to the Security Council within thirty days of adoption of this resolution, *further decides* that, if the Committee has not acted, then the Security Council will complete action to adjust the measures within seven days of receiving that report, and *directs* the Committee to update this list every 12 months;

Transportation

6. *Decides* that the Committee may designate vessels for which it has information indicating they are, or have been, related to activities prohibited by resolutions 1718 (2006), 1874 (2009), 2087 (2013), 2094 (2013), 2270 (2016), 2321 (2016), 2356 (2017), or this resolution and all Member States shall prohibit the entry into their ports of such designated vessels, unless entry is required in the case of emergency or in the case of return to its port of origination, or unless the Committee determines in advance that such entry is required for humanitarian purposes or any other purposes consistent with the objectives of resolutions 1718 (2006), 1874 (2009), 2087 (2013), 2094 (2013), 2270 (2016), 2321 (2016), 2356 (2017), or this resolution;

7. *Clarifies* that the measures set forth in paragraph 20 of resolution 2270 (2016) and paragraph 9 of resolution 2321 (2016), requiring States to prohibit their nationals, persons subject to their jurisdiction and entities incorporated in their territory or subject to their jurisdiction from owning, leasing, operating any vessel flagged by the DPRK, without exception, unless the Committee approves on a case-by-case basis in advance, apply to chartering vessels flagged by the DPRK;

Sectoral

8. *Decides* that paragraph 26 of resolution 2321 (2016) shall be replaced by the following:

"*Decides* that the DPRK shall not supply, sell or transfer, directly or indirectly, from its territory or by its nationals or using its flag vessels or aircraft, coal, iron, and iron ore, and that all States shall prohibit the procurement of such material from the DPRK by their nationals, or using their flag vessels or aircraft . . .

9. *Decides* that the DPRK shall not supply, sell or transfer, directly or indirectly, from its territory or by its nationals or using its flag vessels or aircraft, seafood (including fish, crustaceans, mollusks, and other aquatic invertebrates in all forms), and that all States shall prohibit the procurement of such items from the DPRK by their nationals, or using their flag vessels or aircraft, whether or not originating in the territory of the DPRK, and further *decides* that for sales and transactions of seafood (including fish, crustaceans, mollusks, and other aquatic invertebrates in all forms) for which written contracts have been finalized prior to the adoption of this resolution, all States may allow those shipments to be imported into their territories up to 30 days from the date of adoption of this resolution with notification provided to the Committee containing details on those imports by no later than 45 days after the date of adoption of this resolution;

10. *Decides* that the DPRK shall not supply, sell or transfer, directly or indirectly, from its territory or by its nationals or using its flag vessels or aircraft, lead and lead ore, and that all States shall prohibit the procurement of such items from the DPRK by their nationals, or using their flag vessels or aircraft, whether or not originating in the territory of the DPRK, and further *decides* that for sales and transactions of lead and lead ore for which written contracts have been finalized prior to the adoption of this resolution, all States may allow those shipments to be imported

into their territories up to 30 days from the date of adoption of this resolution with notification provided to the Committee containing details on those imports by no later than 45 days after the date of adoption of this resolution;

11. *Expresses concern* that DPRK nationals frequently work in other States for the purpose of generating foreign export earnings that the DPRK uses to support its prohibited nuclear and ballistic missile programs, *decides* that all Member States shall not exceed on any date after the date of adoption of this resolution the total number of work authorizations for DPRK nationals provided in their jurisdictions at the time of the adoption of this resolution . . .

Financial

12. *Decides* that States shall prohibit, by their nationals or in their territories, the opening of new joint ventures or cooperative entities with DPRK entities or individuals, or the expansion of existing joint ventures through additional investments, whether or not acting for or on behalf of the government of the DPRK, unless such joint ventures or cooperative entities have been approved by the Committee in advance on a case-by-case basis . . .

14. *Clarifies* that companies performing financial services commensurate with those provided by banks are considered financial institutions for the purposes of implementing paragraph 11 of resolution 2094 (2013), paragraphs 33 and 34 of resolution 2270 (2016), and paragraph 33 of resolution 2321 (2016);

Chemical Weapons

15. *Recalls* paragraph 24 of resolution 2270 (2016), *decides* that the DPRK shall not deploy or use chemical weapons, and *urgently calls upon* the DPRK to accede to the Convention on the Prohibition of the Development, Production, Stockpiling and Use of Chemical Weapons and Their Destruction, and then to immediately comply with its provisions . . .

Impact on the People of the DPRK

17. *Regrets* the DPRK's massive diversion of its scarce resources toward its development of nuclear weapons and a number of expensive ballistic missile programs, *notes* the findings of the United Nations Office for the Coordination of Humanitarian Assistance that well over half of the people in the DPRK suffer from major insecurities in food and medical care, including a very large number of pregnant and lactating women and under-five children who are at risk of malnutrition and nearly a quarter of its total population suffering from chronic malnutrition, and, in this context, *expresses* deep concern at the grave hardship to which the people in the DPRK are subjected;

[The Sanctions Implementation section, detailing how the sanctions included will be carried out and monitored, and the Political section, emphasizing the United Nation's ongoing concern surrounding the North Korean nuclear program, have been omitted.]

[Annexes I and II, listing the names of individuals and organizations added to the sanctions list, have been omitted.]

SOURCE: United Nations Security Council. "Resolution 2371 (2017)." August 5, 2017. http://www.un.org/ga/search/view_doc.asp?symbol=S/RES/2371%282017%29.

UN Limits Export of North Korean Products, Movement of North Korean Citizens

September 11, 2017

Resolution 2375 (2017)

Adopted by the Security Council at its 8042nd meeting, on 11 September 2017

The Security Council,

Recalling its previous relevant resolutions . . .

Reaffirming that proliferation of nuclear, chemical and biological weapons, as well as their means of delivery, constitutes a threat to international peace and security,

Expressing its gravest concern at the nuclear test by the Democratic People's Republic of Korea ("the DPRK") on September 2, 2017 . . .

Expressing its gravest concern that the DPRK's ongoing nuclear- and ballistic missile-related activities have destabilized the region and beyond, and *determining* that there continues to exist a clear threat to international peace and security,

Underscoring its concern that developments on the Korean Peninsula could have dangerous, large-scale regional security implications,

Underscoring its commitment to the sovereignty, territorial integrity, and political independence of all States in accordance with the Charter, and *recalling* the purposes and principles of the Charter of the United Nations,

Expressing also its desire for a peaceful and diplomatic solution to the situation, and *reiterating* its welcoming of efforts by Council members as well as other Member States to facilitate a peaceful and comprehensive solution through dialogue,

Underlining the need to ensure international peace and security, and ensure lasting stability in north-east Asia at large and to resolve the situation through peaceful, diplomatic and political means,

Acting under Chapter VII of the Charter of the United Nations, and taking measures under its Article 41,

1. *Condemns* in the strongest terms the nuclear test conducted by the DPRK on September 2 of 2017 in violation and flagrant disregard of the Security Council's resolutions;

2. *Reaffirms* its decisions that the DPRK shall not conduct any further launches that use ballistic missile technology, nuclear tests, or any other provocation; shall immediately suspend all activities related to its ballistic missile program and in this context re-establish its pre-existing commitments to a moratorium on all missile launches; shall immediately abandon all nuclear weapons and existing nuclear programs in a complete, verifiable and irreversible manner, and immediately cease all related activities; and shall abandon any other existing weapons of mass destruction and ballistic missile programs in a complete, verifiable and irreversible manner;

Designations

3. *Decides* that the measures specified in paragraph 8 (d) of resolution 1718 (2006) shall apply also to the individual and entities listed in Annex I and II of this resolution and to any individuals or entities acting on their behalf or at their direction, and to entities owned or controlled by them, including through illicit means, and *decides* further that the measures specified in paragraph 8 (e) of resolution 1718 (2006) shall also apply to the individual listed in Annex I of this resolution and to individuals acting on their behalf or at their direction; . . .

Maritime Interdiction of Cargo Vessels

7. *Calls upon* all Member States to inspect vessels with the consent of the flag State, on the high seas, if they have information that provides reasonable grounds to believe that the cargo of such vessels contains items the supply, sale, transfer or export . . .

9. *Requires* any Member State, when it does not receive the cooperation of a flag State of a vessel pursuant to paragraph 8 above, to submit promptly to the Committee a report containing relevant details regarding the incident, the vessel and the flag State, and *requests* the Committee to release on a regular basis information regarding these vessels and flag States involved . . .

11. *Decides* that all Member States shall prohibit their nationals, persons subject to their jurisdiction, entities incorporated in their territory or subject to their jurisdiction, and vessels flying their flag, from facilitating or engaging in ship-to-ship transfers to or from DPRK-flagged vessels of any goods or items that are being supplied, sold, or transferred to or from the DPRK . . .

Sectoral

13. *Decides* that all Member States shall prohibit the direct or indirect supply, sale or transfer to the DPRK, through their territories or by their nationals, or using their flag vessels or aircraft, and whether or not originating in their territories, of all condensates and natural gas liquids, and *decides* that the DPRK shall not procure such materials;

14. *Decides* that all Member States shall prohibit the direct or indirect supply, sale or transfer to the DPRK, through their territories or by their nationals, or using their flag vessels or aircraft, and whether or not originating in their territories, of all refined petroleum products, *decides* that the DPRK shall not procure such products, *decides* that this provision shall not apply with respect to procurement by the DPRK or the direct or indirect supply, sale or transfer to the DPRK, through their territories or by their nationals, or using their flag vessels or aircraft, and whether or not originating in their territories, of refined petroleum products in the amount of up to 500,000 barrels during an initial period of three months beginning on 1 October 2017 and ending on 31 December 2017 . . .

15. *Decides* that all Member States shall not supply, sell, or transfer to the DPRK in any period of twelve months after the date of adoption of this resolution an amount of crude oil that is in excess of the amount that the Member State supplied, sold or transferred in the period of twelve months prior to adoption of this resolution, unless the Committee approves in advance on a case-by-case basis a shipment of crude oil is exclusively for livelihood purposes of DPRK nationals and unrelated to the DPRK's nuclear or ballistic missile programmes or other activities . . .

16. *Decides* that the DPRK shall not supply, sell or transfer, directly or indirectly, from its territory or by its nationals or using its flag vessels or aircraft, textiles (including but not limited to fabrics and partially or fully completed apparel products), and that all States shall prohibit the procurement of such items from the DPRK by their nationals, or using their flag vessels or aircraft, whether or not originating in the territory of the DPRK, unless the Committee approves on a case-by-case basis in advance . . .

17. *Decides* that all Member States shall not provide work authorizations for DPRK nationals in their jurisdictions in connection with admission to their territories unless the Committee determines on a case-by-case basis in advance that employment of DPRK nationals in a member state's jurisdiction is required for the delivery of humanitarian assistance, denuclearization or any other purpose consistent with the objectives of resolutions 1718 (2006), 1874 (2009), 2087 (2013), 2094 (2013), 2270 (2016), 2321 (2016), 2356 (2017), 2371 (2017), or this resolution . . .

Joint Ventures

18. *Decides* that States shall prohibit, by their nationals or in their territories, the opening, maintenance, and operation of all joint ventures or cooperative entities, new and existing, with DPRK entities or individuals, whether or not acting for or on behalf of the government of the DPRK, unless such joint ventures or cooperative entities, in particular those that are non-commercial, public utility infrastructure projects not generating profit, have been approved by the Committee in advance on a case-by-case basis . . .

Sanctions Implementation

19. *Decides* that Member States shall report to the Security Council within ninety days of the adoption of this resolution, and thereafter upon request by the Committee,

on concrete measures they have taken in order to implement effectively the provisions of this resolution . . .

20. *Calls upon* all Member States to redouble efforts to implement in full the measures in resolutions 1718 (2006), 1874 (2009), 2087 (2013), 2094 (2013), 2270 (2016), 2321 (2016), 2356 (2017), 2371 (2017), and this resolution and to cooperate with each other in doing so, particularly with respect to inspecting, detecting and seizing items the transfer of which is prohibited by these resolutions . . .

22. *Decides* to authorize all Member States to, and that all Member States shall, seize and dispose . . . of items the supply, sale, transfer, or export of which is prohibited by resolutions 1718 (2006), 1874 (2009), 2087 (2013), 2094 (2013), 2270 (2016), 2321 (2016), 2356 (2017), 2371 (2017), or this resolution that are identified in inspections, in a manner that is not inconsistent with their obligations under applicable Security Council resolutions . . .

[The Political section, outlining ongoing concern and monitoring of North Korea's nuclear program, has been omitted.]

[Annexes I and II, listing the names of individuals and businesses targeted for sanctions, have been omitted.]

SOURCE: United Nations Security Council. "Resolution 2375 (2017)." September 11, 2017. https://www.un.org/ga/search/view_doc.asp?symbol=S/RES/2375%282017%29.

President Trump Issues Executive Order Expanding Sanctions against North Korea

DOCUMENT

September 21, 2017

. . . I, DONALD J. TRUMP, President of the United States of America, find that:

The provocative, destabilizing, and repressive actions and policies of the Government of North Korea, including its intercontinental ballistic missile launches of July 3 and July 28, 2017, and its nuclear test of September 2, 2017, each of which violated its obligations under numerous UNSCRs and contravened its commitments under the September 19, 2005, Joint Statement of the Six-Party Talks; its commission of serious human rights abuses; and its use of funds generated through international trade to support its nuclear and missile programs and weapons proliferation, constitute a continuing threat to the national security, foreign policy, and economy of the United States, and a disturbance of the international relations of the United States.

In order to take further steps with respect to the national emergency declared in Executive Order 13466 of June 26, 2008, as modified in scope by and relied upon for additional steps in subsequent Executive Orders, I hereby find, determine, and order:

Section 1. (a) All property and interests in property that are in the United States, that hereafter come within the United States, or that are or hereafter come within the possession or control of any United States person of the following persons are blocked and may not be transferred, paid, exported, withdrawn, or otherwise dealt in:

Any person determined by the Secretary of the Treasury, in consultation with the Secretary of State:

    (i)   to operate in the construction, energy, financial services, fishing, information technology, manufacturing, medical, mining, textiles, or transportation industries in North Korea;

   (ii)   to own, control, or operate any port in North Korea, including any seaport, airport, or land port of entry;

  (iii)   to have engaged in at least one significant importation from or exportation to North Korea of any goods, services, or technology;

  (iv)   to be a North Korean person, including a North Korean person that has engaged in commercial activity that generates revenue for the Government of North Korea or the Workers' Party of Korea; (v) to have materially assisted, sponsored, or provided financial, material, or technological support for, or goods or services to or in support of, any person whose property and interests in property are blocked pursuant to this order; or

  (vi)   to be owned or controlled by, or to have acted or purported to act for or on behalf of, directly or indirectly, any person whose property and interests in property are blocked pursuant to this order.

(b)   The prohibitions in subsection (a) of this section apply except to the extent provided by statutes, or in regulations, orders, directives, or licenses that may be issued pursuant to this order, and notwithstanding any contract entered into or any license or permit granted before the effective date of this order. The prohibitions in subsection (a) of this section are in addition to export control authorities implemented by the Department of Commerce.

(c)   I hereby determine that the making of donations of the types of articles specified in section 203(b)(2) of IEEPA (50 U.S.C. 1702(b)(2)) by, to, or for the benefit of any person whose property and interests in property are blocked pursuant to subsection (a) of this section would seriously impair my ability to deal with the national emergency declared in Executive Order 13466, and I hereby prohibit such donations as provided by subsection (a) of this section.

(d)   The prohibitions in subsection (a) of this section include:

    (i)   the making of any contribution or provision of funds, goods, or services by, to, or for the benefit of any person whose property and interests in property are blocked pursuant to subsection (a) of this section; and

   (ii)   the receipt of any contribution or provision of funds, goods, or services from any such person.

Sec. 2. (a) No aircraft in which a foreign person has an interest that has landed at a place in North Korea may land at a place in the United States within 180 days after departure from North Korea.

(b) No vessel in which a foreign person has an interest that has called at a port in North Korea within the previous 180 days, and no vessel in which a foreign person has an interest that has engaged in a ship-to-ship transfer with such a vessel within the previous 180 days, may call at a port in the United States.

(c) The prohibitions in subsections (a) and (b) of this section apply except to the extent provided by statutes, or in regulations, orders, directives, or licenses that may be issued pursuant to this order, and notwithstanding any contract entered into or any license or permit granted before the effective date of this order.

Sec. 3. (a) All funds that are in the United States, that hereafter come within the United States, or that are or hereafter come within the possession or control of any United States person and that originate from, are destined for, or pass through a foreign bank account that has been determined by the Secretary of the Treasury to be owned or controlled by a North Korean person, or to have been used to transfer funds in which any North Korean person has an interest, are blocked and may not be transferred, paid, exported, withdrawn, or otherwise dealt in.

(b) No United States person, wherever located, may approve, finance, facilitate, or guarantee a transaction by a foreign person where the transaction by that foreign person would be prohibited by subsection (a) of this section if performed by a United States person or within the United States.

(c) The prohibitions in subsections (a) and (b) of this section apply except to the extent provided by statutes, or in regulations, orders, directives, or licenses that may be issued pursuant to this order, and notwithstanding any contract entered into or any license or permit granted before the effective date of this order.

Sec. 4. (a) The Secretary of the Treasury, in consultation with the Secretary of State, is hereby authorized to impose on a foreign financial institution the sanctions described in subsection (b) of this section upon determining that the foreign financial institution has, on or after the effective date of this order:

  (i) knowingly conducted or facilitated any significant transaction on behalf of any person whose property and interests in property are blocked pursuant to Executive Order 13551 of August 30, 2010, Executive Order 13687 of January 2, 2015, Executive Order 13722 of March 15, 2016, or this order, or of any person whose property and interests in property are blocked pursuant to Executive Order 13382 in connection with North Korea-related activities; or

  (ii) knowingly conducted or facilitated any significant transaction in connection with trade with North Korea.

(b) With respect to any foreign financial institution determined by the Secretary of the Treasury, in consultation with the Secretary of State, in accordance with this section to meet the criteria set forth in subsection (a)(i) or (a)(ii) of this section, the Secretary of the Treasury may:

  (i) prohibit the opening and prohibit or impose strict conditions on the maintenance of correspondent accounts or payable-through accounts in the United States; or

(ii)   block all property and interests in property that are in the United States, that hereafter come within the United States, or that are or hereafter come within the possession or control of any United States person of such foreign financial institution, and provide that such property and interests in property may not be transferred, paid, exported, withdrawn, or otherwise dealt in.

(c)   The prohibitions in subsection (b) of this section apply except to the extent provided by statutes, or in regulations, orders, directives, or licenses that may be issued pursuant to this order, and notwithstanding any contract entered into or any license or permit granted before the effective date of this order.

(d)   I hereby determine that the making of donations of the types of articles specified in section 203(b)(2) of IEEPA (50 U.S.C. 1702(b)(2)) by, to, or for the benefit of any person whose property and interests in property are blocked pursuant to subsection (b)(ii) of this section would seriously impair my ability to deal with the national emergency declared in Executive Order 13466, and I hereby prohibit such donations as provided by subsection (b)(ii) of this section.

(e)   The prohibitions in subsection (b)(ii) of this section include:

(i)   the making of any contribution or provision of funds, goods, or services by, to, or for the benefit of any person whose property and interests in property are blocked pursuant to subsection (b)(ii) of this section; and (ii) the receipt of any contribution or provision of funds, goods, or services from any such person.

Sec. 5. The unrestricted immigrant and nonimmigrant entry into the United States of aliens determined to meet one or more of the criteria in section 1(a) of this order would be detrimental to the interests of the United States, and the entry of such persons into the United States, as immigrants or nonimmigrants, is therefore hereby suspended. Such persons shall be treated as persons covered by section 1 of Proclamation 8693 of July 24, 2011 (Suspension of Entry of Aliens Subject to United Nations Security Council Travel Bans and International Emergency Economic Powers Act Sanctions).

Sec. 6. (a) Any transaction that evades or avoids, has the purpose of evading or avoiding, causes a violation of, or attempts to violate any of the prohibitions set forth in this order is prohibited.

(b)   Any conspiracy formed to violate any of the prohibitions set forth in this order is prohibited.

Sec. 7. Nothing in this order shall prohibit transactions for the conduct of the official business of the Federal Government or the United Nations (including its specialized agencies, programmes, funds, and related organizations) by employees, grantees, or contractors thereof.

[Section 8, providing definitions for terms outlined in the order, has been omitted.]

Sec. 9. For those persons whose property and interests in property are blocked pursuant to this order who might have a constitutional presence in the United States, I find that because of the ability to transfer funds or other assets instantaneously, prior notice to such persons of measures to be taken pursuant to this order would render those measures ineffectual. I therefore determine that for these measures to be effective in addressing the national emergency declared in Executive Order 13466, there need be no prior notice of a listing or determination made pursuant to this order . . . .

DONALD J. TRUMP
The White House,
September 21, 2017.

SOURCE: Executive Office of the President. "Executive Order 13810—Imposing Additional Sanctions with Respect to North Korea." September 21, 2017. *Compilation of Presidential Documents* 2017, no. 00675 (September 21, 2017). https://www.gpo.gov/fdsys/pkg/DCPD-201700675/pdf/DCPD-201700675.pdf.

OTHER HISTORIC DOCUMENTS OF INTEREST

FROM PREVIOUS *HISTORIC DOCUMENTS*

House and Senate Vote on Affordable Care Act Repeal

MARCH 24, JULY 20 AND 28, AND OCTOBER 12, 2017

On March 23, 2010, then-President Barack Obama signed into law the Patient Protection and Affordable Care Act (ACA), also known as Obamacare. Since then, the law had faced stiff criticism and political attacks from Republicans who promised to repeal and replace the landmark legislation. Republicans had their best chance to do so following the 2016 election, when they took control of Congress and the White House, but the effort proved harder than expected. An organized opposition spearheaded by activists, advocates, medical industry professionals, and Democrats kept the effort's potentially negative impact at the forefront of the debate. In conjunction, factions in the House Republican caucus, a seemingly disinterested president, and a slim Senate majority threatened to sink the health care repeal effort before it got off the ground. House Speaker Paul Ryan, R-Wis., led the charge, pushing through and then pulling from the floor the American Health Care Act (AHCA). Despite eventual passage of the AHCA, the ACA proved resilient as the Senate was unable to pass its own bill—the Better Care Reconciliation Act (BCRA) and the two chambers could not reach a consensus. Despite a decision by Republican leadership to move the health care repeal effort to the backburner, President Donald Trump forged ahead with an executive order to begin altering key provisions of the ACA.

HOUSE REPEAL EFFORT STALLS BUT CLEARS A KEY HURDLE

When the ACA was signed into law in 2010, it promised to increase access to health insurance for low income Americans. Since its initial debate in Congress, the law faced criticism from Republicans who promised to work to eliminate the law. But with a Democrat in the White House, Republican repeal efforts never seriously threatened the ACA. That calculus changed with the 2016 election; with the backing of President Trump, Speaker Ryan, and Senate Majority Leader Mitch McConnell, R-Ken., Republicans finally moved ahead with their chief campaign promise: repealing and replacing Obamacare.

On January 10, 2017, just days before his inauguration, Trump set down a marker for Congressional Republicans: repeal Obamacare "sometime next week." "We have to get to business," he said, adding, "Obamacare has been a catastrophic event." Specifically, Trump called on Congress to pass a bill that would repeal and simultaneously replace the ACA, rather than repealing the law and later seeking a replacement. Two months later, Republicans unveiled the first effort of the 115th Congress to repeal and replace Obamacare. The AHCA was primarily aimed at repealing several key provisions of the ACA and cutting federal funding for health care, including curtailing government spending on other health care programs, including Medicare.

Critics of AHCA focused on the bill's overall impact on the American health insurance marketplace. Democrats, doctors, health insurance companies, medical professionals, and consumer advocates, among others, argued that the bill would increase the number of uninsured and cut millions of dollars from programs for low income Americans. The non-partisan Congressional Budget Office (CBO) score reinforced these criticisms, projecting that the AHCA would increase the number of uninsured people by 23 million over ten years, decrease the federal budget deficit by $119 billion during that period mainly by cutting Medicaid coverage for lower income Americans, and cut taxes largely for the wealthy. Congressional Republicans were also criticized for their approach to drafting the AHCA with an unprecedented level of secrecy, raising bipartisan alarms about transparency. Negatively impacting the bill's prospects, several prominent Republicans publicly spoke out against the bill; three Republicans from the conservative Freedom Caucus voted against it in committee. Despite mounting pressure, Republicans moved forward with their bill.

On March 24, Congressional leaders scheduled a vote on the AHCA only to pull it from the floor amid pressure from the party's more conservative members. At a press conference to announce that the bill would not be put to a vote on the House floor, Speaker Ryan laid blame at "growing pains" as the Republican caucus transitioned from an opposition party to a governing party. "This is a setback. No two ways about it," Speaker Ryan said. "But it is not the end of the story. Because I know that every man and woman in this conference is now motivated more than ever to step up our game to deliver on our promises." Speaker Ryan added, "Obamacare is the law of the land" and will remain so "for the foreseeable future."

From the White House, President Trump echoed Speaker Ryan's sentiments and argued that Obamacare was failing. "I've been saying for the last year and a half that the best thing we can do politically speaking is let Obamacare explode," President Trump said, adding that Democrats should support efforts to fix Obamacare. "I honestly believe the Democrats will come to us and say, look, let's get together and get a great health care bill or plan that's really great for the people of our country. And I think that's going to happen." He refused to blame the Republican caucus or its leadership, only mentioning that he was "disappointed" in more intransigent caucus members. "I'm a little surprised, to be honest with you. We really had it. It was pretty much there within grasp. But I'll tell you what's going to come out of it is a better bill."

Despite this initial setback, Republicans continued to focus on repealing and replacing Obamacare. Two months after the initial failure of the AHCA, House Republicans announced that they had amended the bill to include additional funding to subsidize insurance for individuals with preexisting conditions. On May 4, 2017, the House voted in favor of repealing the ACA and passing the AHCA by a 217–213 vote. Republicans were quickly bussed from Capitol Hill to the Rose Garden at the White House to celebrate their legislative victory.

Senate Drafts, Debates the BCRA

While House Republicans celebrated, Senate Republicans began drafting their own repeal legislation that they hoped would prove easier to pass than the House companion bill. To sidestep a Democratic filibuster, which would require a sixty-vote threshold to defeat, Senate Republicans announced their intention to use the budget reconciliation process to pass Obamacare. The reconciliation process would allow the chamber to pass legislation with a simple majority but placed strict limits on what could and could not pass. Senate leaders said they would not take up the AHCA but instead draft similar legislation that, while focused on repealing the ACA, sought to include more funding for health insurance subsidies and maintain funding for Medicare and opioid substance abuse prevention. However, a constant with the House and Senate efforts was the secretive process.

Sen. McConnell entrusted thirteen male Republican senators to begin drafting the bill outside of public view. A bipartisan chorus of critics railed against efforts to transform the American health care system and a sixth of the U.S. economy without a single hearing or an open drafting session, while key Republican female senators criticized the proposed cuts to women's health care without a female voice on the drafting committee. "I've said from Day 1, and I'll say it again," said Republican Sen. Bob Corker, R-Tenn., "the process is better if you do it in public, and that people get buy-in along the way and understand what's going on. Obviously, that's not the route that is being taken." Democrats were more pointed. "They're ashamed of the bill," Senate Minority Leader Chuck Schumer, D-N.Y., said. "If they liked the bill, they'd have brass bands marching down the middle of small-town America saying what a great bill it is. But they know it isn't," Schumer remarked.

Adding to the pressure, President Trump began to distance himself from his own party's repeal efforts. While past presidents have spent their political capital to push their legislative priorities—reaching millions from the bully pulpit, hosting town halls, lobbying representatives on Capitol Hill, and inviting key senators to dinner—Trump was more disengaged from the legislative process. He even derided the House repeal as "mean" despite hosting a Rose Garden ceremony to celebrate the same bill.

Senate leadership unveiled their first version of the BCRA on June 22 and tentatively scheduled a floor vote for the following week. Among the proposed changes, BCRA would repeal Obamacare's individual mandate that required each American to have health insurance or pay a penalty, drastically cut back federal support of Medicaid, and eliminate taxes on the wealthy and health insurers. Several key conservative Republican senators—Rand Paul, R-Ken., Ted Cruz, R-Texas, Ron Johnson, R-Wis., and Mike Lee, R-Utah—announced their opposition while swing Republican votes including Sens. Dean Heller, R-Nev., and Susan Collins, R-Maine, also initially withheld support. The opposition led to repeated delays in bringing the bill for a vote, and Republican leaders walked a fine line, attempting to appease hardline conservative voices such as Cruz and Lee, who demanded a full repeal, while also maintaining funding for subsidies, Medicaid, and women's health care to win the votes of more moderate senators. Ultimately, Senate Republicans could not reconcile their differences. BCRA was pulled from the Senate floor just five days after McConnell announced it.

A second, slightly revised version of BCRA found a similar fate a month later. Sens. Collins and Paul announced their intention to oppose the bill and vote to block debate on July 25. A week later, Sens. Mike Lee, R-Utah, and Jerry Moran, R-Kan., said they too would block a vote to proceed, explaining that the bill did not go far enough to roll back regulations and taxes imposed by the ACA. Once again, Republican leaders were unable to whip their caucus, leaving Obamacare in place.

Obamacare Repeal Efforts Come to an End

Despite the embarrassing setback and revolt in his caucus, McConnell pressed forward with repeal efforts. First, Senate leaders pushed the Obamacare Repeal and Reconciliation Act, also known as the "partial repeal," which would eliminate the ACA's coverage provisions, including the individual mandate and Medicaid expansion, while leaving in place insurance market reforms. As estimated by the CBO, 32 million people would lose their health insurance by 2026, the most of any of the Republican proposals, and the bill failed a simple majority vote.

On July 27, Republican leaders unveiled another proposal: the "skinny repeal." They made no changes to the Medicaid program, but eliminated the ACA's insurance regulations and lowered premiums. The CBO estimated that 16 million fewer Americans would have health insurance in 2026 and premiums would be roughly 20 percent higher, compared to current law. Senate leaders believed this effort, while a more modest proposal, proved the most likely to proceed.

In the early hours of July 28, the Senate began voting on the scaled-down plan. Sens. Collins and Lisa Murkowski, R-Alaska, voted against the bill, citing opposition to deep cuts to women's health care. However, Senate leaders remained confident they had the necessary votes. As the Senate parliamentarian announced the votes, Sen. McCain, who had just returned to the Senate after receiving a diagnosis of brain cancer, walked onto the Senate floor, turned to the parliamentarian, and gave a thumb down gesture, casting the decisive vote to defeat the Senate proposal. The bill failed 49–51.

Sen. McCain, one of the most senior Republican senators, explained in a statement that his decision rested on two issues: that the repeal effort was not meaningful reform and that the Senate broke "regular order" in pushing their efforts. "From the beginning, I have believed that Obamacare should be repealed and replaced with a solution that increases competition, lowers costs, and improves care for the American people. The so-called 'skinny repeal' amendment the Senate voted on today would not accomplish those goals," McCain said. "We must now return to the correct way of legislating and send the bill back to committee, hold hearings, receive input from both sides of the aisle, heed the recommendations of nation's governors, and produce a bill that finally delivers affordable health care for the American people."

President Trump Takes Action on ACA

After McCain's "no" vote, Republican Congressional leaders announced that their caucus would shelve the health care repeal effort and move on to reforming the tax code. President Trump, however, took matters into his own hands, announcing on Twitter on October 10, "Since Congress can't get its act together on HealthCare, I will be using the power of the pen to give great HealthCare to many people—FAST." Trump followed his tweet with an October 12 executive order he billed as "Obamacare relief" that would bring affordable health insurance coverage to millions more Americans. The executive order directed federal agencies to work toward finding methods to introduce more competition and choice into the health insurance market. Trump cited the possibility of allowing individuals or small businesses to purchase group health insurance through associations, or allowing the possibility of purchasing health coverage across state lines. Americans would also be able to purchase short-term health insurance plans that do not have to comply with some Obamacare policies, namely, the requirement to offer insurance to those with preexisting conditions. This allows an insurance company to offer lower priced plans, which are typically attractive to younger, healthier Americans. To this point, concerns were raised that such an offer would siphon younger Americans out of larger insurance pools and drastically raise prices for those who are sick or have preexisting conditions. Most notably, however, Trump called for the end of insurance subsidies used by many Americans to help offset the cost of care.

While Trump has the power to offer or amend direction, he cannot alone dismantle laws such as Obamacare through an executive order and would still require the assistance of Congress to enact more reforms. On October 17, a bipartisan group of senators announced that they had agreed in principle to reinstate the subsidy payments for at least two years. While encouraging Congress to continue working to fully repeal Obamacare, the president did offer support to what he called a "short-term solution" in the Senate. Ultimately, the biggest blow to Obamacare came in December, when the House and Senate passed a tax overhaul plan that eliminated the law's individual mandate—requiring all Americans to have health insurance or pay a penalty—starting in 2019.

—Robert Howard

Following are the text of remarks from President Donald Trump on March 24, 2017, regarding health care reform legislation; March 24, 2017, remarks from House Speaker Paul Ryan, R-Wis., on health care reform legislation; a July 20, 2017, statement from President Trump calling on the Senate to pass health care reform legislation; a statement from Sen. John McCain, R-Ariz., on July 28, 2017, regarding his "no" vote on health care reform; and an October 12, 2017, executive order offering direction on amending the ACA.

DOCUMENT

President Trump Addresses Health Care Reform Efforts

March 24, 2017

Thank you very much. We were very close, and it was a very, very tight margin. We had no Democrat support. We had no votes from the Democrats. They weren't going to give us a single vote, so it's a very difficult thing to do.

I've been saying for the last year and a half that the best thing we can do, politically speaking, is let Obamacare explode. It is exploding right now. It's—many States have big problems—almost all States have big problems. I was in Tennessee the other day, and they've lost half of their State in terms of an insurer; they have no insurer. And that's happening to many other places. I was in Kentucky the other day, and similar things are happening.

So Obamacare is exploding. With no Democrat support, we couldn't quite get there. We're just a very small number of votes short in terms of getting our bill passed. Lot of people don't realize how good our bill was because they were viewing phase one. But when you add phase two—which was mostly the signings of Secretary Price, who's behind me—and you add phase three, which I think we would have gotten—it became a great bill. Premiums would have gone down, and it would have been very stable, it would have been very strong. But that's okay.

But we were very, very close. And again, I think what will happen is Obamacare, unfortunately, will explode. It's going to have a very bad year. Last year, you had over a hundred percent increases in various places. In Arizona, I understand it's going up very rapidly again like it did last year; last year it was 116 percent. Many places, 50, 60, 70 percent, I guess it averaged—whatever the average was—very, very high. And this year should be much worse for Obamacare.

So what would be really good, with no Democrat support, if the Democrats, when it explodes—which it will soon—if they got together with us and got a real health care bill. I'd be totally open to it. And I think that's going to happen. I think the losers are Nancy

Pelosi and Chuck Schumer because now they own Obamacare. They own it—hundred percent own it.

And this is not a Republican health care, this is not anything but a Democrat health care. And they have Obamacare for a little while longer, until it ceases to exist, which it will at some point in the near future. And just remember: This is not our bill, this is their bill.

Now, when they all become civilized and get together and try and work out a great health care bill for the people of this country, we're open to it. We're totally open to it.

I want to thank the Republican Party. I want to thank Paul Ryan; he worked very, very hard, I will tell you that. He worked very, very hard. Tom Price and Mike Pence—who's right here—our Vice President, our great Vice President. Everybody worked hard. I worked as a team player and would have loved to have seen it passed. But again, I think you know I was very clear, because I think there wasn't a speech I made, or very few, where I didn't mention that perhaps the best thing that can happen is exactly what happened today, because we'll end up with a truly great health care bill in the future, after this mess known as Obamacare explodes.

So I want to thank everybody for being here. It will go very smoothly, I really believe. I think this is something—it certainly was an interesting period of time. We all learned a lot. We learned a lot about loyalty. We learned a lot about the vote-getting process. We learned a lot about some very arcane rules in, obviously, both the Senate and in the House. So it's been—certainly for me, it's been a very interesting experience. But in the end, I think it's going to be an experience that leads to an even better health care plan. So thank you all very much. And I'll see you soon.

[The question and answer section with members of the media has been omitted.]

SOURCE: Executive Office of the President. "Remarks on Health Care Reform Legislation and an Exchange With Reporters." March 24, 2017. *Compilation of Presidential Documents* 2017, no. 00196 (March 24, 2017). https://www.gpo.gov/fdsys/pkg/DCPD-201700196/pdf/DCPD-201700196.pdf.

House Speaker Ryan Remarks on Inability to Pass ACA Repeal

DOCUMENT

March 24, 2017

Today, House Speaker Paul Ryan (R-WI) delivered the following remarks on the American Health Care Act:

"You've all heard me say this before: Moving from an opposition party to a governing party comes with growing pains. And well, we're feeling those growing pains today.

"We came really close today, but we came up short. I spoke to the president just a little while ago, and I told him the best thing that I think to do is to pull this bill, and he agreed with that decision. I will not sugar coat this: This is a disappointing day for us. Doing big things is hard. All of us. All of us—myself included—we will need time to reflect on how we got to this moment, what we could have done to do it better.

"But ultimately, this all kind of comes down to a choice. Are all of us willing to give a little to get something done? Are we willing to say yes to the good—to the very good—even if it's not the perfect? Because if we're willing to do that, we still have such an incredible opportunity in front of us.

"There remains so much that we can do to help improve people's lives. And we will.

"Because, I got to tell you, that's why I'm here. And I know it's why every member of this conference is here: to make this a better country. We want American families to feel more confident in their lot in life. We want the next generation to know that, yes, the best days of this country are still ahead of us.

"I'm really proud of the bill that we produced. It would make a dramatic improvement in our health care system and provide relief to people hurting under Obamacare. And what's probably most troubling is the worst is yet to come with Obamacare.

"I'm also proud of the long, inclusive, member-driven process that we had. Any member who wanted to engage constructively, to offer ideas, to improve this bill, they could. And I want to thank so many members who helped make this bill better. A lot of our members put a lot of hard work into this.

"I also want to thank the president, I want to thank the vice president, I want to thank Tom Price, Mick Mulvaney, and the entire White House team. The president gave his all in this effort. He did everything he possibly could to help people see the opportunity that we have with this bill. He's really been fantastic.

"Still, we have to do better. And we will. I absolutely believe that. This is a setback. No two ways about it. But it is not the end of this story.

"Because I know that every man and woman in this conference is now motivated more than ever to step up our game. To deliver on our promises. I know that every one is committed to seizing this incredible opportunity that we have. And I sure am."

SOURCE: Office of Speaker Paul Ryan. "Speaker Ryan's Remarks from Today's Press Conference." March 24, 2017. http://www.speaker.gov/press-release/speaker-ryans-remarks-todays-press-conference.

President Trump Calls on Senate to Pass Health Care Legislation

July 20, 2017

Yesterday, I met with Republican Senators at the White House and told them that now is the time for action. Obamacare was a big lie. "You can keep your doctor"—lie. "You can keep your plan"—lie. Now, people are hurting, and inaction is not an option. We must repeal and replace this disaster. The Senate should not leave for summer recess until it has passed a plan to give our people great healthcare. I'm ready to act; I have pen in hand. I'll sign the legislation into law, and then we can celebrate for the American people.

SOURCE: Executive Office of the President. "Statement on Health Care Reform Legislation." July 20, 2017. *Compilation of Presidential Documents* 2017, no. 00484 (July 20, 2017). https://www.gpo.gov/fdsys/pkg/DCPD-201700484/pdf/DCPD-201700484.pdf.

Sen. McCain Votes "No" on Health Care Reform

DOCUMENT

July 28, 2017

U.S. Senator John McCain (R-AZ) released the following statement today on voting "no" on the so-called "skinny repeal" of Obamacare:

"From the beginning, I have believed that Obamacare should be repealed and replaced with a solution that increases competition, lowers costs, and improves care for the American people. The so-called 'skinny repeal' amendment the Senate voted on today would not accomplish those goals. While the amendment would have repealed some of Obamacare's most burdensome regulations, it offered no replacement to actually reform our health care system and deliver affordable, quality health care to our citizens. The Speaker's statement that the House would be 'willing' to go to conference does not ease my concern that this shell of a bill could be taken up and passed at any time.

"I've stated time and time again that one of the major failures of Obamacare was that it was rammed through Congress by Democrats on a strict-party line basis without a single Republican vote. We should not make the mistakes of the past that has led to Obamacare's collapse, including in my home state of Arizona where premiums are skyrocketing and health care providers are fleeing the marketplace. We must now return to the correct way of legislating and send the bill back to committee, hold hearings, receive input from both sides of aisle, heed the recommendations of nation's governors, and produce a bill that finally delivers affordable health care for the American people. We must do the hard work our citizens expect of us and deserve."

SOURCE: Office of Senator John McCain. "Statement by Senator John McCain on Voting 'No' on 'Skinny Repeal.'" July 28, 2017. https://www.mccain.senate.gov/public/index.cfm/press-releases?ID=A952CCCA-66D2-4570-9D57-514561BF3D4D.

President Trump Issues Executive Order on ACA

DOCUMENT

October 12, 2017

By the authority vested in me as President by the Constitution and the laws of the United States of America, it is hereby ordered as follows:

Section 1. Policy. (a) It shall be the policy of the executive branch, to the extent consistent with law, to facilitate the purchase of insurance across State lines and the development and operation of a healthcare system that provides high-quality care at affordable prices for the American people. The Patient Protection and Affordable

Care Act (PPACA), however, has severely limited the choice of healthcare options available to many Americans and has produced large premium increases in many State individual markets for health insurance. The average exchange premium in the 39 States that are using www.healthcare.gov in 2017 is more than double the average overall individual market premium recorded in 2013. The PPACA has also largely failed to provide meaningful choice or competition between insurers, resulting in one-third of America's counties having only one insurer offering coverage on their applicable government-run exchange in 2017.

(b) Among the myriad areas where current regulations limit choice and competition, my Administration will prioritize three areas for improvement in the near term: association health plans (AHPs), short-term, limited-duration insurance (STLDI), and health reimbursement arrangements (HRAs).

    (i) Large employers often are able to obtain better terms on health insurance for their employees than small employers because of their larger pools of insurable individuals across which they can spread risk and administrative costs. Expanding access to AHPs can help small businesses overcome this competitive disadvantage by allowing them to group together to self-insure or purchase large group health insurance. Expanding access to AHPs will also allow more small businesses to avoid many of the PPACA's costly requirements. Expanding access to AHPs would provide more affordable health insurance options to many Americans, including hourly wage earners, farmers, and the employees of small businesses and entrepreneurs that fuel economic growth.

    (ii) STLDI is exempt from the onerous and expensive insurance mandates and regulations included in title I of the PPACA. This can make it an appealing and affordable alternative to government-run exchanges for many people without coverage available to them through their workplaces. The previous administration took steps to restrict access to this market by reducing the allowable coverage period from less than 12 months to less than 3 months and by preventing any extensions selected by the policyholder beyond 3 months of total coverage.

    (iii) HRAs are tax-advantaged, account-based arrangements that employers can establish for employees to give employees more flexibility and choices regarding their healthcare. Expanding the flexibility and use of HRAs would provide many Americans, including employees who work at small businesses, with more options for financing their healthcare.

(c) My Administration will also continue to focus on promoting competition in healthcare markets and limiting excessive consolidation throughout the healthcare system. To the extent consistent with law, government rules and guidelines affecting the United States healthcare system should:

    (i) expand the availability of and access to alternatives to expensive, mandate-laden PPACA insurance, including AHPs, STLDI, and HRAs;

    (ii) re-inject competition into healthcare markets by lowering barriers to entry, limiting excessive consolidation, and preventing abuses of market power; and

(iii) improve access to and the quality of information that Americans need to make informed healthcare decisions, including data about healthcare prices and outcomes, while minimizing reporting burdens on affected plans, providers, or payers.

Sec. 2. Expanded Access to Association Health Plans. Within 60 days of the date of this order, the Secretary of Labor shall consider proposing regulations or revising guidance, consistent with law, to expand access to health coverage by allowing more employers to form AHPs. To the extent permitted by law and supported by sound policy, the Secretary should consider expanding the conditions that satisfy the commonality-of-interest requirements under current Department of Labor advisory opinions interpreting the definition of an "employer" under section 3(5) of the Employee Retirement Income Security Act of 1974. The Secretary of Labor should also consider ways to promote AHP formation on the basis of common geography or industry.

Sec. 3. Expanded Availability of Short-Term, Limited-Duration Insurance. Within 60 days of the date of this order, the Secretaries of the Treasury, Labor, and Health and Human Services shall consider proposing regulations or revising guidance, consistent with law, to expand the availability of STLDI. To the extent permitted by law and supported by sound policy, the Secretaries should consider allowing such insurance to cover longer periods and be renewed by the consumer.

Sec. 4. Expanded Availability and Permitted Use of Health Reimbursement Arrangements. Within 120 days of the date of this order, the Secretaries of the Treasury, Labor, and Health and Human Services shall consider proposing regulations or revising guidance, to the extent permitted by law and supported by sound policy, to increase the usability of HRAs, to expand employers' ability to offer HRAs to their employees, and to allow HRAs to be used in conjunction with nongroup coverage.

Sec. 5. Public Comment. The Secretaries shall consider and evaluate public comments on any regulations proposed under sections 2 through 4 of this order.

Sec. 6. Reports. Within 180 days of the date of this order, and every 2 years thereafter, the Secretary of Health and Human Services, in consultation with the Secretaries of the Treasury and Labor and the Federal Trade Commission, shall provide a report to the President that:

(a) details the extent to which existing State and Federal laws, regulations, guidance, requirements, and policies fail to conform to the policies set forth in section 1 of this order; and

(b) identifies actions that States or the Federal Government could take in furtherance of the policies set forth in section 1 of this order.

Sec. 7. General Provisions. (a) Nothing in this order shall be construed to impair or otherwise affect:

(i) the authority granted by law to an executive department or agency, or the head thereof; or

(ii) the functions of the Director of the Office of Management and Budget relating to budgetary, administrative, or legislative proposals.

(b) This order shall be implemented consistent with applicable law and subject to the availability of appropriations.

(c) This order is not intended to, and does not, create any right or benefit, substantive or procedural, enforceable at law or in equity by any party against the United States, its departments, agencies, or entities, its officers, employees, or agents, or any other person.

DONALD J. TRUMP
The White House,
October 12, 2017.

SOURCE: Executive Office of the President. "Executive Order 13813—Promoting Healthcare Choice and Competition across the United States." October 12, 2017. *Compilation of Presidential Documents* 2017, no. 00742 (October 12, 2017). https://www.gpo.gov/fdsys/pkg/DCPD-201700742/pdf/DCPD-201700742.pdf.

OTHER HISTORIC DOCUMENTS OF INTEREST

FROM THIS VOLUME

- President Trump Addresses a Joint Session of Congress; Democratic Response, p. 140

FROM PREVIOUS HISTORIC DOCUMENTS

- Donald Trump Elected U.S. President, *2016*, p. 612
- Supreme Court Upholds Affordable Care Act Subsidies, *2015*, p. 293
- Supreme Court Rules on Affordable Care Act, *2012*, p. 292
- Health Care Reform Signed into Law, *2010*, p. 83

British Prime Minister Triggers Exit from European Union

MARCH 29, 2017

After the shock 2016 referendum in which a slim majority of British voters opted for the United Kingdom to leave the European Union, the UK government proceeded to give effect to that vote in 2017. Answers to key questions gradually emerged: When would talks begin, how would they be structured, how long would they last, when would the United Kingdom leave. However, what future relationship Britain would have with the European Union was less clear. The Brexit debate evolved into more of a "when and how" rather than an "if," although there were still some hardcore "Remain" holdouts. Meanwhile, the European Union (EU) steadied its ship and succeeded in forging a unified negotiating stance for the talks. The political climate in Europe also calmed somewhat after a series of elections in France, Germany, and the Netherlands in which anti-EU parties, while making significant gains, failed to win outright in any member state.

BONES OF BREXIT COME TOGETHER

At the close of 2016, it was still unclear whether the UK's Conservative Party–led government would seek the assent of the Parliament in Westminster when it launched the Brexit negotiation. The UK Supreme Court answered that question for them in a January 24, 2017, ruling that insisted Parliament's approval was needed to start the talks. The government prepared the necessary legislation, which on March 13 passed comfortably in both legislative chambers—the House of Commons and the House of Lords. The Brexit referendum of June 23, 2016, had created such political momentum that many parliamentarians who had campaigned for Remain the previous year voted to give the green light to the Brexit negotiations now. The parliamentary debates focused on details such as the rights, post-Brexit, of millions of EU citizens living in the United Kingdom and whether the Parliament needed to give its consent to the planned future UK–EU deal.

Under Article 50 of the EU Treaty, an EU member state may start the process of leaving the EU by formally notifying the European Council, the branch of the EU's government that represents the member states. The United Kingdom took this historic step—thereby becoming the first EU member to invoke the article—on March 29 when the UK Ambassador to the European Union handed the Article 50 letter to Council President Donald Tusk. The same day, UK Prime Minister Theresa May addressed the UK Parliament, giving lawmakers the blueprint of how her government intended to approach the Brexit.

"This is an historic moment from which there can be no turning back," said May. "Leaving the European Union presents us with a unique opportunity. It is this generation's chance to shape a brighter future for our country," she added. May reassured that a final Brexit deal would be presented to Parliament for a vote before coming into force.

Underscoring that Brexit would result in a return of political power, she said, "We will ... bring an end to the jurisdiction of the European Court of Justice in Britain," the EU's Luxembourg-based judicial arm. Lawmaking powers would, post-Brexit, reside solely in the UK Parliament in Westminster and the devolved assemblies of Northern Ireland and Wales and parliament of Scotland that were set up in the late 1990s. Prime Minister May said that while the aforementioned devolved governments would be consulted on the Brexit negotiations, "we will negotiate as one United Kingdom," meaning they would have no veto powers over the process. Turning to the relationship between Northern Ireland, which is part of the United Kingdom, and the Republic of Ireland in the south, an independent state that is remaining in the European Union, she said she wanted to keep the common travel area between north and south of the island. Touching on the hot button issue of the referendum, she said, "We will control immigration" to the United Kingdom.

As for the UK's trade relations with the European Union post-Brexit, she said, "We will no longer be members of the Single Market." That was an important clarification because many of the Remain side, while they acknowledged the Brexit referendum result should be respected, argued that the United Kingdom could still remain part of the EU's single market even as it withdrew from the EU's institutional and budgetary structures. Norway and Iceland, for example, were in the single market but were not EU member states. But May excluded this option, mindful that remaining in the single market would require the United Kingdom to continue applying the majority of EU legislation, the one difference being it would no longer have a say in the writing of those laws.

Air of Uncertainty, Suspicion Surrounds Early Talks

In EU headquarters in Brussels, the triggering of Article 50 enabled it to put the Brexit wheels in motion. The bloc was determined to have a strong, unified negotiating stance. Step one required the European Commission, the EU's executive arm, to be granted negotiating authority and provided guidelines by the European Council; this happened on May 22. In December 2016, the Commission tapped Michel Barnier, France's representative on the twenty-eight–member body (one Commissioner per member state) its Brexit chief negotiator. Giving Barnier sole authority to conduct the negotiations was a strategic move aimed at ensuring that UK negotiators could not play different member states against each other to secure a more favorable deal.

The negotiations opened in Brussels on June 19. With six decades of experience negotiating international agreements, the Commission was comfortable in the driving seat. The United Kingdom, by contrast, had not negotiated a free trade agreement with another country for more than four decades, having ceded that authority to the Commission when it joined the European Union in 1973. The Commission scored a quick success when the United Kingdom conceded to the Commission's proposed structure for the talks. According to this structure, the two would have to make "significant progress" on three key "divorce" issues before discussing future trade relations, and the UK was most eager to discuss the trade issues. The top divorce items were how much money the UK government would give the European Union under an exit deal, the rights of EU citizens living in the UK post-Brexit, and maintaining free travel and trade between northern and southern Ireland under the 1998 Northern Ireland peace accord.

The UK's chief negotiator, David Davis, was appointed by May in July 2016 after she replaced David Cameron as Prime Minister. Davis had always been a strong supporter of Brexit, in contrast to May who supported—albeit tepidly—the Remain side in the referendum. Another key figure in Brexit negotiations was UK foreign minister, Boris Johnson. Relatively late in the referendum campaign, Johnson weighed in on the Leave side, giving it a valuable boost in the final weeks. Chancellor of the Exchequer (finance minister) Philip Hammond was an important figure, too. Unlike Davis and Johnson, Hammond had backed the Remain campaign and post-referendum was sympathetic to concerns voiced by the UK business community about the economic damage that could be done were the United Kingdom to leave the single market. As the Brexit negotiations got underway, Hammond continued to spar with Johnson and Davis on strategy.

The process set out under Article 50 had arguably given the upper hand to the European Union in the negotiations. Article 50 stipulates that negotiations should take two years at most. If no agreement is reached by then, the exiting country leaves anyway—thus losing full access to the single market—unless the remaining twenty-seven EU countries unanimously agree to extend the talks. A "no-deal Brexit" scenario started to seem like a real possibility as the monthly negotiating rounds took place and it became apparent that the European Union was in no mood to concede anything, knowing it could simply run out the clock and let the United Kingdom leave with nothing.

This dynamic played out, for example, in the so-called divorce bill, the financial settlement that the European Union demanded from the United Kingdom, which is likely to run into tens of billions of euros. Prime Minister May at first said that the United Kingdom had no legal obligation to pay any such settlement to the EU. Foreign Minister Johnson added that the European Union could "go whistle" if it kept demanding "extortionate" sums. EU chief negotiator Barnier replied sternly, "I'm not hearing any whistling, just the clock ticking."

Mood Improves, Talks Inch Forward

In a bid to ease tensions, Prime Minster May gave a speech in Florence in September where she made concessions on key EU demands. She accepted that the United Kingdom would pay an exit bill, with the precise amount to be negotiated. She also gave the firmest commitments so far about protecting the rights of EU citizens living in the United Kingdom and gave assurances there would be no physical infrastructure erected to separate northern and southern Ireland. After the speech, the Prime Minister received a warmer reception than when she attended an EU leaders' summit in October. The leaders signaled they were amenable to letting the talks proceed to Phase 2 (future trade arrangements) in the coming months as long as progress continued to be made on Phase 1 issues. German Chancellor Angela Merkel struck a slightly more conciliatory tone than French President Emanuel Macron, while Dutch Prime Minister Mark Rutte underscored the need to agree on the financial settlement.

The political sands shifted significantly over the course of 2017 following a series of national elections in EU member countries. In the wake of the Brexit vote, there had been a palpable fear of contagion among EU governments as anti-immigrant, anti-EU, populist parties continued to rise in the polls. There was speculation about the European Union's future should such parties win an election and move to take their respective countries out. The biggest test case came in France where Marine Le Pen, leader of the National Front and a strident critic of the European Union, was running for president. Le Pen progressed to the second-round vote but Macron, a pro-EU centrist, heavily defeated her in the final vote in May. In Germany, the anti-EU Alternative for Germany saw a big increase in its vote share in September's elections, coming third place overall. However, Chancellor

Merkel's center-right, pro-EU Christian Democrats emerged the largest party and was set to return to power through a coalition government with the left-leaning Greens and centrist Free Democrats.

By the latter half of 2017, a sense of calm was returning to the European Union. Economic growth had picked up, the 2015–2016 mass refugee influx had slowed, and there no longer seemed to be an imminent threat of another member country exiting the bloc. As for the United Kingdom, while there was growing consensus that Brexit would actually happen, there was also considerable anxiety over the country's future post-Brexit. Prime Minister May saw her overall parliamentary majority disappear in a snap election she called in June and became reliant on parliamentarians from the Democratic Unionist Party of Northern Ireland to stay in power. She faced rumblings of dissent from within her Conservative Party along with constant rumors of leadership challenges. Nevertheless, she seemed determined to stay on and deliver a Brexit deal by the fall of 2018.

—Brian Beary

Following is the text of a letter dated March 29, 2017, from British Prime Minister Theresa May to European Council President Donald Tusk announcing the intent of the United Kingdom to exit the European Union; and a statement delivered by Prime Minister May before the UK Parliament on March 29, 2017, regarding the letter sent to Tusk.

British Prime Minister Informs EU of Britain's Intent to Leave the Body

March 29, 2017

Dear President Tusk

On 23 June last year, the people of the United Kingdom voted to leave the European Union. As I have said before, that decision was no rejection of the values we share as fellow Europeans. Nor was it an attempt to do harm to the European Union or any of the remaining member states. On the contrary, the United Kingdom wants the European Union to succeed and prosper. Instead, the referendum was a vote to restore, as we see it, our national self-determination. We are leaving the European Union, but we are not leaving Europe—and we want to remain committed partners and allies to our friends across the continent.

Earlier this month, the United Kingdom Parliament confirmed the result of the referendum by voting with clear and convincing majorities in both of its Houses for the European Union (Notification of Withdrawal) Bill. The Bill was passed by Parliament on 13 March and it received Royal Assent from Her Majesty The Queen and became an Act of Parliament on 16 March.

Today, therefore, I am writing to give effect to the democratic decision of the people of the United Kingdom. I hereby notify the European Council in accordance with Article 50(2) of the Treaty on European Union of the United Kingdom's intention to withdraw from the European Union. In addition, in accordance with the same Article 50(2) as applied by Article 106a of the Treaty Establishing the European Atomic Energy Community, I hereby notify the European Council of the United Kingdom's intention to withdraw from the European Atomic Energy Community. References in this letter to the European Union should therefore be taken to include a reference to the European Atomic Energy Community.

This letter sets out the approach of Her Majesty's Government to the discussions we will have about the United Kingdom's departure from the European Union and about the deep and special partnership we hope to enjoy—as your closest friend and neighbour—with the European Union once we leave. We believe that these objectives are in the interests not only of the United Kingdom but of the European Union and the wider world too.

It is in the best interests of both the United Kingdom and the European Union that we should use the forthcoming process to deliver these objectives in a fair and orderly manner, and with as little disruption as possible on each side. We want to make sure that Europe remains strong and prosperous and is capable of projecting its values, leading in the world, and defending itself from security threats. We want the United Kingdom, through a new deep and special partnership with a strong European Union, to play its full part in achieving these goals. We therefore believe it is necessary to agree the terms of our future partnership alongside those of our withdrawal from the European Union.

The Government wants to approach our discussions with ambition, giving citizens and businesses in the United Kingdom and the European Union—and indeed from third countries around the world—as much certainty as possible, as early as possible.

I would like to propose some principles that may help to shape our coming discussions, but before I do so, I should update you on the process we will be undertaking at home, in the United Kingdom.

The process in the United Kingdom

As I have announced already, the Government will bring forward legislation that will repeal the Act of Parliament—the European Communities Act 1972—that gives effect to EU law in our country. This legislation will, wherever practical and appropriate, in effect convert the body of existing European Union law (the "acquis") into UK law. This means there will be certainty for UK citizens and for anybody from the European Union who does business in the United Kingdom. The Government will consult on how we design and implement this legislation, and we will publish a White Paper tomorrow. We also intend to bring forward several other pieces of legislation that address specific issues relating to our departure from the European Union, also with a view to ensuring continuity and certainty, in particular for businesses. We will of course continue to fulfil our responsibilities as a member state while we remain a member of the European Union, and the legislation we propose will not come into effect until we leave.

From the start and throughout the discussions, we will negotiate as one United Kingdom, taking due account of the specific interests of every nation and region of the UK as we do so. When it comes to the return of powers back to the United Kingdom, we will consult fully on which powers should reside in Westminster and which should be devolved to Scotland, Wales and Northern Ireland. But it is the expectation of the Government that the outcome of this process will be a significant increase in the decision-making power of each devolved administration.

Negotiations between the United Kingdom and the European Union

The United Kingdom wants to agree with the European Union a deep and special partnership that takes in both economic and security cooperation. To achieve this, we believe it is necessary to agree the terms of our future partnership alongside those of our withdrawal from the EU.

If, however, we leave the European Union without an agreement the default position is that we would have to trade on World Trade Organisation terms. In security terms a failure to reach agreement would mean our cooperation in the fight against crime and terrorism would be weakened. In this kind of scenario, both the United Kingdom and the European Union would of course cope with the change, but it is not the outcome that either side should seek. We must therefore work hard to avoid that outcome.

It is for these reasons that we want to be able to agree a deep and special partnership, taking in both economic and security cooperation, but it is also because we want to play our part in making sure that Europe remains strong and prosperous and able to lead in the world, projecting its values and defending itself from security threats. And we want the United Kingdom to play its full part in realising that vision for our continent.

Proposed principles for our discussions

Looking ahead to the discussions which we will soon begin, I would like to suggest some principles that we might agree to help make sure that the process is as smooth and successful as possible.

    i. **We should engage with one another constructively and respectfully, in a spirit of sincere cooperation.** Since I became Prime Minister of the United Kingdom I have listened carefully to you, to my fellow EU Heads of Government and the Presidents of the European Commission and Parliament. That is why the United Kingdom does not seek membership of the single market: we understand and respect your position that the four freedoms of the single market are indivisible and there can be no "cherry picking". We also understand that there will be consequences for the UK of leaving the EU: we know that we will lose influence over the rules that affect the European economy. We also know that UK companies will, as they trade within the EU, have to align with rules agreed by institutions of which we are no longer a part—just as UK companies do in other overseas markets.

    ii. **We should always put our citizens first.** There is obvious complexity in the discussions we are about to undertake, but we should remember that at the heart of our talks are the interests of all our citizens. There are, for example, many citizens of the remaining member states living in the United Kingdom, and UK citizens living elsewhere in the European Union, and we should aim to strike an early agreement about their rights.

    iii. **We should work towards securing a comprehensive agreement.** We want to agree a deep and special partnership between the UK and the EU, taking in both economic and security cooperation. We will need to discuss how we determine a fair settlement of the UK's rights and obligations as a departing member state, in accordance with the law and in the spirit of the United Kingdom's continuing partnership with the EU. But we believe it is necessary to agree the terms of our future partnership alongside those of our withdrawal from the EU.

iv. **We should work together to minimise disruption and give as much certainty as possible.** Investors, businesses and citizens in both the UK and across the remaining 27 member states—and those from third countries around the world—want to be able to plan. In order to avoid any cliff-edge as we move from our current relationship to our future partnership, people and businesses in both the UK and the EU would benefit from implementation periods to adjust in a smooth and orderly way to new arrangements. It would help both sides to minimise unnecessary disruption if we agree this principle early in the process.

v. **In particular, we must pay attention to the UK's unique relationship with the Republic of Ireland and the importance of the peace process in Northern Ireland.** The Republic of Ireland is the only EU member state with a land border with the United Kingdom. We want to avoid a return to a hard border between our two countries, to be able to maintain the Common Travel Area between us, and to make sure that the UK's withdrawal from the EU does not harm the Republic of Ireland. We also have an important responsibility to make sure that nothing is done to jeopardise the peace process in Northern Ireland, and to continue to uphold the Belfast Agreement.

vi. **We should begin technical talks on detailed policy areas as soon as possible, but we should prioritise the biggest challenges.** Agreeing a high-level approach to the issues arising from our withdrawal will of course be an early priority. But we also propose a bold and ambitious Free Trade Agreement between the United Kingdom and the European Union. This should be of greater scope and ambition than any such agreement before it so that it covers sectors crucial to our linked economies such as financial services and network industries. This will require detailed technical talks, but as the UK is an existing EU member state, both sides have regulatory frameworks and standards that already match. We should therefore prioritise how we manage the evolution of our regulatory frameworks to maintain a fair and open trading environment, and how we resolve disputes. On the scope of the partnership between us—on both economic and security matters—my officials will put forward detailed proposals for deep, broad and dynamic cooperation.

vii. **We should continue to work together to advance and protect our shared European values.** Perhaps now more than ever, the world needs the liberal, democratic values of Europe. We want to play our part to ensure that Europe remains strong and prosperous and able to lead in the world, projecting its values and defending itself from security threats.

The task before us

As I have said, the Government of the United Kingdom wants to agree a deep and special partnership between the UK and the EU, taking in both economic and security cooperation. At a time when the growth of global trade is slowing and there are signs that protectionist instincts are on the rise in many parts of the world, Europe has a responsibility to stand up for free trade in the interest of all our citizens. Likewise, Europe's security is more fragile today than at any time since the end of the Cold War. Weakening our cooperation for the prosperity and protection of our citizens would be a costly mistake. The United Kingdom's objectives for our future partnership remain those set out in my Lancaster House speech of 17 January and the subsequent White Paper published on 2 February.

We recognise that it will be a challenge to reach such a comprehensive agreement within the two-year period set out for withdrawal discussions in the Treaty. But we believe it is necessary to agree the terms of our future partnership alongside those of our withdrawal from the EU. We start from a unique position in these discussions—close regulatory alignment, trust in one another's institutions, and a spirit of cooperation stretching back decades. It is for these reasons, and because the future partnership between the UK and the EU is of such importance to both sides, that I am sure it can be agreed in the time period set out by the Treaty.

The task before us is momentous but it should not be beyond us. After all, the institutions and the leaders of the European Union have succeeded in bringing together a continent blighted by war into a union of peaceful nations, and supported the transition of dictatorships to democracy. Together, I know we are capable of reaching an agreement about the UK's rights and obligations as a departing member state, while establishing a deep and special partnership that contributes towards the prosperity, security and global power of our continent.

Yours sincerely,
Theresa May

SOURCE: United Kingdom Prime Minister's Office. 10 Downing Street. "Prime Minister's Letter to European Council President Donald Tusk." March 29, 2017. https://www.gov.uk/government/uploads/system/uploads/attachment_data/file/604079/Prime_Ministers_letter_to_European_Council_President_Donald_Tusk.pdf.

Prime Minister May Addresses Parliament on Brexit

March 29, 2017

Thank you Mr Speaker.

Today the government acts on the democratic will of the British people. And it acts, too, on the clear and convincing position of this House.

A few minutes ago in Brussels, the United Kingdom's Permanent Representative to the EU handed a letter to the President of the European Council on my behalf, confirming the government's decision to invoke Article 50 of the Treaty on European Union.

The Article 50 process is now underway. And in accordance with the wishes of the British people, the United Kingdom is leaving the European Union.

This is an historic moment from which there can be no turning back. Britain is leaving the European Union. We are going to make our own decisions and our own laws. We are going to take control of the things that matter most to us. And we are going to take this opportunity to build a stronger, fairer Britain—a country that our children and grandchildren are proud to call home. That is our ambition and our opportunity. That is what this government is determined to do.

Mr Speaker, at moments like these—great turning points in our national story—the choices we make define the character of our nation. We can choose to say the task ahead is too great. We can choose to turn our face to the past and believe it can't be done. Or we can look forward with optimism and hope—and to believe in the enduring power of the British spirit.

I choose to believe in Britain and that our best days lie ahead. And I do so because I am confident that we have the vision and the plan to use this moment to build a better Britain. For leaving the European Union presents us with a unique opportunity. It is this generation's chance to shape a brighter future for our country. A chance to step back and ask ourselves what kind of country we want to be.

My answer is clear. I want the United Kingdom to emerge from this period of change stronger, fairer, more united and more outward-looking than ever before. I want us to be a secure, prosperous, tolerant country—a magnet for international talent and a home to the pioneers and innovators who will shape the world ahead.

I want us to be a truly Global Britain—the best friend and neighbour to our European partners, but a country that reaches beyond the borders of Europe too. A country that goes out into the world to build relationships with old friends and new allies alike.

And that is why I have set out a clear and ambitious plan for the negotiations ahead. It is a plan for a new deep and special partnership between Britain and the European Union. A partnership of values. A partnership of interests. A partnership based on co-operation in areas such as security and economic affairs. And a partnership that works in the best interests of the United Kingdom, the European Union and the wider world.

Because perhaps now more than ever, the world needs the liberal, democratic values of Europe—values that this United Kingdom shares. And that is why, while we are leaving the institutions of the European Union, we are not leaving Europe. We will remain a close friend and ally. We will be a committed partner. We will play our part to ensure that Europe is able to project its values and defend itself from security threats. And we will do all that we can to help the European Union prosper and succeed.

So Mr Speaker, in the letter that has been delivered to President Tusk today—copies of which I have placed in the library of the House—I have been clear that the deep and special partnership we seek is in the best interests of the United Kingdom and of the European Union too.

I have been clear that we will work constructively—in a spirit of sincere co-operation—to bring this partnership into being. And I have been clear that we should seek to agree the terms of this future partnership alongside those of our withdrawal, within the next 2 years.

I am ambitious for Britain. And the objectives I have set out for these negotiations remain. We will deliver certainty wherever possible so that business, the public sector and everybody else has as much clarity as we can provide as we move through the process. It is why, tomorrow, we will publish a White Paper confirming our plans to convert the 'acquis' into British law, so that everyone will know where they stand.

And it is why I have been clear that the government will put the final deal that is agreed between the UK and the EU to a vote in both Houses of Parliament before it comes into force. We will take control of our own laws and bring an end to the jurisdiction of the

European Court of Justice in Britain. Leaving the European Union will mean that our laws will be made in Westminster, Edinburgh, Cardiff and Belfast. And those laws will be interpreted by judges not in Luxembourg, but in courts across this country.

We will strengthen the Union of the 4 nations that comprise our United Kingdom. We will negotiate as one United Kingdom, taking account of the specific interests of every nation and region of the UK and when it comes to the powers that we will take back from Europe, we will consult fully on which powers should reside in Westminster and which should be passed on to the devolved administrations.

But Mr Speaker, no decisions currently taken by the devolved administrations will be removed from them. And it is the expectation of the government that the devolved administrations in Scotland, Wales and Northern Ireland will see a significant increase in their decision-making power as a result of this process.

We want to maintain the common travel area with the Republic of Ireland. There should be no return to the borders of the past. We will control immigration so that we continue to attract the brightest and the best to work or study in Britain, but manage the process properly so that our immigration system serves the national interest.

We seek to guarantee the rights of EU citizens who are already living in Britain, and the rights of British nationals in other member states as early as we can. That is set out very clearly in the letter as an early priority for the talks ahead. We will ensure that workers' rights are fully protected and maintained. Indeed, under my leadership, not only will the government protect the rights of workers, we will build on them.

We will pursue a bold and ambitious free trade agreement with the European Union that allows for the freest possible trade in goods and services between Britain and the EU's member states; that gives British companies the maximum freedom to trade with and operate within European markets; and that lets European businesses do the same in Britain.

Because European leaders have said many times that we cannot 'cherry pick' and remain members of the single market without accepting the 4 freedoms that are indivisible. We respect that position. And as accepting those freedoms is incompatible with the democratically expressed will of the British people, we will no longer be members of the single market.

We are going to make sure that we can strike trade agreements with countries from outside the European Union too. Because important though our trade with the EU is and will remain, it is clear that the UK needs to increase significantly its trade with the fastest growing export markets in the world.

We hope to continue to collaborate with our European partners in the areas of science, education, research and technology, so that the UK is one of the best places for science and innovation. We seek continued co-operation with our European partners in important areas such as crime, terrorism and foreign affairs.

And it is our aim to deliver a smooth and orderly Brexit—reaching an agreement about our future partnership by the time the 2-year Article 50 process has concluded, then moving into a phased process of implementation in which Britain, the EU institutions and member states prepare for the new arrangements that will exist between us.

Mr Speaker, we understand that there will be consequences for the UK of leaving the EU. We know that we will lose influence over the rules that affect the European economy. We know that UK companies that trade with the EU will have to align with rules agreed by institutions of which we are no longer a part, just as we do in other overseas markets. We accept that.

However, we approach these talks constructively, respectfully, and in a spirit of sincere co-operation. For it is in the interests of both the United Kingdom and the European Union that we should use this process to deliver our objectives in a fair and orderly manner. It is in the interests of both the United Kingdom and the European Union that there should be as little disruption as possible. And it is in the interests of both the United Kingdom and the European Union that Europe should remain strong, prosperous and capable of projecting its values in the world.

At a time when the growth of global trade is slowing and there are signs that protectionist instincts are on the rise in many parts of the world, Europe has a responsibility to stand up for free trade in the interests of all our citizens.

With Europe's security more fragile today than at any time since the end of the Cold War, weakening our co-operation and failing to stand up for European values would be a costly mistake.

Our vote to leave the EU was no rejection of the values that we share as fellow Europeans. As a European country, we will continue to play our part in promoting and supporting those values—during the negotiations and once they are done.

We will continue to be reliable partners, willing allies and close friends. We want to continue to buy goods and services from the EU, and sell them ours. We want to trade with them as freely as possible, and work with one another to make sure we are all safer, more secure and more prosperous through continued friendship.

Indeed, in an increasingly unstable world, we must continue to forge the closest possible security co-operation to keep our people safe. We face the same global threats from terrorism and extremism. That message was only reinforced by the abhorrent attack on Westminster Bridge and this place last week.

So there should be no reason why we should not agree a new deep and special partnership between the UK and the EU that works for us all.

Mr Speaker, I know that this is a day of celebration for some and disappointment for others. The referendum last June was divisive at times. Not everyone shared the same point of view, or voted in the same way. The arguments on both side were passionate.

But, Mr Speaker, when I sit around the negotiating table in the months ahead, I will represent every person in the whole United Kingdom—young and old, rich and poor, city, town, country and all the villages and hamlets in between.

And yes, those EU nationals who have made this country their home and it is my fierce determination to get the right deal for every single person in this country. For as we face the opportunities ahead of us on this momentous journey, our shared values, interests and ambitions can—and must—bring us together.

We all want to see a Britain that is stronger than it is today. We all want a country that is fairer so that everyone has the chance to succeed. We all want a nation that is safe and secure for our children and grandchildren. We all want to live in a truly Global Britain that gets out and builds relationships with old friends and new allies around the world.

These are the ambitions of this government's Plan for Britain. Ambitions that unite us, so that we are no longer defined by the vote we cast, but by our determination to make a success of the result.

We are one great union of people and nations with a proud history and a bright future. And now that the decision to leave has been made—and the process is underway—it is time to come together. For this great national moment needs a great national effort. An effort to shape a stronger future for Britain.

So let us do so together. Let us come together and work together. Let us together choose to believe in Britain with optimism and hope. For if we do, we can make the most of the opportunities ahead. We can together make a success of this moment. And we can together build a stronger, fairer, better Britain—a Britain our children and grandchildren are proud to call home.

I commend this statement to the House.

SOURCE: United Kingdom Prime Minister's Office. 10 Downing Street. "Prime Minister's Commons Statement on Triggering Article 50." March 29, 2017. https://www.gov.uk/government/speeches/prime-ministers-commons-statement-on-triggering-article-50.

OTHER HISTORIC DOCUMENTS OF INTEREST

FROM THIS VOLUME

▪ Leaders of France, Germany, and the UK Respond to National Elections, p. 260

FROM PREVIOUS HISTORIC DOCUMENTS

▪ Britons Vote to Exit the European Union, 2016, p. 280

April

Turkish President Responds to Referendum and State of Emergency

APRIL 5, 16, AND 17, AND JULY 14 AND 17, 2017

On April 16, 2017, in an historic decision, Turkish voters declared their preference for a presidential system of government over the parliamentary democracy that had been in place since 1982. The change would give sweeping new powers to President Recep Tayyip Erdoğan, who critics argued would enforce authoritarian rule in the nation. The referendum further soured relations between Turkey and the European Union (EU), as well as its former North Atlantic Treaty Organization (NATO) ally, the United States.

CHANGES TO THE TURKISH CONSTITUTION

The current Turkish constitution went into force in 1982, following a coup that took back control of the country from the military. At that time, a parliamentary system of government was established that vested most of the rule-making and budgetary authority with members of parliament and the prime minister, while the president and Council of Ministers were the de facto heads of state with the president holding only marginal executive authority. Amending the constitution to support a presidential system of government was first proposed by the country's Minister of Justice in 2005, and was backed by Erdoğan, who at that time was serving as prime minister. It would be twelve years, however, before Erdoğan's Justice and Development Party (AKP) had enough support and seats in parliament to ensure the measure's passage.

In January 2017, parliament approved the eighteen proposed amendments to the constitution that would be consolidated under one referendum and put before the voters. The yes/no vote asked citizens whether they preferred to maintain a parliamentary form of government or transition to a presidential system. The proposed amendments would make a number of significant changes to Turkish government. The role of prime minister would be eliminated and replaced by one or more vice presidents, at the discretion of the president. The president would become the head of state and head of the executive and would be given power to appoint cabinet ministers, set the budget, choose a majority of senior judges, and enact laws. These powers would allow him to unilaterally make the decision to declare a state of emergency or dismiss parliament. However, because presidential and parliamentary elections would be tied to one another, if the president chose to dismiss parliament, it would also trigger a presidential election. The president, who would be chosen by the people, would no longer be required to separate himself from his party, and would be limited to two five-year terms.

Under the proposed constitutional amendments, the number of members of parliament would increase from 550 to 600, and, although there was agreement among critics of the amendments that parliament would become the rubber stamp of the president so long as his party held a majority of the seats, some limits were put in place regarding what the president could and could not decree. For example, the president would be barred from contradicting any civil rights enshrined in the nation's constitution, nor could he overturn any laws or decrees that require action by parliament under the current constitution. But, should the president send a bill back to parliament for reconsideration, parliament would need an absolute majority rather than a simple majority for re-passage. Parliament would still be permitted to begin impeachment proceedings against the president, but doing so would become more difficult and require strong backing from the body's members.

The referendum was supported by Erdoğan's AKP and the far-right Nationalist Movement Party (MHP), while opposition primarily came from the Republican People's Party (CHP) and pro-Kurdish People's Democratic Party (HDP). Supporters believed that the referendum would allow for a more streamlined government in which laws and regulations could be more easily enacted without the need for a coalition government. Erdoğan publicly argued that the constitutional reform would allow him to implement measures to improve national security that he felt had deteriorated after a failed coup attempt in July 2016. Opponents, however, saw the referendum as an attempt to consolidate power in the executive and eliminate a system of checks and balances, something both the president and his advisors rejected. "Can such a scenario be politically abused? Certainly," said Mehmet Uçum, the president's chief judicial consultant. "But if that turns out to be the case, the problem could be solved by going back to the people, calling for a new election."

An Historic Referendum

An estimated forty-eight million Turkish citizens cast ballots on April 16. Despite polls leading up to the vote indicating that the referendum would pass with a vast majority, once all votes were tallied, only 51 percent voted in favor of amending the constitution. After learning of its passage, Erdoğan said the nation would be "enacting the most important governmental reform of our history," while Prime Minister Binali Yildirim said the government would "use this result as best as we can—for the wealth and peace of our people." Opponents of the referendum immediately called for a recount after ballot box stuffing and other irregularities were caught on camera. HDP claimed there was "manipulation of 3 to 4 percentage points" of the outcome.

European election monitors said the vote was conducted on "an unlevel playing field" and did not meet international election standards. "We . . . noted a considerable imbalance in the campaign, due—among other things—to the active involvement of the president, several leading national officials, and many local public officials in the 'yes' campaign," said Tana de Zulueta, the mission chief of the Organization for Security and Cooperation in Europe (OSCE) Office for Democratic Institutions and Human Rights (ODIHR), adding, "Our team observed the misuse of administrative resources, and the obstruction of efforts by parties and civil society organizations supporting the 'no' campaign." OSCE also noted that many voters had difficulty reaching the polls because the nearly year-long state of emergency had forced them to flee their homes. Erdoğan rejected the criticisms and told international observers to "know your place." He also dismissed assertions that the referendum could mark the end of Turkey's bid to join the European Union, which the president called "not so important." Erdoğan further noted that he might choose to hold a vote of the Turkish people to decide whether the government should rescind Turkey's EU application.

The changes to the constitution were set to go into effect in 2019 and would reset Erdoğan's term at that point. Erdoğan was the first directly elected president in Turkish history, after winning the election in 2014, and had previously served as prime minister from 2003 to 2014. If Erdoğan were to continue to be popularly elected, he could hold his seat until 2029. However, if snap elections were called by parliament toward the end of his second term as president, the revised constitution would allow Erdoğan (or any sitting president nearing the end of a second term) to run for a third term.

TURKEY'S RELATIONSHIP WITH THE WORLD

Since a state of emergency was declared in July 2016—and extended through 2017—following a coup attempt to overthrow Erdoğan's government, tens of thousands have been arrested, convicted, or fired from government positions for alleged connection to the coup. This move was seen by many in the Western world as a violation of human rights intended only to increase Erdoğan's power. In November 2016, the European Union announced that it would indefinitely suspend negotiations with Turkey regarding its entry into the body because of the current state of affairs. Erdoğan blamed the EU's decision on what he viewed as the body's anti-Muslim leadership. "They have racism. They have Islamophobia and the like. They are not honest," the president claimed. Erdoğan further hurt Turkey's relationship with Europe after accusing the German and Dutch governments of Nazism for failing to allow his AKP to hold rallies in those countries—both of which have large Turkish expat populations—in support of the referendum. Perhaps a final blow to Turkey's relationship with Europe was Erdoğan's announcement at a referendum victory rally of his intent to reinstate the death penalty. The practice was outlawed in Turkey in 2004 as part of its bid to join the European Union; the body does not extend membership to any country where the practice is in use.

Turkey's relationship with the United States progressively soured as well. The two NATO members had at one time worked together to eliminate terrorist networks in the Middle East, and had been aligned in their fight against the Syrian regime. However, the United States under President Donald Trump continued to support, and even armed, the Kurdish People's Protection Unit (YPG), a group that fights alongside the Syrian Democratic Forces (SDF) who are trying to rid the region of the Islamic State of Iraq and the Levant (ISIL) and overthrow the authoritarian Syrian government. Turkey, however, viewed the YPG as part of the Kurdistan Workers' Party (PKK), a group it declared to be a terrorist organization. The United States and Turkey also had an ongoing dispute related to the July 2016 coup attempt. The Turkish government blamed Muslim cleric Fethullah Gülen, who was living in Pennsylvania, for orchestrating the coup and demanded that the United States extradite him for trial. The United States, in turn, requested compelling legal evidence of Gülen's involvement, but did not receive any. Erdoğan expressed dismay at both the U.S.'s refusal for extradition and international response to ongoing states of emergency enacted since the coup, saying he had expected Turkey's allies "to side with human rights, legitimate political will and the elected government." Without a close relationship with the United States or European Union, Turkey has increasingly turned toward Russia and Iran, especially with regard to handling the crisis in Syria, a change in alliance that is of particular concern to the West.

—Heather Kerrigan

Following are five press releases from the Office of Turkish President Recep Tayyip Erdoğan on April 5, 2017, regarding European Union member states; on April 16, 2017, on the passage of the constitutional referendum; and on April 17, July 14, and July 17, 2017, regarding the ongoing state of emergency in Turkey.

Turkish President on Relationship with the EU

April 5, 2017

Drawing attention to anti-Turkey developments in some European countries in his speech at a mass opening ceremony in Bursa, President Erdoğan said: "We are embracing and upholding democracy, human rights and freedoms not because the European countries want so, but because our citizens deserve them. And we are doing this better than they do. Turkey will duly respond to those who resort to any method and means to attack it. As we keep on standing up not falling down, they are running out of breath."

President Recep Tayyip Erdoğan addressed a large crowd of citizens at a mass opening ceremony of the newly-built facilities in the province of Bursa. Also present at the ceremony were First Lady Emine Erdoğan, Minister of Labor and Social Security Mehmet Müezzinoğlu and members of the parliament.

"THEY HAVE KEPT US WAITING AT THE EU DOOR"

Reminding some European countries' remarks that they don't want the new system of government Turkey is to switch to after April 16, President Erdoğan said: "We would be surprised if they wanted. Because we know very well how long they have kept us waiting at the EU door."

Countries which cannot even be compared with Turkey have been made a member of the EU, President Erdoğan underlined, adding that it has become clear that they don't approve of Turkey's membership because 99% of its population is made up of Muslims. The President said: "We haven't said these so far, but will say from now on. They are in favor of separation. They have racism. They have Islamophobia and the like. They are not honest. They are not frank. We used to understand what they actually were when they were laughing at our face, but we didn't tell. But from now on, we will tell. We will tell to their faces."

"EUROPE HAS OPENED ALL ITS DOORS WIDE OPEN TO THE TERRORIST ORGANIZATION PARTISANS"

President Erdoğan stated: "They are harboring the PKK and the FETO (Fetullah Terrorist Organization) on their lands and refusing to extradite their members. And while that is the case, they still unabashedly request extradition from us. No offence, but our judiciary is just as fair as yours. And when we don't hand over the names they request, they freak out. As long as I hold this post, I don't clear the way for it. Europe has opened all its doors wipe open to the terrorist organization partisans while banning entry to our ministers. They are hoisting a banner picturing me with a gun pointed at my temple, and moreover, they are doing this under the escort of the Swiss police. Are we still to remain silent? That is why I am saying 'yes' on April 16. This is not a personal issue, but it is all about holding to account those who disrespected this nation. These terrorists are roaming freely across Europe, aren't they? Pay attention, the doors are open to them. But the doors are closed to yea-sayers. Their ministers and deputies are freely conducting propaganda in favor of 'no.' We will talk to you after April 16."

Stressing that Turkey now has Ankara criteria and no longer needs the EU criteria, President Erdoğan said: "We are embracing and upholding democracy, human rights and freedoms not because the European countries want so, but because our citizens deserve them. And we are doing this better than they do. Turkey will duly respond to those who resort to any method and means to attack it. As we keep on standing up not falling down, they are running out of breath. Today's sick man is the European Union."

"EUROPE'S FUTURE LIES IN OUR CITIZENS LIVING THERE"

"They will be faced with an aging continent whose incomes decline, debts increase, trade volume shrinks, and investment environment deteriorates. And then they will see who needs whom," warned President Erdoğan, and continued: "They cannot cover up this picture by cancelling our ministers' meetings or by attacking our citizens with dogs and horses. Europe's future lies in our citizens living there."

CHEMICAL ATTACK IN IDLIB

Describing the struggle carried out by dint of terrorist organizations as the most immoral struggle of the world, President Erdoğan noted that Turkey confronted this immorality at every stage of its history. The President, in reference to the use of chemical weapons by Assad in the Syrian city of Idlib, underscored that more than 100 people, half of them children, were martyred. Criticizing the UN for its silence in the face of the chemical attack, President Erdoğan said: "We are taking into our country from there whomever we can and providing treatment. We are making everything in our power. Yet, even this is not enough for me. I am sad. They are our kids, our brothers and sisters. I am sorry as a father. The situation of these children is tearing our heart out. We will do everything in our power."

Following the ceremony, President Erdoğan paid a visit to Bursa Governorate, where he was briefed on the works and services in the city.

SOURCE: Presidency of the Republic of Turkey. "Today's Sick Man Is the European Union." April 5, 2017. https://www.tccb.gov.tr/en/news/542/74629/bugunun-hasta-adami-artik-avrupa-birligidir.html.

Turkish President on Passage of Constitutional Referendum

April 16, 2017

President Erdoğan said: "This constitutional change is no ordinary change. It is different and very meaningful. For the first time in its history, Turkey has decided such an important change by the will of the Grand National Assembly of Turkey and people. For first time in the history of the Republic, we have changed our governmental system through civilian politics," in a post-referendum speech in Istanbul.

President Recep Tayyip Erdoğan held a press conference on the outcome of the referendum on constitutional reform.

"I EXPRESS MY GRATITUDE TO EACH INDIVIDUAL OF OUR PEOPLE"

Wishing in his statement at Huber Villa that they outcome of the April 16 referendum may yield beneficial results for the country and the people, President Erdoğan said: "Our people once again went to the polls in a distinct maturity and expressed with their free will their view on the constitutional change, adopted by the Grand National Assembly of Turkey."

"I express my gratitude to each and every individual of our people, regardless of how they voted, who went to the polling stations to protect their national will. Turkey has the power to overcome all kinds of problems, difficulties and crises as long as it upholds people's choices. We have seen very clearly its last example during the July 15 coup attempt. The April 16 referendum is a very significant sign that our people have defended its future," President Erdoğan said.

"TURKEY MADE A HISTORIC DECISION ON ITS SYSTEM OF GOVERNMENT"

Underscoring that Turkey has made a historic decision on its system of government, which has been a matter of discussion for 200 years, President Erdoğan noted that a decision to change the system of government was made today.

Thanking those, who voted 'yes' in the referendum, President Erdoğan said: "The fact that the outcome of the referendum is 'yes' shows that our people accepts the Presidential System of Government, which is also valuable to us."

"FOR FIRST TIME, WE HAVE CHANGED OUR GOVERNMENTAL SYSTEM THROUGH CIVILIAN MEANS"

The President stated: "This constitutional change is no ordinary change. It is different and very meaningful. For the first time in its history, Turkey has decided such an important change by the will of the Grand National Assembly of Turkey and people. In the past, our constitutions and system of government shaped by them were determined under extraordinary conditions such as the War of Independence and its aftermath, and coup periods. For first time in the history of the Republic, we have changed our governmental system through civilian politics, which is of paramount importance."

"April 16 is a victory for all Turkey with everyone who voted 'yes' and 'no', with its 80 million population, 81 provinces and its 780,000 square kilometers of land. Our citizens living abroad are also an important part of this victory," the President said.

"CHANGES WILL COME INTO EFFECT ON NOVEMBER 3, 2019"

Stating that all articles of the constitutional reform does not come into effect at once, President Erdoğan said: "Especially the changes related to the Presidential System of Government will come into effect after the elections on November 3, 2019. We have a lot to do until then."

"WE WOULD LIKE OTHER COUNTRIES AND ORGANIZATIONS TO RESPECT OUR PEOPLE'S DECISION"

"We would like other countries and organizations to respect our people's decision. We expect especially the countries we see as our allies to exert effort to develop their ties with our country in line with our sensitivities, our fight against terrorism in particular," President Erdoğan said.

SOURCE: Presidency of the Republic of Turkey. "Turkey Has Upheld Its Democracy." April 16, 2017. https://www.tccb.gov.tr/en/news/542/74790/turkiye-demokrasisine-sahip-cikti.html.

National Security Council Recommends Extension of State of Emergency

April 17, 2017

A statement, issued after the National Security Council meeting, chaired by President Recep Tayyip Erdoğan, read: "It has been decided to advise to extend the state of emergency in order to ensure the continuity of the measures taken to protect our democracy, the rule of law, and the rights and freedoms of our citizens."

President Recep Tayyip Erdoğan chaired the National Security Council meeting at the Presidential Complex. A written statement was released following the meeting.

Voicing pleasure that the April 16 referendum on constitutional amendments was held in a climate of peace and security across the country, the statement thanked all institutions and security personnel, who contributed to it.

Regarding the state of emergency, the statement read: "It has been decided to advise to extend the State of Emergency in order to ensure the continuity of the measures taken to protect our democracy, the rule of law, and the rights and freedoms of our citizens."

SOURCE: Presidency of the Republic of Turkey. "National Security Council Advises to Extend State of Emergency." April 17, 2017. https://www.tccb.gov.tr/en/news/542/74806/national-security-council-con venes-at-the-presidential-complex.html.

Turkish President on Fight against Terrorism

July 14, 2017

Making a speech at a panel on 'July 15 and Human Rights,' President Erdoğan, with regard to discussions about the ongoing state of emergency, said: "We will lift the state

of emergency when all the disturbances come to an end. We will lift the state of emergency once we achieve the goal in the fight against terror. No one should expect us to lift it before these are done."

President Recep Tayyip Erdoğan spoke at a panel on 'July 15 and Human Rights'.

"JULY 15 IS A FIRST IN THE HISTORY OF WORLD DEMOCRACY"

Describing the aim of the coup plotters as to empty the streets and squares by violently attacking the people with modern weaponry and then to capture the country in a short time, President Erdoğan stressed that coup plotters couldn't achieve this objective of theirs, and continued: "That is because our nation stood firmly against tanks rather than escape. Our nation chased the coup plotters rather than hide from their killing machines. The July 15 is a first in the history of world democracy."

Recalling that Fetullah Terrorist Organization (FETO)'s leader Fetullah Gülen unashamedly said "I will go to Turkey if the US lets me," in an interview with a US media outlet, President Erdoğan stated: "I had called you before, why didn't you come back then? Do you have the heart to do so? You know what the consequences will be if you arrive. As the nation, we will not forgive those who mercilessly took this step putting millions of lives in danger."

"THE JULY 15 WAS AIMED AT TAKING THE NATION AND THE STATE HOSTAGE"

Stressing that the July 15 coup attempt was way different from the May 27, March 12, September 12 and February 28 coups Turkey had previously faced, President Erdoğan said: "The July 15 was not aimed at seizing the control of the state, but at taking the nation and the state hostage totally. Having seen this fact, our people, who hadn't physically resisted the previous coups notwithstanding their disapproval, rushed to the streets on July 15 at the cost of their own lives. Our nation couldn't show this reaction during Menderes' term, yet they, thanks be to Allah, immediately responded to our call."

"JULY 15 WAS AN INVASION ATTEMPT AT THE HANDS OF PAWNS BOUGHT FOR ONE DOLLAR"

"The aim of July 15 was the same as that of those who attacked the Dardanelles ferociously and that of those who invaded our country starting from İzmir to the environs of Ankara. July 15 was an invasion attempt at the hands of pawns bought for one dollar," President Erdoğan underlined, and stressed that the coup plotters' brutal attitude against the nation and the bloodshed they inflicted showed clearly what their true intention was.

President Erdoğan added that Turkey, which has been fighting terrorism for years without compromising on human rights, came under attack on the night of July 15 and that, July 15, therefore, was a grave violation of human rights.

"WE WERE IMMENSELY DISTURBED BY THE DEEP SILENCE MANY COUNTRIES FELL IN ON JULY 15"

Noting that all the coup plotters that were killed died in the clashes while they were attempting to murder other people resisting them, but that despite this situation it was still Turkey that was accused, President Erdoğan said: "The interest and sympathy, which were denied to our citizens who were massacred and wounded and whose freedoms were restricted by coup plotters, were shown to coup plotters at the highest level after the incidents were suppressed. We were immensely disturbed by the deep silence many countries, whom we had expected to side with human rights, legitimate political will and the elected government, fell in on the night of July 15 or the following day."

Drawing attention to discussions about the ongoing state of emergency that was declared following the coup attempt, President Erdoğan added: "We will lift the state of emergency when all the disturbances come to an end. We will lift the state of emergency once we achieve the goal in the fight against terror. No one should expect us to lift it before these are done."

SOURCE: Presidency of the Republic of Turkey. "We Will Lift the State of Emergency once We Achieve the Goal in the Fight against Terror." July 14, 2017. https://www.tccb.gov.tr/en/news/542/79927/terorle-mucadelede-hedefe-ulastigimiz-zaman-ohali-kaldiracagiz.html.

Turkish National Security Council Advises Extension of State of Emergency

July 17, 2017

A statement, issued after the National Security Council (NSC) meeting chaired by President Recep Tayyip Erdoğan, read: "The state of emergency, implemented across the country within the scope of the fight against all terrorist organizations, the FETO/PSS, PKK/PYD-YPG, DAESH in particular, has been assessed; it has been decided to advise to extend the state of emergency in order to ensure the continuation of the measures, aimed at protecting our democracy, the rule of law and our citizens' rights and freedoms."

President Recep Tayyip Erdoğan chaired the National Security Council meeting at the Presidential Complex. A written statement was released following the meeting.

The statement conveyed that the NSC was briefed on the events, enthusiastically held at home and abroad with the participation of millions of citizens on the first anniversary of the defeat of the treasonous coup attempt, staged on 15 July 2016, and that the NSC remembered July 15 martyrs with grace and saluted all veterans with gratitude and appreciation on the occasion of the "Democracy and National Unity Day".

The statement underscored that the courageous soldiers, security officers and citizens, who died a martyr for the perpetuity of the country and the state, would never be forgotten, and that their memories were cherished with respect and grace. It was stated that the measures, taken in line with the law against all sorts of threats to the country's national security, the FETO/PSS, PKK/PYD-YPG, DAESH terrorist organizations in particular, and the struggle, conducted both at home and abroad in order to put an end to terrorism, were discussed extensively.

DETERMINATION IN THE FIGHT AGAINST TERROR

Highlighting that various narcotic drugs, seized during operations conducted to ensure citizens' peace and security, revealed once again the true face of the separatist terrorist organization, the statement read: "Assassinations of civilians and innocent people, representatives of political parties in particular, committed by the blood-thirsty terrorist organization and its extensions, clearly have shown that the organization's sole purpose is to wipe out anyone who is not with them."

"The fact that weapons and ammunition, given by certain allied countries to the PYD-YPG terrorist organization, have been seized from the PKK terrorist organization confirms once again Turkey's rightness in its insistent warning and objection that these are in fact the same organization although they appear under different names," the statement underscored. "It has been underlined that it cannot be possible for the region to find peace and security unless the double standards towards terrorist organizations are abandoned. Our call to the international community to abide by the commitments, made in order to reach a consensus in the fight against terror, has been reiterated. It has been underscored once again that necessary action will continue to be taken in line with international law in case a threat to our southern borders, originating from Syria and Iraq, is identified and harassment and attack take place, and that establishment of a terror state along Turkey's borders will never be allowed, and that the PKK/PYD-YPG terrorist organizations cannot be legitimized by bringing forward its struggle against another terrorist organization, DAESH."

CYPRUS CONFERENCE IN SWITZERLAND

The statement noted that the referendum decision taken by the Northern Iraq Regional Administration cannot be implemented—de jure and de facto—and that this attempt is a grave mistake and will lead to undesired consequences. "It has been assessed that preserving Iraq's territorial integrity and political unity depends on establishing enduring stability, peace, security and prosperity in the region. Retaking of Mosul from DAESH has been welcomed. It has been expressed that Turkey, along with the international community, is ready to undertake all kinds of responsibilities to rebuild the city. Also, it has been stated that the protection of Turkmen presence in Iraq and their rights is being monitored closely."

"The Cyprus Conference in Switzerland and its results have been evaluated," the statement read, underscoring the determination to protect the rights and interests of the Turkish Republic of Northern Cyprus and Turkey within the framework of Turkey's principal rights over the natural resources in Eastern Mediterranean. "The state of emergency, implemented across the country within the scope of the fight against all terrorist organizations, the FETO/PSS, PKK/PYD-YPG, DAESH in particular, has been assessed; it has been decided to advise to extend the state of emergency in order to ensure the continuation of the measures, aimed at protecting our democracy, the rule of law and our citizens' rights and freedoms."

SOURCE: Presidency of the Republic of Turkey. "NSC Advises to Extend State of Emergency." July 17, 2017. https://www.tccb.gov.tr/en/news/542/79947/national-security-council-convenes-at-the-presidential-complex.html.

OTHER HISTORIC DOCUMENTS OF INTEREST

FROM THIS VOLUME

FROM PREVIOUS *HISTORIC DOCUMENTS*

President Trump, United Nations Respond to Chemical Attack in Syria

APRIL 6, 7, AND 11, AND SEPTEMBER 6, 2017

On April 4, 2017, the Syrian Air Force launched an attack on rebels in Khan Shaykhun, Syria; the latest by the Syrian government in the six-year civil war. Unlike other traditional bombing runs, however, this attack was more pernicious—bombs filled with toxic chemicals rained down on rebel positions, turning the rebel-held area into a toxic kill zone. More than 80 people, including civilian women and children, died in the attack, because aid workers collapsed before reaching the injured. Doctors, civilians, and watchdog groups all quickly labeled it as a chemical attack, possibly with the deadly nerve agent sarin. Western leaders, including United Nations (UN) Secretary-General António Guterres and U.S. President Donald Trump, immediately denounced the attack and the Syrian government and called on the government's patrons, Iran and Russia, to cut support to the embattled regime. Syrian President Bashar al-Assad denied responsibility, instead asserting that the rebel forces launched the attack, while Russia claimed government warplanes hit a rebel cache of chemicals. Western leaders launched retaliatory strikes, hoping to signal that chemical attacks would not be condoned. The scale and brazenness of the attack threatened an already fragile cease-fire between the government and the rebel forces and imperiled UN attempts to broker further peace talks.

A DEADLY CHEMICAL ATTACK, SIGNS OF NERVE AGENT

Early in the morning on April 4, 2017, Syrian warplanes launched a bombing raid on rebel-held areas in Khan Shaykhun in northern Syria. Aid workers and civilians rushed to help those hit after the bombs landed, finding civilians and rebels dead or gasping for air. Photographs and videos posted online by residents showed children and older adults struggling to breathe or lying motionless as rescue workers ripped off their clothes and hosed them down with water. In one video, at least ten children lay motionless under a quilt.

The attack was the latest in an escalating civil war between the Syrian government, led by Syrian President Assad, and rebel insurgents. While the war had raged for six years, an attack of this magnitude had only come once, four years earlier. Similarly, Syrian warplanes had targeted civilians and insurgents alike with a deadly chemical attack, operating outside the legal bounds of traditional warfare. Hours after the attack, warplanes again appeared in the skies of the rebel-held territory. This time, the Syrian military targeted a clinic treating victims of the earlier attack, who were forced to smaller hospitals and clinics after an airstrike badly damaged the region's largest hospital two days earlier.

Unlike earlier strikes, this attack was different, according to local doctors, activists, and residents. While chlorine chemical attacks had almost become commonplace in northern Syria, none of the injured or dead exhibited symptoms associated with a chlorine attack. Chlorine typically only kills a handful of people, usually those in tightly enclosed areas, and dissipates into the air quickly. This strike, however, killed dozens, including those in the open air. Victims' pupils were reduced to pencil-point dots, while others were found foaming at the mouth. Taken together, watchdog groups and residents believed the attack involved the nerve agent known as sarin.

The attack was the deadliest chemical attack in Syria since the Syrian military launched a sarin attack in the Damascus suburbs, in which more than 1,000 people were killed according to the Syrian opposition. As with the attack on civilians in Khan Shaykhun, the government denied using chemical weapons, asserting that insurgents used chemicals to frame the government.

THE WORLD RESPONDS

The West quickly condemned the attack and launched retaliatory strikes of their own. President Trump, speaking from his South Florida club Mar-a-Lago, labeled the attack "a horrible chemical weapons attack on innocent civilians" and accused the Syrian government of being the instigator, saying, "Using a deadly nerve agent, Asad [sic] choked out the lives of helpless men, women, and children. It was a slow and brutal death for so many," adding, "No child of God should ever suffer such horror."

President Trump announced that he had authorized targeted military strikes on the airfield in Syria from where the attacks had launched. "It is in this vital national security interest of the United States to prevent and deter the spread and use of deadly chemical weapons," he said. "There can be no dispute that Syria used banned chemical weapons, violated its obligations under the Chemical Weapons Convention, and ignored the urging of the UN Security Council." President Trump called on other nations to join the United States in working to end the Syrian civil war and combat terrorism together.

The United Nations condemned the attack in similarly strong terms yet called for restraint. Secretary General Guterres called the attacks "abhorrent" but warned against escalating the conflict to "avoid any acts that could deepen the suffering of the Syrian people." He went on, "These events underscore my belief that there is no other way to solve the conflict than through a political solution," adding, "I call on the parties to urgently renew their commitment to making progress in the Geneva talks." Despite this call, it remained unlikely the UN Security Council would reach a political solution to the conflict. Partisan divide over assigning blame for the Syrian war has paralyzed its members almost since the conflict began in 2011.

In the face of overwhelming evidence of his military's involvement in the attacks, Assad denied responsibility, despite reports from international observers such as Human Rights Watch that the Syrian government possessed the ability, technical knowledge, and motive to carry out the attack. His military instead accused the rebel forces of attacking their own targets and said the insurgents had accused the army of using toxic weapons "every time they fail to achieve the goals of their sponsors."

Meanwhile, Syria's main ally remained supportive. For years, Russia propped up the Syrian regime, providing financial, military, and political backing for President Assad. A permanent member of the UN Security Council, Russia stymied any international resolution to hold the Syrian regime accountable for their role in the civil war. This time was no different. Despite widespread condemnation from the United Nations, Western leaders, and international humanitarian groups, Russia refused to fault Syria for the attack. Instead, Russian state agents contended that Syrian warplanes launched traditional munitions that struck insurgent chemical caches and maintained that it had no military role in the strike.

Western diplomatic agencies, however, argued that Russian officials were trying to evade responsibility because Russia and Iran guaranteed Syria would adhere to a cease-fire that Russia had helped organize.

Days following the attack, the United States released a declassified report outlining evidence against the Syrian government and Russia's role in sowing confusion around the attack. According to the report, the Syrian and Russian governments "have sought to confuse the world community about who is responsible for using chemical weapons against the Syrian people in this and earlier attacks." The report specifically noted that the governments of Syria and Russia rely on disinformation and "false narratives" concluding that "Moscow's response to the April 4 attack follows a familiar pattern of its responses to other egregious actions; it spins out multiple conflicting accounts in order to create confusion and sow doubt within the international community."

THE WEST RETALIATES

Western leaders intensified their pressure on Syria in the days following the chemical attack, launching political and military assaults on the Syrian regime. The night of the attack, France, the United Kingdom, and the United States pushed the UN Security Council to adopt a resolution that condemned the attack and ordered the Syrian government to provide to international investigators all flight logs, flight plans, and names of commanders in charge of air operations. The resolution failed to pass following a veto by Russia. Meanwhile, U.S. Secretary of State Rex Tillerson pressured Syria's two biggest allies, Russia and Iran, to exercise "their influence over the Syrian regime and to guarantee that this sort of horrific attack never happens again." Secretary Tillerson also laid blame for the attack at the feet of both nations. "Russia and Iran also bear great moral responsibility for these deaths," Tillerson said.

The United States paired its political pressure with military strikes against the Syrian government. Two days after the chemical attack, the destroyers USS Porter and USS Ross in the eastern Mediterranean launched fifty-nine Tomahawk missiles against the Shayrat Airbase near Homs, Syria. Defense officials called the attack "a one-off" that targeted aircraft, hardened aircraft shelters, petroleum and logistical storage, ammunition supply bunkers, air defense systems, and radars. To avoid collateral damage, American leaders notified Russian forces in advance of the strike. According to the Pentagon, "U.S. military planners took precautions to minimize risk to Russian or Syrian personnel located at the airfield."

Despite the advance warning, Russia leaders condemned the U.S. airstrikes and stressed that they would only serve to escalate the conflict. In a statement ahead of the strikes, Russian deputy UN Envoy Vladimir Safronkov said, "We have to think about negative consequences, negative consequences, and all the responsibility if military action occurred will be on shoulders of those who initiated such doubtful and tragic enterprise." After the strikes, Russia said the attacks violated international law and warned that they would do significant damage to relations between Russia and the United States.

U.S. officials ignored the threat from Russia and framed the strikes as a message to the world that the president was not willing to stand by as the Assad regime attacked its own people. "This clearly indicates the president is willing to take decisive action when called for," Secretary Tillerson said. According to Secretary Tillerson, President Trump concluded after seeing the results of the chemical attack that the United States could no longer "turn a blind eye." "The more we fail to respond to the use of these weapons, the more we begin to normalize their use," he continued. U.S. Defense Secretary Jim Mattis echoed

Secretary Tillerson's comments, stating that the strike was a signal to President Assad, Russia, and Iran that the United States intended to use military force if Syria continued to use chemical weapons. National Security Advisor H. R. McMaster added that the strikes would not eliminate the threat of chemical weapons but would degrade President Assad's ability to use them. According to McMaster, the military specifically avoided an alleged sarin gas facility at the airfield.

In the months following the attack, evidence continued to mount that the Syrian government authorized the chemical attacks. The UN's Independent International Commission of Inquiry on the Syrian Arab Republic announced in September that a Sukhoi 22 aircraft operated by the Syrian Air Force carried out the attack, one of at least twenty such chemical attacks carried out by Syrian government forces from March 2013 to April 2017. While watchdog groups and western intelligence agencies reached similar conclusions before the United Nations' report, the panel's report carried more weight in the eyes of the international community making it harder for the Syrian government and its allies to dismiss.

A Fragile Cease-Fire Unravels

The attacks came during a fragile, often nominal cease-fire between the Syrian government and rebel forces negotiated by Russia, Turkey, and Iran. At the same time, the United Nations was in the process of brokering peace talks. However, the scale and brazenness of the attack imperiled both. Further actions by the Assad regime in the months that followed the chemical attack, including the forced removal of civilians, government efforts to cut off 600,000 people from food and medical supplies, and indiscriminate bombardment, all but shuttered the efforts to end the conflict. Meanwhile, western allies, led by the United States, escalated their bombings against military targets and terrorist organizations in Syria. By the close of 2017, the Syrian civil war showed little sign of abating.

—Robert Howard

Following is a statement by U.S. President Donald Trump delivered on April 6, 2017, announcing military operations in Syria; a statement delivered on April 7, 2017, by United Nations Secretary-General Guterres condemning the chemical attacks in Syria; a report declassified by the National Security Council on April 11, 2017, about the chemical attack; and an excerpt from the UN Independent International Commission of Inquiry on the Syrian Arab Republic's report of September 6, 2017, in which it concluded that Syria's government used chemical weapons against civilians.

President Trump Remarks on U.S. Military Operations in Syria

April 6, 2017

My fellow Americans, on Tuesday, Syrian dictator Bashar al-Asad *[sic]* launched a horrible chemical weapons attack on innocent civilians. Using a deadly nerve agent, Asad *[sic]* choked out the lives of helpless men, women, and children. It was a slow and brutal death for so many. Even beautiful babies were cruelly murdered in this very barbaric attack. No child of God should ever suffer such horror.

Tonight I ordered a targeted military strike on the airfield in Syria from where the chemical attack was launched. It is in this vital national security interest of the United States to prevent and deter the spread and use of deadly chemical weapons. There can be no dispute that Syria used banned chemical weapons, violated its obligations under the Chemical Weapons Convention, and ignored the urging of the U.N. Security Council.

Years of previous attempts at changing Asad's [sic] behavior have all failed and failed very dramatically. As a result, the refugee crisis continues to deepen, and the region continues to destabilize, threatening the United States and its allies.

Tonight I call on all civilized nations to join us in seeking to end the slaughter and bloodshed in Syria and also to end terrorism of all kinds and all types. We ask for God's wisdom as we face the challenge of our very troubled world. We pray for the lives of the wounded and for the souls of those who have passed. And we hope that as long as America stands for justice, then peace and harmony will, in the end, prevail.

Goodnight. And God bless America and the entire world. Thank you.

SOURCE: Executive Office of the President. "Remarks on United States Military Operations in Syria from Palm Beach, Florida." April 6, 2017. *Compilation of Presidential Documents* 2017, no. 00238 (April 6, 2017). https://www.gpo.gov/fdsys/pkg/DCPD-201700238/pdf/DCPD-201700238.pdf.

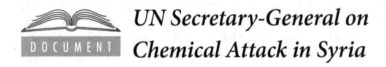

UN Secretary-General on Chemical Attack in Syria

April 7, 2017

I continue to follow the situation in Syria closely and with grave concern.

I was abhorred by the chemical weapons attack in Khan Shaykhun, Syria, and the death and injury of many innocent civilians.

I have long stated that there needs to be accountability for such crimes, in line with existing international norms and Security Council resolutions.

I have been following reports of the air strikes against the Shayrat Airbase in Syria conducted by the United States.

Mindful of the risk of escalation, I appeal for restraint to avoid any acts that could deepen the suffering of the Syrian people.

These events underscore my belief that there is no other way to solve the conflict than through a political solution. I call on the parties to urgently renew their commitment to making progress in the Geneva talks.

A political solution also remains essential for progress in the fight against terrorism.

The Security Council has the primary responsibility for international peace and security. I call on the Council to unite and exercise that responsibility.

For too long, international law has been ignored in the Syrian conflict, and it is our shared duty to uphold international standards of humanity. This is a prerequisite to ending the unrelenting suffering of the people of Syria.

SOURCE: United Nations. "Secretary-General's Statement on Syria." April 7, 2017. https://www.un.org/sg/en/content/sg/statement/2017-04-07/secretary-generals-statement-syria.

National Security Council Report on the Chemical Weapons Attack

April 11, 2017

The United States is confident that the Syrian regime conducted a chemical weapons attack, using the nerve agent sarin, against its own people in the town of Khan Shaykhun in southern Idlib Province on April 4, 2017. According to observers at the scene, the attack resulted in at least 50 and up to 100 fatalities (including many children), with hundreds of additional injuries.

We have confidence in our assessment because we have signals intelligence and geospatial intelligence, laboratory analysis of physiological samples collected from multiple victims, as well as a significant body of credible open source reporting, that tells a clear and consistent story. We cannot publicly release all available intelligence on this attack due to the need to protect sources and methods, but the following includes an unclassified summary of the U.S. Intelligence Community's analysis of this attack.

[The following section summarizing the U.S. intelligence community's assessment of the attack has been omitted.]

Refuting the False Narratives

The Syrian regime and its primary backer, Russia, have sought to confuse the world community about who is responsible for using chemical weapons against the Syrian people in this and earlier attacks. Initially, Moscow dismissed the allegations of a chemical weapons attack in Khan Shaykhun, claiming the attack was a "prank of a provocative nature" and that all evidence was fabricated. It is clear, however, that the Syrian opposition could not manufacture this quantity and variety of videos and other reporting from both the attack site and medical facilities in Syria and Turkey while deceiving both media observers and intelligence agencies.

Moscow has since claimed that the release of chemicals was caused by a regime airstrike on a terrorist ammunition depot in the eastern suburbs of Khan Shaykhun. However, a Syrian military source told Russian state media on April 4 that regime forces had not carried out any airstrike in Khan Shaykhun, contradicting Russia's claim. An open source video also shows where we believe the chemical munition landed—not on a facility filled with weapons, but in the middle of a street in the northern section of Khan Shaykhun. Commercial satellite imagery of that site from April 6, after the allegation, shows a crater in the road that corresponds to the open source video.

Moscow has suggested that terrorists had been using the alleged ammunition depot to produce and store shells containing toxic gas that they then used in Iraq, adding that both Iraq and international organizations have confirmed the use of such weapons by militants. While it is widely accepted that the Islamic State of Iraq and Syria (ISIS) has repeatedly used sulfur mustard on the battlefield, there are no indications that ISIS was responsible for this incident or that the attack involved chemicals in possession.

Moscow suggested this airstrike occurred between 11:30 AM and 12:30 PM local time on April 4, disregarding that allegations first appeared on social media close to 7:00 AM local time that morning, when we know regime aircraft were operating over Khan

Shaykhun. In addition, observed munition remnants at the crater and staining around the impact point are consistent with a munition that functioned, but structures nearest to the impact crater did not sustain damage that would be expected from a conventional high-explosive payload. Instead, the damage is more consistent with a chemical munition.

The Syrian regime has used other chemical agents in attacks against civilians in opposition held areas in the past, including the use of sulfur mustard in Aleppo in late 2016. Russia has alleged that video footage from April 4 indicated that victims from this attack showed the same of poisoning as victims in Aleppo last fall, implying that something other than a nerve agent was used in Khan Shaykhun. However, victims of the attack on April 4 displayed tell-tale signs of nerve agent exposure, including pinpoint pupils, foaming at the nose and mouth, and twitching, all of which are inconsistent with exposure to sulfur mustard.

Russia's allegations fit with a pattern of deflecting blame from the regime and attempting to undermine the credibility of its opponents. Russia and Syria, in multiple instances since mid-2016, have blamed the opposition for chemical use in attacks. Yet similar to the Russian narrative for the attack on Khan Shaykhun, most Russian allegations have lacked specific or credible information. Last November, for instance, senior Russian officials used an image from a widely publicized regime chemical weapons attack in 2013 on social media platforms to publicly allege chemical weapons use by the opposition. In May 2016, Russian officials made a similar claim using an image from a video game. In October 2016, Moscow also claimed terrorists used chlorine and white phosphorus in Aleppo, even though pro-Russian media footage from the attack site showed no sign of chlorine use. In fact, our intelligence from the same day suggests that neither of Russia's accounts was accurate and that the regime may have mistakenly used chlorine on its own forces. Russia's contradictory and erroneous reports appear to have been intended to confuse the situation and to obfuscate on behalf of the regime.

Moscow's allegations typically have been timed to distract the international community from Syria's ongoing use of chemical weapons—such as the claims earlier this week—or to counter the findings from the Organization for the Prohibition of Chemical Weapons (OPCW)-United Nations (UN) Joint Investigative Mechanism (JIM), which confirmed in August and October 2016 reports that the Syrian regime has continued to use chemical weapons on multiple occasions long after it committed to relinquish its arsenal in 2013. Russia has also questioned the impartial findings of the body that Russia helped to establish—and was even willing to go so far as to suggest that the Assad regime should investigate itself for the use of chemical weapons.

Moscow's response to the April 4 attack follows a familiar pattern of its responses to other egregious actions; it spins out multiple, conflicting accounts in order to create confusion and sow doubt within the international community.

International Condemnation and a Time for Action

The Assad regime's brutal use of chemical weapons is unacceptable and poses a clear threat to the national security interests of the United States and the international community. Use of weapons of mass destruction by any actor lowers the threshold for others that may seek to follow suit and raises the possibility that they may be used against the United States, our allies or partners, or any other nation around the world.

The United States calls on the world community in the strongest possible terms to stand with us in making an unambiguous statement that this behavior will not be tolerated. This is a critical—we must demonstrate that subterfuge and false facts hold no weight, that excuses by those shielding their allies are making the world a more dangerous place, and that the Syrian regime's use of chemical weapons will not be permitted to continue.

SOURCE: National Security Council. "The Assad Regime's Use of Chemical Weapons on April 4, 2017." April 11, 2017.

UN Independent International Commission of Inquiry on the Syrian Arab Republic Report

September 6, 2017

[All footnotes, the introduction, and sections detailing political and military developments as well as attacks against civilian populations, children, and protected objects have been omitted.]

VI. USE OF CHEMICAL WEAPONS

67. Between March 2013 and March 2017, the Commission documented 25 incidents of chemical weapons use in the Syrian Arab Republic, of which 20 were perpetrated by government forces and used primarily against civilians. During the reporting period, government forces further used chemical weapons against civilians in the town of Khan Shaykhun, in Al-Latamneh, located approximately 11 kilometres south of Khan Shaykhun, and in eastern Ghouta.

68. While Khan Shaykhun and Al-Latamneh are controlled by Hay'at Tahrir al-Sham, Ahrar-al-Sham and various Free Syrian Army groups, eastern Ghouta is primarily controlled by Jaish al-Islam and Faylaq al-Rahman. At the time of the use of chemical weapons in Khan Shaykhun and Al-Latamneh, Syrian and Russian forces were conducting an aerial campaign against Hay'at Tahrir al-Sham and armed groups in northern Hamah and southern Idlib.

69. At around 6.30 a.m. on 30 March—five days after the chlorine attack on Al-Latamneh hospital by Syrian forces (see para. 64 above)—an unidentified warplane dropped two bombs in an agricultural field south of Al-Latamneh village. Interviewees recalled how the first bomb made almost no sound but released a "toxic material" absent any particular smell, while the second bomb caused a loud explosion. As a result of the former, at least 85 people suffered from respiratory difficulties, loss of consciousness, red eyes and impaired vision. Among the injured were 12 male farmers located 300 metres away from the impact point, 2 of them minors. Nine medical personnel who treated patients without protection also fell ill.

70. While the Commission is unable to identify the exact agent to which the victims of the 30 March incident were exposed, interviewees described certain symptoms,

including a very low pulse in one case, and contracted pupils, suffocation, nausea and spasms in another, that indicate poisoning by a phosphor-organic chemical, such as a pesticide or a nerve agent. The absence of a characteristic chlorine odour, coupled with secondary intoxications among medical personnel treating victims, supports the conclusion that a toxic chemical other than chlorine was employed. Given that Syrian and Russian forces were conducting an aerial campaign in the area, the absence of indications that Russian forces have ever used chemical weapons in the Syrian Arab Republic, and the repeated use of chemical weapons by the Syrian air force, there are reasonable grounds to conclude that the Syrian air force used chemical weapons in Al-Latamneh on 30 March.

71. As part of its offensive to fully besiege Barza, Tishreen and Qabun (see annex III, para. 3), three rockets were launched on the afternoon of 29 March from government forces positions into a residential area of central Qabun municipality, close to the Al-Hayat hospital, as well as into neighbouring Tishreen. One of the rockets released a white cloud in Qabun and witnesses recalled the spread of gas, which smelled strongly of domestic chlorine. Thirty-five persons were injured, including one woman and two children. Victims exhibited symptoms consistent with chlorine exposure, including respiratory difficulties, coughing and runny noses. The most serious cases were treated with hydrocortisone l and oxygen. On 7 April, shortly after midday, Al-Hayat hospital received two men suffering from milder manifestations of the same symptoms. In the first week of July, government forces used chlorine against Faylaq ar-Rahman fighters in Damascus on three occasions: on 1 July in Ayn Tarma, on 2 July in Zamalka and on 6 July in Jowbar. In total, 46 fighters suffered from red eyes, hypoxia, rhinorrhoea, spastic cough and bronchial secretions.

72. The gravest allegation of the use of chemical weapons by Syrian forces during the reporting period was in Khan Shaykhun. In the early morning of 4 April, public reports emerged that air strikes had released sarin in the town. Dozens of civilians were reported killed and hundreds more injured. Russian and Syrian officials denied that Syrian forces had used chemical weapons, explaining that air strikes conducted by Syrian forces at 11.30 a.m. that day had struck a terrorist chemical weapons depot.

73. To establish the facts surrounding these allegations, the Commission sent a note verbale on 7 April to the Permanent Representative of the Syrian Arab Republic to the United Nations Office at Geneva and specialized institutions in Switzerland requesting information from the Government. At the time of writing, no response has been received. The Commission conducted 43 interviews with eyewitnesses, victims, first responders and medical workers. It also collected satellite imagery, photographs of bomb remnants, early warning reports and videos of the area allegedly affected by the air strikes. The Commission also took into account the findings of the Organisation for the Prohibition of Chemical Weapons report on the results of its fact-finding mission. Below is a summary of the Commission's findings, elaborated in full in annex II.

74. Interviewees and early warning reports indicate that a Sukhoi 22 (Su-22) aircraft conducted four air strikes in Khan Shaykhun at around 6.45 a.m. Only Syrian forces operate such aircraft. The Commission identified three conventional

bombs, likely OFAB-100-120, and one chemical bomb. Eyewitnesses recalled that the latter bomb made less noise and produced less smoke than the others. Photographs of weapon remnants depict a chemical aerial bomb of a type manufactured in the former Soviet Union.

75. The chemical bomb killed at least 83 persons, including 28 children and 23 women, and injured another 293 persons, including 103 children. On the basis of samples obtained during autopsies and from individuals undergoing treatment in a neighbouring country, those who undertook the fact-finding mission of the Organisation for the Prohibition of Chemical Weapons concluded that the victims had been exposed to sarin or a sarin-like substance. The extensive information independently collected by the Commission on symptoms suffered by victims is consistent with sarin exposure.

76. Interviewees denied the presence of a weapons depot near the impact point of the chemical bomb. The Commission notes that it is extremely unlikely that an air strike would release sarin potentially stored inside such a structure in amounts sufficient to explain the number of casualties recorded. First, if such a depot had been destroyed by an air strike, the explosion would have burnt off most of the agent inside the building or forced it into the rubble where it would have been absorbed, rather than released in significant amounts into the atmosphere. Second, the facility would still be heavily contaminated today, for which there is no evidence. Third, the scenario suggested by Russian and Syrian officials does not explain the timing of the appearance of victims—hours before the time Russian and Syrian officials gave for the strike.

77. In view of the above, the Commission finds that there are reasonable grounds to believe that Syrian forces attacked Khan Shaykhun with a sarin bomb at approximately 6.45 a.m. on 4 April, constituting the war crimes of using chemical weapons and indiscriminate attacks in a civilian inhabited area. The use of sarin by Syrian forces also violates the Convention on the Prohibition of the Development, Production, Stockpiling and Use of Chemical Weapons and on Their Destruction and Security Council resolution 2118 (2013).

[Sections detailing the ongoing investigation and recommendations as well as the annexes have been omitted.]

Source: United Nations Independent International Commission of Inquiry on the Syrian Arab Republic. "Report of the Independent International Commission of Inquiry on the Syrian Arab Republic." September 6, 2017. http://www.ohchr.org/Documents/HRBodies/HRCouncil/CoISyria/A_HRC_36_55_EN.docx.

Other Historic Documents of Interest

From previous *Historic Documents*

- Aleppo Returned to Syrian Government Control; Russia Backs New Trilateral Talks, *2016*, p. 655
- Syria Peace Talks Begin, *2016*, p. 68

- United Nations Issues Report regarding the Ongoing Crisis in Syria, *2015*, p. 583
- United Nations-Brokered Syrian Peace Talks Conclude without Agreement, *2014*, p. 31
- President Obama Remarks on Conflict in Syria, *2013*, p. 411

U.S. Airstrikes in Afghanistan; Pentagon Sends Additional Troops

APRIL 13, JUNE 14, AND AUGUST 21, 2017

In the first half of 2017, President Donald Trump provided more leeway to the Pentagon and military commanders on the ground in combat zones to make decisions and carry out operations they believe best suited to the mission in Afghanistan. On April 13, the U.S.-led coalition in the Middle Eastern nation used this authority to drop America's largest non-nuclear weapon to destroy Islamic State of Iraq and the Levant (ISIL) tunnels near the Pakistan border. And in June, it was declared that the Secretary of Defense would be given the authority to set troop levels in Afghanistan. It was not until August that President Trump gave a more complete picture of how his administration would operate in Afghanistan. In a major shift from his former statements, the president decided to leave U.S. troops in the country to fight terrorist elements.

MOTHER OF ALL BOMBS DROPPED IN AFGHANISTAN

On April 13, the U.S. military targeted ISIL strongholds in Nangarhar province in Afghanistan (near the Pakistan border) with a 21,600-lb. bomb that was nicknamed the Mother of All Bombs (MOAB). The strike hit ISIL tunnels in an area where fighting had intensified during the previous week. According to the Afghan Defense Ministry, MOAB killed ninety-four ISIL fighters; no civilians were harmed. ISIL, however, denied that any of its fighters were killed in the attack.

First tested in 2003, the MOAB had not yet been used in combat. This particular strike was necessitated, according to Gen. John Nicholson, commander of U.S. and coalition forces in Afghanistan, by ISIL's expanded use of bunkers and tunnels, and because the particular region in Afghanistan was difficult to attack on foot due to both the terrain and landmines placed by ISIL fighters. "This is the right munition to reduce these obstacles and maintain the momentum of our offensive," he said. Gen. Nicolson also noted that use of the MOAB should be seen as a sign that coalition forces in Afghanistan "will not relent in our mission to destroy [ISIL] . . . there will be no sanctuary for terrorists."

The dropping of MOAB was supported by the Afghan government and military. A statement released by Afghan President Ashraf Ghani's office noted that "Afghan and foreign troops closely coordinated this operation and were extra cautious to avoid any civilian casualties." The nation's former president, Hamid Karzai, however, weighed in on Twitter that the United States was using Afghanistan "as a testing ground for new and dangerous weapons" and cautioned, "It is upon us, Afghans, to stop the USA."

PENTAGON GIVEN CONTROL OF TROOP LEVELS

In June, it was revealed that President Trump had given the Pentagon, under the leadership of Secretary of Defense Gen. Jim Mattis, control over troop levels in the war in

Afghanistan, a fight that was entering its sixteenth year. Secretary Mattis said this new responsibility "will enable our military to have greater agility to conduct operations, recognizing our military posture there is part of a broader regional context." Mattis cautioned that, despite calls from generals in Afghanistan for thousands of more boots on the ground, "[t]he delegation of this authority does not in itself change the force levels for Afghanistan. Rather, it ensures the Department of Defense can facilitate our missions and align our commitment to the rapidly evolving security situation, giving our troops greater latitude to provide air power and other vital support."

At the time of the Pentagon's announcement, there were 8,400 troops in Afghanistan, down significantly from 100,000 at the height of the U.S.-led invasion. Combat operations in Afghanistan ended at the close of 2014, and troops remaining in the country were there to conduct counterterrorism missions as well as train and advise Afghan troops as they battled terrorist networks in the country. In late August, Gen. Nicholson announced that more American troops would be sent to Afghanistan and that they would remain in the country to advise and train Afghan forces without a timeline for withdrawal. The number of troops was rumored by news outlets to be around 4,000, although the Pentagon did not make the total count immediately available.

Trump Discusses Afghanistan Strategy

On August 21, President Trump gave the first address of his presidency that outlined his intended strategy for U.S. intervention in Afghanistan. The president shared that his initial instinct had been to pull all troops out of the country, but that, after speaking with his advisors, he determined it would be best to work toward an "honorable" exit, and one that shifted the focus from nation building to ending the terrorist threat in the country. "I share the American people's frustration," Trump said. "I also share their frustration over a foreign policy that has spent too much time, energy, money, and most importantly, lives, trying to rebuild countries in our own image instead of pursuing our security interests above all other considerations." Trump noted that his decision to remain was also tied to the threat posed by ISIL and other terrorist organizations operating within the region, outside Afghanistan's borders. "We must stop the resurgence of safe havens that enable terrorists to threaten America, and we must prevent nuclear weapons and materials from coming into the hands of terrorists and being used against us or anywhere in the world for that matter," the president said.

While the decision to remain in Afghanistan marked a major departure from campaign rhetoric and pronouncements early in the first year of his presidency, Trump did caution that the United States "commitment is not unlimited, and our support is not a blank check." He called on the government and people of Afghanistan "to take ownership of their future, to govern their society, and to achieve an everlasting peace. We are a partner and a friend, but we will not dictate to the Afghan people how to live or how to govern their own complex society. We are not nation-building again. We are killing terrorists." Afghan President Ghani welcomed the new U.S. strategy, noting that basing the mission on conditions rather than a timetable made clear U.S. support for Afghanistan and would help increase the capacity of Afghan troops. The North Atlantic Treaty Organization (NATO) and U.S. allies in the region such as the United Kingdom similarly welcomed a conditions-based approach. "We have to stay the course in Afghanistan," said Michael Fallon, Britain's Defense Secretary, to decrease threats to the west posed by terrorist organizations in the region.

—Heather Kerrigan

Following is a statement from the U.S. Department of Defense on April 13, 2017, regarding the bombing and destruction of a terrorist stronghold in Afghanistan; a June 14, 2017, statement by Secretary of Defense Jim Mattis on the authority to change the number of troops in Afghanistan; and August 21, 2017, remarks by President Donald Trump on military strategy in Afghanistan.

Defense Department Announces Destruction of Terrorist Stronghold in Afghanistan

April 13, 2017

At 7:32 p.m. local time today, U.S. Forces Afghanistan conducted a strike on an Islamic State of Iraq and Syria-Khorasan tunnel complex in Achin district, Nangarhar province, Afghanistan, as part of ongoing efforts to defeat ISIS-K in Afghanistan, according to a U.S. Forces Afghanistan news release.

ISIS-K, also known as the Khorasan group, is based in the Afghanistan-Pakistan region and is composed primarily of former members of Tehrik-e Taliban Pakistan and the Afghan Taliban.

The strike used a GBU-43/B Massive Ordnance Air Blast bomb dropped from a U.S. aircraft. The strike was designed to minimize the risk to Afghan and U.S. forces conducting clearing operations in the area while maximizing the destruction of ISIS-K fighters and facilities.

"As ISIS-K's losses have mounted, they are using [improvised bombs], bunkers and tunnels to thicken their defense," said Army Gen. John W. Nicholson, commander of U.S. Forces Afghanistan. "This is the right munition to reduce these obstacles and maintain the momentum of our offensive against ISIS-K."

U.S. forces took every precaution to avoid civilian casualties with this strike and will continue offensive operations until ISIS-K is destroyed in Afghanistan.

SOURCE: U.S. Defense Department. "U.S. Bombs, Destroys Khorasan Group Stronghold in Afghanistan." April 13, 2017. https://www.defense.gov/News/Article/Article/1151139/us-bombs-destroys-khorasan-group-stronghold-in-afghanistan/.

Secretary of Defense Announces Change in Troop Strategy

June 14, 2017

Yesterday afternoon, the President directed the Department of Defense to set troop levels in Afghanistan. This will enable our military to have greater agility to conduct operations, recognizing our military posture there is part of a broader regional context.

Thanks to the vigilance and skill of the U.S. military and our many allies and partners, horrors on the scale of Sept. 11, 2001, have not been repeated on our shores. However, the danger continues to evolve and that danger requires a commitment to defeat terrorist organizations that threaten the United States, other nations, and the people of Afghanistan. For example, ISIS has established a branch, al-Qaeda and other terrorist groups remain active inside Afghanistan, and the Taliban continue to pose a challenge to the democratically elected government.

This administration will not repeat the mistakes of the past. We cannot allow Afghanistan to once again become a launching point for attacks on our homeland or on our allies.

We are making progress in degrading these groups, but their defeat will come about only by giving our men and women on the ground the support and the authorities they need to win.

The delegation of this authority does not in itself change the force levels for Afghanistan. Rather, it ensures the Department of Defense can facilitate our missions and align our commitment to the rapidly evolving security situation, giving our troops greater latitude to provide air power and other vital support. Our core mission will remain the same: to train, advise and assist Afghan forces. We are there to help defeat a common enemy and ensure Afghan forces can safeguard the future of their country.

This decision is part of a broader strategy we are developing that addresses our role in Afghanistan and beyond. We will present this to the President in the coming weeks. We will continue to work with our allies and we will ask more of them.

Working with the Afghan government and our allies and partners, we will achieve victory against the terrorists abroad, protect our borders at home, and keep America safe.

Source: U.S. Defense Department. "Statement by Secretary of Defense Jim Mattis on Afghanistan Troop Levels." June 14, 2017. https://www.defense.gov/News/News-Releases/News-Release-View/Article/1214597/statement-by-secretary-of-defense-jim-mattis-on-afghanistan-troop-levels/.

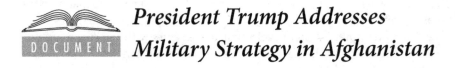

President Trump Addresses Military Strategy in Afghanistan

August 21, 2017

Thank you very much. Thank you. Please be seated.

Vice President Pence, Secretary of State Tillerson, members of the Cabinet, General Dunford, Deputy Secretary Shanahan, and Colonel Duggan. Most especially, thank you to the men and women of Fort Myer and every member of the United States military at home and abroad. We send our thoughts and prayers to the families of our brave sailors who were injured and lost after a tragic collision at sea, as well as to those conducting the search-and-recovery efforts.

I am here tonight to lay out our path forward in Afghanistan and South Asia. But before I provide the details of our new strategy, I want to say a few words to the servicemembers here with us tonight, to those watching from their posts, and to all Americans listening at home.

Since the founding of our Republic, our country has produced a special class of heroes whose selflessness, courage, and resolve is unmatched in human history. American patriots from every generation have given their last breath on the battlefield for our Nation and for our freedom. Through their lives—and though their lives were cut short, in their deeds they achieved total immortality.

By following the heroic example of those who fought to preserve our republic, we can find the inspiration our country needs to unify, to heal, and to remain one Nation under God. The men and women of our military operate as one team, with one shared mission and one shared sense of purpose. They transcend every line of race, ethnicity, creed, and color to serve together—and sacrifice together—in absolutely perfect cohesion. That is because all servicemembers are brothers and sisters. They're all part of the same family; it's called the American family. They take the same oath, fight for the same flag, and live according to the same law. They are bound together by common purpose, mutual trust, and selfless devotion to our Nation and to each other.

The soldier understands what we, as a Nation, too often forget: that a wound inflicted upon a single member of our community is a wound inflicted upon us all. When one part of America hurts, we all hurt. And when one citizen suffers an injustice, we all suffer together. Loyalty to our Nation demands loyalty to one another. Love for America requires love for all of its people. When we open our hearts to patriotism, there is no room for prejudice, no place for bigotry, and no tolerance for hate.

The young men and women we send to fight our wars abroad deserve to return to a country that is not at war with itself at home. We cannot remain a force for peace in the world if we are not at peace with each other. As we send our bravest to defeat our enemies overseas—and we will always win—let us find the courage to heal our divisions within. Let us make a simple promise to the men and women we ask to fight in our name that, when they return home from battle, they will find a country that has renewed the sacred bonds of love and loyalty that unite us together as one.

Thanks to the vigilance and skill of the American military and of our many allies throughout the world, horrors on the scale of September 11—and nobody can ever forget that—have not been repeated on our shores. But we must also acknowledge the reality I am here to talk about tonight: that nearly 16 years after September 11 attacks, after the extraordinary sacrifice of blood and treasure, the American people are weary of war without victory. Nowhere is this more evident than with the war in Afghanistan, the longest war in American history, 17 years.

I share the American people's frustration. I also share their frustration over a foreign policy that has spent too much time, energy, money, and most importantly, lives trying to rebuild countries in our own image, instead of pursuing our security interests above all other considerations.

That is why, shortly after my Inauguration, I directed Secretary of Defense Mattis and my national security team to undertake a comprehensive review of all strategic options in Afghanistan and South Asia. My original instinct was to pull out, and historically, I like following my instincts. But all my life, I've heard that decisions are much different when you sit behind the desk in the Oval Office, in other words, when you're President of the United States. So I studied Afghanistan in great detail and from every conceivable angle. After many meetings, over many months, we held our final meeting last Friday at Camp David, with my Cabinet and generals, to complete our strategy. I arrived at three fundamental conclusion about America's core interests in Afghanistan.

First, our Nation must seek an honorable and enduring outcome worthy of the tremendous sacrifices that have been made, especially the sacrifices of lives. The men and women who serve our Nation in combat deserve a plan for victory. They deserve the tools they need—and the trust they have earned—to fight and to win.

Second, the consequences of a rapid exit are both predictable and unacceptable. Nine-eleven, the worst terrorist attack in our history, was planned and directed from Afghanistan because that country was ruled by a government that gave comfort and shelter to terrorists. A hasty withdrawal would create a vacuum that terrorists, including ISIS and Al Qaida, would instantly fill, just as happened before September 11.

And as we know, in 2011, America hastily and mistakenly withdrew from Iraq. As a result, our hard-won gains slipped back into the hands of terrorist enemies. Our soldiers watched as cities they had fought for and bled to liberate and won were occupied by a terrorist group called ISIS. The vacuum we created by leaving too soon gave safe haven for ISIS to spread, to grow, recruit, and launch attacks. We cannot repeat in Afghanistan the mistake our leaders made in Iraq.

Third and finally, I concluded that the security threats we face in Afghanistan and the broader region are immense. Today, 20 U.S.-designated foreign terrorist organizations are active in Afghanistan and Pakistan, the highest concentration in any region anywhere in the world. For its part, Pakistan often gives safe haven to agents of chaos, violence, and terror. The threat is worse because Pakistan and India are two nuclear-armed states whose tense relations threaten to spiral into conflict. And that could happen.

No one denies that we have inherited a challenging and troubling situation in Afghanistan and South Asia, but we do not have the luxury of going back in time and making different or better decisions. When I became President, I was given a bad and very complex hand, but I fully knew what I was getting into: big and intricate problems. But one way or another, these problems will be solved—I'm a problem solver—and in the end, we will win. We must address the reality of the world as it exists right now: the threats we face, and the confronting of all of the problems of today and extremely predictable consequences of a hasty withdrawal. We need look no further than last week's vile, vicious attack in Barcelona to understand that terror groups will stop at nothing to commit the mass murder of innocent men, women, and children. You saw it for yourself. Horrible.

As I outlined in my speech in Saudi Arabia 3 months ago, America and our partners are committed to stripping terrorists of their territory, cutting off their funding, and exposing the false allure of their evil ideology. Terrorists who slaughter innocent people will find no glory in this life or the next. They are nothing but thugs and criminals and predators and—that's right—losers. Working alongside our allies, we will break their will, dry up their recruitment, keep them from crossing our borders, and yes, we will defeat them, and we will defeat them handily.

In Afghanistan and Pakistan, America's interests are clear: We must stop the resurgence of safe havens that enable terrorists to threaten America, and we must prevent nuclear weapons and materials from coming into the hands of terrorists and being used against us or anywhere in the world for that matter. But to prosecute this war, we will learn from history. As a result of our comprehensive review, American strategy in Afghanistan and South Asia will change dramatically in the following ways:

A core pillar of our new strategy is a shift from a time-based approach to one based on conditions. I've said it many times how counterproductive it is for the United States to announce in advance the dates we intend to begin or end military options. We will not talk about numbers of troops or our plans for further military activities. Conditions on the ground—not arbitrary timetables—will guide our strategy from now on. America's enemies must never know our plans or believe they can wait us out. I will not say when we are going to attack, but attack we will.

Another fundamental pillar of our new strategy is the integration of all instruments of American power—diplomatic, economic, and military—toward a successful outcome. Someday, after an effective military effort, perhaps it will be possible to have a political settlement that includes elements of the Taliban in Afghanistan, but nobody knows if or when that will ever happen. America will continue its support for the Afghan Government and the Afghan military as they confront the Taliban in the field.

Ultimately, it is up to the people of Afghanistan to take ownership of their future, to govern their society, and to achieve an everlasting peace. We are a partner and a friend, but we will not dictate to the Afghan people how to live or how to govern their own complex society. We are not nation-building again. We are killing terrorists.

The next pillar of our new strategy is to change the approach and how to deal with Pakistan. We can no longer be silent about Pakistan's safe havens for terrorist organizations, the Taliban, and other groups that pose a threat to the region and beyond. Pakistan has much to gain from partnering with our effort in Afghanistan. It has much to lose by continuing to harbor criminals and terrorists.

In the past, Pakistan has been a valued partner. Our militaries have worked together against common enemies. The Pakistani people have suffered greatly from terrorism and extremism. We recognize those contributions and those sacrifices.

But Pakistan has also sheltered the same organizations that try every single day to kill our people. We have been paying Pakistan billions and billions of dollars at the same time they are housing the very terrorists that we are fighting. But that will have to change, and that will change immediately. No partnership can survive a country's harboring of militants and terrorists who target U.S. servicemembers and officials. It is time for Pakistan to demonstrate its commitment to civilization, order, and to peace.

Another critical part of the South Asia strategy for America is to further develop its strategic partnership with India, the world's largest democracy and a key security and economic partner of the United States. We appreciate India's important contributions to stability in Afghanistan, but India makes billions of dollars in trade with the United States, and we want them to help us more with Afghanistan, especially in the area of economic assistance and development. We are committed to pursuing our shared objectives for peace and security in South Asia and the broader Indo-Pacific region.

Finally, my administration will ensure that you, the brave defenders of the American people, will have the necessary tools and rules of engagement to make this strategy work and work effectively and work quickly. I have already lifted restrictions the previous administration placed on our warfighters that prevented the Secretary of Defense and our commanders in the field from fully and swiftly waging battle against the enemy. Micromanagement from Washington, DC, does not win battles. They're won in the field drawing upon the judgment and expertise of wartime commanders and frontline soldiers acting in real time, with real authority, and with a clear mission to defeat the enemy.

That's why we will also expand authority for American Armed Forces to target the terrorist and criminal networks that sow violence and chaos throughout Afghanistan. These killers need to know they have nowhere to hide; that no place is beyond the reach of American might and Americans arms. Retribution will be fast and powerful.

As we lift restrictions and expand authorities in the field, we are already seeing dramatic results in the campaign to defeat ISIS, including the liberation of Mosul in Iraq.

Since my Inauguration, we have achieved record-breaking success in that regard. We will also maximize sanctions and other financial and law enforcement actions against these networks to eliminate their ability to export terror. When America commits its warriors to battle, we must ensure they have every weapon to apply swift, decisive, and overwhelming force.

Our troops will fight to win. We will fight to win. From now on, victory will have a clear definition: attacking our enemies, obliterating ISIS, crushing Al Qaida, preventing the Taliban from taking over Afghanistan, and stopping mass terror attacks against America before they emerge.

We will ask our NATO allies and global partners to support our new strategy with additional troop and funding increases in line with our own. We are confident they will. Since taking office, I have made clear that our allies and partners must contribute much more money to our collective defense, and they have done so.

In this struggle, the heaviest burden will continue to be borne by the good people of Afghanistan and their courageous armed forces. As the Prime Minister of Afghanistan has promised, we are going to participate in economic development to help defray the cost of this war to us. Afghanistan is fighting to defend and secure their country against the same enemies who threaten us. The stronger the Afghan security forces become, the less we will have to do. Afghans will secure and build their own nation and define their own future. We want them to succeed. But we will no longer use American military might to construct democracies in faraway lands or try to rebuild other countries in our own image. Those days are now over. Instead, we will work with allies and partners to protect our shared interests. We are not asking others to change their way of life, but to pursue common goals that allow our children to live better and safer lives. This principled realism will guide our decisions moving forward.

Military power alone will not bring peace to Afghanistan or stop the terrorist threat arising in that country. But strategically applied force aims to create the conditions for a political process to achieve a lasting peace.

America will work with the Afghan Government as long as we see determination and progress. However, our commitment is not unlimited, and our support is not a blank check. The Government of Afghanistan must carry their share of the military, political, and economic burden. The American people expect to see real reforms, real progress, and real results. Our patience is not unlimited. We will keep our eyes wide open.

In abiding by the oath I took on January 20, I will remain steadfast in protecting American lives and American interests. In this effort, we will make common cause with any nation that chooses to stand and fight alongside us against this global threat. Terrorists take heed: America will never let up until you are dealt a lasting defeat.

Under my administration, many billions of dollars more is being spent on our military. And this includes vast amounts being spent on our nuclear arsenal and missile defense.

In every generation, we have faced down evil, and we have always prevailed. We prevailed because we know who we are and what we are fighting for. Not far from where we are gathered tonight, hundreds of thousands of America's greatest patriots lay in eternal rest at Arlington National Cemetery. There is more courage, sacrifice, and love in those hallowed grounds than in any other spot on the face of the Earth.

Many of those who have fought and died in Afghanistan enlisted in the months after September 11, 2001. They volunteered for a simple reason: They loved America, and they were determined to protect her.

Now we must secure the cause for which they gave their lives. We must unite to defend America from its enemies abroad. We must restore the bonds of loyalty among our citizens at home, and we must achieve an honorable and enduring outcome worthy of the enormous price that so many have paid.

Our actions, and in the months to come, all of them will honor the sacrifice of every fallen hero, every family who lost a loved one, and every wounded warrior who shed their blood in defense of our great nation. With our resolve, we will ensure that your service and that your families will bring about the defeat of our enemies and the arrival of peace. We will push onward to victory with power in our hearts, courage in our souls, and everlasting pride in each and every one of you.

Thank you. May God bless our military. And may God bless the United States of America. Thank you very much. Thank you.

SOURCE: Executive Office of the President. "Address to the Nation on United States Strategy in Afghanistan and South Asia from Joint Base Myer-Henderson Hall, Virginia." August 21, 2017. *Compilation of Presidential Documents* 2017, no. 00580 (August 21, 2017). https://www.govinfo.gov/content/pkg/DCPD-201700580/pdf/DCPD-201700580.pdf.

OTHER HISTORIC DOCUMENTS OF INTEREST

FROM THIS VOLUME

FROM PREVIOUS *HISTORIC DOCUMENTS*

May

FBI Director Fired, Testifies before Congress

MAY 9 AND JUNE 8, 2017

On May 9, 2017, President Donald Trump fired Federal Bureau of Investigation (FBI) Director James Comey, a Republican who had previously served as deputy attorney general under President George W. Bush before President Barack Obama appointed him FBI Director in 2013. Comey, who at the time of his termination was leading the FBI's investigation into alleged ties between the Trump campaign and Russian government officials, would go on to state before the Senate Intelligence Committee his belief that he was fired by President Trump over the Russia investigation, an assertion the White House vehemently denied.

COMEY'S PREELECTION ANNOUNCEMENT

On July 5, 2016, four months ahead of the presidential election, Comey announced that the FBI was recommending that the Justice Department not bring charges against former senator and secretary of state Hillary Clinton—who at the time was the Democratic candidate for president—regarding her use of a private e-mail server and associated handling of classified information during her time as Secretary of State. While noting that Clinton was "extremely careless," Comey said it was the FBI's judgment "that no reasonable prosecutor would bring such a case." That is not to say, Comey added, that "a person who engaged in this activity would face no consequences. To the contrary, those individuals are often subject to security or administrative sanctions. But that is not what we are deciding now." Brian Fallon, a spokesperson for Clinton's presidential campaign, said the candidate was "pleased" at the outcome and "as the Secretary has long said, it was a mistake to use her personal email and she would not do it again."

Despite the sigh of relief breathed by the Clinton campaign, on October 28, just one week before the election, in a letter to Congress Comey wrote that the FBI intended to reopen its investigation into Clinton's handling of classified information. "The FBI has learned of the existence of emails that appear to be pertinent to the investigation," Comey wrote, adding, "I am writing to inform you that the investigative team briefed me on this yesterday, and I agreed that the FBI should take appropriate investigative steps designed to allow investigators to review these emails to determine whether they contain classified information, as well as to assess their importance to our investigation." Neither Comey nor the FBI provided any additional information related to the contents of the e-mail or whether the presidential candidate had sent or received the e-mail under review.

On November 6, Comey wrote to members of the House and Senate that the review of e-mail—those found on the computer of disgraced former congressman Anthony Weiner, husband of Clinton's top aide Huma Abedin—did not result in any update to its July opinion that charges should not be filed against Clinton. "Based on our review, we have not changed our conclusions that we expressed in July with respect to Secretary Clinton,"

Comey wrote. Sources with knowledge of the investigation told NPR that the e-mail under review in late October were duplicates or personal e-mail that had already been seen.

Clinton was defeated by Trump on November 8, and in 2017 would blame the Comey memo as a primary reason for her loss. "If the election was on October 27, I'd be your president," Clinton said in an interview with journalist Christiane Amanpour. That view was supported by data collected by some pollsters, including FiveThirtyEight's Nate Silver, who wrote ahead of polls closing on November 8 that Clinton had a 5.7 percentage point lead over Trump on October 28, which fell to 2.9 points by Election Day. On May 3, 2017, at a Senate Judiciary Committee hearing, Comey called the decision to reopen the Clinton investigation less than two weeks before the election "a hard choice" but "the right choice." He noted that he was "mildly nauseous" that he may have impacted the election outcome, but said that he could not be swayed in his decision to reopen the investigation based on the political fortunes of others.

FBI Director Fired

Trump was highly critical of Comey's handling of the Clinton investigation throughout the summer and fall of 2016. But the White House repeatedly claimed following Trump's inauguration that he had utmost confidence in Comey to continue serving as FBI director, even in light of the fact that Comey was leading the FBI's investigation into ties between the Trump campaign and members of the Russian government.

Trump, who frequently denied any connection between his campaign and the Russian government, or any effort on the part of the Russian government to support his candidacy, tweeted on May 8, "The Russia–Trump collusion story is a total hoax, when will this taxpayer funded charade end?" Less than twenty-four hours after that tweet, the president fired Comey, citing a recommendation from Attorney General Jeff Sessions and Deputy Attorney General Rod Rosenstein. In his letter to Comey, Trump wrote, "While I greatly appreciate you informing me, on three separate occasions, that I am not under investigation, I nevertheless concur with the judgement of the Department of Justice that you are not able to effectively lead the bureau." The White House also released the memo written by Rosenstein that the president had referred to in his initial reasoning behind the firing, which read, "I cannot defend the director's handling of the conclusion of the investigation of Secretary Clinton's emails, and I do not understand his refusal to accept the nearly universal judgement that he was mistaken."

Trump would go on to say on May 10 and 11 that Comey was fired because "he wasn't doing a good job" and that he had decided to fire the FBI director prior to ever receiving the recommendation from the Justice Department. Trump also noted in an interview with NBC News that he was thinking of "the Russia thing" when he made the decision to fire the FBI director. "When I decided to just do it, I said to myself, I said, 'you know, this Russia thing with Trump and Russia is a made up story, it's an excuse by the Democrats for having lost an election that they should have won.'" White House Deputy Press Secretary Sarah Huckabee Sanders said the White House hoped that "by removing Director Comey" they had taken steps to bring the Russia investigation to a "conclusion with integrity."

Andrew McCabe immediately took over as acting FBI director, and on May 11, in a testimony before the Senate Intelligence Committee, would refute Trump's assertion that Comey had "lost the support" of FBI employees. Comey, McCabe said, "enjoyed broad support within the FBI and does to this day." Christopher Wray was formally nominated to permanently replace Comey on June 26 and was approved by the Senate on August 1.

DEMOCRATS AND REPUBLICANS CRITICIZE FIRING

Reaction from both Democrats and Republicans was swift. Despite anger over the timing of the October 2016 reopening of the investigation into Clinton's handling of classified information, few Democrats lined up to support the president's decision. "This is Nixonian," said Sen. Bob Casey, D-Penn., while subsequently calling on Rosenstein to "immediately appoint a special counsel to continue the Trump/Russia investigation." Sen. Ed Markey, D-Mass., said the firing of the FBI director indicated that the country was "careening ever closer to a Constitutional crisis, and this development only underscores why we must appoint a special prosecutor to fully investigate any dealings the Trump campaign or administration had with Russia." Similarly, many Republicans were united in a belief that the decision to fire Comey could appear to some as a means to cover up or end the investigation into any connection between the Trump campaign and the Russian government. "I've spent the last several hours trying to find an acceptable rationale for the timing of Comey's firing. I just can't do it." Sen. Jeff Flake, R-Ariz., wrote on Twitter. Dozens of members of Congress would eventually join the call for an independent investigation into links between Trump's associates and the Russian government.

Mainstream media outlets also questioned the timing of the president's decision. *The New York Times* editorial board wrote on May 9, "The explanation for this shocking move . . . is impossible to take at face value", and that the decision "decisively crippled the FBI's ability to carry out an investigation of him and his associates." The editorial board went on, "By firing the FBI director, James Comey, late Tuesday afternoon, President Trump has cast grave doubt on the viability of any further investigation into what could be one of the biggest political scandals in the country's history . . . Mr. Comey was fired because he was leading an active investigation that could bring down a president." The editorial drew a comparison between Trump's move and President Richard Nixon's 1973 Saturday Night Massacre when he fired the special prosecutor investigating the Watergate break in.

The growing chorus of calls for an independent investigation into ties between Trump advisors and the Russian government resulted on May 17 in Deputy Attorney General Rosenstein appointing former FBI director Robert Mueller as special counsel to oversee the Russia investigation. That same day, President Trump insinuated in a tweet that there may have been recordings of his conversations with Comey in the Oval Office that would clear the president of any wrongdoing with regard to both Comey's dismissal and the Russia investigation. Just one day earlier, *The New York Times* had reported that, based on documents leaked to the paper, Comey had written extensive memos from each conversation he had with the president, both in person and by phone. A bipartisan group of lawmakers called on Trump and the White House to make available to the House Intelligence Committee any tapes that existed, but on June 22 Trump denied his knowledge of any such recordings, tweeting, "I have no idea . . . whether there are 'tapes' or recordings of my conversations with James Comey, but I did not make, and do not have, any such recordings."

COMEY TESTIFIES BEFORE CONGRESS

On June 8, Comey was called to testify before the Senate Intelligence Committee in relation to its ongoing investigation into alleged ties between the Trump campaign and the Russian government. Comey admitted at the start that he was the one who leaked the memos to *The New York Times*—through a friend—about the detailed notes he kept regarding his meetings with Trump. Comey said he leaked the documents in hopes that it would "prompt the appointment of a special counsel." Asked for further explanation, Comey said he documented his conversations because he "was honestly concerned [Trump] might lie" about them. "I knew there might come a day when I might need a record of what happened" to defend himself and the FBI, Comey said. "My impression is something big is about to happen. I need to remember every word that is spoken."

One specific memo penned by Comey indicated that on February 14 the president asked of Comey, in reference to the investigation into former national security adviser Michael Flynn, "I hope you can see your way clear of letting this go, to letting Flynn go. He is a good guy. I hope you can let this go." When asked what he thought that meant, Comey said he "took it as a direction . . . this is what he wants me to do." Comey added, "I had understood the President to be requesting that we drop any investigation of Flynn in connection with false statements about his conversations with the Russian ambassador in December. I did not understand the President to be talking about the broader investigation into Russia or possible links to his campaign." Comey said his "common sense" told him that the president was "looking to get something in exchange for granting my request to stay on the job." Asked why he thought he was fired, Comey replied that he took "the president at his word that I was fired because of the Russia investigation." Asked his opinion on whether he thought Trump colluded with Russia, Comey replied, "I don't think I should answer in an open setting." Comey also faced questioning on his opinion of whether Trump's February 14 comments amounted to obstruction of justice, but said it was not for him to decide "but that's a conclusion I'm sure the special counsel will work toward, to try and understand what the intention was there and whether that's an offense." Following his public testimony, Comey went into a closed-door meeting with senators on the committee.

On Twitter, Trump accused Comey of "so many false statements and lies" in his testimony. But Trump's lawyer, Marc Kasowitz, said the president felt "completely and totally vindicated" by Comey's testimony. "Mr. Comey's testimony also makes clear that the President never sought to impede the investigation into attempted Russian interference in the 2016 election," Kasowitz said.

—Heather Kerrigan

Following is the text of a letter sent by President Trump to FBI Director James Comey on May 9, 2017, removing Comey from his position, and the accompanying memos from the Attorney General and Deputy Attorney General; and excerpts from the opening statement—as prepared for delivery—from Comey's testimony before the Senate Intelligence Committee on June 8, 2017.

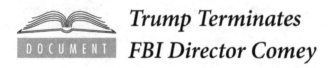

Trump Terminates
FBI Director Comey

May 9, 2017

Dear Director Comey:

I have received the attached letters from the Attorney General and Deputy Attorney General of the United States recommending your dismissal as the Director of the Federal

Bureau of Investigation. I have accepted their recommendation and you are hereby terminated and removed from office, effective immediately.

While I greatly appreciate you informing me, on three separate occasions, that I am not under investigation, I nevertheless concur with the judgment of the Department of Justice that you are not able to effectively lead the Bureau.

It is essential that we find new leadership for the FBI that restores public trust and confidence in its vital law enforcement mission.

I wish you the best of luck in your future endeavors.

DONALD J. TRUMP
The White House,
May 9, 2017.

SOURCE: Executive Office of the President. "Letter to Federal Bureau of Investigation Director James B. Comey, Jr., Informing Him of His Termination and Removal from Office." May 9, 2017. *Compilation of Presidential Documents* 2017, no. 00325 (May 9, 2017). https://www.gpo.gov/fdsys/pkg/DCPD-201700325/pdf/DCPD-201700325.pdf.

Attorney General, Deputy Attorney General Provide Input on Handling of Director Comey

May 9, 2017

President Donald J. Trump
The White House
Washington, DC 20500

Dear Mr. President:

As Attorney General, I am committed to a high level of discipline, integrity, and the rule of law to the Department of Justice—an institution that I deeply respect. Based on my evaluation, and for the reasons expressed by the Deputy Attorney General in the attached memorandum, I have concluded that a fresh start is needed at the leadership of the FBI. It is essential that this Department of Justice clearly reaffirm its commitment to longstanding principles that ensure the integrity and fairness of federal investigations and prosecutions. The Director of the FBI must be someone who follows faithfully the rules and principles of the Department of Justice and who sets the right example for our law enforcement officials and others in the Department. Therefore, I must recommend that you remove Director James B. Comey, Jr. and identify an experienced and qualified individual to lead the great men and women of the FBI.

Sincerely,
Jeff Sessions
Attorney General

***

May 9, 2017

MEMORANDUM FOR THE ATTORNEY GENERAL

FROM: ROD J. ROSENSTEIN
              DEPUTY ATTORNEY GENERAL
SUBJECT: RESTORING PUBLIC CONFIDENCE IN THE FBI

The Federal Bureau of Investigation has long been regarded as our nation's premier federal investigative agency. Over the past year, however, the FBI's reputation and credibility have suffered substantial damage, and it has affected the entire Department of Justice. That is deeply troubling to many Department employees and veterans, legislators and citizens.

The current FBI Director is an articulate and persuasive speaker about leadership and the immutable principles of the Department of Justice. He deserves our appreciation for his public service. As you and I have discussed, however, I cannot defend the Director's handling of the conclusion of the investigation of Secretary Clinton's emails, and I do not understand his refusal to accept the nearly universal judgment that he was mistaken. Almost everyone agrees that the Director made serious mistakes; it is one of the few issues that units people of diverse perspectives.

The Director was wrong to usurp the Attorney General's authority on July 5, 2016, and announce his conclusion that the case should be closed without prosecution. It is not the function of the Director to make such an announcement. At most, the Director should have said the FBI had completed its investigation and presented its findings to federal prosecutors. The Director now defends his decision by asserting that he believed Attorney General Loretta Lynch had a conflict. But the FBI Director is never empowered to supplant federal prosecutors and assume command of the Justice Department. There is a well-established process for other officials to step in when a conflict requires the recusal of the Attorney General. On July 5, however, the Director announced his own conclusions about the nation's most sensitive criminal investigation, without the authorization of duly appointed Justice Department leaders.

Compounding the error, the Director ignored another longstanding principle: we do not hold press conferences to release derogatory information about the subject of a declined criminal investigation. Derogatory information sometimes is disclosed in the course of criminal investigations and prosecutions, but we never release it gratuitously. The Director laid out his version of the facts for the news media as if it were a closing argument, but without a trial. It is a textbook example of what federal prosecutors and agents are taught not to do.

In response to skeptical questions at a congressional hearing, the Director defended his remarks by saying that his "goal was to say what is true. What did we do, what did we find, what do we think about it." But the goal of a federal criminal investigation is not to announce our thoughts at a press conference. The goal is to determine whether there is sufficient evidence to justify a federal criminal prosecution, then allow a federal prosecutor who exercises authority delegated by the Attorney General to make a prosecutorial decision, and then—if prosecution is warranted—let the judge and jury determine the facts. We sometimes release information about closed investigations in appropriate ways, but the FBI does not do it sua sponte.

Concerning his letter to the Congress on October 28, 2016, the Director cast his decision as a choice between whether he would "speak" about the FBI's decision to investigate the newly-discovered email messages or "conceal" it. "Conceal" is a loaded term that misstates the issue. When federal agents and prosecutors quietly open a criminal investigation, we are not concealing anything; we are simply following the longstanding policy that we refrain from publicizing non-public information. In that context, silence is not concealment.

My perspective on these issues is shared by former Attorneys General and Deputy Attorneys General from different eras and both political parties. Judge Laurence Silberman, who served as Deputy Attorney General under President Ford, wrote that "it is not the bureau's responsibility to opine on whether a matter should be prosecuted." Silberman believes that the Director's "performance was so inappropriate for an FBI director that [he] doubt[s] the bureau will ever completely recover." Jamie Gorclick, Deputy Attorney General under President Clinton, joined with Larry Thompson, Deputy Attorney General under President George W. Bush, to opine that the Director had "chosen personally to restrike the balance between transparency and fairness, departing from the department's traditions." They concluded that the Director violated the obligation to "preserve, protect and defend" the tradition of the Department and the FBI.

Former Attorney General Michael Mukasey, who served under President George W. Bush, observed that the Director "stepped way outside his job in disclosing the recommendation in that fashion" because the FBI director "doesn't make that decision." Alberto Gonzales, who also served as Attorney General under President George W. Bush, called the decision "an error in judgment." Eric Holder, who served as Deputy Attorney General under President Clinton and Attorney General under President Obama, said that the Director's decision "was incorrect. It violated long-standing Justice Department policies and traditions. And it ran counter to guidance that I put in place four years ago laying out the proper way to conduct investigations during an election season." Holder concluded that the Director "broke with these fundamental principles" and "negatively affected public trust in both the Justice Department and the FBI."

Former Deputy Attorneys General Gorelick and Thompson described the unusual events as "real-time, raw-take transparency taken to its illogical limit, a kind of reality TV of federal criminal investigation," that is "antithetical to the interests of justice."

Donald Ayer, who served as Deputy Attorney General under President George H.W. Bush, along with other former Justice Department officials, was "astonished and perplexed" by the decision to "break[] with longstanding practices followed by officials of both parties during past elections." Ayer's letter noted, "Perhaps most troubling . . . is the precedent set by this departure from the Department's widely-respected, non-partisan traditions."

We should reject the departure and return to the traditions.

Although the President has the power to remove an FBI director, the decision should not be taken lightly. I agree with the nearly unanimous opinions of former Department officials. The way the Director handled the conclusion of the email investigation was wrong. As a result, the FBI is unlikely to regain public and congressional trust until it has a Director who understands the gravity of the mistakes and pledges never to repeat them. Having refused to admit his errors, the Director cannot be expected to implement the necessary corrective actions.

Source: The White House. "Letter from the Attorney General to President Trump and Memorandum for the Attorney General from the Deputy Attorney General." May 9, 2017.

Comey Addresses Senate Intelligence Committee

June 8, 2017

Statement for the Record
Senate Select Committee on Intelligence

James B. Comey

June 8, 2017

Chairman Burr, Ranking Member Warner, Members of the Committee. Thank you for inviting me to appear before you today. I was asked to testify today to describe for you my interactions with President-Elect and President Trump on subjects that I understand are of interest to you. I have not included every detail from my conversations with the President, but, to the best of my recollection, I have tried to include information that may be relevant to the Committee.

<u>January 6 Briefing</u>

I first met then-President-Elect Trump on Friday, January 6 in a conference room at Trump Tower in New York. I was there with other Intelligence Community (IC) leaders to brief him and his new national security team on the findings of an IC assessment concerning Russian efforts to interfere in the election. At the conclusion of that briefing, I remained alone with the President- Elect to brief him on some personally sensitive aspects of the information assembled during the assessment.

The IC leadership thought it important, for a variety of reasons, to alert the incoming President to the existence of this material, even though it was salacious and unverified. Among those reasons were: (1) we knew the media was about to publicly report the material and we believed the IC should not keep knowledge of the material and its imminent release from the President-Elect; and (2) to the extent there was some effort to compromise an incoming President, we could blunt any such effort with a defensive briefing.

The Director of National Intelligence asked that I personally do this portion of the briefing because I was staying in my position and because the material implicated the FBI's counter-intelligence responsibilities. We also agreed I would do it alone to minimize potential embarrassment to the President-Elect. Although we agreed it made sense for me to do the briefing, the FBI's leadership and I were concerned that the briefing might create a situation where a new President came into office uncertain about whether the FBI was conducting a counter-intelligence investigation of his personal conduct.

It is important to understand that FBI counter-intelligence investigations are different than the more-commonly known criminal investigative work. The Bureau's goal in a counter-intelligence investigation is to understand the technical and human methods that hostile foreign powers are using to influence the United States or to steal our secrets. The FBI uses that understanding to disrupt those efforts. Sometimes disruption takes the form of alerting a person who is targeted for recruitment or influence by the foreign power.

Sometimes it involves hardening a computer system that is being attacked. Sometimes it involves "turning" the recruited person into a double-agent, or publicly calling out the behavior with sanctions or expulsions of embassy-based intelligence officers. On occasion, criminal prosecution is used to disrupt intelligence activities.

Because the nature of the hostile foreign nation is well known, counter-intelligence investigations tend to be centered on individuals the FBI suspects to be witting or unwitting agents of that foreign power. When the FBI develops reason to believe an American has been targeted for recruitment by a foreign power or is covertly acting as an agent of the foreign power, the FBI will "open an investigation" on that American and use legal authorities to try to learn more about the nature of any relationship with the foreign power so it can be disrupted.

In that context, prior to the January 6 meeting, I discussed with the FBI's leadership team whether I should be prepared to assure President-Elect Trump that we were not investigating him personally. That was true; we did not have an open counter-intelligence case on him. We agreed I should do so if circumstances warranted. During our one-on-one meeting at Trump Tower, based on President-Elect Trump's reaction to the briefing and without him directly asking the question, I offered that assurance.

I felt compelled to document my first conversation with the President-Elect in a memo. To ensure accuracy, I began to type it on a laptop in an FBI vehicle outside Trump Tower the moment I walked out of the meeting. Creating written records immediately after one-on-one conversations with Mr. Trump was my practice from that point forward. This had not been my practice in the past. I spoke alone with President Obama twice in person (and never on the phone) – once in 2015 to discuss law enforcement policy issues and a second time, briefly, for him to say goodbye in late 2016. In neither of those circumstances did I memorialize the discussions. I can recall nine one-on-one conversations with President Trump in four months – three in person and six on the phone.

January 27 Dinner

The President and I had dinner on Friday, January 27 at 6:30 pm in the Green Room at the White House. He had called me at lunchtime that day and invited me to dinner that night, saying he was going to invite my whole family, but decided to have just me this time, with the whole family coming the next time. It was unclear from the conversation who else would be at the dinner, although I assumed there would be others.

It turned out to be just the two of us, seated at a small oval table in the center of the Green Room. Two Navy stewards waited on us, only entering the room to serve food and drinks.

The President began by asking me whether I wanted to stay on as FBI Director, which I found strange because he had already told me twice in earlier conversations that he hoped I would stay, and I had assured him that I intended to. He said that lots of people wanted my job and, given the abuse I had taken during the previous year, he would understand if I wanted to walk away.

My instincts told me that the one-on-one setting, and the pretense that this was our first discussion about my position, meant the dinner was, at least in part, an effort to have me ask for my job and create some sort of patronage relationship. That concerned me greatly, given the FBI's traditionally independent status in the executive branch.

I replied that I loved my work and intended to stay and serve out my ten-year term as Director. And then, because the set-up made me uneasy, I added that I was not "reliable" in the way politicians use that word, but he could always count on me to tell him the truth. I added that I was not on anybody's side politically and could not be counted on in the traditional political sense, a stance I said was in his best interest as the President.

A few moments later, the President said, "I need loyalty, I expect loyalty." I didn't move, speak, or change my facial expression in any way during the awkward silence that followed. We simply looked at each other in silence. The conversation then moved on, but he returned to the subject near the end of our dinner.

At one point, I explained why it was so important that the FBI and the Department of Justice be independent of the White House. I said it was a paradox: Throughout history, some Presidents have decided that because "problems" come from Justice, they should try to hold the Department close. But blurring those boundaries ultimately makes the problems worse by undermining public trust in the institutions and their work.

Near the end of our dinner, the President returned to the subject of my job, saying he was very glad I wanted to stay, adding that he had heard great things about me from Jim Mattis, Jeff Sessions, and many others. He then said, "I need loyalty." I replied, "You will always get honesty from me." He paused and then said, "That's what I want, honest loyalty." I paused, and then said, "You will get that from me." As I wrote in the memo I created immediately after the dinner, it is possible we understood the phrase "honest loyalty" differently, but I decided it wouldn't be productive to push it further. The—honest loyalty—had helped end a very awkward conversation and my explanations had made clear what he should expect.

During the dinner, the President returned to the salacious material I had briefed him about on January 6, and, as he had done previously, expressed his disgust for the allegations and strongly denied them. He said he was considering ordering me to investigate the alleged incident to prove it didn't happen. I replied that he should give that careful thought because it might create a narrative that we were investigating him personally, which we weren't, and because it was very difficult to prove a negative. He said he would think about it and asked me to think about it.

As was my practice for conversations with President Trump, I wrote a detailed memo about the dinner immediately afterwards and shared it with the senior leadership team of the FBI.

February 14 Oval Office Meeting

On February 14, I went to the Oval Office for a scheduled counter-terrorism briefing of the President. He sat behind the desk and a group of us sat in a semi-circle of about six chairs facing him on the other side of the desk. The Vice President, Deputy Director of the CIA, Director of the National Counter-Terrorism Center, Secretary of Homeland Security, the Attorney General, and I were in the semi-circle of chairs. I was directly facing the President, sitting between the Deputy CIA Director and the Director of NCTC. There were quite a few others in the room, sitting behind us on couches and chairs.

The President signaled the end of the briefing by thanking the group and telling them all that he wanted to speak to me alone. I stayed in my chair. As the participants started to leave the Oval Office, the Attorney General lingered by my chair, but the President thanked him and said he wanted to speak only with me. The last person to leave was Jared Kushner, who also stood by my chair and exchanged pleasantries with me. The President then excused him, saying he wanted to speak with me.

When the door by the grandfather clock closed, and we were alone, the President began by saying, "I want to talk about Mike Flynn." Flynn had resigned the previous day. The President began by saying Flynn hadn't done anything wrong in speaking with the Russians, but he had to let him go because he had misled the Vice President. He added that he had other concerns about Flynn, which he did not then specify.

The President then made a long series of comments about the problem with leaks of classified information—a concern I shared and still share. After he had spoken for a few minutes about leaks, Reince Priebus leaned in through the door by the grandfather clock and I could see a group of people waiting behind him. The President waved at him to close the door, saying he would be done shortly. The door closed.

The President then returned to the topic of Mike Flynn, saying, "He is a good guy and has been through a lot." He repeated that Flynn hadn't done anything wrong on his calls with the Russians, but had misled the Vice President. He then said, "I hope you can see your way clear to letting this go, to letting Flynn go. He is a good guy. I hope you can let this go." I replied only that "he is a good guy." (In fact, I had a positive experience dealing with Mike Flynn when he was a colleague as Director of the Defense Intelligence Agency at the beginning of my term at FBI.) I did not say I would "let this go."

The President returned briefly to the problem of leaks. I then got up and left out the door by the grandfather clock, making my way through the large group of people waiting there, including Mr. Priebus and the Vice President.

I immediately prepared an unclassified memo of the conversation about Flynn and discussed the matter with FBI senior leadership. I had understood the President to be requesting that we drop any investigation of Flynn in connection with false statements about his conversations with the Russian ambassador in December. I did not understand the President to be talking about the broader investigation into Russia or possible links to his campaign. I could be wrong, but I took him to be focusing on what had just happened with Flynn's departure and the controversy around his account of his phone calls. Regardless, it was very concerning, given the FBI's role as an independent investigative agency.

The FBI leadership team agreed with me that it was important not to infect the investigative team with the President's request, which we did not intend to abide. We also concluded that, given that it was a one-on-one conversation, there was nothing available to corroborate my account. We concluded it made little sense to report it to Attorney General Sessions, who we expected would likely recuse himself from involvement in Russia-related investigations. (He did so two weeks later.) The Deputy Attorney General's role was then filled in an acting capacity by a United States Attorney, who would also not be long in the role. After discussing the matter, we decided to keep it very closely held, resolving to figure out what to do with it down the road as our investigation progressed. The investigation moved ahead at full speed, with none of the investigative team members—or the Department of Justice lawyers supporting them—aware of the President's request.

Shortly afterwards, I spoke with Attorney General Sessions in person to pass along the President's concerns about leaks. I took the opportunity to implore the Attorney General to prevent any future direct communication between the President and me. I told the AG that what had just happened—him being asked to leave while the FBI Director, who reports to the AG, remained behind—was inappropriate and should never happen. He did not reply. For the reasons discussed above, I did not mention that the President broached the FBI's potential investigation of General Flynn.

March 30 Phone Call

On the morning of March 30, the President called me at the FBI. He described the Russia investigation as "a cloud" that was impairing his ability to act on behalf of the country. He said he had nothing to do with Russia, had not been involved with hookers in Russia, and had always assumed he was being recorded when in Russia. He asked what we could do to "lift the cloud." I responded that we were investigating the matter as quickly as we could, and that there would be great benefit, if we didn't find anything, to our having done the work well. He agreed, but then re-emphasized the problems this was causing him.

Then the President asked why there had been a congressional hearing about Russia the previous week—at which I had, as the Department of Justice directed, confirmed the investigation into possible coordination between Russia and the Trump campaign. I explained the demands from the leadership of both parties in Congress for more information, and that Senator Grassley had even held up the confirmation of the Deputy Attorney General until we briefed him in detail on the investigation. I explained that we had briefed the leadership of Congress on exactly which individuals we were investigating and that we had told those Congressional leaders that we were not personally investigating President Trump. I reminded him I had previously told him that. He repeatedly told me, "We need to get that fact out." (I did not tell the President that the FBI and the Department of Justice had been reluctant to make public statements that we did not have an open case on President Trump for a number of reasons, most importantly because it would create a duty to correct, should that change.)

The President went on to say that if there were some "satellite" associates of his who did something wrong, it would be good to find that out, but that he hadn't done anything wrong and hoped I would find a way to get it out that we weren't investigating him.

In an abrupt shift, he turned the conversation to FBI Deputy Director Andrew McCabe, saying he hadn't brought up "the McCabe thing" because I had said McCabe was honorable, although McAuliffe was close to the Clintons and had given him (I think he meant Deputy Director McCabe's wife) campaign money. Although I didn't understand why the President was bringing this up, I repeated that Mr. McCabe was an honorable person.

He finished by stressing "the cloud" that was interfering with his ability to make deals for the country and said he hoped I could find a way to get out that he wasn't being investigated. I told him I would see what we could do, and that we would do our investigative work well and as quickly as we could.

Immediately after that conversation, I called Acting Deputy Attorney General Dana Boente (AG Sessions had by then recused himself on all Russia-related matters), to report the substance of the call from the President, and said I would await his guidance. I did not hear back from him before the President called me again two weeks later.

April 11 Phone Call

On the morning of April 11, the President called me and asked what I had done about his request that I "get out" that he is not personally under investigation. I replied that I had passed his request to the Acting Deputy Attorney General, but I had not heard back. He replied that "the cloud" was getting in the way of his ability to do his job. He said that perhaps he would have his people reach out to the Acting Deputy Attorney General. I said that was the way his request should be handled. I said the White House Counsel should contact the leadership of DOJ to make the request, which was the traditional channel.

He said he would do that and added, "Because I have been very loyal to you, very loyal; we had that thing you know." I did not reply or ask him what he meant by "that thing." I said only that the way to handle it was to have the White House Counsel call the Acting Deputy Attorney General. He said that was what he would do and the call ended.

That was the last time I spoke with President Trump.

SOURCE: Senate Select Committee on Intelligence. "Statement for the Record – James B. Comey." June 8, 2017. https://www.intelligence.senate.gov/sites/default/files/documents/os-jcomey-060817.pdf.

OTHER HISTORIC DOCUMENTS OF INTEREST

FROM THIS VOLUME

- Director of National Intelligence Declassifies Report on Russian Interference in 2016 U.S. Election, p. 12
- Former FBI Director Robert Mueller Appointed Special Counsel on U.S. Election–Russia Investigation, Issues Indictments, p. 270

FROM PREVIOUS *HISTORIC DOCUMENTS*

- President-Elect Donald Trump Forms Transition Team; Nominates Senior Administration Officials, *2016*, p. 631
- Donald Trump Elected U.S. President, *2016*, p. 612
- CIA and FBI Release Findings on Russian Involvement in U.S. Election, *2016*, p. 511

Leaders of France, Germany, and the UK Respond to National Elections

MAY 15, JUNE 9, AND NOVEMBER 21, 2017

France, Germany, and the United Kingdom held national elections in close succession from spring to fall of 2017. In France and Germany, there was an uptick in support for populist and anti-immigrant candidates and parties, although more moderate, centrist parties won the most votes. France elected a new president, Emmanuel Macron, who emerged as a charismatic new figure on the global stage, while Germany looked set to retain longtime Chancellor Angela Merkel though her standing was diminished. In the United Kingdom, the election was dominated by the imminent negotiations to terminate the country's near half-century membership in the twenty-eight nation European Union (EU). The Conservative Prime Minister, Theresa May, called the election prematurely, hoping to bolster her parliamentary majority but the move backfired when her party actually lost seats—and its majority.

Fresh Face for France

Of the three elections, France was the only one where a new leader emerged. The thirty-nine-year-old Macron was a relative newcomer to politics. He served a stint as economics minister before setting up his own party, Forward! (*En Marche!*) in 2016. With his win, Macron upstaged Marine Le Pen, leader of the far right National Front who many had expected would be the big story of the election. Since coming in a respectable third place in the 2012 presidential election with 18 percent of the vote, Le Pen had fixed her focus firmly on the 2017 ballot. The daughter of National Front founder and longtime leader, Jean-Marie Le Pen, she worked assiduously to rid the party of some of his embarrassing political baggage, such as his comments dismissing the Holocaust as a "detail" of history. But, like her father's, her platform was heavily anti-immigrant, anti-Muslim, and anti-European Union. She advocated pulling France out of the multinational body and expressed admiration for both Russia's President Vladimir Putin and U.S. President Donald Trump.

Until Macron formally announced his candidacy in November 2016, the established parties scrambled to find candidates with charisma comparable to Le Pen. Meanwhile, she consolidated her support, notably capitalizing on the shocking terrorist attacks in Paris in November 2015 and Nice in July 2016 that killed more than 200 civilians. Outgoing President François Hollande's popularity had dipped so low that he declined to run for reelection. Hollande's center left socialist party tapped Benoît Hamon instead; however, he also failed to gain traction with voters. The center right Republicans nominated a former French prime minister, François Fillon, but his candidacy ran into trouble in early 2017 due to a nepotism scandal. A populist left-wing candidate, Jean-Luc Mélenchon, enjoyed a surge in support, mainly at the expense of Hamon.

In the first round of voting on April 23, turnout was 78 percent. Macron came first place with 24 percent of votes cast, Le Pen came second with 22 percent, while Fillon and Mélenchon came third and fourth, respectively, a percentage point or two behind Le Pen. Hamon came a disappointing fifth, winning just 6 percent. The top two candidates, Macron and Le Pen, proceeded to a runoff vote on May 7. In the end, Macron scored a convincing win, taking 66 percent to Le Pen's 34 percent. Despite her loss, it was still the highest score the National Front ever attained in a presidential contest.

In his inaugural speech, Macron said, "The world and Europe needs France more than ever." France had been doubting itself for decades, and his mission was to restore its self-confidence, he said. Macron pledged to make France a leader in responding to major global issues, including migration, climate change, the resurgence in authoritarianism, excesses of capitalism, and terrorism. He followed up his presidential win with an equally impressive victory for his party in parliamentary elections in June.

A More Fragile UK Government Braces for Brexit

The ghost of Brexit had lurked over the United Kingdom ever since the June 2016 referendum in which 52 percent of voters opted for the country to leave the European Union. Then-Prime Minister David Cameron, who had called the referendum and campaigned for the United Kingdom to stay inside the European Union, resigned after the shock result. The Conservative parliamentary party then elected Theresa May to succeed him as party leader and, consequently, Prime Minister. Labour, the main opposition party, was also plunged into similar turmoil by the Brexit vote. While its members were generally more pro-EU than May's Conservatives, Labour leader Jeremy Corbyn had sent mixed messages when campaigning on the Remain side. In the summer of 2016, Corbyn faced down a revolt from more pro-European parliamentary colleagues by easily winning a leadership vote among the grassroots membership, taking 62 percent of the vote.

However, by early 2017, the splits within Labour were taking their toll and the Conservatives were well ahead in opinion polls, spurring Prime Minister May to call an election for June 8. May could have waited until 2020 to call the election but she calculated that a snap vote could boost her majority, just seventeen, in the 650-seat House of Commons. On March 29, May had formally notified the European Union that the United Kingdom was leaving the bloc and Brexit talks were due to start in June. With tough negotiations and votes ahead, May was banking on an increased majority that would give her a much-needed cushion. But things did not go as planned.

On the campaign trail, May often appeared ill-at-ease mingling with ordinary voters, in contrast to Labour leader Corbyn who was more in his element in grassroots settings. Brexit was a top campaign issue throughout. While majorities of Conservatives and Labour parliamentarians had backed the Remain side prior to the referendum, the pro-Brexit result shifted the political sands so that now most elected representatives from both parties either were advancing Brexit or acquiescing. The UK Independence Party (UKIP), the pivotal force in bringing about the Brexit referendum, was ironically now struggling. Established in the early 1990s with the sole purpose of taking the United Kingdom out of the European Union, the referendum created something of a sense of 'mission accomplished' causing UKIP to hemorrhage support both to Labour and the Conservatives.

Election day was a shock for Prime Minister May. The Conservatives, instead of expanding its majority, lost it, while Labour gained 30 seats. The Conservatives remained the largest party in parliament with 318 seats to Labour's 262. The other big loser was the Scottish

National Party (SNP), the party whose main goal was for Scotland to become an independent country. In the 2015 UK election, the SNP had won a remarkable fifty-six out of Scotland's fifty-nine seats in the UK parliament. But in 2017, by contrast, the SNP lost 13 percentage points and twenty-one seats, although it still won a majority of Scottish seats. In response to the surprise dip, the SNP leader Nicola Sturgeon put on hold her plan to hold a new referendum on Scottish independence in 2018. A Scottish independence referendum in 2014 had resulted in 55 percent of voters opting for Scotland to stay in the United Kingdom.

In Northern Ireland, there was a surge in support for the two more hardline parties, the pro-UK Democratic Unionist Party (DUP) and pro-Ireland Sinn Fein, at the expense of the more moderate, Irish-leaning Social Democratic and Labour Party (SDLP) and UK-leaning Ulster Unionist Party (UUP). Having won ten seats, the DUP was perfectly poised to put the Conservatives back in government, the Conservatives being seven seats shy of an overall majority. Brexit dominated the Northern Ireland campaign because it raised the specter of a new border being erected to separate northern (outside the EU) and southern (inside the EU) Ireland. Pro-Irish voices fiercely opposed such an idea, whereas the DUP's priority was to keep Northern Ireland an integral part of the United Kingdom.

Following the election, May said, "This government will guide the country through the crucial Brexit talks that begin in just 10 days," underscoring how the issue was set to overshadow all others in the immediate future. Of the new Conservative-DUP partnership, May noted that "our two parties have enjoyed a strong relationship over many years." But the partnership made it harder for May to be impartial in Northern Ireland because it empowered the DUP to bring down her government at any time, thus giving it huge leverage in the Brexit talks on the Irish border.

Merkel's Grip Loosens, Far Right Enters Parliament

The parliamentary elections in Germany were scheduled for September 24. Chancellor Angela Merkel looked on course to win a fourth successive term as leader, having first been elected in 2005. Her center-right Christian Democratic Union (CDU) and its sister party, the Bavaria-based Christian Social Union (CSU), had lost support since its 41.5 percent win in the previous election in 2013 but were still the largest party in the polls. A distant second place was the center left Social Democratic Party (SPD), which had nominated Martin Schulz, former president of the European Parliament, as its candidate.

This was the country's first national election since a million refugees fleeing Syria's civil war arrived on Germany's doorstep over a few frantic months in 2015. The CDU-CSU and SPD had, from 2013 to 2017, been in a so-called grand coalition government together, so they felt compelled to stand behind the government's decision to admit the refugees. This created an opening for the newest force in German politics, the Alternative for Germany (AfD) party. AfD was founded in 2013 on a platform that opposed the EU bailouts to deeply indebted Mediterranean countries like Greece. AfD narrowly missed entering in the German parliament in 2013, winning 4.7 percent of the vote, just below the 5 percent threshold parties must clear to get seats. The Syrian refugee crisis led AfD to shift its focus to opposing Muslim immigration to Germany. Three other parties were on course to clear the 5 percent threshold, too: the environmentalist Green Party, pro-business Free Democrats (FDP), and The Left, a far-left party.

The results were disappointing for Chancellor Merkel. CDU-CSU dropped to 33 percent but remained the largest bloc. The result was worse for the SPD, which won 20 percent, its lowest score since World War II. The big winner was the AfD, which won

13 percent of the vote, making it the third largest party in parliament. The Greens, Left, and FDP all secured seats in parliament, scoring about 10 percent of votes each. This made for a more fragmented Bundestag, with seven parties and six parliamentary groups.

The first coalition talks took place between the CDU-CSU, Greens, and FDP. The media dubbed this prospective partnership as a "Jamaica Coalition" because the three parties' colors (black for CDU-CSU, green for Greens, and yellow for FDP) were the same as on the Jamaican flag. On November 19, however, it was announced to widespread shock that these negotiations had collapsed. The sticking point was refugee and migration policy, with the FDP walking out of the talks.

Meanwhile, the German parliament elected Wolfgang Schäuble, a longtime finance minister of Chancellor Merkel, as its president. Commenting on the unexpected turn of events, Schäuble said, "The collapse of the coalition talks shows us more clearly that a Parliament reflecting the diversity of society in this way will find it more difficult to form majorities." He added, "The mandate from the electorate also imposes a duty on all of us to form majorities to help create a government that can govern." With the Jamaica Coalition a nonstarter, CDU-CSU and SPD began talks to forge a new grand coalition. SPD leader Schulz had ruled out this option after the election, given how poorly his party performed, but now there was no other mathematical way to form a majority. Amid the political uncertainty, Schäuble sought to reassure his fellow Germans, saying, "It is a testing time, but it is not a national crisis."

—Brian Beary

Following is the text of a speech by newly elected French President Emmanuel Macron on May 15, 2017; a statement on June 9, 2017, by British Prime Minister Theresa May following the general election; and a speech by German Bundestag President Dr. Wolfgang Schäuble regarding the formation of a coalition government ahead of the opening of a new session of parliament on November 21, 2017.

French President Delivers Speech upon His Election

May 15, 2017

Ladies and gentlemen,

On May 7, as you reminded us, the French chose hope and the spirit of conquest.

The whole world watched our presidential election. Everywhere, people wondered whether the French would in turn decide to retreat to the illusory past, if they would make a break with the affairs of the world, exit the scene of History, succumb to the mistrust of democracy and the spirit of division and turn their backs on the Enlightenment, or if on the contrary they would embrace the future, collectively regain momentum, and reaffirm their faith in the values which have made them a great people.

On May 7, the French made a choice. May they here be thanked.

The responsibility that they have entrusted to me is an honor, and I am aware of its significance.

The world and Europe, today more than ever, need France. They need a France who is strong and confident in its destiny. They need a France who bears the voice of freedom and solidarity aloft. They need a France who can invent the future.

The world needs what French women and men have always taught: the audacity of freedom, the imperative of equality, the will for fraternity.

But, for decades, France has doubted herself. She feels threatened in her culture, in her social model, her closely held beliefs. She is doubtful of everything that has made her.

For this reason my presidential term will be guided by two requirements.

The first will be to restore to the French this self-confidence, weakened for too long. Let me reassure you, I did not think for one second that it would recover as if by magic on the evening of May 7. It will be a slow, demanding, yet indispensable, task.

It will be up to me to convince the French that our country, which today seems crippled by the sometimes contrary winds of the course of the world, carries in her heart all the resources to stand at the forefront of the world's nations.

I will convince our compatriots that the power of France is not declining, but that we are on the cusp of an extraordinary rebirth, because we hold between our hands all the assets which will make and which make the great powers of the 21st century.

To that end, I will yield nothing on the commitments I made to the French people. Everything which contributes to the strength of France and its prosperity will be implemented: work will be freed, businesses will be supported, and initiative will be encouraged.

Culture and education, through which emancipation is built, creation and innovation, will be at the heart of my actions.

The French women and men who feel forgotten by this vast movement of the world must find themselves better protected. Everything which forges our national solidarity will be restored, reinvented, reinvigorated. Equality in the face of life's misfortunes will be strengthened.

Everything which makes France a safe country, where one can live without fear, will be amplified. The secular character of the Republic will be defended; our police force, our intelligence services, our armies comforted.

Europe, which we need, will be renewed rekindled, because it protects us and allows us to uphold our values in the world.

Our institutions, decried by some, must recover in the eyes of the French the effectiveness which has guaranteed their continuity. Because I believe in the institutions of the Fifth Republic and will do everything in my power to ensure they function according to the spirit which gave birth to them. To that end, I will ensure that our country experiences a renewal of democratic vitality. Citizens will have a say. They will be listened to.

In the pursuit of this objective I will need help from one and all. The responsibility of all the elites—political, economic, social, religious—and of all the appointed bodies of the French nation, will be called upon. We can no longer hide behind sometimes outdated customs or practices. We must recover the deepest meaning, the dignity of what today brings us together: to act in a just and effective way for our people.

France is strong only if it is prosperous. France is a model for the world only if it is exemplary.

And this is my second requirement.

Because we will have restored in the French their taste for the future and their pride in what they are, the whole world will pay attention to what France has to say.

Because we will overcome our fears and our anguish together, we will give, together, the example of a people who can affirm its values and its principles, which are those of democracy and the Republic.

The efforts of my predecessors in this direction were remarkable and I want to pay tribute to them here.

I am thinking of General de Gaulle, who worked to rebuild France and restore her stature among nations. I am thinking of George Pompidou, who made our country a major industrial power. Of Valery Giscard d'Estaing, who led France and her society into modernity. Of François Mitterrand, who accompanied the reconciliation of the French and European dreams. Of Jacques Chirac, giving us the status of a nation able to stand up to the claims of the sabre-rattlers. In Nicolas Sarkozy, working tirelessly to solve the financial crisis that had so violently struck the world. And I am thinking of course of François Hollande, acting as a pioneer with the Paris climate agreement and protecting the French in a world struck by terrorism.

Their achievements, especially in recent decades, were too often hampered by a poisonous internal atmosphere, by the despondency of French women and men feeling unfairly disadvantaged, downgraded, or forgotten. What France had to say to the world has sometimes been weakened by a national situation crippled by anxiety, or even mistrust.

Today, ladies and gentlemen, the time has come for France to rise to the occasion. The division and the fractures that run through our society must be overcome, be they economic, social, political or moral; because the world expects us to be solid, strong and clear-sighted.

France's mission in the world is eminent. We will shoulder all our responsibilities to bring, each time it is necessary, an appropriate response to major contemporary crises. Whether it be the migration crisis, the climate challenge, authoritarian excesses, the excesses of global capitalism, and of course terrorism; nothing now strikes one place while sparing others. We are all connected. We are all neighbors.

France will take care always to be on the side of freedom and human rights, but always to build peace in the long term.

We have a considerable role to play: to correct the excesses of the course of the world, and to ensure the defense of freedom. This is our vocation. To do this, we need a more efficient, more democratic, more political Europe, because it is the instrument of our power and our sovereignty. I will work towards this.

Geography has shrunk significantly. But time has accelerated. We are living through a period which will determine the destiny of France for decades to come. We will not fight only for this generation, but for the generations to come. It is incumbent on all of us, here and now, to decide on the world in which these generations will live. This is perhaps our greatest responsibility.

We have to build the world our youth deserves.

I know that the French, at this time, expect much of me. They are right because the mandate they are entrusting to me gives them the right to place the utmost demands on me. I am very aware of this.

No ground will be yielded to the easy option or to compromise. Nothing will weaken my resolve. Nothing will make me give up defending, at all times and in all places, the best interests of France.

I will, at the same time, have an ongoing commitment to reconcile and bring the French together.

The trust that French women and men have shown me fills me with immense energy. The deep certainty that we can, together, write one of the most beautiful pages of our History will support my action.

In these moments when everything could change, the French people have always known how to find the energy, the judgement, the spirit of harmony to build profound change. This is where we are. It is for this mission that I will humbly serve our people.

I know I can count on all of our compatriots to carry out the substantial and exhilarating task that awaits us.

As for me, I will set to work this very evening.

Long live the Republic. Long live France.

SOURCE: President of the French Republic. "Speech by the President of the Republic." May 15, 2017. http://www.elysee.fr/declarations/article/discours-d-investiture-du-president-de-la-republique/.

British Prime Minister Remarks on *General Election*

June 9, 2017

I have just been to see Her Majesty the Queen, and I will now form a government—a government that can provide certainty and lead Britain forward at this critical time for our country.

This government will guide the country through the crucial Brexit talks that begin in just 10 days, and deliver on the will of the British people by taking the United Kingdom out of the European Union.

It will work to keep our nation safe and secure by delivering the change that I set out following the appalling attacks in Manchester and London—cracking down on the ideology of Islamist extremism and all those who support it. And giving the police and the authorities the powers they need to keep our country safe.

The government I lead will put fairness and opportunity at the heart of everything we do, so that we fulfil the promise of Brexit together and—over the next 5 years—build a country in which no one and no community is left behind.

A country in which prosperity and opportunity are shared right across this United Kingdom.

What the country needs more than ever is certainty, and having secured the largest number of votes and the greatest number of seats in the general election, it is clear that only the Conservative & Unionist Party has the legitimacy and ability to provide that certainty by commanding a majority in the House of Commons.

As we do, we will continue to work with our friends and allies in the Democratic Unionist Party in particular. Our 2 parties have enjoyed a strong relationship over many years, and this gives me the confidence to believe that we will be able to work together in the interests of the whole United Kingdom.

This will allow us to come together as a country and channel our energies towards a successful Brexit deal that works for everyone in this country—securing a new partnership with the EU which guarantees our long-term prosperity.

That's what people voted for last June.

That's what we will deliver.

Now let's get to work.

SOURCE: United Kingdom Prime Minister's Office. 10 Downing Street. "PM Statement: General Election 2017." June 9, 2017. https://www.gov.uk/government/speeches/pm-statement-general-election-2017.

President of the German Bundestag
on Formation of a Government

November 21, 2017

Ladies and gentlemen,

This is a special sitting—unquestionably so—not only because it is the first regular sitting since the Bundestag was constituted on 24 October, no less than four weeks ago.

All of us have been affected by the collapse of the coalition talks on Sunday. This applies to everyone who was directly involved in the talks but also to the citizens of our country and, not least, to us, their elected parliamentary representatives.

As the reasons for the failure of these talks are discussed, questions arise as to where we go from here—legitimate questions. It is also understandable that people are concerned—concerned about the political capacity and stability of our country.

Since the outcome of the election of 24 September became clear, we have known that the task facing us was not an easy one, that lengthy negotiations lay ahead. It is not without good reason that today's agenda includes the appointment of a Main Committee—as happened four years ago, incidentally, in a different constellation. This is how we ensure that the Bundestag performs its functions properly and responsibly until a government is formed.

It was clearly evident from the constituent sitting that a Parliament with seven parties in six parliamentary groups will be a more colourful political assembly engaging in livelier debates. The collapse of the coalition talks shows us more clearly that a Parliament reflecting the diversity of society in this way will find it more difficult to form majorities. Democracy, however, requires majorities, and our desire for a stable system also requires sustainable majorities.

As our Basic Law says, all state authority is derived from the people. The people spoke in the election. We, their elected representatives, must now react and do so responsibly.

There is now a great deal of talk about a mandate from the electorate. Every elected Member of Parliament feels bound by that mandate. But what is the mandate we have received from the voters? It is not as simple and clear-cut as it may seem.

Every political party, every Member of Parliament, all of us feel duty-bound to implement the substance of the programmes we promoted during the electoral campaign. But the fact is that the mandate from the electorate also imposes a duty on all of us to form majorities, to help create a government that can govern. Opinions may differ as to how the country should be governed, but there is no doubt that it must be governed. Both of these duties make up the mandate with which the voters have entrusted us. As politically responsible individuals, we must respond conscientiously to both.

In so responding, parties may conclude, on mature reflection, that they do not wish to enter into an alliance with others. That must be possible. But that decision must also be coherently explained, so as to avoid any impression of a desire to abdicate responsibility.

Voters have duties too. They must exercise their capacity to form judgements, be prepared to weigh up arguments and be fair to those who accept responsibility.

There is also a need for those who shape and express public opinion to develop understanding of the complexity of the task, the diversity of interests, opinions and sensitivities and the limitations and finite nature of reality and to be aware that these factors compel us to compromise and seek majority decisions. That is how I put it in my speech at the constituent sitting. These things cannot be done overnight, especially not in view of the complex problems that confront us in many areas today, and certainly not when we are faced with the need to examine details.

There is also a need for understanding of the tightrope walk required of all those who exercise responsibility, which may even involve abandoning parts of their own electoral manifesto for the sake of tenable compromises. That is not 'capitulation', nor is it a lack of firm principles. It is the only way to form majorities and the coalitions that are needed to sustain them. It is a strenuous process for everyone. Reaching agreement through mutual concessions requires courage. Yet it is the only way to preserve the capacity to take political decisions, and that, after all, is what people rightly expect of their politicians, of us.

Let me repeat that the responsibility to cherish these foundations of our parliamentary democracy is incumbent on all of us, electors and elected.

Ladies and gentlemen,

We now have an exceptional situation, as the Federal President emphasised yesterday in his statement. It is a testing time, but it is not a national crisis. We should not overdramatise the task by drawing inappropriate historical comparisons. The task is great, but it is achievable.

Our Basic Law sets the rules. They are unequivocal and astute, and within the bounds of those constitutional requirements we shall all have to exercise our responsibility.

Under Article 63 of the Basic Law, it is the duty of the Federal President to propose a Federal Chancellor for election by the Bundestag. Yesterday President Steinmeier announced his intention of holding discussions with the heads of the organs of our Constitution and talks with the chairs of various political parties. He rightly demands that parties must be willing to engage with each other.

In the meantime, we have an executive government—that is the constitutional, prudent and appropriate transitional solution. And we have a Parliament that is able to act—through its overseeing bodies and through today's appointment of a Main Committee, of the Petitions Committee and of the Committee for the Scrutiny of Elections, Immunity and the Rules of Procedure; a Parliament, moreover, in which each of us can exercise his or her rights as a representative of the people.

We bear joint responsibility for our country—and not only for our country. Europe needs a capable Germany. The reactions from abroad have shown that Europe and many countries in the wider world are waiting for us. The challenges are great. Just as we ourselves need strong partners, our neighbours also want our country alongside them as a reliable partner.

To sum up, the mandate from the electorate means exercising responsibility for our country in Europe and in the world at large. To do that, we need majorities as well as a government that can govern.

Source: German Bundestag. "Speech Delivered prior to the Start of Business." November 21, 2017. https://www.bundestag.de/en/documents/textarchive/kw47-schaeuble-inhalt/532284.

OTHER HISTORIC DOCUMENTS OF INTEREST

FROM THIS VOLUME

FROM PREVIOUS *HISTORIC DOCUMENTS*

Former FBI Director Robert Mueller Appointed Special Counsel on U.S. Election–Russia Investigation, Issues Indictments

MAY 17, OCTOBER 5 AND 30, AND DECEMBER 1, 2017

On May 17, 2017, the Department of Justice announced its intent to appoint former Federal Bureau of Investigation (FBI) director Robert Mueller as special counsel to lead an investigation into possible ties between the campaign of President Donald Trump and members of the Russian government. The move came just a week after Trump fired FBI Director James Comey, a decision that resulted in outcry from both Democrats and Republicans. Despite various attempts to undermine his investigation, by the end of 2017, Mueller's work resulted in two guilty pleas of lying to the FBI by former Trump campaign foreign policy adviser George Papadopoulos and senior adviser Michael Flynn, as well as indictments against former national security advisor Paul Manafort and his business partner Rick Gates on charges ranging from money laundering to failure to register as a foreign agent to conspiracy against the United States. Democrats were hopeful that the investigation would uncover evidence that the Trump campaign did collude with the Russian government to secure his election, while the White House and many Republicans were certain that the president and his closest associates would be cleared of any wrong doing. It was expected that Mueller's investigation would last at least through 2018.

ROSENSTEIN APPOINTS A SPECIAL COUNSEL

Both during his campaign and after his election, President Trump made no secret of his distaste for FBI Director Comey and the way in which he carried out the FBI's investigation into former secretary of state Hillary Clinton's handling of classified information through her private e-mail server. But it was not until May 9 that Trump wrote a letter to the FBI director relieving him of his duties. In testimony before Congress, Comey stated that he felt he was fired by Trump because of the ongoing investigation into his campaign's alleged connections to the Russian government. After his firing, a growing chorus of Democrats called for an independent investigation into the Trump campaign's possible ties with the Russian government. Sen. Chuck Schumer, D-N.Y., said that the failure to do so would cause "every American" to "rightly suspect that the decision to fire Director Comey was part of a cover-up."

On May 17, the Department of Justice answered those requests when Deputy Attorney General Rod Rosenstein announced he would appoint Mueller as special counsel to lead an investigation into the Trump-Russia connection; Rosenstein made the announcement as Acting Attorney General because Attorney General Jeff Sessions recused himself in

March from any Justice Department inquiries into the 2016 presidential election. Rosenstein said he determined that a special counsel was necessary "in order for the American people to have full confidence in the outcome" of the FBI's investigation into the Trump–Russia link, but noted that the "decision is not the finding that crimes have been committed or that any prosecution is warranted." Then-President George W. Bush first appointed Mueller, a former federal prosecutor, as FBI director in 2001, and he stayed on with the administration of President Barack Obama before Comey replaced him in 2013. In accepting the position, Mueller said he would "discharge it to the best of my ability."

The newly appointed special counsel was "authorized to conduct the investigation confirmed by then-FBI Director James B. Comey in testimony before the House Permanent Select Committee on Intelligence on March 20, 2017" to include "any links and/or coordination between the Russian government and individuals associated with the campaign of President Donald Trump." The order also stated, "If the special counsel believes it is necessary and appropriate, the special counsel is authorized to prosecute federal crimes arising from the investigation of these matters." The counsel would receive money and staff from the Justice Department to carry out its efforts.

In response to the appointment of a special counsel, President Trump stated that "a thorough investigation will confirm what we already know—there was no collusion between my campaign and any foreign entity. I look forward to this matter concluding quickly." On Twitter, however, the president expressed a deeper frustration that there was no special counsel named to investigate what he called "the illegal acts that took place in the Clinton campaign & Obama Administration." He also tweeted that allegations of collusion were "the single greatest witch hunt of a politician in American history."

Democrats welcomed Mueller's appointment. "Former Director Mueller is exactly the right kind of individual for this job. I now have significantly greater confidence that the investigation will follow the facts wherever they lead," Schumer said. Republicans overwhelmingly rejected the necessity of the special counsel prior to Mueller's appointment. However, once he was selected, many began voicing their support. "Right thing to do and the right choice," Rep. Barbara Comstock, R-Va., tweeted, while Rep. Ryan Costello, R-Penn., said it was "one less question we have to answer about an extremely confusing and contentious issue." Rep. Jason Chaffetz, R-Utah, chair of the House Oversight Committee was supportive of Mueller's credentials, but said, "I don't think they should have appointed someone," and asked, "Where is the actual crime that they think they need a special prosecutor to prosecute?" Congressional leaders were also quick to note that the ongoing House and Senate committee investigations into the alleged links between the Trump campaign and Russia would continue alongside Mueller's investigation.

MUELLER TEAM HANDS DOWN FIRST INDICTMENTS

The work of the Mueller team was largely kept secret, with rampant speculation about whether any charges would result from the investigation and who would be the first charged. The Mueller investigation issued its first indictments on October 30 in a thirty-one page, twelve-count charge against Paul Manafort, Trump's former campaign manager, and Richard Gates, Manafort's former business partner. The charges included money laundering, false statements to the Justice Department, failure to register as a foreign agent under the Foreign Agent Registration Act, failure to file reports regarding foreign bank and financial accounts, and acts of conspiracy against the United States. In part, the charges alleged that from 2006 through at least 2015, Manafort and Gates conducted lobbying activities on behalf of a pro-Russian political party in the Ukraine, a group that was headed by former Ukrainian president Victor Yanukovych, an ally of Russian President Vladimir Putin. They made tens of millions of dollars in income from these efforts, which they hid from U.S. authorities to avoid paying taxes by laundering the money through various domestic and foreign corporations and bank accounts. To further cover up their illegal activities, the indictment alleges that when contacted by the Justice Department in 2016 about their lobbying activities and earnings, both Manafort and Gates provided knowingly false and misleading statements. Both Gates and Manafort pleaded not guilty to the charges after surrendering to the FBI. Bond was set at $10 million for Manafort and $5 million for Gates; both men agreed to home detention while awaiting trial.

Taken together, the charges did not add up to collusion between the Trump campaign and the Russian government, but were largely viewed in the media as a tactic to put pressure on Trump and his associates as the investigation continued. If convicted, Gates and Manafort could receive decades in federal prison sentences. In a White House press briefing on the same day the indictments were released, Press Secretary Sarah Huckabee Sanders said they were indicative of what the White House had said "from day one. There's been no evidence of Trump-Russia collusion, and nothing in the indictment today changes that at all."

On the day Manafort and Gates surrendered, a charging document was unsealed that listed charges against former Trump campaign foreign policy adviser George Papadopoulos, who had pleaded guilty in September to making false statements to the FBI. According to the statement of charges, Papadopoulos had lied to the FBI about his attempts to coordinate meetings between the Trump campaign and individuals with connections to the Russian government. The court filing indicated that Papadopoulos had originally told the FBI he was not part of the Trump campaign when an "overseas professor" told him that he had information on Democratic presidential nominee Clinton that could be used against her; specifically, this individual had access to "thousands of emails" sent to or received by the former secretary of state. This information was actually obtained in April 2016, during Papadopoulos' time with the campaign. Papadopoulos also told the FBI that the individual he had spoken with in Russia was insignificant, although the court filing indicates he "understood the professor to have substantial connections to high-level Russian government officials." He further failed to disclose to the FBI that the professor had introduced him to someone with a connection to the Russian Ministry of Foreign Affairs and that he had been directed by a "Campaign Supervisor" to travel to Russia for an off-the-record meeting with the Ministry of Foreign Affairs. (That trip never took place.) In September, Papadopoulos agreed to plead guilty to one count of lying to authorities in exchange for his cooperation with the ongoing investigation. The White House downplayed the situation and Papadopoulos' connection to the president, calling him a low-level volunteer, and saying that the charges had "nothing to do with the activities of the campaign, it has to do with his failure to tell the truth."

FORMER NATIONAL SECURITY ADVISER PLEADS GUILTY

Less than one month after the Manafort, Gates, and Papadopoulos charges were made public, the Mueller team released charges against Michael Flynn, a member of the Trump campaign and transition team, for lying to the FBI. Flynn had served as National Security Advisor in the Trump administration for less than one month before stepping down over misleading statements he made to Vice President Mike Pence regarding his interactions with the Russian ambassador during the transition. According to the charge, Flynn asked then-Russian Ambassador Sergey Kislyak not to respond to U.S. sanctions against Russia issued on December 28, 2016, by the Obama administration, and to help delay or defeat a United Nations Security Council vote regarding Israeli settlements. According to the brief statement of charges, Flynn had been directed to make such contact with Kislyak by "a very senior member of the Presidential Transition Team." Flynn spoke with Kislyak on both December 22 and 29, 2016, and kept the "very senior member" apprised of the conversations. However, when interviewed by the FBI on January 24, 2017, Flynn denied such conversations took place. Media reports indicated that the "very senior member" may have been the president's senior adviser and son-in-law, Jared Kushner. Although no charges were brought against Kushner by the end of 2017, his legal team began seeking a crisis communications firm two weeks after Flynn pleaded guilty.

Flynn pleaded guilty to one count of lying to the FBI in exchange for his cooperation with the ongoing Mueller investigation. If convicted, Flynn would face a maximum of five years in prison. Flynn stated, after surrendering to the FBI that his actions "were wrong, and, through my faith in God, I am working to set things right. My guilty plea and agreement to cooperate with the Special Counsel's Office reflect a decision I made in the best interests of my family and our country. I accept full responsibility for my actions." For his cooperation, Flynn will not be charged with or prosecuted for other federal crimes committed, such as misreported foreign lobbying filings related to his work for Turkey.

White House lawyer Ty Cobb issued a statement after the charges were released, saying, "Nothing about the guilty plea or the charge implicates anyone other than Mr. Flynn. The conclusion of this phase of the Special Counsel's work demonstrates that the Special Counsel is moving with all deliberate speed and clears the way for a prompt and reasonable conclusion." The statement also characterized Flynn as a "former Obama administration official." Flynn had served as head of the Defense Intelligence Agency before being fired by the Obama administration for poor management; the administration would reportedly go on to warn the Trump transition team against hiring Flynn.

ATTEMPTS TO UNDERMINE THE MUELLER INVESTIGATION

By law, Mueller is permitted to investigate whether someone is trying to subvert the investigation; however, there was no public indication that he was doing so. The investigation did face multiple attempts to discredit its work, primarily from Republicans, the Trump administration, and right-wing media organizations. It is worth noting, however, that the White House continued to cooperate with the investigation throughout 2017, and many White House staffers and key presidential aides were interviewed by Mueller's team.

Two major stories came to light in December 2017 that were used as talking points by those opposed to the investigation. First, on December 12, text messages between FBI Agent Peter Strzok and FBI lawyer Lisa Page, both of whom had previously worked on the Mueller investigation team, were released. The messages, obtained through an ethics investigation by the Justice Department's inspector general, were politically charged and displayed a clear displeasure over Trump's candidacy and ultimate victory. "God, Trump is a loathsome human," Page texted on March 4, 2016, and later, after Trump's election, Page wrote that she had purchased the book "All the President's Men" because she "needed to brush up on Watergate." After their release, Democrats largely painted the issue as overblown, but Rep. Bob Goodlatte, R-Va., chair of the House Judiciary Committee, said they showed "the magnitude of this insider bias on Mr. Mueller's team." Rep. Louie Gohmert, R-Tex., echoed those remarks, noting, "This is disgusting political bias and there's no way that could not affect a person's work."

Soon after the text messages were made public, Mueller's team was again in the spotlight, this time for evidence it had acquired as part of its investigation. In question were e-mails sent and received by the Trump presidential transition team (PTT), which the Mueller team requested and received through the General Services Administration (GSA). The content of these e-mails was used in the questioning of special counsel witnesses, many of whom worked inside the White House. Kory Langhofer, general counsel for Trump for America (TFA), wrote in a letter to the chairs of the Senate Committee on Homeland Security and Government Affairs and the House Committee on Oversight and Government Reform that the e-mails were "private, privileged materials," not government property and that the Mueller team was violating the Presidential Transition Act of 1963 in using them in the investigation. "TFA owned and controlled the PTT emails and data," Langhofer wrote, "and GSA had no right to access or control the records but was simply serving as Trump For America's records custodian." The letter went on to suggest that the career GSA staff who provided the e-mail may have been politically motivated to do so. Mueller's team held firm that they were acting well within the bounds of the law. "When we have obtained emails in the course of our ongoing criminal investigation, we have secured either the account owner's consent or appropriate criminal process," Mueller's team asserted. At issue was whether all e-mail ending in a .gov extension and stored on a government server, as the e-mail in this case did, are public record or whether the @ptt.gov e-mail are privileged because they belong to the transition team and not a government official.

Frequently, the idea was floated that Trump would remove Mueller from his duties. Some Democratic senators even went as far as to attempt pushing legislation that would legally protect Mueller and his team from dismissal until the conclusion of the investigation. Not only would such a dismissal likely cause a major uproar from both Democrats and Republicans, it would also subvert the power of the Justice Department because Mueller reports to, and could only be fired by, Rosenstein (or anyone who might take his place in the event he was removed from or left his position). Without the ability to dismiss Mueller, the White House took a separate tact, expressing hope that the investigation would reach a conclusion by the close of 2017 (which it did not), one that would clear Trump of any wrongdoing. Despite attempts to cast doubt on the investigation, Deputy Attorney General Rosenstein remained a supporter throughout 2017. "I know what he's doing," he told members of the House Judiciary Committee. "If I felt he was doing something inappropriate, I would take action."

—Heather Kerrigan

Following is the text of the May 17, 2017, order appointing a special counsel to investigate any links between the Russian government and the campaign of President Donald Trump; the October 5, 2017, statement of offense against George Papadopoulos; the October 30, 2017, indictment against Paul Manafort and Rick Gates; and the December 1, 2017, statement of offense against Michael Flynn.

Justice Department
Appoints Special Counsel

May 17, 2017

ORDER NO. 3915-2017

APPOINTMENT OF SPECIAL COUNSEL
TO INVESTIGATE RUSSIAN INTERFERENCE WITH THE 2016 PRESIDENTIAL
ELECTION AND RELATED MATTERS

By virtue of the authority vested in me as Acting Attorney General, including 28 U.S.C. §§ 509, 510, and 515, in order to discharge my responsibility to provide supervision and management of the Department of Justice, and to ensure a full and thorough investigation of the Russian government efforts to interfere in the 2016 presidential election, I hereby order as follows:

(a) Robert S. Mueller III is appointed to serve as Special Counsel for the United States Department of Justice.

(b) The Special Counsel is authorized to conduct the investigation confirmed by then-FBI Director James B. Comey in testimony before the House Permanent Select Committee on Intelligence on March 20, 2017, including:

   (i) any links and/or coordination between the Russian government and individuals associated with the campaign of President Donald Trump; and

   (ii) any matters that arose or may arise directly from the investigation; and

   (iii) any other matters within the scope of 28 C.F.R. § 600.4(a).

(c) If the Special Counsel believes it is necessary and appropriate, the Special Counsel is authorized to prosecute federal crimes arising from the investigation of these matters.

(d) Sections 600.4 through 600.10 of Title 28 of the Code of Federal Regulations are applicable to the Special Counsel.

Rod J. Rosenstein
Acting Attorney General

SOURCE: U.S. Justice Department. Order No. 3915-2017. "Appointment of Special Counsel to Investigate Russian Interference with the 2016 Presidential Election and Related Matters." May 17, 2017. https://www.justice.gov/opa/press-release/file/967231/download.

George Papadopoulos
Statement of Offense

October 5, 2017

[Footnotes have been omitted.]

UNITED STATES DISTRICT COURT
FOR THE DISTRICT OF COLUMBIA

UNITED STATES OF AMERICA

v.

GEORGE PAPADOPOULOS, Defendant.

Criminal No: 17 Cr. 182 (RDM) SEALED

Violation: 18 U.S.C. § 1001 (False Statements)

STATEMENT OF THE OFFENSE

Pursuant to Federal Rule of Criminal Procedure 11, the United States of America and the defendant, GEORGE PAPADOPOULOS, stipulate and agree that the following facts are true and accurate. These facts do not constitute all of the facts known to the parties concerning the charged offense; they are being submitted to demonstrate that sufficient facts exist that the defendant committed the offense to which he is pleading guilty.

I. Overview

1. The defendant, GEORGE PAPADOPOULOS, who served as a foreign policy advisor for the presidential campaign of Donald J. Trump (the "Campaign"), made material false statements and material omissions during an interview with the Federal Bureau of Investigation that took place on January 27, 2017. At the time of the interview, the FBI had an open investigation into the Russian government's efforts to interfere in the 2016 presidential election, including the nature of any links between individuals associated with the Campaign and the Russian government, and whether there was any coordination between the Campaign and Russia's efforts. The FBI opened and coordinated the investigation in Washington, DC.

2. Defendant PAPADOPOULOS made the following material false statements and material omissions to the FBI:

   a. Defendant PAPADOPOULOS claimed that his interactions with an overseas professor, who defendant PAPADOPOULOS understood to have substantial connections to Russian government officials, occurred before defendant PAPADOPOULOS became a foreign policy adviser to the Campaign. Defendant PAPADOPOULOS acknowledged that the professor had told him about the Russians possessing "dirt" on then-candidate Hillary Clinton in the form of "thousands of emails," but stated multiple times that he learned that information prior to joining the Campaign. In truth and in fact, however, defendant PAPADOPOULOS learned he would be an advisor to the Campaign in early March, and met the professor on or about March 14, 2016; the professor only took interest in defendant PAPADOPOULOS because of his status with the Campaign; and the professor told defendant PAPADOPOULOS about the "thousands of emails" on or about April 26, 2016, when defendant PAPADOPOULOS had been a foreign policy adviser to the Campaign for over a month.

b. Defendant PAPADOPOULOS further told the investigating agents that the professor was "a nothing" and "just a guy talk[ing] up connections or some-thing." In truth and in fact, however, defendant PAPADOPOULOS understood that the professor had substantial connections to Russian government officials (and had met with some of those officials in Moscow immediately prior to tell-ing defendant PAPADOPOULOS about the "thousands of emails") and, over a period of months, defendant PAPADOPOULOS repeatedly sought to use the professor's Russian connections in an effort to arrange a meeting between the Campaign and Russian government officials.

c. Defendant PAPADOPOULOS claimed he met a certain female Russian national before he joined the Campaign and that their communications consisted of emails such as, "'Hi, how are you?'" In truth and in fact, how-ever, defendant PAPADOPOULOS met the female Russian national on or about March 24, 2016, after he had become an adviser to the Campaign; he believed that she had connections to Russian government officials; and he sought to use her Russian connections over a period of months in an effort to arrange a meeting between the Campaign and Russian government officials.

3. Through his false statements and omissions, defendant PAPADOPOULOS impeded the FBI's ongoing investigation into the existence of any links or coor-dination between individuals associated with the Campaign and the Russian gov-ernment's efforts to interfere with the 2016 presidential election.

II. Timeline of Selected Events

PAPADOPOULOS's Role on the Campaign

4. In early March 2016, defendant PAPADOPOULOS learned he would be a for-eign policy advisor for the Campaign. Defendant PAPADOPOULOS was living in London, England, at the time. Based on a conversation that took place on or about March 6, 2016, with a supervisory campaign official (the "Campaign Supervisor"), defendant PAPADOPOULOS understood that a principal foreign policy focus of the Campaign was an improved U.S. relationship with Russia.

PAPADOPOULOS's Introduction to the Professor and the Female Russian National

5. On or about March 14, 2016, while traveling in Italy, defendant PAPADOPOULOS met an individual who was a professor based in London (the "Professor"). Initially, the Professor seemed uninterested in defendant PAPADOPOULOS. However, after defendant PAPADOPOULOS informed the Professor about his joining the Campaign, the Professor appeared to take great interest in defendant PAPADOPOULOS. Defendant PAPADOPOULOS was interested in the Professor because, among other reasons, the Professor claimed to have substantial connections with Russian government officials, which defendant PAPADOPOULOS thought could increase his importance as a policy advisor to the Campaign.

6. On or about March 21, 2016, the Campaign told *The Washington Post* that defendant PAPADOPOULOS was one of five named foreign policy advisors for the Campaign.

7. On or about March 24, 2016, defendant PAPADOPOULOS met with the Professor in London. The Professor brought with him a female Russian national (the "Female Russian National"), introduced to defendant PAPADOPOULOS as a relative of Russian President Vladimir Putin with connections to senior Russian government officials.

PAPADOPOULOS Pursues His Contacts with the Professor and the Female Russian National

8. Following his March 24, 2016 meeting with the Professor and the Female Russian National, defendant PAPADOPOULOS emailed the Campaign Supervisor and several members of the Campaign's foreign policy team and stated that he had just met with his "good friend" the Professor, who had introduced him to the Female Russian National (described by defendant PAPADOPOULOS in the email as "Putin's niece") and the Russian Ambassador in London. Defendant PAPADOPOULOS stated that the topic of their discussion was "to arrange a meeting between us and the Russian leadership to discuss U.S.-Russia ties under President Trump." The Campaign Supervisor responded that he would "work it through the campaign," but that no commitments should be made at that point. The Campaign Supervisor added: "Great work."

9. On or about March 31, 2016, defendant PAPADOPOULOS attended a "national security meeting" in Washington, D.C., with then-candidate Trump and other foreign policy advisors for the Campaign. When defendant PAPADOPOULOS introduced himself to the group, he stated, in sum and substance, that he had connections that could help arrange a meeting between then-candidate Trump and President Putin.

10. After his trip to Washington, D.C., defendant PAPADOPOULOS worked with the Professor and the Female Russian National to arrange a meeting between the Campaign and the Russian government, and took steps to advise the Campaign of his progress.

a. In early April 2016, defendant PAPADOPOULOS sent multiple emails to other members of the Campaign's foreign policy team regarding his contacts with "the Russians" and his "outreach to Russia."

b. On or about April 10, 2016, defendant PAPADOPOULOS emailed the Female Russian National, who responded the next day, on or about April 11, 2016, that she "would be very pleased to support your initiatives between our two countries." Defendant PAPADOPOULOS then asked the Female Russian National, in an email cc'ing the Professor, about setting up "a potential foreign policy trip to Russia."

c. The Professor responded to defendant PAPADOPOULOS's email later that day, on or about April 11, 2016: "This is already been agreed. I am flying to Moscow on the 18th for a Valdai meeting, plus other meetings at the Duma." The Duma is a Russian government legislative assembly.

d. The Female Russian National responded: "I have already alerted my personal links to our conversation and your request. . . . As mentioned we are all very excited by the possibility of a good relationship with Mr. Trump. The Russian Federation would love to welcome him once his candidature would be officially announced."

The Professor Introduces PAPADOPOULOS to a Russian National Connected to the Russian Ministry of Foreign Affairs

11. On or about April 18, 2016, the Professor introduced defendant PAPADOPOULOS over email to an individual in Moscow (the "Russian MFA Connection") who told defendant PAPADOPOULOS he had connections to the Russian Ministry of Foreign Affairs. The MFA is the executive entity in Russia responsible for Russian foreign relations. Over the next several weeks, defendant PAPADOPOULOS and the Russian MFA Connection had multiple conversations over Skype and email about setting "the groundwork" for a "potential" meeting between the Campaign and Russian government officials.

12. On or about April 22, 2016, the Russian MFA Connection sent defendant PAPADOPOULOS an email thanking him "for an extensive talk" and proposing "to meet in London or in Moscow." Defendant PAPADOPOULOS replied by suggesting that "we set one up here in London with the Ambassador as well to discuss a process moving forward."

13. On or about April 25, 2016, defendant PAPADOPOULOS emailed a senior policy advisor for the Campaign (the "Senior Policy Advisor"): "The Russian government has an open invitation by Putin for Mr. Trump to meet him when he is ready. The advantage of being in London is that these governments tend to speak a bit more openly in 'neutral' cities."

PAPADOPOULOS Learns that the Russians Have "Dirt" on Clinton

14. On or about April 26, 2016, defendant PAPADOPOULOS met the Professor for breakfast at a London hotel. During this meeting, the Professor told defendant

PAPADOPOULOS that he had just returned from a trip to Moscow where he had met with high-level Russian government officials. The Professor told defendant PAPADOPOULOS that on that trip he (the Professor) learned that the Russians had obtained "dirt" on then-candidate Clinton. The Professor told defendant PAPADOPOULOS, as defendant PAPADOPOULOS later described to the FBI, that "They [the Russians] have dirt on her"; "the Russians had emails of Clinton"; "they have thousands of emails."

15. Following that conversation, defendant PAPADOPOULOS continued to correspond with Campaign officials, and continued to communicate with the Professor and the Russian MFA Connection, in an effort to arrange a meeting between the Campaign and the Russian government.

    a. For example, the day after his meeting at the hotel with the Professor, on or about April 27, 2016, defendant PAPADOPOULOS emailed the Senior Policy Advisor: "Have some interesting messages coming in from Moscow about a trip when the time is right."

    b. Also on or about April 27, 2016, defendant PAPADOPOULOS emailed a high-ranking official of the Campaign (the "High-Ranking Campaign Official") "to discuss Russia's interest in hosting Mr. Trump. Have been receiving a lot of calls over the last month about Putin wanting to host him and the team when the time is right."

    c. On or about April 30, 2016, defendant PAPADOPOULOS thanked the Professor for his "critical help" in arranging a meeting between the Campaign and the Russian government, and remarked: "It's history making if it happens."

PAPADOPOULOS Shares Information from the Russian MFA Connection

16. On or about May 4, 2016, the Russian MFA Connection sent an email (the "May 4 MFA Email") to defendant PAPADOPOULOS and the Professor that stated: "I have just talked to my colleagues from the MFA. The[y] are open for cooperation. One of the options is to make a meeting for you at the North America Desk, if you are in Moscow." Defendant PAPADOPOULOS responded that he was "[g]lad the MFA is interested." Defendant PAPADOPOULOS forwarded the May 4 MFA Email to the High-Ranking Campaign Official, adding: "What do you think? Is this something we want to move forward with?" The next day, on or about May 5, 2016, defendant PAPADOPOULOS had a phone call with the Campaign Supervisor, and then forwarded the May 4 MFA Email to him, adding to the top of the email: "Russia updates."

17. On or about May 13, 2016, the Professor emailed defendant PAPADOPOULOS with "an update" of what they had discussed in their "recent conversations," including: "We will continue to liaise through you with the Russian counterparts in terms of what is needed for a high level meeting of Mr. Trump with the Russian Federation."

18. The next day, on or about May 14, 2016, defendant PAPADOPOULOS emailed the High-Ranking Campaign Official and stated that the "Russian government[] ha[s] also relayed to me that they are interested in hosting Mr. Trump."

19. On or about May 21, 2016, defendant PAPADOPOULOS emailed another high-ranking Campaign official, with the subject line "Request from Russia to meet Mr. Trump." The email included the May 4 MFA Email and added: "Russia has been eager to meet Mr. Trump for quite sometime and have been reaching out to me to discuss."

20. On or about June 1, 2016, defendant PAPADOPOULOS emailed the High-Ranking Campaign Official and asked about Russia. The High-Ranking Campaign Official referred him to the Campaign Supervisor because "he is running point." Defendant PAPADOPOULOS then emailed the Campaign Supervisor, with the subject line "Re: Messages from Russia": "I have the Russian MFA asking me if Mr. Trump is interested in visiting Russia at some point. Wanted to pass this info along to you for you to decide what's best to do with it and what message I should send (or to ignore)."

21. From mid-June through mid-August 2016, PAPADOPOULOS pursued an "off the record" meeting between one or more Campaign representatives and "members of President Putin's office and the MFA."

    a. For example, on or about June 19, 2016, after several email and Skype exchanges with the Russian MFA Connection, defendant PAPADOPOULOS emailed the High-Ranking Campaign Official, with the subject line "New message from Russia": "The Russian ministry of foreign affairs messaged and said that if Mr. Trump is unable to make it to Russia, if a campaign rep (me or someone else) can make it for meetings? I am willing to make the trip off the record if it's in the interest of Mr. Trump and the campaign to meet specific people."

    b. After several weeks of further communications regarding a potential "off the record" meeting with Russian officials, on or about August 15, 2016, the Campaign Supervisor told defendant PAPADOPOULOS that "I would encourage you" and another foreign policy advisor to the Campaign to "make the trip[], if it is feasible."

    c. The trip proposed by defendant PAPADOPOULOS did not take place.

The Defendant's False Statements to the FBI

22. On or about January 27, 2017, defendant PAPADOPOULOS agreed to be interviewed by agents from the FBI.

23. The agents informed defendant PAPADOPOULOS that the FBI was investigating interference by the Russian government in the 2016 presidential election and whether any individuals related to the Campaign were involved. The agents further informed defendant PAPADOPOULOS that he needed to be truthful and warned that he could get "in trouble" if he lied. The agents also advised him that lying to them "is a federal offense." They confirmed that the interview was "completely voluntary."

24. During the course of the interview, defendant PAPADOPOULOS made numerous false statements and omitted material facts regarding the conduct and communications described above, and, in particular, lied about the extent, timing, and nature of his communications with the Professor, the Female Russian National, and the Russian MFA Connection.

False Statement: PAPADOPOULOS Met the Professor and Learned About Russian "Dirt" Before He Joined the Campaign

25. During his interview with the FBI, defendant PAPADOPOULOS acknowledged that he met the Professor and that the Professor told him the Russians had "dirt" on then-candidate Clinton in the form of "thousands of emails," but defendant PAPADOPOULOS stated multiple times that those communications occurred prior to when he joined the Campaign. Defendant PAPADOPOULOS told the FBI: "This isn't like he [the Professor]'s messaging me while I'm in April with Trump"; "I wasn't even on the Trump team, that wasn't even on the radar"; "I wasn't even on Trump's orbit[] at this time"; and "This was a year ago, this was before I even got with Trump." He also said it was a "very strange coincidence" to be told of the "dirt" before he started working for the Campaign.

26. In truth and in fact, however, and as set forth above, defendant PAPADOPOULOS met the Professor for the first time on or about March 14, 2016, after defendant PAPADOPOULOS had already learned he would be a foreign policy advisor for the Campaign; the Professor showed interest in defendant PAPADOPOULOS only after learning of his role on the Campaign; and the Professor told defendant PAPADOPOULOS about the Russians possessing "dirt" on then-candidate Clinton in late April 2016, more than a month after defendant PAPADOPOULOS had joined the Campaign.

False Statement: PAPADOPOULOS's Contacts with the Professor Were Inconsequential

27. During his interview with the FBI, defendant PAPADOPOULOS also made false statements in an effort to minimize the extent and importance of his communications with the Professor. For example, defendant PAPADOPOULOS stated that "[the Professor]'s a nothing," that he thought the Professor was "just a guy talk[ing] up connections or something," and that he believed the Professor was "BS'ing to be completely honest with you."

28. In truth and in fact, however, defendant PAPADOPOULOS understood the Professor to have substantial connections to high-level Russian government officials and that the Professor spoke with some of those officials in Moscow before telling defendant PAPADOPOULOS about the "dirt." Defendant PAPADOPOULOS also engaged in extensive communications over a period of months with the Professor regarding foreign policy issues for the Campaign, including efforts to arrange a "history making" meeting between the Campaign and Russian government officials.

29. In addition, defendant PAPADOPOULOS failed to inform investigators that the Professor had introduced him to the Russian MFA Connection, despite being asked if he had met with Russian nationals or "[a]nyone with a Russian accent" during the Campaign. Indeed, while defendant PAPADOPOULOS told the FBI that he was involved in meetings and did "shuttle diplomacy" with officials from several other countries during the Campaign, he omitted the entire course of

conduct with the Professor and the Russian MFA Connection regarding his efforts to establish meetings between the Campaign and Russian government officials.

False Statement: PAPADOPOULOS Met the Female Russian National Before He Joined the Campaign, and His Contacts with Her Were Inconsequential

30. During his interview with the FBI, defendant PAPADOPOULOS also falsely claimed that he met the Female Russian National before he joined the Campaign, and falsely told the FBI that he had "no" relationship at all with the Female Russian National. He stated that the extent of their communications was her sending emails—"Just, 'Hi, how are you?'" "That's it."

31. In truth and in fact, however, defendant PAPADOPOULOS met the Female Russian National on or about March 24, 2016, after he had joined the Campaign; he believed that the Female Russian National had connections to high-level Russian government officials and could help him arrange a potential foreign policy trip to Russia; and during the Campaign be emailed and spoke over Skype on numerous occasions with the Female Russian National about the potential foreign policy trip to Russia.

IV. Events Following PAPADOPOULOS January 27, 2017 Interview with the FBI

32. The FBI interviewed defendant PAPADOPOULOS again on February 16, 2017. His counsel was present for the interview. During the interview, defendant PAPADOPOULOS reiterated his purported willingness to cooperate with the investigation.

33. The next day, on or about February 17, 2017, defendant PAPADOPOULOS deactivated his Facebook account, which he had maintained since approximately August 2005 and which contained information about communications he had with the Professor and the Russian MFA Connection. Shortly after be deactivated his account, PAPADOPOULOS created a new Facebook account that did not contain the communications with the Professor and the Russian MFA Connection.

34. On or about February 23, 2017, defendant PAPADOPOULOS ceased using his cell phone number and began using a new number.

35. On July 27, 2017, defendant PAPADOPOULOS was arrested upon his arrival at Dulles International Airport. Following his arrest, defendant PAPADOPOULOS met with the Government on numerous occasions to provide information and answer questions.

ROBERT S. MUELLER, III
Special Counsel

[The Defendant's Acceptance and Attorney's Acknowledgement has been omitted.]

Source: U.S. Justice Department. *United States of America v. George Papadopoulos.* Filed October 5, 2017. https://www.justice.gov/file/1007346/download.

![book icon with "DOCUMENT" label]

Paul Manafort and Rick Gates Indicted on Multiple Counts

October 30, 2017

IN THE UNITED STATES DISTRICT COURT
FOR THE DISTRICT OF COLUMBIA

UNITED STATES OF AMERICA

v.

PAUL J. MANAFORT, JR. and
RICHARD W. GATES III, Defendants.

Criminal No. (18 U.S.C. §§ 2, 371, 981 (a)(1)(C), 982, 1001(a), 1956(h), and 3551 et seq.; 22 U.S.C. §§ 612(a), 618(a)(1), and 618(a)(2); 28 U.S.C. § 2461(c); 31 U.S.C. §§ 5314 and 5322(b))

INDICTMENT

The Grand Jury for the District of Columbia charges:

Introduction

At all times relevant to this Indictment:

1. Defendants PAUL J. MANAFORT, JR., (MANAFORT) and RICHARD W. GATES III (GATES) served for years as political consultants and lobbyists. Between at least 2006 and 2015, MANAFORT and GATES acted as unregistered agents of the Government of Ukraine, the Party of Regions (a Ukrainian political party whose leader Victor Yanukovych was President from 2010 to 2014), Yanukovych, and the Opposition Bloc (a successor to the Party of Regions that formed in 2014 when Yanukovych fled to Russia). MANAFORT and GATES generated tens of millions of dollars in income as a result of their Ukraine work. In order to hide Ukraine payments from United States authorities, from approximately 2006 through at least 2016, MANAFORT and GATES laundered the money through scores of United States and foreign corporations, partnerships, and bank accounts.

2. In furtherance of the scheme, MANAFORT and GATES funneled millions of dollars in payments into foreign nominee companies and bank accounts, opened by them and their accomplices in nominee names and in various foreign countries, including Cyprus, Saint Vincent & the Grenadines (Grenadines), and the Seychelles. MANAFORT and GATES hid the existence of the foreign companies and bank accounts, falsely and repeatedly reporting to their tax preparers and to the United States that they had no foreign bank accounts.

3. In furtherance of the scheme, MANAFORT and GATES concealed from the United States their work as agents of, and millions of dollars in payments from, Ukraine and its political parties and leaders. Because MANAFORT and GATES, among other things, directed a company to lobby United States officials on behalf of the Government of Ukraine, the President of Ukraine, and Ukrainian political parties, they were required by law to report to the United States their work and fees. MANAFORT and GATES did not do so. Instead, when the Department of Justice sent inquiries to MANAFORT and GATES in 2016 about their activities, MANAFORT and GATES responded with a series of false and misleading statements.

4. In furtherance of the scheme, MANAFORT and GATES used his hidden overseas wealth to enjoy a lavish lifestyle in the United States, without paying taxes on that income. MANAFORT, without reporting the income to his tax preparer or the United States, spent millions of dollars on luxury goods and services for himself and his extended family through payments wired from offshore nominee accounts to United States vendors. MANAFORT also used these offshore accounts to purchase multi-million dollar properties in the United States. MANAFORT then borrowed millions of dollars in loans using these properties as collateral, thereby obtaining cash in the United States without reporting and paying taxes on the income. In order to increase the amount of money he could access in the United States, MANAFORT defrauded the institutions that loaned money on these properties so that they would lend him more money at more favorable rates than he would otherwise be able to obtain.

5. GATES aided MANAFORT in obtaining money from these offshore accounts, which he was instrumental in opening. Like MANAFORT, GATES used money from these offshore accounts to pay for his personal expenses, including his mortgage, children's tuition, and interior decorating of his Virginia residence.

6. In total, more than $75,000,000 flowed through the offshore accounts. MANAFORT laundered more than $18,000,000, which was used by him to buy property, goods, and services in the United States, income that he concealed from the United States Treasury, the Department of Justice, and others. GATES transferred more than $3,000,000 from the offshore accounts to other accounts that he controlled.

[The section of the indictment outlining the individuals and parties referred to in the charges, as well as tables listing the entities owned by MANAFORT and GATES, have been omitted.]

The Scheme

14. Between in or around 2008 and 2017, both dates being approximate and inclusive, in the District of Columbia and elsewhere, MANAFORT and GATES devised and intended to devise, and executed and attempted to execute, a scheme and artifice to defraud, and to obtain money and property by means of false and fraudulent pretenses, representations, and promises from the United States, banks, and other financial institutions. As part of the scheme, MANAFORT and GATES repeatedly provided false information to financial bookkeepers, tax accountants, and legal counsel, among others.

[The details of the alleged illegal activity carried out by Manafort and Gates, and the associated tables, have been omitted.]

Statutory Allegations

COUNT ONE
(Conspiracy Against the United States)

... 38. From in or about and between 2006 and 2017, both dates being approximate and inclusive, in the District of Columbia and elsewhere, the defendants, PAUL J. MANAFORT, JR., and RICHARD W. GATES III, together with others, knowingly and intentionally conspired to defraud the United States by impeding, impairing, obstructing, and defeating the lawful governmental functions of a government agency, namely the Department of Justice and the Department of the Treasury, and to commit offenses against the United States, to wit, the violations of law charged in Counts Three through Six and Ten through Twelve. ...

COUNT TWO
(Conspiracy to Launder Money)

... 41. In or around and between 2006 and 2016, both dates being approximate and inclusive, in the District of Columbia and elsewhere, the defendants, PAUL J. MANAFORT, JR., and RICHARD W. GATES III, together with others, did knowingly and intentionally conspire to:

(a) transport, transmit, and transfer monetary instruments and funds from places outside the United States to and through places in the United States and from places in the United States to and through places outside the United States, with the intent to promote the carrying on of specified unlawful activity, to wit: a felony violation of the FARA ... and

(b) conduct financial transactions, affecting interstate and foreign commerce, knowing that the property involved in the financial transactions would represent the proceeds of some form of unlawful activity, and the transactions in fact would involve the proceeds of Specified Unlawful Activity, knowing such financial transactions were designed in whole and in part (i) to engage in conduct constituting a violation of sections 7201 and 7206 of the Internal Revenue Code of 1986, and (ii) to conceal and disguise in nature, location, source, ownership, and control of the proceeds of the Specified Unlawful Activity ...

COUNTS THREE THROUGH SIX
(Failure To File Reports Of Foreign Bank And
Financial Accounts For Calendar Years 2011-2014)

... 43. On the filing due dates listed below, in the District of Columbia and elsewhere, the defendant PAUL J. MANAFORT, JR., unlawfully, willfully, and knowingly did fail to file with the Department of the Treasury an FBAR disclosing that he has a financial interest in, and signature and other authority over, a bank, securities, and other financial account in a foreign country, which had an aggregate value of more than $10,000, while violating another law of the United States and as part of pattern of illegal activity involving more than $100,000 in a 12-month period, during the years listed below:

[The table listing the number of counts of failure to file a disclosure has been omitted.]

COUNTS SEVEN THROUGH NINE

(Failure To File Reports Of Foreign Bank and Financial

Accounts For Calendar Years 2011-2013)

. . . 45. On the filing due dates listed below, in the District of Columbia and elsewhere, the defendant RICHARD W. GATES III, unlawfully, willfully, and knowingly did fail to file with the Department of the Treasury an FBAR disclosing that he has a financial interest in, and signature and other authority over, a bank, securities, and other financial account in a foreign country, which had an aggregate value of more than $10,000, while violating another law of the United States and as part of a pattern of illegal activity involving more than $100,000 in a 12-month period, during the years listed below:

[The table listing the number of counts of failure to file a disclosure has been omitted.]

COUNT TEN

(Unregistered Agent Of A Foreign Principal)

. . . 47. From in or about and between 2008 and 2014, both dates being approximate and inclusive, within the District of Columbia and elsewhere, the defendants PAUL J. MANAFORT, JR., and RICHARD W. GATES III knowingly and willfully, without registering with the Attorney General as required by law, acted as agents of a foreign principal, to wit, the Government of Ukraine, the Party of Regions, and Yanukovych.

COUNT ELEVEN

(False and Misleading FARA Statements)

. . . 49. On or about November 23, 2016 and February 10, 2017, within the District of Columbia and elsewhere, the defendants PAUL J. MANAFORT, JR., and RICHARD W. GATES III knowingly and willfully caused to be made a false statement of a material fact, and omitted a material fact necessary to make the statements therein not misleading, in a document filed and furnished to the Attorney General under the provisions of FARA, to wit the underlined statements:

- "[DMI]'s efforts on behalf of the Party of Regions and Opposition Bloc did not include meetings or outreach within the U.S."

- "[N]either [DMI] nor Messrs. Manafort or Gates had any agreement with the [Centre] to provide services."

- "[DMI] did not provide the [Centre], at the request of members of the Party of Regions, with a list of potential U.S.-based consultants—including [Company A and Company B]—for the [Centre]'s reference and further consideration. [The Centre] then contracted directly with [Company A and Company B] to provide services within the United States for which these entities registered under the Lobbying Disclosure Act."

- "To Gates' recollection, these efforts included providing policy briefings to the [Centre] and its consultants on key initiatives and political developments in Ukraine, including participation in and/or coordination of related conference calls and meetings. Although Gates recalls interacting with [the Centre]'s consultants regarding efforts in the Ukraine and Europe, neither Gates nor Mr. Manafort recall meeting with or conducting outreach to U.S. government officials or U.S. media outlets on behalf of [the Centre], nor do they recall being party to, arranging, or facilitating any such communications. Rather, it is the recollection and understanding of Messrs. Gates and Manafort that such communications would been have facilitated and conducted by the [Centre]'s U.S. consultants, as directed by the [Centre], pursuant to the agreement reached between those parties (to which [DMI] was not a party)."

- "[A] search has been conducted for correspondence containing additional information related to the matters described in [the government's] Letters. However, as a result of [DMI's] Email Retention Policy, which does not retain communications beyond thirty days, the search has returned no responsive communications."

COUNT TWELVE

(False Statements)

. . . 51. On or about November 23, 2016 and February 10, 2017, within the District of Columbia and elsewhere, in a matter within the jurisdiction of the executive branch of the Government of the United States, the defendants PAUL J. MANAFORT, JR., and RICHARD W. GATES III knowingly and willfully did cause another: to falsify, conceal, and cover up by a scheme and device a material fact; to make materially false, fictitious, and fraudulent statements and representation; and to make and use a false writing and document knowing the same to contain materially false, fictitious, and fraudulent statement, to wit, the statements in the November 23, 2016 and February 10, 2017 submissions to the Department of Justice . . .

[The portion of the indictment outlining the property subject to forfeiture by Manafort and Gates has been omitted.]

Robert S. Mueller, III
Special Counsel
Department of Justice

SOURCE: U.S. Justice Department. *United States of America v. Paul J. Manafort Jr. and Richard W. Gates III.* Filed October 30, 2017. https://www.justice.gov/file/1007271/download.

Michael Flynn Pleads
Guilty to Lying to the FBI

December 1, 2017

UNITED STATES DISTRICT COURT

FOR THE DISTRICT OF COLUMBIA

UNITED STATES OF AMERICA

v.

MICHAEL T. FLYNN, Defendant.

Violation: 18 U.S.C. § 1001 (False Statements)

STATEMENT OF THE OFFENSE

Pursuant to Federal Rule of Criminal Procedure 11, the United States of America and the defendant, MICHAEL T. FLYNN, stipulate and agree that the following facts are true and accurate. These facts do not constitute all of the facts known to the parties concerning the charged offense; they are being submitted to demonstrate that sufficient facts exist that the defendant committed the offense to which he is pleading guilty.

1. The defendant, MICHAEL T. FLYNN, who served as a surrogate and national security advisor for the presidential campaign of Donald J. Trump ("Campaign"), as a senior member of President-Elect Trump's Transition Team ("Presidential Transition Team"), and as the National Security Advisor to President Trump, made materially false statements and omissions during an interview with the Federal Bureau of Investigation ("FBI") on January 24, 2017, in Washington, D.C. At the time of the interview, the FBI had an open investigation into the Government of Russia's ("Russia") efforts to interfere in the 2016 presidential election, including the nature of any links between individuals associated with the Campaign and Russia, and whether there was any coordination between the Campaign and Russia's efforts.

2. FLYNN's false statements and omissions impeded and otherwise had a material impact on the FBI's ongoing investigation into the existence of any links or coordination between individuals associated with the Campaign and Russia's efforts to interfere with the 2016 presidential election.

False Statements Regarding FLYNN's Request to the Russian Ambassador that Russia Refrain from Escalating the Situation in Response to U.S. Sanctions against Russia

3. On or about January 24, 2017, FLYNN agreed to be interviewed by agents from the FBI ("January 24 voluntary interview"). During the interview, FLYNN falsely stated that he did not ask Russia's Ambassador to the United States ("Russian

Ambassador") to refrain from escalating the situation in response to sanctions that the United States had imposed against Russia. FLYNN also falsely stated that he did not remember a follow-up conversation in which the Russian Ambassador stated that Russia had chosen to moderate its response to those sanctions as a result of FLYNN's request. In truth and in fact, however, FLYNN then and there knew that the following had occurred:

a. On or about December 28, 2016, then-President Barack Obama signed Executive Order 13757, which was to take effect the following day. The executive order announced sanctions against Russia in response to that government's actions intended to interfere with the 2016 presidential election ("U.S. Sanctions").

b. On or about December 28, 2016, the Russian Ambassador contacted FLYNN.

c. On or about December 29, 2016, FLYNN called a senior official of the Presidential Transition Team ("PTT official"), who was with other senior members of the Presidential Transition Team at the Mar-a-Lago resort in Palm Beach, Florida, to discuss what, if anything, to communicate to the Russian Ambassador about the U.S. Sanctions. On that call, FLYNN and the PTT official discussed the U.S. Sanctions, including the potential impact of those sanctions on the incoming administration's foreign policy goals. The PTT official and FLYNN also discussed that the members of the Presidential Transition Team at Mar-a-Lago did not want Russia to escalate the situation.

d. Immediately after his phone call with the PTT official, FLYNN called the Russian Ambassador and requested that Russia not escalate the situation and only respond to the U.S. Sanctions in a reciprocal manner.

e. Shortly after his phone call with the Russian Ambassador, FLYNN spoke with the PTT official to report on the substance of his call with the Russian Ambassador, including their discussion of the U.S. Sanctions.

f. On or about December 30, 2016, Russian President Vladimir Putin released a statement indicating that Russia would not take retaliatory measures in response to the U.S. Sanctions at that time.

g. On or about December 31, 2016, the Russian Ambassador called FLYNN and informed him that Russia had chosen not to retaliate in response to FLYNN's request.

h. After his phone call with the Russian Ambassador, FLYNN spoke with senior members of the Presidential Transition Team about FLYNN's conversations with the Russian Ambassador regarding the U.S. Sanctions and Russia's decision not to escalate the situation.

False Statements Regarding FLYNN's Request that Foreign Officials Vote Against or Delay a United Nations Security Council Resolution

4. During the January 24 voluntary interview, FLYNN made additional false statements about calls he made to Russia and several other countries regarding a resolution submitted by Egypt to the United Nations Security Council on December 21, 2016.

Specifically FLYNN falsely stated that he only asked the countries' positions on the vote, and that he did not request that any of the countries take any particular action on the resolution. FLYNN also falsely stated that the Russian Ambassador never described to him Russia's response to FLYNN's request regarding the resolution. In truth and in fact, however, FLYNN then and there knew that the following had occurred:

a. On or about December 21, 2016, Egypt submitted a resolution to the United Nations Security Council on the issue of Israeli settlements ("resolution"). The United Nations Security Council was scheduled to vote on the resolution the following day.

b. On or about December 22, 2016, a very senior member of the Presidential Transition Team directed FLYNN to contact officials from foreign governments, including Russia, to learn where each government stood on the resolution and to influence those governments to delay the vote or defeat the resolution.

c. On or about December 22, 2016, FLYNN contacted the Russian Ambassador about the pending vote. FLYNN informed the Russian Ambassador about the incoming administration's opposition to the resolution, and requested that Russia vote against or delay the resolution.

d. On or about December 23, 2016, FLYNN again spoke with the Russian Ambassador, who informed FLYNN that if it came to a vote Russia would not vote against the resolution.

Other False Statements Regarding FLYNN's Contacts with Foreign Governments

5. On March 7, 2017, FLYNN filed multiple documents with the Department of Justice pursuant to the Foreign Agents Registration Act ("FARA") pertaining to a project performed by him and his company, the Flynn Intel Group, Inc. ("FIG"), for the principal benefit of the Republic of Turkey ("Turkey project"). In the FARA filings, FLYNN made materially false statements and omissions, including by falsely stating that (a) FIG did not know whether or the extent to which the Republic of Turkey was involved in the Turkey project, (b) the Turkey project was focused on improving U.S. business organizations' confidence regarding doing business in Turkey, and (c) an op-ed by FLYNN published in *the Hill* on November 8, 2016, was written at his own initiative; and by omitting that officials from the Republic of Turkey provided supervision and direction over the Turkey project.

ROBERT S. MUELLER, III
Special Counsel

[The Defendant's Acceptance and Attorney's Acknowledgment have been omitted.]

Source: U.S. Justice Department. *United States of America v. Michael T. Flynn.* Filed December 1, 2017. https://www.justice.gov/file/1015126/download.

OTHER HISTORIC DOCUMENTS OF INTEREST

FROM THIS VOLUME

FROM PREVIOUS *HISTORIC DOCUMENTS*

Supreme Court Rules on Gerrymandering

MAY 22, 2017

In a major ruling on racial gerrymandering, on May 22, 2017, the United States Supreme Court, in *Cooper v. Harris*, struck down two congressional districts in North Carolina after finding that racial considerations unconstitutionally predominated in their design. Gerrymandering, defined as the manipulation of electoral boundaries to benefit and entrench the party that controls the redistricting process, is not new. Its name dates to 1812 when a governor named "Gerry" created a district that was shaped like a "salamander," and the resulting mash-up has been used to describe contorted voting districts ever since. Despite its somewhat silly name, many have argued that gerrymandering poses a threat to representational democracy, particularly now that the United States' increasingly partisan politics is on a collision course with technological advances in data mining and computer mapping, which are making possible the use of mass data to finely dice a community's voters and draw precise boundary lines to manipulate the outcome of elections. As is often said, voters in a democracy should choose their politicians, politicians should not choose their voters.

Supreme Court decisions over the past few decades have divided gerrymandering into two categories: racial and partisan. Precedents have been clear that race-based gerrymandering can be unconstitutional, but the courts have been less willing to intervene when the redistricting is for strictly partisan purposes without regard to race. The ruling in *Cooper v. Harris* involved race-based gerrymandering; the Republican-dominated North Carolina legislature tried to pack tens of thousands of extra black voters into two already safely Democratic districts. The Court, in an opinion written by Justice Elena Kagan, struck down the districts, clearly reasserting that the Equal Protection clause of the Fourteenth Amendment to the Constitution bars a state from racially gerrymandering legislative districts, absent compelling reasons. Going forward, new language in the opinion is likely to make it harder for states, particularly southern states where racial and partisan lines run together, to redraw districts along racial lines while claiming that the goal was partisan rather than race-based gerrymandering.

NORTH CAROLINA'S CONGRESSIONAL DISTRICTS

As required by the Constitution, every ten years the federal government takes a census of everyone in the country. States then use these numbers to design congressional districts of roughly equal numbers of people, as required by the principle of one person-one vote. While some states have a process to draw the maps involving independent commissions, courts, or a balanced mix of legislators, others, including Florida, Michigan, Pennsylvania, North Carolina, Ohio, Texas, and Virginia, allow for single party control of the redistricting process. North Carolina is a battleground state, almost evenly split between Democrats and Republicans, with highly contested statewide elections. Following the 2010 Census, the Republican-led state legislature in North Carolina redrew district lines within the state. Before the redistricting, North Carolina sent seven Democratic and six Republican representatives to Washington; after the redistricting, in 2012, with roughly the same number voting for each party, the state elected three Democrats and ten Republicans.

Cooper v. Harris involved a challenge to the most recent redistricting of North Carolina's voting Districts 1 and 12, both of which include substantial populations of black voters, and both, as Justice Kagan wrote, "have quite the history before this Court." In the past twenty-five years, challenges involving these same two districts have been up to the Supreme Court multiple times. In the 1990s, the Democratic Party controlled the state legislature and used race to gerrymander these two districts into tortured shapes. When Republican voters sued, the legislature argued that, while it was racial gerrymandering, it was doing so to create majority-minority districts to comply with the Voting Rights Act, which bars states from diluting minority voting power. The Supreme Court ruled that relying on race in this way violated the Equal Protection Clause of the Constitution. When the state responded with a new districting plan, it was again challenged. This time, the Supreme Court found that racial considerations did not predominate in the design. Rather, this time the map was found to be the result of a "political gerrymander" designed to engineer a safe seat for Democrats, "without regard to race." The Court has ruled repeatedly that race-based redistricting raises constitutional concerns, but has resisted interfering when the redistricting is done for partisan purposes.

After the 2010 Census, a Republican-controlled state legislature made significant alterations to both District 1 and District 12. It added a "finger-like extension" into heavily black areas to add 100,000 new people to District 1 and it narrowed the already "snakelike body" of District 12 to lose 50,000 white voters and added areas at either end to add 35,000 black voters. Critics argued that the legislature was trying to pack as many African American voters as possible into already predominately Democratic districts to limit the number of districts that could be won by Democrats. Registered voters in each district sued North Carolina officials, complaining of impermissible racial gerrymanders. A three-judge panel at the federal trial court held both districts unconstitutional and the parties appealed directly to the Supreme Court.

THE COURT STRIKES DOWN TWO GERRYMANDERED CONGRESSIONAL DISTRICTS

Justice Kagan wrote the majority opinion, joined by Justices Clarence Thomas, Ruth Bader Ginsburg, Stephen G. Breyer, and Sonia Sotomayor. Chief Justice John G. Roberts, Jr., and Justices Samuel A. Alito, Jr., and Anthony M. Kennedy agreed with the majority in rejecting District 1 but dissented about District 12, and Justice Neil M. Gorsuch, who had not been on the Court at the time of the oral arguments, took no part in the decision.

Justice Kagan laid out the precedents involving racial gerrymandering cases. While it is the job of the states to design congressional districts, the Equal Protection clause of the Fourteenth Amendment prohibits the use of "race as the predominant factor in drawing district lines unless it has a compelling reason." Turning first to District 1, the Court focused on uncontested evidence in the record showing that the state's mapmakers had a racial target when redrawing the boundaries of this district; they were told that the new district must have "a majority black voting age population." The chief mapmaker testified that he did not, as he usually would have, respect county or precinct divisions, because "the more important thing" was to create a majority-minority district. Based on the evidence, the Court affirmed the lower court's opinion that District 1 is "a textbook example" of race-based districting. The next question then was whether the racial gerrymandering nevertheless served a compelling interest. Here, North Carolina argued that it had purposefully drawn District 1 as a majority-minority district to comply with the requirements of the Voting Rights Act of 1965, which prohibits vote dilution. However, one of the elements of a vote dilution violation is that the district's "whites vote sufficiently as a bloc . . . to defeat the minority's preferred candidate." No evidence of this "effective white bloc-voting" existed in District 1. On the contrary, in the past two decades, with an African American population between 46 percent and 48 percent, a "meaningful number of white voters joined a politically cohesive black community to elect that group's favored candidate" in landslide elections. It was, Justice Kagan wrote, "an extraordinarily safe district for African-American preferred candidates." The Court found no evidence to support the necessity of racial gerrymandering; it affirmed the district court's conclusion that North Carolina's District 1 was unconstitutional.

Turning to District 12, here the state made no attempt to justify race-based districting, but, rather, flat out denied that race "played the slightest role in" the redesign of the district's boundaries. Only political and partisan concerns were involved, they argued. In other words, the state argued, its mapmakers intended "to 'pack' District 12 with Democrats, not African-Americans." Justice Kagan recognized that the trial court faces a "formidable task" when it tries to "assess whether the plaintiffs have managed to disentangle race from politics and prove that the former drove a district's lines" as it is clear that "racial identification is highly correlated with political affiliation." But the Supreme Court's job, she wrote, is easier because it must affirm the district court decision as long as it is "plausible." Here, she continued, the district court held a trial calling live witnesses and evaluated their credibility and did not clearly err in reaching its finding that race not politics predominated in this redistricting. Kagan also rejected the state's position that the plaintiffs had to produce an alternative legislative map showing how the state could satisfy its asserted political goals while improving racial balance. While recognizing that such a map could be helpful, she nevertheless ruled that other kinds of evidence, such as testimony from lawmakers and experts, could also be sufficient to show racial gerrymandering.

Some election law experts have focused on a footnote in Justice Kagan's opinion that may blur the distinction between racial and partisan gerrymandering, particularly in states in which race and party are closely entwined. This, some predict could make future legal challenges easier. In this footnote, Justice Kagan wrote that when both racial and partisan considerations drive redistricting, it violates the Constitution if the state includes voters in a district "predominantly because of their race, regardless of their ultimate objective in taking that step." She explained further that "the sorting of voters on the grounds of their race remains suspect even if race is meant to function as a proxy for other (including political) characteristics."

Interestingly, the justices did not split along usual ideological lines in this case. Decided 5–3, the majority was mostly composed of the Court's more liberal justices with one, highly unusual and surprising addition. Justice Thomas, one of the, if not *the*, most consistently conservative justices on the court, voted with the liberal block, but not because of any change of position. He has unfailingly voted against any kind of race-based governmental action, advocating a strictly race-blind interpretation of the equal protection requirements of the Constitution. In the 1990s, he opposed race-conscious redistricting by majority-Democratic legislatures designed to increase African American representation. While liberals and conservatives appear to have switched opinions on racial gerrymandering, he has not moved.

REACTION TO THE DECISION AND POTENTIAL IMPACT

Legal scholars debate whether the result in this case was merely the application of established legal precedent, or whether it changed the rules in a way that will make it easier to challenge redistricting that is based partially on race and partially on political affiliation. But, either way, Democrats welcomed the result. Former Attorney General Eric H. Holder Jr., who is now the chairman of the National Democratic Redistricting Committee, released a statement calling this opinion "a watershed moment in the fight to end racial gerrymandering." He described North Carolina's maps as "among the worst racial gerrymanders in the nation" and said that the ruling "sends a stark message to legislatures and governors around the country: Racial gerrymandering is illegal and will be struck down in a court of law." Republican reaction focused on the difficulty for legislatures to operate in a changing legal environment. Robin Hayes, chair of North Carolina's Republican Party, questioned "how any legislature can perform this task when the rules change constantly from case to case, often after the fact." He added, "It is also important to note that this ruling does not impact our current congressional map, which we also believe is fair and legal." Those current maps were drawn in response to the lower court's ruling in *Cooper v. Harris* and will be used in the 2018 election. However, they have also been challenged in court, this time for partisan gerrymandering, and these challenges will be heard by the Court in June 2018.

The historical significance of the Court's racial gerrymandering decision in *Cooper v. Harris* is likely to be overshadowed by the decision in its next gerrymandering case. On October 3, 2017, the Supreme Court heard oral arguments in *Gill v. Whitford*, a challenge to a particularly extreme partisan gerrymandering of legislative districts in Wisconsin following the 2010 Census. After winning control of the state assembly in the 2010 elections, the Republican-controlled legislature developed new legislative maps in a secret process. In the next election, Democratic candidates won a majority of the votes counted, but the Republicans, because of how the district lines were drawn, won a 60–39 seat advantage in the State Assembly. This case will present the Supreme Court with the historic opportunity to potentially strike down, for the first time, a legislative map due to purely partisan gerrymandering.

—Melissa Feinberg

> *Following are excerpts from the case of* Cooper v. Harris, *in which the Supreme Court ruled 5–3 on May 22, 2017, that two North Carolina congressional districts had been unconstitutionally gerrymandered on a racial basis.*

DOCUMENT   *Cooper v. Harris*

May 22, 2017

[Most footnotes have been omitted.]

SUPREME COURT OF THE UNITED STATES

No. 15–1262

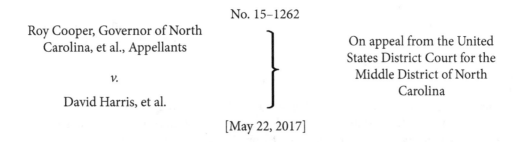

Roy Cooper, Governor of North Carolina, et al., Appellants

v.

David Harris, et al.

On appeal from the United States District Court for the Middle District of North Carolina

[May 22, 2017]

JUSTICE KAGAN delivered the opinion of the Court.

The Constitution entrusts States with the job of designing congressional districts. But it also imposes an important constraint: A State may not use race as the predominant factor in drawing district lines unless it has a compelling reason. In this case, a three-judge District Court ruled that North Carolina officials violated that bar when they created two districts whose voting-age populations were majority black. Applying a deferential standard of review to the factual findings underlying that decision, we affirm.

I

A

The Equal Protection Clause of the Fourteenth Amendment limits racial gerrymanders in legislative districting plans. It prevents a State, in the absence of "sufficient justification," from "separating its citizens into different voting districts on the basis of race." *Bethune-Hill v. Virginia State Bd. of Elections*, 580 U. S. ___, ___ (2017) (slip op., at 6) (internal quotation marks and alteration omitted). When a voter sues state officials for drawing such race-based lines, our decisions call for a two-step analysis.

First, the plaintiff must prove that "race was the predominant factor motivating the legislature's decision to place a significant number of voters within or without a particular district." *Miller v. Johnson*, 515 U. S. 900, 916 (1995). That entails demonstrating that the legislature "subordinated" other factors—compactness, respect for political subdivisions, partisan advantage, what have you—to "racial considerations." Ibid. The plaintiff may make the required showing through "direct evidence" of legislative intent, "circumstantial evidence of a district's shape and demographics," or a mix of both. Ibid.

Second, if racial considerations predominated over others, the design of the district must withstand strict scrutiny. See *Bethune-Hill*, 580 U. S., at ___ (slip op., at 13). The burden thus shifts to the State to prove that its race-based sorting of voters serves a "compelling interest" and is "narrowly tailored" to that end. Ibid. This Court has long assumed that one compelling interest is complying with operative provisions of the Voting Rights Act of 1965 (VRA or Act), 79 Stat. 437, as amended, 52 U. S. C. §10301 et seq. See, e.g., *Shaw v. Hunt*, 517 U. S. 899, 915 (1996) (Shaw II).

[The remainder of Section I, outlining the background and facts in the case, and the entirety of Section II, in which the Court responds to each side's arguments, has been omitted.]

III

With that out of the way, we turn to the merits of this case, beginning (appropriately enough) with District 1. As noted above, the court below found that race furnished the predominant rationale for that district's redesign. And it held that the State's interest in complying with the VRA could not justify that consideration of race. We uphold both conclusions.

A

Uncontested evidence in the record shows that the State's mapmakers, in considering District 1, purposefully established a racial target: African-Americans should make up no less than a majority of the voting-age population. See 159 F. Supp. 3d, at 611–614. Senator Rucho and Representative Lewis were not coy in expressing that goal. They repeatedly told their colleagues that District 1 had to be majority-minority, so as to comply with the VRA. During a Senate debate, for example, Rucho explained that District 1 "must include a sufficient number of African-Americans" to make it "a majority black district." App. 689–690. Similarly, Lewis informed the House and Senate redistricting committees that the district must have "a majority black voting age population." Id., at 610. And that objective was communicated in no uncertain terms to the legislators' consultant. Dr. Hofeller testified multiple times at trial that Rucho and Lewis instructed him "to draw [District 1] with a [BVAP] in excess of 50 percent." 159 F. Supp. 3d, at 613; see, e.g., ibid. ("Once again, my instructions [were] that the district had to be drawn at above 50 percent").

Hofeller followed those directions to the letter, such that the 50%-plus racial target "had a direct and significant impact" on District 1's configuration. *Alabama*, 575 U. S., at __ (slip op., at 17). In particular, Hofeller moved the district's borders to encompass the heavily black parts of Durham (and only those parts), thus taking in tens of thousands of additional African-American voters. That change and similar ones, made (in his words) to ensure that the district's racial composition would "add[] up correctly," deviated from the districting practices he otherwise would have followed. App. 2802. Hofeller candidly admitted that point: For example, he testified, he sometimes could not respect county or precinct lines as he wished because "the more important thing" was to create a majority-minority district. Id., at 2807; see id., at 2809. The result is a district with stark racial borders: Within the same counties, the portions that fall inside District 1 have black populations two to three times larger than the portions placed in neighboring districts. See Brief for United States as *Amicus Curiae* 19; cf. *Alabama*, 575 U. S., at ___–___ (slip op., at 17–18) (relying on similar evidence to find racial predominance).

Faced with this body of evidence—showing an announced racial target that subordinated other districting criteria and produced boundaries amplifying divisions between blacks and whites—the District Court did not clearly err in finding that race predominated in drawing District 1. Indeed, as all three judges recognized, the court could hardly have concluded anything but. See 159 F. Supp. 3d, at 611 (calling District 1 a "textbook example" of race-based districting).

B

The more substantial question is whether District 1 can survive the strict scrutiny applied to racial gerrymanders. As noted earlier, we have long assumed that complying with the

VRA is a compelling interest. And we have held that race-based districting is narrowly tailored to that objective if a State had "good reasons" for thinking that the Act demanded such steps. North Carolina argues that District 1 passes muster under that standard: The General Assembly (so says the State) had "good reasons to believe it needed to draw [District 1] as a majority-minority district to avoid Section 2 liability" for vote dilution. Brief for Appellants 52. We now turn to that defense.

This Court identified, in *Thornburg v. Gingles*, three threshold conditions for proving vote dilution under §2 of the VRA. See 478 U. S., at 50–51. First, a "minority group" must be "sufficiently large and geographically compact to constitute a majority" in some reasonably configured legislative district. Id., at 50. Second, the minority group must be "politically cohesive." Id., at 51. And third, a district's white majority must "vote[] sufficiently as a bloc" to usually "defeat the minority's preferred candidate." Ibid. Those three showings, we have explained, are needed to establish that "the minority [group] has the potential to elect a representative of its own choice" in a possible district, but that racially polarized voting prevents it from doing so in the district as actually drawn because it is "submerg[ed] in a larger white voting population." *Growe v. Emison*, 507 U. S. 25, 40 (1993). If a State has good reason to think that all the "*Gingles* preconditions" are met, then so too it has good reason to believe that §2 requires drawing a majority-minority district. See Bush v. Vera, 517 U. S. 952, 978 (1996) (plurality opinion). But if not, then not.

Here, electoral history provided no evidence that a §2 plaintiff could demonstrate the third Gingles prerequisite—effective white bloc-voting. For most of the twenty years prior to the new plan's adoption, African-Americans had made up less than a majority of District 1's voters; the district's BVAP usually hovered between 46% and 48%. See 159 F. Supp. 3d, at 606; App. 312. Yet throughout those two decades, as the District Court noted, District 1 was "an extraordinarily safe district for African-American preferred candidates." 159 F. Supp. 3d, at 626. In the *closest* election during that period, African-Americans' candidate of choice received 59% of the total vote; in other years, the share of the vote garnered by those candidates rose to as much as 70%. See supra, at 5. Those victories (indeed, landslides) occurred because the district's white population did *not* "vote[] sufficiently as a bloc" to thwart black voters' preference, *Gingles*, 478 U. S., at 51; rather, a meaningful number of white voters joined a politically cohesive black community to elect that group's favored candidate. In the lingo of voting law, District 1 functioned, election year in and election year out, as a "crossover" district, in which members of the majority help a "large enough" minority to elect its candidate of choice. *Bartlett v. Strickland*, 556 U. S. 1, 13 (2009) (plurality opinion). When voters act in that way, "[i]t is difficult to see how the majority-bloc-voting requirement could be met"—and hence how §2 liability could be established. Id., at 16. So experience gave the State no reason to think that the VRA required it to ramp up District 1's BVAP. . . .

In sum: Although States enjoy leeway to take race-based actions reasonably judged necessary under a proper interpretation of the VRA, that latitude cannot rescue District 1. We by no means "insist that a state legislature, when redistricting, determine precisely what percent minority population [§2 of the VRA] demands." Ibid. But neither will we approve a racial gerrymander whose necessity is supported by no evidence and whose *raison d'être* is a legal mistake. Accordingly, we uphold the District Court's conclusion that North Carolina's use of race as the predominant factor in designing District 1 does not withstand strict scrutiny.

IV

We now look west to District 12, making its fifth(!) appearance before this Court. This time, the district's legality turns, and turns solely, on which of two possible reasons predominantly explains its most recent reconfiguration. The plaintiffs contended at trial that the General Assembly chose voters for District 12, as for District 1, because of their race; more particularly, they urged that the Assembly intentionally increased District 12's BVAP in the name of ensuring preclearance under the VRA's §5. But North Carolina declined to mount any defense (similar to the one we have just considered for District 1) that §5's requirements in fact justified race-based changes to District 12—perhaps because §5 could not reasonably be understood to have done so, see n. 10, infra. Instead, the State altogether denied that racial considerations accounted for (or, indeed, played the slightest role in) District 12's redesign. According to the State's version of events, Senator Rucho, Representative Lewis, and Dr. Hofeller moved voters in and out of the district as part of a "strictly" political gerrymander, without regard to race. 6 Record 1011. The mapmakers drew their lines, in other words, to "pack" District 12 with Democrats, not African Americans. After hearing evidence supporting both parties' accounts, the District Court accepted the plaintiffs'.

Getting to the bottom of a dispute like this one poses special challenges for a trial court. In the more usual case alleging a racial gerrymander—where no one has raised a partisanship defense—the court can make real headway by exploring the challenged district's conformity to traditional districting principles, such as compactness and respect for county lines. In *Shaw II*, for example, this Court emphasized the "highly irregular" shape of then District 12 in concluding that race predominated in its design. 517 U. S., at 905 (internal quotation marks omitted). But such evidence loses much of its value when the State asserts partisanship as a defense, because a bizarre shape—as of the new District 12—can arise from a "political motivation" as well as a racial one. *Cromartie I*, 526 U. S., at 547, n. 3. And crucially, political and racial reasons are capable of yielding similar oddities in a district's boundaries. That is because, of course, "racial identification is highly correlated with political affiliation." *Cromartie II*, 532 U. S., at 243. As a result of those redistricting realities, a trial court has a formidable task: It must make "a sensitive inquiry" into all "circumstantial and direct evidence of intent" to assess whether the plaintiffs have managed to disentangle race from politics and prove that the former drove a district's lines. *Cromartie I*, 526 U. S., at 546 (internal quotation marks omitted).[1]

Our job is different—and generally easier. As described earlier, we review a district court's finding as to racial predominance only for clear error, except when the court made a legal mistake. See supra, at 3–4. Under that standard of review, we affirm the court's finding so long as it is "plausible"; we reverse only when "left with the definite and firm conviction that a mistake has been committed." *Anderson*, 470 U. S., at 573–574; see supra, at 4. And in deciding which side of that line to come down on, we give singular deference to a

---

1. As earlier noted, that inquiry is satisfied when legislators have "place[d] a significant number of voters within or without" a district predominantly because of their race, regardless of their ultimate objective in taking that step. See supra, at 2, and n. 1. So, for example, if legislators use race as their predominant districting criterion with the end goal of advancing their partisan interests—perhaps thinking that a proposed district is more "sellable" as a race-based VRA compliance measure than as a political gerrymander and will accomplish much the same thing—their action still triggers strict scrutiny. See *Vera*, 517 U. S., at 968–970 (plurality opinion). In other words, the sorting of voters on the grounds of their race remains suspect even if race is meant to function as a proxy for other (including political) characteristics. See *Miller*, 515 U. S., at 914.

trial court's judgments about the credibility of witnesses. See Fed. Rule Civ. Proc. 52(a)(6). That is proper, we have explained, because the various cues that "bear so heavily on the listener's understanding of and belief in what is said" are lost on an appellate court later sifting through a paper record. *Anderson*, 470 U. S., at 575.

In light of those principles, we uphold the District Court's finding of racial predominance respecting District 12. The evidence offered at trial, including live witness testimony subject to credibility determinations, adequately supports the conclusion that race, not politics, accounted for the district's reconfiguration. And no error of law infected that judgment: Contrary to North Carolina's view, the District Court had no call to dismiss this challenge just because the plaintiffs did not proffer an alternative design for District 12 as circumstantial evidence of the legislature's intent.

[Additional analysis presented by the Court has been omitted.]

V

Applying a clear error standard, we uphold the District Court's conclusions that racial considerations predominated in designing both District 1 and District 12. For District 12, that is all we must do, because North Carolina has made no attempt to justify race-based districting there. For District 1, we further uphold the District Court's decision that §2 of the VRA gave North Carolina no good reason to reshuffle voters because of their race. We accordingly affirm the judgment of the District Court.

It is so ordered.

JUSTICE GORSUCH took no part in the consideration or decision of this case.

[Maps of the North Carolina districts in question have been omitted.]

JUSTICE THOMAS, concurring.

I join the opinion of the Court because it correctly applies our precedents under the Constitution and the Voting Rights Act of 1965 (VRA), 52 U. S. C. §10301 et seq. I write briefly to explain the additional grounds on which I would affirm the three-judge District Court and to note my agreement, in particular, with the Court's clear-error analysis.

As to District 1, I think North Carolina's concession that it created the district as a majority-black district is by itself sufficient to trigger strict scrutiny. See Brief for Appellants 44; see also, e.g., *Bethune-Hill v. Virginia State Bd. of Elections*, 580 U. S. ___, ___–___ (2017) (slip op., at 1–2) (THOMAS, J., concurring in judgment in part and dissenting in part). I also think that North Carolina cannot satisfy strict scrutiny based on its efforts to comply with §2 of the VRA. See ante, at 12. In my view, §2 does not apply to redistricting and therefore cannot justify a racial gerrymander. See *Holder v. Hall*, 512 U. S. 874, 922–923 (1994) (THOMAS, J., concurring in judgment).

As to District 12, I agree with the Court that the District Court did not clearly err when it determined that race was North Carolina's predominant motive in drawing the district. See ante, at 21. This is the same conclusion I reached when we last reviewed District 12. *Easley v. Cromartie*, 532 U. S. 234, 267 (2001) (Cromartie II) (dissenting opinion). The Court reached the contrary conclusion in *Cromartie II* only by misapplying our deferential standard for reviewing factual findings. See id., at 259– 262. Today's decision does not repeat *Cromartie II*'s error, and indeed it confines that case to its particular facts. It thus represents a welcome course correction to this Court's application of the clear-error standard.

[The opinion of Justices Alito and Kennedy, and Chief Justice Roberts, concurring in part and dissenting in part, has been omitted.]

SOURCE: Supreme Court of the United States. *Cooper v. Harris.* 581 U.S.__(2017). https://www.supreme court.gov/opinions/16pdf/15-1262_db8e.pdf.

OTHER HISTORIC DOCUMENTS OF INTEREST

FROM PREVIOUS *HISTORIC DOCUMENTS*

- Supreme Court Rules on Voting Rights Act, *2013*, p. 284

Philippine President Establishes Martial Law

MAY 23, 2017

Following his declaration of a state of emergency in 2016, Philippine President Rodrigo Duterte established martial law and suspended habeas corpus in the southern region of Mindanao in May 2017. This latest declaration sought to help the military combat ongoing terrorist threats from Muslim insurgent groups that have attacked both government and civilian targets in their pursuit of greater autonomy from the central government.

A Decades-Long Conflict

Violent internal conflicts between the Philippine government and Muslim insurgencies have marked the last several decades of the overwhelmingly Catholic country's history, with Muslim groups seeking to establish an independent Islamic state. The Mindanao island group, located in the southern part of the country, is the home to several terrorist organizations and has been particularly impacted by the violence.

Abu Sayyaf is the best known among these groups. Founded in 1991 and previously linked to al-Qaeda, the group's leader, Isnilon Hapilon, has pledged allegiance to the Islamic State in the Levant (ISIL) and declared himself amir of the South East Asian caliphate. In addition to bombings and assassinations, Abu Sayyaf carried out kidnappings and demanded ransoms. In some instances, the group beheaded male victims whose ransoms were not paid and those who do not believe in Islam. Abu Sayyaf is allied with several other insurgent organizations, including the Maute group, which also pledged allegiance to ISIL and became nationally known after raiding a prison and freeing twenty-three inmates in Marawi City on Mindanao in August 2016.

Duterte has pledged to "destroy" Abu Sayyaf and has sent the military to conduct operations against the group in the regions where it is based. The president also declared a state of emergency in September 2016, following an attack on a market in Davao City that killed 14 people. Abu Sayyaf claimed responsibility for the attack, which has also been linked to the Maute group. Amid the state of emergency, Duterte issued guidelines for the military and Philippine National Police to "undertake all necessary measures to suppress any and all forms of lawless violence in Mindanao and prevent the spread and escalation thereof elsewhere in the country."

Martial Law Declared

On May 23, 2017, Duterte issued Proclamation 55, declaring a state of martial law and suspending habeas corpus in the Mindanao island group. Martial law gave the government the ability to use its military to enforce laws and to detain people for long periods without specific charges. The proclamation cited various attacks by the Maute, including violence that had broken out the same day in Marawi City, to explain the need for martial law. "This recent attack shows the capability of the Maute group and other rebel groups to sow terror, and cause death and damage to property not only in Lanao del Sur but also in other parts of Mindanao," it read.

Earlier in the day, the Maute fired on Philippine soldiers, took over a hospital and a jail, set up checkpoints throughout Marawi City, burned government and private buildings, and held a priest and several church patrons hostage. They also raised the ISIL flag over the city. Military officials stated that the attack was carried out in response to a failed army raid of an apartment where fifteen Islamic militants were reportedly hiding; the soldiers were on a mission to capture Hapilon, who they believed to be in the apartment.

The Philippine Constitution gives the president, with approval from Congress, the authority to declare martial law for up to sixty days to stop an invasion or rebellion. Most lawmakers supported martial law; however, several opposition lawmakers argued it was unconstitutional and petitioned the Supreme Court to review and nullify the declaration. The lawmakers claimed that no invasion or rebellion had taken place that required the declaration of martial law and that Duterte's proclamation contained "fatal inaccuracies and falsities." The Court unanimously upheld Duterte's declaration in a ruling on July 4.

A CONTROVERSIAL EXTENSION

The conflict in Marawi City continued into the summer. The Philippine military conducted air strikes, bombing suspected terrorist targets in and around the city, with U.S. Special Forces providing support to help end the siege. As of July 20, military officials reported that roughly 427 militants, ninety-nine government officials, and forty-five civilians had been killed in the fighting.

Five days before Proclamation 55 was set to expire, Duterte sent a letter to the Philippine Congress requesting that martial law be extended until the end of the year, stating that it was necessary to continue fighting militants in Marawi City. Duterte said that about 220 militants remained in the city—a much higher number than the sixty insurgents cited by the military—and said that terrorist leaders had survived the military's attacks on the area. Separately, Duterte told reporters that insurgents were holding about 300 Filipinos. Congress overwhelmingly approved the request in a special joint session, with 240 of 267 lawmakers voting against it. Duterte's opponents claimed the extension was unnecessary and would be used by the president to return the Philippines to authoritarian rule. (The country was subject to fourteen years of martial law under the former dictator, President Ferdinand Marcos.) "Extending martial law can unmask the Duterte government's real political intentions to apply authoritarian rule in the country, like the way he ruled Davao City for 20 years as a city mayor," said Rommel Banlaoi, chair of Philippine Institute for Peace, Violence, and Terrorism Research.

Duterte further fanned these concerns during a speech to the military on September 2, when he indicated that he might not lift martial law at year's end. "I was thinking that we could, you know, lift it earlier, but the way it looks, there is a spillover of violence in the ARMM [Autonomous Region of Muslim Mindanao] and Buldon," he said. "Let us see, if it is to the interest of the country, and if I will lift it, I will lift it. But if not, then we'll just continue with the martial law." However, Duterte appeared to reverse course later in the month, stating on September 21 that martial law would be lifted "when it's safe here in Mindanao," noting that the government would also need to "clean up" the area, including by removing any remaining explosive devices, before the area could be deemed safe.

—Linda Grimm

Following is Proclamation No. 55, issued by Philippine President Rodrigo Rao Duterte on May 23, 2017, declaring martial law and the suspension of habeas corpus.

Declaration of Martial Law and Suspension of Habeas Corpus in Mindanao

DOCUMENT

May 23, 2017

Whereas, Proclamation No. 55, series of 2016, was issued on 04 September 2016 declaring a state of national emergency on account of lawless violence in Mindanao;

Whereas, Section 18, Article VII of the Constitution provides that "xxx in case of invasion or rebellion, when the public safety requires it, he (the President) may, for a period not exceeding sixty days, suspend the privilege of the write of habeas corpus or place the Philippines or any part thereof under martial law xxx";

Whereas, Article 135 of the Revised Penal Code, as amended by R.A. No. 6968, provides that "the crime of rebellion or insurrection is committed by rising and taking arms against the Government for the purpose of removing from the allegiance to said Government or its laws, the territory of the Republic of the Philippines or any part thereof, of any body of land, naval or other armed forces, or depriving the Chief Executive or the Legislature, wholly or partially, of any of their powers or prerogatives";

Whereas, part of the reasons for the issuance of Proclamation No. 55 was the series of violent acts committed by the Maute terrorist group such as the attack on the military outpost in Butig, Lanao del Sur in February 2016, killing and wounding several soldiers, and the mass jailbreak in Marawi City in August 2016, freeing their arrested comrades and other detainees;

Whereas, today, 23 May 2017, the same Maute terrorist group has taken over a hospital in Marawi City, Lanao del Sur, established several checkpoints within the City, burned down certain government and private facilities and inflicted casualties on the part of the Government forces, and started flying the flag of the Islamic State of Iraq and Syria (ISIS) in several areas, thereby openly attempting to remove from the allegiance to the Philippine Government this part of Mindanao and deprive the Chief Executive of his powers and prerogatives to enforce the laws of the land and to maintain pubic order and safety in Mindanao, constituting the crime of rebellion; and

Whereas, this recent attack shows the capability of the Maute group and other rebel groups to sow terror, and cause death and damage to property not only in Lanao del Sur but also in other parts of Mindanao.

Now, therefore, I, Rodrigo Roa Duterte, President of the Republic of the Philippines, by virtue of the powers vested in me by the Constitution and by law, do hereby proclaim, as follows:

Section 1. There is hereby declared a state of martial law in the Mindanao group of islands for a period not exceeding sixty days, effective as of the date hereof.

Section 2. The privilege of the writ of habeas corpus shall likewise be suspended in the aforesaid area for the duration of the state of martial law.

Done in the Russian Federation, this 23rd day of May in the year of our Lord, Two Thousand and Seventeen.

SOURCE: Republic of the Philippines Official Gazette. "Proclamation No. 216: Declaring a State of Martial Law and Suspending the Privilege of the Writ of Habeas Corpus in the Whole of Mindanao." May 23, 2017. http://www.officialgazette.gov.ph/downloads/2017/05may/20170523-PROC-216-RRD.pdf.

OTHER HISTORIC DOCUMENTS OF INTEREST

FROM PREVIOUS *HISTORIC DOCUMENTS*

Same-Sex Marriage Legalized in Taiwan, Germany, Malta, and Australia

MAY 24, JUNE 30, JULY 12, AND DECEMBER 4, 2017

In 2017, the international LGBTQ community celebrated several legislative victories that legalized same-sex marriage in Germany, Malta, and Australia. Additionally, Taiwan became the first Asian country to make a major step toward legalizing same-sex marriage when its highest court ruled that defining marriage as between one man and one woman violated the island's constitution. With most of these victories, however, came challenges. Many conservatives, for example, pushed back on shifting cultural traditions. Meanwhile, LGBTQ activists in some cases criticized political developments for falling short of desired goals.

TAIWAN COURT RULES ON SAME-SEX MARRIAGE

As the world gained new LGBTQ leaders in 2017, some countries also made significant steps toward legalizing same-sex marriage. Taiwan led the way on May 24, when its highest court, known as the Judicial Yuan, declared that the island's Civil Code definition of marriage between one man and one woman violates the constitution and citizens' rights to equality. The decision resulted from a lawsuit filed by LGBTQ activist Chi Chia-wei after the Taiwanese government rejected his application for a marriage license. The city government of Taipei also supported the lawsuit, calling for a review of the Civil Code after additional plaintiffs sued the municipality for rejecting their marriage applications.

The Judicial Yuan's landmark decision gave the parliament, or Legislative Yuan, two years to either amend the existing civil code or pass new laws to abide by the ruling. If the legislative body does not take action after two years, the court ruled that same-sex couples can marry automatically. Should parliament follow through with the court's order, Taiwan would become the first government in Asia to legalize same-sex marriage, potentially boosting similar movements in Vietnam, China, and Cambodia.

Despite the ruling and the LGBTQ-friendly Democratic Progressive Party holding a majority in the Legislative Yuan, political opposition and a divided public posed a challenge to legislators seeking changes to Taiwanese law. Forty-six percent of the country supported same-sex marriage while forty-five percent opposed it, and legislative elections loom in 2018. Meanwhile, conservative groups committed to use lobbying and the ballot box to restrict passage of any laws related to same-sex marriage, citing the unfairness of judicial overreach. Democratic Progressive Party legislators previously tried to pass same-sex marriage bills at the end of 2016, but their momentum deteriorated in early 2017 as opposition forces threatened to mobilize voters against lawmakers. Conservative backlash also strongly influenced the political platform of Taiwanese President Tsai Ing-wen, who originally declared her support for same-sex marriage after taking office in 2016, but tempered her position amid mass protests and increased persecution of the LGBTQ community.

The ruling presented the Legislative Yuan with several options. In the most progressive scenario, parliament could amend the Civil Code in favor of same-sex couples while also extending rights related to adoption, parenting, inheritance, and decision making in medical emergencies. Alternatively, the parliament could take a more cautious path by simply changing gender language in the Civil Code and not extending other rights and equal treatment. By the end of the year, the Legislative Yuan had still not acted to codify the court's ruling, generating frustration among the country's LGBTQ activists.

LEGALIZATION OF SAME-SEX MARRIAGE IN GERMANY

About one month after the Judicial Yuan's decision, Germany's Lower House of Parliament voted 393 to 226 in favor of same-sex marriage and adoption on June 30, 2017. The legislation marked a reversal for Prime Minister Angela Merkel and her political party, the center-right Christian Democratic Union (CDU), which originally stood in opposition to same-sex marriage, citing the Constitution and cultural traditions within the country. The CDU's stance on the issue ran counter to public opinion for years. Several polls measuring public opinion estimated that between 70 percent and 85 percent of Germans supported same-sex marriage, and the country legalized civil unions in 2001. Despite the CDU's opposition, a handful of legislators and prominent party members supported the proposition, including Merkel's chief of staff and defense minister.

Merkel, who still voted no on the proposition with many of her party members, pushed the vote through quickly, ahead of the parliament's summer recess. Merkel's decision came after the left-leaning Social Democratic, Free Democratic, and Green parties threatened to make the legislation a condition for future coalition-building with Merkel's CDU. She called on lawmakers to vote according to their consciences and claimed the vote would permanently end the culture war on the issue. The speed with which the legislation moved through the house angered many members of Merkel's party, who could eventually challenge the measure in Constitutional Court.

Though German LGBTQ activists raised some concerns over nuanced limitations to same-sex adoption in the proposition, its passage prompted emotional celebrations at the Bradenburg Gate in Berlin. The law took effect in the fall, and Karl Kreile and Bodo Monde became the first same-sex couple to legally marry in Germany on October 1, 2017.

LEGALIZATION OF SAME-SEX MARRIAGE IN MALTA

Malta rounded out a progressive summer for LGBTQ politics when lawmakers introduced same-sex marriage legislation on July 12, 2017. The legislation provides for these marriages by amending language within the Marriage Act, a regulation dating back to 1975. Lawmakers replaced "husband" and "wife," for example, with the gender-neutral term of "spouse." Similarly, terms such as "parents" and "surname at birth" have replaced words such as "father," "mother," and "maiden name." The legislation fulfilled Prime Minister Joseph Muscat's major campaign promise that a same-sex marriage bill would be the first law brought before the legislative body in his second term. Equity Minister Helena Dalli also played a crucial role in pushing the law through.

Malta's accomplishment signals its incredible transformation and perhaps the most impressive LGBTQ victory in the world this year. The deeply religious Roman Catholic country of roughly 417,000 people is heavily influenced by the Catholic Church and has a history of socially conservative policies. However, Malta's 2004 admission into the EU and a 2011 bill allowing divorce began a domino effect for the country that encouraged the Maltese to tackle other social issues. The country permitted civil unions and same-sex adoption in 2014, banned invasive surgery on intersex citizens in 2015, and became the first nation in the world to ban gay conversion therapy in 2016. Intense opposition from the Catholic Church on most of these issues failed to halt the Maltese wave of social liberalism, including the amendment to the Marriage Act, which passed in the country's parliament by an almost unanimous margin of sixty-six to one.

AUSTRALIA LEGALIZES SAME-SEX MARRIAGE

A final win for LGBTQ civil rights in 2017 came late in the year when, following approval from the Senate, Australia's House of Representatives voted overwhelmingly on December 7, 2017, to pass a bill legalizing same-sex marriage, with just four representatives opposing it. The new law, which changed the definition of marriage to "the union of two people," also extended equal treatment in cases of government benefits, employment, and taxes.

Unlike other countries that legalized same-sex marriage in 2017, Australia's vote resulted from a nonbinding national referendum in the fall, in which 12.7 million Australians participated and 61.6 percent voted in favor of same-sex marriage. LGBTQ activists originally criticized the referendum, pushed by Prime Minister Malcolm Turnbull, as a stall tactic to pacify far-right members of his center-right Liberal Party. Yet Turnbull saw the decision as an opportunity to obtain a mandate on a shift in social policy that many of his partisan colleagues opposed. Turnbull, a longtime supporter of same-sex marriage, voted yes on the measure, claiming it to be "an issue of fundamental fairness." Speaking before the House of Representatives on December 4, Turnbull argued, "A society which promotes freedom and equality under the law should accord gay men and women the right to marry. We now recognise same-sex couples in every other aspect of the law—financial, medical, adoption—but we have not yet given them the right to call their relationship a marriage."

The referendum did not come without its controversy, because same-sex marriage supporters felt burdened by the AUD$122 million price tag for the legally superfluous poll. Additionally, they noted the referendum unleashed a deluge of hate and fear mongering, emotionally impacting many LGBTQ citizens and their families. As Senator Penny Wong described, "Our very identity has been the subject of public scrutiny and public debate. . . . Through this campaign, we have seen the best of our country and also the worst."

In December, however, proponents hailed the legislature's decision and celebrated throughout the country. Overcome with relief, many viewed the development as long overdue, since Australia's parliament failed twenty-two times since 2004 to pass similar bills. Though a few opposing lawmakers attempted to stifle the expansive legislation through amendments ensuring protections for religious freedom, they ultimately failed to do so. In general, the development saw rare moments of bipartisan consensus and celebration. On the days and hours leading up to the vote, politicians on the left and right embraced the decision with emotional speeches and even a marriage proposal by a gay Parliament member. The country's first legal same-sex marriages are expected to begin in January.

—Andrew Jacobs

Following is a press release from the Judicial Yuan Republic of China (Taiwan) from May 24, 2017, on its ruling legalizing same-sex marriage; excerpted deliberations from the German Bundestag concerning same-sex marriage from June 30, 2017; a press release issued by the Maltese government on July 12, 2017, announcing the Maltese Parliament's approval of the Marriage Equality Bill; and remarks delivered by Australian Prime Minister Malcolm Turnbull to the House of Representatives on December 4, 2017, urging lawmakers to vote in favor of same-sex marriage.

Judicial Yuan Issues Same-Sex Marriage Ruling

May 24, 2017

On the consolidated petitions of Huei-Tai-12674 filed by Chia-Wei Chi and Huei-Tai-12771 filed by the Taipei City Government, regarding the constitutionality of same-sex marriage, the Constitutional Court announces the J.Y. Interpretation No. 748 at 4 PM on May 24, 2017.

NOTE: This press release constitutes no part of the Interpretation but is prepared by the Clerk's Office of the Constitutional Court, for the convenience of the reader.

The rulings of the Court are as follows:

(1)   The provisions of Chapter 2 on Marriage of Part IV on Family of the Civil Code do not allow two persons of the same sex to create a permanent union of intimate and exclusive nature for the committed purpose of managing a life together. The said provisions, to the extent of such failure, are in violation of both the people's freedom of marriage as protected by Article 22 and the people's right to equality as guaranteed by Article 7 of the Constitution.

(2)   The authorities concerned shall amend or enact relevant laws, in accordance with the ruling of this Interpretation, within two years from the issuance of this Interpretation. It is within the discretion of the authorities concerned to determine the formality for achieving the equal protection of the freedom of marriage.

(3)   If relevant laws are not amended or enacted within the said two years, two persons of the same sex who intend to create the said permanent union shall be allowed to have their marriage registration effectuated at the authorities in charge of household registration, by submitting a written document signed by two or more witnesses in accordance with the said Marriage Chapter.

The main reasons of this Interpretation are as follows:

(1)   For more than three decades, Petitioner Chia-Wei Chi has been appealing to the legislative, executive, and judicial departments for the right to same-sex

marriage. After more than a decade, the Legislative Yuan is still unable to complete its legislative process on those bills regarding same-sex marriage. This case involves the very controversial social and political issues of whether homosexuals shall enjoy the equal protection of the same freedom of marriage as heterosexuals. The representative body is to enact or revise the relevant laws in due time. Nevertheless, the timetable for such legislative solution is hardly predictable now and yet these petitions involve the protection of people's fundamental rights. It is the constitutional duty of this Court to render a binding judicial decision, in time, on issues concerning the safeguarding of constitutional basic values such as the protection of people's constitutional rights and the free democratic constitutional order.

(2)   Those prior J.Y. Interpretations mentioning "husband and wife" or "a man and a woman", in terms of the factual backgrounds of the original cases from which they arose, were made within the context of opposite-sex marriage. Thus far, this Court has not made any Interpretation on the issue of whether two persons of the same sex are allowed to marry each other.

(3)   Unspoused persons eligible to marry shall have their freedom to marry, which includes the freedom to decide "whether to marry" and "whom to marry" (see J.Y. Interpretation No. 362). Such decisional autonomy is vital to the sound development of personality and safeguarding of human dignity, and therefore is a fundamental right to be protected by Article 22 of the Constitution.

(4)   Creation of a permanent union of intimate and exclusive nature for the committed purpose of managing a life together by two persons of the same sex will not affect the application of the Marriage Chapter to the union of two persons of the opposite sex. Nor will it alter the social order established upon the existing opposite-sex marriage. Furthermore, the freedom of marriage for two persons of the same sex, once legally recognized, will constitute the collective basis, together with opposite-sex marriage, for a stable society. The need, capability, willingness and longing, in both physical and psychological senses, for creating such permanent unions of intimate and exclusive nature are equally essential to homosexuals and heterosexuals, given the importance of the freedom of marriage to the sound development of personality and safeguarding of human dignity. Both types of union shall be protected by the freedom of marriage under Article 22 of the Constitution. The current provisions of the Marriage Chapter do not allow two persons of the same sex to create a permanent union of intimate and exclusive nature for the committed purpose of managing a life together. This is obviously a gross legislative flaw. To such extent, the provisions of the Marriage Chapter are incompatible with the spirit and meaning of the freedom of marriage as protected by Article 22 of the Constitution.

(5)   Article 7 of the Constitution provides, "All citizens of the Republic of China, irrespective of sex, religion, race, class, or party affiliation, shall be equal before the law." The five classifications of impermissible discrimination set forth in the said Article are only exemplified, neither enumerated nor exhausted. Therefore, different treatment based on other classifications, such as disability or sexual orientation, shall also be governed by the right to equality under the said Article.

(6)   Sexual orientation is an immutable characteristic that is resistant to change. The contributing factors to sexual orientation may include physical and psychological elements, living experience, and the social environment. Major medical associations have stated that homosexuality is not a disease. In our country, homosexuals were once denied by social tradition and custom in the past. As a result, they have long been locked in the closet and suffered various forms of de facto or de jure exclusion or discrimination. Besides, homosexuals, because of the demographic structure, have been a discrete and insular minority in the society. Impacted by stereotypes, they have been among those lacking political power for a long time, unable to overturn their legally disadvantaged status through ordinary democratic process. Accordingly, in determining the constitutionality of different treatment based on sexual orientation, a heightened standard shall be applied.

(7)   The Marriage Chapter does not set forth the capability to procreate as a requirement for concluding an opposite-sex marriage. Nor does it provide that a marriage is void or voidable, or a divorce decree may be issued, if either party is unable or unwilling to procreate after marriage. Accordingly, reproduction is obviously not an essential element of marriage. The fact that two persons of the same sex are incapable of natural procreation is the same as the result of two opposite-sex persons' inability, in an objective sense, or unwillingness, in a subjective sense, to procreate. Disallowing two persons of the same sex to marry, for the sake of their inability to reproduce, is a different treatment having no apparent rational basis.

(8)   The basic ethical orders built upon the existing institution of opposite-sex marriage will remain unaffected, even if we allow two persons of the same sex to enter into a legally recognized marriage pursuant to the formal and substantive requirements of the Marriage Chapter, as long as they are subject to the rights and obligations of both parties during the marriage and after the marriage ends. Disallowing two persons of the same sex to marry, for the sake of safeguarding basic ethical orders, is a different treatment, also obviously having no rational basis. Such different treatment is incompatible with the spirit and meaning of the right to equality as protected by Article 7 of the Constitution.

(9)   The authorities concerned shall complete the amendment or enactment of relevant laws in accordance with the ruling of this Interpretation, within two years after the announcement of this Interpretation. It is within the discretion of the authorities concerned to determine the formality (for example, revision of the Marriage Chapter, enactment of a special Chapter in Part IV on Family of the Civil Code, enactment of a special law, or other formality) for achieving the equal protection of the freedom of marriage for two persons of the same sex.

(10)   If the amendment or enactment of relevant laws is not completed within the said two-year timeframe, two persons of the same sex who intend to create a permanent union of intimate and exclusive nature for the committed purpose of managing a life together may, pursuant to the provisions of the Marriage Chapter, apply for marriage registration to the authorities in charge of household registration, by submitting a document signed by two or more witnesses. Any such two persons, once registered, shall be accorded the status of a legally recognized couple, and then enjoy the rights and bear the obligations arising on couples.

Justice Jui-Ming Huang recused himself and took no part in the deliberation, oral arguments or the decision of this case.

Justice Horng-Shya Huang filed a dissenting opinion in part. Justice Chen-Huan Wu filed a dissenting opinion.

SOURCE: Judicial Yuan Republic of China (Taiwan). "Press Release on the Same-Sex Marriage Case." May 24, 2017. http://jirs.judicial.gov.tw/GNNWS/NNWSS002.asp?id=267570.

German Bundestag Discusses Same-Sex Marriage Legislation

June 30, 2017

DRAFT BUNDESRAT LAW PERMITTING SAME-SEX MARRIAGE

A. Problem and goal

Marriage is still denied to same-sex couples, a fact that constitutes a concrete and symbolic discrimination against people based on their sexual identity. However, the public debate following the referendum in the Republic of Ireland on the permission for marriage of same-sex couples has once again made it clear that, in view of the social change and the resulting change in the understanding of marriage, there are no justifiable reasons to treat homosexual and heterosexual couples differently and to continue to impede same-sex marriage. Moreover, same-sex couples are still comparatively at a disadvantage in a number of legal areas, despite the introduction of the Institute of Registered Partnerships in 2001. This applies primarily to the right of adoption.

B. Solution

It is clarified by supplementing § 1353 of the German Civil Code (BGB) that same-sex persons can also enter into a marriage. The rights of the churches and religious communities remain unaffected by this new legal regulation. . . .

[A letter from Angela Merkel to the President of the Bundestag and the articles of the law have been omitted.]

Justification

[References to federal court cases have been omitted.]

A. General Part

On 22 March 2013, the Bundesrat had already drafted a bill to introduce the right to marry for persons of the same sex and submitted it to the German Bundestag, BR-Drucksache 193/13 (decision). However, the draft bill has been subjected to discontinuity due to the expiry of the legislative term.

Article 6, paragraph 1 of the constitution stipulates: "Marriage and family are under special protection of the government." According to the case-law of the Federal Constitutional Court, this provision guarantees marriage as an institution, among other things. The legislature must therefore observe the essential structural principles determining the institution of marriage. These structural principles have been derived by the Federal Constitutional Court from the established, traditional forms of life in connection with the freedom character of Article 6, paragraph 1 of the constitution and other constitutional norms. However, Article 6 (1) of the constitution does not guarantee marriage in an abstract manner, but rather in the constitutionally guided form that corresponds to the prevailing views expressed authoritatively in the statutory provisions.

Accordingly, the constitution protects marriage as a supportive and responsible communion, independent of the family—in contrast to the Weimar constitution, which saw marriage as the basis of the family and emphasized the reproductive function. For this reason, childless marriage is also protected under Article 6 of the constitution.

According to the traditional understanding of marriage, the gender difference between the spouses was of particular importance. For a long time, it was also regarded as a necessary precondition for marriage within the meaning of Article 6, paragraph 1 of the constitution, so that same-sex partnerships were excluded from the concept of marriage. When the constitution was passed, homosexuality was considered immoral and was prohibited under criminal law in §§ 175 ff. of the Criminal Law. Inclusion of homosexuals in the protection against discrimination under the constitution or even recognition of same-sex couples was at that time beyond the realm of imagination across all party boundaries. It was not until 1969, when the total prohibition of male homosexuality under criminal law was lifted, that legal practice changed and social stigma gradually declined.

In a decision by a chamber of the Federal Constitutional Court in 1993, it ruled that "sufficient evidence for a fundamental change in the understanding of marriage in the sense that sexual difference no longer had any formative significance" had not been presented. The court therefore refused to allow marriage for homosexuals for reasons of constitution and left it to the legislature to take further steps for the legal recognition of homosexual couples. This did not rule out a future change in the understanding of marriage, which allows marriage to be permitted for same-sex partnerships.

For some time now, there has been sufficient evidence of a fundamental change in the traditional understanding of marriage, which, in view of the legislature's freedom of discretion, allows the introduction of the right to marry persons of the same sex under constitutional law. The jurisprudence of the Federal Constitutional Court permits a change in meaning if either new facts appear that are not covered by the statutory regulation or facts have changed as a result of being included in the overall development. As a result, the meaning of a constitutional law norm can change without altering its text. The limit, however, lies in the meaning and purpose of the constitutional norm, which in the case of Article 6 (1) of the constitution, permits a considerable change in values.

First, there has been a fundamental change in the understanding of marriage following the establishment of the legal institution of a civil union. Today's population no longer differentiates between marriage and civil union. Marriage and the establishment of a civil union are called "marriage" without distinction. We also do not differentiate between "married" and "partnered" any more, but instead we talk without discrimination about the fact that they are "married" in the case of spouses and life partners. The public also assumes, as a matter of course, that spouses and partners have the same duties and rights, even though this really only applies to their duties. According to current opinion polls, the majority are in favour of allowing same-sex couples to marry.

The legal equivalence of registered life partnerships with married couples, as intended by the Registered Life Partnership Act, has also been understood in large parts of the law. Nevertheless, it has been the Federal Constitutional Court that has complained on several occasions about a continuing unequal treatment.

On 7 May 2013, for example, the Federal Constitutional Court declared the unequal treatment of registered life partners and spouses with regard to the splitting of spouses with respect to the income tax law and on 19 February 2013, the non-admission of the successive adoption of adopted children of a registered life partner by the other life partner to be incompatible with the constitution. These decisions are in line with the decisions of the Federal Constitutional Court, which have objected to legal regulations that contain an unequal treatment of registered life partnership and marriage.

The legislature has contributed to this change in the understanding of marriage through the Act amending the Transsexual Law of 17 July 2009 (Federal Law Gazette I, p. 1978). By this law § 8 paragraph 1 number 2 of the Transsexual Law was deleted without substitution because the Federal Constitutional Court had declared the provision null and void. This provision had allowed the legal change of marital status of a married transsexual only if the latter had previously been divorced. The legislature could have reacted differently to the ruling of the Federal Constitutional Court. The Federal Constitutional Court had expressly granted it the possibility of stipulating that the legal relationship established as "marriage" should be continued with the same rights and obligations, but under a different label, among other things. This would enable the legislature to defend the strict heterosexual aspect of marriage. The legislature did not attach any decisive importance to this aspect and allowed same-sex marriages by deleting § 8 paragraph 1 point 2 of the Transsexual Law. As a result, legal same-sex marriages already exist in Germany.

Furthermore, it should be noted that the Federal Constitutional Court also generally acknowledges and takes note of social change in the interpretation of Article 6 of the constitution. For example, it declared a submission by the district court of Schweinfurt to be inadmissible in which this court essentially claimed that parents within the meaning of Article 6, paragraph 2, first sentence, of the constitution could not be same-sex life partners, because this provision speaks of a "natural" right of parents, to which in the court's opinion homosexual persons should not be entitled. The Federal Constitutional Court briefly expands on this: "Apart from the fact that the court has not dealt with the history of the origins of Article 6 of the constitution and any conclusions drawn thereof regarding the ownership of parental rights, nor with a possible change in the legal understanding of parenthood that could influence the interpretation of Article 6 of the constitution, it has dealt insufficiently with the case-law of the Federal Constitutional Court and the views expressed in the literature on the question as to who is competent to bear the right of parenthood." In addition, the Federal Constitutional Court points to its case-law, according to which natural parenthood has no priority over legal and social-family parenthood. This also shows how social change—including decisions taken by the legislature—affects the interpretation of Article 6 of the constitution. Whatever has been possible here with respect to the concept of family and parenting should also be possible with respect to marriage. The Schweinfurt District Court may surely have still found supporters for its interpretation in the 19th century, but this is no longer the case today.

Finally, the legal systems of other countries provide further evidence that the concept that spouses must be of different genders is obsolete. Recently, the Republic of Ireland allowed marriage between same-sex couples. Civil marriage has been allowed for same-sex marriages in Belgium, the Netherlands, France, Luxembourg, Finland, Canada, South Africa, Spain, Norway, Sweden, Portugal, Iceland, Denmark, Argentina, Brazil, Uruguay, New Zealand, Scotland, England and Wales, 41 states in the United States and the District of Columbia, as well as in two states and Mexico's capital city. Same-sex marriages are also recognized in Israel.

In addition, constitutional courts from some of the above-mentioned U.S. states, Canadian provinces and South Africa have even forced marriages to be permitted between same-sex couples against the decisions of the local legislature, in order to avoid discrimination. These courts also took note of the thought, which can be found in the case-law of the Federal Constitutional Court, that marriage was historically based on a mixed gender concept in all western states. Nevertheless, they concluded that the exclusion of same-sex couples from marriage was incompatible with the constitutional principles of respect for private autonomy and equality before the law. Finally, the Massachusetts Supreme Judicial Court pointed out the example that legal marriage between white and black Americans had not been possible in parts of the USA for decades and centuries, and drew a parallel to this constellation, since in both constellations there were no factual reasons for differentiation.

Similar counter-arguments were also raised in European countries for same-sex couples when marriage was permitted. Marriage is a union between a man and a woman, it was so and it should remain so. What the advocates emphasized was that marriage—like family—is a dynamic social category and recalled that in the past, marriage between Catholics and Protestants was prohibited, just as indissolubility was one of the structural principles of marriage, for example.

Apart from the theoretical doubts regarding the observance of the structural principles of a changing family law institution, the introduction of a simple legal right to marry for persons of the same sex cannot affect the institutional guarantee enshrined in Article 6, paragraph 1 of the constitution. No dimension of this fundamental right is violated by it, and to this extent the objective function of Article 6 of the constitution may neither be exploited nor abused against the subjective rights of other holders of fundamental rights.

With the permission of marriage to same-sex couples, there is no need to keep the legal institution of registered life partnership open for new registrations—even in view of the fact that it includes the same obligations as marriage, but not the full rights (e.g., right of adoption). Therefore, new registrations of life partnership will no longer be possible. The already registered partnerships will, on the other hand, continue to exist, unless the partners transform them into a marriage. . . .

[A description of the law amendments has been omitted.]

Statement by the Federal Government

The Federal Government states the following on the draft law of the Bundesrat:

The Federal Government is convinced that same-sex partnerships also embody values that are fundamental to our society.

For 14 years, same-sex partners have been able to establish a legal framework for their relationship in the Federal Republic of Germany. To this end, the Life Partnership

Act came into force on 1 August 2001. In order to remedy the unfavourable position of life partners, further adjustments were made in the following period, including changes in inheritance and real estate transfer tax, civil servants' rights and the right of adoption.

The Federal Government aims to end existing discrimination against same-sex life partnerships and people on the basis of their sexual identity in all areas of society. This includes the elimination of legal regulations that make same-sex partnerships unfavourable.

Following the implementation of the Federal Constitutional Court ruling on successive adoption, the Federal Government has therefore initiated a draft bill to streamline the rights of life partners, which has been passed by the legislative bodies.

The Federal Government will closely follow further discussion on legal policy.

SOURCE: German Bundestag. "Second and Third Recommendations on the Draft Bill Introduced by the Federal Council for the Introduction of the Right to Marry Persons of the Same Sex." June 30, 2017. Translated by SAGE Publishing. http://dip21.bundestag.de/dip21/btd/18/066/1806665.pdf.

DOCUMENT

Maltese Parliament Approves Marriage Equality Bill

July 12, 2017

The Maltese Parliament approved the Marriage Equality Bill during its third and final reading, making Malta the 25th country in the world, and the 15th in Europe, to approve such a law. This was the first law which Government moved in Parliament during this new legislature, as promised by Prime Minister Joseph Muscat.

The aim of this law is that of modernising marriage law through the mainstreaming of equality for all. This means that the institution of marriage is now fully gender neutral to ensure that lesbian, gay, bisexual, trans, intersex, and genderqueer (LGBTIQ) persons are free to contract a marriage with their loved ones, be they of the same or a different sex, and also to parent children without having unnecessary references to their gender or biological make-up on their children's birth certificates.

It also means that all discrepancies between husband and wife have now been removed. For example, both are now free to adopt or take on their partner's surname without distinction. Their siblings would then take on the family surname that the couple chooses on their marriage day.

During the process towards the adoption of the Bill, a lot of the discussion centred on whether it was necessary to convert civil marriage to a fully gender neutral institution. Government insisted that this was necessary in order to respect the anti-discrimination provisions in the country's Constitution adopted in 2014 relative to sexual orientation and gender identity. Additionally, Government indicated that both the Civil Unions Act, and the Cohabitation Act adopted in 2014 and 2016 respectively are both gender neutral, and that marriage should not be an exception.

A celebration organised by the Government of Malta and the LGBTIQ Consultative Council (a government instituted body consisting of representatives of all LGBTIQ civil society organisations) was held in front of the Auberge de Castille, the seat of the Prime Minister's Office.

SOURCE: Government of Malta. "Maltese Parliament Approves Marriage Equality Bill." July 12, 2017. https://gov.mt/en/Government/Press%20Releases/Pages/2017/July/12/pr171689.aspx.

Remarks by Australian Prime Minister Turnbull in Favor of Same-Sex Marriage Bill

December 4, 2017

Thank you Mr Speaker.

It's time for us to get on with it.

The Australian people have said 'yes' to marriage equality, 'yes' to fairness, 'yes' to commitment, 'yes' to love. The time has now come to make that equality a reality.

Now this is momentous social reform and the road to this day has been long and arduous. It's littered with injustice, dealt out to men and women who dared to confess their love.

Not so long ago homosexuality was a crime in this country. Slowly—too slowly—Parliament and people have changed their attitudes towards gay men and women, extended basic rights. Homosexuality was decriminalized. Gay Australians were allowed to serve in the military . . .

But the issue of marriage remained.

Now the message it *[sic]* today, to every gay person in this nation, is clear; we love you. We respect you. Your relationship is recognised by the Commonwealth as legitimate and honorable as anybody else's. You belong . . .

I am very firmly of the view Mr Speaker, that families are the foundation of our society. We would be a stronger society if more people were married and by that I mean formally, legally married and fewer were divorced . . .

I have to say that I am utterly unpersuaded by the proposition that my marriage to Lucy or indeed any marriage, is undermined by two gay men or women setting up house down the road whether it is called a marriage or not. Let's be honest to each other; the threat to traditional marriage is not from gay people. It is a lack of loving commitment, whether it is found in the form of neglect, indifference, cruelty or adultery to name just a few manifestations of that loveless desert in which too many marriages come to grief. If the threat to marriage today is lack of commitment, then surely other couples making and maintaining that commitment sets a good example, rather than a bad one.

Are not gay people who seek the right to marry, to formalise their commitment to each other, holding up a mirror to heterosexuals who regrettably, in my view at least, are marrying less frequently and divorce more often . . .

Mr Speaker, as I said at the start of this marriage survey, this is an issue of fundamental fairness.

A society which promotes freedom and equality under the law should accord gay men and women the right to marry.

We now recognise same-sex couples in every other aspect of the law—financial, medical, adoption—but we have not yet given them the right to call their relationship a marriage.

Now, this distinction will end with the passage of this Bill and of course, it ends with the emphatic endorsement of an enormous majority of Australians.

The postal survey was one of the most remarkable political events in my lifetime—and I believe in the lifetime of many Australians . . .

But above all the credit is due to the Australian people, 80 per cent of whom cast a vote. Now that was remarkable. Nobody predicted that or expected that. In a general election, where we actually fine you if you don't vote, the participation rate is only a little bit above 90 per cent. This was a remarkable turnout and it proved what we always said; that Australians wanted to have their say.

Now, that outcome, that survey Mr Speaker, had many opponents, most notably on the other side of this chamber.

In fact, this moment would've come far sooner if the Opposition had supported our original plebiscite proposal in this Parliament . . .

Now, Mr Speaker, the best thing about the result has been the tremendous affirmation of same sex couples and indeed all gay Australians, in the result.

In voting 'yes', Australians have thrown their arms around their fellow Australians who are gay and said clearly: "We accept you and we accept your relationship."

I hope that in that positive affirmation, the most positive you could have in a democracy, same sex couples take comfort in the acceptance and love of their fellow Australians.

Now Mr Speaker, there were many who voted against the change, but I know that they will accept and respect the democratic outcome of this process. They voted 'no' for many different reasons. Some believe homosexuality itself is sinful, others simply wanted to keep the legal definition of marriage as it has been for thousands of years.

Now, I respect the vote of every Australian—both 'yes' and 'no'—and we made sure they could be heard and I recognise the fundamental importance of ensuring freedom of religion and speech are protected. The Bill has been designed, as Senator Smith said in the Senate when he moved it, to ensure religious freedom is protected and I do not believe that the Bill threatens our cherished religious freedoms. There is nothing in the Bill for example, which prevents anyone from maintaining or adhering to the teaching of their church on marriage or morality.

But we must not fail to recognise that there is sincere, heartfelt anxiety about the Bill's impact on religious freedom. That is why I will support several amendments to the Bill which will provide that additional reassurance in respect of these fundamental rights and freedoms . . .

We are united in our diversity, our values of mutual respect have made Australia the most harmonious, the most successful multicultural society on the planet.

Australians have shown by the enormous turnout, they're deeply engaged with this issue and they have voted overwhelmingly for a country built on equality, where the law does not discriminate against you on the basis of your sexual orientation, any more than on the basis of your race or religion or gender.

So today is a day of which every Australian should be proud.

Proud that we can conduct and did conduct, despite all the naysayers, a very civil debate.

Proud that given the opportunity to vote, far from being apathetic as the naysayers predicted, we participated in such enormous numbers.

This is a day to be especially proud that all of our friends, our colleagues, our neighbours, our brothers, our sisters, can marry the people they love.

And for those who voted 'no' and remain disappointed with the result, a day to be proud that your voices were heard and that you have a Government that ensured your voices were heard, as you wanted. They were counted and that ultimately, as you acknowledged, the majority was decisive.

The postal survey gave the ultimate democratic seal to this historic change.

Now Mr Speaker, I commend all the men and women who fought for decades to bring this reform about . . .

But most of all, to same-sex couples in Australia; you are equal, you are respected, you are loved.

I commend the Bill to the house.

SOURCE: Prime Minister of Australia. "Second Reading Speech: Marriage Amendment (Definition and Religious Freedoms) Bill 2017." December 4, 2017. https://www.pm.gov.au/media/second-reading-speech-marriage-amendment-definition-and-religious-freedoms-bill-2017.

OTHER HISTORIC DOCUMENTS OF INTEREST

FROM PREVIOUS *HISTORIC DOCUMENTS*

June

United States Withdraws from the Paris Climate Accord

JUNE 1, 2016

Carbon emissions related to human industrial activity contribute significantly to climate change. Without dramatic measures to reduce emissions this century, climate change poses profound risks to planetary systems that support human populations. According to the UN, geopolitical instability with new burdens on economies and governments will likely result from effects of climate change such as stronger and more frequent natural disasters, increased flooding and drought, potential crop failure, sea level rise, spread of disease, and species extinction.

During his campaign, President Donald Trump labeled climate change a "hoax" perpetrated by China to hinder U.S. economic growth. Embracing isolationist influences, he delivered on a campaign promise to put "America first," and in a bold assertion of this rhetoric, Trump announced a plan to withdraw the United States from the historic Paris Climate Agreement. One of the most significant pieces of international diplomacy in recent years, the ambitious goal it put forth draws strength from solidarity among world leaders. Abdication of American leadership on this global issue would weaken years of careful negotiations and alter the United States' position in international conversations surrounding environmental policy.

AN HISTORIC AGREEMENT: THE PARIS CLIMATE ACCORD

In 1992, the United Nations Framework Convention on Climate Change (UNFCCC) laid the foundation for all future climate diplomacy. The Paris accord is the culmination of two decades of negotiations surrounding carbon emissions, climate change mitigation, and financial dimensions of sustainable development. Adopted in December 2015 in France, and effective November 4, 2016, the accord puts forth a global goal of reduced carbon emissions to avoid warming of 2°C (3.6°F) above preindustrial levels. The 2°C threshold was adopted as the tipping point beyond which impacts to the climate system would likely be catastrophic and irreversible. (Earth has warmed about 1°C since 1880. A "business as usual" scenario would likely result in 4°C warming by 2100.)

The agreement was hailed as a turning point in global climate diplomacy with an unprecedented level of support: 195 countries had signed on by November 2016. Only two—Nicaragua, which argued the terms were not strong enough, and war-torn Syria—did not sign the agreement. Widely seen as balanced and transparent, the deliberately "bottom-up" approach requires each country to set its own voluntary, nonbinding targets, contributing to the collective global goal, with progress to be reported and stronger goals set on a five-year cycle. No specific regulations are imposed, and abiding by the accord requires only an ongoing effort to contribute to global emission reductions. While pledges cannot be weakened once committed, no country is penalized for failing to meet its goal.

The accord is meant to send an economic signal, to steer the global economy away from "business as usual" by encouraging economic divestment from fossil fuels and promoting strong growth and investment in renewable energy.

Twenty-five years of UNFCCC discussions have encompassed the scientific, geopolitical, financial, and moral implications of climate change. Economic and geographic divides between affluent and developing regions are such that countries most vulnerable to effects of climate change are generally those that are least responsible for causing it. Global consensus on climate action requires accounting for this stark difference in historic responsibility, current circumstances, and future ambitions. The Green Climate Fund was established as a financial mechanism under UNFCCC to support capacity building for mitigation and adaptation. This is achieved by affluent and industrialized nations collectively mobilizing significant financial resources to promote climate-resilient development in vulnerable regions aligned with each country's goals. Of the global collective $10.3 billion, then-President Barack Obama had pledged $3 billion from the United States, about a third of which had been delivered.

President Trump Announces America's Exit from the Accord

On June 1, 2017, President Trump announced that he planned to withdraw the United States from the Paris Accord. He perceived the agreement, and the global solidarity it represents, to be a pernicious economic and ideological threat to American sovereignty. When the agreement was signed, President Obama had pledged a U.S. reduction of emissions by 17 percent below 2005 levels by 2020. Trump defended his decision to exit by citing a widely disputed figure, claiming that such a reduction would result in 2.7 million American jobs lost by 2025, with particular harm to oil, gas, and coal industries. He remarked, "It would once have been unthinkable that an international agreement could prevent the United States from conducting its own domestic affairs." Ignoring the fact that the U.S. is the second largest national source of carbon emissions, he said that he "could not . . . support a deal that punished the U.S. and that poses no punishment for the world's great polluters."

On August 4, 2017, the State Department issued a notification to the United Nations outlining the administration's intentions to leave the accord. The document has no legal weight and does not initiate the United States' departure, since a party can withdraw only after three years from the accord coming into effect and with one year's notice. The United States cannot officially start the withdrawal process until 2019, then could officially exit November 4, 2020. Although the State Department continued to participate in UNFCCC meetings, the president indicated that the United States will "cease all implementation." This includes discontinuing support for the Green Climate Fund, which Trump asserted was costing the United States "a vast fortune." Despite Paris commitments being nonbinding and voluntary, Trump suggested that the United States would seek a "better deal," without specifying what this might entail. The administration maintained that it supports lowering emissions "while promoting economic growth and ensuring energy security." The State Department's notice also calls for working with other nations to help them "access and use fossil fuels more cleanly and efficiently." The administration left the door open to reengaging with the accord, if terms more favorable for the United States could be found.

A Reproachful Global Response

The move was backed by some congressional Republicans such as Senate Majority Leader Mitch McConnell, R-Ken., who described it as a "significant blow to the Obama administration's assault on domestic energy production." However, Democratic lawmakers, international officials, business leaders, and the general public responded with alarm at the denial of established science as well as shortsighted rejection of economic opportunity. Former Vice President Al Gore called the move "reckless and indefensible," and Senate Minority Leader Chuck Schumer, D-N.Y., remarked that it was "a devastating failure of historic proportions."

Within hours of the announcement, Germany, France, and Italy released a joint statement asserting that the accord is not open to any renegotiation. They were joined by many heads of state around the world reaffirming their commitments to sustainable development. The unyielding response of global leaders came amid a surge of condemnation for the United States' decision to renege on the agreement after decades of climate leadership. While Trump declared that he was elected to "represent the people of Pittsburg not Paris," Pittsburg mayor Bill Peduto tweeted to reassure the world that his city "will follow the guidelines of the Paris Agreement for our people, our economy & future."

In the following days and weeks, more than 2,500 mayors, governors, corporate leaders, and university presidents representing all fifty states signaled their commitments to sustainable development. In an open letter titled "We Are Still In," signatories vowed to support climate action and uphold commitments made in Paris. Along with California governor Jerry Brown, former New York City mayor Michael Bloomberg, whose organization pledged $200 million to help U.S. cities solve key problems including climate change, created a complimentary initiative called America's Pledge, which seeks to "compile and quantify" commitments by states, cities, and businesses to reduce greenhouse gas emissions in accordance with the goals of the Paris agreement. Bloomberg also partnered with Maroš Šefčovič, the vice president of the European Commission, to form the Global Covenant of Mayors for Climate & Energy, through which mayors from nearly 7,500 cities around the world are working "to address the causes and consequences of global climate change." Šefčovič has noted that if necessary, the accord will bypass the White House and work directly with states to ensure progress in the absence of leadership from Washington. Since June, Syria and Nicaragua had both joined the accord, isolating the United States as the only government on Earth to reject terms of the agreement. Despite actions by municipal and state officials to circumvent the White House for stronger representation, the Trump administration's position has not changed.

Undermining Environmental Progress

A Yale University study published in May 2017 found that the majority of Americans across the political spectrum supported the accord. Prominent demonstrations such as the March for Science and People's Climate March (both in April 2017) were precipitated by widespread concern among scientists and environmental activists, with heightened awareness among the general public regarding the new administration's attitudes toward environmental policy. Trump rejected well-established tenets of climate science and emphasized that his priorities lie with the American fossil fuel industry by appointing proponents to key cabinet positions.

His first year in office was marked by an anticipated, but abrupt, shift in the nation's approach to environmental policy, and his rejection of the Paris agreement was the most dramatic of a series of actions taken to undermine his predecessor's environmental legacy. To reflect the new leadership's approach to environmental policy, climate data and other information on environmental science were removed from the White House and agency websites. The administration, with a Republican Congress, has aggressively endeavored to limit the amount of federal funding available for scientific and environmental objectives, while targeting environmental regulations perceived as taxing to the fossil fuel industry. Trump has pursued expansion of oil and gas extraction into ecologically sensitive areas and public lands, ordered a review of national monuments, dismissed key science advisors in federal agencies, and put forward a host of similar anti-environmental policies and procedures.

Curbing emissions from coal-fired plants was a central component of Obama's steps toward the Paris targets. Declaring an "end to the war on coal," Trump signed an Energy Independence Executive Order to review the Clean Power Plan, the centerpiece of Obama's efforts to address climate change, and other "job-killing regulations." (Coal jobs have decreased by 25 percent since 2008, in large part due to policies aimed at reducing emissions, while jobs in renewable energy have expanded.) Trump's insistence on promoting fossil fuels goes against economic interest, as former executive secretary of UNFCCC, Christiana Figueres, pointed out, "Trying to make fossil fuels remain competitive in the face of a booming clean renewable power sector . . . is going against the flow of economics."

Sustainable Development: High Stakes and an Uncertain Future

If the United States had remained in the Paris agreement, it likely would not have met emission targets, given Trump's approach to environmental policy. Other signatories understood climate change to be a profound and immediate global threat requiring effective, coordinated contributions to collective solutions. Since the United States is the second largest source of carbon pollution, the Paris accord will not be effective in the end without American involvement.

Prominent American political figures lamented both the United States' forfeiture of future long-term economic opportunity and rejection of long-standing diplomatic relationships. George Shultz, former Secretary of State during the administration of President Ronald Reagan, penned a May 9, 2017, op-ed for the *New York Times* in which he wrote, "If America fails to honor a global agreement that it helped forge, the repercussions will undercut our diplomatic priorities across the globe." In a rare offering of his political views since leaving the White House, President Obama effectively said, *we're still in*: "The nations that remain in the Paris agreement will be the nations that reap the benefits in jobs and industries created. . . . Even in the absence of American leadership, I'm confident that our states, cities, and businesses will step up and do even more to lead the way."

Trump was not among the heads of state invited to participate in the 2017 climate talks in Germany, but the United States was represented by a State Department delegation to ensure that all future policy options remain open. The "We Are Still In" coalition also participated in the sessions, and a spokesman for UN Secretary General António Guterres made clear that any reengagement by the Trump administration would be welcome, emphasizing the need for U.S. leadership on sustainable development.

The final decision to support or reject American commitments to global climate action at a federal level will be decided by American voters in the next presidential election. While the lack of leadership from Washington changes the tone of discussions, the accord's deliberate "bottom up" structure and foundation of global solidarity foster the kind of diplomatic environment necessary for inclusion of American involvement, with or without federal support.

—Megan Howes

The following are excerpts from a transcript of remarks by President Donald Trump and Environmental Protection Agency Administrator Scott Pruitt on June 1, 2017, regarding the decision to withdraw the United States from the Paris Climate Agreement; and the text of a joint statement by France, Germany, and Italy regarding the U.S. decision to leave the Paris Climate Agreement, also on June 1, 2017.

President Trump Announces Withdrawal from Paris Agreement

June 1, 2017

. . . One by one, we are keeping the promises I made to American people during my campaign for President, whether it's cutting job-killing regulations; appointing and confirming a tremendous Supreme Court Justice, putting in place tough new ethics rules, achieving a record reduction in illegal immigration on our southern border, or bringing jobs, plants, and factories back into the United States at numbers which no one until this point thought even possible. And believe me, we've just begun. The fruits of our labor will be seen very shortly even more so.

Paris Agreement on Climate Change

On these issues and so many more, we're following through on our commitments. And I don't want anything to get in our way. I am fighting every day for the great people of this country. Therefore, in order to fulfill my solemn duty to protect America and its citizens, the United States will withdraw from the Paris climate accord—[*applause*]—thank you, thank you—but begin negotiations to reenter either the Paris accord or an—really entirely new transaction on terms that are fair to the United States, its businesses, its workers, its people, its taxpayers. So we're getting out. But we will start to negotiate, and we will see if we can make a deal that's fair. And if we can, that's great. And if we can't, that's fine.

As President, I can put no other consideration before the well-being of American citizens. The Paris climate accord is simply the latest example of Washington entering into an agreement that disadvantages the United States to the exclusive benefit of other countries, leaving American workers—who I love—and taxpayers to absorb the cost in terms of lost jobs, lower wages, shuttered factories, and vastly diminished economic production.

Thus, as of today, the United States will cease all implementation of the nonbinding Paris accord and the draconian financial and economic burdens the agreement imposes on our country. This includes ending the implementation of the nationally determined contribution and, very importantly, the Green Climate Fund which is costing the United States a vast fortune.

Compliance with the terms of the Paris accord and the onerous energy restrictions it has placed on the United States could cost America as much as 2.7 million lost jobs by 2025 according to the National Economic Research Associates. This includes 440,000 fewer manufacturing jobs—not what we need; believe me, this is not what we need—including automobile jobs, and the further decimation of vital American industries on which countless communities rely. They rely for so much, and we would be giving them so little.

According to this same study, by 2040, compliance with the commitments put into place by the previous administration would cut production for the following sectors: paper, down 12 percent; cement, down 23 percent; iron and steel, down 38 percent; coal—and I happen to love the coal miners—down 86 percent; natural gas, down 31 percent. The cost to the economy at this time would be close to $3 trillion in lost GDP and 6½ million industrial jobs, while households would have $7,000 less income and, in many cases, much worse than that.

Not only does this deal subject our citizens to harsh economic restrictions, it fails to live up to our environmental ideals. As someone who cares deeply about the environment, which I do, I cannot in good conscience support a deal that punishes the United States—which is what it does—the world's leader in environmental protection, while imposing no meaningful obligations on the world's leading polluters.

For example, under the agreement, China will be able to increase these emissions by a staggering number of years, 13. They can do whatever they want for 13 years. Not us. India makes its participation contingent on receiving billions and billions and billions of dollars in foreign aid from developed countries. There are many other examples. But the bottom line is that the Paris accord is very unfair, at the highest level, to the United States.

Further, while the current agreement effectively blocks the development of clean coal in America—which it does, and the mines are starting to open up. We're having a big opening in 2 weeks. Pennsylvania, Ohio, West Virginia, so many places. A big opening of a brand-new mine. It's unheard of. For many, many years, that hasn't happened. They asked me if I'd go. I'm going to try.

China will be allowed to build hundreds of additional coal plants. So we can't build the plants, but they can, according to this agreement. India will be allowed to double its coal production by 2020. Think of it: India can double their coal production. We're supposed get rid of ours. Even Europe is allowed to continue construction of coal plants. In short, the agreement doesn't eliminate coal jobs, it just transfers those jobs out of America and the United States and ships them to foreign countries.

This agreement is less about the climate and more about other countries gaining a financial advantage over the United States. The rest of the world applauded when we signed the Paris Agreement—they went wild; they were so happy—for the simple reason that it put our country, the United States of America, which we all love, at a very, very big economic disadvantage. A cynic would say the obvious reason for economic competitors and their wish to see us remain in the agreement is so that we continue to suffer this self-inflicted major economic wound. We would find it very hard to compete with other countries from other parts of the world.

We have among the most abundant energy reserves on the planet, sufficient to lift millions of America's poorest workers out of poverty. Yet, under this agreement, we are effectively putting these reserves under lock and key, taking away the great wealth of our Nation—it's great wealth, it's phenomenal wealth; not so long ago, we had no idea we had such wealth—and leaving millions and millions of families trapped in poverty and joblessness.

The agreement is a massive redistribution of United States wealth to other countries. At 1-percent growth, renewable sources of energy can meet some of our domestic demand, but at 3- or 4-percent growth, which I expect, we need all forms of available American energy, or our country will be at grave risk of brownouts and blackouts, our businesses will come to a halt in many cases, and the American family will suffer the consequences in the form of lost jobs and a very diminished quality of life.

Even if the Paris Agreement were implemented in full, with total compliance from all nations, it is estimated it would only produce a two-tenths of one degree—think of that; this much—Celsius reduction in global temperature by the year 2100. Tiny, tiny amount. In fact, 14 days of carbon emissions from China alone would wipe out the gains from America—and this is an incredible statistic—would totally wipe out the gains from America's expected reductions in the year 2030, after we have had to spend billions and billions of dollars, lost jobs, closed factories, and suffered much higher energy costs for our businesses and for our homes.

As the Wall Street Journal wrote this morning: "The reality is that withdrawing is in America's economic interest and won't matter much to the climate." The United States, under the Trump administration, will continue to be the cleanest and most environmentally friendly country on Earth. We'll be the cleanest. We're going to have the cleanest air. We're going to have the cleanest water. We will be environmentally friendly, but we're not going to put our businesses out of work, and we're not going to lose our jobs. We're going to grow; we're going to grow rapidly.

And I think you just read—it just came out minutes ago, the small business report—small businesses as of just now are booming, hiring people. One of the best reports they've seen in many years.

I'm willing to immediately work with Democratic leaders to either negotiate our way back into Paris, under the terms that are fair to the United States and its workers, or to negotiate a new deal that protects our country and its taxpayers.

So if the obstructionists want to get together with me, let's make them nonobstructionists. We will all sit down, and we will get back into the deal. And we'll make it good, and we won't be closing up our factories, and we won't be losing our jobs. And we'll sit down with the Democrats and all of the people that represent either the Paris accord or something that we can do that's much better than the Paris accord. And I think the people of our country will be thrilled, and I think then the people of the world will be thrilled. But until we do that, we're out of the agreement.

I will work to ensure that America remains the world's leader on environmental issues, but under a framework that is fair and where the burdens and responsibilities are equally shared among the many nations all around the world.

No responsible leader can put the workers—and the people—of their country at this debilitating and tremendous disadvantage. The fact that the Paris deal hamstrings the United States, while empowering some of the world's top polluting countries, should dispel any doubt as to the real reason why foreign lobbyists wish to keep our magnificent country tied up and bound down by this agreement: It's to give their country an economic edge over the United States. That's not going to happen while I'm President. I'm sorry.

My job as President is to do everything within my power to give America a level playing field and to create the economic, regulatory, and tax structures that make America the most prosperous and productive country on Earth and with the highest standard of living and the highest standard of environmental protection.

Our tax bill is moving along in Congress, and I believe it's doing very well. I think a lot of people will be very pleasantly surprised. The Republicans are working very, very hard. We'd love to have support from the Democrats, but we may have to go it alone. But it's going very well.

The Paris Agreement handicaps the United States economy in order to win praise from the very foreign capitals and global activists that have long sought to gain wealth at our country's expense. They don't put America first. I do, and I always will.

The same nations asking us to stay in the agreement are the countries that have collectively cost America trillions of dollars through tough trade practices and, in many cases, lax contributions to our critical military alliance. You see what's happening. It's pretty obvious to those that want to keep an open mind.

At what point does America get demeaned? At what point do they start laughing at us as a country? We want fair treatment for its citizens, and we want fair treatment for our taxpayers. We don't want other leaders and other countries laughing at us anymore. And they won't be. They won't be.

I was elected to represent the citizens of Pittsburgh, not Paris. I promised I would exit or renegotiate any deal which fails to serve America's interests. Many trade deals will soon be under renegotiation. Very rarely do we have a deal that works for this country, but they'll soon be under renegotiation. The process has begun from day one. But now we're down to business.

Beyond the severe energy restrictions inflicted by the Paris accord, it includes yet another scheme to redistribute wealth out of the United States through the so-called Green Climate Fund—nice name—which calls for developed countries to send $100 billion to developing countries all on top of America's existing and massive foreign aid payments. So we're going to be paying billions and billions and billions of dollars, and we're already way ahead of anybody else. Many of the other countries haven't spent anything, and many of them will never pay one dime.

The Green Fund would likely obligate the United States to commit potentially tens of billions of dollars of which the United States has already handed over $1 billion—nobody else is even close; most of them haven't even paid anything—including funds raided out of America's budget for the war against terrorism. That's where they came. Believe me, they didn't come from me. They came just before I came into office. Not good. And not good the way they took the money.

In 2015, the United Nation's departing top climate officials reportedly described the $100 billion per year as "peanuts" and stated that "the $100 billion is the tail that wags the dog." In 2015, the Green Climate Fund's Executive Director reportedly stated that estimated funding needed would increase to $450 billion per year after 2020. And nobody even knows where the money is going to. Nobody has been able to say, where is it going to?

Of course, the world's top polluters have no affirmative obligations under the Green Fund, which we terminated. America is $20 trillion in debt. Cash-strapped cities cannot hire enough police officers or fix vital infrastructure. Millions of our citizens are out of work. And yet, under the Paris accord, billions of dollars that ought to be invested right here in America will be sent to the very countries that have taken our factories and our jobs away from us. So think of that.

There are serious legal and constitutional issues as well. Foreign leaders in Europe, Asia, and across the world should not have more to say with respect to the U.S. economy than our own citizens and their elected representatives. Thus, our withdrawal from the agreement represents a reassertion of America's sovereignty. Our Constitution is unique among all the nations of the world, and it is my highest obligation and greatest honor to protect it. And I will.

Staying in the agreement could also pose serious obstacles for the United States as we begin the process of unlocking the restrictions on America's abundant energy reserves, which we have started very strongly. It would once have been unthinkable that an international agreement could prevent the United States from conducting its own domestic economic affairs, but this is the new reality we face if we do not leave the agreement or if we do not negotiate a far better deal.

The risks grow as historically these agreements only tend to become more and more ambitious over time. In other words, the Paris framework is a starting point—as bad as it is—not an end point. And exiting the agreement protects the United States from future intrusions on the United States sovereignty and massive future legal liability. Believe me, we have massive legal liability if we stay in.

As President, I have one obligation, and that obligation is to the American people. The Paris accord would undermine our economy, hamstring our workers, weaken our sovereignty, impose unacceptable legal risk, and put us at a permanent disadvantage to the other countries of the world. It is time to exit the Paris accord and time to pursue a new deal that protects the environment, our companies, our citizens, and our country.

It is time to put Youngstown, Ohio, Detroit, Michigan, and Pittsburgh, Pennsylvania—along with many, many other locations within our great country—before Paris, France. It is time to make America great again. Thank you. Thank you. Thank you very much.

Thank you. Thank you very much. Thank you very much. Very important. I'd like to ask Scott Pruitt, who most of you know and respect, as I do, just to say a few words.

Scott, please.

Environmental Protection Agency Administrator E. Scott Pruitt. Thank you, Mr. President. Your decision today to exit the Paris accord reflects your unflinching commitment to put America first.

And by exiting, you're fulfilling yet one more campaign promise to the American people. Please know that I am thankful for your fortitude, your courage, and your steadfastness as you serve and lead our country.

America finally has a leader who answers only to the people—not to the special interests who have had their way for way too long. In everything you do, Mr. President, you're fighting for the forgotten men and women across this country. You're a champion for the hard-working citizens all across this land who just want a Government that listens to them and represents their interest.

You have promised to put America first in all that you do, and you've done that in any number of ways, from trade, to national security, to protecting our border, to rightsizing Washington, DC. And today you've put America first with regard to international agreements and the environment.

This is an historic restoration of American economic independence—one that will benefit the working class, the working poor, and working people of all stripes. With this action, you have declared that the people are rulers of this country once again. And it should be noted that we as a Nation do it better than anyone in the world in striking the balance between growing our economy, growing jobs while also being a good steward of our environment.

We owe no apologies to other nations for our environmental stewardship. After all, before the Paris Accord was ever signed, America had reduced its CO_2 footprint to levels from the early 1990s. In fact, between the years 2000 and 2014, the United States reduced its carbon emissions by 18-plus percent. And this was accomplished not through government mandate, but accomplished through innovation and technology of the American private sector.

For that reason, Mr. President, you have corrected a view that was paramount in Paris that somehow the United States should penalize its own economy, be apologetic, lead with our chin, while the rest of world does little. Other nations talk a good game; we lead with action—not words.

Our efforts, Mr. President, as you know, should be on exporting our technology, our innovation, to nations who seek to reduce their CO2 footprint to learn from us. That should be our focus versus agreeing to unachievable targets that harm our economy and the American people.

Mr. President, it takes courage, it takes commitment to say no to the plaudits of men while doing what's right by the American people. You have that courage, and the American people can take comfort because you have their backs.

Thank you, Mr. President.

SOURCE: Executive Office of the President. "Remarks Announcing United States Withdrawal from the United Nations Framework Convention on Climate Change Paris Agreement." June 1, 2017. *Compilation of Presidential Documents* 2017, no. 00373 (June 1, 2017). https://www.gpo.gov/fdsys/pkg/DCPD-201700373/pdf/DCPD-201700373.pdf.

DOCUMENT

France, Germany, and Italy Respond to U.S. Departure from Paris Agreement

June 1, 2017

"We, the Heads of State and of Government of France, Germany and Italy, take note with regret of the decision by the United States of America to withdraw from the universal agreement on climate change.

"The Paris Agreement remains a cornerstone in the cooperation between our countries, for effectively and timely tackling climate change and for implementing the 2030 Agenda sustainable development goals.

"We deem the momentum generated in Paris in December 2015 irreversible and we firmly believe that the Paris Agreement cannot be renegotiated, since it is a vital instrument for our planet, societies and economies.

"We are convinced that the implementation of the Paris Agreement offers substantial economic opportunities for prosperity and growth in our countries and on a global scale.

"We therefore reaffirm our strongest commitment to swiftly implement the Paris Agreement, including its climate finance goals and we encourage all our partners to speed up their action to combat climate change.

"We will step up efforts to support developing countries, in particular the poorest and most vulnerable, in achieving their mitigation and adaptation goals."

SOURCE: The Federal Government of Germany. "Statement on the United States of America's Announcement to Withdraw from the Paris Agreement on Climate Change." June 1, 2017. https://www.bundesregier ung.de/Content/EN/Pressemitteilungen/BPA/2017/2017-06-01-joint-statement_en.html?nn=709674.

OTHER HISTORIC DOCUMENTS OF INTEREST

FROM PREVIOUS *HISTORIC DOCUMENTS*

Two States File Emoluments Lawsuit against President Trump

JUNE 12, 2017

As the owner of a global company with extensive business holdings, President Donald Trump faced considerable pressure to liquidate his assets or place them in a blind trust to avoid any conflicts of interest while in office. Trump's decision to retain ownership of his company prompted the attorneys general of Maryland and the District of Columbia to file a federal lawsuit against the president that alleged numerous violations of the Foreign and Domestic Emoluments Clauses of the Constitution. The suit was one of three filed in 2017 claiming Emoluments Clause violations. In each case, the U.S. Justice Department has argued that the Emoluments Clauses do not apply to the president's business transactions.

TRUMP ANNOUNCES PLAN TO AVOID CONFLICTS OF INTEREST

Trump's ownership of hundreds of businesses worldwide through his company, The Trump Organization, raised questions about potential conflicts of interest when he became president—particularly whether foreign governments would attempt to influence Trump policy through business deals or by patronizing Trump hotels, casinos, golf courses, and other businesses. Ethics experts, including the U.S. Office of Government Ethics, urged Trump to completely divest from his company or establish a blind trust for his assets to avoid such conflicts. (The creator of a blind trust does not know what the trust's holdings are or how the assets are managed.)

On January 11, 2017, Trump and lawyer Sheri Dillon announced that the president planned to retain ownership of his businesses, meaning he would still benefit from them financially, but that he would resign from oversight positions and remove himself from the businesses' day-to-day operations. Trump's various businesses were placed in a trust—but not a blind trust—that is overseen by an independent ethics officer and is managed by his two sons, as well as The Trump Organization CFO Allen Weisselberg. Additionally, The Trump Organization hired a chief compliance officer to ensure the company did not exploit the presidency for profit. Trump said he would not discuss the businesses with his sons, though he would still receive profit and loss reports, and pledged to donate all profits resulting from foreign government patronage of his hotels to the U.S. Treasury.

Dillon added that The Trump Organization would not enter into any new foreign licensing agreements, deals with foreign officials, or deals with the U.S. government while Trump was president, and that new domestic projects would be undertaken only once they had been approved by the trust's ethics officer. Dillon defended the decision not to create a blind trust, claiming it was unrealistic for a family-owned company. She also said that much of Trump's wealth was in the form of assets that could not be easily sold, such as real estate holdings, or deals that would be difficult to undo, adding that divestment would hurt Trump financially. "President-elect Trump should not be expected to destroy the company he built," she said. "This plan offers a suitable alternative to address the concerns of the American people."

Trump's plan was immediately criticized by the ethics experts and others who had called for a blind trust. Walter Schaub, Jr., director of the U.S. Office of Government Ethics, said the plan was "wholly inadequate" and "meaningless from a conflict of interest perspective." Trump countered these critics by claiming he had done more than he was required to do.

Lawsuits Allege Constitutional Violations

On June 12, the attorneys general of Maryland and the District of Columbia filed a lawsuit against Trump in the U.S. District Court for the District of Maryland, Greenbelt Division, alleging "unprecedented constitutional violations by the President that have injured and threaten to cause continuing injury to the District of Columbia and the State of Maryland and their respective residents." The lawsuit centered on claims that through his ownership of his various businesses, Trump had violated the Foreign and Domestic Emoluments Clauses of the U.S. Constitution. The Foreign Emoluments Clause prohibits any "Person holding any Office of Profit or Trust" from accepting "any present, Emolument, Office, or Title, of any kind whatever, from any King, Prince or foreign State" without Congress's consent. Similarly, the Domestic Emoluments Clause allows a president to be paid a salary while in office but otherwise prevents him from receiving "any other emolument from the United States, or any of them." The clauses are intended to prevent the corruption of government leaders.

In their filing, the attorneys general argued that Trump's continued ownership of his company "renders him deeply enmeshed with a legion of foreign and domestic government actors." The filing continued:

> "Whatever the sincerity of the persons involved, foreign and domestic officials are put in the position of considering whether offering benefits to businesses associated with the President is important to maintaining goodwill. And irrespective of whether such benefits affect the President's decision-making or shift his foreign or domestic policy, uncertainty about whether the President is acting in the best interests of the American people, or rather for his own ends or personal enrichment, inflicts lasting harm on our democracy."

The filing went on to list Trump's alleged violations of the Emoluments Clauses, which included leases of Trump properties to foreign government-owned entities; purchases of condos in Trump properties by foreign governments or foreign government-controlled entities; hotel accommodations, restaurant purchases, and the use of event venues by foreign governments and diplomats at properties owned, operated, or licensed by Trump in the United States; payments from foreign government-owned broadcasters related to "The Apprentice" television show and its spinoffs; and the General Services Administration's lease of the building that houses the Trump International Hotel in Washington, D.C. to The Trump Organization. The filing claimed that, as government entities with taxation and regulatory authority over businesses and real estate, Maryland and the District of Columbia are "harmed by perceived and/or actual pressure to grant special treatment" to Trump and his businesses "or else be placed at a disadvantage vis-à-vis other states and governments that have granted or will grant such special treatment." The two state governments further argued that they had been directly harmed by the president's violations of the Emoluments Clauses because they are also proprietors of businesses that compete with that of Trump.

The lawsuit was one of three brought against Trump by parties alleging Emoluments Clause violations. Three days after Trump took office, Citizens for Responsibility and Ethics in Washington (CREW) filed a similar lawsuit claiming that Trump was "submerged in conflicts of interest due to foreign government spending at the D.C. hotel." CREW filed an amended lawsuit on April 18, adding luxury hotel event booker Jill Phaneuf and Restaurant Opportunities Centers (ROC) United—an organization representing more than 25,000 restaurant workers and 200 restaurants—as plaintiffs. Phaneuf and ROC United claimed that Trump's businesses were unfair competition. Additionally, on June 14, 196 Democratic members of Congress filed suit alleging Foreign Emoluments Clause violations. Led by Connecticut Sen. Richard Blumenthal and Michigan Rep. John Conyers, the lawmakers asked the U.S. District Court for the District of Columbia to enjoin the president from "accepting any benefits from foreign states without first obtaining Congressional consent." The filing argued that Trump "has chosen to accept numerous benefits from foreign states without first seeking or obtaining congressional approval." The filing went on to state that by denying Congress the opportunity to give or withhold its consent, Trump had "thwarted the transparency that the 'Consent of the Congress' provision was designed to provide." Members of Congress, the filing stated, "must have the opportunity to cast a binding vote that gives or withholds their 'Consent.'" The CREW and congressional lawsuits cited Foreign Emoluments Clause violations such as China granting trademarks to The Trump Organization, Trump Tower rent paid by the Industrial & Commercial Bank of China and the Abu Dhabi Tourism & Culture Authority, and events held at the Trump International Hotel by the Kuwait Embassy and a lobbying firm representing Saudi Arabia.

TRUMP RESPONDS

Lawyers for the president denied that Trump had violated the Constitution, arguing that fair-market transactions, such as when a foreign delegation pays the market rate to stay at a hotel, are allowed by the Emoluments Clauses. Dillon made a similar argument when announcing Trump's business plan in January, stating that the Emoluments Clauses apply to gifts but not business transactions.

White House Press Secretary Sean Spicer dismissed the lawsuit filed by the Maryland and District of Columbia attorneys general, saying it was "not hard to conclude that partisan politics may be one of the motivations," and Trump declared that CREW's lawsuit was "totally without merit." The U.S. Justice Department filed motions to dismiss all three cases. Filing in response to the CREW lawsuit, federal attorneys argued that "the Emolument Clauses apply only to the receipt of compensation for personal services and to the receipt of honors and gifts based on official position. They do not prohibit any company in which the President has any financial interest from doing business with any foreign, federal, or state instrumentality." In the case of Maryland and the District of Columbia, the Justice Department filing claimed that neither government had standing to sue, nor had they demonstrated actual damages incurred because of Trump's businesses. In particular, the filing stated, "They assume that the operation of a single luxury hotel in downtown Washington, D.C., would have an extraordinarily wide-ranging impact on D.C.'s and Maryland's economies." Federal attorneys also filed a motion to dismiss the congressional lawsuit, arguing that lawmakers were attempting to circumvent the legislative process and were going through the courts because they were unable to pass legislation finding the president in violation of the Emoluments Clauses. "Plaintiffs could not convince their own colleagues in Congress to take the actions they desired, and now seek the aid of the Judiciary to circumvent the legislative process prescribed by the Constitution," they wrote.

On October 18, the U.S. District Court for the Southern District of New York held a preliminary hearing on the CREW lawsuit. Judge George Daniels ultimately dismissed the lawsuit, ruling on December 21 that the plaintiffs lacked standing and that the issue of emoluments violations should be dealt with by Congress, not the courts.

A preliminary hearing in the case of Maryland and the District of Columbia has been set for January 25, 2018. A hearing date has not yet been set for the congressional lawsuit.

—Linda Grimm

Following is an excerpt from the District of Columbia and Maryland Attorneys General lawsuit against President Donald Trump, filed June 12, 2017, in the U.S. District Court for the District of Maryland, Greenbelt Division, alleging Emoluments Clause violations.

D.C. and Maryland Sue President Trump for Emoluments Clause Violations

June 12, 2017

IN THE UNITED STATES DISTRICT COURT FOR THE DISTRICT OF MARYLAND
Greenbelt Division

THE DISTRICT OF COLUMBIA
441 Fourth Street, N.W.
Washington, D.C. 20001,

and

THE STATE OF MARYLAND
200 Saint Paul Place, 20th Floor
Baltimore, Maryland 21202,
Plaintiffs,

v.

DONALD J. TRUMP, in his official capacity as President of the United States of America
1600 Pennsylvania Avenue, N.W.
Washington, D.C. 20500,
Defendant.

[Sections I, II, and III, detailing the nature of the action, parties to the lawsuit, and legal background in the case, and all footnotes have been omitted.]

IV. RELEVANT FACTS

A. The defendant's Foreign Emoluments Clause violations

29. Following the defendant's inauguration, he continues to own and control hundreds of businesses throughout the world, including hotels and other properties. His business empire comprises a multitude of different corporations, limited-liability companies, limited partnerships, and other entities that he owns or controls, in whole or in part, operating in the United States and at least 20 foreign countries. His businesses are loosely organized under an umbrella known as the "Trump Organization," consisting of the Trump Organization LLC d/b/a The Trump Organization and The Trump Organization, Inc., both of which are owned solely by him. But his interests also include scores of other entities not directly owned by either Trump Organization entity but that he personally owns, owns through other entities, and/ or controls. The defendant also has several licensing agreements that provide continuing flows of income. Through these entities and agreements, he personally benefits from business dealings, and is (and will be) enriched by any business in which the entities he owns or controls engage with foreign governments, instrumentalities, and officials.

30. On January 11, 2017, the defendant announced a plan to turn "leadership and management" of the Trump Organization over to his sons Eric Trump and Donald Trump Jr., as well as a longtime company executive. But the plan did not include relinquishing ownership of his businesses or establishing a blind trust.

31. The defendant continues to own—and be well aware of the activities of—the Trump Organization and other corporations, limited-liability companies, limited partnerships, and other entities in which he retains an ownership interest. Although he formed a trust to hold his business assets, he may obtain distributions from his trust at any time.

32. The defendant's son, Eric Trump (who is also an advisor to the defendant's trust), initially indicated that he would not communicate with his father concerning his business interests. Eric Trump has now acknowledged, however, that he will provide business updates to the President on at least a quarterly basis.

33. The defendant has neither sought nor received "Consent of the Congress" with respect to his receipt of presents or emoluments from foreign government officials, entities, or instrumentalities.

The District of Columbia's Trump International Hotel

34. The Trump International Hotel Washington, D.C. is located on Pennsylvania Avenue, N.W., just blocks from the White House. The defendant owns and controls this hotel through various entities.

35. The defendant, through entities he owns, receives payments made to the Trump International Hotel by guests who stay in hotel rooms and patrons who use the hotel venues or other goods or services in the hotel . . .

37. Since the election, the Trump International Hotel has specifically marketed itself to the diplomatic community. On one occasion, barely a week after the election, it held an event where it pitched the hotel to about 100 foreign diplomats. The hotel also hired a "director of diplomatic sales" to facilitate business with foreign states and their diplomats and agents, luring the director away from a competing hotel in Washington.

38. In addition, the defendant has repeatedly appeared at the hotel since his election, adding further media attention to the property and raising its public profile. Several figures in his administration, including Treasury Secretary Steve Mnuchin and Small Business Administration Administrator Linda McMahon, have also lived or continue to live in the hotel . . .

40. The Embassy of Kuwait, a foreign state, held its National Day celebration at the Trump International Hotel on February 22, 2017. Upon information and belief, Kuwait paid for the venue, food, and other services provided in connection with the celebration. The cost has been estimated at $40,000 to $60,000. Before the election, a "save the date" reservation had been made with the Four Seasons hotel, where the event had previously been held. According to one report, the Embassy of Kuwait moved the event under pressure from the Trump Organization (though Kuwait's ambassador to the United States denied being pressured). As a result, the Trump International Hotel or its controlling entities have received one or more payments from Kuwait after 12:01 pm on January 20, 2017.

41. Between January 23 and 26, 2017 and during February 2017, the Kingdom of Saudi Arabia, a foreign state, spent thousands of dollars on rooms, catering, and parking at the Trump International Hotel. . . . Some of the payments were made after the defendant's inauguration as President. Upon information and belief, Saudi Arabia paid at least $250 per night for each of the rooms it rented through its agent between January 23 and 26, 2017, and paid the hotel for meals and other services provided in connection with the stay. Saudi Arabia paid for individuals to have dinner at the hotel on January 23 and both breakfast and dinner on January 24. . . . Upon information and belief, Saudi Arabia paid the hotel through its agent for similar expenses associated with a visit in mid-February. As a result, the Trump International Hotel or its controlling entities have received one or more payments from Saudi Arabia, through its agent, after 12:01 pm on January 20, 2017.

42. On or about April 6, 2017, Kaha Imnadze, the Ambassador and Permanent Representative of Georgia to the United Nations, stayed at the Trump International Hotel and then tweeted his compliments about the hotel. Upon information and belief, the government of Georgia, a foreign state, paid the hotel for his room and other services provided in connection with his stay. As a result, the Trump International Hotel or its controlling entities have received one or more payments from Georgia after 12:01 pm on January 20, 2017 . . .

46. Prior to taking office, President Trump's attorney promised that all profits earned from foreign governments would be donated to the U.S. Treasury. The Trump Organization later admitted, however, that it was not tracking all payments that it received from foreign governments, and that it plans only to estimate, rather than calculate, such payments.

New York's Trump Tower

47. Trump Tower is a mixed-use skyscraper on Fifth Avenue in New York City. Through the use of various entities, the defendant owns and controls Trump Tower and, through entities he owns, receives payments made to Trump Tower by tenants.

48. One of the largest tenants of Trump Tower is the Industrial and Commercial Bank of China ('ICBC'), which is a Chinese majority-state-owned enterprise. As such, ICBC is an instrumentality of a foreign state.

49. After 12:01 pm on January 20, 2017, Trump Tower or its controlling entities have received one or more payments from ICBC under its lease. Trump Tower or its controlling entities will continue to receive regular payments from ICBC under its lease agreement . . .

51. The term of ICBC's Trump Tower lease runs until October 2019, before the end of the defendant's term. As a result, any negotiations for a renewal or extension of the lease will occur while he is serving as President.

52. Trump Grill is a restaurant located inside Trump Tower that the defendant owns through various business entities. Upon information and belief, tenants of Trump Tower, including officials of China and other countries, have dined at Trump Grill as a result of their tenancy in the Tower and the foreign states themselves may host events there. Accordingly, foreign states or their instrumentalities likely have paid or will pay for services at Trump Grill. The defendant has and will continue to receive payments from various foreign states through Trump Grill.

New York's Trump World Tower

53. Trump World Tower is a skyscraper on United Nations Plaza in New York City, containing condominium units. Through the use of various entities, the defendant manages and controls Trump World Tower and, through entities he owns, receives payments made by residents of the Trump World Tower for common charges and handles rental transactions involving condominium units.

54. In 2001, the Kingdom of Saudi Arabia paid $4.5 million to purchase a floor of Trump World Tower. The annual common charges for building amenities for the floor totaled $85,585 at the time. As of 2003, the most recent year for which information is publicly available, the Kingdom of Saudi Arabia paid monthly common charges of about $7,398—or $88,781 per year. The floor currently belongs to the Kingdom of Saudi Arabia for use by the Saudi Mission to the United Nations, which upon information and belief continues to pay common charges to the defendant . . .

56. The Kingdom of Saudi Arabia is a foreign state, and the Saudi Mission to the United Nations is an instrumentality of a foreign state.

57. In 2002, the Permanent Mission of India to the United Nations, an instrumentality of a foreign state, paid $5.1 million to purchase two units in Trump World Tower from the defendant. As of 2003, the most recent year for which information is publicly available, the Mission paid monthly common charges of approximately $3,639—or $43,670 per year. The units continue to belong to the Mission, which upon information and belief continues to pay common charges to the defendant.

58. In 2009, the Permanent Mission of Afghanistan to the United Nations, an instrumentality of a foreign state, paid $4.235 million to purchase a unit in Trump World Tower. As of 2003, the most recent year for which information is publicly available, the common monthly charges for the unit purchased by the Mission were approximately $2,090 per month—or $25,085 per year. The unit continues to belong to the Mission, which upon information and belief continues to pay common charges to the defendant.

59. In 2002, the Permanent Mission of Qatar to the United Nations, an instrumentality of a foreign state, paid $1,995,000 to purchase a unit in Trump World Tower, and in 2012, it paid $8.375 million to purchase two additional units in Trump World Tower. As of 2003, the most recent year for which information is publicly available, the common monthly charges for the units purchased by the Mission were a total of approximately $5,660 per month—or $67,920 per year. The units continue to belong to the Mission, which upon information and belief still pays common charges to the defendant.

60. The defendant, through entities he owns, receives payments made to Trump World Tower by tenants and owners of units in the building through their payment of common charges and other fees. On information and belief, these payments include management and other fees paid to the building's management company, an entity owned by the defendant.

61. Trump World Tower or its controlling entities will continue to receive regular common charge payments from Saudi Arabia, India, Afghanistan, and Qatar, and those payments will flow to the defendant . . .

Chinese Trademarks

64. The defendant began to seek trademark protection in China for the use of his name in connection with building construction services in 2006. His application was rejected by the Trademark Office, and he subsequently lost his appeals to the Trademark Review and Adjudication Board, the Beijing Intermediate People's Court, and the Beijing High People's Court. The defendant suffered his most recent court defeat in May 2015, the month before he declared his candidacy for President.

65. Three weeks after his election, on December 2, 2016, the defendant spoke directly with Taiwanese President Tsai Ing-wen. That conversation broke longstanding protocol and suggested that the defendant might end the "One China" policy that the United States had observed for decades. The defendant further indicated before taking office that he might end the One China policy unless some benefit were received in exchange.

66. On February 9, 2017, however, the defendant spoke with Chinese President Xi Jinping and pledged to honor the One China policy. Five days later, on February 14, 2017, China reversed its prior course and gave the defendant trademark protection.

67. Chinese law prohibits awarding trademarks that are "the same as or similar to the name of leaders of national, regional, or international political organizations."

68. Even though China had denied the defendant trademark protection for more than ten years, including in a ruling from an appellate court, and despite Chinese law

barring the use of foreign leaders' names as trademarks, China reversed course and decided to grant the defendant the trademark he had sought and valued. But China did so only after he had been elected President, questioned the One China policy, was sworn in, and then re-affirmed the One China policy.

69. The trademarks have considerable value because they give the Trump Organization the sole right to profit from the Trump brand in China. China's granting of these trademarks constitutes a present or emolument provided to the defendant . . .

International Versions and Distribution of "The Apprentice" and Its Spinoffs

71. The defendant earns royalties and other payments from the distribution in other countries of the television program "The Apprentice" and its spinoffs (including "The Celebrity Apprentice" and "The New Celebrity Apprentice," for which he is still an executive producer), and also from international versions of the programs produced in other countries. In some instances, these payments originate from foreign governments or their agents or instrumentalities. For instance, the defendant is paid for a version of the program "The Apprentice" that airs in the United Kingdom, as the network that broadcasts "The Apprentice" and spinoff shows in the United Kingdom is an instrumentality of a foreign state.

72. After 12:01 pm on January 20, 2017, the defendant has received and will continue to receive payments from foreign states via their payments for "The Apprentice" or its spinoffs and international versions. Such payments constitute presents or emoluments that the defendant has accepted and will accept from a foreign state . . .

B. The Defendant's Domestic Emoluments Clause Violations

79. As alleged above, the defendant owns and controls hundreds of businesses throughout the country, including hotels and other properties. The defendant personally benefits from the business dealings of these entities and agreements associated with them, and is and will be enriched by their business with state governments or federal agencies within the scope of the Domestic Emoluments Clause.

The District of Columbia's Trump International Hotel

80. On August 5, 2013, Trump Old Post Office LLC, a business entity owned primarily by the defendant, signed a 60-year lease with the General Services Administration ("GSA")—an independent agency of the United States, whose administrator is appointed by the President—to open a hotel in the Old Post Office Building in the District of Columbia.

81. More than 76% of Trump Old Post Office LLC is owned by DJT Holdings LLC, which is in turn owned almost entirely by the Donald J. Trump Revocable Trust, of which the defendant is the sole beneficiary. The Trump International Hotel Washington, D.C. is located at this site. The defendant has not divested his interest in the lease since becoming President.

82. Section 37.19 of the Old Post Office lease states: "No... elected official of the Government of the United States . . . shall be admitted to any share or part of

this Lease, or to any benefit that may arise therefrom." A violation of Section 37.19 is a non-monetary breach and a default unless it is remedied within 30 days after notice from the GSA. Accordingly, the defendant has been in breach of the lease with the GSA since 12:01 pm on January 20, 2017, when he became President.

83. Before the defendant's inauguration, the GSA's Deputy Commissioner indicated to Representatives Elijah Cummings, Peter DeFazio, Gerald Connolly, and André Carson that the defendant would be in violation of the lease unless he "fully divests himself of all financial interests in the lease" for the Trump International Hotel, which he has not done. Shortly after the inauguration, Norman Dong, a GSA official appointed by former President Obama, became acting administrator. But less than a day later, the defendant replaced Mr. Dong with Tim Horne, who had coordinated the GSA's transition with the defendant's campaign.

84. Several weeks later, on March 16, 2017, the defendant released a proposed 2018 budget increasing GSA's funding, while cutting all (or nearly all) other non-defense-related agencies' budgets. One week after that, on March 23, the GSA issued a letter stating that—contrary to the lease's plain terms—Trump Old Post Office LLC "is in full compliance with Section 37.19 [of the lease] and, accordingly, the lease is valid and in full force and effect." A significant portion of the letter reviews the purported financial benefits of the lease to the GSA and taxpayers-even though those benefits are immaterial to the question of breach.

85. Attached to the March 23, 2017 letter was an amendment to the agreement governing the business of Trump Old Post Office LLC. This amendment is the basis of the GSA's position that the tenant is in compliance with the lease, but the letter does not explain how the amendment brings the tenant into compliance. In fact, as described above, the amendment does not prevent the defendant from receiving "any benefit" from the lease, and Trump Old Post Office LLC remains in breach of the lease . . .

87. Additionally, the defendant, through entities he owns, is seeking a $32 million historic-preservation tax credit for the Trump International Hotel. Approval of this credit is at the discretion of the National Park Service, an instrumentality of the federal government now under the defendant's authority. If approved, the tax credit would offset approximately 20% of the cost of rehabilitating the building in which the Trump International Hotel is operating.

88. On November 14, 2016, the defendant received approval from the National Park Service for the second phase of the three-step-approval process. If final approval is granted, it may constitute an emolument, in violation of the Domestic Emoluments Clause.

Mar-a-Lago Club

89. The Mar-a-Lago Club is a private club and estate located in Palm Beach, Florida . . . It is owned by the defendant directly or owned by entities that he directly controls.

90. The defendant, through entities he owns, receives payments made to the Mar-a-Lago Club by members and guests who join or visit the club, or rent space there, or pay for other goods or services at the club.

91. Membership in the Mar-a-Lago Club requires payment of an initiation fee of $200,000, plus tax, as well as $14,000 a year in annual dues. This fee was doubled following the defendant's election as President—an increase from $100,000 to $200,000. Since his election, the defendant has also attempted to capitalize on his office by advertising his private property to foreign governments and individuals.

92. The State Department and at least two U.S. Embassies—those located in the United Kingdom and Albania—have promoted the Mar-a-Lago estate and club on their respective websites by posting a 400-word blog post, originally written by Leigh Hartman for a State Department-managed website, "Share America," on April 4, 2017 . . .

97. The defendant has used his official position as President to promote his Mar-a-Lago property. He has designated Mar-a-Lago as the "Winter White House," and also refers to it as the "southern White House." Since taking office, he has visited Mar-a-Lago on at least seven occasions, and has met with a number of foreign leaders there, including Japanese Prime Minister Shinzo Abe and the President of the People's Republic of China, Xi Jinping.

98. Upon information and belief, federal, state, and local governments, or their instrumentalities, have made and will continue to make payments for the use of facilities owned or operated by the defendant for a variety of functions. The defendant will receive a portion of those payments, which constitute emoluments prohibited by the Domestic Emoluments Clause.

99. Although the exact extent of these emoluments is not currently known, examples of current or potential violations include "public pension funds in at least seven U.S. states—but not the State of Maryland or the District of Columbia—that "have invested millions of dollars in an investment fund that owns a New York hotel and pays one of President Donald Trump's companies to run it, according to a Reuters review of public records." And the defendant has received (or will likely receive) a host of other potential emoluments from federal, state, and or local governments.

C. Post-Inauguration Premium for the Defendant's Goods and Services

100. Since the defendant's inauguration as President, goods and services sold by his various Trump businesses have sold at a premium. The defendant's high office gives the Trump brand greater prominence and exposure. Moreover, these goods and services provide (or have the potential to provide) a unique benefit: access to, influence on, and the goodwill of the President of the United States. . . .

[The remainder of Section IV, as well as Sections V and VI, regarding the claims in the case, have been omitted.]

SOURCE: Office of the Maryland Attorney General. *D.C. v. Trump.* June 12, 2017. http://www.maryland attorneygeneral.gov/Pages/Emoluments/DC_v_Trump.pdf.

OTHER HISTORIC DOCUMENTS OF INTEREST

FROM THIS VOLUME

- Donald J. Trump Sworn In as 45th President of the United States, p. 33

FROM PREVIOUS *HISTORIC DOCUMENTS*

- Donald Trump Elected U.S. President, *2016*, p. 612
- President-Elect Donald Trump Forms Transition Team; Nominates Senior Administration Officials, *2016*, p. 631

UNHCR Issues Report on Global Migrants

JUNE 19, 2017

In "Global Trends: Forced Displacement in 2016," the latest installment of its annual report on displaced persons worldwide, the United Nations High Commissioner for Refugees (UNHCR) found that more than 65 million people—including a record number of refugees—had been forcibly displaced due to various political, economic, and social conflicts around the globe. A subsequent UNHCR report underscored the impact of European efforts to strengthen border controls and stem the tide of immigration, highlighting changes in migration that correlate with more restricted access to popular routes from Africa across the Mediterranean Sea.

REPORT FINDINGS

According to UNHCR's "Global Trends" report, 65.6 million people were forcibly displaced at the end of 2016 "as a result of persecution, conflict, violence, or human rights violations." More than 10 million people were newly displaced during the year, including 6.9 million who were displaced within their own countries and 3.4 million new refugees and asylum-seekers. The report noted that while the number of displaced persons only grew by about 300,000 people since 2015—suggesting a slower rate of displacement in 2016, when compared to prior year-to-year increases in the millions—the total was still a record high.

The total included 22.5 million refugees, "the highest number seen since UNHCR was founded" in 1950. The conflict in Syria continued to be the largest source of refugees—about 5.5 million—with 12 million people (65 percent of Syria's population) either internally displaced or living outside the country as refugees. However, South Sudan was found to be the fastest-growing source of displaced people, with the ongoing civil war and dire food shortages leading to an 85 percent increase in the country's refugee population in 2016. In total, 3.3 million people have fled their homes in South Sudan, including more than 1.4 million refugees. For the third consecutive year, Turkey hosted the largest number of refugees worldwide (2.9 million people), followed by Pakistan, Lebanon, Iran, Uganda, and Ethiopia. Nearly 190,000 refugees were admitted for resettlement in thirty-seven countries, with the United States hosting 96,900 of them.

UNHCR's 2016 total also included 40.3 million internally displaced people and 2.8 million asylum-seekers. After Syria, Colombia, Afghanistan, and Iraq had the largest populations of displaced people. Two million new asylum claims were filed in 2016, of which 75,000 were received from children traveling alone or separated from their parents. Germany received the most asylum applications during the year—approximately 722,000—followed by the United States, Italy, and Turkey.

"By any measure this is an unacceptable number," said UN High Commissioner for Refugees Filippo Grandi. "It speaks louder than ever to the need for solidarity and common purpose in preventing and resolving crises, and ensuring together that the world's refugees, internally displaced and asylum-seekers are properly protected and cared for while solutions are pursued."

CHANGES IN MIGRATION PATTERNS

Five months after UNHCR published its "Global Trends" report, the agency released another report detailing shifts in the patterns of migration to Europe in the third quarter of 2017. The report found that the number of migrants arriving in Italy from Libya via the Central Mediterranean Sea route had decreased steadily since July. The timing of the decrease was particularly notable because the summer months are typically the busiest for migrant travel by sea, due to more favorable weather. Although the Central Mediterranean route was still the most popular during the time period studied, the Eastern Mediterranean route, by which migrants arrive in Greece, was the primary entry point into Europe in August and September. Nearly 5,000 migrants arrived in Greece in September—the highest number in one month since March 2016. Additionally, Spain saw a 90 percent increase in the number of migrants it received, by land and sea, during the third quarter. According to the report, all three routes remained dangerous for migrants: By the end of September, nearly 2,700 refugees and migrants died at sea en route to Europe and another 55 died along land routes in Europe or at Europe's borders in 2017.

TIGHTENING ACCESS TO EUROPE

The report linked changing migration patterns in part to the increasing difficulties migrants faced when attempting to travel from Libya, one of the most popular departure points for African migrants, to Italy. News reports indicated that armed groups were preventing some migrants from leaving Libya and locking them up in detention centers. In August, the Libyan Coast Guard announced that foreign ships would be prohibited from operating in Libya's declared search and rescue zone, which it also extended into international waters, without authorization. As a result, NGOs including Médicins Sans Frontiers, Save the Children, and Sea Eye suspended their humanitarian search and rescue efforts in the area, citing concerns about threats to their safety. Such organizations' efforts had already been hampered by a "code of conduct" for NGOs running search and rescue missions that the Italian Parliament passed in July, which included bans on entering Libyan waters except in situations of grave or imminent danger, phone calls to help migrant departures, and transferring rescued migrants to other vessels, as well as a required commitment to allowing armed police onto their ships to monitor the groups' activities. Only three of the eight humanitarian groups operating in the Mediterranean agreed to these terms.

Additionally, the Italian Navy sent two ships to Libya in August to help the Libyan Coast Guard stem the flow of migrants. This followed the European Commission's July adoption of an action plan to reduce the number of migrants traveling to Italy. (Both Italy and Libya had appealed to the EU for assistance.) The plan included measures such as providing increased funding for migration management in Italy; supporting the creation of a Maritime Rescue and Coordination Centre in Libya; working with Libya to strengthen southern border controls; engaging Niger and Mali to help prevent migrants from moving toward Libya; securing readmission agreements with countries of origin and transit; and working with UNHCR and African countries to launch and fund a resettlement initiative.

"The focus of our efforts has to be on solidarity—with those fleeing war and persecution and with our Member States under the most pressure," said European Commission President Jean-Claude Juncker. "At the same time, we need to act, in support of Libya, to fight smugglers and enhance border control to reduce the number of people taking hazardous journeys to Europe."

Efforts by Italy's center-left government to reduce migrant flows came amid growing pressure from parties on the right and center-right, which accused the government of not doing enough to address the issue. Municipal elections held in June resulted in victories for anti-immigrant mayors and local councilors, with the center-right gaining control of twenty-five Italian cities, including Genoa and L'Aquila, which were previously seen as leftist strongholds. Observers questioned whether the results could be a sign of things to come in the national election set for May 2018, in which migration was expected to be a major campaign issue.

Italy's situation reflects broader trends across Europe, where anti-immigrant sentiment has fueled the growing popularity of nationalist political parties and policies. The far-right Alternative for Germany party, which strongly opposes the refugee influx and ran on an anti-immigrant platform, won more than eighty seats in that country's Parliament during the September 2017 national elections—the first time a far-right party held parliamentary seats in more than fifty years. In France, far-right National Front party leader Marine Le Pen was a strong presidential contender, advancing to the runoff against ultimate victor Emmanuel Macron. Immigration concerns also featured prominently in the Brexit referendum in the United Kingdom.

The refugee crisis has also given rise to tougher immigration policies in Europe, including a deal struck between Turkey and the European Union (EU) to stop the flood of refugees traveling from Turkey to Greece. Under the deal, the EU agreed to provide Turkey with €3 billion in humanitarian aid in exchange for Turkey increasing border controls and stopping refugees from boarding ships destined for the Greek islands. The European Commission also signed agreements with Ethiopia, Mali, Niger, Nigeria, and Senegal, under which development aid, trade, and other EU policies were tied to those countries' efforts to return migrants to their country of origin.

Such measures appear to be working. The significant growth of migration to Spain in 2016 highlighted in UNHCR's migration patterns report suggests that migrants are finding other routes to Europe while access to the Central and Eastern Mediterranean routes is further restricted. Additionally, the Italian Ministry of the Interior said that half as many migrants arrived in Italy in July 2017 than in July 2016. According to the International Organization for Migration, the migrant influx slowed even further in the fall, with only 6,000 migrants arriving in Italy in October 2017, compared to 27,000 migrants received in October 2016.

Some critics claim that Europe is simply exporting its immigration problem, or even bribing poorer countries into taking care of the issue for them. Tighter access to Europe has also created a bottleneck of refugees in Libya, where thousands of migrants are held in squalid detention centers run by militiamen and are often deprived of food, forced into labor or sexual exploitation, or subject to abuse and torture. In mid-November, CNN broadcast a report that some migrants were being sold as slaves, prompting a global outcry and protests in London, Paris, and several major African cities. The Libyan government said it is investigating these reports and would bring those responsible to justice.

UN Global Compact on Migration

In September 2016, UN member states came together to unanimously adopt the New York Declaration for Refugees and Migrants, expressing the "political will of world leaders to save lives, protect rights and share responsibility on a global scale." The declaration committed member states to protecting the human rights of refugees and migrants; ensuring that all refugee and migrant children receive an education shortly after arriving in their host country; providing support to countries that rescue, receive, or host large numbers of refugees and migrants; and finding homes for refugees identified by UNHCR as needing resettlement, among other measures. Member states agreed to work toward the development of a global compact that would improve migration governance and establish a framework for "safe, orderly and regular migration in 2018," to include a "more equitable sharing of the burden and responsibility" for hosting refugees. Initial discussions about the global compact began in April 2017.

On December 2, two days before a preparatory meeting of an intergovernmental conference on the compact was set to begin, the United States withdrew from the talks. "While we will continue to engage on a number of fronts at the United Nations, in this case, we simply cannot in good faith support a process that could undermine the sovereign right of the United States to enforce our immigration laws and secure our borders," said Secretary of State Rex Tillerson. UN Ambassador Nikki Haley added that "our decisions on immigration policies must always be made by Americans and Americans alone."

To date, the United States is the only country to have withdrawn from the talks. The preparatory meeting proceeded as planned, with more than 400 delegates from 136 member states and 16 international NGOs participating. According to the UN, intergovernmental negotiations on the substance of the compact are expected to begin in February 2018.

—Linda Grimm

Following are excerpts from a report released by the UN High Commissioner for Refugees on June 19, 2017, detailing global trends in forced displacement in 2016.

UN Releases Global Trends Report on Forcibly Displaced Persons

June 19, 2017

[All footnotes, tables, figures, maps, and infographics, and in-text references to them, have been omitted.]

Chapter 1: Introduction

MORE PEOPLE THAN EVER AFFECTED BY FORCED DISPLACEMENT

Over the past two decades, the global population of forcibly displaced people has grown substantially from 33.9 million in 1997 to 65.6 million in 2016, and it remains at a record high. Most of this increase was concentrated between 2012 and 2015, driven mainly by the Syrian conflict. But this rise also was due to other conflicts in the region such as in Iraq and Yemen, as well as in sub-Saharan Africa including Burundi, the Central African Republic, the Democratic Republic of the Congo, South Sudan, and Sudan. The increase of recent years has led to a major increase in displacement: from about 1 in 160 people a decade ago to 1 in 113 today.

Although still at a record high at the end of 2016, the growth in the number of people who have been forcibly displaced has slowed for the first time in recent years. However, large numbers of people were on the move in 2016 and affected by forced displacement, with many people newly displaced as well as large numbers of returning refugees and IDPs. During the year, 10.3 million people were newly displaced, including 3.4 million who sought protection abroad and 6.9 million people who were forced to flee but remained in their own countries. These 10.3 million new displacements equated to an average of 20 people being newly displaced every minute of every day in 2016. Still, many others returned to their countries or areas of origin to try to rebuild their lives, including 6.5 million internally displaced people (IDPs) and over 550,000 refugees.

Some countries were especially affected by forced displacement in 2016. Syrians continued to be the largest forcibly displaced population, with 12 million people at the end of 2016; that included 5.5 million refugees, 6.3 million IDPs, and nearly 185,000 asylum-seekers. Colombians were the second-largest group, with 7.7 million forcibly displaced, mostly inside their country. A total of 4.7 million Afghans were also forcibly displaced, of whom 1.8 million were IDPs and 2.9 million were refugees or asylum-seekers. Other large displaced populations at the end of 2016—those with over 2 million people displaced, either internally or as refugees or asylum-seekers—were from Iraq (4.2 million), South Sudan (3.3 million), Sudan (2.9 million), the Democratic Republic of the Congo (2.9 million), Somalia (2.6 million), Nigeria (2.5 million), Ukraine (2.1 million), and Yemen (2.1 million) . . .

While the magnitude of forced displacement generated by the conflict in Syria may have overshadowed other crises and conflicts, other emergencies also had deep consequences in 2016.

These continued to cause significant humanitarian needs, especially in the countries least able to respond to them. The war in South Sudan led to a rapid outflow of refugees and many new IDP displacements, accelerating in the second half of the year; overall, the refugee population from South Sudan grew by 85 per cent during the year.

Similarly, the refugee population from Burundi increased by 39 per cent during 2016 while the IDP population in that country quadrupled to 141,200 people. Conflict and violence also continued in Afghanistan, the Central African Republic, the Democratic Republic of the Congo, Eritrea, Iraq, Libya, Sudan, Ukraine, and Yemen, leading to new displacements and inhibiting returns.

In 2016, the South Sudanese refugee crisis was the fastest growing in the world. The large number of infants, children, and pregnant women among the South Sudanese refugees made the humanitarian response particularly challenging. South Sudan and the neighbouring countries are among the poorest and least developed countries in the world, with limited resources to deal with the needs and challenges associated with hosting displaced people.

Although most refugees remained close to home, some moved further afield, often seeking international protection in a small number of countries. In 2015 and 2016, many people risked their lives to cross the Mediterranean Sea in search of safety and protection. As a result, some countries in Europe experienced an increase in their refugee and asylum-seeker population. In Germany, this population rose to 1.3 million people by the end of 2016, while in Sweden it reached 313,300.

Around half of refugees were children in 2016. Without the protection of family or kin, unaccompanied and separated children are particularly at risk of exploitation and abuse. The number of such children who were reported as having applied for asylum reached 75,000 during the year, although this number is considered to be an underestimate.

In 2016, more refugees and IDPs returned to their countries or areas of origin than in 2015. Some half a million refugees returned to their countries of origin in 2016, the majority to Afghanistan, Somalia and Sudan, compared with 201,400 in 2015, but these numbers remained low at only 3 per cent of the overall refugee population. About 6.5 million IDPs returned to their areas of origin, representing 18 per cent of the population. However, the context in which many displaced people returned was complex, leading to concerns that many returns may not be sustainable. Resettlement provided a solution for 189,300 refugees . . .

Chapter 2: Refugees

GLOBAL REFUGEE POPULATION IS HIGHEST ON RECORD

The global refugee population stood at 22.5 million at the end of 2016, including 5.3 million Palestinian refugees under UNRWA's mandate, and is now at the highest level ever recorded. There were 17.2 million refugees under UNHCR's mandate, the focus of this report and, unless otherwise stated, all reference to refugees in this report refers to these refugees.

Overall, the refugee population under UNHCR's mandate increased by some 65 per cent over the past five years. The change in the refugee population is due mainly to refugees returning to their countries of origin and new or continuing conflicts fuelling new refugee outflows. While still growing, the rate of growth is the slowest since 2012. Over the course of 2016, the refugee population increased by 1.1 million or 7 per cent, while in 2015 this figure increased by about 1.7 million (12 per cent) and in 2014 by some 2.2 million (23 per cent).

. . . In 2016, there were about 2.3 million newly recognized refugees. The conflict in Syria dominated figures for newly recognized refugees in 2016 with 824,400 new recognitions, making this the most common country of origin.

However, crises in sub-Saharan Africa also led to significant refugee movement. There were 737,400 newly recognized refugees from South Sudan, mostly in the second half of 2016, followed by Burundi (121,700 newly recognized), Iraq (81,900), Eritrea (69,600), Afghanistan (69,500), and Nigeria (64,700). Offsetting these growth trends, there also were 552,200 refugee returns during the year, as well as approximately 189,300 people resettled and 23,000 known naturalizations of refugees.

Due mainly to the crisis in Syria, the number of refugees in Europe continued to rise. At year-end, Turkey hosted the largest number of refugees (2.9 million, mostly from Syria), while the rest of the European countries hosted 2.3 million refugees. Sub-Saharan Africa hosted a large and growing number of refugees (constituting a 16 per cent increase over 2015), due mainly to refugees from Burundi, the Central African Republic, the Democratic Republic of the Congo, Eritrea, Somalia, South Sudan, and Sudan. In sub-Saharan Africa, the vast majority of refugees remained in the immediately neighbouring countries . . .

[The remaining sections of chapter two and all of chapter three, containing additional data about refugees and discussing solutions for refugees, have been omitted.]

SOUTH SUDAN CONFLICT

Armed conflict combined with economic stagnation, disease, and food insecurity has plunged the world's newest country into a desperate situation. During 2016, more South Sudanese than ever were forced to leave their homes to survive. Conflict displaced about 3.3 million, of whom an estimated 1.9 million remained in South Sudan and 1.4 million fled as refugees to neighboring countries, altogether about 1 out of every 4 South Sudanese has been displaced. More than 99 per cent of this refugee population was hosted in neighbouring countries, with very few seeking protection farther afield.

South Sudan became independent in July 2011, following wars that claimed over 2.5 million lives. Unfortunately, fighting erupted in late 2013 in the streets of the capital, Juba. Before long, the conflict spread to the three states of Greater Upper Nile. Since then, despite numerous talks and ceasefires, hostilities have engulfed the whole country. Large scale violence broke out in Juba in July 2016, which spread across the country, including to the formerly more peaceful areas of Equatoria, and accelerated new displacements.

Major Protection Crisis

This devastating conflict has resulted in a protection crisis, both for the South Sudanese people and the 262,600 refugees living in South Sudan. It is difficult to deliver humanitarian assistance, especially for the most vulnerable groups, under these circumstances. Multiple abuses of human rights have been reported and documented, including violations of international humanitarian law. Many victims have been targeted on the basis of their ethnicity or presumed political allegiances. Incidents include targeted killings of civilians, including children, arbitrary arrests, detention, and alleged torture. There has been widespread destruction of civilian property, hospitals, and schools as well as looting and destruction of humanitarian property including attacks on UN personnel.

Brutal sexual violence has been used on all sides as a tactic of war. UNICEF estimated that 16,000 children have been recruited into armed groups, and that over half of all children have been out of school, the highest proportion in the world. A major economic crisis has developed with escalating food prices and crime.

Displacement in 2016

The IDP population in South Sudan continued to increase from 1.7 million at the beginning of 2016 to 1.9 million at the end. This increase masks the high level of movement, with the outbreak of conflict in Juba in July 2016 a watershed moment; with 752,300 returns largely before the crisis, and 865,000 new displacements throughout the year accelerated by the July crisis. Unfortunately, due to continued warfare and conflict, returning people may still be at risk of violence and further displacement.

More than 224,000 people sought refuge in Protection of Civilians (PoC) sites and many have been there since December 2013. These are IDP settlements on UN premises, often inside UN peacekeeping bases. 60 per cent of residents were children and there were also disproportionately more women, as men often remain to defend their families' livelihoods. The areas of South Sudan worst affected by internal displacement were the former states of Unity, Jonglei, Central Equatoria and Upper Nile.

Over the course of 2016, 739,900 fled South Sudan as refugees and asylum-seekers. Of them, the vast majority went to neighbouring countries, especially Uganda. This population in Uganda increased more than threefold during 2016, from 199,400 to 639,000. The

Ugandan Government provided South Sudanese refugees with plots of land for agricultural purposes and access to all public services, despite a severe shortfall in funding (UNHCR operations were only 33 per cent funded, with a gap of 186 million USD). Uganda also was the first country to apply the Comprehensive Refugee Response Framework linked to the New York Declaration for Refugees and Migrants to support the Government's progressive refugee policies and initiatives.

Other countries hosting South Sudanese refugees included Ethiopia (338,800), Sudan (297,200), Kenya (87,100), the Democratic Republic of the Congo (66,700), the Central African Republic (4,900), and Egypt (2,500).

A Young, Rural Emergency

Two-thirds of refugees from South Sudan were children under the age of 18. Children under the age of five, especially vulnerable to disease and undernutrition, represented nearly 1 in 5 refugees. Older child refugees were at risk of not having their educational needs met. Women made up 63 per cent of the refugee adult population and working age men (aged 18 to 59) were a small minority of the entire refugee population.

This refugee crisis is overwhelmingly rural in nature, with 91 per cent of refugees from South Sudan living in rural locations in countries of asylum.

Conflict Deepening

Unfortunately there was little evidence of a resolution to the conflict in 2016 and UN reports warned of looming food insecurity for 5.5 million people – almost half the total population – by mid-2017. Operational data show that forced displacement continues in 2017 with large numbers of new internal displacements and arrivals to neighbouring countries.

Despite the gravity of this desperate situation, chronic and severe underfunding has reached a point where critical life-saving help has become dangerously compromised. Transit and reception facilities are rapidly becoming overwhelmed. Significant challenges are being faced in providing refugees and IDPs with adequate food rations, health, and educational services.

Chapter 4: Internally Displaced Persons (IDPs)

MANY NEW DISPLACEMENTS AS WELL AS RETURNS OF IDPs

By the end of 2016, 40.3 million people were internally displaced due to armed conflict, generalized violence, or human rights violations. That is almost on a par with the 40.8 million reported the previous year, according to the Internal Displacement Monitoring Centre (IDMC). However, this total figure to some extent masks the enormous upheavals that continued to take place in 2016, with many large-scale new displacements as well as large numbers of people returning to their homes, often under difficult circumstances.

Since the inter-agency cluster approach was introduced in January 2006, IDP statistics have been collected jointly by UNHCR and cluster members. The total number of IDPs, including those in IDP-like situations reported by UNHCR offices also decreased, albeit to a greater extent than estimated by IDMC. (The UNHCR figure is lower than IDMC's global figure, as not all IDP populations were covered by UNHCR or cluster partners.) At the end of 2016, the IDP population reported by UNHCR offices stood at 36.6 million, compared with 37.5 million a year earlier, a decrease of 0.9 million. This number comprised reports by 29 countries where UNHCR was engaged with IDP populations during 2016, compared to 28 countries reporting the previous year. Of the 36.6 million IDPs, 13.9 million were assisted by UNHCR, compared with 13.3 million in 2015.

During 2016, 5.5 million IDPs were newly displaced by conflict and violence in their countries, according to data reported by UNHCR offices. More than 1.3 million people were newly displaced in the Democratic Republic of the Congo, followed by South Sudan (865,000), Libya (630,000), Afghanistan (623,200), Iraq (598,000), and Yemen (467,100). At the same time, 6.5 million IDPs returned to their areas of origin, and IDP numbers decreased by another 3 million as some crossed an international border and become a refugee or due to statistical adjustments . . .

[The remaining sections containing additional data about internally displaced persons have been omitted.]

Chapter 5: Asylum-Seekers

2.8 MILLION PEOPLE WAITING FOR LIFE-CHANGING DECISIONS

By the end of 2016, there were 2.8 million asylum-seekers—people who are seeking international protection but whose refugee status is yet to be determined. While this was a decrease from 2015, most of this change was due to statistical adjustments in South Africa and thus masked the underlying trend of an increasing population of asylum-seekers globally. Some 2.2 million individual applications for asylum or refugee status were submitted to States or UNHCR in 164 countries or territories in 2016, a reduction from 2015 when there were 2.4 million. Of the provisional total of 2.2 million asylum claims, an estimated 2.0 million were initial applications lodged in 'first instance' procedures. The remaining 165,900 claims were submitted at second instance, including with courts or other appellate bodies.

In many countries, UNHCR has been invited to undertake refugee status determination. UNHCR offices in those countries registered 208,100 applications, of which 8,300 were on appeal.

[The remaining sections containing additional data about asylum-seekers have been omitted.]

Chapter 6: Stateless Population

AN 'INVISIBLE PROBLEM'—HARD TO TRACK

Stateless people are not considered as nationals by any State under its law. Statelessness is sometimes referred to as an invisible problem, because stateless people often remain unseen and unheard. They may not be able to go to school, see a doctor, get a job, open a bank account, buy a house, or even get married. Stateless people frequently live in precarious situations on the margins of society, making it a challenge to measure statelessness.

Despite the increasing number of countries engaged in reporting on and enhancing the reliability of their figures, UNHCR was unable to provide comprehensive statistics on stateless people in all countries in 2016. Of the estimated 10 million stateless people around the world, only 3.2 million are captured in this report.

[The remaining paragraphs containing additional data stateless individuals have been omitted.]

Chapter 7: Other Groups or People of Concern

803,000 OTHER PEOPLE NEED UNHCR'S PROTECTION

UNHCR extends its protection or assistance activities to people considered to be 'of concern' but who do not fall into any of the other population or legal categories. In most cases, UNHCR's activities in relation to these people are based on humanitarian grounds. Examples of people helped in this way have included former refugees who were assisted to integrate locally, rejected asylum-seekers whom UNHCR deemed to be in need of humanitarian assistance, and host populations significantly impacted, directly or indirectly, by an influx of displaced people.

There were 803,100 people in this category at the end of 2016. That was a decline from previous years, with over 1 million having been in the 'other of concern' category in 2014, for instance. Of this 2016 population, 180,000 were Ugandan nationals living in refugee-hosting communities benefiting from UNHCR-assisted programmes such as education, health, water, and sanitation, so as to equip the communities to meet the challenges of the arrival of a large number of refugees.

Former refugees also were a key population receiving assistance from UNHCR. These included the 114,200 Afghan returned refugees who continued to face social, economic, and security challenges in their reintegration in Afghanistan, and the over 162,200 naturalized former Burundian refugees in Tanzania who continued to need assistance and protection while being locally integrated. In addition, 80,000 Filipino Muslims living in Sabah in Malaysia were in need of international protection and were considered of concern to UNHCR in 2016.

Forty-seven UNHCR offices reported data on other populations of other groups or populations of concern in 2016.

[The following sections containing additional demographic and location data on displaced persons, as well as the report's appendix with detailed data tables, have been omitted.]

SOURCE: UN High Commissioner for Refugees. "Global Trends: Forced Displacement in 2016." June 19, 2017. http://www.unhcr.org/5943e8a34.

OTHER HISTORIC DOCUMENTS OF INTEREST

FROM THIS VOLUME

From previous *Historic Documents*

Supreme Court Rules on Arkansas Birth Certificate Law

JUNE 26, 2017

In the two years since its historic decision in *Obergefell v. Hodges* (2015) recognizing marriage equality as a constitutional mandate, the Supreme Court has only ruled twice in cases seeking to limit the application of this landmark ruling. Both cases involved state rules determining who can be a child's legal parent, and in both the Supreme Court summarily rejected attempts to treat same-sex marriages differently from opposite-sex marriages. In one of those cases, *Pavan v. Smith*, the Supreme Court released a short, unsigned opinion, this time reversing the Arkansas Supreme Court. At issue was an Arkansas state law that generally required the name of a mother's male spouse to appear on a child's birth certificate, regardless of his biological relationship to the child. The Supreme Court summarily reversed the Arkansas Supreme Court's ruling that had barred same-sex married couples from similarly having both names appear on their children's birth certificates. The unsigned opinion of the Court reaffirmed the central *Obergefell* holding that same-sex couples are constitutionally entitled to marriage "on the same terms and conditions as opposite-sex couples."

LEGAL BACKGROUND: MARRIAGE EQUALITY AND ARKANSAS BIRTH CERTIFICATES

In 2015, the Supreme Court ruled in *Obergefell v. Hodges* that same-sex couples have the right to marry. The historic 5–4 decision, written by Justice Anthony M. Kennedy, held that the Constitution requires recognition of same-sex marriages "on the same terms as accorded to couples of the opposite sex," and it invalidated all state same-sex marriage bans across the nation. The opinion was very clear on the requirement of equal treatment for all marriages "on the same terms and conditions;" in fact, the language "terms and conditions" was repeated many times in the opinion to make clear that same-sex marriage must be treated the same as opposite-sex marriage. States cannot, Justice Kennedy wrote, deny same-sex couples "the constellation of benefits that the States have linked to marriage." He also wrote at length that one reason in favor of recognizing marriage equality was concern for the protection of children being raised by same-sex couples who "provide loving and nurturing homes to their children, whether biological or adopted."

Under the Arkansas Code, Section 20-18-401, when a married woman gives birth she is deemed to be the mother for purposes of birth registration and "the name of [her] husband shall be entered on the certificate as the father of the child." While there are limited exceptions to this rule, it applies even if the married woman conceived by means of artificial insemination by using an anonymous sperm donor, as long as her husband consented to the artificial insemination. Other parts of the law apply to adoption and provide for the sealing of the child's original birth certificate and the issuance of a new one listing the adoptive, nonbiological parents as the parents on a new birth certificate.

Two married same-sex couples living in Arkansas conceived children through anonymous sperm donation. After the births of their babies in 2015, the couples filled out the paperwork for birth certificates listing both spouses as parents. The Arkansas Department of Health refused to list both mothers as parents on the infants' birth certificates. The married couples brought suit in Arkansas state court against the director of the Arkansas Department of Health claiming that its refusal to list them on the birth certificate violated the Supreme Court's decision in *Obergefell v. Hodges*. The trial court agreed with the parents, but, on appeal, in a divided opinion, the Arkansas Supreme Court reversed that judgment. A majority of the court held that the state law "does not run afoul of *Obergefell*" because it rests on the biological relationship of a mother and father to a baby and not on the marital relationship of the spouses. Associate Judge Jo Hart argued, "It does not violate equal protection to acknowledge basic biological truths." Identifying biological parents, to the extent possible, Judge Hart added, served an "important governmental objective" for reasons such as analyzing public health trends and providing medically necessary genetic information to the children. Two justices on the court dissented, citing the rule that "a same-sex married couple is entitled to a birth certificate on the same basis as an opposite-sex married couple."

The couples appealed this ruling to the United States Supreme Court.

The Ruling in *Pavan v. Smith*

On June 26, 2017, the Supreme Court resolved *Pavan v. Smith* with a *per curiam* decision, that is, a decision of the court with no identified author; these types of decisions are usually reserved for dispositions in relatively uncomplicated cases. Here, the Court also ruled summarily, meaning that it did not allow for briefing of the issues or oral argument, but ruled based only on the record below. None of this means that the decision was unanimous, and in this case, Justice Neil M. Gorsuch wrote a brief dissent, which Justices Samuel A. Alito Jr. and Clarence Thomas joined.

The *per curiam* opinion presented the case as clear cut: Arkansas treats two similarly situated married couples differently. When a married woman in Arkansas conceives a baby though artificial insemination, the state will list the name of her spouse on the child's birth certificate, but only if she is in an opposite-sex marriage. As a result, the Court ruled, "Same-sex parents in Arkansas lack the same right as opposite-sex parents to be listed on a child's birth certificate." The opinion illustrated that it matters whose name is on a birth certificate, which it described as "a document often used for important transactions like making medical decisions for a child or enrolling a child in school." Such disparate treatment, the Court concludes, is proscribed by its ruling in *Obergefell* that a state may not "exclude same-sex couples from civil marriage on the same terms and conditions as opposite-sex couples."

The Court rejected the position advanced by the State of Arkansas that *Obergefell* did not apply because birth certificates are not a benefit of marriage, but a record of biology. In its brief to the Arkansas Supreme Court, the state had argued that its laws are generally "designed to ensure biological accuracy" and that the specific rule about artificial insemination is a "narrow departure from a biology-based regime." Arkansas argued that it has rational reasons for a biology-based birth registration system and that the two couples should have limited their challenge to the specific insemination statute rather than the general birth certificate law. The Supreme Court rejected this argument flatly: "Arkansas law makes birth certificates about more than just genetics," by requiring that a husband's name be put on the birth certificate even when the child was conceived through anonymous sperm donation and the husband "is definitely not the biological father." The opinion concludes, "Arkansas has thus chosen to make its birth certificates more than a mere marker of biological relationships: The State uses those certificates to give married parents a form of legal recognition that is not available to unmarried parents. Having made that choice, Arkansas may not, consistent with *Obergefell*, deny married same-sex couples that recognition."

In his dissent, Justice Gorsuch, the newest justice on the Court, did not directly argue against the correctness of *Obergefell*, but took the position that nothing in it spoke to the question of whether a state can establish rules to ensure "that the biological parents of a child are listed on the child's birth certificate." He emphasized the argument made by the Arkansas Court that "rational reasons exist for a biology-based birth registration regime, reasons that in no way offend *Obergefell*—like ensuring government officials can identify public health trends and helping individuals determine their biological lineage, citizenship, or susceptibility to genetic disorders." Some commentators interpreted one sentence in the dissent as a swipe at Justice Anthony M. Kennedy, who wrote the opinion in *Obergefell* and is frequently criticized for opaque decisions. "Nothing in *Obergefell* spoke (let alone clearly) to the question whether . . . the Arkansas code, or a state supreme court decision upholding it, must go," he wrote.

THE FUTURE OF SAME-SEX MARRIAGE CHALLENGES

Organizations that advocate for gay marriage were pleased with this summary reversal of the Arkansas Supreme Court. Susan Sommer, Associate Legal Director and Director of Constitutional Litigation for Lambda Legal, said, "This decisive ruling is strong medicine for states and others that think they can resist the full equality due to same-sex couples and their children, mandated as the law of the land in the Supreme Court's landmark *Obergefell* decision issued exactly two years ago today." However, despite the *Pavan v. Smith* decision's reaffirmation that same-sex marriage is entitled to the same "constellation of benefits" that states have linked to opposite-sex marriage, just a few days after the decision, a defiant Texas Supreme Court, in *Parker v. Pidgeon*, ruled unanimously to allow Houston to deny generally available spousal insurance benefits to the same-sex spouses of its employees. *Obergefell*, the Texas Court held, does not clearly require states to extend spousal benefits to same-sex couples. The case was appealed to the U.S. Supreme Court, which in December decided that it would not hear the case, thus leaving intact the lower court ruling.

The response to a majority of the challenges to *Obergefell* thus far indicate that, at least for now, a majority of the court has little interest in relitigating this historic holding that states must treat all married couples equally and grant them equal access to all the rights, benefits, and responsibilities of marriage. However, Court opinions since *Obergefell* do not resolve all outstanding issues surrounding marriage equality. In fact, on the same day it released the *Pavan v. Smith* decision, the Court agreed to hear a case involving a very different kind of challenge to *Obergefell*. The case, *Masterpiece Cakeshop v. Colorado Civil Rights Commission*, will require addressing whether a Colorado baker who refused to make a wedding cake for a same-sex couple should be exempt from state antidiscrimination law because of his First Amendment speech and religion rights.

—Melissa Feinberg

Following is the text of the Supreme Court's per curiam decision in the case of Pavan v. Smith *in which the Court ruled 6–3 on June 26, 2017, that prohibiting same-sex parents from having both of their names on their child's birth certificate violates the Due Process Clause and Equal Protection Clause of the Constitution.*

DOCUMENT   ## Pavan v. Smith

June 26, 2017

SUPREME COURT OF THE UNITED STATES

No. 16–992

Marisa N. Pavan, et al.

v.

Nathaniel Smith

On petition for writ of certiorari to the Supreme Court of Arkansas

Decided June 26, 2017

PER CURIAM.

As this Court explained in *Obergefell v. Hodges*, 576 U. S. ___ (2015), the Constitution entitles same-sex couples to civil marriage "on the same terms and conditions as opposite-sex couples." Id., at ___ (slip op., at 23). In the decision below, the Arkansas Supreme Court considered the effect of that holding on the State's rules governing the issuance of birth certificates. When a married woman gives birth in Arkansas, state law generally requires the name of the mother's male spouse to appear on the child's birth certificate—regardless of his biological relationship to the child. According to the court below, however, Arkansas need not extend that rule to similarly situated same-sex couples: The State need not, in other words, issue birth certificates including the female spouses of women who give birth in the State. Because that differential treatment infringes *Obergefell*'s commitment to provide same-sex couples "the constellation of benefits that the States have linked to marriage," id., at ___ (slip op., at 17), we reverse the state court's judgment.

The petitioners here are two married same-sex couples who conceived children through anonymous sperm donation. Leigh and Jana Jacobs were married in Iowa in 2010, and Terrah and Marisa Pavan were married in New Hampshire in 2011. Leigh and Terrah each gave birth to a child in Arkansas in 2015. When it came time to secure birth certificates for the newborns, each couple filled out paperwork listing both spouses as parents—Leigh and Jana in one case, Terrah and Marisa in the other. Both times, however, the Arkansas Department of Health issued certificates bearing only the birth mother's name.

The department's decision rested on a provision of Arkansas law, Ark. Code §20-18-401 (2014), that specifies which individuals will appear as parents on a child's state-issued birth certificate. "For the purposes of birth registration," that statute says, "the mother is deemed to be the woman who gives birth to the child." §20-18-401(e). And "[i]f the mother was married at the time of either conception or birth," the statute instructs that "the name of [her] husband shall be entered on the certificate as the father of the child." §20-18-401(f)(1). There are some limited exceptions to the latter rule—for example, another man may appear on the birth certificate if the "mother" and "husband" and "putative father" all file affidavits vouching for the putative father's paternity. Ibid. But as all parties agree, the requirement that a married woman's husband appear on her child's birth certificate applies in cases where the couple conceived by means of artificial insemination with the help of an anonymous sperm donor. See Pet. for Cert. 4; Brief in Opposition 3–4; see also Ark. Code §9-10-201(a) (2015) ("Any child born to a married woman by means of artificial insemination shall be deemed the legitimate natural child of the woman and the woman's husband if the husband consents in writing to the artificial insemination").

The Jacobses and Pavans brought this suit in Arkansas state court against the director of the Arkansas Department of Health—seeking, among other things, a declaration that the State's birth-certificate law violates the Constitution. The trial court agreed, holding that the relevant portions of §20–18–401 are inconsistent with Obergefell because they "categorically prohibi[t] every same-sex married couple . . . from enjoying the same spousal benefits which are available to every opposite-sex married couple." App. to Pet. for Cert. 59a. But a divided Arkansas Supreme Court reversed that judgment, concluding that the statute "pass[es] constitutional muster." 2016 Ark. 437, 505 S. W. 3d 169, 177. In that court's view, "the statute centers on the relationship of the biological mother and the biological father to the child, not on the marital relationship of husband and wife," and so it "does not run afoul of Obergefell." Id., at 178. Two justices dissented from that view, maintaining that under Obergefell "a same-sex married couple is entitled to a birth certificate on the same basis as an opposite-sex married couple." 505 S. W. 3d, at 184 (Brill, C. J., concurring in part and dissenting in part); accord, id., at 190 (Danielson, J., dissenting).

The Arkansas Supreme Court's decision, we conclude, denied married same-sex couples access to the "constellation of benefits that the Stat[e] ha[s] linked to marriage." Obergefell, 576 U. S., at ___ (slip op., at 17). As already explained, when a married woman in Arkansas conceives a child by means of artificial insemination, the State will—indeed, must—list the name of her male spouse on the child's birth certificate. See §20-18-401(f)(1); see also §9-10-201; supra, at 2. And yet state law, as interpreted by the court below, allows Arkansas officials in those very same circumstances to omit a married woman's female spouse from her child's birth certificate. See 505 S. W. 3d, at 177–178. As a result, same-sex parents in Arkansas lack the same right as opposite-sex parents to be listed on a child's birth certificate, a document often used for important transactions like making medical decisions for a child or enrolling a child in school. See Pet. for Cert. 5–7 (listing situations in which a parent might be required to present a child's birth certificate).

Obergefell proscribes such disparate treatment. As we explained there, a State may not "exclude same-sex couples from civil marriage on the same terms and conditions as opposite-sex couples." 576 U. S., at ___ (slip op., at 23). Indeed, in listing those terms and conditions—the "rights, benefits, and responsibilities" to which same-sex couples, no less than opposite-sex couples, must have access—we expressly identified "birth and death certifi-cates." Id., at ___ (slip op., at 17). That was no accident: Several of the plaintiffs in *Obergefell* challenged a State's refusal to recognize their same-sex spouses on their children's birth certificates. See *DeBoer v. Snyder*, 772 F. 3d 388, 398–399 (CA6 2014). In considering those challenges, we held the relevant state laws unconstitutional to the extent they treated same-sex couples differently from opposite-sex couples. See 576 U. S., at ___ (slip op., at 23). That holding applies with equal force to §20-18-401.

Echoing the court below, the State defends its birth certificate law on the ground that being named on a child's birth certificate is not a benefit that attends marriage. Instead, the State insists, a birth certificate is simply a device for recording biological parentage—regardless of whether the child's parents are married. But Arkansas law makes birth cer-tificates about more than just genetics. As already discussed, when an opposite-sex couple conceives a child by way of anonymous sperm donation—just as the petitioners did here—state law requires the placement of the birth mother's husband on the child's birth certifi-cate. See supra, at 2. And that is so even though (as the State concedes) the husband "is definitively not the biological father" in those circumstances. Brief in Opposition 4. Arkansas has thus chosen to make its birth certificates more than a mere marker of bio-logical relationships: The State uses those certificates to give married parents a form of legal recognition that is not available to unmarried parents. Having made that choice, Arkansas may not, consistent with *Obergefell*, deny married same-sex couples that recog-nition. The petition for a writ of certiorari and the pending motions for leave to file briefs as amici curiae are granted. The judgment of the Arkansas Supreme Court is reversed, and the case is remanded for further proceedings not inconsistent with this opinion.

It is so ordered.

JUSTICE GORSUCH, with whom JUSTICE THOMAS and JUSTICE ALITO join, dissenting.

Summary reversal is usually reserved for cases where "the law is settled and stable, the facts are not in dispute, and the decision below is clearly in error." *Schweiker v. Hansen*, 450 U. S. 785, 791 (1981) (Marshall, J., dissenting). Respectfully, I don't believe this case meets that standard.

To be sure, *Obergefell* addressed the question whether a State must recognize same-sex marriages. But nothing in *Obergefell* spoke (let alone clearly) to the question whether §20-18-401 of the Arkansas Code, or a state supreme court decision upholding it, must go. The statute in question establishes a set of rules designed to ensure that the biological parents of a child are listed on the child's birth certificate. Before the state supreme court, the State argued that rational reasons exist for a biology based birth registration regime, reasons that in no way offend *Obergefell*—like ensuring government officials can identify public health trends and helping individuals determine their biological lineage, citizen-ship, or susceptibility to genetic disorders. In an opinion that did not in any way seek to defy but rather earnestly engage *Obergefell*, the state supreme court agreed. And it is very hard to see what is wrong with this conclusion for, just as the state court recognized, nothing in *Obergefell* indicates that a birth registration regime based on biology, one no doubt with many analogues across the country and throughout history, offends the Constitution. To the contrary, to the extent they speak to the question at all, this Court's precedents suggest just the opposite conclusion. See, e.g., *Michael H. v. Gerald D.*, 491 U. S. 110, 124–125 (1989); *Tuan Anh Nguyen v. INS*, 533 U. S. 53, 73 (2001). Neither does anything in today's opinion purport to identify any constitutional problem with a biology based birth registration regime. So whatever else we might do with this case, summary reversal would not exactly seem the obvious course.

What, then, is at work here? If there isn't a problem with a biology based birth registration regime, perhaps the concern lies in this particular regime's exceptions. For it turns out that Arkansas's general rule of registration based on biology does admit of certain more specific exceptions. Most importantly for our purposes, the State acknowledges that §9–10–201 of the Arkansas Code controls how birth certificates are completed in cases of artificial insemination like the one before us. The State acknowledges, too, that this provision, written some time ago, indicates that the mother's husband generally shall be treated as the father—and in this way seemingly anticipates only opposite-sex marital unions.

But if the artificial insemination statute is the concern, it's still hard to see how summary reversal should follow for at least a few reasons. First, petitioners didn't actually challenge §9-10-201 in their lawsuit. Instead, petitioners sought and the trial court granted relief eliminating the State's authority under §20-18-401 to enforce a birth registration regime generally based on biology. On appeal, the state supreme court simply held that this overbroad remedy wasn't commanded by *Obergefell* or the Constitution. And, again, nothing in today's opinion for the Court identifies anything wrong, let alone clearly wrong, in that conclusion. Second, though petitioners' lawsuit didn't challenge §9-10-201, the State has repeatedly conceded that the benefits afforded nonbiological parents under §9-10-201 must be afforded equally to both same-sex and opposite-sex couples. So that in this particular case and all others of its kind, the State agrees, the female spouse of the birth mother must be listed on birth certificates too. Third, further proof still of the state of the law in Arkansas today is the fact that, when it comes to adoption (a situation not present in this case but another one in which Arkansas departs from biology based registration), the State tells us that adopting parents are eligible for placement on birth certificates without respect to sexual orientation.

Given all this, it seems far from clear what here warrants the strong medicine of summary reversal. Indeed, it is not even clear what the Court expects to happen on remand that hasn't happened already. The Court does not offer any remedial suggestion, and none leaps to mind. Perhaps the state supreme court could memorialize the State's concession on §9-10-201, even though that law wasn't fairly challenged and such a chore is hardly the usual reward for seeking faithfully to apply, not evade, this Court's mandates.

I respectfully dissent.

SOURCE: Supreme Court of the United States. *Pavan v. Smith.* 582 U.S.__ (2017). https://www.supreme court.gov/opinions/16pdf/16-992_868c.pdf.

OTHER HISTORIC DOCUMENTS OF INTEREST

FROM PREVIOUS *HISTORIC DOCUMENTS*

■ Supreme Court Legalizes Same-Sex Marriage Nationwide, *2015,* p. 309

Supreme Court Rules on Parochial Schools and Grant Money

JUNE 26, 2017

On June 26, 2017, the Supreme Court held that it was unconstitutional for the state of Missouri to categorically disqualify religious institutions from competing for a playground resurfacing grant. Trinity Lutheran Church Child Learning Center, a church-operated preschool and daycare center, sued the state after being denied the grant to rubberize their school playground surfaces. In *Trinity Lutheran Church of Columbia, Inc. v. Comer*, the Court ruled that this denial violated the church's First Amendment right to free exercise of their religion. The state may not, argued Chief Justice John Roberts, writing for the Court, deny "a qualified religious entity a public benefit solely because of its religious character." This denial was "odious to our Constitution," he concluded, "and cannot stand." The case is not as clear cut as the 7–2 vote and the short, matter-of-fact majority opinion might otherwise indicate. There were multiple opinions including a lengthy dissent written by Justice Sonia Sotomayor, as well as three concurring opinions. Moreover, the majority took the highly unusual step of denying the general constitutional implications of its own opinion by adding a footnote that explicitly limited the reach of the opinion to playground resurfacing. Only four justices agreed with this statement and it is likely that lower courts will look to the opinion for guidance on future issues involving secular aid to religious institutions. In fact, the opinion is likely to have broad implications for future church-state battles, particularly in the context of state funding for a religious organization's secular activity in areas such as school choice and voucher programs.

CHURCH REQUESTS—AND IS DENIED—STATE GRANT FUNDS

Trinity Lutheran Church of Columbia operates a licensed preschool and daycare called the Trinity Lutheran Church Child Learning Center. The Center enrolls about ninety children from age two to five and admits students of any religion. It described its mission as providing "a safe, clean, and attractive school facility in conjunction with an educational program structured to allow a child to grow spiritually, physically, socially and cognitively." Daily religious instruction is incorporated into the center's programs, and it provides a playground with the standard equipment, including slides and swings, that is open to the public during nonschool hours. The surface beneath the equipment is coarse pea gravel, which can lead to injuries when children inevitably fall. Missouri's Department of Natural Resources runs a scrap tire program that provides state grants to help both public and private schools purchase rubber playground surfaces made from recycled tires. In 2012, Trinity applied to this program for a grant to resurface its playground. Its application to the program detailed the benefits of resurfacing to include "increasing access to the playground for all children, including those with disabilities." The Missouri program scores applicants on several criteria, such as the poverty level of the population served and the applicant's plan to promote recycling. Trinity ranked fifth overall among the forty-four applicants in the 2012 program, and the state awarded fourteen grants.

Despite its high score, the state deemed Trinity categorically ineligible for a grant due to the provisions of Article 1, Section 7 of the Missouri Constitution, which states that "no money shall ever be taken from the public treasury, directly or indirectly, in aid of any church, section or denomination of religion." This kind of constitutional provision is called a "Blaine Amendment" and is included in the constitutions of thirty-eight states. Trinity sued in federal court, arguing that the failure of the Missouri-run program to approve its application violates the Free Exercise Clause of the First Amendment. The district court dismissed the case for failure to state a claim, stating that the Free Exercise clause "does not prohibit withholding an affirmative benefit on account of religion." Trinity appealed to the Eighth Circuit Court of Appeals, which affirmed the lower court. The Supreme Court then agreed to hear the case in January 2016, just before the death of Justice Antonin Scalia. It then waited more than a year to schedule oral arguments, making it one of the first cases heard with the new justice, Neil M. Gorsuch.

THE COURT RULES IN THE CHURCH'S FAVOR

Chief Justice Roberts wrote the controlling opinion in this case, joined in full by Justices Anthony M. Kennedy, Samuel A. Alito, Jr., and Elena Kagan. Justices Clarence Thomas and Gorsuch joined all the opinion except for footnote three, and Justice Stephen G. Breyer agreed with the result, but wrote his own concurring opinion. The case presented the question: whether the disqualification of the church from an otherwise neutral and secular playground resurfacing program violated the First Amendment's guarantee of free exercise of religion.

Cases involving religion can be complicated because the First Amendment has two separate clauses that concern the relationship of government to religion that can sometimes be in tension. The amendment provides, in part, "Congress shall make no law respecting an establishment of religion, or prohibiting the free exercise thereof." The Court has recognized that there is, what it refers to as "play in the joints," between what the Establishment Clause will permit and what the Free Exercise will compel. Justice Roberts' opinion reviewed earlier cases to find the basic principle "that denying a generally available benefit solely on account of religious identity imposes a penalty on the free exercise of religion that can be justified only by a state interest 'of the highest order.'" Applying that standard to the case, Justice Roberts finds discrimination against Trinity Church in the state's refusal to allow the church to compete with secular organizations for a grant "solely because it is a church." The Church must choose between being a church and receiving an otherwise generally available government benefit. This, Roberts writes, is a "penalty on the free exercise of religion that must be subjected to the 'most rigorous' scrutiny." The analysis then turns to an evaluation of the state interest underlying the discriminatory policy. Here, Roberts described the interest as "nothing more than Missouri's policy preference for skating as far as possible from religious establishment concerns." This, Roberts writes, "cannot qualify as compelling." For these reasons, the opinion concludes that, despite the seemingly minimal consequence to the state policy, resulting as it does in only "a few extra scraped knees," nevertheless, "the exclusion of Trinity Lutheran from a public benefit for which it is otherwise qualified, solely because it is a church, is odious to our Constitution."

Although this was a 7–2 decision, it did not necessarily reflect a broad consensus of the Court. The Chief Justice did not take the more sweeping position of finding that Missouri's constitutional provision, one shared by a majority of states, was unconstitutional. In fact, the majority opinion went out of its way to limit the impact of its decision with a footnote that read: "This case involves express discrimination based on religious identity with respect to playground resurfacing. We do not address religious uses of funding or other forms of discrimination." Justices Thomas and Gorsuch did not agree to this footnote, writing separately that court cases are resolved on general principles, not "ad hoc improvisations." Gorsuch wrote, "The general principles here do not permit discrimination against religious exercise—whether on the playground or anywhere else." Because the footnote only received four votes, it is not a part of the majority opinion. This adds to the uncertainty about whether future district courts will read the footnote as limiting the application of the case to "playground resurfacing," or whether the decision will be read more broadly as opening the door to more religious groups suing the government for access to funds for a wider range of purposes.

While Justices Thomas and Gorsuch wrote separately to indicate they would have ruled more broadly than the majority, Justice Breyer wrote a separate opinion to indicate that he would have ruled more narrowly. His concurring opinion reached the same result as the majority, but reflected his view that the majority decided more than the case required. He noted that earlier cases had held that the First Amendment clearly does not require cutting off church schools from such "general government services as ordinary police and fire protection." He did not see a significant difference between those government services and a program involving the improvement of school playgrounds meant to benefit the health and safety of children.

Justice Sotomayor, signifying strong disagreement with the majority, read at length from her twenty-seven-page dissent in open court, arguing that much more was at stake in this case than playground resurfacing. The majority opinion marked the first time in our nation's history, she stated, that the Court interpreted the Constitution to compel a state to provide taxpayer funds to a house of worship, a change she described as profoundly altering and weakening "this country's longstanding commitment to a separation of church and state beneficial to both." Justice Ruth Bader Ginsburg joined her dissent.

REACTION TO THE DECISION

Reaction to *Trinity Lutheran v. Comer* was mixed. Advocates for private school voucher programs had been closely watching the case and had hoped for a stronger opinion clearly dismantling state Blaine Amendments, which prevent the transfer of state funds to religious organizations and have been a major roadblock to expansion of school voucher and other educational choice programs in the states. Lily Eskelsen García, the president for the National Education Association, cheered the Supreme Court's narrower decision and released a statement saying that the country's largest teachers' union "applauded the Supreme Court's refusal to accept the invitation of voucher proponents to issue a broad ruling that could place in jeopardy the ability of states to protect their public education system by refusing to divert public school funding to private religious schools." Nevertheless, putting aside the controversial footnote, supporters of easing restrictions on religious institutions' access to government funding found much to like in the majority's reasoning. Michael Bindas, an attorney with the Institute for Justice, an advocate for private-school voucher programs, said, "The court's reasoning sends a strong signal that just as the court would not tolerate the exclusion of a church from a playground resurfacing program, it will not tolerate the exclusion of a child from a school-choice program solely because they want to use a scholarship at a religious school." Likewise, Greg Brock, executive director for the American Federation for Children, said in a statement, "We hope to see future court cases address the broader issue at hand and, hopefully, strike down these discriminatory Blaine Amendments which deny far too many families the widest array of educational options for their children."

Those in favor of a strong separation between church and state found much in the decision disheartening. For example, the Court's opinion left Rev. Barry W. Lynn, executive director of Americans United for Separation of Church and State, with questions. "Lots of churches could use an upgrade. They might have old furnaces or sagging roofs. Are taxpayers now expected to fund these improvements as well? After all, the roof might collapse and harm someone." In his view, "[t]he Founders got it right: Forcing someone to 'help' religion against his or her will is an affront to the right of conscience. Our churches will pay the consequences for this reckless decision to blow a huge hole in the wall between church and state."

—Melissa Feinberg

Following are excerpts from the Supreme Court decision in Trinity Lutheran Church of Columbia, Inc. v. Comer, *in which the Court ruled 7–2 on June 26, 2017, that it was unconstitutional for the state of Missouri to disqualify a religious institution from applying for state grant money to resurface a playground.*

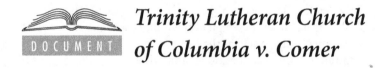

Trinity Lutheran Church of Columbia v. Comer

June 26, 2017

[Most footnotes have been omitted.]

SUPREME COURT OF THE UNITED STATES

No. 15-577

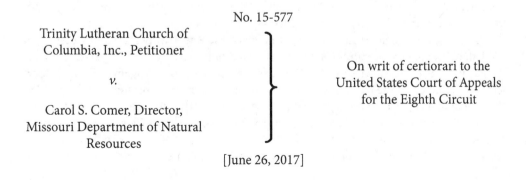

Trinity Lutheran Church of Columbia, Inc., Petitioner

v.

Carol S. Comer, Director, Missouri Department of Natural Resources

On writ of certiorari to the United States Court of Appeals for the Eighth Circuit

[June 26, 2017]

CHIEF JUSTICE ROBERTS delivered the opinion of the Court, except as to footnote 3.

The Missouri Department of Natural Resources offers state grants to help public and private schools, nonprofit daycare centers, and other nonprofit entities purchase rubber playground surfaces made from recycled tires. Trinity Lutheran Church applied for such a grant for its preschool and daycare center and would have received one, but for the fact that Trinity Lutheran is a church. The Department had a policy of categorically disqualifying churches and other religious organizations from receiving grants under its playground resurfacing program. The question presented is whether the Department's policy violated the rights of Trinity Lutheran under the Free Exercise Clause of the First Amendment.

[Sections I and II, outlining the background and facts in the case, have been omitted.]

III

A

The Department's policy expressly discriminates against otherwise eligible recipients by disqualifying them from a public benefit solely because of their religious character. If the cases just described make one thing clear, it is that such a policy imposes a penalty on the free exercise of religion that triggers the most exacting scrutiny. *Lukumi*, 508 U. S., at 546. This conclusion is unremarkable in light of our prior decisions.

Like the disqualification statute in *McDaniel*, the Department's policy puts Trinity Lutheran to a choice: It may participate in an otherwise available benefit program or remain a religious institution. Of course, Trinity Lutheran is free to continue operating as a church, just as *McDaniel* was free to continue being a minister. But that freedom comes at the cost of automatic and absolute exclusion from the benefits of a public program for which the Center is otherwise fully qualified. And when the State conditions a benefit in this way, *McDaniel* says plainly that the State has punished the free exercise of religion: "To condition the availability of benefits . . . upon [a recipient's] willingness to . . . surrender[] his religiously impelled [status] effectively penalizes the free exercise of his constitutional liberties." 435 U. S., at 626 (plurality opinion) (alterations omitted).

The Department contends that merely declining to extend funds to Trinity Lutheran does not *prohibit* the Church from engaging in any religious conduct or otherwise exercising its religious rights. In this sense, says the Department, its policy is unlike the ordinances struck down in *Lukumi*, which outlawed rituals central to Santeria. Here the Department has simply declined to allocate to Trinity Lutheran a subsidy the State had no obligation to provide in the first place. That decision does not meaningfully burden the Church's free exercise rights. And absent any such burden, the argument continues, the Department is free to heed the State's antiestablishment objection to providing funds directly to a church. Brief for Respondent 7–12, 14–16.

It is true the Department has not criminalized the way Trinity Lutheran worships or told the Church that it cannot subscribe to a certain view of the Gospel. But, as the Department itself acknowledges, the Free Exercise Clause protects against "indirect coercion or penalties on the free exercise of religion, not just outright prohibitions." *Lyng*, 485 U. S., at 450. As the Court put it more than 50 years ago, "[i]t is too late in the day to doubt that the liberties of religion and expression may be infringed by the denial of or placing of conditions upon a benefit or privilege." *Sherbert*, 374 U. S., at 404; see also *McDaniel*, 435 U. S., at 633 (Brennan, J., concurring in judgment) (The "proposition—that the law does not interfere with free exercise because it does not directly prohibit religious activity, but merely conditions eligibility for office on its abandonment—is . . . squarely rejected by precedent").

Trinity Lutheran is not claiming any entitlement to a subsidy. It instead asserts a right to participate in a government benefit program without having to disavow its religious character. The "imposition of such a condition upon even a gratuitous benefit inevitably deter[s] or discourage[s] the exercise of First Amendment rights." *Sherbert*, 374 U. S., at 405. The express discrimination against religious exercise here is not the denial of a grant, but rather the refusal to allow the Church—solely because it is a church—to compete with secular organizations for a grant. Cf. *Northeastern Fla. Chapter, Associated Gen. Contractors of America v. Jacksonville*, 508 U. S. 656, 666 (1993) ("[T]he 'injury in fact' is the inability to compete on an equal footing in the bidding process, not the loss of a contract"). Trinity Lutheran is a member of the community too, and the State's decision to exclude it for purposes of this public program must withstand the strictest scrutiny.

B

The Department attempts to get out from under the weight of our precedents by arguing that the free exercise question in this case is instead controlled by our decision in *Locke v. Davey*. It is not. In *Locke*, the State of Washington created a scholarship program to assist high achieving students with the costs of postsecondary education. The scholarships were paid out of the State's general fund, and eligibility was based on criteria such as an applicant's score on college admission tests and family income. While scholarship recipients were free to use the money at accredited religious and non-religious schools alike, they were not permitted to use the funds to pursue a devotional theology degree—one "devotional in nature or designed to induce religious faith." 540 U. S., at 716 (internal quotation marks omitted). Davey was selected for a scholarship but was denied the funds when he refused to certify that he would not use them toward a devotional degree. He sued, arguing that the State's refusal to allow its scholarship money to go toward such degrees violated his free exercise rights.

This Court disagreed. It began by explaining what was not at issue. Washington's selective funding program was not comparable to the free exercise violations found in the "*Lukumi* line of cases," including those striking down laws requiring individuals to "choose between their religious beliefs and receiving a government benefit." *Id.*, at 720–721. At the outset, then, the Court made clear that *Locke* was not like the case now before us.

Washington's restriction on the use of its scholarship funds was different. According to the Court, the State had "merely chosen not to fund a distinct category of instruction." Id., at 721. *Davey* was not denied a scholarship because of who he was; he was denied a scholarship because of what he proposed to do—use the funds to prepare for the ministry. Here there is no question that Trinity Lutheran was denied a grant simply because of what it is—a church.

The Court in *Locke* also stated that Washington's choice was in keeping with the State's antiestablishment interest in not using taxpayer funds to pay for the training of clergy; in fact, the Court could "think of few areas in which a State's antiestablishment interests come more into play." Id., at 722. The claimant in *Locke* sought funding for an "essentially religious endeavor . . . akin to a religious calling as well as an academic pursuit," and opposition to such funding "to support church leaders" lay at the historic core of the Religion

Clauses. Id., at 721–722. Here nothing of the sort can be said about a program to use recycled tires to resurface playgrounds.

Relying on *Locke*, the Department nonetheless emphasizes Missouri's similar constitutional tradition of not furnishing taxpayer money directly to churches. Brief for Respondent 15–16. But *Locke* took account of Washington's antiestablishment interest only after determining, as noted, that the scholarship program did not "require students to choose between their religious beliefs and receiving a government benefit." 540 U. S., at 720–721 (citing *McDaniel*, 435 U. S. 618). As the Court put it, Washington's scholarship program went "a long way toward including religion in its benefits." *Locke*, 540 U. S., at 724. Students in the program were free to use their scholarships at "pervasively religious schools." Ibid. Davey could use his scholarship to pursue a secular degree at one institution while studying devotional theology at another. Id., at 721, n. 4. He could also use his scholarship money to attend a religious college and take devotional theology courses there. Id., at 725. The only thing he could not do was use the scholarship to pursue a degree in that subject.

In this case, there is no dispute that Trinity Lutheran is put to the choice between being a church and receiving a government benefit. The rule is simple: No churches need apply.[1]

C

The State in this case expressly requires Trinity Lutheran to renounce its religious character in order to participate in an otherwise generally available public benefit program, for which it is fully qualified. Our cases make clear that such a condition imposes a penalty on the free exercise of religion that must be subjected to the "most rigorous" scrutiny. *Lukumi*, 508 U. S., at 546.

Under that stringent standard, only a state interest "of the highest order" can justify the Department's discriminatory policy. *McDaniel*, 435 U. S., at 628 (internal quotation marks omitted). Yet the Department offers nothing more than Missouri's policy preference for skating as far as possible from religious establishment concerns. Brief for Respondent 15–16. In the face of the clear infringement on free exercise before us, that interest cannot qualify as compelling. As we said when considering Missouri's same policy preference on a prior occasion, "the state interest asserted here—in achieving greater separation of church and State than is already ensured under the Establishment Clause of the Federal Constitution—is limited by the Free Exercise Clause." *Widmar*, 454 U. S., at 276.

The State has pursued its preferred policy to the point of expressly denying a qualified religious entity a public benefit solely because of its religious character. Under our precedents, that goes too far. The Department's policy violates the Free Exercise Clause.

***

Nearly 200 years ago, a legislator urged the Maryland Assembly to adopt a bill that would end the State's disqualification of Jews from public office:

"If, on account of my religious faith, I am subjected to disqualifications, from which others are free, . . . I cannot but consider myself a persecuted man. . . .

---

1. This case involves express discrimination based on religious identity with respect to playground resurfacing. We do not address religious uses of funding or other forms of discrimination.

An odious exclusion from any of the benefits common to the rest of my fellow-citizens, is a persecution, differing only in degree, but of a nature equally unjustifiable with that, whose instruments are chains and torture." Speech by H. M. Brackenridge, Dec. Sess. 1818, in H. Brackenridge, W. Worthington, & J. Tyson, Speeches in the House of Delegates of Maryland, 64 (1829).

The Missouri Department of Natural Resources has not subjected anyone to chains or torture on account of religion. And the result of the State's policy is nothing so dramatic as the denial of political office. The consequence is, in all likelihood, a few extra scraped knees. But the exclusion of Trinity Lutheran from a public benefit for which it is otherwise qualified, solely because it is a church, is odious to our Constitution all the same, and cannot stand.

The judgment of the United States Court of Appeals for the Eighth Circuit is reversed, and the case is remanded for further proceedings consistent with this opinion.

It is so ordered.

[The opinion of Justice Thomas, with whom Justice Gorsuch joined, concurring in part, has been omitted.]

JUSTICE GORSUCH, with whom JUSTICE THOMAS joins, concurring in part.

[Text outlining the Court's majority opinion has been omitted.]

Second and for similar reasons, I am unable to join the footnoted observation, ante, at 14, n. 3, that "[t]his case involves express discrimination based on religious identity with respect to playground resurfacing." Of course the footnote is entirely correct, but I worry that some might mistakenly read it to suggest that only "playground resurfacing" cases, or only those with some association with children's safety or health, or perhaps some other social good we find sufficiently worthy, are governed by the legal rules recounted in and faithfully applied by the Court's opinion. Such a reading would be unreasonable for our cases are "governed by general principles, rather than ad hoc improvisations." *Elk Grove Unified School Dist. v. Newdow*, 542 U. S. 1, 25 (2004) (Rehnquist, C. J., concurring in judgment). And the general principles here do not permit discrimination against religious exercise—whether on the playground or anywhere else.

JUSTICE BREYER, concurring in the judgment.

I agree with much of what the Court says and with its result. But I find relevant, and would emphasize, the particular nature of the "public benefit" here at issue. . . .

The Court stated in *Everson* that "cutting off church schools from" such "general government services as ordinary police and fire protection . . . is obviously not the purpose of the First Amendment." 330 U. S., at 17–18. Here, the State would cut Trinity Lutheran off from participation in a general program designed to secure or to improve the health and safety of children. I see no significant difference. The fact that the program at issue ultimately funds only a limited number of projects cannot itself justify a religious distinction. Nor is there any administrative or other reason to treat church schools differently. The sole reason advanced that explains the difference is faith. And it is that last-mentioned fact that calls the Free Exercise Clause into play. We need not go further. Public benefits come in many shapes and sizes. I would leave the application of the Free Exercise Clause to other kinds of public benefits for another day.

JUSTICE SOTOMAYOR, with whom JUSTICE GINSBURG joins, dissenting.

To hear the Court tell it, this is a simple case about recycling tires to resurface a playground. The stakes are higher. This case is about nothing less than the relationship between religious institutions and the civil government—that is, between church and state. The Court today profoundly changes that relationship by holding, for the first time, that the Constitution requires the government to provide public funds directly to a church. Its decision slights both our precedents and our history, and its reasoning weakens this country's longstanding commitment to a separation of church and state beneficial to both.

[Section I of the dissent, reviewing the facts in the case, has been omitted.]

II

Properly understood then, this is a case about whether Missouri can decline to fund improvements to the facilities the Church uses to practice and spread its religious views. This Court has repeatedly warned that funding of exactly this kind—payments from the government to a house of worship—would cross the line drawn by the Establishment Clause. See, e.g., *Walz v. Tax Comm'n of City of New York*, 397 U. S. 664, 675 (1970); *Rosenberger v. Rector and Visitors of Univ. of Va.*, 515 U. S. 819, 844 (1995); *Mitchell v. Helms*, 530 U. S. 793, 843–844 (2000) (O'Connor, J., concurring in judgment). So it is surprising that the Court mentions the Establishment Clause only to note the parties' agreement that it "does not prevent Missouri from including Trinity Lutheran in the Scrap Tire Program." Constitutional questions are decided by this Court, not the parties' concessions. The Establishment Clause does not allow Missouri to grant the Church's funding request because the Church uses the Learning Center, including its playground, in conjunction with its religious mission. The Court's silence on this front signals either its misunderstanding of the facts of this case or a startling departure from our precedents.

[Sections II and III, refuting the majority opinion, have been omitted.]

IV

The Religion Clauses of the First Amendment contain a promise from our government and a backstop that disables our government from breaking it. The Free Exercise Clause extends the promise. We each retain our inalienable right to "the free exercise" of religion, to choose for ourselves whether to believe and how to worship. And the Establishment Clause erects the backstop. Government cannot, through the enactment of a "law respecting an establishment of religion," start us down the path to the past, when this right was routinely abridged.

The Court today dismantles a core protection for religious freedom provided in these Clauses. It holds not just that a government may support houses of worship with taxpayer funds, but that—at least in this case and perhaps in others, see ante at 14, n. 3—it must do so whenever it decides to create a funding program. History shows that the Religion Clauses separate the public treasury from religious coffers as one measure to secure the kind of freedom of conscience that benefits both religion and government. If this separation means anything, it means that the government cannot, or at the very least need not, tax its citizens and turn that money over to houses of worship. The Court today blinds itself to the outcome this history requires and leads us instead to a place where separation of church and state is a constitutional slogan, not a constitutional commitment. I dissent.

SOURCE: Supreme Court of the United States. *Trinity Lutheran Church of Columbia, Inc. v. Comer.* 582 U.S.__ (2017). https://www.supremecourt.gov/opinions/16pdf/15-577_khlp.pdf.

OTHER HISTORIC DOCUMENTS OF INTEREST

FROM PREVIOUS *HISTORIC DOCUMENTS*

July

Qatari Diplomatic Crisis

JULY 5, 21, AND 30, 2017

On June 4, 2017, the quartet of United Arab Emirates, Egypt, and Bahrain joined Saudi Arabia in cutting diplomatic ties to Qatar. With the exception of Egypt, all are fellow members with Qatar of the Gulf Cooperation Council (GCC), which has served as a forum for coordinating regional policy since 1981. The quartet claimed that the rupture, which imposed a blockade on trade with Qatar, was a response to Qatari funding and support for terrorist groups, citing quotes attributed to the country's leaders on national websites. Qatar claimed that the quotes, which also spoke approvingly of Iran and Hamas, were planted by hackers orchestrating a disinformation campaign at the behest of the Emirati (UAE) government, possibly with Russian involvement.

ARAB SPRING, U.S. INFLUENCE LEAD TO DIPLOMATIC CRISIS

Notwithstanding recent controversies, the roots of the conflict stem from Qatar's increasing detachment from the Saudi orbit after achieving independence from the United Kingdom in 1971. Its role as a regional maverick was highlighted by its alignment with opposition figures in the aftermath of the Arab Spring of 2011 that targeted longstanding autocratic governments, including Bahrain, a client state of Saudi Arabia. Qatar's Al Jazeera television network was sympathetic to the Bahraini demonstrators, who highlighted enduring complaints of discrimination by the Sunni monarchy toward the island's majority Shia population. While Al Jazeera seldom criticizes the Qatari government, it is seen as a credible alternative source of news in neighboring countries with restricted media environments. Qatar has also been viewed as a destabilizing influence due to its perceived association with the Muslim Brotherhood, the perennial opposition force in Egypt. These issues present more likely provocations for the rupture than the quotes that were leaked on Qatari sites May 24.

Although the blockade of Qatar reflected longstanding grievances, external analysts held that the move would not have proceeded without the approval of the U.S. government. On May 20, 2017, President Donald Trump traveled to Saudi Arabia for his first foreign excursion as president, where he received the full honors of a state visit. When the rupture was announced in June, he appeared to offer his approval on Twitter, countering his own State Department's attempts to deescalate the conflict. The president also seemed to credit himself with influencing the decision: "During my recent trip to the Middle East I stated that there can no longer be funding of Radical Ideology. Leaders pointed to Qatar—look!" His statement obscured the role that other states have had in exporting fundamentalist ideologies, as well as Saudi Arabia and Qatar's shared allegiance to the Salafist tradition of Sunni Islam, also known as Wahhabism.

External observers also noted that the president's son-in-law, Jared Kushner, had advised the president to side with Saudi Arabia after his family's real estate business,

Kushner Companies, failed to secure a $500 million loan from Sheikh Hamad bin Jassim al Thani, a former prime minister and member of the Qatari royal family. In contrast, Saudi investors have supported Trump investments since the 1980s. In May, Saudi Arabia also announced that it would contribute $20 billion to a national infrastructure fund managed by the Blackstone Group, an organization cofounded by Stephen Schwarzman, who led the president's business council.

While support for the Saudi line on Qatar reflected the president's ties to the kingdom, U.S. policymakers voiced concern that his acceptance of the blockade could embolden Saudi Arabia and its allies to press for more dramatic concessions from Qatar, delaying a resolution of the crisis. This proved to be the case. Following a period of mediation by Kuwait, the quartet delivered a list of thirteen objectives in June 2017, which demanded a reversal of recent Qatari policy toward its neighbors within ten days. These included the suspension of the Al Jazeera news network, reduced military cooperation with Turkey, and withdrawal from full diplomatic relations with Iran. The conditions would have been subject to monthly, quarterly, and annual external checks over a period of ten years, but were rejected by Qatar.

Diplomats fear that the impasse could prompt Qatar to reconsider its role as moderating maverick in favor of deeper alliances with Turkey and Iran, Saudi Arabia's rivals for influence in the Gulf. In recent years, America has aimed for a balance of Sunni powers unified in their opposition to Iranian influence. Moreover, Qatar has been seen as a crucial ally. It paid more than $1 billion to help construct the al-Udeid Air Base near its capital, from which the U.S. Central Command has launched operations in Syria, Iraq, and Afghanistan.

The Saudi-led Quartet Defends the Blockade

The development of the diplomatic crisis illustrated risk tolerance and skepticism toward the status quo in both the United States and Saudi administrations following the promotion of the hawkish Mohammed bin Salman as Saudi crown prince in 2015. In 2017, conservative governments in the Gulf calculated that Qatar could be compelled to give up its media operations in the face of an air and land blockade.

In a six-point statement, issued from Cairo on July 5, 2017, the Saudi-led quartet highlighted uncensored expression as their core concern, arguing that it fomented terrorism. The phrase "all forms" was repeated in three of the six points, to encompass any coverage or activity that could encourage extremism indirectly or threaten the government legitimacy within targeted audiences. This inclusive language also alluded to aforementioned arguments that Qatar's soft power initiatives, particularly funding Al Jazeera, were an affront to its neighbors and a threat to their internal stability, as was its support for the Muslim Brotherhood; both of these were obliquely referred to in the fifth point.

The statement closed with a power play, thanking Trump for his "decisive position . . . on the need for an immediate end to the support and elimination of extremism and terrorism and the intolerability of any violations by any party in this regard." In this, the quartet seemed to be informing both Qatar and uninvolved parties that they had greater leverage in the situation due to support from the U.S. president, if not the entire U.S. government, and that resolving the conflict would depend on recognition of their interests.

Qatari Response

On July 21, 2017, the Emir of Qatar, Tamim bin Hamad al Thani, addressed his country-men as the personification of their nation during a "rally the flag" moment in the emirate's history. However, the emir was also focused on international observers and presented Qatar as a beleaguered, but flexible country. Countering his detractors, he criticized attempts to "impose capitulation" on the country and cited the Qatar's record of coop-eration with anti-terror efforts. In separate speeches to foreign audiences through 2017, Qatar's foreign ministry suggested that autocracy modeled on Saudi rule, not contrarian media, was driving radicalization and terrorism.

Turning to the immediate crisis, the emir emphasized that while the whole country had faced the inconvenience of the blockade together, they had also coalesced around an identity as a freethinking and resilient people who implicitly discounted disinformation by hackers and rejected Islamic extremism. The emir argued that diplomacy, not isolation, should be used to resolve conflicts.

More important for government credibility, al Thani affirmed that supplies of staple goods and services were being maintained in the face of the blockade. This was initially facilitated by shipments from Turkey and Iran. By late 2017, relief supplies included air-planes full of cows from the United States, which were destined for a massive climate-controlled indoor farm aimed at bolstering Qatar's dairy supplies and food security. Additional bids for economic diversification were expected as the crisis wore on into 2018, pushing up prices in wealthy emirate.

While the quartet's initial statement had closed with a nod to U.S. influence, the emir's speech concluded with an affirmation of all parties' shared Islamic identity, and Qatari support for the Palestinian people, rather than Hamas, a militant Palestinian group. Earlier quotes attributed to the Qatari government on national sites had praised the group, which is listed as a terrorist organization by several countries.

The Quartet Stands Firm

Discussions within the quartet continued as Qatari concessions failed to materialize. After a meeting in Manama on July 30, the four countries reiterated their call for Qatar to engage based on the six points of their initial statement and the thirteen points sent as a corollary following Kuwaiti mediation. This statement, like the first, implied that perceived interference in the affairs of other states was a greater offense than inspiring terrorism and that reconciliation depended on Qatar dismantling its media empire and related tools for soft power influence. Dovetailing with Qatar's pious sign-off on July 21, the quartet closed by raising concern that Qatar had blocked its nationals from perform-ing the Hajj pilgrimage in Saudi Arabia and affirmed that Qatari pilgrims were welcome in the kingdom.

An enduring stalemate appeared increasingly likely in 2018, with the quartet and Qatar respectively claiming geopolitical and moral advantage in the conflict. If the Russians had indeed interfered by aiding Emirati attempts to hack the Qatari government, their efforts rewarded them with a frozen conflict within the usual roster of U.S. allies in the region. This also benefited Russian allies in Syria and Iran. In addition to complicating American interests in the region, the rift between the Qataris and the Saudi axis could undermine the kingdom's influence in the long term, granting Turkey and Iran greater sway with a previously unaligned country in the Gulf. On a more prosaic level, the impasse may force the Qataris to focus their policies on practical concerns, with soft power campaigns back-burnered in favor of troubleshooting supply risks, route access, and economic diversification. If the blockade results in Qatar's retreat from regional affairs, the Saudis may still get what they wanted after all.

—Anastazia Clouting

Following is the text of two statements by the foreign ministers of Saudi Arabia, Egypt, the United Arab Emirates, and Bahrain, on July 5 and July 30, 2017, regarding the diplomatic crisis with Qatar; and the text of a tweet from the government of Qatar regarding the ongoing diplomatic crisis, on July 21, 2017.

Foreign Ministers Discuss Qatari Diplomatic Crisis

July 5, 2017

The foreign ministers of the four Arab countries, Saudi Arabia, Egypt, the United Arab Emirates and Bahrain issued a joint statement following their meeting in Cairo today on the Qatari crisis.

Following is the text of the statement read by the Egyptian Foreign Minister Sameh Shukri:

"The Ministers of Foreign Affairs of Egypt, Kingdom of Saudi Arabia, United Arab Emirates and Kingdom of Bahrain met in Cairo on Wednesday, the 5th of July 2017 to consult on the ongoing efforts to stop the State of Qatar's support for extremism and terrorism and its interference in the internal affairs of Arab countries and the threats against Arab national security and international peace and security due to Qatar's policies.

"It was stressed that the position of the four countries is based on the importance of adherence to international conventions, charters and resolutions as well as the principles stipulated in the charters of the United Nations, the Arab League and the Organization of Islamic Cooperation in addition to the conventions on combating international terrorism with emphasis on the following principles:

Commitment to combat extremism and terrorism in all its forms and to prevent their financing or the provision of safe havens.

Prohibiting all acts of incitement and all forms of expression which spread, incite, promote or justify hatred and violence.

Full commitment to Riyadh Agreement 2013 and the supplementary agreement and its executive mechanism for 2014 within the framework of the Gulf Cooperation Council (GCC) for Arab States.

Commitment to all the outcomes of the Arab-Islamic-US Summit held in Riyadh in May 2017.

Refrain from interfering in the internal affairs of States and from supporting illegal entities.

The responsibility of all States of international community to confront all forms of extremism and terrorism as a threat to international peace and security.

"The four countries affirmed that supporting extremism, terrorism and interfering in the internal affairs of the Arab countries is a matter that cannot be tolerated or procrastinated and that the list of demands made to the State of Qatar came within the framework of ensuring adherence to the six principles outlined above, protecting Arab national security, maintaining international peace and security, combating extremism and terrorism and providing appropriate circumstances to reach a political settlement of the region's crises where it is no longer possible to tolerate the destructive role being played by the State of Qatar.

"The four Arab countries stressed that the measures taken and sustained by them are the result of the violation by the State of Qatar of its obligations and commitments under international law and its continued interference in the affairs of the Arab States and its support for extremism and terrorism and the consequent threats to the security of the region.

"The four countries expressed their thanks and appreciation to Sheikh Sabah Al-Ahmad Al-Sabah, Emir of the State of Kuwait, for his efforts and endeavor to resolve the crisis with the State of Qatar and expressed sorrow over negligence, lack of seriousness and the negative response received by the State of Qatar to deal with the roots of the problem and not ready to reconsider its policies and practices, reflecting a lack of understanding of the gravity of the situation,"

"The four countries stressed their keenness on the importance of the relationship between the Arab peoples and the deep appreciation to the Qatari people, expressing the hope that wisdom would prevail and the State of Qatar may make the right decision.

"The four countries stressed that the time has come for the international community to shoulder its responsibility to put an end to the support of extremism and terrorism and that there is no room for any entity or party involved in practicing, supporting or financing of extremism and terrorism in the international community or to be as a partner in the efforts of peaceful settlement of political crises in the region,

"In this context, the four countries expressed their appreciation for the decisive position adopted by President Donald Trump of the United States of America on the need for an immediate end to the support and elimination of extremism and terrorism and the intolerability of any violations by any party in this regard."

The ministers agreed to follow up the situation and hold their next meeting in Manama.

SOURCE: Royal Embassy of Saudi Arabia in Washington, D.C. "Joint Statement by the Foreign Ministers of Saudi Arabia, Egypt, the United Arab Emirates, and Bahrain." July 5, 2017. https://www.saudiembassy.net/statements/joint-statement-foreign-ministers-saudi-arabia-egypt-united-arab-emirates-and-bahrain.

Qatar Tweets about Emir's Speech on Ongoing Diplomatic Crisis

July 21, 2017

Key points of His Highness The Emir of the State of Qatar's speech

1. The spirit of solidarity, harmony and defiance that had prevailed in the people of Qatar frustrated the hopes of those who banked on the opposite.

2. All those who live in this country have become spokespersons for Qatar.

3. The people have seen through the heavy curtain of concoctions and incitement, to impose capitulation on this country. People do not believe the lies of those who do not respect their minds.

4. Arab and non-Arab countries that have a respected public opinion stood with us, or at least did not stand with the siege.

5. Qatar does not try to impose its opinion on anyone.

6. Since childhood, our children have learned that lying and slander are two of the worst vices.

7. Qatar is fighting terrorism relentlessly and without compromises, and the international community recognizes this.

8. Differences are resolved through dialogue and negotiation and we should not burden civilians with political differences.

9. This crisis has driven Qatari society not only to explore its human values but also to draw on its sources of strength that lie in its unity, will and determination.

10. The government with its various ministries and state institutions, efficiently dealt with the crisis to cater for all the needs of the population.

11. We are opening our economy to initiatives, investments, production of food, medicine and ultimately to diversify our sources of income.

12. We are not afraid of identifying and correcting our error. This crisis has helped us identify and overcome the shortcomings and obstacles in determining Qatar's national, political, economic and independent identity.

13. We are all passing through this test with honor and dignity, we need diligence, creativity, independent thinking and self-reliance for the future.

14. We are open to dialogue to find solutions to lingering problems, within the framework of respect for the sovereignty and will of each State as mutual undertakings and joint commitments binding all.

15. Qatar stands in solidarity with the Palestinian people, especially people in Al Quds (Jerusalem) and condemns of the closure of the Al-Aqsa Mosque.

SOURCE: Qatar Government Communications Office Twitter Account (@saifaalthani). July 21, 2017. https://twitter.com/saifaalthani/status/888486539126243329/photo/1?ref_src=twsrc%5Etfw&ref_url=http%3A%2F%2Fwww.aljazeera.com%2Fnews%2F2017%2F07%2Fsheikh-tamim-talks-respect-qatar-sovereignty-170721184815998.html.

Foreign Ministers of UAE, Saudi Arabia, Bahrain, and Egypt Issue Statement on Qatar

July 30, 2017

The foreign ministers of the United Arab Emirates, Kingdom of Saudi Arabia, Kingdom of Bahrain and the Arab Republic of Egypt issued the following statement after their joint meeting in Manama Sunday:

-The foreign ministers of the United Arab Emirates, Kingdom of Saudi Arabia, Kingdom of Bahrain and the Arab Republic of Egypt met on July 30th 2017 as part of their continuing consultations on the Qatari crisis and the necessity of Doha stopping its support and funding of terrorism; sheltering and providing safe havens for fugitives and defects convicted of terrorism and its financing in their countries; promoting hatred rhetoric and incitement; and meddling in the internal affairs of the region's countries.

-The ministers praised the efforts made by the King of Bahrain Sheikh Hamad bin Isa Al Khalifa and his warm welcome and hospitality, expressing gratitude at getting informed of his wise vision to ensure common Arab interests and continuation of solidarity between the four countries vis-a-vis all the challenges besetting them.

-The ministers reviewed the latest developments of the Qatari crisis and the communications they conducted over the past period at the regional and international levels, affirming their continued coordination to put an end to terrorism and maintain regional and international peace and security.

-The four nations have underscored the importance of the six guiding principles declared at the Cairo meeting as representing international consensus toward combatting terrorism and extremism, uprooting its funding, and rejecting interference in the internal affairs of other countries, which are all acts that fly in the face of all international laws and conventions, underlining in this regard the importance of enforcing the Riyadh Agreements in 2013 and 2014 which have not been honoured by the State of Qatar.

-The four nations underline the importance of Qatar meeting the 13 anti-terror demands listed by them before in order to achieve security regionally and globally.

-The four nations expressed readiness for dialogue with Qatar with the condition that it declares its sincere willingness to stop funding terrorism and extremism and its commitment to not interfere in other countries' foreign affairs and respond to the 13 demands.

-The four countries stress that all the measures taken against Qatar align with their sovereignty and international law.

-The four states commended the role played by the Emir of the State of Kuwait Sheikh Jaber Al-Ahmad Al-Sabah to resolve the Qatari crisis within an Arab framework.

-The four countries denounced Qatar's measures regarding blocking its nationals from performing Haj this year, lauding the consistent services provided by the Custodian of the Two Holy Mosques to welcome all pilgrims and streamline their religious rituals.

The four ministers agreed to continue consultations and coordination on the issue during their next meetings.

H.H. Sheikh Abdullah bin Zayed Al Nahyan, Minister of Foreign Affairs and International Cooperation represented the UAE during the meeting.

SOURCE: United Arab Emirates Ministry of Foreign Affairs & International Cooperation. "Statement by Foreign Ministers of UAE, Saudi Arabia, Bahrain, Egypt on Qatar." July 30, 2017. https://www.mofa.gov .ae/EN/TheMinistry/TheForeignMinisterWebsite/Pages/30-07-2017-UAE-Qatar.aspx.

OTHER HISTORIC DOCUMENTS OF INTEREST

FROM PREVIOUS *HISTORIC DOCUMENTS*

- Arab Spring: Violent Crackdown on Protesters in Bahrain, *2011*, p. 114

President Trump, Prime Minister Abadi Remark on Liberation of Mosul

JULY 10, 2017

Following a nearly nine-month battle, on July 10, 2017, the Iraqi prime minister declared the city of Mosul liberated from the Islamic State of Iraq and the Levant (ISIL), alternately known as the Islamic State, the Islamic State of Iraq and Syria, and Daesh. The Battle of Mosul resulted in the destruction of infrastructure, deaths of civilians, and hundreds of thousands fleeing their homes, and the Iraqi government struggled throughout 2017 to ensure their safe return and rebuild the city. While the liberation of Mosul marked a major victory for Iraqi Security Forces and the U.S.-led coalition against ISIL, military leaders and government officials cautioned that the terrorist group, while weakened, may try to re-infiltrate the city, requiring security measures to be put in place and leadership better solidified.

THE BATTLE FOR MOSUL BEGINS

Mosul fell into ISIL control in June 2014, and efforts to retake the city through early 2016 were unsuccessful. However, with increased support from U.S.-led coalition troops to provide counterintelligence and logistical support to the Iraqi Security Forces, in addition to much-needed airstrikes, in October 2016 the Battle of Mosul began on the city's eastern outskirts. Iraqi government troops, Kurdish Peshmerga forces, Turkish-backed Sunni fighters, and Shia militia groups were on the ground while coalition forces provided air support.

The forces experienced early successes, liberating dozens of towns and villages on Mosul's border within a couple weeks of the start of the operation. But when troops officially entered Mosul on November 1, they met heavy resistance from ISIL fighters. Troops were forced to move slowly from east to west through the city and had to clear each building on foot due to the difficulty in moving heavy-duty vehicles through tightly packed streets. By December, the Iraqi and coalition forces had only taken control of an estimated 25 percent of the city.

In mid-January, the Iraqi-led effort experienced a major success with the retaking of Mosul University, which coincided with Iraqi troops reaching the Tigris River that bisects Mosul, signaling that they had secured a majority of the eastern half of the city. Military commanders were cautious about the victories, however, because ISIL continued to infiltrate some of the smaller towns and villages in eastern Mosul, and Iraqi security forces were continuously weakened as troops were left behind to provide security in liberated areas and to ward off any ongoing threat from the terrorist group.

IRAQI TROOPS RECLAIM MOSUL'S OLD CITY, DECLARE VICTORY

The military effort to claim the more densely populated western half of the city began on February 18. In anticipation of the assault, ISIL rendered useless the city's airport by carving deep trenches in the runways, preventing coalition forces from using the facility. Air support, which had been relied on heavily during the taking of the eastern portion of the city, also struggled in the west because ISIL fighters had built tunnels throughout the city that allowed them to move undetected. Despite dropping leaflets ahead of the invasion, Iraqi troops also contended with providing secure passage for fleeing civilians each time they moved into a new area of the city. ISIL frequently shot or kidnapped those attempting to escape and used them as human shields.

It was not until early June when the joint forces surrounded and moved into Mosul's Old City, the last territory held by ISIL. Gen. Abdel Ghani al-Asadi, head of the Iraqi special forces, said he expected ISIL to put up a "vicious and tough fight" to maintain their ground, and he promised to be cautious of the estimated 100,000 civilians thought to be trapped in the city. The Iraqi army estimated that 300 ISIL fighters remained in the area, a sharp decrease from the 6,000 fighting for control of Mosul in October 2016. On June 21, one of ISIL's last actions before its fall in Mosul was to bomb the 800-year-old al-Nuri mosque, the site where it had declared its caliphate in June 2014.

On July 10, 2017, Iraqi Prime Minister Haider al-Abadi declared victory in the operation against ISIL in Mosul. "From here, from the heart of the liberated and free Mosul, by the sacrifices of the Iraqis from all the provinces, we declare the great victory for all of Iraq and Iraqis," Abadi said. Lt. Gen. Stephen Townsend, who led the coalition effort against ISIL in Iraq, said the coalition was "proud to stand side-by-side with our Iraqi partners as they celebrate their hard-fought victory." However, Townsend cautioned that "this victory does not mark the end of this evil ideology and the global threat of ISIS. Now it is time for all Iraqis to unite to ensure ISIS is defeated across the rest of Iraq and that the conditions that led to the rise of ISIS in Iraq are not allowed to return again." President Donald Trump agreed that the United States and its partners would "continue to seek the total destruction of ISIS," noting that the liberation of Mosul indicated "its days in Iraq and Syria are numbered."

REBUILDING MOSUL

The Iraqi government will face a multitude of challenges as it rebuilds Mosul. The United Nations estimates that upwards of 5,000 buildings were damaged and 490 destroyed in just the Old City, a densely packed area of Mosul, which may cost more than $1 billion dollars to rebuild. Throughout the rest of the city, infrastructure, including the airport and the bridges connecting eastern and western Mosul over the Tigris River, were destroyed. Hundreds of thousands of the city's former 2.5 million residents were displaced by the fighting, and many attempted to return to the city after it was liberated. The government will also be seeking methods to ensure ISIL fighters do not return to Mosul, as has occurred in many other villages across Iraq that were once declared liberated. This will include working with local leaders and militias to ensure ISIL does not gain a foothold in the city again. The U.S.-led coalition fighting ISIL will be an instrumental part of ensuring ongoing security. "Under Iraqi leadership, the United States and our Coalition partners will continue to work closely with the UN to stabilize liberated areas throughout Mosul, supporting the return of displaced civilians to their homes," said Secretary of State Rex Tillerson. He added, "There is still much work to be done to defeat this enemy. The Global Coalition will continue to stand with our Iraqi partners to ensure that ISIS is defeated wherever it remains in Iraq."

The central Iraqi government also faces a challenge in determining who leads Mosul. Residents of the city, who are primarily Sunni, have long believed that they are left out of the political process dominated by Shias. "We need to start a new page where the Sunnis will be real participants," said Intisar al-Jabbouri, a member of the Iraqi parliament who represents Mosul, adding that her constituents "need to be seen as equal citizens of Iraq and not as second-degree citizens." This will include Abadi and his Shia government choosing governors for the area that represent Sunni interests as well as providing necessary funds for reconstruction, a process that failed to make much headway in 2017. According to the United Nations, by late 2017, thousands of civilians returned to their homes, but recovery in east and west Mosul was vastly different. While those in the eastern portion of the city had reestablished businesses and children returned to school, much of western Mosul, and specifically the Old City, still lay in ruins.

—Heather Kerrigan

Following is the text of a statement by President Donald Trump on July 10, 2017, regarding the liberation of Mosul by Iraqi Security Forces; and the text of a press release from the office of Iraqi Prime Minister Haider al-Abadi, also on July 10, 2017, on the liberation of Mosul.

President Trump Responds to Liberation of Mosul

July 10, 2017

Today, Iraqi Security Forces, supported by the United States and the Global Coalition, liberated the city of Mosul from its long nightmare under the rule of ISIS. We congratulate Prime Minister Haider al-Abadi, the Iraqi Security Forces, and all Iraqis for their victory over terrorists who are the enemies of all civilized people.

We mourn the thousands of Iraqis brutally killed by ISIS and the millions of Iraqis who suffered at the hands of ISIS. We grieve with the Iraqi people for the loss of the heroic soldiers and Peshmerga who gave their lives to restore life to their country, and we honor their sacrifice. We in the United States and the Global Coalition are proud to stand with the Iraqi Security Forces and all those who made this moment of liberation possible.

We have made tremendous progress against ISIS—more in the past 6 months than in the years since ISIS became a major threat. The victory in Mosul, a city where ISIS once proclaimed its so-called "caliphate," signals that its days in Iraq and Syria are numbered. We will continue to seek the total destruction of ISIS.

SOURCE: Executive Office of the President. "Statement on the Liberation of Mosul, Iraq, from the Control of the Islamic State of Iraq and Syria Terrorist Organization." July 10, 2017. *Compilation of Presidential Documents* 2017, no. 00464 (July 10, 2017). https://www.gpo.gov/fdsys/pkg/DCPD-201700464/pdf/DCPD-201700464.pdf.

Iraqi Prime Minister Celebrates Victory in Mosul

July 10, 2017

H.E. Supreme Commander of the armed forces Dr. Haider Al-Abadi declared today, Monday July-10-2017 a decree from here from Old Mosul we announced the Iraqi Great Victory

His Excellency said: From here, from the heart of liberated Mosul, we declare victory to all Iraq and Iraqis, Dear Iraqi fighters, brave fighters, in our unity and our united line, we fought the Daesh, and we were able, through your efforts, sacrifices and blood, to foiled all plans to divide the Iraqis. Today Iraq is more unified than it was,

Our victory today is a victory over brutality and terrorism, and it was announced here from Mosul to the whole world, the end and the failure of the fake state, proclaimed three years ago, and we were able to achieve victory over that state, to the dustbin of history.

Heroes, martyrs and wounded will be in our hearts and minds, we will never forget this favor ever, and grand a tribute to their families,

And we do not forget to congratulate the wise marjieia, his reverend Al-Sistani and the historical jihadist fatwas, and heroes of all victorious forces,

Dear Iraqis, this victory is for you. These operations were planned and accomplished by Iraqis. The Iraqis did not share by the others. The Iraqis fought on the ground.

And they have the right to be proud in front of our people, the world, no fighter fought only Iraqis, and we did not make anyone but the Iraqis, and we thank all the countries that stood with Iraq against Daesh by providing training and logistical support and air support for our fighters on the ground.

We have the task of building and stability, and that needs unity, and as we united in the fighting against Daesh, we must be united for the stability and return of IDPs, and the victory only from God Almighty, the wise Iraq lived victorious.

SOURCE: Prime Minister of Iraq Media Office. "H.E. Supreme Commander of the Armed Forces Dr. Haider Al-Abadi: From Here from Old Mosul We Announced the Iraqi Great Victory." July 10, 2017. http://www.pmo.iq/pme/press2017en/10-7-2017i en.htm.

OTHER HISTORIC DOCUMENTS OF INTEREST

FROM PREVIOUS HISTORIC DOCUMENTS

Controversial Court Reforms in Poland

JULY 24 AND 31, AND DECEMBER 20, 2017

Throughout his campaign for president of Poland, Andrzej Duda promised that, if elected, he would implement what he viewed as much-needed reforms of the Polish judiciary system. According to Duda and his supporters, the current system was inefficient, leaving cases languishing for years before trial, and was also set up in such a way that gave most of the power to Poland's elites. Duda's rhetoric resonated with the portion of the Polish public that believed its leaders were often corrupt and ignored the interests of Poland's middle and lower classes. As president, Duda unexpectedly vetoed proposed court reform measures in July 2017. However, by December he had reached an agreement with parliament over what reforms should be put in place and signed into law two bills that would make drastic changes to the current judicial system and that would place an increasing amount of oversight power with the president and legislature, effectively negating a system of checks and balances. The European Union (EU) quickly denounced the measures as a violation of the rule of law and called on member states to support sanctions against Poland, including a potential removal of its voting rights.

NATIONALIST RULING PARTY ATTEMPTS TO IMPLEMENT JUDICIAL CHANGES

Poland's conservative, nationalist Law and Justice Party (PiS) came to power in 2015 when it won a narrow parliamentary majority of 235 of 460 seats. Since that time, the party faced stiff criticism from other European and Western governments for changes it implemented that appeared to weaken democratic traditions, such as placing greater control over the media and weakening civil liberties. The party has managed to enjoy popularity among the public by investing significant sums of money into social welfare programs that resulted in guaranteed payments for, among others, parents with one or more child in the home. Following years of post-communist rule as the country transitioned to capitalism, welfare programs were anemic at best so any attempt at bolstering the economic wellbeing of Polish citizens was a welcome relief. PiS supporters view the party as antiestablishment and a protection against whom they view as corrupt liberal elites. The party has also carved out a strong position in Polish politics as the anti-immigrant party, a stance that has endeared it to many Poles, especially because EU members have taken in a growing number of migrants. The PiS-led government has continually refused to accept migrants, with Prime Minister Beata Szydlo noting that it is Poland's responsibility to protect their citizens "when political elites in Brussels, blinded by political correctness, won't accept this responsibility."

Despite its popularity at home, PiS came under increasing scrutiny for its growing number of antidemocratic changes, although none received as much attention as those first proposed in the summer of 2017 that would give the president and lawmakers more control over the country's judiciary. Parliament put together a package of bills to make significant changes to the appointment and oversight of Poland's judges. The bills would have immediately dismissed all current members of the Supreme Court and allowed the president to reappoint justices at his discretion to fill the vacant seats. The legislation also would have allowed parliament to select a majority of members of the National Judicial Council (the body that chooses judges) rather than allowing those members to be selected by other judges and would have given power to the Minister of Justice to appoint and dismiss all judicial heads of regional and appeals courts. Supporters of the move publicly stated that it would replace an inefficient system with one that can hear cases faster and, according to the prime minister, would protect Poland "from Polish or from foreign defenders of the interest of the elites."

Polls suggested that three-quarters of Polish citizens did not want to see their court system politicized, and protesters took to the streets calling on President Duda to veto the measures. Under pressure, on July 24, the president announced that he was vetoing the judicial reform package passed by parliament, with the exception of the provision regarding the powers of the Minister of Justice. While calling the bills "largely responsive to social expectations," the president noted that the provisions in the bills needed to be fine-tuned "in order to preserve the independence of the judiciary . . . so that they lay down conditions for the judges to feel free from various types of pressures." On July 31, the president officially sent his vetoes to parliament, with an indication that, as written, "[t]his law would not strengthen the sense of justice." The move came as a surprise and dealt a death blow to the bill package because PiS did not have enough votes in parliament to overturn the vetoes on their own and were unlikely to build a coalition to acquiesce to the bills as written.

PARLIAMENT CONSIDERS REVISED JUDICIARY BILLS

Without enough support to overturn the president's vetoes, PiS members of parliament reconvened to find a more palatable method to reform the nation's judiciary. Duda provided counterproposals to parliament, all of which would have maintained the politicization of Poland's courts and would have divided the power of appointment and firing of justices between the president and parliament. Both Duda's own PiS and other parties in parliament were critical of his proposals, and Duda conceded that he would leave it to the body to decide what would be best for moving the country forward.

In mid-December, the upper and lower houses of parliament introduced new bills to overhaul the nation's judicial system. Taking into account a suggestion from Duda, the bills would require Supreme Court justices to retire at age sixty-five instead of seventy unless an extension was received from the president. In addition, the Supreme Court would be given the authority to review and appeal, as necessary, decisions made by lower courts, even those made during the past two decades. The new rules would also create a disciplinary body within the Supreme Court staffed by nonjudicial individuals to be chosen by parliament's upper house that would address matters involving judges and legal professionals. Finally, members of the National Judicial Council would be chosen by parliament's lower house rather than the judicial community.

Despite heated debate, the legislation passed both chambers overwhelmingly, and President Duda quickly signed the bill package into law on December 20. After signing the legislation, Duda noted his disgust with those who felt the changes would remove judicial independence and politicize the court system. "Please, check in how many countries the executive authorities can influence the selection of judges, including European countries," Duda stated.

EU Body Launches Process to Punish Poland

When the court reforms were first debated in parliament in July, EU leaders were highly critical of the changes and began discussing whether they would invoke the never before used Article 7 of the EU charter to sanction Poland. On December 20, the day Duda signed two court reform bills into law, the European Commission formally asked its members to declare that the changes to the judiciary in Poland represented "a clear risk of a serious breach of the rule of law in Poland" and raised "serious questions . . . about the effective application of EU law." Frans Timmermans, vice president of the European Commission, explained, "Judicial reforms in Poland mean that the country's judiciary is now under the political control of the ruling majority. In the absence of judicial independence, serious questions are raised about the effective application of EU law," adding that the decision to invoke Article 7 was done "for Poland, for Polish citizens."

Prior to a vote taking place, EU government representatives would meet to hear directly from Poland and would be permitted to ask questions to address any concerns. Then at least twenty-two of the twenty-eight member states would need to agree that Poland had violated EU standards for a formal warning to be issued to the nation. They would then need to agree unanimously that Poland was in direct violation of the rule of law before the process could move forward toward sanctions. Measures could include suspending payments to Poland, which as of the end of 2017 was the largest recipient of EU funds, or a suspension of voting rights in the body. Hungary was quick to announce that it would not support any such decision, calling the EU's actions seriously damaging to Polish sovereignty, and making any action against Poland unlikely.

Poland was given three months to implement changes to bring its judiciary in line with EU values, at which time the European Commission could rescind its decision. The changes requested by the Council of Europe included maintaining the retirement age of Supreme Court judges, removing the power of the president to extend Supreme Court terms, eliminating the power of the Minister of Justice to appoint judges, and restoring the independence of the Constitutional Tribunal. Polish leaders showed no desire to reverse their stance. "This decision has no merit. It is in our opinion a purely political decision," said Beata Mazurek, a spokesperson for PiS, while Polish Foreign Minister Witold Waszczykowski called it "an attempt to stigmatise Poland and push us aside when key decisions are made in the EU."

—Heather Kerrigan

Following is the text of a statement delivered by Polish President Andrzej Duda on July 24, 2017, on his plan to reform Poland's judiciary; a press release from the Polish president's office, issued on July 31, 2017, announcing the president's decision to veto two bills from parliament related to court reform; a December 20, 2017, press release from the Polish president's office announcing the official signing of judiciary reform bills; and a December 20, 2017, announcement from the European Commission proposing the use of Article 7 to sanction Poland for a breach of rule of law.

Polish President Speaks about Attempt to Reform Judiciary System

July 24, 2017

Dear Compatriots, Ladies and Gentlemen!

Back in my presidential campaign on many occasions did I reiterate that President of the Republic of Poland should serve two grand causes: should serve the Polish nation, and should serve the Polish state. It is incumbent on the President to seek the nation's prosperity and to spare no effort to contribute to its well-being, and also security. Likewise, it is incumbent on the President to take care of the quality of the state and of its institutions in their functioning.

The administration of justice is one of such institutions who feature especially importantly in the social and political system. The quality of the functioning of the former determines the level of trust placed by the society in the state and its institutions. In recent years, the demand for the reform of administration of justice has been repeatedly heard. Unfortunately, there are many people who have been wronged by the administration of justice, and harbour a deep sense of injustice. The society expects form judges that they will be professional, will be ethical and perfectly honest, that they will deliver judgments in line with their oath of office: impartially and in line with their conscience. But it is also expected that they will always be mindful of the fact that they administer justice to people, that a judge will be able to see a human person who stands before him in a sheer expectation of justice beyond the pile of files on his desk.

Without reform of the administration of justice there is no way to build a just state, i.e. the one which affords equal treatment to all citizens, the one which commands confidence of the Polish people. Changes are absolutely essential: on the procedural and formal platform, but also the ethical one.

The package of bills to reform the system of justice, as it was prepared by the Parliament, has been largely responsive to social expectations. Nevertheless, as President, I could not approve them, and I have made use of my right of veto since their require to be fine-tuned with the Constitution in order to preserve the independence of the judiciary; that however without the sense of absolute supremacy and impunity; so that they lay down conditions for the judges to feel free from various types of pressures.

Bearing this in mind in the nearest future I will submit new versions of bills to reform the judiciary. I believe that these amended bills will be adopted by the Polish Parliament in a possibly nearest future and that a wise pro-state and, foremostly, pro-social reform of the administration of justice will become an accomplished fact. This is what the people are expecting.

For almost two years, the camp of the good change has been reforming the country in such a way so as to make Poland more citizens-friendly. I am deeply convinced that a reform of the judiciary, one which is thoroughly and wisely prepared, will further contribute to our pursuits of the Home Country's welfare: as a state that is strong and just, the state which respects and protects an ordinary citizen.

After all, its is [sic] our shared dream to live in a free, democratic, secure and prosperous country.

Thank you very much.

SOURCE: President of the Republic of Poland. "President: I Will Present New Versions of Judiciary Reforms." July 24, 2017. http://www.president.pl/en/news/art,509,president-i-will-present-new-versions-of-judiciary-reforms-.html.

President Duda Vetoes Judiciary Bills

July 31, 2017

President Andrzej Duda on Monday sent to the Sejm (lower house) his decisions on the vetoing of two bills, on the Supreme Court and the National Judicial Council, presidential spokesman Krzysztof Łapiński said.

The President signed his decisions to veto the two bills on Monday, July 24. He then stressed that he was guided by sense of responsibility for the Polish state. He also announced he would prepare his own draft laws.

President Duda said at the time that the Supreme Court and the National Judiciary Council bills needed amending, as the Prosecutor General should not interfere with courts to the extent provided for by the bills. Substantiating his decision, the president said that "in the Polish constitutional tradition" the Prosecutor General had never had any oversight powers over the Supreme Court, or the power to decide who can be a judge of the Supreme Court.

He also suggested that the mode and rules of work of the Supreme Court should not be determined by the Prosecutor General "by drawing up the court's internal regulations", the President said when announcing his decision to veto the bills.

The President did sign into law a bill on the common courts system. The law gave the Justice Minister greater say over the appointment of court heads and made the assignment of cases to judges random.

The vetoing of the bills means they are referred for reconsideration to the Sejm. The Chamber may reject presidential veto by a three-fifths majority vote in the presence of at least half of the statutory number of deputies, whereupon the President signs it into law within 7 days.

SOURCE: President of the Republic of Poland. "Vetoed Bills Sent back to Parliament." July 31, 2017. http://www.president.pl/en/news/art,512,vetoed-bills-sent-back-to-parliament-.html.

President Duda Signs Judiciary Reforms into Law

December 20, 2017

Polish President Andrzej Duda on Wednesday signed into law two bills reforming the country's key judicial bodies. The two bills reform the Supreme Court (SN) and the National Judicial Council (KRS).

President Duda has prepared his own SN and KRS bills after he vetoed the ruling party Law and Justice's (PiS) July legislation reforming the two institutions.

The president stressed they differed significantly from the vetoed drafts. Among other changes, they curbed the justice minister's authority over the SN, increased the number of SN judges and introduced the possibility to appeal any lower court verdict to the top court, he enumerated.

Andrzej Duda said he was "disgusted" to hear voices, including ones from the judicial community, that the new system infringed upon judicial independence and politicised the justice system.

"Please, check in how many countries the executive authorities can influence the selection of judges, including European countries," Andrzej Duda said, adding that in the United States the president nominated Supreme Court justices, with the Senate confirming them.

The president said that the principle of checks and balances was extremely important, as opposed to the tripartite separation of powers alone, and stressed the new solutions democratised the state.

Under the KRS law, the body's 15 members elected from among judges will be chosen for a four-year term by the Sejm (lower house), and not by the judicial community itself, as has been the case until now.

Each Sejm caucus will be entitled to name up to nine candidates, and a Sejm committee will draw up a list of 15 names, with each caucus having at least one candidate among them. The lower house will then vote on the list, with a three-fifths' majority required. If such backing is not garnered, the Sejm will vote again on the same list, but this time, an absolute majority will be required.

As for the SN bill, it will make every valid ruling of a Polish court—including past verdicts going back 20 years—subject to a possible appeal ("an extraordinary complaint") to the SN.

In addition, two new chambers will be set up at the SN, to deal with extraordinary control and public affairs, as well as disciplinary matters, respectively. They will include lay judges elected by the Senate. The latter chamber will be tasked with treating disciplinary cases involving judges and other legal professionals. Finally, the retirement age for SN judges will be lowered from 70 to 65, although the president will be allowed to let them work past this limit.

SOURCE: President of the Republic of Poland. "President Signs Judiciary Reforms." December 20, 2017. http://www.president.pl/en/news/art,636,president-signs-judiciary-reforms.html.

EU Proposes Sanctioning Poland over Judicial Reforms

December 20, 2017

Despite repeated efforts, for almost two years, to engage the Polish authorities in a constructive dialogue in the context of the Rule of Law Framework, the Commission has today concluded that there is a clear risk of a serious breach of the rule of law in Poland.

The Commission is therefore proposing to the Council to adopt a decision under Article 7(1) of the Treaty on European Union . . .

The European Commission is taking action to protect the rule of law in Europe. Judicial reforms in Poland mean that the country's judiciary is now under the political control of the ruling majority. In the absence of judicial independence, serious questions are raised about the effective application of EU law, from the protection of investments to the mutual recognition of decisions in areas as diverse as child custody disputes or the execution of European Arrest Warrants.

The Commission has also today issued a complementary (4th) Rule of Law Recommendation, **setting out clearly the steps that the Polish authorities can take to remedy the current situation**. Should the Polish authorities implement the recommended actions, the Commission is ready, in close consultation with the European Parliament and the Council, to reconsider its Reasoned Proposal.

Furthermore, the Commission has decided to take the next step in its infringement procedure against Poland for **breaches of EU law** by the Law on the Ordinary Courts Organisation, referring Poland to the Court of Justice of the European Union.

Whilst taking these unprecedented measures, the **Commission maintains its offer for a constructive dialogue** to remedy the current situation.

1. Reasoned Proposal for a Council Decision

Over a period of two years, the Polish authorities have adopted more than 13 laws affecting the entire structure of the justice system in Poland, impacting the Constitutional Tribunal, Supreme Court, ordinary courts, National Council for the Judiciary, prosecution service and National School of Judiciary. The common pattern is that the executive and legislative branches have been systematically enabled to politically interfere in the composition, powers, administration and functioning of the judicial branch.

The Reasoned Proposal sets out the Commission's concerns, recalling the steps taken under the Rule of Law Framework and the numerous contacts with the Polish authorities to try to identify a solution, and invites the Council to find that there is a clear risk of a serious breach of the rule of law. The concerns relate specifically to the lack of an independent and legitimate constitutional review and judicial independence.

Should the Polish authorities implement the remedial actions set out in the Rule of Law Recommendation accompanying its Reasoned Proposal, the Commission is ready to reconsider the Reasoned Proposal.

2. Rule of Law Recommendation

The Rule of Law Recommendation adopted today complements three previous Recommendations, adopted on 27 July 2016, 21 December 2016 and 27 July 2017. Today's Recommendation focuses on the fresh concerns raised by the new law on the Supreme Court adopted by the Polish Parliament on 15 December 2017 and the law on the National Council for the Judiciary adopted on 15 December 2017. The Polish authorities have still not addressed the concerns identified in the first three Commission Recommendations, which remain valid.

Today's Recommendation clearly sets out a set of actions that need to be taken by the Polish authorities to address its concerns. The Polish authorities are invited to:

- Amend the Supreme Court law, not apply a lowered retirement age to current judges, remove the discretionary power of the President to prolong the mandate of Supreme Court judges, and remove the extraordinary appeal procedure, which includes a power to reopen final judgments taken years earlier;

- Amend the law on the National Council for the Judiciary, to not terminate the mandate of judges-members, and ensure that the new appointment regime continues to guarantee the election of judges-members by their peers;

- Amend or withdraw the law on Ordinary Courts Organisation, in particular to remove the new retirement regime for judges including the discretionary powers of the Minister of Justice to prolong the mandate of judges and to appoint and dismiss presidents of courts;

- Restore the independence and legitimacy of the Constitutional Tribunal, by ensuring that its judges, President and Vice-President are lawfully elected and by ensuring that all its judgements are published and fully implemented;

- Refrain from actions and public statements which could further undermine the legitimacy of the judiciary.

3. INFRINGEMENT PROCEDURE ON THE BASIS OF EU LAW

The College of Commissioners also decided to refer the Polish Government to the European Court of Justice for breach of EU law, concerning the **Law on the Ordinary Courts** and, specifically, the retirement regime it introduces.

The Commission's key legal concern identified in this law relates to the discrimination on the basis of gender due to the introduction of a different retirement age for female judges (60 years) and male judges (65 years). This is contrary to Article 157 of the Treaty on the Functioning of the European Union (TFEU) and Directive 2006/54 on gender equality in employment.

In its referral to the European Court of Justice, the Commission will also raise the linked concern that the independence of Polish courts will be undermined by the fact that the Minister of Justice has been given a discretionary power to prolong the mandate of judges which have reached retirement age (see Article 19(1) TEU in combination with Article 47 of the EU Charter of Fundamental Rights).

NEXT STEPS

The Commission's Recommendation invites the Polish authorities to address the problems within three months, and to inform the Commission of the steps taken to that effect. The Commission stands ready to pursue a constructive dialogue with the Polish Government. Should the Polish authorities implement the recommended actions, the Commission is ready, in close consultation with the European Parliament and the Council, to reconsider its Reasoned Proposal.

Under Article 7(1) TEU, the Council must hear Poland's position and obtain the consent of the European Parliament (on the basis of Article 354 TFEU, the European Parliament shall act by a two-thirds majority of votes cast, representing the majority of its component Members), before adopting a Decision by a four-fifths majority (22 of 27 Members of the Council entitled to vote on the basis of Article 354 TFEU), determining that there is a clear risk of a serious breach of the rule of law. The Council may also address recommendations to Poland, acting in accordance with the same voting procedure.

BACKGROUND

Article 7(1) of the Treaty on European Union provides for the Council, acting by a majority of four fifths of its members, to determine that there is a clear risk of a serious breach by a Member State of the common values referred to in Article 2 of the Treaty (see Annex II). The Commission can trigger this process by a reasoned proposal.

The rule of law is one of the common values upon which the European Union is founded. It is enshrined in Article 2 of the Treaty on European Union. The European Commission, together with the European Parliament and the Council, is responsible under the Treaties for guaranteeing the respect of the rule of law as a fundamental value of our Union and making sure that EU law, values and principles are respected.

It is up to Poland to identify its own model for its justice system, but it should do so in a way that respects the rule of law; this requires it to safeguard the independence of the judiciary, separation of powers and legal certainty.

A breach of the rule of law in one Member State has an effect on all Member States and the Union as a whole. First, because the independence of the judiciary—free from undue political interference—is a value that reflects the concept of European democracy we have built up together, heeding the lessons of the past. Second, because when the rule of law in any Member State is put into question, the functioning of the Union as a whole, in particular with regard to Justice and Home Affairs cooperation and the functioning of the Internal Market, is put into question too.

The European Commission opened a dialogue with the Polish Authorities in January 2016 under the Rule of Law Framework (see Memo for more details). The Framework—introduced by the Commission on 11 March 2014—has three stages (see graphic in Annex 1). The entire process is based on a continuous dialogue between the Commission and the Member State concerned. The Commission keeps the European Parliament and Council regularly and closely informed. The Commission has attempted to work constructively with the Polish authorities, as they have passed more than 13 laws impacting the Constitutional Tribunal, Supreme Court, ordinary courts, national Council for the Judiciary, prosecution service and National School of Judiciary.

The European Parliament has consistently supported the Commission's concerns, including in the three Resolutions of 13 April 2016, 14 September 2016 and 15 November 2017. In addition, on 16 May 2017, the Commission informed the General Affairs Council of the situation in Poland. A very broad majority of Member States supported the Commission's role and efforts to address this issue, and called upon the Polish Government to resume the dialogue with the Commission. The Commission provided a further update to the General Affairs Council on 25 September 2017, and there was broad agreement on the need for Poland to engage in a dialogue to find a solution.

A wide range of other actors at European and international levels have expressed their deep concern about the reform of the Polish justice system: representatives of the judiciary across Europe, including the Network of Presidents of the Supreme Judicial Courts of the European Union and the European Network of Councils for the Judiciary, the Venice Commission, the Commissioner for Human Rights of the Council of Europe, the United Nations Human Rights Committee as well as numerous civil society organisations such as Amnesty International and the Human Rights and Democracy Network.

[Annexes I and II have been omitted.]

SOURCE: European Commission. "Rule of Law: European Commission Acts to Defend Judicial Independence in Poland." December 20, 2017. http://europa.eu/rapid/press-release_IP-17-5367_en.htm.

OTHER HISTORIC DOCUMENTS OF INTEREST

FROM PREVIOUS *HISTORIC DOCUMENTS*

- European Court of Human Rights Rules on Poland's Involvement with CIA Secret Prisons, *2014*, p. 362

President Trump Announces Transgender Military Ban

JULY 26, AND AUGUST 25 AND 28, 2017

In the summer of 2017, President Donald Trump initiated another reversal of a policy implemented by President Barack Obama's administration when he announced that transgender individuals would no longer be able to serve openly in the U.S. military. While praised by some conservatives, many across the political spectrum condemned the change, including LGBT organizations that filed lawsuits challenging the constitutionality of what they deemed a discriminatory policy.

TRUMP SIGNALS CHANGE IN POLICY

Trump first announced the sudden change in policy via Twitter on July 26, tweeting that the U.S. would no longer "accept or allow" transgender individuals to serve in the military. Trump wrote that the military "must be focused on decisive and overwhelming victory" and "cannot be burdened with the tremendous medical costs and disruption" that having transgender troops would entail. Press Secretary Sarah Huckabee Sanders later stated that the president had concluded that having transgender people serving openly "erodes military readiness and unit cohesion."

Trump's announcement amounted to a reversal of an Obama administration policy, announced in June 2016, that said transgender individuals currently enlisted in the military could begin serving openly and that "service members may no longer be involuntarily separated, discharged, or denied reenlistment solely on the basis of gender identity." The policy also authorized the use of military resources to provide medical care related to gender transition, including gender reassignment surgery, and called for enlistment to be opened to transgendered individuals by July 1, 2017. Shortly before the deadline, the U.S. Defense Department extended it to January 1, 2018, to allow more time to study the issue and prepare for the change.

Trump's move was widely characterized as a hasty decision, with no details available from either the White House or the Defense Department on how the change in policy would be implemented and how troops who were already enlisted would be impacted by the shift. Some speculated that the change was motivated by White House concern that conservative opposition to using taxpayer money for gender reassignment surgery and related health expenses might derail a $790 billion defense spending bill being debated on Capitol Hill, to which some Republicans wanted to add provisions preventing such expenditures by the Defense Department.

Reactions to Trump's announcement were swift and divided. Many conservatives praised Trump. "AFA applauds President Trump for his courageous decision to end the usage of our military for social engineering and political correctness," said Tim Wildmon, president of the American Family Association. Others did not. Senate Armed Services

Committee Chairman John McCain, R-Ariz., said, "There is no reason to force service members who are able to fight, train and deploy to leave the military—regardless of their gender identity." LGBT organizations widely condemned the policy. "This heinous and disgusting action endangers the lives of American service members, undermines military readiness and makes our country less safe," said Chad Griffin, president of the Human Rights Campaign.

Trump Issues Memo on Transgender Individuals in the Military

On August 25, Trump issued an official memo directing the Secretaries of Defense and Homeland Security to return to the pre-June 2016 policies around transgender troops "until such time as a sufficient basis exists upon which to conclude that terminating that policy and practice" would not negatively impact the military. "In my judgment," the memo read, "the previous Administration failed to identify a sufficient basis to conclude that terminating the Departments' longstanding policy and practice would not hinder military effectiveness and lethality, disrupt unit cohesion, or tax military resources, and there remain meaningful concerns that further study is needed to ensure that continued implementation of last year's policy change would not have those negative effects." The new directive was set to take effect on January 1, 2018, with the memo calling on the Departments of Defense and Homeland Security to submit to the president a plan for implementing the reversal and for addressing transgender individuals currently serving openly in the military. Until that plan was developed, the memo stated, no action should be taken against those individuals.

LGBT Organizations File Suit on Behalf of Service Members

The memo set off another wave of outrage and condemnation among LGBT advocates and prompted several organizations to file lawsuits challenging the policy on behalf of transgender service members and recruits. Among these suits was one filed in the U.S. District Court for the District of Maryland on August 28 by the American Civil Liberties Union (ACLU) and Covington & Burling LLP. According to a press release issued by the ACLU, the filing claimed that Trump's policy "violates the constitutional guarantees of equal protection and substantive due process by singling out transgender individuals for unequal and discriminatory treatment" and was based on "uninformed speculation, myths and stereotypes, moral disapproval, and a bare desire to harm this already vulnerable group." Josh Block, a senior staff attorney for the ACLU's LGBT & HIV Project, said that "each and every claim made by President Trump to justify this ban can be easily debunked by the conclusions drawn from the Department of Defense's own review process."

Block was referring to a study conducted by the RAND Corporation that estimated there are roughly 1,300 to 6,600 transgender individuals among the active duty military—out of a total troop population of 1.3 million—and that thirty to 140 of these individuals would seek hormone treatment while another twenty-five to 130 would seek gender transition surgery. These treatments were projected to cost $2.4 million to $8.4 million annually, or no more than a 0.13% increase in the military's total health care costs. These estimates led RAND Corporation to conclude that allowing transgender troops to serve openly would "have minimal impact on readiness and health care costs" and "little or no impact on unit cohesion, operational effectiveness or readiness."

Two other lawsuits—one by GLBTQ Legal Advocates & Defenders (GLAAD) and the National Center for Lesbian Rights, and one by Lambda Legal and OutServe-SLDN—were also filed in August. The U.S. Justice Department argued that each of these cases should be dismissed because none of the plaintiffs had been affected by a policy change yet, noting that the Defense Department was in the middle of its review period and no troops would be discharged until that review was complete.

On October 30, the U.S. District Court for the District of Columbia granted a partial injunction in the GLAAD case, ruling that a ban on new transgender troops enlisting could not be enforced while the case was being reviewed in court, though the court did not block the government from ending payments for gender reassignment treatment. On November 21, the judge presiding over the ACLU case similarly issued a preliminary injunction against the ban, characterizing it as "capricious, arbitrary and unqualified" and stating that it likely violated the Constitution's equal protection provisions. The injunction blocked both the ban on enlisting new transgender troops and the ban on gender reassignment treatments. On December 11, the U.S. District Court for the Western District of Washington became the third court to issue an injunction. That same day, the D.C. court issued a second ruling, affirming that its October injunction should remain in place, meaning that the Defense Department needed to allow transgender individuals to enlist in the military beginning January 1, 2018. The Justice Department is in the process of appealing this ruling.

—Linda Grimm

Following are the series of tweets by President Donald Trump on July 26, 2017, announcing his decision to ban transgender individuals from serving in the military; a memo issued by President Trump on August 25, 2017, prohibiting openly transgender Americans from serving in the military; and a press release from the American Civil Liberties Union on August 28, 2017, announcing a lawsuit challenging the president's ban.

President Trump Tweets about Transgender Individuals in the Military

July 26, 2017

After consultation with my Generals and military experts, please be advised that the United States Government will not accept or allow. . . .

. . . Transgender individuals to serve in any capacity in the U.S. Military. Our military must be focused on decisive and overwhelming. . . .

. . . victory and cannot be burdened with the tremendous medical costs and disruption that transgender in the military would entail. Thank you

SOURCE: Donald J. Trump (@realDonaldTrump). Twitter posts, July 26, 2017. https://twit ter.com/realdonaldtrump/status/890193981585444864?lang=en, https://twitter.com/realdonaldtrump/status/890196164313833472?lang=en, and https://twitter.com/realdonaldtrump/status/890197095151546369?lang=en.

President Trump Issues Memorandum on Military Service by Transgender Individuals

DOCUMENT

August 25, 2017

Memorandum for the Secretary of Defense and the Secretary of Homeland Security

Subject: Military Service by Transgender Individuals

Section 1. Policy. (a) Until June 2016, the Department of Defense (DoD) and the Department of Homeland Security (DHS) (collectively, the Departments) generally prohibited openly transgender individuals from accession into the United States military and authorized the discharge of such individuals. Shortly before President Obama left office, however, his Administration dismantled the Departments' established framework by permitting transgender individuals to serve openly in the military, authorizing the use of the Departments' resources to fund sex-reassignment surgical procedures, and permitting accession of such individuals after July 1, 2017. The Secretary of Defense and the Secretary of Homeland Security have since extended the deadline to alter the currently effective accession policy to January 1, 2018, while the Departments continue to study the issue.

In my judgment, the previous Administration failed to identify a sufficient basis to conclude that terminating the Departments' longstanding policy and practice would not hinder military effectiveness and lethality, disrupt unit cohesion, or tax military resources, and there remain meaningful concerns that further study is needed to ensure that continued implementation of last year's policy change would not have those negative effects.

(b) Accordingly, by the authority vested in me as President and as Commander in Chief of the Armed Forces of the United States under the Constitution and the laws of the United States of America, including Article II of the Constitution, I am directing the Secretary of Defense, and the Secretary of Homeland Security with respect to the U.S. Coast Guard, to return to the longstanding policy and practice on military service by transgender individuals that was in place prior to June 2016 until such time as a sufficient basis exists upon which to conclude that terminating that policy and practice would not have the negative effects discussed above. The Secretary of Defense, after consulting with the Secretary of Homeland Security, may advise me at any time, in writing, that a change to this policy is warranted.

Sec. 2. Directives. The Secretary of Defense, and the Secretary of Homeland Security with respect to the U.S. Coast Guard, shall:

(a) maintain the currently effective policy regarding accession of transgender individuals into military service beyond January 1, 2018, until such time as the

Secretary of Defense, after consulting with the Secretary of Homeland Security, provides a recommendation to the contrary that I find convincing; and

(b) halt all use of DoD or DHS resources to fund sex-reassignment surgical procedures for military personnel, except to the extent necessary to protect the health of an individual who has already begun a course of treatment to reassign his or her sex.

Sec. 3. Effective Dates and Implementation. Section 2(a) of this memorandum shall take effect on January 1, 2018. Sections 1(b) and 2(b) of this memorandum shall take effect on March 23, 2018. By February 21, 2018, the Secretary of Defense, in consultation with the Secretary of Homeland Security, shall submit to me a plan for implementing both the general policy set forth in section 1(b) of this memorandum and the specific directives set forth in section 2 of this emorandum. The implementation plan shall adhere to the determinations of the Secretary of Defense, made in consultation with the Secretary of Homeland Security, as to what steps are appropriate and consistent with military effectiveness and lethality, budgetary constraints, and applicable law. As part of the implementation plan, the Secretary of Defense, in consultation with the Secretary of Homeland Security, shall determine how to address transgender individuals currently serving in the United States military. Until the Secretary has made that determination, no action may be taken against such individuals under the policy set forth in section 1(b) of this memorandum.

Sec. 4. Severability. If any provision of this memorandum, or the application of any provision of this memorandum, is held to be invalid, the remainder of this memorandum and other dissimilar applications of the provision shall not be affected.

Sec. 5. General Provisions. (a) Nothing in this memorandum shall be construed to impair or otherwise affect:

(i)   the authority granted by law to an executive department or agency, or the head thereof; or

(ii) the functions of the Director of the Office of Management and Budget relating to budgetary, administrative, or legislative proposals.

(b) This memorandum shall be implemented consistent with applicable law and subject to the availability of appropriations.

(c) This memorandum is not intended to, and does not, create any right or benefit, substantive or procedural, enforceable at law or in equity by any party against the United States, its departments, agencies, or entities, its officers, employees, or agents, or any other person.

(d) The Secretary of Defense is authorized and directed to publish this memorandum in the Federal Register.

DONALD J. TRUMP

SOURCE: Executive Office of the President. "Memorandum on Military Service by Transgender Individuals." August 25, 2017. *Compilation of Presidential Documents* 2017, no. 00587 (August 25, 2017). https://www.gpo.gov/fdsys/pkg/DCPD-201700587/pdf/DCPD-201700587.pdf.

ACLU Files Lawsuit Challenging Transgender Service Member Ban

August 28, 2017

MARYLAND—The American Civil Liberties Union and Covington & Burling LLP today filed a lawsuit against the Trump administration challenging the president's directive banning transgender service members from continuing to serve in the military or receiving medically necessary health care, and banning men and women who are transgender from enlisting.

The lawsuit was filed on behalf of the ACLU of Maryland and six current members of the armed forces who are transgender: Petty Officer First Class Brock Stone, Senior Airman John Doe, Airman First Class Seven Ero George, Petty Officer First Class Teagan Gilbert, Staff Sergeant Kate Cole, and Technical Sergeant Tommie Parker.

In the lawsuit, the ACLU argues that the ban violates the constitutional guarantees of equal protection and substantive due process by singling out transgender individuals for unequal and discriminatory treatment. The lawsuit argues that the ban discriminates based on sex and transgender status and that the ban is based on uninformed speculation, myths and stereotypes, moral disapproval, and a bare desire to harm this already vulnerable group.

"Each and every claim made by President Trump to justify this ban can be easily debunked by the conclusions drawn from the Department of Defense's own review process. Allowing men and women who are transgender to serve openly and providing them with necessary health care does nothing to harm military readiness or unit cohesion," said Josh Block, senior staff attorney with the ACLU's LGBT & HIV Project. "Men and women who are transgender with the courage and capacity to serve deserve more from their commander-in-chief."

At the culmination of a thorough process, the Department of Defense concluded in 2016 that there was no basis for the military to exclude transgender individuals from openly serving their country, subject to the same fitness requirements as other service members. This review process carefully considered and rejected the notion that medical costs, military readiness, or other factors presented any reason to discriminate against transgender service members, many of whom had already been serving with honor in silence for years.

For example, Petty Officer First Class Brock Stone has served in the U.S. Navy for 9 years, including a nine-month deployment to Afghanistan. He has received extensive and costly training and is skilled in his field. He has devoted and risked his life for the United States and is seeking nothing more than the ability to continue to do so on the same terms as his fellow officers.

The other individual plaintiffs are:

- Staff Sergeant Cole has served in the U.S. Army for almost 10 years, including a one-year deployment to Afghanistan where she served as a team leader and designated marksman.

- Senior Airman Doe has served for approximately six years on active duty in the U.S. Air Force, where he was awarded "Airman of the Year" for his flight and hopes to serve in the armed forces for his entire career.

- Airman First Class George is a member of the Air National Guard. He is training as a nurse and intends to pursue a commission in the U.S. Army.

- Petty Officer First Class Gilbert has served in the U.S. Navy for 13 years, including a one-year deployment to Afghanistan, and currently serves as an Information Technology specialist.

- Technical Sergeant Parker served in the Marine Corps for four years and has served in the Air National Guard for 16 years, currently as a fuel technician.

The plaintiffs are represented by the ACLU, the ACLU of Maryland, and Covington & Burling LLP.

SOURCE: American Civil Liberties Union. "ACLU Files Lawsuit Challenging Trump's Transgender Service Member Ban." August 28, 2017. https://www.aclu.org/news/aclu-files-lawsuit-challenging-trumps-transgender-service-member-ban.

OTHER HISTORIC DOCUMENTS OF INTEREST

FROM PREVIOUS *HISTORIC DOCUMENTS*

Pakistan Prime Minister Removed from Office

JULY 28, 2017

In 2017, allegations that Prime Minister Nawaz Sharif and several of his family members were hiding assets and not fully disclosing sources of income divided Pakistan. While Sharif's supporters rallied to his defense, in some instances claiming a conspiracy against the prime minister, opposition parties called loudly for his resignation. The allegations prompted a federal investigation of Sharif and his finances, the findings of which played a major role in leading the Supreme Court of Pakistan to rule that Sharif should be disqualified and removed from office.

Panama Papers Prompt Corruption Probe

The April 2016 release of the Panama Papers spurred the corruption probe into Sharif and his family. The documents leaked from Panama-based law firm Mossack Fonseca revealed widespread use of offshore bank accounts and companies by politicians, business leaders, and celebrities worldwide, giving rise to conflict of interest accusations and allegations of illicit financial activity. While Sharif was not named in the Panama Papers, his children Hassan Nawaz Sharif, Hussain Nawaz Sharif, and Maryam Nawaz Sharif were. The documents showed that Sharif's children were involved in shell companies based in the British Virgin Islands through which they owned expensive apartments in London—homes that the Sharifs would not have been able to afford with their known income. Additionally, the apartments were bought in the early 1990s, when Sharif's children would have been minors, leading many to assume that the prime minister had made the purchases and prompting allegations that he was involved in financial wrongdoing and money laundering.

The Panama Papers allegations were the latest political challenge Sharif faced in his colorful history as prime minister. In 1993, in the middle of the first of his three, nonconsecutive terms in office, Sharif was removed by then-President Ghulam Ishaq Khan and the Pakistani military, which has exerted significant control in the country since Pakistan gained its independence from Britain in 1947. Sharif was reelected in 1997 but was overthrown two years later in a coup led by General Pervez Musharraf after Sharif fired him from his position as leader of the Pakistani army. In 2000, Sharif was found guilty of orchestrating the hijacking of Gen. Musharraf's plane, terrorism, and corruption and was sentenced to life in prison. However, the Saudi royal family struck a deal with the Pakistani government that allowed Sharif to go into exile in Saudi Arabia with eighteen of his family members. Sharif was elected once again in 2013.

Since his latest election, Sharif faced repeated calls from Imran Khan, the leader of the opposition Pakistan Tehreek-e-Insaf political party, to step down. In 2014, for example, Khan and cleric Muhammad Tahir-ul Qadri led more than 40,000 people to Pakistan's "red zone" (the area of the capital of Islamabad where the National Assembly, official residence of the prime minister, and various Western embassies are located) to call for Sharif's resignation for alleged election rigging. The protest began in mid-August and continued in the form of a sit-in outside the National Assembly into November. Khan seized on the Panama Papers news as another reason to pressure Sharif, with his party pushing the prime minister to provide documentation proving that the apartment purchases were made legitimately. Khan planned to lead thousands of supporters to "lock down" the capital of Islamabad in protest on November 1, 2016, until Sharif stepped down or faced corruption charges. However, Khan called off the protest after the Supreme Court of Pakistan said it would form a commission to investigate the allegations against Sharif. In the days leading up to the planned protest, at least 1,500 of Khan's supporters were arrested in clashes with police.

Supreme Court Forms Joint Investigation Team

The Supreme Court began hearing petitions against Sharif in November 2016. On April 20, 2017, a five-member panel of the court ruled 3–2 that Sharif could remain in office but ordered the creation of a Joint Investigation Team (JIT) to investigate Sharif's finances and report on their findings within sixty days. The team included representatives of the Federal Investigation Agency, National Accountability Bureau, Security & Exchange Commission of Pakistan, State Bank of Pakistan, Inter-Services Intelligence, and Military Intelligence.

The JIT completed its investigation and submitted its report on July 11, concluding that the Sharif family was living beyond their means and accusing the prime minister and his three children named in the Panama Papers of hiding their assets, perjury, and forgery. Among their accusations, the JIT said Sharif's daughter Maryam had forged a trust deed for the apartments that listed her as a trustee only and not an owner of the two offshore companies that bought the apartments. Investigators noted that the deed was written using a Microsoft Word font that was not available until 2007, even though it was dated 2006. Investigators also stated that a letter providing information about the Sharif family's financials purportedly sent by a Qatari royal whose family had done business with Sharif's father was fake.

The report sparked a major outcry in Pakistan, with opposition parties coming together to call for Sharif's resignation. Sharif and his supporters denied the allegations. Sharif called the report a "pack of lies" and claimed that the wealth used to purchase the London homes had been legally acquired through his family's long-held private businesses before he became a politician. Sharif also claimed that the investigation was the result of a conspiracy against him, with some supporters implying that the intelligence community had given the JIT evidence against the Sharif family and others stating that the military supported his removal from office. "We know very well what the crime of Nawaz Sharif and the Muslim League is," said Minister for Railways Khawaja Saad Rafiq. "What do we ask for? We ask for civilian supremacy in Pakistan." Zafarullah Khan, Minister of State for Law and Justice, claimed the materials gathered by the JIT "don't have evidentiary value" and labeled the charges as "a political case" driven by opposition parties who were "using the shoulder of the courts to have a judicial coup."

Sharif Disqualified from Holding Office

Hearings in the Sharif case began on July 17. Eleven days later, the Supreme Court issued a unanimous ruling removing Sharif from office and disqualifying him from public office for ten years. The court also removed Sharif's son-in-law, Mohammad Safdar, from office as a National Assembly member for corruption.

The ruling cited Articles 62 and 63 of the Pakistani Constitution, which disqualify a lawmaker from holding office if they are found to be dishonest. The court found that Sharif had tried to conceal his assets and stated that the Sharif family and their lawyers had not provided satisfactory documentation of their finances and that some of the materials they provided were fake. The ruling cited as evidence of his dishonesty Sharif's failure to disclose monthly income from a company his son owned in the United Arab Emirates when filing papers for the 2013 election, though Sharif and his lawyers argued that the prime minister never received that salary.

The court referred all investigative materials to the National Accountability Bureau and ordered that criminal charges against Sharif, his three children, Safdar, and Finance Minister Ishaq Dar be filed before the Accountability Court within six weeks and directed the court to issue a ruling within six months of the charges being filed.

Sharif submitted his resignation immediately following the ruling, though he said he did not "understand the grounds for my dismissal," adding, "I am only content that I was not disqualified on the grounds of alleged corruption." Sharif's supporters remained loyal despite the ruling. "Nawaz Sharif will continue to rule the public's hearts, even after being disqualified to hold office by the Supreme Court," said Information Minister Maryam Aurangzeb. "This decision is not surprising but we are disappointed." Opposition leader Khan celebrated the ruling, calling it a victory for Pakistan. "Our struggle proves that mighty people in our country can also be held accountable now," he said. He also declared, "Today onward, big thieves will be caught." (Notably, Khan is also being investigated by the Supreme Court for allegedly failing to disclose some sources of income. Khan denies the charges.)

INTERIM PRIME MINISTER SELECTED

Sharif had one year left of his five-year term at the time of the Supreme Court's ruling, meaning that his party, the Pakistan Muslim League-Nawaz, must select an interim prime minister to serve until the 2018 elections. Sharif's daughter Maryam had widely been expected to succeed him, but her involvement in the corruption case made this no longer possible.

On July 29, the day after the Supreme Court issued its ruling, Sharif proposed that his younger brother Shahbaz become the next prime minister. At the time, Shahbaz was serving as the chief minister of Punjab province. To become prime minister, he would first have to resign that post and win a special by-election for his brother's former seat in the National Assembly. Since this process was expected to take about forty-five days, Sharif proposed that Minister for Petroleum and Natural Resources Shahid Khaqan Abbasi serve as interim prime minister.

Abbasi was elected as prime minister on August 1, handily winning 221 of 342 votes from the National Assembly. A week later, Sharif said his brother would remain in office in Punjab province rather than run for the National Assembly. Various reports indicated that party leaders thought Shahbaz would be better able to help the party maintain control in Punjab province, which, as the most populous province in the country, has more seats in the National Assembly than all other provinces and federal areas combined, if he remained chief executive.

Abbasi continues to serve as prime minister. General elections have been scheduled for July 15, 2018.

—Linda Grimm

Following are excerpts from the text of the Supreme Court of Pakistan's ruling, issued July 28, 2017, disqualifying Prime Minister Nawaz Sharif from office for failure to disclose assets.

Supreme Court of Pakistan Disqualifies Sharif from Office

July 28, 2017

JUDGEMENT

EJAZ AFZAL KHAN, J. - This judgment is in continuation of our judgments dated 20.04.2017 in Constitution Petitions No. 29, 30 of 2016 and Constitution Petition No. 03 of 2017

[The April 20, 2017, judgements have been omitted.]

3. The JIT undertook the task thus assigned and submitted a complete investigation report on 10.07.2017. Parties to the proceedings were provided the report of the JIT and a weeks' time to go through it. Khawaja Harris Ahmed, learned Sr. ASC appearing on behalf of respondent No. 1 submitted a CMA expressing his reservations about the report. Dr. Tariq Hassan, learned ASC for respondent No. 10 also filed a CMA expressing his reservations about the report. Learned ASC appearing for petitioner in Const. P. No. 29 of 2016, Sheikh Rasheed Ahmed, petitioner appearing in person in Const. P. No. 30 of 2016 and learned ASC appearing for the petitioner in Const. P. No. 03 of 2017, by picking up the thread from where they left off, sought to canvass at the bar that the JIT has collected sufficient evidence proving that respondent No. 1, his dependents and benamidars own, possess and have acquired assets which are disproportionate to their known sources of income; that neither respondent No. 1 nor any of his dependents or benamidars before or during the course of investigation could account for these assets, therefore, he has become disqualified to be a Member of Parliament. They further stated that certified copies of the correspondence between Mr. Errol George, Director Financial Investigating Agency and the Anti-Money Laundering Officer of Mossack Fonseca & Co. (B.V.I.) Limited collected through Mutual Legal Assistance prove that respondent No. 6 is the beneficial owner of the Avenfield apartments, therefore, the document showing her as trustee is a fabrication on the face of it for which she is liable to be proceeded against for forgery and using forged documents; that use of Calibri Font,

which became commercially available in 2007, in the preparation of the trust deed in February 2006 is another circumstance leading to the inference that it was forged and fabricated; that narrative of Tariq Shafi vis-à-vis receipt of AED 12 million from sale of 25% shares of Ahli Steel Mills formerly known as Gulf Steel Mills is false on the face of it which has been confirmed by the JIT in its report; that whatever has been stated in Qatri letters remained unsubstantiated as the Qatri Prince neither appeared before the JIT nor ever stated his point of view through any other legally recognizable means; that respondents were given ample opportunities to provide the trail of money and answer the questions asked in the order of the Court dated 20.04.2017 but they throughout have been evasive; that the discrepancies between the first Qatri letter and affidavit of Mr. Tariq Shafi show that neither of them is credible; that the spreadsheet attached with the second Qatri letter too is of no help to the respondents as it is neither signed nor supported by any documentary evidence; that the entire story about trail of money is seriously marred by inconsistencies surfacing in the statements of the respondents recorded by the JIT; that story of transporting machinery from Dubai to Jeddah and thereby establishing Azizia Steel Company Limited still awaits proof; that how the entire amount running to SAR 63.10 million could be utilized by respondent No. 7 notwithstanding he was entitled to only 1/3rd finds no explanation therefor, the sources establishing Hill Metal Establishment have not been proved; that failure of respondent No. 1 to disclose his assets deposited in his account on account of his being Chairman of Capital FZE would also call for his disqualification, as it being an asset for all legal and practical purposes was required to be disclosed under Section 12(2)(f) of the Representation of the People Act, 1976; that the respondent denied withdrawal of salary, but payment of salaries to all employees electronically, through the Wage Protection System, under Ministerial Resolution No. (788) for 2009 on Wage Protection used by United Arab Emirates Ministry of Labour and Rules 11(6) and 11(7) of the Jebel Ali Free Zone Rules, would belie his stance; that the assets of respondents No. 7 and 8 have surprisingly grown manifold overnight notwithstanding all of their business enterprises run in loss; that the facts and figures showing inflow and outflow of Hill Metals Establishment also appear to be fudged and fabricated when seen in the light of the material collected during the course of investigation by the JIT; that material already brought on the record and collected through the JIT leave no doubt that the assets of respondent No. 1, his children and benamidars are disproportionate to their known sources of income and that their failure to satisfactorily account for them would inevitably entail disqualification of respondent No. 1 in terms of Section 9(a)(v) of the National Accountability Bureau Ordinance, 1999.

4. Learned Sr. ASC appearing for Respondent No. 1 contended that JIT overstepped its mandate by reopening the case of Hudabiya Paper Mills when it was not so directed by the Court; that another investigation or inquiry shall also be barred by the principle of double jeopardy when the Reference relating to the said Mills was quashed in the case of Hudabiya Paper Mills Limited. Vs. Federation of Pakistan (PLD 2016 Lahore 667); that no evidence has been collected by the JIT showing respondent No.1 to have any nexus with the Avenfield apartments, Hill Metals Establishment, Flagship Investment Limited or any other business concern run by respondent no. 7 and 8; that all the material collected and finding

given by the JIT do not deserve any consideration inasmuch as they are beyond the scope of investigation authorized by the order of this Court; that the investigation conducted by the JIT cannot be said to be fair and just when none of the respondents was questioned about or confronted with any of the documents tending to incriminate them and that the JIT exceeded its authority while obtaining documents from abroad by engaging the firm of the persons happening to be their near and dear. Such exercise, the learned Sr. ASC added, cannot be termed as Mutual Legal Assistance by any interpretation nor can the documents thus obtained be vested with any sanctity in terms of Section 21(g) of the National Accountability Bureau Ordinance, 1999. He next contended that no weight could be given to the finding of the JIT when it is not supported by any authentic document. An investigation of this type, the learned Sr. ASC added, which is a farce and a breach of due process cannot form basis of any adverse verdict against respondent No. 1. The learned Sr. ASC to support his contention placed reliance on the cases of Khalid Aziz Vs. The State (2011 SCMR 136) and Muhammad Arshad and others. Vs. The State and others (PLD 2011 SC 350).

5. Learned ASC appearing on behalf of respondents No. 6, 7, 8 and 9 contended that Avenfield apartments are owned and possessed by respondent No. 7, and that the trail of money and the way it has culminated in the acquisition of the Avenfield apartments stand explained by Qatri letters; that respondent No. 6 besides being a trustee of the apartments at some stage of time has not been their beneficial owner, therefore, the correspondence between Errol George, Director FIA and Mossack Fonseca & Co. (B.V.I.) Limited or the certified copies thereof obtained through an MLA request cannot be relied upon unless proved in accordance with law and that the JIT report and the material collected by it during the course of investigation per se cannot form basis of a judgment in a proceeding under Article 184(3) of the Constitution of the Islamic Republic of Pakistan.

6. Learned ASC appearing on behalf of respondent No. 10 contended that assets of respondent No. 10 have been audited and examined from time to time but no irregularity was ever found in any of them; that the respondent has accounted for whatever assets he owns, possesses or has acquired; that his assets were also subject matter of Reference No. 5 of 2000 which was quashed in the case of Hudabiya Paper Mills Limited. Vs. Federation of Pakistan (supra); that another criminal proceeding cannot be initiated when everything has been accounted for down to the rupee. The learned ASC by producing the income tax returns from 2007 to 2016, wealth tax returns from 1981-1982 to 2000-2001 and from 2009 to 2016 contended that every asset is property vouched and documented; that the finding of the JIT has no legal or factual basis; that no conclusion much less sweeping can be drawn on the basis of such report; that 91 times increase in his assets from 1992-1993 to 2008-2009 shown in the JIT's report is based on miscalculation; that the respondent cannot be impaled on the same charge by imputing a wrongdoing without any tangible evidence; that failure on the part of the FBR to provide the relevant record cannot be construed to the detriment of the respondent when it has been with the NAB Authorities throughout and that with this background in view, it would be rather unjust to thrust the respondent in another treadmill of tiresome trial before the Accountability Court.

7. We have carefully gone through the record, the report submitted by the JIT and considered the submissions of the learned ASCs, Sr. ASC of the parties as well as the learned Additional Attorney General for Pakistan.

8. We have already dealt with the background of the case and detailed submissions of the learned ASCs for the parties in paras 1 to 12 of the majority judgment authored by one of us (Ejaz Afzal Khan, J) and notes written by my learned brothers Mr. Justice Sh. Azmat Saeed and Mr. Justice Ijaz ul Ahsan . . .

9. A careful examination of the material so far collected reveals that a prima facie triable case under Section 9, 10 and 15 of the Ordinance is made out against respondents No. 1, 6, 7 and 8 vis-à-vis the following assets:-

"(i)   Flagship Investments Limited.

(ii)   Hartstone Properties Limited;

(iii) Que Holdings Limited;

(iv)   Quint Eaton Place 2 Limited;

(v)   Quint Saloane Limited (formerly Quint Eaton Place Limited).

(vi)   Quaint Limited;

(vii) Flagship Securities Limited;

(viii) Quint Gloucester Place Limited;

(ix)   Quint Paddington Limited (formerly Rivates Estates Limited);

(x)   Flagship Developments Limited;

(xi)   Alanna Services Limited (BVI);

(xii) Lankin SA (BVI);

(xiii) Chadron Inc;

(xiv) Ansbacher Inc;

(xv)   Coomber Inc; and

(xvi) Capital FZE (Dubai)."

So is the case against respondent No. 10 vis-à-vis 91 times increase (from Rs.9.11 million to 831.70 million) in his assets within a short span of time . . .

12. The argument that the JIT overstepped its authority by reopening the case of Hudabiya Paper Mills when Reference No. 5 was quashed by the High Court does not appear to be correct as the JIT has simply made recommendations in this behalf which can better be dealt with by this Court if and when an appeal, before this Court, as has been undertaken by Special Prosecutor NAB, is filed and a view to the contrary is taken by this Court.

13. The next question emerging for the consideration of this Court is whether respondent No. 1 as a Chairman of the Board of Capital FZE is entitled to salaries and whether the salaries if not withdrawn being receivable as such constitute

assets which require disclosure in terms of Section 12(2) of the Representation of the People Act, 1976 and whether his failure to disclose them would entail his disqualification? The word asset has not been defined in the Representation of the People Act, 1976, ("ROPA"), therefore, its ordinary meaning has to be considered for the purposes of this case. The word asset as defined in Black's Law Dictionary means and contemplates *"an asset can be (i) something physical such as cash, machinery, inventory, land and building (ii) an enforceable claim against others such as accounts receivable (iii) rights such as copyright, patent trademark etc (iv) an assumption such as goodwill"*. The definition of the word receivable as used in the above mentioned definition as given in the Black's Law Dictionary is also relevant which means and contemplates *"any collectible whether or not it is currently due. That which is due and owing a person or company. In book keeping, the name of an account which reflects a debt due. Accounts receivable a claim against a debtor usually arising from sales or services rendered"*. The word 'receivable' also has similar ring and connotation according to Business Dictionary which reads as under:

> *"Accounting term for amount due from a customer, employee, supplier (as a rebate or refund) or any other party. Receivables are classified as accounts receivable, notes receivable etc and represent an asset of the firm"*.

The definitions reproduced above leave no doubt that a salary not withdrawn would nevertheless be receivable and as such would constitute an asset for all legal and practical purposes. When it is an asset for all legal and practical purposes, it was required to be disclosed by respondent No. 1 in his nomination papers in terms of Section 12(2) of the ROPA. When we confronted, the learned Sr. ASC for respondent No. 1, whether the said respondent has ever acquired work permit (Iqama) in Dubai, remained Chairman of the Board of Capital FZE and was entitled to salary as such, his reply was in the affirmative with the only addition that respondent No. 1 never withdrew any salary . . .

It has not been denied that respondent No. 1 being Chairman of the Board of Capital FZE was entitled to salary, therefore, the statement that he did not withdraw the salary would not prevent the un-withdrawn salary from being receivable, hence an asset. When the un-withdrawn salary as being receivable is an asset it was required to be disclosed by respondent No. 1 in his nomination papers for the Elections of 2013 in terms of Section 12(2)(f) of the ROPA. Where respondent No. 1 did not disclose his aforesaid assets, it would amount to furnishing a false declaration on solemn affirmation in violation of the law mentioned above, therefore, he is not honest in terms of Section 99(1)(f) of the ROPA and Article 62(1)(f) of the Constitution of the Islamic Republic of Pakistan.

14. As a sequel to what has been discussed in paragraphs 7 to 11 the following directions are made:

    i)   The National Accountability Bureau (NAB) shall within six weeks from the date of this judgment prepare and file before the Accountability Court, Rawalpindi/Islamabad, the following References, on the basis of the material collected and referred to by the Joint Investigating Team (JIT) in its report and such other material as may be available with the Federal Investigating Agency (FIA) and NAB having any nexus with the assets or which may subsequently become available including material that may come before it pursuant to the Mutual Legal Assistance requests sent by the JIT to different jurisdictions:

a)   Reference against Mian Muhammad Nawaz Sharif (Respondent No. 1), Maryam Nawaz Sharif (Maryam Safdar) (Respondent No. 6), Hussain Nawaz Sharif (Respondent No. 7), Hassan Nawaz Sharif (Respondent No. 8) and Capt. (Retd) Muhammad Safdar (Respondent No. 9) relating to the Avenfield properties (Flats No. 16, 16-A, 17 and 17-A Avenfield House, Park Lane, London, United Kingdom). In preparing and filing this Reference, the NAB shall also consider the material already collected during the course of investigations conducted earlier.

b)   Reference against respondents No. 1, 7 and 8 regarding Azizia Steel Company and Hill Metal Establishment, as indicated above;

c)   Reference against respondents No. 1, 7 and 8 regarding the Companies mentioned in paragraph 9 above;

d)   Reference against respondent No. 10 for possessing assets and funds beyond his known sources of income, as discussed in paragraph 9 above;

e)   NAB shall also include in the proceedings all other persons including Sheikh Saeed, Musa Ghani, Kashif Masood Qazi, Javaid Kiyani and Saeed Ahmed, who have any direct or indirect nexus or connection with the actions of respondents No. 1, 6, 7, 8 and 10 leading to acquisition of assets and funds beyond their known sources of income;

f)   NAB may file supplementary Reference(s) if and when any other asset, which is not prima facie reasonably accounted for, is discovered;

g)   The Accountability Court shall proceed with and decide the aforesaid References within a period of six months from the date of filing such References; and

h)   In case the Accountability Court finds any deed, document or affidavit filed by or on behalf of the respondent(s) or any other person to be fake, false, forged or fabricated, it shall take appropriate action against the concerned person(s) in accordance with law.

15. As a sequel to what has been discussed in paragraphs 13 above, the following declaration and direction is issued:

i)   It is hereby declared that having failed to disclose his un-withdrawn receivables constituting assets from Capital FZE, Jebel Ali, UAE in his nomination papers filed for the General Elections held in 2013 in terms of Section 12(2)(f) of the Representation of the People Act, 1976 (ROPA), and having furnished a false declaration under solemn affirmation respondent No. 1 Mian Muhammad Nawaz Sharif is not honest in terms of Section 99(f) of ROPA and Article 62(1)(f) of the Constitution of the Islamic Republic of Pakistan, 1973, therefore, he is disqualified to be a Member of the Majlis-e-Shoora (Parliament);

ii) The Election Commission of Pakistan shall issue a notification disqualifying respondent No. 1 Mian Muhammad Nawaz Sharif from being a Member of the Majlis-e-Shoora (Parliament) with immediate effect, whereafter he shall cease to be the Prime Minister of Pakistan; and

iii) The President of the Islamic Republic of Pakistan is required to take all necessary steps under the Constitution to ensure continuation of the democratic process.

16. The Hon'ble Chief Justice of Pakistan is requested to nominate an Hon'ble Judge of this Court to supervise and monitor implementation of this judgment in letter and spirit and oversee the proceedings conducted by the NAB and the Accountability Court in the above matters. . . .

19. These petitions are thus disposed of in the terms mentioned above.

SOURCE: Supreme Court of Pakistan. "Constitution Petition No. 29 of 2016 Etc." July 28, 2017. http:// www.supremecourt.gov.pk/web/user_files/File/Const.P._29_2016_28072016.pdf.

OTHER HISTORIC DOCUMENTS OF INTEREST

FROM PREVIOUS *HISTORIC DOCUMENTS*

- Mossack Fonseca, International Officials Respond to Leak of "Panama Papers," *2016*, p. 199
- Resignation of Pakistani President Musharraf, *2008*, p. 359
- Pakistani Leaders on the Political Situation in Pakistan, *2007*, p. 648
- Pakistani General Musharraf on Military Coup, *1999*, p. 624

August

U.S. Government Seeks to Impose New Immigration Limits

AUGUST 2 AND 25, AND SEPTEMBER 5, 2017

President Donald Trump campaigned extensively on promises to take a harder line on immigration policy and, once elected, he moved rapidly to deliver on these promises. In his first few months as president, he barred visitors from certain Muslim-majority countries from entering the United States, limited the number of admitted refugees, increased the number of Immigration and Customs Enforcement (ICE) agents, and encouraged an increase in the number of immigration arrests and deportations. The president extended his tough stance on immigration and used his authority to pardon Arizona sheriff, Joe Arpaio, who gained national notoriety for unconstitutional immigration arrests, among other questionable law enforcement practices. In late 2017, Trump came up against an Obama-era policy, known as Deferred Action for Childhood Arrivals (DACA), concerning immigrants who had been brought to the country illegally as children. The president frequently changed his public stance on how to deal with the so-called "Dreamers," frustrating those on the right and left who were trying to secure a bipartisan agreement to handle these immigrants.

THE RAISE ACT

On August 2, 2017, President Trump publicly endorsed immigration legislation proposed by Sen. Tom Cotton, R-Ark., and Sen. David Perdue, R-Ga. The Reforming American Immigration for Strong Employment (RAISE) Act, would, if passed, usher in far-reaching changes including the complete elimination of some of the most widely relied on avenues of legal immigration, the initiation of a merit-based system for green cards, and drastic reductions in the number of refugees admitted each year. These changes would cut legal immigration to the United States by 50 percent over the next decade.

Multiple provisions of the RAISE Act would limit legal immigration. First, the act eliminates the Diversity Visa Program, which currently awards 50,000 visas a year through a lottery-based program meant to encourage immigration from countries with "historically low rates of immigration to the United States." Millions enter every year for the chance to apply for a visa and only a small percentage are accepted, in recent years primarily from African countries. Sens. Cotton and Perdue described the program as "plagued with fraud, advances no economic or humanitarian interest, and does not even promote diversity."

The RAISE Act would also limit so-called 'chain migration,' the method by which immigrants can sponsor their family members to join them. Under current law, citizens can petition for parents, siblings, and married children to get legal residency, and those with green cards can sponsor spouses and unmarried children for permanent residency status. Once a petition is accepted, however, because of numerical limits, the family members can wait in line for years, even decades, until their number is called. The RAISE Act would stop all preferences for siblings and adult children.

The new law would also create a new point system to rank applicants for green cards. In his remarks on the legislation, President Trump described this as "merit-based" immigration, designed to replace the current "low-skilled system." Points, the president said, are given to "favor applicants who can speak English, physically support themselves and their families, and demonstrate skills that will contribute to our economy."

Proponents of the bill, like co-sponsor Sen. Cotton, argued that the current system must change because unskilled immigrants push down wages and compete with Americans for jobs. "For some people, they may think that that's a symbol of America's virtue and generosity," he said. "I think it's a symbol that we're not committed to working-class Americans. And we need to change that." The bill, however, garnered little support in Congress. Democrats and immigration rights groups denounced it, and it was not widely supported by Republicans. Sen. Lindsey Graham, R-S.C., said that agriculture and tourism were the top industries in his state and "if this proposal were to become law, it would be devastating to our state's economy, which relies on this immigrant work force."

Many in the tech industry, who had been lobbying for more high-skilled immigration, nevertheless pushed back against the RAISE Act. Senior editor at WIRED, Issie Lapowsky, wrote that "such a point system looks like it would benefit the tech industry by prioritizing high-skilled immigrants," but "it includes no provisions to actually expand the number of high-skilled visas that the tech industry has been clamoring for. What's more, it would force immigrants who do make the cut to kiss their families goodbye, which could lead more of them to choose to bypass the U.S. in favor of Canada, as some skilled workers are already doing."

THE PRESIDENT PARDONS ARIZONA SHERIFF JOE ARPAIO

On August 25, 2017, President Trump issued a pardon to the long-serving and controversial former sheriff of Maricopa County, Arizona, Joe Arpaio, who often referred to himself as "America's toughest sheriff." A federal court had convicted, but not yet sentenced, him for intentionally disobeying a federal court order to stop making unconstitutional immigration arrests. "He's done a great job for the people of Arizona. He's very strong on borders, very strong on illegal immigration," President Trump said at a press conference, explaining his pardon, adding, "I thought he was treated unbelievably unfairly."

The eighty-five-year-old Arpaio had served for almost twenty-four years as sheriff in an Arizona county that includes most of Phoenix. During that time, he earned a national reputation for his hardline immigration stance and for creating a brutal Tent City Jail that he referred to as his own concentration camp. Prisoners in these camps endured limited meals, chain gangs, temperatures that often exceeded 140 degrees, and the highest prison suicide rate in the country. The sheriff was an early supporter of candidate Trump and had been one of the first to join his "birther" movement; Trump praised Arpaio in 2011 when he announced the formation of a "posse" that went to Hawaii to investigate then-President Barack Obama's birth certificate.

In 2007, a class action lawsuit, *Melendres v. Arpaio*, alleged that Sheriff Arpaio ordered racially discriminatory traffic stops, targeting Latinos without any constitutionally necessary individualized suspicion or cause. In 2013, U.S. District Judge G. Murray Snow, after a lengthy trial, found the sheriff had systematically targeted Latinos for traffic stops and illegal detention in violation of the Constitution and ordered him to end the illegal practices. Sheriff

Arpaio willfully violated the court order and was charged with criminal contempt of court. The contempt case was transferred to a different district court judge in Phoenix, Judge Susan Bolton, who held a five-day bench trial. "Not only did Defendant abdicate responsibility," she wrote in the July 31, 2017, order finding Arpaio guilty of criminal contempt, "he announced to the world and to his subordinates that he was going to continue business as usual no matter who said otherwise." The conviction carried a possible punishment of up to one year in prison, and the judge set the date for a sentencing hearing on October 5, 2017.

Before he could be sentenced, however, President Trump, making his first use of the presidential clemency power, pardoned Arpaio, ending any chance that he would spend time in prison. This move drew an outcry from civil rights groups and lawmakers of both parties. The American Civil Liberties Union (ACLU) called the pardon a "presidential endorsement of racism." Others, including Sen. John McCain, R-Ariz., emphasized the erosion of the rule of law. McCain said in a statement, "No one is above the law and the individuals entrusted with the privilege of being sworn law officers should always seek to be beyond reproach in their commitment to fairly enforcing the laws they swore to uphold. . . . The President has the authority to make this pardon, but doing so at this time undermines his claim for the respect of rule of law as Mr. Arpaio has shown no remorse for his actions." Others applauded the pardon. James Fotis, president of the National Center for Police Defense, released a statement supporting the pardon. "President Trump," he said, "recognized Sheriff Arpaio was doing his job, following the law, and this is why he deserves to be pardoned."

The presiding judge in Sheriff Arpaio's contempt case accepted the pardon, but in an October 20 ruling, rejected arguments from his lawyers and the Justice Department that Arpaio was entitled to have all rulings in the case vacated, including the guilty verdict. In a decision that is likely to be appealed, she ruled that the pardon mooted the sentence and entry of judgment but left the conviction in place. "The Court found Defendant guilty of criminal contempt. The President issued the pardon. Defendant accepted. The pardon undoubtedly spared Defendant from any punishment that might otherwise have been imposed. It did not, however, 'revise the historical facts' of this case," she said.

On January 9, 2018, Arpaio announced his intent to run for the Senate seat of retiring Arizona Sen. Jeff Flake.

DEFERRED ACTION FOR CHILDHOOD ARRIVALS POLICY

On September 5, 2017, Attorney General Jeff Sessions announced "the program known as DACA, that was effectuated under the Obama Administration, is being rescinded." President Trump then released a statement formally ending DACA and ordering "an orderly transition and wind-down" of the program that had provided temporary status to approximately 800,000 undocumented immigrants who had been brought to the United States as children, often referred to as Dreamers.

President Obama created DACA program in 2012 through an executive order after broader immigration reform legislation had repeatedly failed to pass through the Congress. The DACA program allowed certain undocumented immigrants who had been brought illegally into the country as children by their parents to be able to live and work without fear of deportation for a renewable two-year period. To be eligible for DACA, applicants must have entered the United States before they turned sixteen and be under age thirty-one as of June 15, 2012. They were screened for any criminal history and must be currently in school, have a high school diploma, or have served in the military.

Republican congressional leaders objected to the executive order, arguing that the Constitution provides that only Congress can create laws. In 2014, when the Obama administration tried to expand DACA, a coalition of states filed suit arguing that the president had overstepped the authority of the executive branch and the Fifth Circuit Court of Appeals agreed, declaring the expansion of DACA unconstitutional. The Supreme Court, down a justice after the death of Justice Antonin Scalia, deadlocked, leaving the lower court's ruling in place. The original DACA was not part of this lawsuit, but the courts' rulings left it legally vulnerable. With President Trump in the White House and his newly appointed Supreme Court Justice, Neil Gorsuch, likely to vote with the conservative justices to overturn DACA, a group of ten Republican state attorneys general threatened that they would file suit to halt DACA if President Trump did not act to end it by September 5.

Against this backdrop, President Trump moved to end DACA, which he once called "one of the most unconstitutional actions ever undertaken by a president." In his statement, he referred to the program as an "end run around Congress" and said that his Attorney General, as well as "other top legal experts," had advised him that it "cannot be successfully defended in court." He did not end the program effective immediately, but rather, in what he called a "gradual process" with permits beginning to expire in six months. This six-month delay, he said, would "provide a window of opportunity for Congress to finally act."

In the following weeks, multiple lawsuits were filed around the country challenging Trump's order to end DACA. On January 9, 2018, U.S. District Judge William Alsup in San Francisco, in a case brought by the attorneys general of California, Maine, Maryland, and Minnesota, and the University of California, issued a nationwide injunction blocking the Trump administration from terminating DACA pending a final resolution in the court case. The White House called the injunction "outrageous" and said that it would appeal.

At the same time, a deeply divided Congress had made little progress in advancing legislation to make the provisions of DACA into law, despite public opinion polls that showed as many as 86 percent of Americans in favor of letting the Dreamers stay and broad bipartisan support for them in Congress. As a January 19, 2018, deadline approached for Congress to pass a spending bill to keep the government open, the fight to extend government funding morphed into a fight about immigration policy with DACA at its core. Democrats held the position that a solution to DACA must be a part of any federal budget deal. With Congress scrambling for a DACA deal, the deadline passed and the government shutdown. After three days of acrimonious negotiations, Democrats and Republicans agreed to a three-week funding extension that included a promise from Senate Majority Leader Mitch McConnell to bring DACA legislation to the floor for a vote no later than February 8, 2018; a second, brief, shutdown pushed this deadline to February 12. Congress was ultimately unable to agree on a fix. The president promised—without a definitive timeline—to revisit the issue, leaving Dreamers in limbo.

—Melissa Feinberg

Following is the text of a statement by Attorney General Jeff Sessions on August 2, 2017, in support of the RAISE Act; President Donald Trump's August 2, 2017, remarks on immigration; an August 25, 2017, statement from the White House announcing Trump's decision to pardon Arizona Sheriff Joe Arpaio; and the text of a statement by President Trump on September 5, 2017, announcing his decision to end the DACA program.

Attorney General Sessions Provides Support to RAISE Act

August 2, 2017

Attorney General Jeff Sessions today issued the following statement on the RAISE Act:

"This proposal will help the Department of Justice perform its duties to uphold our nation's immigration law and end the unlawful abuse of our public benefits program that undermine U.S. taxpayers. The higher entry standards established in this proposal will allow authorities to do a more thorough job reviewing applicants for entry, therefore protecting the security of the U.S. homeland. The additional time spent on vetting each application as a result of this legislation will also ensure that each application serves the national interest.

"The American people deserve a lawful immigration system that promotes our national interest. The RAISE Act would give us a more merit-based immigration system that admits the best and the brightest around the world while making it harder for people to come here illegally. The bill would end programs known to be rife with fraud and abuse and finally improve the vetting process, making our country—and working-class wages— much safer and stronger."

SOURCE: U.S. Justice Department. "Statement by Attorney General Sessions on the RAISE Act." August 2, 2017. https://www.justice.gov/opa/pr/statement-attorney-general-sessions-raise-act.

President Trump Responds to the RAISE Act

August 2, 2017

Thank you very much. It's great to be here today to unveil legislation that would represent the most significant reform to our immigration system in a half a century. I want to thank Senators Tom Cotton and David Perdue for their tremendous work in putting together this historic and very vital proposal.

As a candidate, I campaigned on creating a merit-based immigration system that protects U.S. workers and taxpayers, and that is why we are here today. Merit-based.

The RAISE Act—R–A–I–S–E—the RAISE Act will reduce poverty, increase wages, and save taxpayers billions and billions of dollars. It will do this by changing the way the United States issues green cards to nationals from other countries. Green cards provide permanent residency, work authorization, and fast track to citizenship.

For decades, the United States was operated and has operated a very low-skilled immigration system, issuing record numbers of green cards to low-wage immigrants. This policy has placed substantial pressure on American workers, taxpayers, and community resources. Among those hit the hardest in recent years have been immigrants and, very importantly, minority workers competing for jobs against brand new arrivals. And it has not been fair to our people, to our citizens, to our workers.

The RAISE Act ends chain migration and replaces our low-skilled system with a new points-based system for receiving a green card. This competitive application process will favor applicants who can speak English, financially support themselves and their families, and demonstrate skills that will contribute to our economy.

The RAISE Act prevents new migrants and new immigrants from collecting welfare and protects U.S. workers from being displaced. And that's a very big thing. They're not going to come in and just immediately go and collect welfare. That doesn't happen under the RAISE Act. They can't do that. Crucially, the green card reforms in the RAISE Act will give American workers a pay raise by reducing unskilled immigration.

This legislation will not only restore our competitive edge in the 21st century, but it will restore the sacred bonds of trust between America and its citizens. This legislation demonstrates our compassion for struggling American families who deserve an immigration system that puts their needs first and that puts America first.

Finally, the reforms in the RAISE Act will help ensure that newcomers to our wonderful country will be assimilated, will succeed, and will achieve the American Dream.

I'd like now to invite Senator Cotton and Senator Perdue to say a few words. Thank you. Thank you very much.

[At this point, Sens. Thomas B. Cotton and David A. Perdue, Jr., made brief remarks. The President then concluded as follows.]

Thank you, David. I just want to state that, as you probably have noticed, the stock market hit an alltime record high today, over 22,000. We've picked up, substantially now, more than $4 trillion in net worth in terms of our country, our stocks, our companies. We have a growth rate—a GDP—which has been much higher than, as you know, anybody anticipated, except maybe us. But then, it's going to go up. It's going to go higher too. We're doing a job.

And you're going to see, jobs are pouring back into the country. The factories and plants are coming back into the country. We're going to start making product in America again. And that's happening all over. As I mentioned yesterday, Foxconn is going to spend $10 billion in Wisconsin and other places. And I think the $10 billion is going to end up being $30 billion. They make the iPhones for Apple and others, and it is a truly incredible company.

So we have a lot of things happening that are really great. But again, today the stock market hit the highest level that it has ever been, and our country is doing very well.

I just want to thank you all. Tom and David are going to be outside. They're going to speak to you at length about what we're going to do with respect to this aspect of immigration. I think it's going to be very, very important, the biggest in 50 years—biggest change in 50 years.

Thank you all very much.

SOURCE: Executive Office of the President. "Remarks on Immigration Reform Legislation." August 2, 2017. *Compilation of Presidential Documents* 2017, no. 00557 (August 2, 2017). https://www.gpo.gov/fdsys/pkg/DCPD-201700557/pdf/DCPD-201700557.pdf.

White House Statement on Arpaio Pardon

August 25, 2017

Today, President Donald J. Trump granted a Presidential pardon to Joe Arpaio, former Sheriff of Maricopa County, Arizona. Arpaio's life and career, which began at the age of 18 when he enlisted in the military after the outbreak of the Korean War, exemplify selfless public service. After serving in the Army, Arpaio became a police officer in Washington, D.C. and Las Vegas, NV and later served as a Special Agent for the Drug Enforcement Administration (DEA), formerly the Bureau of Narcotics. After 25 years of admirable service, Arpaio went on to lead the DEA's branch in Arizona.

In 1992, the problems facing his community pulled Arpaio out of retirement to return to law enforcement. He ran and won a campaign to become Sheriff of Maricopa County. Throughout his time as Sheriff, Arpaio continued his life's work of protecting the public from the scourges of crime and illegal immigration. Sheriff Joe Arpaio is now eighty-five years old, and after more than fifty years of admirable service to our Nation, he is worthy candidate for a Presidential pardon.

SOURCE: The White House. "President Trump Pardons Sheriff Joe Arpaio." August 25, 2017. https://www .whitehouse.gov/briefings-statements/president-trump-pardons-sheriff-joe-arpaio.

Trump Rescinds DACA Program

September 5, 2017

As President, my highest duty is to defend the American people and the Constitution of the United States of America. At the same time, I do not favor punishing children, most of whom are now adults, for the actions of their parents. But we must also recognize that we are a nation of opportunity because we are a nation of laws. The legislative branch, not the executive branch, writes these laws; this is the bedrock of our Constitutional system, which I took a solemn oath to preserve, protect, and defend.

In June of 2012, President Obama bypassed Congress to give work permits, social security numbers, and Federal benefits to approximately 800,000 illegal immigrants currently between the ages of 15 and 36. The typical recipients of this executive amnesty, known as DACA, are in their twenties. Legislation offering these same benefits had been introduced in Congress on numerous occasions and rejected each time.

In referencing the idea of creating new immigration rules unilaterally, President Obama admitted that "I can't just do these things by myself." And yet that is exactly what he did, making an end run around Congress and violating the core tenets that sustain our Republic. Officials from 10 States are suing over the program, requiring my administration to make a decision regarding its legality. The Attorney General of the United States, the Attorneys General of many States, and virtually all other top legal experts have advised that the program is unlawful and unconstitutional and cannot be successfully defended in court.

There can be no path to principled immigration reform if the executive branch is able to rewrite or nullify Federal laws at will. The temporary implementation of DACA by the Obama administration, after Congress repeatedly rejected this amnesty-first approach, also helped spur a humanitarian crisis: the massive surge of unaccompanied minors from Central America including, in some cases, young people who would become members of violent gangs throughout our country, such as MS-13. Only by the reliable enforcement of immigration law can we produce safe communities, a robust middle class, and economic fairness for all Americans.

Therefore, in the best interests of our country, and in keeping with the obligations of my office, the Department of Homeland Security will begin an orderly transition and wind-down of DACA, one that provides minimum disruption. While new applications for work permits will not be accepted, all existing work permits will be honored until their date of expiration up to 2 full years from today. Furthermore, applications already in the pipeline will be processed, as will renewal applications for those facing near-term expiration. This is a gradual process, not a sudden phaseout. Permits will not begin to expire for another 6 months and will remain active for up to 24 months. Thus, in effect, I am not going to just cut DACA off, but rather provide a window of opportunity for Congress to finally act.

Our enforcement priorities remain unchanged. We are focused on criminals, security threats, recent border crossers, visa overstays, and repeat violators. I have advised the Department of Homeland Security that DACA recipients are not enforcement priorities unless they are criminals, are involved in criminal activity, or are members of a gang.

The decades-long failure of Washington, DC, to enforce Federal immigration law has had both predictable and tragic consequences: lower wages and higher unemployment for American workers, substantial burdens on local schools and hospitals, the illicit entry of dangerous drugs and criminal cartels, and many billions of dollars a year in costs paid for by U.S. taxpayers. Yet few in Washington expressed any compassion for the millions of Americans victimized by this unfair system. Before we ask what is fair to illegal immigrants, we must also ask what is fair to American families, students, taxpayers, and jobseekers.

Congress now has the opportunity to advance responsible immigration reform that puts American jobs and American security first. We are facing the symptom of a larger problem, illegal immigration, along with the many other chronic immigration problems Washington has left unsolved. We must reform our green card system, which now favors low-skilled immigration and puts immense strain on U.S. taxpayers. We must base future immigration on merit; we want those coming into the country to be able to support themselves financially, to contribute to our economy, and to love our country and the values it stands for. Under a merit-based system, citizens will enjoy higher employment, rising wages, and a stronger middle class. Senators Tom Cotton and David Perdue have introduced the RAISE Act, which would establish this merit-based system and produce lasting gains for the American people. I look forward to working with Republicans and Democrats in Congress to finally address all of these issues in a manner that puts the hard-working citizens of our country first.

As I've said before, we will resolve the DACA issue with heart and compassion—but through the lawful Democratic process—while at the same time ensuring that any immigration reform we adopt provides enduring benefits for the American citizens we were elected to serve. We must also have heart and compassion for unemployed, struggling, and forgotten Americans.

Above all else, we must remember that young Americans have dreams too. Being in government means setting priorities. Our first and highest priority in advancing immigration reform must be to improve jobs, wages, and security for American workers and their families. It is now time for Congress to act.

SOURCE: Executive Office of the President. "Statement on Deferred Action for Childhood Arrivals Policy." September 5, 2017. *Compilation of Presidential Documents* 2017, no. 00609 (September 5, 2017). https://www.gpo.gov/fdsys/pkg/DCPD-201700609/pdf/DCPD-201700609.pdf.

OTHER HISTORIC DOCUMENTS OF INTEREST

FROM THIS VOLUME

- President Trump Issues Immigration Orders, p. 42

FROM PREVIOUS *HISTORIC DOCUMENTS*

- Federal Court Rules on Obama Administration Immigration Plan, *2015*, p. 628
- Federal Leaders Remark on Immigration Reform, *2013*, p. 229
- Secretary of Homeland Security Amends Immigration Policy, *2012*, p. 255

South African Political Parties Issue Statements on No Confidence Vote against President Zuma

---

AUGUST 8 AND 9, 2017

Three years after voters elected him to a second term as president of South Africa, Jacob Zuma faced the biggest threat to his presidency: a vote of no confidence in the South African National Assembly. While the August 2017 vote was the fourth vote of no confidence President Zuma faced since taking office in 2009, it represented his political rivals' best attempt to bring change to the South African government. The measure was introduced by the Democratic Alliance (DA) over what it considered years of mismanagement and corruption under Zuma's leadership. A successful vote of no confidence would have forced the immediate resignation of President Zuma and his cabinet, but the measure narrowly failed. However, Zuma ultimately resigned amid significant public pressure from the African National Congress (ANC), the political party he led, to step down.

The Threat to President Zuma's Government

On August 8, 2017, President Zuma faced the biggest threat to this presidency. The South African parliament, led by opposition leader Mmusi Maimane of the DA, introduced a vote of no confidence to oust the president and his entire cabinet. While President Zuma had faced—and prevailed over—three earlier votes of no confidence, this motion was different in that the scope of frustration with President Zuma had peaked and his rivals had successfully orchestrated the first secret ballot to challenge the president, which they saw as their best attempt to oust him from power.

In the months leading up to the motion, a broad coalition united around shared frustrations surrounding longstanding scandals involving corruption and mismanagement of the nation's economy. Opposition party members, including the Economic Freedom Fighters, DA, Inkatha Freedom Party, National Freedom Party, and the Freedom Front Plus, stood together to call for the end of the president's reign. The president's own party, which had dominated South Africa's representative government since the end of apartheid in 1994, appeared fractured. And President Zuma's political rivals successfully convinced the speaker of parliament and ANC member, Baleka Mbete, to allow a secret ballot, which opponents hoped would give disaffected ANC members cover to vote against President Zuma without fear of reprisal. For many South Africans and their parliamentary representatives, President Zuma's corruption and mismanagement of the federal government signaled a desperate need for change.

ALLEGATIONS OF CORRUPTION AND
INCOMPETENCE PLAGUE SOUTH AFRICA

Since taking office, President Zuma's administration was plagued by charges of corruption and incompetence. Critics held that his government's practices, including steps to enrich the president using taxpayer dollars, siphoned public funds from critical public works projects and laid bare his dismissive attitude to norms meant to protect the young African democracy. Others charged President Zuma with mishandling fundamental issues, such as employment and poverty, and failing to invest in adequate energy, water, and road infrastructure.

President Zuma's political critics were not alone in their negative view of his presidency. For years, President Zuma rebuffed calls for him to refund the South African government for home improvements he said were necessary to his office. The lavish building projects, among them a chicken coop, a cattle enclosure, an amphitheater, a swimming pool, a visitor center, and a helipad, were necessary for his safety and his ability to execute the duties of his office, the president maintained. The nation's Supreme Court disagreed. A year prior to the fourth vote of no confidence, the country's highest court reprimanded President Zuma for corrupt practices related to these taxpayer-funded home improvements. In a humiliating rebuke to President Zuma, the Constitutional Court's eleven justices ruled unanimously that the president had "failed to uphold, defend and respect the Constitution as the supreme law of the land." The justices ordered President Zuma to repay 246 million rand ($16.7 million) to the South African treasury and censured the executive for flouting democratic norms.

Aside from corruption charges, critics attacked the president for mismanaging basic issues. South Africa's economy, Africa's second largest and most sophisticated, suffered from persistent unemployment and fiscal irresponsibility. The nation's unemployment rate hovered above 20 percent throughout President Zuma's second term, rising to a high of 27 percent in 2016, and while living conditions improved since the demise of apartheid, the gains have slowed. Economic growth in 2017 was the slowest since the 2009 global recession. Rising debt threatened to crowd out public investment and spending, and in the spring of 2017 South Africa's credit rating was downgraded to "junk" status, sending the rand tumbling.

South Africa's investment in public infrastructure also languished under President Zuma. Citizens routinely lacked adequate electricity, water, and functioning roads, frustrating South Africans and slowing economic growth and private investment. Rolling blackouts and daily outages signaled a deep power crisis, threatening key industries and households. Eskom, the troubled state utility plagued by mismanagement and lack of investment, struggled to maintain the aging, under-maintained infrastructure. Meanwhile, labor unrest, including a five-month wage strike in the platinum industry—an important sector of South Africa's economy—and a separate dispute involving 220,000 metalworkers and engineers, further undercut economic growth. The lagging economy, mismanagement, and public corruption charges set the stage for a contentious showdown between an obstinate president and his emboldened political rivals.

ZUMA BEATS VOTE OF NO CONFIDENCE

As the legislature gathered to debate and eventually vote by secret ballot on President Zuma's future, crowds amassed in Cape Town, the seat of the legislature. Protesters and supporters alike listened to the proceedings, which were streamed and broadcast live, while thousands gathered in the major cities of Johannesburg and Pretoria. President Zuma's supporters pointed to potential chaos should the motion succeed rather than defending the president's policy decisions and tenure. At a rally for ANC loyalists outside City Hall in Cape Town, the spot where Nelson Mandela addressed huge crowds after being released from prison in 1990, activist Nobuntu Kuse bellowed, "This is where our democracy began. The ANC freed this country. We aren't going anywhere."

Inside the legislature, both sides fiercely debated the motion. President Zuma's opponents said the vote was essential to restoring confidence in the government and improving the economy. "Economic resources keep shrinking and our economy is not growing, thus resulting in huge job losses and relegating the majority of South Africans to utter despair," said Nhlanhlakayise Moses Khubisa, the leader of the tiny National Freedom Party. Repeatedly, critics invoked President Zuma's corruption charges and his link to the Guptas, a powerful South African family with extensive business holdings. Mangosuthu Buthelezi, the leader of the Inkatha Freedom Party, argued that under President Zuma the country was for sale "to the highest bidder." DA leader Maimane, who introduced the motion, asked members to put the country ahead of political allegiance. In a speech pitched in moral terms, Maimane implored members to stand up to oppression and corruption: "I never imagined that one day I would be here, in this Parliament, fighting a new form of oppression—a corrupt system that keeps our people imprisoned in poverty." He continued, invoking the plight of the poor across South Africa, "I've heard of parents abandoning their babies, and I have heard of good people turning to crime out of sheer desperation." Maimane ended his speech asking members to vote their conscience. Other parliamentarians, including former ANC members, sought to drive a wedge between President Zuma and the ANC in the hopes of convincing other ANC members to break with their president. "We are not here today to remove the democratically elected government of the ANC, which was voted for by our people in 2014," said Julius Malema, the leader of the Economic Freedom Fighters party, referring to the last national election. Malema reminded his colleagues that the vote was "not against the ANC" but against its leader, "the most corrupt individual in this country."

Despite a near unified opposition, a secret ballot, and a seemingly fractured ANC, President Zuma survived the no confidence motion. The final vote fell only twenty votes shy—177 lawmakers voted yes, 198 voted no, and nine abstained—a much narrower margin than expected. Most important, the vote revealed the truly shaky ground President Zuma occupied with members of his own party. The ANC controlled 249 seats in the 400-member National Assembly, the lower and more powerful house of South Africa's parliament, and many of those members had voted against their party's leader.

ANC, Democratic Alliance React to Vote of No Confidence

Following the vote, President Zuma addressed joyous supporters rallying outside the legislature in Cape Town. The president called the vote a victory, noting, "The ANC is supported by the overwhelming majority" of South Africans. Despite his narrow margin of victory, the president offered a public face of confidence and exuberance. The ANC echoed the president's comments in a statement delivered after the vote. The party's spokesperson, Zizi Kodwa, congratulated the parliament for "its robust engagement in the National Assembly today" and labeled the vote a victory for representative government. "The biggest victor of today's event is our constitutional dispensation," Kodwa said. "It once again reaffirms the ANC's position as the leader of society in that the country's MP's are able to exercise this critical constitutional provision aimed at safeguarding our democracy," he added. Addressing their political rivals, including the DA, the ANC stated, "We reject the craven opportunism and hypocrisy of members of the political opposition who have consistently sought to portray our MP's as unprincipled and cowardly" and reaffirmed its commitment to "work across all structures of government to deliver on our electoral mandate of delivering a better life for all."

Opposition leaders struck a decidedly different chord and signaled the necessity of dramatic action to bring about change. The DA proclaimed the day after the vote that the ANC had lost the people's mandate. "The ANC may have won in the No Confidence motion in Parliament yesterday, but it has lost the confidence of the country," Maimane said. "South Africa now needs a new beginning." Not content to wait until fresh elections, Maimane called for parliament to be dissolved and new election to be held immediately. Maimane concluded, "South Africa is now truly on the cusp of renewal and change. And that change cannot come soon enough." Despite his impassioned call, the DA would need to rely on the ruling ANC to dissolve Congress, a farfetched scenario no matter President Zuma's winnowing support.

A Short-Lived Victory Sets the Stage for Future Change

President Zuma survived the motion of no confidence but emerged bruised with sagging political support within his own party. Despite labeling the vote a victory, it was clear that South Africans' confidence in the president, including those in the ANC, had fallen to its lowest point. Four months after the vote of no confidence was defeated, the ANC replaced President Zuma with his deputy, Cyril Ramaphosa. Then on February 13, 2018, the ANC National Executive Committee asked Zuma to resign and said it would schedule a no confidence vote in parliament later in the week. Zuma resigned on February 14, and Ramaphosa was elected as South Africa's new president on February 15.

—Robert Howard

Following is the text of a statement delivered by ANC spokesperson Zizi Kodwa on August 8, 2017, following the unsuccessful vote of no confidence against President Jacob Zuma; and the text of a statement delivered by DA leader Mmusi Maimane at a press conference in Cape Town on August 9, 2017.

DOCUMENT

African National Congress Responds to Vote of No Confidence

August 8, 2017

The African National Congress (ANC) congratulates the Parliament of the Republic of South Africa for its robust engagement in the National Assembly today that resulted in the resounding defeat of the motion of no confidence in President Zuma and our Cabinet.

The ANC regards it as paramount that not just our elected representatives, but all South Africans; are able to engage on the most critical issues facing our country without fear of favour.

The biggest victor of today's event is our constitutional dispensation. It once again reaffirms the ANC's position as the leader of society in that the country's MP's are able to exercise this critical constitutional provision aimed at safeguarding our democracy.

Whilst the ANC has consistently noted the numerous challenges facing our democracy as presented by the political opposition—at the same time we cannot lose sight of the record of success and achievement under the ANC government as presented by ANC MP's in today's debate.

It is only through robust engagement and constant dialogue that we will be able to address and overcome the challenges facing our country, such as we have witnessed today.

The ANC has always retained the utmost faith in its deployed cadres in government. They are men and women of principle who owe their position to an overwhelming public mandate given to the ANC in successive elections since democracy.

We reject the craven opportunism and hypocrisy of members of the political opposition who have consistently sought to portray our MP's as unprincipled and cowardly.

Our MP's carry with them the aspirations of the electorate—and whether this motion of no confidence had been put to the vote via secret or open ballot, the ANC is confident our MP's will have acted in the best interests of our country.

Our elected representatives will continue to work across all structures of government to deliver on our electoral mandate of delivering a better life for all.

As Africa's oldest liberation movement, the ANC is a resilient movement, and South Africa is a resilient country. Despite the challenges we face as a country, we remain steadfast in our commitment to entrench the gains of our democracy. Most importantly, we remain resolute in our determination to accelerate transformation for the betterment of the lives of all our people.

The ANC calls on all sectors of society, even those with whom our views diverge, to work with us to realize this vision of radical socio-economic transformation for all our people.

SOURCE: African National Congress. "ANC Statement on Vote of No Confidence in the National Assembly." August 8, 2017. http://www.anc.org.za/content/anc-statement-vote-no-confidence-national-assembly.

DOCUMENT

Democratic Alliance Issues Statement on Failed Vote of No Confidence

August 9, 2017

On behalf of the Democratic Alliance (DA), I would like to pay tribute to all the women in our nation on this Women's Day. We must all work together to build a society in which women are celebrated and can flourish and lead in our society—not where women are victims of abuse, violence and worsening poverty.

The ANC may have won in the No Confidence motion in Parliament yesterday, but it has lost the confidence of the country.

Yesterday, Jacob Zuma survived yet again, protected by the party that elected him twice and shielded him from accountability countless times. South Africa now needs a new beginning.

We believe the voters should now have the chance to express their opinion about the conduct of the ANC in defending Jacob Zuma. In short, we believe that Parliament should be dissolved now so that the country can hold an early election.

We are sure that the ANC has lost the confidence of the majority of South Africans. We say, bring it on! Let's fight an election for the future of our country, and let's do it now. By the time Jacob Zuma has destroyed the ANC completely, and the country, it will be too late. Let's let the country choose a new beginning, now.

As such, the DA has taken a decision—in terms of Section 50 of the Constitution—to move a motion in the National Assembly to dissolve Parliament and for an early general election to be held. Section 50 of our Constitution states that the President must dissolve the National Assembly if the Assembly has adopted a resolution to dissolve with a supporting vote of a majority of its members, and three years have passed since the Assembly was elected.

Yesterday was an historic moment for our nation, as it was the first time in 23 years of democracy that such a number of ANC MPs broke rank and voted with the opposition in defiance of the party line. Between 30 and 40 ANC MPs voted with a united opposition to signal a disapproval of, and lack of confidence in, the sitting President and his leadership. Jacob Zuma has brought the country, and his own party, to its knees.

The significance of this outcome cannot be overstated. President Zuma survived only because members of parliament in the ANC voted for their own survival, and in support and defence of corruption, looting, and state capture.

Yesterday's vote made it clear to all South Africans that the divide in our country is not racial or political. It is between those who support and defend corruption, and those who are against it in all its forms. The ANC has shown yet again which side it is on.

Opposition parties are coming together to fight the evil of corruption in the ANC and those in the ANC who voted with us yesterday are coming to the realisation day by day that their future is with us. Now is the time for us to come together to save our country.

We believe that following yesterday's Motion of No Confidence, Parliament requires a fresh mandate, and that mandate ought to be given by the voters through the ballot box. This motion will be tabled in Parliament tomorrow, 10 August 2017, and we will ensure it is debated and voted on as soon as practically possible.

It is the DA's view that this is the most appropriate way to ensure a legitimate government is in place, one which the people of South Africa have full confidence in. Moreover, we call on those within the ANC—who are against corruption, looting and state capture, to vote in support of our motion to dissolve Parliament.

In addition to this motion, the DA will continue with its legal action against Jacob Zuma and his group of corrupt friends. We will see him in court next month—on 14 & 15 September, where he will have to defend himself in the Supreme Court of Appeal against the 783 charges of fraud, corruption and racketeering he still faces.

The DA has also filed an intervening application in the matter currently before the Constitutional Court on procedures to be followed in impeachment proceedings against the President. This case forms a part of a wider push to ensure that President Zuma, as well as future heads of State, are held to account.

South Africa cannot wait for December—that is a pipe dream. The change we need, and the new beginning we all want, will not come from an ANC elective conference in

December. We need a new government, and a new beginning, now! That's why we need fresh elections and a fresh mandate.

As proud South Africans, we must remain hopeful. This is not the end for our young democracy, it is the new beginning. South Africa is now truly on the cusp of renewal and change. And that change cannot come soon enough.

The people of South Africa—not compromised ANC politicians—must be given the choice as to who leads our country towards the dream of a united, non-racial and prosperous South Africa for all.

SOURCE: Democratic Alliance. "ANC Has Lost the Confidence of the Country: We Need an Election!" August 9, 2017. https://www.da.org.za/2017/08/anc-lost-confidence-country-need-election.

OTHER HISTORIC DOCUMENTS OF INTEREST

FROM PREVIOUS HISTORIC DOCUMENTS

Sonic Attacks on U.S. Diplomats in Cuba Suspected

AUGUST 9, SEPTEMBER 29, AND OCTOBER 3, 2017

In the summer of 2017, reports that some U.S. government personnel in Cuba had suffered from unexplained hearing loss and other unusual medical symptoms began surfacing. The news that these symptoms appeared to develop after the Americans heard various noises in their homes and hotel rooms led to rampant speculation that they had been the target of sonic attacks. Some U.S. officials were quick to blame the Cuban government for the purported attacks, despite Cuba's strong denials, while others suggested that Russia, a long-time ally of Cuba's Communist government, may be involved. To date, U.S. and Cuban investigations have not resulted in any concrete findings, yet the ongoing speculation and finger-pointing has fueled tensions between the two countries, particularly as President Donald Trump has placed new restrictions on U.S.–Cuba relations.

U.S. Diplomats in Cuba Report Concussion-like Symptoms

Amid swirling reports about U.S. diplomats' mysterious medical issues in the summer of 2017, State Department spokeswoman Heather Nauert confirmed on August 9 that some "incidents" had been reported by U.S. personnel, dating back to late 2016, and that several diplomats had to be brought back to the United States or had chosen to end their tours early as a result. Later in the month, Nauert revealed that at least sixteen U.S. employees in Cuba had experienced medical symptoms and had received treatment in the United States and Cuba. This number rose to twenty-one by the end of September, and twenty-four in November, with the most recent "medically confirmed" case occurring on August 21, according to the State Department.

The Americans involved in these incidents reported various symptoms, including "ear complaints, hearing loss, dizziness, headache, fatigue, cognitive issues, and difficulty sleeping," according to a statement by U.S. Secretary of State Rex Tillerson, symptoms that some officials also described as concussion-like. The Americans also reported hearing various sounds, such as high-pitched chirps, grating metal, or humming—often late at night, and sometimes accompanied by vibrations—prior to developing these symptoms. The Canadian Foreign Ministry reported that some of its personnel in Cuba had been similarly affected.

Nauert told reporters that the United States had "multiple agencies and departments" investigating the incidents and that the Cuban government was cooperating, but said that officials did not yet know the cause of the symptoms. "We're not assigning responsibility at this point," she said.

Sonic Attacks Suspected

The seeming link between the Americans' symptoms and the noises they reported hearing led to widespread speculation that they had been the target of a sonic attack and that a covert sound device had been placed in or near their homes and hotel rooms. Some were quick to blame the Cuban government, citing a history of Cuban officials' harassment of U.S. diplomats prior to the restoration of U.S.–Cuba diplomatic ties in 2015 under President Barack Obama. "The Cuban government has been harassing U.S. personnel working in Havana for decades. This has not stopped with President Obama's appeasement," said Sen. Marco Rubio, R-Fla. "Personal harm to U.S. officials shows the extent the Castro regime will go and clearly violates international norms." Trump also said he believed Cuba was responsible. Others questioned whether a third party may have been involved, noting Russia's long-standing alliance with Cuba and use of radio waves during the Cold War to disrupt U.S. intelligence-gathering activities. Moscow, or even a rogue element within the Cuban intelligence community, could be attempting to disrupt warmer U.S.–Cuba relations, they suggested.

However, many acoustic experts said it was highly unlikely that the symptoms reported were caused by a sonic weapon. Some sound devices are used by the U.S. military for defense, but they produce extremely loud sounds that would be impossible to miss. Ultrasound waves, which are a higher frequency than what humans can hear, are unable to travel long distances, can be weakened by the kind of humidity characteristic to Cuba, and would be deflected by walls or closed windows. An ultrasound weapon would need to be huge to use the waves at a distance, and experts questioned the likelihood that a small ultrasound emitter could be placed in something like a pillowcase without being discovered. Some research has been done by the U.S. military and private companies on the use of infrasound—sound waves that are a frequency lower than what humans can hear—as a weapon, but these waves are difficult to focus and use in a small area.

Cuba Denies Involvement

Cuban officials vehemently denied any responsibility for the attacks. "Cuba has never perpetrated nor will it ever perpetrate actions of this sort," said Cuban Foreign Minister Bruno Rodriguez in a speech to the United Nations. "Cuba has never allowed nor will it ever allow its territory to be used by third parties with that purpose." A statement from the Cuban Ministry of Foreign Affairs reaffirmed that "Cuba complies rigorously and seriously with all its obligations arising from the 1961 Vienna Convention on Diplomatic Relations in connection with the protection and inviolability of diplomatic agents and the premises of diplomatic missions." The Ministry also said that Cuba "took this issue with the utmost seriousness and acted expeditiously and professionally in order to clarify the facts of this situation, initiating a comprehensive, priority and urgent investigation on the indications of the highest level of the Cuban government." Cuba had established an "inter-institutional expert committee" to investigate the incidents, expanded and reinforced embassy and diplomatic residence security, and established new channels for direct communication between the U.S. embassy and Cuba's Department of Diplomatic Security, it added.

Some Cuban officials suggested the attacks were fabricated to justify President Donald Trump's rollback of Obama-era changes in U.S.–Cuba relations. In June, Trump reversed parts of what he considered Obama's "terrible and misguided deal" with Cuba, placing new restrictions on Americans' travel to and business dealings with the country. For example, Americans are now prohibited from doing business with a company controlled by the Cuban military or intelligence or security services. Americans are also no longer able to plan their own private trips to Cuba and must go through a government-approved tour company to book cultural and educational travel. Rodriguez said the U.S. was "deliberately lying" about the attacks and was using the incidents as "a political pretext for damaging bilateral relations and eliminating the progress made" during Obama's administration, adding that the range of symptoms reported by U.S. personnel suggested there was not a single cause.

Cuban officials also accused the United States of not sharing the diplomats' medical records or any other evidence with them. The Cubans claimed they had searched the hotel rooms and neighborhoods where many of the diplomats lived, analyzed air and soil samples, and researched insects and toxic chemicals that could have been responsible for the Americans' symptoms. "We've been unable to find anything to prove this situation exists or ever existed," Lt. Col. Jorge Alazo, head of the criminal division of the Interior Ministry, told NBC News.

STATE DEPARTMENT RECALLS, EXPELS DIPLOMATS

On September 29, the State Department announced it had ordered the departure of all nonemergency personnel and family members from Cuba. "Until the Government of Cuba can ensure the safety of our diplomats in Cuba, our Embassy will be reduced to emergency personnel in order to minimize the number of diplomats at risk of exposure to harm," said Tillerson. "The Department does not have definitive answers on the cause or source of the attacks and is unable to recommend a means to mitigate exposure." The State Department also issued a travel warning advising U.S. citizens to avoid journeying to Cuba, though the agency acknowledged there was no evidence that attacks had targeted private citizens. A few days later, the State Department expelled fifteen officials from the Cuban Embassy in Washington, D.C. Tillerson attributed the decision to "Cuba's failure to take appropriate steps to protect our diplomats in accordance with its obligations under the Vienna Convention." He noted that the United States would continue to maintain diplomatic relations with Cuba. Despite these announcements, the State Department declined to say the Cuban government was responsible for the Americans' health issues, though Tillerson said he was "convinced these were targeted attacks" and that Cuba probably knew who was responsible and could make them stop.

Investigations into the incidents are ongoing. The Federal Bureau of Investigation released an interim report from its investigation on January 4, 2018, stating that the agency has not yet found evidence that sound waves were responsible for the Americans' medical issues. Also in January 2018, the State Department launched an Accountability Review Board to investigate the purported attacks. Testifying on Capitol Hill, Acting Assistant Director for Diplomatic Security Todd Brown said that the agency was exploring whether exposure to a virus caused the Americans' to fall ill, in addition to considering sonic attacks.

—Linda Grimm

Following is a statement from Cuba's Ministry of Foreign Affairs from August 9, 2017, responding to the diplomatic situation; a statement from U.S. Secretary of State Rex Tillerson from September 29, 2017, on the U.S. response to attacks on government personnel in Cuba; and a statement by Secretary Tillerson from October 3, 2017, on the expulsion of Cuban diplomats from the embassy in Washington, D.C.

Cuban Ministry of Foreign Affairs
Responds to Sonic Attack Allegations

August 9, 2017

On 17 February this year, the United States Embassy in Havana and the Department of State informed the Ministry of Foreign Affairs of the occurrence of some alleged incidents affecting some officials of that diplomatic mission and their families.

Cuba took this issue with the utmost seriousness and acted expeditiously and professionally in order to clarify the facts of this situation, initiating a comprehensive, priority and urgent investigation on the indications of the highest level of the Cuban government. To this end, it conveyed to the United States Embassy the need for information-sharing and proposed to establish cooperation between the competent authorities of both countries.

The Cuban authorities set up an inter-institutional expert committee for the analysis of the facts; expanded and reinforced the protection and security measures of the mission, its staff and diplomatic residences; and new channels were made available for direct communication between the Embassy and the Department of Diplomatic Security.

In this context, on 23 May, the Department of State informed the Cuban Embassy in Washington of the decision that two Cuban diplomats leave the United States territory. This led to a protest by the Ministry of Foreign Affairs due to this unjustified and unsubstantiated decision.

The Ministry of Foreign Affairs reaffirms that Cuba complies rigorously and seriously with all its obligations arising from the 1961 Vienna Convention on Diplomatic Relations in connection with the protection and inviolability of diplomatic agents and the premises of diplomatic missions.

Our country's impeccable track record in this area is recognized internationally and Cuba is universally considered as a safe destination for both visitors and foreign diplomats, including Americans.

The Ministry categorically emphasizes that Cuba has never, nor would it ever, allow that the Cuban territory be used for any action against accredited diplomatic agents or their families, without exception. Moreover, it reiterates its willingness to cooperate in the clarification of this situation.

Havana, 9 August 2017.

SOURCE: Cuba's Representative Office Abroad. "Statement by the Ministry of Foreign Affairs of Cuba." August 11, 2017. http://misiones.minrex.gob.cu/en/articulo/statement-ministry-foreign-affairs-cuba-4.

Secretary Tillerson Statement on U.S.
Response to Attacks on Personnel in Cuba

September 29, 2017

Over the past several months, 21 U.S. Embassy employees have suffered a variety of injuries from attacks of an unknown nature. The affected individuals have exhibited a range of physical symptoms, including ear complaints, hearing loss, dizziness, headache, fatigue, cognitive issues, and difficulty sleeping. Investigators have been unable to determine who is responsible or what is causing these attacks.

On September 29, the Department ordered the departure of non-emergency personnel assigned to the U.S. Embassy in Havana, as well as all family members. Until the Government of Cuba can ensure the safety of our diplomats in Cuba, our Embassy will be reduced to emergency personnel in order to minimize the number of diplomats at risk of exposure to harm.

In conjunction with the ordered departure of our diplomatic personnel, the Department has issued a Travel Warning advising U.S. citizens to avoid travel to Cuba and informing them of our decision to draw down our diplomatic staff. We have no reports that private U.S. citizens have been affected, but the attacks are known to have occurred in U.S. diplomatic residences and hotels frequented by U.S. citizens. The Department does not have definitive answers on the cause or source of the attacks and is unable to recommend a means to mitigate exposure.

The decision to reduce our diplomatic presence in Havana was made to ensure the safety of our personnel. We maintain diplomatic relations with Cuba, and our work in Cuba continues to be guided by the national security and foreign policy interests of the United States. Cuba has told us it will continue to investigate these attacks and we will continue to cooperate with them in this effort.

The health, safety, and well-being of our Embassy community is our greatest concern. We will continue to aggressively investigate these attacks until the matter is resolved.

SOURCE: U.S. State Department. "Actions Taken in Response to Attacks on U.S. Government Personnel in Cuba." September 29, 2017. https://cu.usembassy.gov/actions-taken-response-attacks-u-s-government-personnel-cuba.

Secretary Tillerson Statement on the Expulsion of Cuban Officials from the U.S.

October 3, 2017

On October 3, the Department of State informed the Government of Cuba that it was ordering the departure of 15 of its officials from its embassy in Washington, D.C. The decision was made due to Cuba's failure to take appropriate steps to protect our diplomats in accordance with its obligations under the Vienna Convention. This order will ensure equity in our respective diplomatic operations.

On September 29, the Department ordered the departure of non-emergency personnel assigned to the U.S. Embassy in Havana, as well as all family members. Until the Government of Cuba can ensure the safety of our diplomats in Cuba, our embassy will be reduced to emergency personnel to minimize the number of diplomats at risk of exposure to harm.

We continue to maintain diplomatic relations with Cuba, and will continue to cooperate with Cuba as we pursue the investigation into these attacks.

Source: U.S. State Department. "On the Expulsion of Cuban Officials from the United States." October 3, 2017. https://cu.usembassy.gov/expulsion-cuban-officials-united-states.

Other Historic Documents of Interest

From previous *Historic Documents*

- President Obama on Historic Visits to Cuba and Hiroshima, *2016*, p. 158
- United States and Cuban Officials Remark on Renewed Relations, *2015*, p. 181
- President Obama on Restoring Diplomatic Relations with Cuba, *2014*, p. 619

Neo-Nazi Protest in Charlottesville

AUGUST 14, 15, AND 16, 2017

In August 2017, Charlottesville, Virginia, found itself in the national spotlight as white supremacists and white nationalists converged on the city for a rally against officials' plans to remove a statue of Civil War Gen. Robert E. Lee from a local park. Rally goers and counter protestors clashed violently, and one counter protestor was killed, prompting a major public outcry and condemnations from local, state, and federal officials. The violence occurred during a roiling national debate over whether Confederate statues, monuments, and other memorials should be removed from public spaces as symbols of racism, or preserved as part of U.S. history and culture. The incident also exposed President Donald Trump to significant criticism for his seeming reluctance to condemn the white supremacist and white nationalist groups involved and disavow the support of alt-right groups.

RALLY GOERS, COUNTER PROTESTORS CLASH IN CHARLOTTESVILLE

Organized by white nationalist Jason Kessler—known locally for protesting Charlottesville's status as a sanctuary city—the Unite the Right rally was planned for August 12, 2017. The rally was intended to protest the Charlottesville City Council's decision in February 2017 to sell a statue of Gen. Lee located in a city park. City officials had deliberated for more than a year about what to do with the statue after an African American high school student started a petition to have the statue removed in March 2016. Two months later, the council established a special commission to consider what to do with the statue. The commission recommended that the statue be relocated or changed to include "new accurate historical information," leading to the council's vote to sell the statue. Opponents of the council's decision, including the Virginia chapter of the Sons of Confederate Veterans, sued the council in March 2017, winning a temporary injunction to prevent the move. Richard Spencer, president of the white supremacist think tank the National Policy Institute, led a march in Charlottesville in May to protest the statue's removal. This was followed by a Klu Klux Klan rally in July that ended in clashes between Klan members and counter protestors as well as the arrest of more than twenty people.

Kessler's Unite the Right rally was set to take place in Emancipation Park, formerly Lee Park and home to the contested statue. The night before, approximately 250 white supremacists and white nationalists marched through the University of Virginia (UVA) campus, carrying tiki torches and chanting slogans such as "White lives matter" and "You will not replace us." The group marched to a statue of Thomas Jefferson, founder of UVA, where they encountered about thirty counter protestors. The two groups engaged in fighting but eventually dispersed. University leadership quickly sought to distance the school from the incident. "I strongly condemn the unprovoked assault on members of our community," said UVA President Teresa Sullivan. "The violence displayed on the grounds is intolerable and is entirely inconsistent with the university's values."

The day of the rally, protestors began gathering early in the morning, with media reports indicating that some carried shields, clubs, or guns. Counter protestors, comprised of religious and community leaders, Black Lives Matter activists, and anti-fascist groups, also converged near the park. Virginia State Police and Charlottesville police were stationed around Emancipation Park, except for one side. As rally goers approached that side of the park, they met a line of counter protestors blocking their path and began to fight their way through. Chaos ensued, with protestors punching, swinging clubs, using pepper spray, and throwing rocks and bottles. The police did not intervene until about twenty minutes into the altercation. "At 11:22, we declared an unlawful assembly. We quelled the disturbance at that point," explained Virginia Secretary of Public Safety and Homeland Security Brian Moran after the incident. Virginia Gov. Terry McAuliffe declared a state of emergency, and the Virginia National Guard was dispatched to the park to help clear the area. As the crowd dispersed and began to make their way to other parts of the city, the day turned deadly: Rally goer James Alex Fields Jr. drove his car into a crowd of counter protestors, killing Charlottesville native Heather Heyer and injuring at least nineteen other people.

Responding to the tragedy and the day's events, McAuliffe said he had a message for "all the white supremacists and the Nazis" who came to Charlottesville for the rally. "Go home," he said. "You are not wanted in this great commonwealth." The City of Charlottesville and the Charlottesville City Council issued a statement of condolence, honoring Heyer and two state policemen who died in a helicopter crash as they were helping respond to the incident. "This senseless act of violence rips a hole in our collective hearts," the statement read. "While it will never make up for the loss of a member of our community, we will pursue charges against the driver of the vehicle that caused her death and are confident justice will prevail."

Two days after the rally, McAuliffe convened an emergency cabinet meeting to discuss next steps for "healing our community and confronting the racism that stubbornly remains in our nation." The governor said he had directed the formation of a commission "to make actionable recommendations for executive and legislative solutions to advance our mission of reconciliation, unity, and public safety." He added that he was also directing a review of how the state's government issued rally permits, prepared law enforcement to respond to similar incidents, and coordinated with local and federal officials. McAuliffe also called on the federal government to "focus on the threat of domestic terrorism especially when it comes from beyond state lines."

The Lee statue and another of Gen. "Stonewall" Jackson were covered with black tarps as a sign of mourning for Heyer's death. Fields was charged with second-degree murder, and the U.S. Department of Justice announced it was launching a civil rights investigation into Heyer's death, in coordination with the Federal Bureau of Investigation and the U.S. Attorney for the Western District of Virginia.

Those involved in the rally remained defiant. "You think that we're going to back down to this kind of behavior to you and your little provincial town?" asked Spencer, who was scheduled to speak at the Charlottesville rally. "No. We are going to make Charlottesville the center of the universe."

TRUMP RESPONDS

In the wake of the Charlottesville protest, the nation looked to President Donald Trump for his reaction to the deadly events. Speaking before a bill signing the day of the rally,

Trump said, "We condemn in the strongest possible terms this egregious display of hatred, bigotry and violence on many sides, on many sides." Trump's use of the phrase "many sides" opened him to immediate criticism for not specifically condemning the white nationalists and white supremacists involved and for seemingly equating the counter protestors with those groups. "From the beginning, President Trump has sheltered and encouraged the forces of bigotry and discrimination," said House Minority Leader Nancy Pelosi, D-Calif. "There is only one side to be on when a white supremacist mob brutalizes and murders in America. The American people deserve a president who understands that." Sen. John McCain, R-Ariz., declared on Twitter, "There's no moral equivalency between racists & Americans standing up to defy hate & bigotry. The President of the United States should say so."

Some claimed that by not addressing the white supremacist groups directly, Trump was essentially endorsing their actions. The statement also appeared to affirm Trump's connection to the "alt-right," a collection of conservatives and fringe groups that pursues nationalist policies and has been accused of promoting racist and xenophobic ideologies. Trump's installation of Steve Bannon, the executive chair of the far-fight Breitbart News and self-proclaimed alt-right leader, as CEO of his presidential campaign and then as chief White House strategist, firmly established this connection in the minds of many. Some have also pointed to white supremacists' praise of Trump and the president's refusal to disavow them as proof of his implicit support for their views. "When [former Ku Klux Klan Imperial Wizard] David Duke and white supremacists cheer your remarks, you're doing it very, very wrong," said Sen. Chuck Schumer, D-N.Y. In fact, the day of the Unite the Right rally, Duke linked the protest to Trump's election. "We are going to fulfill the promises of Donald Trump," he said. "That's what we believed in, that's why we voted for Donald Trump because he said he's going to take our country back and that's what we're going to do."

Amid mounting criticism, Trump issued a second statement during a public appearance on August 14. "Racism is evil and those who cause violence in its name are criminals and thugs, including the KKK, neo-Nazis, white supremacists and other hate groups," he said. If Trump offered no further comment on the Charlottesville incident, his critics may have been assuaged. However, during a press conference on August 15, the president doubled down on his original statement. "There are two sides to a story," he told reporters. "You had a group on one side that was bad and you had a group on the other side that was also very violent. Nobody wants to say it, but I will say it right now." Trump noted that counter protestors "came charging with clubs in their hands" and did not have a permit to be at Emancipation Park. When asked why he waited two days to condemn white supremacist groups by name, Trump said, "I wanted to make sure, unlike most politicians, that what I said was correct, not make a quick statement." Trump lamented the removal of Confederate statues from public spaces and questioned whether statues of George Washington and Thomas Jefferson would be removed next because they owned slaves. "Where does it stop?" he asked. He also lashed out at the media, saying, "If the press were not fake, and if it was honest, the press would have said what I said was very nice."

These remarks prompted a fresh outcry from Trump's critics and led others to distance themselves from the president. At least eighteen charities cancelled or moved events that had been scheduled to take place at Trump's Mar-a-Lago resort in Florida. Dissatisfaction with the president's response also led business executives serving on Trump's American Manufacturing Council and Strategic and Policy Forum to resign in protest. Explaining her decision to step down from the council, Campbell Soup Co.

President and CEO Denise Morrison said, "Racism and murder are unequivocally reprehensible and are not morally equivalent to anything else that happened in Charlottesville. . . . I believe the President should have been—and still needs to be—unambiguous on that point. Following yesterday's remarks from the President, I cannot remain on the Manufacturing Jobs Initiative." Both groups were eventually dissolved, but not before the president lashed out at departing executives on Twitter. "For every CEO that drops out of the Manufacturing Council, I have many to take their place. Grandstanders should not have gone on," he wrote.

The Debate over Confederate Symbols

The drama that unfolded in Charlottesville over the planned removal of a Confederate statue reflected the challenge facing state and local officials as they considered what to do with statues, monuments, and other symbols of the Confederacy found in public spaces amid a growing national debate about whether such symbols ought to be removed or preserved. This debate picked up steam in 2015 after Dylann Roof killed nine African American parishioners at a historically black church in Charleston, South Carolina, in what was later ruled a hate crime. The shooting fueled calls for the removal of Confederate flags from public spaces, leading to the controversial decision by South Carolina Gov. Nikki Haley to take down the Confederate flag that had flown over the state capitol for more than fifty years. Focus soon shifted from flags to statues and other monuments to Confederate leaders and soldiers.

The debate over Confederate symbols is primarily divided into two camps: those who claim they are symbols of racism and should be taken down, and those who claim that their removal is tantamount to ignoring or rewriting U.S. history. Those who favor removal note that the statues and other memorials were not erected immediately after the Civil War; most were instead built in the early 1900s when states were implementing Jim Crow laws to segregate white and black populations and in the 1950s and 1960s as a way to push back on the Civil Rights Movement. They also argue that the Confederacy fought the Civil War to preserve slavery, which should not be commemorated or celebrated. On the other side, those who support preserving the monuments say they represent Southern pride and commemorate the fight to preserve states' rights, not a pro-slavery movement.

According to the Southern Poverty Law Center, there were approximately 1,500 Confederate place names and symbols in the United States in 2016. Between the Roof shooting in 2015 and April 2016, about sixty of these were removed or renamed. State and local officials took similar actions throughout 2017. In New Orleans, four Confederate monuments were taken down in May, prompting a series of protests, though none as violent as in Charlottesville. "These monuments celebrate a fictional, sanitized Confederacy ignoring the death, ignoring the enslavement, ignoring the terror that it actually stood for," said New Orleans Mayor Mitch Landrieu. In June, Levar Stoney, mayor of Richmond, Virginia, announced that Confederate statues along the city's famed Monument Avenue would remain in place but a committee would be established to help "redefine the false narrative" of the statues and provide more historical context.

Charlottesville motivated further, rapid action by state and local officials. Days after the rally, Baltimore Mayor Catherine Pugh had four Confederate monuments "quickly and quietly" removed overnight. Maryland Gov. Larry Hogan called for a statue of Supreme Court Justice Roger Taney to be removed from the state house grounds. (Taney wrote the majority opinion in the Dred Scott decision that upheld slavery and denied

African Americans citizenship.) North Carolina Gov. Roy Cooper called on the state legislature to repeal a law preventing the removal or relocation of monuments and asked the Department of Natural and Cultural Resources to evaluate the costs and logistics for removing Confederate monuments from state property. In the meantime, protestors took matters into their own hands and pulled down a Confederate monument in Durham, North Carolina. Jim Gray, mayor of Lexington, Kentucky, announced plans to remove two Confederate statues from their location near a historic statehouse. In Florida, the Jacksonville City Council asked city officials to conduct an inventory of Confederate symbols on public property to inform a plan for relocating them, and the United Daughters of the Confederacy had a monument to Confederate soldiers removed from Gainesville's downtown. Busts of Lee and Jackson were removed from the City University of New York's Hall of Fame for Great Americans, and the University of Texas removed three Confederate statues from its campus.

—Linda Grimm

Following is a statement by Virginia Governor Terry McAuliffe from August 14, 2017, on next steps to be taken by the state government after the Charlottesville protest; a statement by President Donald Trump from August 14, 2017, in response to the protest; excerpts from an exchange between Trump and reporters on August 15, 2017, in which the president answered questions about the situation in Charlottesville; and a statement of condolence from the City of Charlottesville and Charlottesville City Council from August 16, 2017.

Governor McAuliffe on the Events in Charlottesville

August 14, 2017

Governor Terry McAuliffe released the statement below regarding the next steps he and his administration will take following the events this past weekend in Charlottesville, VA:

"Today, I convened an emergency cabinet meeting to discuss the next steps we, as a commonwealth, must take in order to begin the arduous process of healing our community and confronting the racism that stubbornly remains in our nation. The events of this weekend have only strengthened our resolve to combat hatred and bigotry, and I want Virginia to be a leader in the national conversation about how we move forward. I have directed my team to impanel a commission with representatives from community organizations, faith leaders, and law enforcement to make actionable recommendations for executive and legislative solutions to advance our mission of reconciliation, unity, and public safety.

"Also, while we continue to grieve and support the families of those who lost their lives, we must learn from this tragic event to prevent a recurrence in our community or elsewhere. In that spirit, I also directed my team to conduct an extensive review that will include how we issue rally permits, law enforcement preparation and response, and coordination at the local, state, and federal level. In addition, the federal government must focus on the threat of domestic terrorism especially when it comes from beyond state lines.

"Finally, I commend our Virginia State Police and National Guard personnel, who worked in support of the City of Charlottesville, for their tireless work this weekend under very challenging and volatile circumstances. Without their extensive preparations and measured actions, we would be facing a far more grave situation today."

Source: Virginia Governor Ralph S. Northam. "Governor McAuliffe Statement on Next Steps after Events in Charlottesville." August 14, 2017. https://governor.virginia.gov/newsroom/newsarticle?articleId=20931.

President Trump Remarks on the Situation in Charlottesville

August 14, 2017

We will be discussing economic issues in greater detail later this afternoon, but based on the events that took place over the weekend in Charlottesville, Virginia, I would like to provide the Nation with an update on the ongoing Federal response to the horrific attack and violence that was witnessed by everyone.

I just met with FBI Director Christopher Wray and Attorney General Jeff Sessions. The Department of Justice has opened a civil rights investigation into the deadly car attack that killed one innocent American and wounded 20 others. To anyone who acted criminally in this weekend's racist violence, you will be held fully accountable. Justice will be delivered.

As I said on Saturday, we condemn in the strongest possible terms this egregious display of hatred, bigotry, and violence. It has no place in America. And as I have said many times before, no matter the color of our skin, we all live under the same laws, we all salute the same great flag, and we are all made by the same almighty God. We must love each other, show affection for each other, and unite together in condemnation of hatred, bigotry, and violence. We must rediscover the bonds of love and loyalty that bring us together as Americans.

Racism is evil. And those who cause violence in its name are criminals and thugs, including the KKK, neo-Nazis, White supremacists, and other hate groups that are repugnant to everything we hold dear as Americans. We are a nation founded on the truth that all of us are created equal. We are equal in the eyes of our Creator, we are equal under the law, and we are equal under our Constitution. Those who spread violence in the name of bigotry strike at the very core of America.

Two days ago, a young American woman, Heather Heyer, was tragically killed. Her death fills us with grief, and we send her family our thoughts, our prayers, and our love. We also mourn the two Virginia State troopers who died in service to their community, their commonwealth, and their country. Troopers Jay Cullen and Berke Bates exemplify the very best of America, and our hearts go out to their families, their friends, and every member of American law enforcement.

These three fallen Americans embody the goodness and decency of our Nation. In times such as these, America has always shown its true character: responding to hate with love, division with unity, and violence with an unwavering resolve for justice.

As a candidate, I promised to restore law and order to our country, and our Federal law enforcement agencies are following through on that pledge. We will spare no resource in fighting so that every American child can grow up free from violence and fear. We will defend and protect the sacred rights of all Americans, and we will work together so that every citizen in this blessed land is free to follow their dreams in their hearts, and to express the love and joy in their souls.

Thank you, God bless you, and God bless America. Thank you very much.

SOURCE: Executive Office of the President. "Remarks on the Situation in Charlottesville, Virginia." August 14, 2017. *Compilation of Presidential Documents* 2017, no. 00570 (August 14, 2017). https://www.gpo.gov/fdsys/pkg/DCPD-201700570/pdf/DCPD-201700570.pdf.

President Trump Speaks to Reporters about Charlottesville

August 15, 2017

[The following exchanges with reporters have been excerpted from the transcript of a press conference on infrastructure to focus on the president's Charlottesville-specific comments.]

Q.   Let me ask you, Mr. President, why did you wait so long to blast neo-Nazis? . . .

The President. I didn't wait long . . .

Q.   You waited 2 days—

The President. I didn't wait long.

Q.   Forty-eight hours.

The President. I wanted to make sure, unlike most politicians, that what I said was correct, not make a quick statement. The statement I made on Saturday, the first statement, was a fine statement. But you don't make statements that direct unless you know the fact. It takes a little while to get the facts. You still don't know the facts. And it's a very, very important process to me, and it's a very important statement. So I don't want to go quickly and just make a statement for the sake of making a political statement. I want to know the facts . . .

As I said on—remember, Saturday—"We condemn in the strongest possible terms this egregious display of hatred, bigotry, and violence. It has no place in America." And then, I went on from there. Now, here's the thing . . . When I make a statement, I like to be correct. I want the facts. This event just happened. In fact, a lot of the event didn't even happen yet, as we were speaking. This event just happened. Before I make a statement, I need the facts. So I don't want to rush into a statement. So making the statement when I made it was excellent. In fact, the young woman, who I hear is a fantastic young woman, and it was on NBC . . . her mother wrote me and said through, I guess, Twitter, social media, the nicest things. And I very much appreciated that. I hear she was a fine—really, actually, an incredible—young woman. But her mother, on Twitter, thanked me for what I said . . . And honestly, if the press were not fake, and if it was honest, the press would have said what I said was very nice. But unlike you, and . . . unlike the media, before I make a statement, I like to know the facts.

Q.   Why do Nazis like you—[inaudible]—these statements?

The President. They don't. They don't . . .

Q.   Richard Spencer has praised you. David Duke has praised you.

The President. How about a couple of infrastructure questions?

Q.   The CEO of Walmart said you missed a critical opportunity—

The President. Say it. What?

Q.   The CEO of Walmart said you missed a critical opportunity to help bring the country together. Did you?

The President. Not at all. I think the country—look, you take a look. I've created over a million jobs since I'm President. The country is booming. The stock market is setting records. We have the highest employment numbers we've ever had in the history of our country. We're doing record business. We have the highest levels of enthusiasm. So the head of Walmart, who I know—who's a very nice guy—was making a political statement. I mean, ask him how he's doing—

Q.   So if you had to do it again—[inaudible]?

The President. I'd do it the same way. And you know why? Because I want to make sure, when I make a statement, that the statement is correct . . . There was no way of making a correct statement that early. . . .

I didn't know David Duke was there. I wanted to see the facts. And the facts, as they started coming out, were very well stated. In fact, everybody said: "His statement was beautiful. If he would have made it sooner, that would have been good." I couldn't have made it sooner because I didn't know all of the facts. Frankly, people still don't know all of the facts.

It was very important—excuse me, excuse me—it was very important to me to get the facts out and correctly. Because if I would have made a fast statement—and the first statement was made without knowing much, other than what we were seeing. The second statement was made after, with knowledge, with great knowledge . . .

Q.   Was this terrorism? . . .

The President. Well, I think the driver of the car is a disgrace to himself, his family, and this country. And that is—you can call it terrorism. You can call it murder. You can call it whatever you want. I would just call it as "the fastest one to come up with a good verdict." That's what I'd call it. Because there is a question: Is it murder? Is it terrorism? And then, you get into legal semantics. The driver of the car is a murderer. And what he did was a horrible, horrible, inexcusable thing . . .

Q.   Senator McCain said that the alt-right is behind these attacks, and he linked that same group to those who perpetrated the attack in Charlottesville.

The President. Well, I don't know. I can't tell you. I'm sure Senator McCain must know what he's talking about. But when you say the alt-right, define "alt-right" to me. You define it. Go ahead . . .

Q.   Senator McCain defined them as the same group—

The President. Okay, what about the alt-left that came charging at them—excuse me, what about the alt-left that came charging at the, as you say, the alt-right? Do they have any semblance of guilt? . . . Let me ask you this: What about the fact they came charging—that they came charging with clubs in their hands, swinging clubs? Do they have any problem? I think they do. So, you know, as far as I'm concerned, that was a horrible, horrible day . . .

Q.   Is the alt-left as bad as White supremacists?

The President. I will tell you something. I watched those very closely, much more closely than you people watched it. And you have—you had a group on one side that was bad, and you had a group on the other side that was also very violent. And nobody wants to say that, but I'll say it right now. You had a group on the other side that came charging in, without a permit, and they were very, very violent.

Q.   Is the alt-left as bad as Nazis?

The President. Those people—all of those people—excuse me, I've condemned neo-Nazis. I've condemned many different groups. But not all of those people were neo-Nazis, believe me. Not all of those people were White supremacists by any stretch . . . Those people were also there because they wanted to protest the taking down of a statue, Robert E. Lee.

Q.   Should that statue be taken down?

The President. So—excuse me. And you take a look at some of the groups, and you'd see—and you'd know it if you were honest reporters, which in many cases you're not—but many of those people were there to protest the taking down of the statue of Robert E. Lee. So this week, it's Robert E. Lee. I noticed that Stonewall Jackson is coming down. I wonder, is it George Washington next week? And is it Thomas Jefferson the week after? You know, you really do have to ask yourself, where does it stop? . . .

Q.   Should statues of Robert E. Lee stay up?

The President. I would say that's up to a local town, community, or the Federal Government, depending on where it is located.

Q.   How concerned are you about race relations in America? And do you think things have gotten worse or better since you took office?

The President. I think they've gotten better or the same. I—look, they've been frayed for a long time. And you can ask President Obama about that, because he'd make speeches about it. But I believe that the fact that I brought in—it will be soon—millions of jobs—you see where companies are moving back into our country—I think that's going to have a tremendous, positive impact on race relations . . .

Q.   Mr. President, are you putting what you're calling the alt-left and White supremacists on the same moral plane?

The President. I'm not putting anybody on a moral plane. What I'm saying is this: You had a group on one side, and you had a group on the other, and they came at each other with clubs. And it was vicious, and it was horrible. And it was a horrible thing to watch. But there is another side. There was a group on this side. You can call them the left—you've just called them the left—that came violently attacking the other group. So you can say what you want, but that's the way it is.

Q.   You said there was hatred, there was violence on both sides. Are the—

The President. Well, I do think there's blame—yes, I think there's blame on both sides.

Q.   Is there bigotry on both sides?

The President. If you look at both sides, I think there's blame on both sides. And I have no doubt about it, and you don't have any doubt about it either . . .

Q.   But as for bigotry, the neo-Nazis started this. They showed up in Charlottesville to protest the removal of that statue—

The President. Excuse me, excuse me. They didn't put themselves down as you do, and you had some very bad people in that group, but you also had people that were very fine people, on both sides . . . I saw the same pictures as you did. You had people in that group that were there to protest the taking down of, to them, a very, very important statue and the renaming of a park from Robert E. Lee to another name.

Q.   George Washington and Robert E. Lee are not the same, Mr. President.

The President. No, George Washington was a slave owner . . . So will George Washington now lose his status? Are we going to take down . . . statues to George Washington? . . . How about Thomas Jefferson? What do you think of Thomas Jefferson? . . . Are we going to take down the statue? Because he was a major slave owner. Now, are we going to take down his statue? . . .

So you know what, it's fine. You're changing history. You're changing culture. And you had people—and I'm not talking about the neo-Nazis and the White nationalists, because they should be condemned totally—but you had many people in that group other than neo-Nazis and White nationalists. Okay? And the press has treated them absolutely unfairly . . .

Now, in the other group also, you had some fine people. But you also had troublemakers, and you see them come with the black outfits and with the helmets and with the baseball bats. You had a lot of bad people in the other group . . .

Q.   Sir, I'm sorry. I just didn't understand what you were saying. You were saying the press has treated White nationalists unfairly?

The President. No . . . There were people in that rally—and I looked the night before—if you look, there were people protesting very quietly the taking down of the statue of Robert E. Lee. I'm sure in that group there were some bad ones. The following day it looked like they had some rough, bad people: neo-Nazis, White nationalists, whatever you want to call them. But you had a lot of people in that group that were there to innocently protest, and very legally protest—because you know, I don't know if you know, they had a permit. The other group didn't have a permit. So I only tell you this: There are two sides to a story. I thought what took place was a horrible moment for our country, a horrible moment. But there are two sides to the country . . .

SOURCE: Executive Office of the President. "Remarks on Infrastructure and an Exchange with Reporters in New York City." August 15, 2017. *Compilation of Presidential Documents* 2017, no. 00573 (August 15, 2017). https://www.gpo.gov/fdsys/pkg/DCPD-201700573/pdf/DCPD-201700573.pdf.

Condolence Statement from the City of Charlottesville

August 16, 2017

Statement of Condolence on the Deaths of Heather D. Heyer, 32, of Charlottesville, Va., Lieutenant H. Jay Cullen, 48, of Midlothian, Va., and Trooper-Pilot Berke M. M. Bates of Quinton, Va.

The City of Charlottesville and Charlottesville City Council send our thoughts to the families of the three Virginia residents who lost their lives yesterday, August 12, 2017.

Charlottesville resident Heather Heyer was struck down by a vehicle while exercising her peaceful first-amendment right to speech. This senseless act of violence rips a hole in our collective hearts. While it will never make up for the loss of a member of our community, we will pursue charges against the driver of the vehicle that caused her death and are confident justice will prevail.

Virginia State Police Lieutenant H. Jay Cullen and Trooper-Pilot Berke M. M. Bates were working with the Charlottesville Police and their brothers and sisters in the Virginia State Police to help ensure the safety of the many city residents and visitors who were in Charlottesville yesterday. These men gave their lives in the line of duty and our gratitude to them cannot be overstated.

On behalf of the City of Charlottesville and all of our citizens, we send our deepest condolences to the families and friends of Ms. Heyer, Lieutenant Cullen and Trooper-Pilot Bates. Their loss is a loss for all of us and we mourn with you.

Source: City of Charlottesville, Virginia. "A Statement of Condolence from the City of Charlottesville and City Council." August 16, 2017. http://www.charlottesville.org/Home/Components/News/News/8422/635?npage=2.

OTHER HISTORIC DOCUMENTS OF INTEREST

FROM PREVIOUS *HISTORIC DOCUMENTS*

United Nations Responds to Flooding in India, Nepal, and Bangladesh

AUGUST 24, SEPTEMBER 1 AND 2, 2017

Weeks of exceptionally heavy rains during South Asia's 2017 monsoon season led to catastrophic flooding in India, Nepal, and Bangladesh in August and September. Across the three countries, more than 45 million people were affected, as hundreds of thousands of homes and millions of acres of rural farmland were damaged or destroyed. Following the disaster, the United Nations (UN) coordinated with governments and other humanitarian organizations to provide supplies and information about avoiding disease to affected areas.

Monsoon Rains Devastate South Asia

South Asia's monsoon season typically stretches from June to September each year, marked by heavy rainfall and the potential for landslides and flash flooding. While some loss of life and destruction of property is reported each monsoon season, international relief organizations stated that the flooding caused by the 2017 monsoons was far worse than in recent years.

Data released by the UN Office for the Coordination of Humanitarian Affairs (OCHA) on August 24 indicated that nearly 41 million people across Bangladesh, India, and Nepal had been affected by flooding and landslides and at least 900 people were killed. By September, the death toll had increased to at least 1,288 with more than 45 million people affected, according to a report from the UN Children's Fund (UNICEF).

According to Bangladesh's Meteorological Department, roughly one week's worth of average monsoon season rain fell during a few hours on August 11, when rainfall peaked in that country. UNICEF reported that more than 8 million people were affected by the resulting floods, including about 3 million children. An estimated 696,169 houses were damaged or destroyed, including more than 2,000 schools. Roughly one third of the country was reported to be underwater, with the International Federation of the Red Cross and the Red Crescent stating it was the worst flooding Bangladesh had seen in forty years. The government reported that thirty-one districts in the northern, north eastern, and central parts of the country were impacted by flooding, stating that the Kurigram and Chimari districts in the north were the hardest hit.

An estimated 1.7 million Nepalese people were impacted by the flooding, including 680,000 children. More than 185,000 homes were damaged or destroyed, as were nearly 2,000 schools. Thirty-two of the country's seventy-five districts were reportedly affected by what the Ministry of Home Affairs said was the heaviest recorded rainfall in central and western Nepal in sixty years. The Terai district in southern Nepal suffered the most, with flooding reported across more than 80 percent of the district's land. This area is home to some of Nepal's poorest people, many of whom are subsistence farmers, which raised questions about Nepal's food security. A UNICEF report stated that a Rapid Nutrition Assessment conducted in August found a Global Acute Malnutrition rate of nearly 24 percent among children aged six months to five years in the Terai district, or about twice as high as it was before the flooding.

More than 31 million people in India—more than 12 million of whom were children—were affected by the flooding. Approximately 805,000 homes were damaged, as were nearly 15,500 schools. The Assam, Bihar, West Bengal, and Uttar Pradesh states in northern India suffered the most, and Mumbai recorded the worst flooding it had seen since 2005 when roughly 500 people were killed. The impact of the floods underscored India's lack of preparedness to prevent and respond to such a disaster. A report released in July 2017 by India's federal auditor found that most of the country's states had not identified or assessed flood-prone regions and that tens of millions of dollars that had been allocated for flood management efforts had not been spent. Furthermore, the report found that only 349 of the country's more than 4,800 large dams were functioning. In addition, flood prevention measures recommended by a government-established committee following the 2005 flooding in Mumbai have only been partially implemented. Some local officials pushed back on criticism of their flood preparation efforts. "If you get a whole year's rain in one to two days, how will you handle it?" asked Anirudh Kumar, a representative of Bihar state's disaster management department. "No preparation and planning will work."

UN Secretary-General António Guterres expressed his condolences to the flooding victims via a statement by his spokesperson. "The Secretary-General is saddened by the loss of life and the devastation caused by widespread floods and landslides," the statement read, adding that he "salutes the respective Governments' leadership in responding to the needs of those affected."

UN Coordinates Humanitarian Response

At the end of August, OCHA reported that various UN agencies were working with the governments of the affected countries to deliver aid, as were local humanitarian agencies, the International Federation of the Red Cross and Red Crescent, and private sector companies. In Bangladesh, for example, nearly 2,000 local medical teams were deployed while the government distributed cash and food aid to flood victims. The government also allocated $1.1 million to aid efforts and another $1.2 million for housing reconstruction. In India, flood relief camps were set up to provide food and shelter for those who lost their homes. Prime Minister Narendra Modi announced a 20 billion rupee relief package to help fund rehabilitation and reconstruction efforts, as well as flood mitigation. The UN collaborated with the Nepalese government and other NGOs to provide food, medical services, and hygiene kits to flood victims, and 27,000 security personnel and civil servants were mobilized to assist with relief efforts. The government gave more than $11.3 million to affected areas for nonfood relief and announced a plan to provide cash disbursements to families whose homes were completely destroyed. Another $16.2 million in humanitarian aid was pledged by other governments and nonprofit organizations.

UNICEF was among the UN agencies working with partners on the ground to provide aid to the affected countries. UNICEF estimated that 16 million children were impacted by the floods and in need of urgent support. "Millions of children have seen their lives swept away by these devastating floods," said Jean Gough, UNICEF's regional director or South Asia. "Children have lost their homes, schools and even friends and loved ones." UNICEF officials emphasized that the most pressing needs were ensuring children had access to food, clean water, hygiene supplies to help prevent the spread of disease, and safe places to play at shelters. UNICEF also said it was "absolutely critical" to get children back in school to give them a "sense of stability."

In Bangladesh, UNICEF distributed emergency hygiene kits and water purification tablets to help prevent the spread of water-borne diseases. According to Bangladesh's Director of General Health Services, more than 13,000 cases of water-borne disease linked to the flooding—including acute diarrhea, eye infections, skin diseases, and respiratory infections—had been reported as of September 1. UNICEF also participated in a Humanitarian Coordination Task Team with members of the Bangladeshi government and other humanitarian organizations, which met on August 30 to develop a flood response plan targeting 330,000 people in need of assistance across six districts. In Nepal, UNICEF supplied medical tents and surgical kits to affected communities, as well as basic needs such as buckets, tarps, and blankets. In India, UNICEF worked with the government to coordinate relief efforts in Bihar and Assam states, with UNICEF providing educational materials about safe drinking water and handwashing practices to residents of those states.

The UN World Food Programme (WFP) also partnered with local NGOs to distribute emergency food supplies to more than 200,000 people in Bangladesh and announced plans to help provide cash assistance to 100,000 of the "poorest and most vulnerable" to buy food and other necessities. "Many flood survivors have lost everything: their homes, their possessions, their crops," said Christa Räder, WFP's country director for Bangladesh. "People need food right now, and the full impact on longer-term food security threatens to be devastating." Nearly half of Bangladesh's labor force is concentrated in the agricultural sector, with sustenance farming widespread in the country's northern regions. According to the Bangladeshi government, roughly 62,000 hectares of cropland were completely damaged while another 531 million hectares were partially damaged by the floods. Bangladeshi officials encouraged farmers to return to their homes as soon as the flood waters receded to try and save their crops. "Farmers still have around 20 days to re-cultivate rice plants," said Reaz Ahmed, director general of Bangladesh's Department of Disaster Management. "The government is providing them seed, saplings and fertilizers."

FLASH FLOODS HIT KARACHI

Pakistan was the next South Asian country to hit by heavy monsoon rains, with flash flooding reported in the coastal city of Karachi—Pakistan's most populous city—at the beginning of September. The Karachi Meteorological Department reported that Karachi typically receives about twenty millimeters of rain each September, but it received ninety-seven millimeters of rain on August 30 alone. Downpours led to flooding in the city's northern and western districts, as well as electricity blackouts and the collapse of some buildings and roads. At least twenty-three people were killed, mostly by electrocution when they came in contact with electrified flood waters. Prime Minister Shahid Khaqan Abbasi directed the army and paramilitary Pakistan Rangers to help clear roads and reestablish communications infrastructure. The army and navy distributed water pumps to help drain parts of the city, and the navy sent boats and divers to assist with rescue and relief operations.

—Linda Grimm

Following is a press release from the UN Office for the Coordination of Humanitarian Affairs from August 24, 2017, describing the impact of and relief efforts in response to flooding in South Asia; a statement from UN Secretary-General António Guterres's spokesperson on September 1, 2017, in response to the floods; and a September 2, 2017, report from the United Nations Children's Fund on the number of children affected by the floods.

DOCUMENT   ## UN Agencies Aid Those in South Asia

August 24, 2017

United Nations humanitarian agencies are working with the Government and partners in Nepal to bring in clean water, food, shelter and medical aid for some of the 41 million people affected by flooding and landslides in South Asia.

Nearly a thousand people have been killed, and tens of thousands of homes, schools and hospitals have been destroyed in Bangladesh, India and Nepal.

"There is the possibility that the situation could deteriorate further as rains continue in some flood-affected areas and flood waters move south," the UN Office for the Coordination of Humanitarian Affairs (OCHA) today said in an updated note.

In Bangladesh, nearly 2,000 local medical teams have been deployed, even as one-third of the country is reportedly underwater. Aid workers are concerned about water-borne diseases, such as diarrhoea and malaria.

"Their most urgent concern is to accessing safe water and sanitation facilities," OCHA said earlier this week, citing national authorities.

It also warned of dangers to women and children, who are at increased risk for abuse, violence and sexual harassment.

In India, rescue operations are ongoing in many flood-affected areas, with those stranded being rescued by helicopter.

Flood relief camps have been established for those displaced by the disaster where they are being provided with food and shelter, OCHA said.

The Government recently announced additional funding for relief, rehabilitation, reconstruction and flood mitigation.

In addition to people suffering, Indian authorities also reported large parts of a famous wildlife reserve park destroyed, with endangered animals killed.

SOURCE: United Nations. "UN Agencies Aid Millions Affected by Flooding, Landslides in South Asia." August 24, 2017. http://www.un.org/apps/news/story.asp?NewsID=57403#.Wmc8VqinE2y.

UN Secretary-General Responds to Flooding

September 1, 2017

The Secretary-General is saddened by the loss of life and the devastation caused by widespread floods and landslides due to torrential monsoon rains in Bangladesh, India and Nepal.

The Secretary-General extends his condolences to the Governments and the people of Bangladesh, India and Nepal and salutes the respective Governments' leadership in responding to the needs of those affected.

The United Nations remains ready to support the relief efforts.

Eri Kaneko, Associate Spokesperson for the Secretary-General

SOURCE: United Nations Secretary-General. "Statement Attributable to the Spokesperson for the Secretary-General on Flooding in Bangladesh, India and Nepal." September 1, 2017. https://www.un.org/sg/en/content/sg/statement/2017-09-01/statement-attributable-spokesperson-secretary-general-flooding.

UNICEF Reports on Children Impacted by Flooding

September 2, 2017

The United Nations Children's Fund (UNICEF) said today that an estimated 16 million children are in urgent need of life-saving support in the wake of torrential monsoon rains and catastrophic flooding in Nepal, India and Bangladesh.

"Millions of children have seen their lives swept away by these devastating floods," said Jean Gough, UNICEF Regional Director for South Asia. "Children have lost their homes, schools and even friends and loved ones. There is a danger the worst could still be to come as rains continue and flood waters move south," she added.

UNICEF is on the ground working in close coordination with respective governments and humanitarian partners in the South Asian countries to scale up its responses and respond to immediate needs of affected children and their families.

Since mid-August, there have been at least 1,288 reported deaths, with over 45 million people estimated to be affected.

Many areas remain inaccessible due to damage to roads, bridges, railways and airports. The most urgent needs for children are clean water, hygiene supplies to prevent the spread of disease, food supplies and safe places in evacuation centres for children to play.

"Massive damage to school infrastructure and supplies also mean hundreds of thousands of children may miss weeks or months of school," said Gough. "Getting children back into school is absolutely critical in establishing a sense of stability for children during times of crisis and provides a sense of normality when everything else is being turned upside down."

In Bangladesh alone, more than 8 million people have been affected by flooding, including around 3 million children. An estimated 696,169 houses have been damaged or destroyed and 2,292 primary and community schools have been damaged by high water. There have already been more than 13,035 cases of water-borne diseases in the country.

In Nepal, 1.7 million people, including 680,000 children, have been affected with 352,738 displaced from their homes. More than 185,126 homes have been damaged or destroyed in addition to 1,958 schools, affecting the education of 253,605 children.

In India, four states in northern India have been extensively affected by the flooding, affecting over 31 million people including 12.33 million children. Some 805,183 houses are either partially or fully damaged and 15,455 schools have been damaged, disrupting the education of nearly one million students. Further heavy rains in Mumbai resulted in at least five deaths by drowning and three people including two children died due to house collapse.

SOURCE: United Nations. "16 Million Children Affected by Massive Flooding in South Asia – UNICEF." September 2, 2017. http://www.un.org/apps/news/story.asp?NewsID=57455#.Wmc8RKinE2x.

OTHER HISTORIC DOCUMENTS OF INTEREST

FROM PREVIOUS *HISTORIC DOCUMENTS*

- United Nations and Nepalese Officials Remark on Earthquake and Recovery, *2015*, p. 222

President Trump, Vice President Pence Visit Texas, Florida, and Puerto Rico after Hurricanes

AUGUST 29, SEPTEMBER 14, AND OCTOBER 6, 2017

An active 2017 Atlantic hurricane season had devastating effects on the southern United States and Puerto Rico. Residents of Texas, Louisiana, and Florida faced severe flooding that destroyed homes and cut power after Hurricanes Harvey and Irma. Puerto Rico's infrastructure was largely wiped out by Hurricanes Irma and Maria, and by the end of 2017, some residents still lacked access to power and clean water. Federal government response to Hurricanes Harvey and Irma was swift but was slow to reach Puerto Rico following Hurricane Maria, sparking intense criticism of the Trump administration.

HURRICANE HARVEY CAUSES SEVERE FLOODING

Hurricane Harvey, the eighth named storm of the 2017 Atlantic hurricane season, made landfall in Texas on August 25 as a Category 4 storm. The National Hurricane Center ranks hurricanes on a scale of one to five, five being the strongest. A Category 4 hurricane is categorized as one in which wind speeds range from 130 to 156 miles per hour, at which speed trees are uprooted, windows are blown out, and power lines are downed.

In January 2018, the National Hurricane Center released a report documenting Harvey's strength and damage, noting, "Harvey was the most significant tropical cyclone rainfall event in United States history, both in scope and peak rainfall amounts, since reliable rainfall records began around the 1880s." Nederland, Texas, a small town in the eastern part of the state, had the highest reported rain total at 60.58 inches. (The highest U.S. rainfall total prior to Hurricane Harvey was in 1950 in Hawaii at fifty-two inches.) Harris County, where the city of Houston is located, and Galveston County, which includes the island off Texas' southeast coast, were the hardest hit. Sixty-eight deaths were directly attributed to the storm, more than half of which occurred in Harris County. Most of those deaths were caused by drowning in the floodwaters. An additional thirty-five were considered indirect deaths, caused by factors such as motor vehicle accidents, downed power lines, house fires, and heart attacks.

Hurricane Harvey also impacted Louisiana, with peak rainfall amounts around 23.71 inches, and produced fifty-seven tornadoes in the Houston metropolitan area, Alabama, Louisiana, Mississippi, and Tennessee. In the Houston metropolitan area, some 300,000 structures were flooded, 500,000 cars were flooded, 336,000 individuals lost power, and 40,000 individuals were evacuated to shelters. In total, National Oceanic and Atmospheric Administration (NOAA) estimated that the damage from Hurricane Harvey could range from $90 billion to $160 billion; the midpoint estimate of $125 billion would make it the second costliest hurricane in U.S. history after 2005's Hurricane Katrina that hit Louisiana and caused $160 billion in damage. Two researchers at Ball State University estimated the damage to commercial and public property in the Houston metropolitan area alone to be closer to $198 billion.

The federal government prepared its storm response before Harvey ever made landfall, stationing supplies, Federal Emergency Management Agency (FEMA), and National Guard personnel in the Texas areas expected to be hardest hit. President Donald Trump, First Lady Melania Trump, and members of the president's cabinet visited Houston on August 29, 2017, to meet with Governor Greg Abbot and local members of Congress to discuss storm damage and recovery efforts. The president noted that while the storm had passed, the recovery would be long term. While on the ground, the president's team outlined how the federal government would aid in recovery, including ensuring affected residents had access to medical care and pharmacies, that home and business loans were readily available to those with lost income and property, and that funding could be obtained for infrastructure redevelopment.

Hurricane Irma Hits Caribbean, Florida, and Puerto Rico

Hurricane Irma carved a destructive path through a string of Caribbean islands in early September—including Cuba where it was the first Category 5 storm to hit the island since the 1920s—before making landfall in the United States, first in the Virgin Islands, then Puerto Rico, and then twice in Florida (once in the Florida Keys and then again on the mainland). The Caribbean islands Irma hit experienced extreme devastation. "There are shipwrecks everywhere, destroyed houses everywhere, torn-off roofs everywhere," said Saint Martin's President Daniel Gibbs. In Barbuda, a majority of the island's housing was destroyed and nearly all plant life uprooted. An estimated 60 percent of Puerto Rico was left without power. Dozens were killed across the areas where the storm made landfall.

Early predictions of the storm indicated that it could hit Tampa or Miami, potentially putting those cities entirely underwater, but a last-minute westward shift saved major metropolitan areas from enduring extensive damage. However, despite weakening to a Category 2 hurricane before hitting Florida, the storm brought with it significant storm surges. "Do not think the storm is over when the wind slows down," warned Florida Governor Rick Scott. "The storm surge will rush in and it could kill you." Scott, along with many other governors along the country's southeastern coast, declared a state of emergency and ordered the evacuation of 6.5 million Florida residents—primarily those on barrier islands and low-lying coastal areas—the largest evacuation in the state's history.

Irma was different from many other tropical cyclones because of the amount of time the storm lingered while maintaining its strength. Irma was the longest-lived Atlantic hurricane since 2004 and spent three days in the ocean as a Category 5 storm, the longest that strength has ever been sustained since tracking began in 1966. The storm also clocked 185-mile-per-hour sustained winds in the open ocean. The storm was unique in that it formed not in the warm waters of the Gulf of Mexico and Caribbean, but in the cooler waters further east.

Because FEMA had provided a significant amount of funding to those impacted by Hurricane Harvey just weeks earlier, Irma's anticipated destruction required the Trump administration to request an emergency $8 billion in funding from Congress. The House and Senate ultimately provided $15.3 billion in additional monies to FEMA for hurricane recovery efforts. Governor Scott met with President Trump, local members of Congress, and the president's cabinet on September 14 to tour hurricane-affected areas and discuss the ongoing response. Governor Scott praised the assistance offered by the federal government thus far, but cautioned that the state had a long way to go. "We're not done today. We're going to work hard. I know the Federal Government will continue to be a partner, our locals will, our State will. We're going to make sure—we're going to continue to be a strong, resilient State," Scott said.

Puerto Rico Residents Continue to Suffer from Hurricane Maria

Hurricane Maria hit the island of Puerto Rico on September 20 as a Category 4 storm with sustained winds of 155 miles per hour and was the most intense storm there since 1928. It battered the island for thirty hours before moving back out into the ocean, dropping thirty inches of rain in some parts of Puerto Rico. For an island that was still reeling from the effects of Hurricane Irma, Maria dealt a significant blow, knocking out any remaining electricity, telephone lines, and cellphone service; leaving most residents without access to clean water; and destroying 80 percent to 90 percent of structures in some towns.

Maria caused an estimated $90 billion in damage in Puerto Rico alone. The official death toll from the storm was recorded as sixty-four; however, reports from aid organizations operating on the island and independent media investigations indicate that the total is likely higher than 1,000. Because of this, Puerto Rico's Governor Ricardo Roselló ordered a recount in mid-December. The governor, who asked for immediate assistance from Congress and the president, called the island-wide devastation a "humanitarian crisis." Because of the destruction of an estimated 70,000 to 75,000 homes and damage to another 300,000, many Puerto Ricans relocated to the United States once planes and boats began leaving the island's shores. According to FEMA, 10,000 individuals received federal assistance to stay in hotel rooms across forty-two states through at least mid-March 2018.

The Trump administration was roundly criticized for its slow response to the damage done by Hurricane Maria in Puerto Rico. The president waited six days to hold a Situation Room meeting on the hurricane, and orders to deploy the east coast's only navy hospital ship did not come until September 26. Some believed the president was treating the residents of the island, a territory of the United States, as secondary to those residing within the fifty states. The mayor of San Juan frequently criticized the president, who responded that the mayor had "such poor leadership ability" and that Puerto Ricans "want everything to be done for them when it should be a community effort."

When he toured the hurricane damage, Vice President Mike Pence attempted to assure the people of Puerto Rico that the federal government would do everything in its power to aid in recovery efforts. "I say to you we will be here for the long haul. We will be here until all the people can say with one voice: Puerto Rico se levanta. Puerto Rico is rising," Pence said. "When one part of America cries out for help, we come together. And I believe in my heart that when the history of this time and this crisis is recorded in Puerto Rico, this will be a chapter when Americans stood by Americans and delivered on that promise," he added.

Despite the vice president's promises, by the end of 2017, an estimated 35 percent of the island was still without power and 14 percent lacked access to water. On January 30, 2018, FEMA announced that, due to the reopening of some businesses and supermarkets, it would withdraw some aid from the island and end its distribution of food, water, and medical supplies. Puerto Rican officials felt the move was premature. "We were not informed that supplies would stop arriving, nor did the Government of Puerto Rico agree with this action," said Hector Pesquera, the Puerto Rican government's State Coordinating Officer. FEMA, however, countered that by continuing to provide emergency assistance, it was discouraging residents from patronizing local markets, thus impacting the ability of the island to return to economic normalcy. However, due to growing outcry from Puerto Rican leaders and members of Congress, on January 31, 2018, FEMA reversed its decision and said it would "continue to support the Government of Puerto Rico to meet the needs they identify."

—Heather Kerrigan

Following is the text of remarks delivered by federal officials at a press briefing on August 29, 2017, regarding Hurricane Harvey relief efforts; the text of remarks delivered by members of the federal government on September 14, 2017, in response to Hurricane Irma; and the text of a statement delivered by Vice President Mike Pence on October 6, 2017, in Puerto Rico following Hurricane Maria.

DOCUMENT

President Trump, Federal Officials Address Hurricane Harvey Recovery

August 29, 2017

The President. And I have to say this: Under great pressure, this State has really responded. And, hopefully, you can think the Government—the Federal Government—has really done its job, because we've enjoyed working with you. Even though these are really trying times, we've enjoyed it very much, Governor. I want to thank you.

Governor Gregory W. Abbott of Texas. Well, thank you. If I could, Mr. President, I want you to know the gratitude that Texans have for you. We're honored to have you here in the Lone Star State. I wish it were not under these circumstances.

But we are able to be where we are today, in the aftermath of this catastrophic storm that we faced. And it's really been two storms: It was a hurricane that turned into one of the most immense floods ever suffered by the United States. People's lives have been on the line, and I've been able to see firsthand your care and your compassion for the people of Texas.

You—I've had the opportunity—for those who only get to see what happens on the front lines, you need to know what happens behind the scenes. And behind the scenes, the President has shown both care, compassion, and direction and commitment, from the very beginning when the storm was still way out in the ocean. He helped Texas get prepared, providing us every resource and tool that we needed so that we could have a plan to respond to the catastrophe that was coming. And then, after the hurricane came onshore, and after the flooding began in Houston, we were in communication, either you and I almost every day, or you and myself and your tremendous Cabinet members who have bent over backwards to assist us.

And then, on our flight from Corpus Christi to Austin, you could see his genuine compassion, as we saw videos of what was going on in Houston, Texas, with the rising water and our fellow Texans suffering, the President was heartbroken about what he saw, and he's committed to ensuring that Texas will rebuild, because that's the American way. We take care of each other. We've seen that with Texans helping Texans, with Americans helping Americans. And, Mr. President, we're stronger, better, and better prepared because of your leadership from the very beginning. And I want to thank you.

The President. Thank you. And I want to just say hello—Elaine Duke is here someplace. Elaine, fantastic job. And Brock has been incredible. And from your standpoint, Nim and the whole group have been—and Steve, who I just met—Steve—and the job that they've done getting along. Number one, they like each other, very important. [*Laughter*] And number two, they respect each other. And the job that all of these groups have done getting along is—in terms of coordination, has been really incredible, and everyone is talking about it.

The sad thing is that this is long term. Nobody has ever seen anything this long, and nobody has ever seen this much water, in particular. The wind was pretty horrific, but the water has never been seen like this, to the extent.

And it's maybe someday going to disappear. We keep waiting. We have 3 of our great—4 of our great Congressmen right here, and we want to appreciate—we really appreciate you being here. We're going to be working with Congress on helping out the State of Texas. It's going to be a costly proposition, because again, and probably—Ted Cruz is here. And, Senator, thank you very much—Senator Cornyn. And we'll be working with these characters over here—[*laughter*]—and I think we'll come through with the really— the right solution.

But probably, there's never been anything so expensive in our country's history. There's never been anything so historic in terms of damage and in terms of ferocity as what we've witnessed with Harvey. Sounds like such an innocent name, Ben, right? But it's not. [*Laughter*] It's not innocent. It's not innocent.

I also want to thank my people. Ben Carson, as you know, is here from HUD, and Linda is—Linda McMahon from Small Business. And I say this is not small business, Linda, this is big business. When you add it all up, you're going to be giving away many, many millions of dollars to help people out. And Tom Price, as you know is—Dr. Tom Price, who is—you have your people in the field, Tom.

In fact, you may say a couple of words. And then, I'll ask Linda, and I'll ask Ben, and then I think we'll get on to Nim and to Brock and everybody.

Tom.

Secretary of Health and Human Services Thomas E. Price. Sure. Thanks, Mr. President. As you said, this is a historic proportions storm and flood. The challenge that we have, obviously, is to get the resources to the individuals that are stranded right now, make certain that the evacuees have a place to go. From an HHS standpoint, our responsibilities are medical and veterinary and mortuary. And there will be all of the above.

The challenge that we have in the long term is that most individuals who suffer from these suffer from not being able to get the medical care that they need after the—when the sun comes out. So trying to make certain that we've got pharmacies staffed, make certain that dialysis units are up, make certain that folks are getting the electricity to their homes so the oxygen concentrators and the like are able to be utilized. And then, just chronic disease—making certain the folks can get to their doctor when they aren't in their hometown and get the treatment that they need.

But we're staffed up and ready to go. We've got four Federal medical stations that—two are up and running and two on the way. And we've another four or five that are stationed beyond after that, depending on where folks need services—

The President. And they're big ones.

Secretary Price. Yes, sir. Yes. So we're here for you.

The President. Thank you very much. Thank you, Tom. Linda.

Small Business Administration Administrator Linda E. McMahon. Well, SBA has its main disaster relief office in the Dallas-Fort Worth area, so we have 900 people there permanently. We have 600 available in the surge. There will be—they're already coming in. I actually did get a note on the plane from Corpus there that we made the first home loan approval from this disaster.

So I was glad that we're already up and running.

We will be making home loans, business loans. We'll be making loans for those folks who have lost income and also the opportunity to replace plant property and equipment and inventories. So we're up and ready to go.

The President. Thank you very much. And Ben Carson from HUD.

Secretary of Housing and Urban Development Benjamin S. Carson, Sr. Well, thank you, Mr. President. Thank you for your leadership and Mrs. First Lady also. Compassion permeates everything that's been done, and it's been great working with everybody. And, Governor, you're one of the people that I admire the most.

Gov. Abbott. Thank you, Secretary.

Secretary Carson. Brock is doing a fantastic job, and Elaine. Everybody that we've been working with is fantastic.

And what we've been trying to do is make sure that we go from the phase of rescue and reaction to the phase of recovery and a smooth transition. We're also going to be assisting State and local governments in reallocation of Federal assets to the disaster relief. Looking at granting immediate foreclosure relief; insurance—mortgage insurance, as well as insurance for rehabilitation, through the Section 203(k) program, Section 108 loan guarantees for infrastructure, for economic development, and for a host of things; and also disseminating information, which is so critical. The masses frequently become confused. We're working very hard to get rid of some of the regulatory burden so that we can get things done very quickly. Linda and I will be working on that to make sure that we get what we need to the people.

And I want everybody to know that we're in this for the long run, and we know that once the water recedes, that's where our work really begins. And we're going to be at it until we finish the job.

The President. Thank you, Ben, very much. I appreciate it.

So, Nim, why don't you take over along with Brock, and we can [go] through some of the different things that we're going to be doing.

[At this point, the briefing continued, but no transcript was provided.]

SOURCE: Executive Office of the President. "Remarks at Briefing on Hurricane Harvey Relief Efforts in Austin, Texas." August 29, 2017. *Compilation of Presidential Documents* 2017, no. 00594 (August 29, 2017). https://www.gpo.gov/fdsys/pkg/DCPD-201700594/pdf/DCPD-201700594.pdf.

Federal Officials Discuss Hurricane Irma Relief Efforts

September 14, 2017

The President. Well, I just want to thank everybody. I came down to see FEMA, to see the Coast Guard, to see the Army, the Marines, everybody—the Navy. The job that everybody has done is incredible. And I know you're also in the process, but to think of the incredible power of that storm. And while people unfortunately passed, it was such a small number that nobody would have—people thought thousands and thousands of people may have their lives ended. And the number is a very small number, which is a great tribute to you.

Also in the fact that I know in the case of FEMA and the case of Coast Guard, the job you've done in saving people, saving lives. As an example, in Harvey in Texas, we talked—over 16,000 lives. And nobody would even understand that, it's hard to even imagine, and down here the same thing.

So I want to thank, everybody. You guys have been—I don't want to see you next week in another place, okay? [*Laughter*] We've seen you enough.

Participant. Yes, sir, Mr. President.

The President. But I just want to thank everybody, the first responders, on behalf of myself, our Vice President. Melania really wanted to be with us; she's really—it has really touched her heart what's gone on. And we've seen the devastation. We're going to see some more of it now unfortunately. And I have to say that your Governor—where is our Governor here? Rick Scott. The job he's done is incredible, and I guess I've been very lucky, because, you know, you have a great Governor in Texas; you have a great Governor in Florida. The job that Rick has done is being talked about all over.

And to think that—and I must say, Florida Power and Light—where's Eric?
Eric. Where's Eric? Come here, Eric. Eric, great job.

Florida Power and Light Co. President and Chief Executive Officer Eric E. Silagy. Thank you.

The President. But get going, Eric. I will say they're way ahead of schedule. There are more electrical people in this State, I think, than ever accumulated anywhere in the world is what I read before.

Mr. Silagy. It's big.

The President. It's from all over the country they came, and I've never seen—you've never seen anything——

Mr. Silagy. No, we haven't.

The President. Mobilized all over. I see Pam Bondi, who has done such an incredible job stopping certain little problems before they start and actually getting some of the companies to put up a lot of money.

Florida State Attorney General Pamela J. Bondi. They've been great.

The President. So the attorney general, I want to thank you, Pam. Fantastic job. Really fantastic job.

Elaine—where's Elaine Duke? Elaine Duke and—where's our Brock? Don't lose him, okay, Elaine, please. [*Laughter*] I have to say that Brock, working with your Governor, working with Pam, working with Elaine, working, by the way, with Marco Rubio, who is around here someplace.

It's a team like very few people have seen, and I want to thank everybody. Marco, I want to thank you a lot; you were really helpful.

Senator Marco A. Rubio. Thank you.

The President. And I just—again, I have to say that, what do I know? But I hope this man right here, Rick Scott, runs for the Senate. I don't know what he's going to do. [*Laughter*] But I know that at a certain point it ends for you, and we can't let it end. So I hope he runs for Senate. Who knows what he is going to do?

Again, I came down to say hello to you folks and to say hello to you folks. And the First Lady and myself, this is an honor for us to be here. We're now going to tour some of the areas.

And as Rick said, we have been very, very fast, and we had to be. We were signing papers as the storm was coming in, and that's never happened before. But, Rick, thank you very much, really great job. And, Brock, everybody, thank you very much. We have a great—Rick Perry here.

Secretary of Energy J. Richard Perry. We've got your back, sir.

The President. We have Energy. We have Linda—Linda McMahon, we have so many people, so many of the Cabinet members, because they're going to help. I want to thank Mike Pence. He is—in fact, I'd like you to say a few words.

[*At this point, Vice President Michael R. Pence made brief remarks, concluding as follows.*]

Vice President Pence. And as the President has said, we're with you today, we're going to be with you tomorrow, and we're going to be with you until Florida rebuilds bigger and better than ever before. So thank you.

The President. Just one word on a very important subject, so your power is, I mean literally, Rick, it's going on as we speak. It's going way ahead of schedule, weeks ahead of schedule. And much of it—most of it, I guess outside of the Keys, where we have a very special problem, but we're working hard on that. That's a very, very special problem. That was just dead-center, but we're working very hard on that. And we have a lot of goods out there, a lot of water, a lot of food, a lot of everything.

But I'd like to ask your Governor to say a few words. Again, he's been absolutely outstanding. Thank you.

Rick.

[Governor Richard L. Scott of Florida made brief remarks, concluding as follows.]

Governor Scott. So we have a lot of work to do. This is not—we're not done today. We're going to work hard. I know the Federal Government will continue to be a partner, our locals will, our State will. We're going to make sure—we're going to continue to be a strong, resilient State.

I want to thank from the bottom of my heart, everybody's prayers to help us get through this.

The President. So we are now going to be making a tour of the areas. We're going to see some of the folks and make sure they're happy, because we're trying to keep it as happy as we can under the circumstances. In many cases, they lost their homes, and it's a tough situation. So we're going to go see a lot of the folks.

And I will tell you again, I want to thank you. I want to thank the military. Just incredible. So thank everybody, and we'll see you later.

Media, we appreciate you being so understanding. It's been a very tough period of time even for you folks, and we really do appreciate your understanding. This has been a difficult situation.

As Rick knows, almost all of the roads are now open, and the ports are just about open. What we had to do to get some of those ports open, people wouldn't even believe that we did it so quickly. So we're very proud of the job that everybody around here has done.

Thank you all. Thank you very much. We'll see you later. Thank you.

SOURCE: Executive Office of the President. "Remarks during a Briefing on Hurricane Irma Relief Efforts in Fort Meyers, Florida." September 14, 2017. *Compilation of Presidential Documents* 2017, no. 00636 (September 14, 2017). https://www.gpo.gov/fdsys/pkg/DCPD-201700636/pdf/DCPD-201700636.pdf.

Vice President Pence Speaks on Puerto Rico Hurricane Recovery Efforts

October 6, 2017

THE VICE PRESIDENT: Father Pena, all of the members of this extraordinary church, a 24-hour church that knows that the light is never gone. (Laughter.) It is a great honor and joy for my wife, Karen, and I to be here at Parroquia Santa Bernadita, a place of vibrant faith that is impressing the people of Puerto Rico and the world. (Applause.)

To my fellow Americans in the room, I bring you greetings from a man who was here just two days ago, the 45th President of the United States of America who sent me to say, we are with you today. We will be with you tomorrow. We will be with you every day until Puerto Rico rebuilds and recovers bigger and better than ever before—President Donald Trump. (Applause.)

And let me express a word of appreciation on behalf of President Trump for your governor. Governor Rossello and his wonderful wife, Beatrice, who is only eight months pregnant. I told your governor in one of our recent video conferences that Puerto Rico is impressing America and impressing the world. And Governor Rossello, you and your family's commitment, your determination, your vision for Puerto Rico is inspiring our country. And I commend you for that, and I thank you. (Applause.)

And let me assure you that Puerto Rico has a tenacious advocate in Washington, D.C. She is known as your resident commissioner, but we just call her Congresswoman Jennifer Gonzalez. She is amazing. (Applause.)

And thank you, all. Thank you for such a warm welcome today. I must tell you that the hearts of the American people have been breaking for people across these islands. Karen and I were in the U.S. Virgin Islands earlier today. And the President directed me to be with you this week to make sure that people all across Puerto Rico not just in this great city, but in places like Utuado (ph,) Arracebo (ph,) Coma Rio (ph)—all the cities and towns and promises across this land know, as President Trump said, we will get through this, and we will get through this together for everyone on Puerto Rico. (Applause.)

And on the President's behalf, I say to you we will be here for the long haul. We will be here until all the people can say with one voice: Puerto Rico se levanta. (Applause.)

Puerto Rico is rising. It's rising on the resilience of the good people of Puerto Rico. It's rising on the commitment of the American people whose hands and feet are in the form of our armed forces, in the form of FEMA, and the more than 15,000 federal personnel that are on the ground. And it rises in the form of faith that your governor so eloquently described.

And it's to that faith we repair and we say in this place of worship that first and foremost, we remember those who've lost loved ones in these storms. The Bible tells us that the Lord is close to the broken-hearted. And let that be our prayer for all of those who have lost loved ones and may yet learn of loss as time goes forward.

Our commitment to Puerto Rico, I trust is demonstrated by the President and the First Lady's presence—Karen and my presence here today. But as Jennifer kindly mentioned, I'm honored to be joined by the Secretary of Transportation, Elaine Chao. (Applause.) The Acting Secretary of Health and Human Services Don Wright. (Applause.) And the still new Surgeon General of the United States, Dr. Jerome Adams, who has been in the islands for a week. (Applause.)

The President often says that in America and among the American people when one hurts, we all hurt; when one struggles, we all struggle. When one part of America cries out for help, we come together. And I believe in my heart that when the history of this time and this crisis is recorded in Puerto Rico, this will be a chapter when Americans stood by Americans and delivered on that promise. (Applause.)

With the strong leadership of Governor Rossello, federal officials were here before the storm even arrived, during the storm. I spoke to our FEMA leadership in the region who explained to me that this was a rare occasion where FEMA personnel were sheltering in place during a Category 5 hurricane, not once but twice. We're proud of the efforts of FEMA. We're proud of our team on the ground. Nearly a month and a half, one hurricane after another, federal emergency management personnel across this region and across the country have made all of America proud. (Applause.)

And we're proud of the Armed Forces of the United States of America, including the National Guard of Puerto Rico. (Applause.)

It is remarkable to think of those patriots in the Puerto Rican National Guard, many of whom suffered loss in their homes, in their communities, but still answered the governor's call, stepped forward to come alongside neighbors and friends in their hour of need.

With the strong leadership of Governor Rossello, strong support of local officials at every level, and the support of those nearly 15,000 federal officials and armed forces, I'm pleased to report to you at this present we've delivered 7 million meals, 6 million liters of water. We are—we have a presence here of 14 Navy and Coast Guard ships, the USNS Comfort has arrived. And we have been making steady progress—steady progress opening roads and opening commerce and restoring basic infrastructure. But we have a long way to go.

President Trump and I know this; our entire team does. The people of Puerto Rico can be assured that we will be with you every step of the way. We will see this challenge through. While we've made progress, commercial flights resumed; 75 percent of gas stations up and running; electricity to around 50 hospitals and dialysis centers. We know there is so much work to do. But I stand before you today with confidence that this work will be done because I have faith. I have faith in the leadership of Puerto Rico, of Governor Rossello, of all of your leadership at the local level and those that represent you in Washington, D.C., and those that serve you in uniform at every level.

I have faith in all the American citizens across Puerto Rico who have come alongside neighbors and friends in acts of kindness and charity. I have faith in President Trump's leadership, his determination to stand by Puerto Rico in this challenging time. And I have faith that all of the American people stand today committed to see Puerto Rico through because we are all unidos por Puerto Rico. (Applause.)

And lastly, as Father Pena mentioned, I have that other kind of faith. I have faith that He in who the people of Puerto Rico have placed their trust for generations past is still with us today as our refuge and our strength, and that as Puerto Rico and its people do as you've done throughout your history, as you continue to build on that rock, that the rains may come down, the winds will blow and beat against the house, but the house will not fall because it's built upon the rock. (Applause.)

And on that rock of faith, we know Puerto Rico will rise again. The U.S. Virgin Islands will rise again, as President Trump loves to say, bigger and better than ever before.

And so let me say with confidence, with your continued generosity to your neighbors, with the strong leadership of Puerto Rico at every level, with the dedication of American officials from our armed forces to FEMA, the generosity of Americans who at this very hour are finding ways to help and contribute to the renewal of this region, and with the leadership of President Donald Trump in the White House, and with God's help, I know in my heart of hearts Cochi (ph) will sing loudly once again. (Applause.) And the best days for Puerto Rico and for all of America are yet to come.

Thank you. God bless all of you. God bless Puerto Rico and may God bless the United States of America. (Applause.)

SOURCE: The White House. "Remarks by the Vice President at Santa Bernadita, San Juan, PR." October 6, 2017. https://www.whitehouse.gov/briefings-statements/remarks-vice-president-santa-bernadita-san-juan-pr.

OTHER HISTORIC DOCUMENTS OF INTEREST

FROM PREVIOUS *HISTORIC DOCUMENTS*

September

Kenyan Court Discounts
Election Results

SEPTEMBER 1, 2017

Kenya's August 2017 general election pitted current president Uhuru Kenyatta against former prime minister Raila Odinga, who was making his fourth run at the seat. Despite Kenya's electoral body declaring Kenyatta the victor, on September 1, based on an appeal by Odinga, the country's Supreme Court threw out the election results and ordered that a second vote be held within two months. Before fresh elections could be held, Odinga dropped out of the race, citing a belief that the vote was being held in violation of the nation's constitution because the electoral body had not called for new party nominations after the September 1 ruling. Despite Odinga's withdrawal, the vote proceeded on October 26, and Kenyatta was declared the victor with 98 percent of the vote. Shortly thereafter, Odinga's opposition party announced its intent to form a parallel government and hold new elections.

KENYATTA WINS FIRST ROUND OF VOTING

On August 8, 2017, Kenya held its second presidential election since the violence-stricken 2007 poll that resulted in a power-sharing agreement enshrined in the country's constitution. That agreement attempted to move the country from a presidential system of government to more of a parliamentary one in which the prime minister would hold primary executive authority. The agreement, however, was incomplete and left in place a mixed presidential–parliamentary system with a president and prime minister sharing power, although not always peacefully. During the 2017 general election, voters would choose the president, members of parliament, local governors, and other elected officials. In the presidential race, incumbent Kenyatta faced off against former prime minister Odinga of the National Super Alliance (NASA).

Although the election took place with relatively few reports of violence, according to Human Rights Watch, Kenyan security forces carried out intimidation campaigns ahead of the vote to deter Kenyan's from going to the polls, specifically those who did not support the president's Jubilee Party of Kenya. The Carter Center, which had an observation mission in the country for the election led by former U.S. secretary of state John Kerry commended "the people of Kenya for the remarkable patience and resolve they demonstrated during the Aug. 8 elections for president. . . . In an impressive display of their commitment to the democratic process, Kenyans were undeterred by long lines and cast their ballots in a generally calm and peaceful atmosphere."

The larger concern about the election came in regards to the electronic transmission of results from the local polling stations to the 290 constituency tallying locations, which proved unreliable and required that the nation's election body, the Independent Electoral and Boundaries Commission (IEBC), ask for paper copies of the results to be tallied instead. Ultimately, on August 11, the IEBC declared Kenyatta the victor with 54 percent of the vote to Odinga's 45 percent. Due to the balloting concern, Odinga said he would not accept the results of the vote.

SUPREME COURT NULLIFIES ELECTION RESULTS

One week after the August 11 announcement, just as he had done after losing to Kenyatta in the 2013 election, Odinga and his opposition supporters filed a formal complaint with Kenya's Supreme Court. In its filing, Odinga's NASA party asserted that some vote tallies were rigged and that official documents transmitting the election results from each polling station were faked. These documents are expected to be signed by members of each party supervising the polling station, but according to the filing, of 25,000 results forms reviewed by NASA, 14,000 had errors that brought their authenticity into question. "The nature and extent of the flaws and irregularities so significantly affected the results that the IEBC cannot accurately and verifiably determine the number of votes any of the candidates received," the petition read.

On September 1, the Supreme Court issued its ruling with four of six justices voting to uphold Odinga's petition. In its finding, the court noted that the IEBC "failed, neglected or refused to conduct the Presidential Election in a manner consistent with the dictates of the Constitution and . . . the Laws of Kenya." The court also agreed with Odinga's assertion of irregularities in the transmission in election results and found that both "the irregularities and illegalities affected the integrity of the election." Ultimately, the court ruled, "A declaration is hereby issued that the Presidential Election held on 8th August 2017 was not conducted in accordance with the Constitution and the applicable law rendering the declared result invalid, null and void."

Two members of the Kenyan Supreme Court issued separate dissenting opinions. The first, written by Justice Njoki Ndungu, stated that he did not believe Odinga presented "material evidence, to the standard required, to upset the results." The justice further contended that Odinga did not challenge the results of the vote, but rather the method through which the results were transmitted from the polling stations to the IEBC. "How . . . can a process used to transmit those results for tallying upset the will of the electorate?" Ndungu asked. Justice Jackton Boma Ojwang reached a similar conclusion in his dissent, disagreeing with the majority's assertion that the transmission of the results could invalidate the results of an election that was conducted fairly. "There is not an iota of merit in invalidating the clear expression of the Kenyan people's democratic will, which was recorded on 8th August, 2017," Justice Ojwang wrote. The electoral process, he argued, "had all the vital features of merit" as acknowledge by both Kenyan and international observers. "To disregard such outstanding features of merit in the just-concluded elections, is to overlook the most basic democratic principles which safeguard the electors' entitlement to choose their public office-holders," Ojwang found.

Odinga celebrated the court's ruling. "For the first time in the history of African democratization, a ruling has been made by a court nullifying the election of a president." Kenyatta, who disagreed with the ruling, agreed to respect the court's decision and asked the public to remain calm as the nation moved toward a new election date.

ODINGA WITHDRAWS, VOTING PROCEEDS

In its ruling, the court ordered that a new election be held within sixty days, and it was scheduled by the IEBC for October 26. In a shocking move, on October 10, Odinga withdrew from the race, announcing that he would boycott the vote and urging his supporters to do the same. "We have come to the conclusion that there is no intention on the part of the IEBC to undertake any changes to its operations and personnel," Odinga said. "All indications are that the election scheduled for 26 October will be worse than the previous one." Odinga supporters quickly took to the streets, and on October 12, Kenyatta's government banned protests in what it called a bid to protect "Kenyans and their property." Further, the government announced, Odinga's NASA party would be held liable for any damage caused during the protests. The decision riled supporters of Odinga, who had in the past accused the president of using violence and repression to maintain his government's hold on power, despite promising a more free and fair society when he first came to power in 2013.

Protests continued despite the ban, and according to a joint report by Human Rights Watch and Amnesty International, up to fifty civilians had been killed by police between the first and second votes. The reports of violence across the country led the European Union to withdraw some of its election monitors, and a member of the IEBC resigned and fled to the United States amid death threats shortly before the October vote.

On October 26, of the nation's 19.6 million registered voters, only one-third turned out for the re-vote, which Odinga said represented a "vote of no confidence" for Kenyatta. Security concerns resulted in the suspension of voting by the IEBC in twenty-five constituencies in the western portion of the country, an Odinga stronghold. According to the IEBC, the results in these locations would not have impacted the final outcome of the election, which Kenyatta won with 98 percent of the vote. IEBC Chair Wafula Chebukati called the polling "a free, fair, and credible election." Odinga, however, continued to push his supporters to form a "national resistance movement" to "restore democracy." Odinga told supporters shortly after the results were announced, "This election must not stand. . . . It will make a complete mockery of elections and might well be the end of the ballot as a means of instituting government in Kenya. It will completely destroy public confidence in the vote."

Opposition to Kenyatta's Victory Continues

Under the nation's constitution, the Kenyan Supreme Court has the authority to consider any challenges to election results. Only two petitions were received regarding the October election, one of which was submitted by Harun Mwau, a member of parliament, who argued that the IEBC violated the law by failing to call for new nominations of candidates after the September 1 nullification of the election results. Notably, Odinga himself did not submit a challenge to the October results. On November 20, the court rejected both petitions, stating that they were "not merited."

The opposition boycotted Kenyatta's November 28 swearing in, and Odinga announced that he would be inaugurated himself on December 12 at a counter swearing-in. During his inaugural address, Kenyatta spoke directly to his competitors, stating that he would "endeavor to incorporate some of their ideas. The election was not a contest between a good dream and a bad dream. It was a contest between two competing visions. I will devote my time and energy to build bridges, to unite and bring prosperity to all Kenyans."

On December 10, NASA delayed Odinga's swearing-in, saying that "our resolve has not changed. Specifically, we wish to reiterate that any national dialogue must have electoral justice on the agenda. We are not interested in sharing illegitimate dictatorial power." In early January 2018, NASA announced that the swearing-in would be held on January 30, to be followed by the unveiling of the opposition government's leadership. The event proceeded as expected, despite a January 24 court filing by the nation's

Attorney General, Githu Muigai, to prohibit the counter swearing-in. Following the swearing in, a number of members of parliament who attended were arrested, three television stations that had planned to stream the event were suspended, and ruling Jubilee party leaders began calling for Odinga's arrest to end what they saw as a political insurgency.

—Heather Kerrigan

Following is the text of the majority opinion and two dissenting opinions of the Kenyan Supreme Court, issued on September 1, 2017, overturning the results of the August 8, 2017, presidential election.

Supreme Court Overturns Election Results with Two Dissenting Opinions

September 1, 2017

REPUBLIC OF KENYA

IN THE SUPREME COURT OF KENYA AT NAIROBI

(Coram: Maraga, CJ & P, Mwilu, DCJ & V-P, Ojwang, Wanjala, Njoki S. Ndung'u and Lenaola, SCJJ)

ELECTION PETITION NO. 1 OF 2017

-BETWEEN-

1. RAILA AMOLO ODINGA . . . 1ST PETITIONER

2. STEPHEN KALONZO MUSYOKA . . . 2ND PETITIONER

-AND-

1. INDEPENDENT ELECTORAL AND BOUNDARIES COMMISSION . . . 1ST RESPONDENT

2. CHAIRPERSON, INDEPENDENT ELECTORAL AND BOUNDARIES COMMISSION . . . 2ND RESPONDENT

3. H.E. UHURU MUIGAI KENYATTA . . . 3RD RESPONDENT

DETERMINATION OF PETITION WITHOUT REASONS

(Pursuant to Rule 23(1) of the Supreme Court (Presidential Election Rules) 2017

[1] The hearing of this Petition was concluded on Tuesday, 29th August 2017 well after 9.00 p.m. The Judges thereafter retreated to deliberate on the following issues for determination as crafted by the court:

(i) Whether the 2017 Presidential Election was conducted in accordance with the principles laid down in the Constitution and the law relating to elections.

(ii) Whether there were irregularities and illegalities committed in the conduct of the 2017 Presidential Election.

(iii) If there were irregularities and illegalities, what was their impact, if any, on the integrity of the election?

(iv) What consequential orders, declarations and reliefs should this court grant, if any?

[2] Having carefully considered the above issues, the following is the majority decision of the court with two Judges (J.B Ojwang and N. S. Ndung'u SCJJ) dissenting:

(i) As to whether the 2017 Presidential Election was conducted in accordance with the principles laid down in the Constitution and the law relating to elections, upon considering inter alia Articles 10, 38, 81 and 86 of the Constitution as well as, Sections 39(1C), 44, 44A and 83 of the Elections Act, the decision of the court is that the 1st Respondent failed, neglected or refused to conduct the Presidential Election in a manner consistent with the dictates of the Constitution and *inter alia* the Elections Act, Chapter 7 of the Laws of Kenya.

(ii) As to whether there were irregularities and illegalities committed in the conduct of the 2017 Presidential Election, the court was satisfied that the 1st Respondent committed irregularities and illegalities *inter alia*, in the transmission of results, particulars and the substance of which will be given in the detailed and reasoned Judgment of the court. The court however found no evidence of misconduct on the part of the 3rd Respondent.

(iii) As to whether the irregularities and illegalities affected the integrity of the election, the court was satisfied that they did and thereby impugning the integrity of the entire Presidential Election.

[3] Consequent upon the above findings, and as to what orders, declarations and reliefs this court should grant, the following are the orders of the court pursuant to Article 140(2) and (3) of the Constitution and Rule 22 of the Supreme Court (Presidential Election) Rules:

(i) *A declaration is hereby issued that the Presidential Election held on 8th August 2017 was not conducted in accordance with the Constitution and the applicable law rendering the declared result invalid, null and void;*

(ii) *A declaration is hereby issued that the 3rd Respondent was not validly declared as the President elect and that the declaration is invalid, null and void;*

(iii) An order is hereby issued directing the 1st Respondent to organize and conduct a fresh Presidential Election in strict conformity with the Constitution and the applicable election laws within 60 days of this determination under Article 140(3) of the Constitution.

(iv) Regarding costs, each party shall bear its own costs.

[4] A detailed Judgment containing the reasons for this decision and the dissents will be issued within 21 days of this determination in conformity with Rule 23(1) of the Supreme Court (Presidential Elections) Rules, 2017 as it is otherwise impossible with the limited time the court has, to do so.

[5] It is so ordered.

DATED AND DELIVERED AT NAIROBI THIS 1ST DAY OF SEPTEMBER, 2017

D. K. Maraga

Chief Justice & President of the Supreme Court

P. M. Mwilu

Deputy Chief Justice & Vice President of the Supreme Court

J. B. Ojwang

Justice of the Supreme Court

S. C. Wanjala

Justice of the Supreme Court

N. S. Ndung'u

Justice of the Supreme Court

Lenaola

Justice of the Supreme Court

SUMMARISED DISSENTING OPINION OF OJWANG, SCJ.

[1] It is not necessary in this summarized Judgment—which is to be followed by a fully detailed and reasoned decision on an occasion already signalled by the Chief Justice and President of the Court—to give the comprehensive facts, submissions and legal principles bearing upon the instant petition.

[2] The important petition, which seeks the annulment of Kenya's Presidential election results emanating from the General Elections of 8th August, 2017, is focused on a limited number of contentions: (a) that the said Presidential Election was not conducted in accordance with the relevant principles of the Constitution; (b) that the said Presidential Election was compromised by certain illegalities and irregularities; (c) that, consequently, the said General Election lacked integrity, and ought to be invalidated.

[3]   Whereas the substance of the case founded on illegality and irregularity rests on the voting-results electronic transmission process, there is substantial information showing that, by law, the conduct of the election should have been mainly manual, and only partially electronic. Hardly any conclusive evidence has been adduced in this regard, which demonstrates such a manifestation of irregularity as to justify the invalidation of the election results.

[4]   As regards the invocation of the Constitution as a basis for annulling the electoral process, only general attributions of impropriety have been made, and furthermore, without adherence to the prescription that the task of interpreting the Constitution with finality, rests with no one but the Courts—in this case, with this Supreme Court.

[5]   Much of the evidence which the majority opinion adopts, is largely unascertained, apart from standing in contradiction to substantial, more credible evidence.

[6]   In such a marginal state of merits in the case challenging the conduct of elections on 8th August, 2017, it is clear to me beyond peradventure, that there is not an iota of merit in invalidating the clear expression of the Kenyan people's democratic will, which was recorded on 8th August, 2017.

[7]   The procedural law for assuring the integrity of elections is abundantly set out in the Elections Act, 2011 (Act No. 11 of 2011), and in the Electoral Code of Conduct; and the relevant provisions were conscientiously applied by the Independent Electoral and Boundaries Commission, which fully provided for the role of international and local observers, as well as agents, in the conduct of the Presidential Election. The resulting electoral process had all the vital features of merit, as all the observers publicly acknowledge.

[8]   To disregard such outstanding features of merit in the just-concluded elections, is to overlook the most basic democratic principles which safeguard the electors' entitlement to choose their public office-holders.

[9]   In summarized form, I hereby record, without equivocation, my dissent from the Judgment given by the numerical majority of the Supreme Court Bench. For my part, I would dismiss in its entirety the petition which came up before us, as it was devoid of requisite supporting evidence, just as it did not rest upon the pillars of the Constitution, the ordinary law, or the pertinent elements inherent in the configuration of a democratic election.

[10]   In accordance with the terms of Section 26(2) of the Supreme Court Act, 2011 (Act No. 7 of 2011), I hereby reserve the detailed, reasoned edition of my opinion, to be delivered within the next 21 days.

....

J.B. OJWANG

JUSTICE OF THE SUPREME COURT

DATE and **DELIVERED** at **NAIROBI** this 1st day of September, 2017.

SUMMARISED DISSENTING OPINION OF NJOKI NDUNGU, SCJ.

[1] The Court has rendered its Judgement by a majority. I am however, of a different opinion. At the heart of democracy are, the people, whose will constitute the strand of governance that we have chosen as a country. On 8th August, 2017, millions of Kenyans from all walks of life yielded to the call of democracy and queued for many hours to fulfil their duty to our Republic by delegating their sovereign power to their democratically elected representatives. This was an exercise that was hailed by many regional and international observers as largely, free, fair, credible and peaceful. That duty stands sacred and is only to be upset if there is any compelling reason to do so. That reason must affect the outcome of the election.

[2] The election was managed by the 1st Respondent chaired by the 2nd Respondent who were assisted by hundreds of others to execute the mandate of the Commission under Article 88 of the Constitution. At the end of the process, the 2nd Respondent, in accordance with Article 138 (10) of the Constitution, declared the result of the election. Having received more than half of all the votes cast in the election and at least twenty-five percent of the votes cast in each of more than half of the Counties, the 3rd Respondent was declared President-elect.

[3] The case revolved around three fundamental questions:

(i) whether the election was conducted in accordance with the Constitution and the law? (ii) whether there were illegalities committed during the conduct of the election and (iii) if there were irregularities and illegalities, what was the integrity of the election? In answer to these three issues, my opinion is that the election was indeed conducted in accordance with the Constitution and the law. In fact, the 1st and 2nd Respondents to my satisfaction demonstrated that they had adhered to the directions given by the Court of Appeal in the case of *Independent Electoral and Boundaries Commission vs. Maina Kiai & 5 Others*, Civil Appeal No. 105 of 2017 (the *Maina Kiai* case). The Court of Appeal in this case cautioned, and I agree, that the results declared at the polling station are **final**. In fact, the polling station is at the heart of any election. It is what happens there that is to be assessed and that is why its outcome is final.

[4] In any election, the ordinary Kenyan voter will ask themselves the following questions?

(1) Was there a problem with registration of voters?

(2) Were voters properly identified at the polling station

(3) Were voters allowed to cast their ballots peacefully and within good time?

(4) Were the votes cast-counted, declared and verified at the polling station to the satisfaction of all parties?

If the answer to all these questions is in the affirmative, then the election has been conducted properly.

[5] The Petitioners in my view did not present material evidence, to the standard required, to upset the results returned to the National Tallying Centre by the presiding officers in Forms 34A. Those results, counted and agreed upon by Agents at the polling station were not challenged. What was fiercely contested was the mode through which those results were transmitted from the polling station to the National Tallying Centre. The 1st and 2nd Respondents urged that transmission was conducted in line with the directions by the Court of Appeal in the *Maina Kiai* case. This process yielded the results that were streamed onto the portal and which, were not sufficiently impugned during the trial. The decision of the voter at the primary locale of the election, that is the polling station was unchallenged. *How then can a process used to transmit those results for tallying upset the will of the electorate?* It was not proved that the voter's will during the conduct of elections, was so affected by any irregularities cited so as to place this Court or the country in doubt as to what the result of the election was. Challenges which are to be expected during the conduct of any election. However, those challenges which occurred, (and in my opinion, none of which occurred deliberately or in bad faith, and which fell particularly outside the remit of the voter and his/her will)—ought not to supplant the voter's exercise of their right of suffrage.

[6] In summary, I respectfully disagree with the decision of the majority, and in accordance with Section 26(2) of the Supreme Court Act, 2011, and will issue my full dissenting Judgment within 21 days.

DATED and **DELIVERED** at **NAIROBI** this 1st day of September, 2017

....

N. S. NDUNGU

JUSTICE OF THE SUPREME COURT

SOURCE: Supreme Court of the Republic of Kenya. "Election Petition No. 1 of 2017." September 1, 2017. http://kenyalaw.org/caselaw/cases/view/140478/.

OTHER HISTORIC DOCUMENTS OF INTEREST

FROM PREVIOUS *HISTORIC DOCUMENTS*

Census Bureau Releases Annual Report on Poverty in the United States

SEPTEMBER 12, 2017

In September 2017, the United States Census Bureau released its annual report on the number of Americans living in poverty, along with its supplemental measure of these statistics, designed to take into account, among other factors, government safety net programs such as food stamps and cash benefits. Both reports noted a slight decline in the rate of those in poverty for the second consecutive year, bringing the number in line with 2007 figures, the year before the most recent recession began. The decline in the nation's poverty rate was coupled with a rise in median household income and further decline in the number of Americans without health insurance coverage.

RATE AND NUMBER OF AMERICANS IN POVERTY DECREASES

The 2017 release of the annual Census Bureau report *Income and Poverty in the United States* marked the publication's fiftieth anniversary. The report indicated a decrease of 0.8 percentage points in the official poverty rate from 13.5 percent 2015 to 12.7 percent 2016; the number of individuals in poverty fell by 2.5 million to 40.6 million. As defined by the Office of Management and Budget, the 2016 poverty threshold was $24,563 for a family of four or $12,228 for an individual. According to the Census report, "At 12.7 percent, the 2016 poverty rate is not statistically different from 2007 (12.5 percent), the year before the most recent recession." That fact is notable, because it indicates that the economy has regained much of what it lost during the 2007 to 2009 recession.

Further indicative of an improving economy, in 2016 almost no demographic group experienced a statistically significant increase in poverty, and, in fact, for most demographic groups the poverty rate declined. For those aged eighteen to sixty-four, the poverty rate decreased from 12.4 percent in 2015 to 11.6 percent, or 22.8 million people, in 2016. Those over age sixty-five were the only demographic group to experience an increase in the number of people in poverty (although not statistically significant), rising 0.4 percent, or 367,000 individuals, from 2015 to 2016. In 2015, 19.7 percent of children under age eighteen were in poverty, and that rate declined to 18 percent, or around 13.3 million children, in 2016. Children represented 32.6 percent of people in poverty in 2016, despite representing only 23 percent of the total U.S. population.

The poverty rate decreased in two of the four Census regions, but was not statistically different in the Midwest or West from 2015 to 2016. In the Northeast, the poverty rate fell from 12.4 percent, or 6.9 million people, in 2015 to 10.8 percent, or 6 million individuals, in 2016. The South continued to have the highest poverty rate at 14.1 percent, or 17 million individuals, although this was down from 15.3 percent, or 18.3 million individuals, in 2015.

Among racial groups, the poverty rate for non-Hispanic whites was 8.8 percent, or 17.3 million individuals, which was not statistically different from 2015. This group accounted for 42.5 percent of all people in poverty in the United States in 2016. Similarly, Asians did not experience a statistically different poverty rate from 2015 to 2016. The poverty rate for blacks decreased from 24.1 percent, or 10 million people, in 2015 to 22 percent, or 9.2 million individuals, in 2016. And for Hispanics, the poverty rate fell from 21.4 percent, or 12.1 million individuals, in 2015 to 19.4 percent, or 11.1 million individuals, in 2016.

The number of shared households, those with one or more additional non-household member, spouse, or partner aged eighteen or older—not counting those enrolled in school—was 19.4 percent, or 24.6 million households, in spring 2017. This was not a statistically significant change from 2016's 24.1 million shared households. However, the rate remained well above the 2007 prerecession level of 19.7 million households. According to the report, it can be difficult to fully determine the impact shared households have on the overall poverty rate. For example, young adults aged twenty-five to thirty-four living with their parents in 2017 had an official 2016 poverty rate of 7.3 percent, but if poverty status was determined based solely on the income of that individual, the rate would have been 36.1 percent.

Median household income was $59,039 in 2016, up 3.2 percent over 2015, marking the second consecutive increase in this metric. According to Jared Bernstein, senior fellow at the Center on Budget and Policy Priorities, growth in median income is likely due to more Americans returning to work or moving from part-time to full-time employment rather than from companies offering raises. The Census report supported this, indicating that median household income was driven up by an increase of 2.2 million in the number of individuals working full-time year-round with earnings from 2015 to 2016.

When the Census Bureau released its annual metrics on income and poverty, it also released a separate report on health insurance coverage. This report found that in 2016, 28.1 million, or 8.8 percent, of Americans did not have health insurance. This marked a decrease from 29 million, or 9.1 percent, since 2015. The number and rate of uninsured Americans has consistently declined since major provisions of the Affordable Care Act (ACA) were enacted in 2014. For comparison, in 2013, the year before most ACA policies took effect, 41.8 million Americans lacked health insurance coverage.

Supplemental Report

The official Census estimate of poverty does not account for food stamps, cash assistance, tax credits, and a variety of other government safety-net programs, all of which can have a significant impact on the number of Americans considered impoverished. The official estimate also does not account for children under the age of fifteen who are unrelated to anyone in their household. In 2010, the Census released its first supplemental poverty report, which was hailed as a more accurate method for determining the number of Americans living in poverty by taking into account government assistance programs and expenses such as health insurance, childcare, housing, job expenses including transportation, and nontraditional children, such as those in foster care.

Released at the same time as the official report, the supplemental report recorded a poverty rate of 14 percent, higher than the official rate of 12.7 percent, but down from the 14.5 percent supplemental rate recorded in 2015. In 2016, the supplemental report found 44.8 million people in poverty, while the official number was 40.6 million. Poverty rates were lower under the supplemental definition than the official definition for a number of groups, including children who had an 18 percent poverty rate under the official definition and 15.1 percent under the supplemental.

The supplemental poverty report shows the impact of social programs on the number and rate of those in poverty. For example, Social Security benefits kept 26.1 million Americans out of poverty, while the Supplemental Nutrition Assistance Program (SNAP), commonly referred to as food stamps, kept 3.6 million out of poverty, and refundable tax credits lifted 8.2 million out of poverty. The supplemental report was released at a time when Republicans, who controlled the House, Senate, and White House, were discussing methods to rollback federally funded safety net programs. The report, said John Bouman, president of the Sargent Shriver National Center on Poverty Law, "comes as the president and congressional Republicans are advancing a cruel policy agenda that would decimate key anti-poverty programs, like federal food assistance and refundable tax credits." If the proposed changes to these programs were to become law, Bouman said, "they would undermine the quality of life and chances at upward mobility of millions of struggling Americans." However, that view was not universal. Such programs, said Michael Tanner, a senior fellow at the Cato Institute, "are making poverty less miserable but they're not enabling people to rise above poverty."

INCOME INEQUALITY REMAINS

Although historical comparisons can be difficult due to the changes made in the calculations by the Census Bureau over the years, 2016 marked the highest median income ever recorded, and there was improvement across many groups. However, income inequality remains evident. Those in the top 20 percent of income earners accounted for 51.5 percent of all income earned in 2016, while those in the bottom 20 percent made up 3.5 percent of all income earned. During the past decade, those in the top 20 percent experienced an increase in household income of nearly $14,000, while those in the bottom 20 percent saw their income fall by $571. When adjusted for inflation, middle-income households have not experienced a statistically significant change in income since prior to the most recent recession in 2007, and they are only beginning to see higher incomes than in 1999 after the tech boom.

There is also significant variance in the poverty rate among different demographic groups. Although not a statistically significant difference from 2015, the median earnings of full-time male workers was $51,640, while females had a median full-time income of $41,554. This did mark a 1.1 percentage point increase in the female-to-male ratio, the first time the ratio marked an annual increase in a decade. Even so, women are far more likely than men to live below the poverty level, especially when single householders are taken into account. Male householders with no partner present had a poverty rate of 13.1 percent in 2016, while females without a partner who were considered the single head of household had a poverty rate of 26.6 percent.

Unsurprisingly, education appears to be one of the primary drivers in determining whether a person will be impoverished or not. In 2016, those aged twenty-five and older without a high school diploma had a poverty rate of 24.8 percent, while those with a high school diploma had a poverty rate of 13.3 percent. Among Americans with at least a bachelor's degree, 4.5 percent were in poverty. Those without a high school diploma, or those who only hold a high school diploma, are more likely to work low-skill, low-wage jobs than are their degree-holding counterparts.

Some economists worry that, despite minor gains being made among low-income earners, women, and minorities, the current labor market may be as good as it gets, signaling that future income growth could be slow. "We are already at a 16-year low in unemployment. The likelihood of significant job growth from here is limited," said Peter Atwater, president of Financial Insyghts.

—Heather Kerrigan

Following are excerpts from the U.S. Census Bureau report on poverty in the United States, released on September 12, 2017; and excerpts from the U.S. Census Bureau supplemental poverty report also released on September 12, 2017.

Census Bureau Report on Poverty in the United States

DOCUMENT

September 12, 2017

[All portions of the report not corresponding to poverty, as well as tables, graphs, and footnotes, and references to them, have been omitted.]

POVERTY IN THE UNITED STATES

Highlights

- The official poverty rate in 2016 was 12.7 percent, down 0.8 percentage points from 13.5 percent in 2015. This is the second consecutive annual decline in poverty. Since 2014, the poverty rate has fallen 2.1 percentage points from 14.8 percent to 12.7 percent.

- In 2016 there were 40.6 million people in poverty, 2.5 million less than in 2015 and 6.0 million fewer than in 2014.

- The poverty rate in 2016 (12.7 percent) was not significantly higher than the poverty rate in 2007 (12.5 percent), the year before the most recent recession.

- For most demographic groups, the number of people in poverty decreased from 2015. Adults aged 65 and older were the only population group . . . to experience an increase in the number of people in poverty.

- Between 2015 and 2016, the poverty rate for children under age 18 declined from 19.7 percent to 18.0 percent. The poverty rate for adults aged 18 to 64 declined from 12.4 percent to 11.6 percent. The poverty rate for adults aged 65 and older was 9.3 percent in 2016, not statistically different from the rate in 2015.

Race and Hispanic Origin

The poverty rate for non-Hispanic Whites was 8.8 percent in 2016 with 17.3 million individuals in poverty. Neither the poverty rate nor the number in poverty was statistically different from 2015. Non-Hispanic Whites accounted for 61.0 percent of the total population and 42.5 percent of the people in poverty.

The poverty rate for Blacks decreased to 22.0 percent in 2016, down from 24.1 percent in 2015. The number of Blacks in poverty decreased to 9.2 million, down from 10.0 million. For Asians, the 2016 poverty rate and the number in poverty was 10.1 percent and 1.9 million. Neither estimate for Asians was statistically different from 2015. The poverty rate for Hispanics decreased to 19.4 percent in 2016, down from 21.4 percent in 2015. The number of Hispanics in poverty decreased to 11.1 million, down from 12.1 million.

Age

Between 2015 and 2016, the poverty rate for people aged 18 to 64 decreased to 11.6 percent, down from 12.4 percent. The number of people in this age group in poverty declined to 22.8 million, down from 24.4 million. For people aged 65 and older, the 2016 poverty rate (9.3 percent) was not statistically different from 2015 while the number in poverty increased from 4.2 million to 4.6 million.

For children under age 18, 18.0 percent and 13.3 million were in poverty in 2016, down from 19.7 percent and 14.5 million in 2015. Children represented 23.0 percent of the total population and 32.6 percent of the people in poverty.

Related children are people under age 18 related to the householder by birth, marriage, or adoption, who are not themselves householders or spouses of householders. The poverty rate and the number in poverty for related children under age 18 were 17.6 percent and 12.8 million in 2016, down from 19.2 percent and 14.0 million in 2015. For related children in married-couple families, 8.4 percent and 4.2 million were in poverty in 2016, down from 9.8 percent and 4.8 million in 2015. For related children in families with a female householder, 42.1 percent and 7.6 million were in poverty in 2016, not statistically different from 2015. The 2016 poverty estimates for related children in male-householder families, 19.9 percent and 1.0 million, reflect a decline from 25.9 percent and 1.3 million in 2015.

The poverty rate and the number in poverty for related children under age 6 were 19.5 percent and 4.6 million in 2016, down from 21.0 percent and 4.9 million in 2015. About half (49.1 percent) of related children under age 6 in families with a female householder were in poverty. This was more than four times the rate of their counterparts in married-couple families (9.5 percent).

Sex

In 2016, 11.3 percent of males were in poverty, down from 12.2 percent in 2015. About 14.0 percent of females were in poverty in 2016, down from 14.8 percent in 2015.

Gender differences in poverty rates were more pronounced for those aged 18 to 64. The poverty rate for women aged 18 to 64 was 13.4 percent, while the poverty rate for men aged 18 to 64 was 9.7 percent. The poverty rate for women aged 65 and older was 10.6 percent, while the poverty rate for men aged 65 and older was 7.6 percent. For children under age 18, the poverty rate for girls was 18.4 percent while the poverty rate for boys was 17.6 percent.

Nativity

The poverty rate and the number in poverty for the native-born population decreased to 12.3 percent and 34.0 million in 2016, down from 13.1 percent and 36.0 million in 2015.

Among the foreign-born population, 15.1 percent and 6.6 million were in poverty in 2016, down from 16.6 percent and 7.2 million in 2015.

The poverty rate in 2016 for foreign-born naturalized citizens (10.0 percent) was lower than poverty rates for noncitizens and native-born citizens (19.5 percent and 12.3 percent, respectively). The poverty rate for foreign-born naturalized citizens fell from 11.2 percent in 2015 while the number of foreign-born naturalized citizens in poverty in 2016 was 2.0 million, not statistically different from 2015. The poverty rate for those who were not U.S. citizens decreased in 2016 to 19.5 percent, down from 21.3 percent in 2015. About 4.6 million noncitizens were in poverty in 2016, not statistically different from 2015. Within the foreign-born population in 2016, 46.6 percent were naturalized U.S. citizens, while the remaining were not citizens of the United States.

Region

The 2016 poverty rate and number in poverty for the Northeast was 10.8 percent and 6.0 million, down from 12.4 percent and 6.9 million in 2015. For the South, the 2016 poverty rate was 14.1 percent, down from 15.3 percent in 2015, while the number in poverty decreased to 17.0 million from 18.3 million. In 2016, the Midwest poverty rate and the number in poverty was 11.7 percent and 7.8 million, not statistically different from 2015. The poverty rate for the West in 2016 was 12.8 percent and the number in poverty was 9.8 million, not statistically different from 2015. The South had the highest poverty rate in 2016 relative to the other three regions.

Residence

Inside metropolitan statistical areas, the poverty rate decreased to 12.2 percent in 2016, down from 13.0 percent in 2015. The number in poverty decreased to 33.7 million, down from 35.7 million. Among those living outside metropolitan statistical areas, the poverty rate was 15.8 percent in 2016, not statistically different from 2015. However, the number in poverty decreased to 6.9 million, down from 7.4 million.

The 2016 poverty rate for those living inside metropolitan areas but not in principal cities was 10.0 percent, down from 10.8 percent in 2015. The number in poverty decreased to 17.2 million from 18.4 million. Among those who lived in principal cities, the 2016 poverty rate was 15.9 percent, down from 16.8 percent in 2015. The number in poverty was 16.6 million, not statistically different from 2015.

Within metropolitan areas, a higher percentage of people in poverty lived in principal cities in 2016 than outside of principal cities. While 37.7 percent of all people living in metropolitan areas in 2016 lived in principal cities, 49.1 percent of poor people in metropolitan areas lived in principal cities.

Work Experience

In 2016, 5.8 percent of workers aged 18 to 64 were in poverty, a decline from 6.3 percent in 2015. For those who worked full-time, year-round, 2.2 percent were in poverty in 2016, not statistically different from 2015. Those working less than full-time, year-round had a poverty rate in 2016 of 14.7 percent, down from 15.5 percent in 2015.

Among those aged 18 to 64 who did not work at least one week during the calendar year, the poverty rate decreased to 30.5 percent in 2016 from 31.8 percent in 2015. Those who did not work at least one week in 2016 represented 23.4 percent of all people aged 18 to 64, while they made up 61.6 percent of people aged 18 to 64 in poverty.

Disability Status

For people aged 18 to 64 with a disability, the poverty rate in 2016 was 26.8 percent, down from 28.5 percent in 2015. The number in poverty was 4.1 million, not statistically different from 2015. For people aged 18 to 64 without a disability, the poverty rate and the number in poverty decreased to 10.3 percent and 18.6 million in 2016, down from 11.0 percent and 20.0 million in 2015.

Among people aged 18 to 64, those with a disability represented 7.8 percent of all people, compared with 18.1 percent of people aged 18 to 64 in poverty.

Educational Attainment

Between 2015 and 2016, the only educational attainment group to have a decline in poverty were those without a high school diploma. In 2016, 24.8 percent of people aged 25 and older without a high school diploma were in poverty, a decline from 26.3 percent in 2015. The 2016 poverty rate for those with a high school diploma but with no college was 13.3 percent, not statistically different from 2015. For those with some college but no degree, 9.4 percent were in poverty in 2016, not statistically different from 2015.

Among people with at least a bachelor's degree, 4.5 percent were in poverty in 2016, not statistically different from 2015. People with at least a bachelor's degree in 2016 represented 34.2 percent of all people aged 25 and older, compared with 14.6 percent of people aged 25 and older in poverty.

Families

The poverty rate for families in 2016 was 9.8 percent, representing 8.1 million families, a decline from 10.4 percent and 8.6 million families in 2015.

For married-couple families, neither the poverty rate nor the number in poverty showed any statistical change between 2015 and 2016. For married-couple families, 5.1 percent were in poverty in 2016, representing 3.1 million families. The poverty rate and the number in poverty decreased for families with a female householder, to 26.6 percent and 4.1 million in 2016, down from 28.2 percent and 4.4 million in 2015. The poverty rate also decreased for families with a male householder. For families with a male householder, the poverty rate in 2016 was 13.1 percent, a decline from 14.9 percent in 2015. The number of families with a male householder in poverty was 847,000 in 2016, down from 939,000 in 2015.

Depth of Poverty

Categorizing a person as "in poverty" or "not in poverty" is one way to describe his or her economic situation. The income-to-poverty ratio and the income deficit or surplus describe additional aspects of economic well-being. While the poverty rate shows the proportion of people with income below the relevant poverty threshold, the income-to-poverty ratio gauges the depth of poverty and shows how close a family's income is to its poverty threshold. The income-to-poverty ratio is reported as a percentage that compares a family's or an unrelated individual's income with the applicable threshold. For example, a family with an income-to-poverty ratio of 125 percent has income that is 25 percent above its poverty threshold.

The income deficit or surplus shows how many dollars a family's or an individual's income is below (or above) their poverty threshold. For those with an income deficit, the measure is an estimate of the dollar amount necessary to raise a family's or a person's income to their poverty threshold.

Ratio of Income to Poverty

. . . In 2016, 18.5 million people reported family income below one-half of their poverty threshold. They represented 5.8 percent of all people and 45.6 percent of those in poverty. Approximately 17.0 percent of individuals had family income below 125 percent of their threshold, 21.2 percent had family income below 150 percent of their poverty threshold while 29.8 percent had family income below 200 percent of their threshold.

Of the 18.5 million people in 2016 with family income below one-half of their poverty threshold, 6.0 million were children under age 18, 10.9 million were aged 18 to 64, and 1.6 million were aged 65 years and older. The demographic makeup of the population differs at varying degrees of poverty. In 2016 children represented:

- 23.0 percent of the overall population.

- 20.0 percent of the people in families with income at or above 200 percent of their poverty threshold.

- 28.3 percent of people in families with income between 100 percent and less than 200 percent of their poverty threshold.

- 32.6 percent of people in families below 50 percent of their poverty threshold.

By comparison, people aged 65 and older represented:

- 15.4 percent of the overall population.

- 15.3 percent of people in families with income at or above 200 percent of their poverty threshold.

- 19.1 percent of people in families between 100 percent and less than 200 percent of their poverty threshold.

- 8.7 percent of people in families below 50 percent of their poverty threshold.

Income Deficit

The income deficit for families in poverty (the difference in dollars between a family's income and its poverty threshold) averaged $10,505 in 2016, higher than the income deficit for families in poverty in 2015 ($10,246). The average income deficit was larger for families with a female householder ($11,139) than for married-couple families ($9,991).

The average per capita income deficit was also larger for families with a female householder ($3,313) than for married-couple families ($2,749). For unrelated individuals, the average income deficit for those in poverty was $6,815 in 2016. The $6,632 deficit for unrelated women was lower than the $7,060 deficit for unrelated men.

Shared Households

Shared households are defined as households that include at least one "additional" adult, a person aged 18 or older, who is not the householder, spouse, or cohabiting partner of the householder. Adults aged 18 to 24 who are enrolled in school are not counted as additional adults.

In 2017, the percentage of shared households remained higher than in 2007, the year before the most recent recession. In 2007, 17.0 percent of all households were shared households, totaling 19.7 million shared households. In 2017, 19.4 percent of all households were shared households, totaling 24.6 million shared households.

Between 2016 and 2017, the number of shared households increased from 24.1 million to 24.6 million households while the percentage of shared households (19.4 percent) was not statistically different.

In 2017, an estimated 28.0 percent (12.4 million) of adults aged 25 to 34 were additional adults in someone else's household, neither of which was statistically different from 2016. Of young adults aged 25 to 34, 16.1 percent (7.1 million) lived with their parents in 2017, neither estimate statistically different from 2016.

It is difficult to assess the precise impact of household sharing on overall poverty rates. Adults aged 25 to 34 living with their parents in 2017 had an official 2016 poverty rate of 7.3 percent (when the entire family's income is compared with the threshold that includes the young adult as a member of the family). However, if poverty status had been determined using only the young adult's own income, 36.1 percent of those aged 25 to 34 would have been below the poverty threshold for a single person under age 65. Although 6.9 percent of families including at least one adult child of the householder were in poverty in 2016, the poverty rate for these families would have increased to 12.5 percent if the young adult were not living in—and contributing to—the household.

SOURCE: U.S. Census Bureau. "Income and Poverty in the United States: 2016." September 12, 2017. https://census.gov/content/dam/Census/library/publications/2017/demo/P60-259.pdf.

Census Bureau Report on
Supplemental Poverty Measures

September 12, 2017

[All figures, tables (except Table A-2), graphics, and references to them, have been omitted. Only the sections related to poverty estimates, poverty rates, and the effect of non-cash benefits have been included below.]

POVERTY ESTIMATES FOR 2016: OFFICIAL AND SPM

... 14.0 percent of people were poor using the SPM definition of poverty, higher than the 12.7 percent using the official definition of poverty with the comparable universe.* While for most groups, SPM rates were higher than official poverty rates, the SPM shows lower poverty rates for children and individuals living in cohabiting partner units. Official and

---

*Appendix Table A-2 contains rates for a more extensive list of demographic groups.

Table A-2. Number and Percentage of People in Poverty by Different Poverty Measures: 2016

(Numbers in thousands, margin of error in thousands or percentage points as appropriate. For information on confidentially protection, sampling error, nonsampling error, and definitions, see www2.census.gov/programs-surveys/cps/techdocs/cpsmar17.pdf)

Characteristic	Number** (in thousands)	Official**				SPM				Difference	
		Number		Percent		Number		Percent			
		Estimate	Margin of error† (±)	Estimate	Margin of error† (±)	Estimate	Margin of error† (±)	Estimate	Margin of error† (±)	Number	Percent
All people	320,372	40,706	735	12.7	0.2	44,752	810	14.0	0.3	*4,046	*1.3
Sex											
Male	156,939	17,739	396	11.3	0.3	20,693	438	13.2	0.3	*2,954	*1.9
Female	163,433	22,967	458	14.1	0.3	24,059	476	14.7	0.3	*1,092	*0.7
Age											
Under 18 years	74,047	13,344	366	18.0	0.5	11,281	349	15.2	0.5	*−2,062	*−2.8
18 to 64 years	197,051	22,795	473	11.6	0.2	26,303	571	13.3	0.3	*3,508	*1.8
65 years and older	49,274	4,568	198	9.3	0.4	7,168	235	14.5	0.5	*2,600	*5.3
Type of Unit											
Married couple	192,344	11,257	501	5.9	0.3	16,516	601	8.6	0.3	*5,260	*2.7
Cohabiting partners	24,994	6,576	345	26.3	1.0	3,261	284	13.0	1.0	*−3,314	*−13.3
Female reference person	42,758	11,647	510	27.2	1.0	11,655	498	27.3	1.0	7	Z
Male reference person	15,030	1,814	196	12.1	1.2	2,635	258	17.5	1.6	*821	*5.5
Unrelated individuals	45,246	9,413	324	20.8	0.6	10,685	343	23.6	0.6	*1,272	*2.8

(Continued)

(Continued)

Characteristic	Number** (in thousands)	Official** Number Estimate	Official** Number Margin of error† (±)	Official** Percent Estimate	Official** Percent Margin of error† (±)	SPM Number Estimate	SPM Number Margin of error† (±)	SPM Percent Estimate	SPM Percent Margin of error† (±)	Difference Number	Difference Percent
Race¹ and Hispanic Origin											
White	246,310	27,174	546	11.0	0.2	30,717	617	12.5	0.3	*3,543	*1.4
White, not Hispanic	195,453	17,304	494	8.9	0.3	19,446	564	9.9	0.3	*2,142	*1.1
Black	42,040	9,248	388	22.0	0.9	9,086	390	21.6	0.9	-162	-0.4
Asian	18,897	1,917	176	10.1	0.9	2,774	204	14.7	1.1	*857	*4.5
Hispanic (any race)	57,670	11,160	399	19.4	0.7	12,670	432	22.0	0.7	*1,511	*2.6
Nativity											
Native born	276,518	34,079	666	12.3	0.2	35,515	728	12.8	0.3	*1,437	*0.5
Foreign born	43,854	6,627	269	15.1	0.6	9,237	325	21.1	0.7	*2,609	*6.0
Naturalized citizen	20,409	2,045	143	10.0	0.7	3,205	171	15.7	0.8	*1,160	*5.7
Not a citizen	23,445	4,582	223	19.5	0.9	6,032	263	25.7	1.0	*1,449	*6.2
Educational Attainment											
Total aged 25 and older	216,921	22,636	425	10.4	0.2	27,929	503	12.9	0.2	*5,293	*2.4
No high school diploma	22,541	5,599	214	24.8	0.8	6,356	227	28.2	0.8	*757	*3.4

Characteristic	Number** (in thousands)	Official**				SPM				Difference	
		Number		Percent		Number		Percent			
		Estimate	Margin of error[†] (±)	Estimate	Margin of error[†] (±)	Estimate	Margin of error[†] (±)	Estimate	Margin of error[†] (±)	Number	Percent
High school, no college	62,512	8,309	250	13.3	0.4	10,139	317	16.2	0.5	*1,830	*2.9
Some college	57,765	5,430	202	9.4	0.3	6,615	251	11.5	0.4	*1,184	*2.1
Bachelor's degree or higher	74,103	3,299	167	4.5	0.2	4,819	225	6.5	0.3	*1,521	*2.1
Tenure											
Owner	210,698	14,761	496	7.0	0.2	19,149	611	9.1	0.3	*4,388	*2.1
Owner/mortgage	136,731	6,739	350	4.9	0.2	10,122	461	7.4	0.3	*3,383	*2.5
Owner/no mortgage/rent free	77,320	8,891	399	11.5	0.5	9,825	417	12.7	0.5	*934	*1.2
Renter	106,321	25,077	695	23.6	0.6	24,806	703	23.3	0.6	-271	-0.3
Residence											
Inside metropolitan statistical areas	276,816	33,808	832	12.2	0.3	39,125	843	14.1	0.3	*5,317	*1.9
Inside principal cities	104,295	16,598	646	15.9	0.5	18,057	669	17.3	0.5	*1,459	*1.4
Outside principal cities	172,521	17,211	575	10.0	0.3	21,068	656	12.2	0.3	*3,858	*2.2
Outside metropolitan statistical areas[2]	43,556	6,898	604	15.8	0.9	5,627	501	12.9	0.7	*-1,271	*-2.9

(Continued)

(Continued)

Characteristic	Number** (in thousands)	Official**				SPM				Difference	
		Number		Percent		Number		Percent			
		Estimate	Margin of error† (±)	Estimate	Margin of error† (±)	Estimate	Margin of error† (±)	Estimate	Margin of error† (±)	Number	Percent
Region											
Northeast	55,558	5,982	352	10.8	0.6	6,874	320	12.4	0.6	*892	*1.6
Midwest	67,016	7,829	358	11.7	0.5	7,424	361	11.1	0.5	*–406	*–0.6
South	121,325	17,056	523	14.1	0.4	17,966	616	14.8	0.5	*909	*0.7
West	76,473	9,838	375	12.9	0.5	12,489	452	16.3	0.6	*2,650	*3.5
Health Insurance Coverage											
With private insurance	216,203	11,635	421	5.4	0.2	17,898	545	8.3	0.3	*6,264	*2.9
With public, no private insurance	76,117	22,446	553	29.5	0.6	19,646	510	25.8	0.6	*–2,799	*–3.7
Not insured	28,052	6,626	261	23.6	0.9	7,208	268	25.7	0.9	*582	*2.1
Work Experience											
Total 18 to 64 years	197,051	22,795	473	11.6	0.2	26,303	571	13.3	0.3	*3,508	*1.8
All workers	150,904	8,743	254	5.8	0.2	12,111	361	8.0	0.2	*3,368	*2.2
Worked full-time, year-round	107,781	2,416	131	2.2	0.1	5,099	207	4.7	0.2	*2,683	*2.5
Less than full-time, year-round	43,123	6,327	223	14.7	0.5	7,012	258	16.3	0.6	*685	*1.6

Characteristic	Number** (in thousands) Estimate	Official**				SPM				Difference	
		Number		Percent		Number		Percent		Number	Percent
		Estimate	Margin of error[†] (±)	Estimate	Margin of error[†] (±)	Estimate	Margin of error[†] (±)	Estimate	Margin of error[†] (±)	Number	Percent
Did not work at least 1 week	46,148	14,052	381	30.5	0.7	14,193	395	30.8	0.7	141	0.3
Disability Status[3]											
Total 18 to 64 years	197,051	22,795	473	11.6	0.2	26,303	571	13.3	0.3	*3,508	*1.8
With a disability	15,405	4,123	191	26.8	1.1	3,905	182	25.4	1.0	*-218	*-1.4
With no disability	180,783	18,629	409	10.3	0.2	22,350	533	12.4	0.3	*3,720	*2.1

* An asterisk preceding an estimate indicates change is statistically different from zero at the 90 percent confidence level.

** Includes unrelated individuals under the age of 15.

[†] The margin of error (MOE) is a measure of an estimate's variability. The larger the MOE in relation to the size of the estimate, the less reliable the estimate.

This number, when added to and subtracted from the estimate, forms the 90 percent confidence interval. The MOEs shown in this table are based on standard errors calculated using replicate weights. For more information, see "Standard Errors and Their Use" at <ww2.census.gov/library/publications/2017/demo/p60-259sa.pdf>.

Z Represents or rounds to zero.

[1]Federal surveys give respondents the option of reporting more than one race. Therefore, two basic ways of defining a race group are possible. A group such as Asian may be defined as those who reported Asian and no other race (the race-alone or single-race concept) or as those who reported Asian regardless of whether they also reported another race (the race-alone-or-in-combination concept). This table shows data using the first approach (race alone). The use of the single-race population does not imply that it is the preferred method of presenting or analyzing data. The Census Bureau uses a variety of approaches. Information on people who reported more than one race, such as White and American Indian and Alaska Native or Asian and Black or African American, is available from the 2010 Census through American FactFinder. About 2.9 percent of people reported more than one race in the 2010 Census. Data for American Indians and Alaska Natives, Native Hawaiians and Other Pacific Islanders, and those reporting two or more races are not shown separately.

[2]The "Outside metropolitan statistical areas" category includes both micropolitan statistical areas and territory outside of metropolitan and micropolitan statistical areas. For more information, see "About Metropolitan and Micropolitan Statistical Areas" at <www.census.gov/population/metro>.

[3]The sum of those with and without a disability does not equal the total because disability status is not defined for individuals in the U.S.A. Armed Forces.

NOTE: Details may not sum to totals due to rounding.

SOURCES: U.S. Census Bureau, Current Population Survey, 2017 Annual Social and Economic Supplement.

SPM poverty rates for individuals living in female reference person units, Blacks, and individuals who did not work were not statistically different. Note that poverty rates for those aged 65 and over were higher under the SPM compared with the official measure. This partially reflects that the official thresholds are set lower for units with householders in this age group, while the SPM thresholds do not vary by age.

Next, we show the official measure and the SPM over the 8 years for which we have estimates. The charts show two values for 2013, one using the traditional income questions comparable to SPM estimates from 2009–2012, and the second using the redesigned income questions used for this report and comparable to the 2014–2016 estimates presented here. Figure 4 shows the official measure (with the comparable universe) and the SPM across 8 years. The SPM has ranged from 0.6 to 1.3 percentage points higher than the official measure since 2009.

Figure 5 shows the poverty rate using both measures for children and for those aged 65 and over. For the first time since 2010, in 2016 there was a statistically significant increase in SPM poverty rates for one of the major age categories. This increase in poverty for individuals aged 65 and over can be seen in both the official and SPM rates, although the increase in the rate is not statistically significant in the official measure.

Poverty Rates by State: Official and SPM

To create state-level estimates using the CPS ASEC, the Census Bureau recommends using 3-year averages for additional statistical reliability. . . . The 3-year average poverty rates for the United States for the years 2014, 2015, and 2016 were 13.7 percent with the official measure and 14.7 percent using the SPM.

While the SPM national poverty rate is higher than the official, that difference varies by geographic area. . . .

The 13 states for which the SPM rates were higher than the official poverty rates were California, Colorado, Connecticut, Florida, Hawaii, Illinois, Maryland, Massachusetts, Nevada, New Hampshire, New Jersey, New York, and Virginia. The SPM rate for the District of Columbia was also higher. Higher SPM rates by state may occur for many reasons. Geographic adjustments for housing costs and/or different mixes of housing tenure may result in higher SPM thresholds. Higher nondiscretionary expenses, such as taxes or medical expenses, may also drive higher SPM rates.

The 20 states where SPM rates were lower than the official poverty rates were Alabama, Arkansas, Idaho, Iowa, Kansas, Kentucky, Louisiana, Maine, Michigan, Mississippi, Montana, New Mexico, North Carolina, Ohio, Oklahoma, South Carolina, South Dakota, Tennessee, Vermont, and West Virginia. Lower SPM rates would occur due to lower thresholds reflecting lower housing costs, a different mix of housing tenure, or more generous noncash benefits.

Those 17 states that were not statistically different under the two measures include Alaska, Arizona, Delaware, Georgia, Indiana, Minnesota, Missouri, Nebraska, North Dakota, Oregon, Pennsylvania, Rhode Island, Texas, Utah, Washington, Wisconsin, and Wyoming. . . .

The SPM and the Effect of Cash and Noncash Transfers, Taxes, and Other Nondiscretionary Expenses

This section moves away from comparing the SPM with the official measure and looks only at the SPM. This analysis allows one to gauge the effects of taxes and transfers and other necessary expenses using the SPM as a measure of economic well-being.

The official poverty measure takes account of cash benefits from the government (e.g., Social Security and Unemployment Insurance benefits, Supplemental Security Income [SSI], public assistance benefits, such as Temporary Assistance for Needy Families, and workers' compensation benefits), but does not take account of taxes or noncash benefits aimed at improving the economic situation of the poor. Besides taking account of cash benefits and necessary expenses, such as medical expenses and expenses related to work, the SPM also accounts for taxes and noncash transfers. An important contribution of the SPM is that it allows us to gauge the potential magnitude of the effect of tax credits and transfers in alleviating poverty. We can also examine the effects of nondiscretionary expenses, such as work and medical expenses.

Figure 8 shows the effect that various additions and subtractions had on the number of people who would have been considered poor in 2016, holding all else the same and assuming no behavioral changes. Additions and subtractions are shown for the total population and by three age groups. Additions shown in the figure include cash benefits, also accounted for in the official measure, as well as noncash benefits, included only in the SPM. This allows us to examine the effects of government transfers on poverty estimates. Since child support paid is subtracted from income, we also examine the effect of child support received on alleviating poverty. Child support payments received are counted as income in both the official measure and the SPM.

Figure 8 allows us to compare the effect of transfers, both cash and noncash, and nondiscretionary expenses on numbers of individuals in poverty, all else equal. Social Security transfers and refundable tax credits had the largest impacts, preventing 26.1 million and 8.1 million individuals, respectively, from falling into poverty. Medical expenses were the largest contributor to increasing the number of individuals in poverty. . . .

Removing one item from the calculation of SPM resources and recalculating poverty rates shows, for example, that Social Security benefits decrease the SPM rate by 8.1 percentage points, from 22.1 percent to 14.0 percent. This means that with Social Security benefits, 26.1 million fewer people are living below the poverty line. By including refundable tax credits (the Earned Income Tax Credit [EITC] and the refundable portion of the child tax credit) in resources, 8.1 million fewer people are considered poor, all else constant. On the other hand, when the SPM subtracts amounts paid for child support, income and payroll taxes, work-related expenses, and medical expenses, the number and percentage in poverty are higher. Subtracting medical expenses from income, the SPM rate is 3.3 percentage points higher. In numbers, 10.5 million more people are classified as poor.

In comparison to 2015, the 2016 impacts on poverty of refundable tax credits, the Supplemental Nutrition Assistance Program (SNAP), child support received, and workers' compensation, each declined in absolute and relative terms. From 2015 to 2016, refundable tax credits lifted 0.8 million fewer individuals out of poverty and SNAP lifted 1 million fewer individuals out of poverty (Appendix Table A-7). Conversely in 2016, including medical expenses and work expenses had a lower impact on poverty. Medical expenses pushed 0.9 million fewer people into poverty in 2016 than 2015, while work expenses pushed 0.6 million fewer people into poverty. . . . In 2016, accounting for refundable tax credits resulted in a 5.9 percentage-point decrease in the child poverty rate, representing 4.4 million children prevented from falling into poverty by the inclusion of these credits. Subtracting medical expenses, such as contributions toward the cost of medical care and health insurance premiums, from the income of families with children resulted in a child poverty rate 2.9 percentage points higher. For the 65-and-over age group, SPM rates increased by about 5.8 percentage points with the subtraction of medical expenses from income.

Adding Social Security benefits lowered poverty rates by 34.8 percentage points for the 65-and-over age group, lifting 17.1 million individuals above the poverty line. In comparison to 2015, the percentage of individuals aged 65 and over kept out of poverty by Social Security declined, from 36.2 percent to 34.8 percent.

Summary

This report provides estimates of the SPM for the United States. The results shown illustrate differences between the official measure of poverty and a poverty measure that takes account of noncash benefits received by families and nondiscretionary expenses that they must pay. The SPM also employs a poverty threshold that is updated by the BLS with information on expenditures for food, clothing, shelter, and utilities. Results showed higher poverty rates using the SPM than the official measure for most groups, with children being an exception with lower poverty rates using the SPM.

The SPM allows us to examine the effect of taxes and non-cash transfers on the poor and on important groups within the population in poverty. Because the SPM includes these items in determining resources, there are lower percentages of the SPM poverty populations in the very high and very low resource categories than we find using the official measure. Since noncash benefits help those in extreme poverty, there were lower percentages of individuals with resources below half the SPM threshold for most groups. In addition, the effect of benefits received from each program and taxes and other nondiscretionary expenses on SPM rates were examined.

SOURCE: U.S. Census Bureau. "The Supplemental Poverty Measure: 2016." September 12, 2017. https://www.census.gov/content/dam/Census/library/publications/2017/demo/p60-261.pdf.

OTHER HISTORIC DOCUMENTS OF INTEREST

FROM THIS VOLUME

- President Trump Addresses a Joint Session of Congress; Democratic Response, p. 140
- House and Senate Vote on Affordable Care Act Repeal, p. 187

FROM PREVIOUS *HISTORIC DOCUMENTS*

- Census Bureau Releases Annual Report on Poverty in the United States, *2016*, p. 455

President Trump Addresses the United Nations.

SEPTEMBER 19, 2017

In his highly anticipated first speech to the United Nations (UN) General Assembly, President Donald Trump struck a markedly different tone from his predecessors and other UN members by directly and bluntly criticizing governments he characterized as "rogue regimes," openly threatening North Korea, and emphasizing the need for states to maintain their sovereignty. Trump also used the speech as a platform to call for reforms at the UN and for other member states to increase their contributions to the organization. His remarks generated sharp rebuttals from the governments he criticized, though some world leaders and U.S. lawmakers praised him for his candid assessment of global threats and challenges.

An Emphasis on National Sovereignty

Trump's remarks to the General Assembly began by echoing the "America first" theme of his presidential campaign. While the president acknowledged the need for UN members to "work together in close harmony and unity to create a more safe and peaceful future for all people," he affirmed that he would always put American first. "The United States will forever be a great friend to the world and especially to its allies. But we can no longer be taken advantage of or enter into a one-sided deal where the United States gets nothing in return," he said. "As long as I hold this office, I will defend America's interests above all else."

Trump's emphasis on sovereignty extended beyond his America first doctrine, with the president arguing that having member states remain strong and independent nations was critical to the UN's success. Trump said that different nations had the right to their own values and culture and that the United Nations should not try to impose global governance on its members. He also stated that the United States does "not seek to impose our way of life on anyone," suggesting the country was no longer interested in nation building. However, analysts later noted that despite this declaration, Trump went on to criticize certain countries for their lack of democracy and was particularly critical of the socialist governments of Cuba and Venezuela.

A Call for UN Reforms

The need for reforms to address bureaucracy and mismanagement at the United Nations and make the organization more accountable and effective was a focus of Trump's speech. The day before his remarks, Trump hosted a reform-focused event at the United Nations with Secretary-General António Guterres, who has also emphasized the need for reform. UN members were invited to attend if they signed a U.S.-drafted ten-point declaration backing Guterres' reform efforts to "simplify procedures and decentralize decisions, with greater transparency, efficiency and accountability." The declaration included a commitment to "reducing mandate duplication, redundancy and overlap, including among the main organs of the United Nations" and "making concrete changes in the United Nations system to better align its work on humanitarian response, development and sustaining peace initiatives." More than 120 countries signed the declaration.

During his General Assembly remarks, Trump thanked Guterres for acknowledging reform was necessary and proposing changes. In making the case for reform, Trump noted that "states that seek to subvert this institution's noble aims have hijacked the very systems that are supposed to advance them. For example, it is a massive source of embarrassment to the United Nations that some governments with egregious human rights records sit on the U.N. Human Rights Council." Trump also took issue with the United States being responsible for what he said was a disproportionate and unfair amount of the UN's budget. The United States contributes 22 percent of the organization's overall budget and pays about 28 percent of the separate peacekeeping budget. The president said the investment would be worthwhile if the UN actually accomplished its goals and said other members needed to play a greater role in the UN, both financially and militarily, to help protect and advance their own regions.

"Rogue Regimes" Identified as Global "Scourge"

Much of Trump's speech was dedicated to sharp attacks on "rogue regimes" that he claimed "violate every principle on which the United Nations is based" and "respect neither their own citizens nor the sovereign rights of their countries," making them "the scourge of our planet today."

North Korea was the first such regime named by Trump. "No one has shown more contempt for other nations and for the well-being of their own people than the depraved regime in North Korea," Trump said. He blamed the North Korean government for starving, imprisoning, torturing, killing, and oppressing its own people. Trump also cited the country's "reckless pursuit" of nuclear weapons as a threat to the entire world and criticized UN member states—without naming them—that continue to trade with North Korea or provide other forms of support that enable it to maintain its nuclear program. Trump acknowledged the UN Security Council—with a special thank you to Russia and China—for unanimously approving two resolutions in August and September that imposed tougher sanctions on North Korea but said "much more" was needed. "The United States has great strength and patience, but if it is forced to defend itself or its allies, we will have no choice but to totally destroy North Korea," Trump threatened, adding that "Rocket Man," a nickname he coined for North Korean Supreme Leader Kim Jong-un, was "on a suicide mission for himself and for his regime." Trump's fiery rhetoric marked a further escalation of a war of words the two leaders had engaged in throughout the year and ramped up in the summer, when Trump warned that North Korea would be met with "fire and fury like the world has never seen" if it continued to threaten the United States.

Iran was next on the president's list of rogue regimes, and was accused by Trump of hiding "a corrupt dictatorship behind the false guise of a democracy." The Iranian government, he said, "has turned a wealthy country with a rich history and culture into an economically depleted rogue state whose chief exports are violence, bloodshed, and chaos. The longest suffering victims of Iran's leaders are, in fact, its own people." Trump criticized Iran for funding Hezbollah, a Lebanon-based Islamic political party that the United States considers a terrorist organization; helping prop up Syrian President Bashar al-Assad's government; feeding the civil war in Yemen; and otherwise undermining peace in the Middle East. Trump declared that Iran should not be allowed to destabilize the region while pursuing nuclear weapons before pivoting to his often-repeated critiques of the Iranian nuclear agreement, which he described as "one of the worst and most one-sided transactions the United States has ever entered into." The United States "cannot abide by an agreement if it provides cover for the eventual construction of a nuclear program," he said. Trump's commentary on the deal fueled further speculation that the United States may decline to certify Iran's compliance with the terms of the accord by an October 15 deadline—a decision that could lead Congress to impose new sanctions on Iran—and withdraw from the deal despite the International Atomic Energy Agency's conclusion at the end of August that Iran was meeting its commitments under the agreement.

Trump next took aim at President Nicolás Maduro's administration in Venezuela. Trump accused Maduro of inflicting "terrible pain and suffering" on the Venezuelan people through his efforts to impose "a failed ideology that has produced poverty and misery everywhere it has been tried." He also criticized Maduro for trying to consolidate his power, an allusion to the Socialist Party–controlled Supreme Court's efforts to strip the National Assembly of its legislative authority and Maduro's push for the election of a National Constituent Assembly that could rewrite the country's constitution and eventually replace the National Assembly. Stating that the United States had already "taken important steps to hold the regime accountable," a reference to several rounds of sanctions imposed on Maduro and other Venezuelan officials over the summer, Trump declared that he was "prepared to take further action" if the government did not embrace reforms and restore democracy. Trump had previously indicated he would not rule out taking military action in Venezuela.

REACTIONS TO THE SPEECH

Trump's speech was considered noteworthy not only because it was his first address to the General Assembly but also because of its stark departure from previous U.S. presidents' remarks at the United Nations. Widely characterized as bellicose and hostile in tone by the media and international analysts, the speech presented what many called a dark and fearful view of a world in which Western civilization faced great peril from the "wicked few." Analysts also noted that it rarely happened that world leaders used their General Assembly speeches to criticize or threaten other countries.

Trump received a muted response from those in the General Assembly hall, with members remaining largely silent during pauses for applause. However, reactions from international leaders and U.S. lawmakers after the speech were much less reserved, particularly among those criticized by Trump. Maduro called Trump "the new Hitler of international politics," and Venezuelan Foreign Minister Jorge Arreaza declared, "No leader can come and question our democracy, can come and question our sovereignty." Iranian Foreign Minister Mohammad Javad Zarif said that "ignorant hate speech belongs in medieval times—not the 21st century UN" and that "fake empathy for Iranians fools no one." North Korean Foreign Minister Ri Yong-ho said his country might test a hydrogen bomb in the Pacific Ocean in response to Trump's threats. Kim Jong-un also released an unprecedented statement in direct response to Trump's remarks. Kim said Trump was "unfit to hold the prerogative of supreme command of a country, and he is surely a rogue and a gangster fond of playing with fire, rather than a politician." Trump's remarks were a "declaration of a war," he said, and convinced him that "the path I chose is correct and that it is the one I have to follow to the last." Kim concluded by saying, "I will surely and definitely tame the mentally deranged U.S. dotard with fire."

Others praised Trump. "In over 30 years in my experience with the UN, I never heard a bolder or more courageous speech," said Israeli Prime Minister Benjamin Netanyahu. Trump "spoke the truth about the great dangers facing our world and issued a powerful call to confront them in order to ensure the future of humanity," he added. Park Soo-hyun, a spokesperson for South Korean President Moon Jae-in, said Trump "expressed a firm and specific stance regarding the important issue of maintaining peace and security now facing the international community and the United Nations."

Reactions within the United States were also mixed and generally split along party lines. Sen. Lindsey Graham, R-S.C., said he was "very impressed" with the speech. "President Trump is right to rally the world to deal with a nuclear-armed North Korea," he said. "He's also right to focus on getting a better deal with Iran regarding their nuclear program, and to push the UN to reform the way it does business." On the other side of the aisle, Sen. Dianne Feinstein, D-Calif., criticized Trump for using the General Assembly speech "as a stage to threaten war," saying, "He missed an opportunity to present any positive actions the UN could take with respect to North Korea, and he launched a diatribe against Iran, again offering no pathway forward. . . . He aims to unify the world through tactics of intimidation, but in reality, he only further isolates the United States."

—Linda Grimm

Following are excerpts from President Donald Trump's speech to the United Nations General Assembly on September 19, 2017.

President Trump Remarks to the United Nations General Assembly

September 19, 2017

Mr. Secretary-General, Mr. President, world leaders, and distinguished delegates: Welcome to New York. It is a profound honor to stand here in my home city, as a representative of the American people, to address the people of the world.

As millions of our citizens continue to suffer the effects of the devastating hurricanes that have struck our country, I want to begin by expressing my appreciation to every leader in this room who has offered assistance and aid. The American people are strong and resilient, and they will emerge from these hardships more determined than ever before.

Fortunately, the United States has done very well since election day last November 8. The stock market is at an all time high, a record. Unemployment is at its lowest level in 16 years, and because of our regulatory and other reforms, we have more people working in the United States today than ever before. Companies are moving back, creating job growth the likes of which our country has not seen in a very long time. And it has just been announced that we will be spending almost $700 billion on our military and defense. Our military will soon be the strongest it has ever been.

For more than 70 years, in times of war and peace, the leaders of nations, movements, and religions have stood before this assembly. Like them, I intend to address some of the very serious threats before us today, but also the enormous potential waiting to be unleashed.

We live in a time of extraordinary opportunity. Breakthroughs in science, technology, and medicine are curing illnesses and solving problems that prior generations thought impossible to solve. But each day also brings news of growing dangers that threaten everything we cherish and value. Terrorists and extremists have gathered strength and spread to every region of the planet. Rogue regimes represented in this body not only support terrorists, but threaten other nations and their own people with the most destructive weapons known to humanity.

Authority—and authoritarian powers seek to collapse the values, the systems, and alliances that prevented conflict and tilted the world toward freedom since World War II. International criminal networks traffic drugs, weapons, people; force dislocation and mass migration; threaten our borders; and new forms of aggression exploit technology to menace our citizens.

To put it simply, we meet at a time of both immense promise and great peril. It is entirely up to us whether we lift the world to new heights or let it fall into a valley of disrepair . . .

Our success depends on a coalition of strong and independent nations that embrace their sovereignty to promote security, prosperity, and peace for themselves and for the world.

We do not expect diverse countries to share the same cultures, traditions, or even systems of government. But we do expect all nations to uphold these two core sovereign duties: to respect the interests of their own people and the rights of every other sovereign nation. This is the beautiful vision of this institution, and this is the foundation for cooperation and success

In America, we do not seek to impose our way of life on anyone, but rather to let it shine as an example for everyone to watch. . . . In America, the people govern, the people rule, and the people are sovereign. I was elected not to take power, but to give power to the American people, where it belongs. In foreign affairs, we are renewing this founding principle of sovereignty. Our Government's first duty is to its people, to our citizens: to serve their needs, to ensure their safety, to preserve their rights, and to defend their values.

As President of the United States, I will always put America first, just like you, as the leaders of your countries, will always, and should always, put your countries first. All responsible leaders have an obligation to serve their own citizens, and the nation-state remains the best vehicle for elevating the human condition. But making a better life for our people also requires us to work together in close harmony and unity to create a more safe and peaceful future for all people.

The United States will forever be a great friend to the world and especially to its allies. But we can no longer be taken advantage of or enter into a one-sided deal where the United States gets nothing in return. As long as I hold this office, I will defend America's interests above all else . . .

If we desire to lift up our citizens, if we aspire to the approval of history, then we must fulfill our sovereign duties to the people we faithfully represent. We must protect our nations, their interests, and their futures. We must reject threats to sovereignty, from the Ukraine to the South China Sea. We must uphold respect for law, respect for borders, and respect for culture, and the peaceful engagement these allow. And just as the founders of this body intended, we must work together and confront together those who threaten us with chaos, turmoil, and terror.

The scourge of our planet today is a small group of rogue regimes that violate every principle on which the United Nations is based. They respect neither their own citizens nor the sovereign rights of their countries. If the righteous many do not confront the wicked few, then evil will triumph. When decent people and nations become bystanders to history, the forces of destruction only gather power and strength.

No one has shown more contempt for other nations and for the well-being of their own people than the depraved regime in North Korea. It is responsible for the starvation deaths of millions of North Koreans, and for the imprisonment, torture, killing, and oppression of countless more. We were all witness to the regime's deadly abuse when an innocent American college student, Otto Warmbier, was returned to America only to die a few days later. We saw it in the assassination of the dictator's brother using banned nerve agents in an international airport. We know it kidnapped a sweet 13-year-old Japanese girl from a beach in her own country to enslave her as a language tutor for North Korea's spies.

If this is not twisted enough, now North Korea's reckless pursuit of nuclear weapons and ballistic missiles threatens the entire world with unthinkable loss of human life. It is an outrage that some nations would not only trade with such a regime, but would arm, supply, and financially support a country that imperils the world with nuclear conflict. No nation on Earth has an interest in seeing this band of criminals arm itself with nuclear weapons and missiles.

The United States has great strength and patience, but if it is forced to defend itself or its allies, we will have no choice but to totally destroy North Korea. Rocket Man is on a suicide mission for himself and for his regime. The United States is ready, willing and able, but hopefully, this will not be necessary. That's what the United Nations is all about; that's what the United Nations is for. Let's see how they do.

It is time for North Korea to realize that the denuclearization is its only acceptable future. The United Nations Security Council recently held two unanimous 15-to-nothing votes adopting hard-hitting resolutions against North Korea, and I want to thank China and Russia for joining the vote to impose sanctions, along with all of the other members of the Security Council. Thank you to all involved. But we must do much more. It is time for all nations to work together to isolate the Kim regime until it ceases its hostile behavior.

We face this decision not only in North Korea. It is far past time for the nations of the world to confront another reckless regime, one that speaks openly of mass murder, vowing death to America, destruction to Israel, and ruin for many leaders and nations in this room. The Iranian Government masks a corrupt dictatorship behind the false guise of a democracy. It has turned a wealthy country with a rich history and culture into an eco-nomically depleted rogue state whose chief exports are violence, bloodshed, and chaos. The longest suffering victims of Iran's leaders are, in fact, its own people.

Rather than use its resources to improve Iranian lives, its oil profits go to fund Hizballah and other terrorists that kill innocent Muslims and attack their peaceful Arab and Israeli neighbors. This wealth, which rightly belongs to Iran's people, also goes to shore up Bashar al Asad's dictatorship, fuel Yemen's civil war, and undermine peace throughout the entire Middle East.

We cannot let a murderous regime continue these destabilizing activities while build-ing dangerous missiles, and we cannot abide by an agreement if it provides cover for the eventual construction of a nuclear program. The Iran deal was one of the worst and most one-sided transactions the United States has ever entered into. Frankly, that deal is an embarrassment to the United States, and I don't think you've heard the last of it, believe me.

It is time for the entire world to join us in demanding that Iran's Government end its pursuit of death and destruction. It is time for the regime to free all Americans and citizens of other nations that they have unjustly detained. And above all, Iran's Government must stop supporting terrorists, begin serving its own people, and respect the sovereign rights of its neighbors . . .

The Iranian regime's support for terror is in stark contrast to the recent commitments of many of its neighbors to fight terrorism and halt its financing. In Saudi Arabia early last year, I was greatly honored to address the leaders of more than 50 Arab and Muslim nations. We agreed that all responsible nations must work together to confront terrorists and the Islamic extremism that inspires them. We will stop radical Islamic terrorism because we cannot allow it to tear up our Nation and, indeed, to tear up the entire world.

We must deny the terrorists safe haven, transit, funding, and any form of support for their vile and sinister ideology. We must drive them out of our nations. It is time to expose and hold responsible those countries who support and finance terror groups like Al Qaida, Hizballah, the Taliban, and others that slaughter innocent people.

The United States and our allies are working together throughout the Middle East to crush the loser terrorists and stop the reemergence of safe havens they use to launch attacks on all of our people. Last month, I announced a new strategy for victory in the fight against this evil in Afghanistan. From now on, our security interests will dictate the length and scope of military operations, not arbitrary benchmarks and timetables set up by politicians. I have also totally changed the rules of engagement in our fight against the Taliban and other terrorist groups. In Syria and Iraq, we have made big gains toward lasting defeat of ISIS. In fact, our country has achieved more against ISIS in the last 8 months than it has in many, many years combined.

We seek the deescalation of the Syrian conflict and a political solution that honors the will of the Syrian people. The actions of the criminal regime of Bashar al-Asad—including the use of chemical weapons against his own citizens, even innocent children—shock the conscience of every decent person. No society can be safe if banned chemical weapons are allowed to spread. That is why the United States carried out a missile strike on the airbase that launched the attack. We appreciate the efforts of United Nations agencies that are providing vital humanitarian assistance in areas liberated from ISIS, and we especially thank Jordan, Turkey, and Lebanon for their role in hosting refugees from the Syrian conflict.

The United States is a compassionate nation and has spent billions and billions of dollars in helping to support this effort. We seek an approach to refugee resettlement that is designed to help these horribly treated people, and which enables their eventual return to their home countries, to be part of the rebuilding process.

For the cost of resettling one refugee in the United States, we can assist more than 10 in their home region. Out of the goodness of our hearts, we offer financial assistance to hosting countries in the region, and we support recent agreements of the G-20 nations that will seek to host refugees as close to their home countries as possible. This is the safe, responsible, and humanitarian approach.

For decades, the United States has dealt with migration challenges here in the Western Hemisphere. We have learned that, over the long term, uncontrolled migration is deeply unfair to both the sending and the receiving countries. For the sending countries, it reduces domestic pressure to pursue needed political and economic reform and drains them of the human capital necessary to motivate and implement those reforms. For the receiving countries, the substantial costs of uncontrolled migration are borne overwhelmingly by low-income citizens whose concerns are often ignored by both media and government.

I want to salute the work of the United Nations in seeking to address the problems that cause people to flee from their homes. The United Nations and African Union led peacekeeping missions to have invaluable contributions in stabilizing conflicts in Africa. The United States continues to lead the world in humanitarian assistance, including famine prevention and relief in South Sudan, Somalia, and northern Nigeria and Yemen . . .

We also thank the Secretary-General for recognizing that the United Nations must reform if it is to be an effective partner in confronting threats to sovereignty, security, and prosperity. Too often, the focus of this organization has not been on results, but on bureaucracy and process. In some cases, states that seek to subvert this institution's noble aims have hijacked the very systems that are supposed to advance them. For example, it is a massive source of embarrassment to the United Nations that some governments with egregious human rights records sit on the U.N. Human Rights Council.

The United States is one out of 193 countries in the United Nations, and yet we pay 22 percent of the entire budget and more. In fact, we pay far more than anybody realizes. The United States bears an unfair cost burden, but to be fair, if it could actually accomplish all of its stated goals, especially the goal of peace, this investment would easily be well worth it.

Major portions of the world are in conflict, and some, in fact, are going to hell. But the powerful people in this room, under the guidance and auspices of the United Nations, can solve many of these vicious and complex problems. The American people hope that one day soon the United Nations can be a much more accountable and effective advocate for human dignity and freedom around the world. In the meantime, we believe that no nation should have to bear a disproportionate share of the burden, militarily or financially. Nations of the world must take a greater role in promoting secure and prosperous societies in their own regions.

That is why in the Western Hemisphere, the United States has stood against the corrupt, destabilizing regime in Cuba and embraced the enduring dream of the Cuban people to live in freedom. My administration recently announced that we will not lift sanctions on the Cuban Government until it makes fundamental reforms.

We have also imposed tough, calibrated sanctions on the socialist Maduro regime in Venezuela, which has brought a once thriving nation to the brink of total collapse. The socialist dictatorship of Nicolas Maduro has inflicted terrible pain and suffering on the good people of that country. This corrupt regime destroyed a prosperous nation by imposing a failed ideology that has produced poverty and misery everywhere it has been tried. To make matters worse, Maduro has defied his own people, stealing power from their elected representatives to preserve his disastrous rule.

The Venezuelan people are starving, and their country is collapsing. Their democratic institutions are being destroyed. This situation is completely unacceptable, and we cannot stand by and watch. As a responsible neighbor and friend, we and all others have a goal. That goal is to help them regain their freedom, recover their country, and restore their democracy. I would like to thank leaders in this room for condemning the regime and providing vital support to the Venezuelan people.

The United States has taken important steps to hold the regime accountable. We are prepared to take further action if the Government of Venezuela persists on its path to impose authoritarian rule on the Venezuelan people. We are fortunate to have incredibly strong and healthy trade relationships with many of the Latin American countries gathered here today. Our economic bond forms a critical foundation for advancing peace and prosperity for all of our people and all of our neighbors. I ask every country represented here today to be prepared to do more to address this very real crisis. We call for the full restoration of democracy and political freedoms in Venezuela . . .

America stands with every person living under a brutal regime. Our respect for sovereignty is also a call for action. All people deserve a government that cares for their safety, their interests, and their well-being, including their prosperity.

In America, we seek stronger ties of business and trade with all nations of good will, but this trade must be fair and it must be reciprocal. For too long, the American people were told that mammoth multinational trade deals, unaccountable international tribunals, and powerful global bureaucracies were the best way to promote their success. But as those promises flowed, millions of jobs vanished and thousands of factories disappeared. Others gamed the system and broke the rules. And our great middle class, once the bedrock of American prosperity, was forgotten and left behind, but they are forgotten no more, and they will never be forgotten again.

While America will pursue cooperation and commerce with other nations, we are renewing our commitment to the first duty of every government: the duty of our citizens. This bond is the source of America's strength and that of every responsible nation represented here today.

If this organization is to have any hope of successfully confronting the challenges before us, it will depend, as President Truman said some 70 years ago, on the "independent strength of its members." If we are to embrace the opportunities of the future and overcome the present dangers together, there can be no substitute for strong, sovereign, and independent nations: nations that are rooted in their histories and invested in their destinies; nations that seek allies to befriend, not enemies to conquer; and most important of all, nations that are home to patriots, to men and women who are willing to sacrifice for their countries, their fellow citizens, and for all that is best in the human spirit . . .

Today, if we do not invest ourselves, our hearts, and our minds in our nations, if we will not build strong families, safe communities, and healthy societies for ourselves, no one can do it for us. We cannot wait for someone else, for faraway countries or far-off bureaucrats—we can't do it. We must solve our problems, to build our prosperity, to secure our futures, or we will build vulnerable to decay, domination, and defeat . . .

The United States of America has been among the greatest forces for good in the history of the world and the greatest defenders of sovereignty, security, and prosperity for all. Now we are calling for a great reawakening of nations, for the revival of their spirits, their pride, their people, and their patriotism. History is asking us whether we are up to the task. Our answer will be a renewal of will, a rediscovery of resolve, and a rebirth of devotion. We need to defeat the enemies of humanity and unlock the potential of life itself . . .

Thank you. God bless you, God bless the nations of the world, and God bless the United States of America. Thank you very much. Thank you.

SOURCE: Executive Office of the President. "Remarks to the United Nations General Assembly in New York City." September 19, 2017. *Compilation of Presidential Documents* 2017, no. 00658 (September 19, 2017). https://www.gpo.gov/fdsys/pkg/DCPD-201700658/pdf/DCPD-201700658.pdf.

OTHER HISTORIC DOCUMENTS OF INTEREST

October

Government Officials Respond to Catalan Independence Referendum

OCTOBER 1 AND 19, 2017

In October 2017, pro-independence politicians in Catalonia, the northeastern region of Spain, made another push for secession by conducting an independence referendum in which 90 percent of voters favored separation from Spain. The federal government, backed by Spain's Constitutional Court, claimed the vote was illegal, and a formal declaration of independence by the Catalan Parliament resulted in Prime Minister Mariano Rajoy dissolving the regional government and calling for snap elections.

Road to the Referendum

Catalonia enjoyed broad autonomy prior to the Spanish Civil War of the late 1930s, but this was significantly repressed by dictator Gen. Francisco Franco, who ruled Spain from 1939 until his death in 1975. The region's autonomy was restored by the Spanish Constitution of 1978 and bolstered by the 2006 Statute of Autonomy of Catalonia, which provides for the region's self-government and jurisdiction over areas such as education, health, commerce, and transportation. Some government functions are shared with the Spanish federal government; the judicial system, for example, is primarily administered by the federal government. Additionally, Catalonia has its own police force, but federal law enforcement is also deployed throughout the region. The Catalan government—known as the Generalitat de Catalunya—is comprised of a regional parliament, president, and executive council.

The roots of the modern Catalan independence movement trace back to a ruling issued by Spain's Constitutional Court in 2010 following a challenge to the Statute of Autonomy brought by the People's Party, the center-right political party that currently leads Spain's government. The court struck down fourteen and limited twenty-seven of the statute's more than 200 articles. Notably, the court wrote that, "The interpretation of the references to 'Catalonia as a nation' and to 'the national reality of Catalonia' in the preamble of the Statute of Autonomy of Catalonia have no legal effect."

The ruling spurred massive protests and prompted Catalonia's political leaders to push for separation from Spain. A symbolic, regional independence referendum was held in November 2014. Less than half of registered voters cast a ballot, but among those who did, nearly 81 percent agreed that Catalonia should be a state and that it should be independent. Pro-independence politicians won a majority of seats in the Catalan Parliament in the 2015 elections, giving separatists additional momentum. The call for independence continued into 2017, and on September 6, the Catalan Parliament passed a law approving an independence referendum. A second law passed on September 8 outlined a legal framework for the region to secede from Spain, should the vote be in favor of separation. In a memo explaining the referendum law, Parliament said it represented "the democratic response to the frustration created by the final attempt . . . to guarantee for the people of Catalonia full recognition, representation and participation in the political, social, economic and cultural life of the Spanish state." The memo went on to state that "every effort was made to find an agreed way for the people of Catalonia to freely decided upon its future" and that "all forms of dialogue and negotiation with the Spanish state" had been exhausted.

Within a week of the laws' passage, the Constitutional Court suspended both while it reviewed their constitutionality. Prime Minister Mariano Rajoy decried the laws as an "intolerable act of disobedience." The federal government claimed the referendum was illegal because Spain's Constitution grants all Spaniards the right to vote in referenda on major issues, meaning Catalan secession should be put to a national rather than regional vote, and called for it to be suspended. (The court eventually ruled on October 17 that the referendum was illegal and against the "indissoluble unity of the Spanish nation.")

REFERENDUM PROCEEDS AMID LAW ENFORCEMENT CRACKDOWN

Despite the court ruling and federal claims of illegality, separatist politicians led by Catalan President Carles Puigdemont pushed ahead with the independence referendum. Puigdemont and Barcelona Mayor Ada Colau (Barcelona is the seat of the Catalan government) asked European Union officials to mediate the referendum, but they declined. European Parliament President Antonio Tajani said it was "a Spanish problem in which we can do little."

In the weeks leading up to the vote, the federal government ordered the national police to raid regional government offices, which resulted in the arrests of fourteen Catalan officials and the seizure of millions of paper ballots, election leaflets and posters, and polling station signage. The police also sealed some polling stations, disabled the software connecting polling stations, and shut down online voting applications to try to stop the referendum. In response, Catalans built barricades near polling places to protect them from police, with reports indicating that doors had been removed from some locations to keep police from bolting them shut, and some camped out at schools to ensure they stayed open. Catalan officials also took measures to circumvent law enforcement, printing ballots privately and changing voting rules to allow voters to cast a ballot at any polling place, regardless of where they were registered.

The referendum took place on October 1, with many Catalans lining up at polling stations hours before they opened. The national police were again dispatched to disrupt the vote, with dozens of polling places closed and others raided. Police also clashed with voters. Photographs of the day showed police punching voters and beating them with batons, dragging people from polling stations by their hair, and fighting with Catalan firefighters and regional police who were trying to protect the polling stations. Witnesses also described national police breaking down polling station doors with axes and firing rubber bullets into crowds. According to Catalonia's health department, at least 760 people were injured during the raids. Spain's Ministry of the Interior reported that at least a dozen police officers were also injured.

Several politicians expressed outrage over the police crackdown and called for Rajoy to resign. Colau said the prime minister "had crossed all red lines" and was "a coward who does not live up to his state responsibilities." Pablo Iglesias, leader of the left-wing party Podemos, said that "if something breaks Spain," it would be the continued efforts of the People's Party and its supporters to "destroy democracy." For his part, Rajoy praised the police for acting with "firmness and serenity" and defended his use of law enforcement. "We have done what was required of us," he said. "We have acted, as I have said from the beginning, according to the law and only according to the law. And we have shown that our democratic state has the resources to defend itself from an attack as serious as the one that was perpetrated with this illegal referendum."

Amid the chaos, 2.26 million Catalans voted in the referendum, according to regional government spokesman Jordi Turull. Of those, 90 percent voted in favor of independence. However, turnout represented only about 42 percent of all registered voters, suggesting that support for independence was not so widespread. In fact, a week before the vote, thousands of people marched in Barcelona to call for a continued union with Spain.

"On this day of hope and suffering, Catalonia's citizens have earned the right to have an independent state in the form of a republic," said Puigdemont after the vote. "My government, in the next few days, will send the results of [the] vote to the Catalan parliament, where the sovereignty of our people lies, so that it can act in accordance with the law of the referendum." The Spanish government continued to dismiss the vote as illegal. At a press conference the same day, Deputy Prime Minister Soraya Sáenz de Santamaría called the referendum "irresponsible" and a "farce," stating that "since it is incompatible with our democratic rules, it could not be held and nor has it been held." Noting the lack of an official census, legal polling stations, or an electoral board, as well as the complaints lodged against the referendum by local officials and citizens, she added that the vote was "a democratic disgrace to the people of Catalonia and to the people of Spain as a whole, who have seen their rights infringed for not agreeing with the aims of the pro-independence forces."

Spain Dissolves Catalan Government

Puigdemont was expected to formally declare Catalonia's independence from Spain during a speech before the Catalan Parliament scheduled for October 10. Instead, Puigdemont claimed a mandate to initiate secession efforts and called for talks with the federal government to discuss Catalonia's future. The next day, Rajoy held an emergency cabinet meeting during which officials agreed to require the Catalan government formally to "confirm whether it has declared or not independence." Analysts speculated the meeting and subsequent announcement was an effort by Rajoy to garner support for invoking Article 155 of the Constitution, which would allow him to suspend Catalonia's autonomy.

Puigdemont wrote to the prime minister on October 16 to call for a meeting to discuss an agreement on regional independence. When the prime minister did not respond, Puigdemont sent a follow-up letter on October 19, reiterating his request and noting that he had not officially declared Catalonia's independence in hopes of having a dialogue. He also accused the Spanish government of increasing its repression of Catalonia, including by arresting representatives from "social institutions of a renowned civic, peaceful and democratic trajectory." Puigdemont wrote, "Given all our efforts and our willingness to dialogue, if the only answer of the Spanish Government is the suspension of self-government, it shows that you are not aware of the problem and that you do not want to enter into dialogue." In closing, he warned that if the government continued to refuse talks and repress the region, Catalonia's Parliament would vote on a formal declaration of independence.

A meeting between Puigdemont and Rajoy did not take place. Puigdemont deferred the decision on independence to the Catalan Parliament, which voted to formally declare independence on October 27. Most pro-union lawmakers walked out ahead of the vote, creating a lopsided result of seventy votes for separation and ten against. Within hours of Parliament's vote, the Spanish Senate voted to invoke Article 155. Rajoy removed Puigdemont, his cabinet, and the director general of Catalonia's police force from office, dissolved the Catalan Parliament and called a snap election, and ordered Catalonia's representative offices overseas closed. "We never wanted to reach this situation, never," said Rajoy. "We believe it is urgent to listen to Catalan citizens, to all of them, so that they can decide their future and nobody can act outside the law on their behalf."

A few days later—and shortly before Spain's attorney general announced he would seek charges of rebellion, sedition, and misuse of public funds against Puigdemont and thirteen members of his administration—the deposed Catalan president and four of his former ministers fled to Belgium. "We are facing a state that only understands the reason of force," said Puigdemont, who explained that if he and his colleagues had stayed in Catalonia "there would have been a violent reaction." An international arrest warrant was issued for the self-exiled officials after they ignored a court order to appear before a Spanish judge. Eight former ministers who did appear in court were arrested. Officials later dropped the arrest warrant to move the case back to Spanish jurisdiction and avoid the extradition process with Belgium.

In the Catalan Parliament election held on December 21, pro-independence parties garnered 47.5 percent of the vote, winning seventy of the Parliament's 135 seats—a slim majority. Notably, the Ciudadanos Party, which wanted Catalonia to remain united with Spain, received the largest share of votes among the competing parties, winning thirty-seven seats. Observers question whether the three separatist parties would be able to come together to form a coalition government, particularly since many of the parties' leaders were either in prison or exile. As of January, Puigdemont was the only candidate for Catalan president; however, he would face charges if he returns to Spain. Rajoy said that Puigdemont cannot govern remotely and threatened that the federal government will continue to run Catalonia via emergency rule if Parliament elects him president.

—Linda Grimm

Following is a statement by Spanish deputy prime minister Soraya Sáenz de Santamaría from October 1, 2017, responding to the Catalan independence referendum; and a letter from Catalan president Carles Puigdemont to Prime Minister Mariano Rajoy from October 19, 2017, requesting a dialogue on regional independence.

Deputy Prime Minister Comments on Catalan Referendum

October 1, 2017

"A very good day to everyone. I appear here before you, on behalf of the government, to assess the situation caused in Catalonia as a result of the decision taken by the Regional Government of Catalonia to maintain its determination to hold an illegal referendum. This attempt was, from the very outset, unconstitutional, anti-democratic but, most importantly, it went against all our standards of co-existence. And, since it is incompatible with our democratic rules, it could not be held and nor has it been held.

The rule of law, applied firmly and proportionally, has thwarted all the plans and intentions of the Regional Government of Catalonia. Prior to today, this attempt did not meet the most basic and elementary democratic requirements. Its backers ignored all the parliamentary rules to try and give an appearance of legality which was immediately suspended by the courts. This attempt is a democratic disgrace to the people of Catalonia and to the people of Spain as a whole, who have seen their rights infringed for not agreeing with the aims of the pro-independence forces.

The Regional Government of Catalonia and those on their side decided to proceed despite receiving no official backing and despite the rule of law eroding any entitlement to hold this referendum. There was no official census, or legally constituted polling stations, or official premises accredited, or electoral board to guarantee the neutrality of the process. They were warned by international bodies that their attempts to proceed with the referendum were discredited. Mayors, regional councillors, public servants, journalists and citizens lodged claims against the anti-democratic methods that they were victims of.

Despite the proven illegality and numerous judicial rulings, they still sought to proceed, and they decided to mobilise their followers to impose their wishes by using children and the elderly without any compunction. Today, after the latest actions by the justice system, they even decided to change the few instructions given by the Regional Government of Catalonia and, in an unprecedented attempt under any democracy, less than an hour before voting was due to take place, they ran roughshod over any attempt at appearing to hold a referendum. The Regional Government of Catalonia has acted in a wholly irresponsible manner, it has tried to eliminate any form of law and justice, and hence, democracy, in Catalonia; but we have seen that the democratic rule of law works and that it has tools at its disposal to ensure that court rulings that protect the rights of everyone are upheld.

The absolute irresponsibility of the Regional Government of Catalonia has had to be replaced by the professionalism of the law enforcement agencies. They have complied with the rulings of the system of justice, they have acted professionally and proportionally. The targets of their actions have never been individuals but the electoral material. They have always sought to protect individual rights and liberties.

I would like to take this opportunity, here before all of you, to acknowledge their efforts at this time. They have complied with their democratic obligation, they have attended to the judicial instructions and the requests for support that the Mossos [Regional Police Force of Catalonia] sent them, and informed the Government Representative in Catalonia accordingly.

No referendum has been held, or any semblance of one. It never made sense to head down this irrational path and it makes no sense to continue doing so. I would ask the Regional Government of Catalonia and the political parties that supports it to stop being irresponsible, and henceforth take on board that what was never legal is now clearly untenable. It makes no sense to continue with this farce which is not heading anywhere. They should stop this right now.

It is in their hands to bring this situation to an end. The people of Catalonia and of Spain as a whole have gone through weeks of great democratic uncertainty. We have seen how some people have sought to bring to an end centuries of a shared way of life and decades of democratic stability, how some people who should be the first to uphold the law have flaunted their disobedience, but Spain is a democracy, a consolidated democracy, a strong democracy in which the rights and liberties of individuals prevail above the personal claims of their governors. These citizens have seen today how their rights have been restored, their shared way of life guaranteed and their liberties protected because this is all a part of living together in a democracy.

I am totally sure that the government and the State institutions as a whole, as has been seen in recent days, work to oversee our democracy, to ensure that the liberties of our citizens are guaranteed and to recover the harmony that exists among all the people of Spain.

Thank you very much."

SOURCE: La Moncloa. "'There Has Been No Referendum or Any Semblance of One,' Says Soraya Sáenz de Santamaría." October 1, 2017. http://www.lamoncloa.gob.es/lang/en/gobierno/news/Paginas/2017/20171001_refesoraya.aspx.

DOCUMENT

Letter from President Puigdemont to Prime Minister Rajoy

October 19, 2017

Dear President Rajoy:

On October 1st, the people of Catalonia decided its independence in a referendum endorsed by a high percentage of voters. A higher percentage than the one that allowed the United Kingdom to start the Brexit process, and with a number of voters in favour larger than the Statute of Autonomy of Catalonia.

On October 10th, the Parliament held a session to assess the outcome of the referendum and its effects. There I proposed to suspend the effects of the popular mandate.

I took this decision to foster the dialogue that political and social institutions and leaders from all over Europe and the rest of the world have repeatedly been asking of you and myself. Similarly, in my letter on Monday, I proposed to hold a meeting with you and it has not yet been attended.

In the same way, the request to stop repression has not been met either. On the contrary, it has increased, resulting in the imprisonment of the president of *Òmnium Cultural* and the president of the Catalan National Assembly, social institutions of a renowned civic, peaceful and democratic trajectory.

This suspension is still in force. The decision to apply Article 155 of the Constitution corresponds to the State Government, with prior authorization from the Senate. Given all our efforts and our willingness to dialogue, if the only answer of the Spanish Government is the suspension of self-government, it shows that you are not aware of the problem and that you do not want to enter into dialogue.

Finally, if the State Government persists in blocking dialogue and the repression continues, the Parliament of Catalonia will proceed, if deemed appropriate, to vote on the formal declaration of independence, which it did not vote on October 10th.

Sincerely,
Carles Puigdemont Casamajó
Barcelona, October 19th 2017

SOURCE: Generalitat de Catalunya (@govern). Twitter post, October 19, 2017. https://twitter.com/govern/status/920985946610372613.

Federal Leaders Respond to Mass Shooting in Las Vegas

OCTOBER 2, 4, AND 6, 2017

As concert goers lined up for the final day of the Route 91 Harvest music festival in Las Vegas, Nevada, Stephen Paddock assembled an arsenal on the 32nd floor of the overlooking Mandalay Bay Resort and Casino, preparing to commit the deadliest mass shooting in the history of the United States. Paddock's preparation, weapons, and vantage point took law enforcement by surprise, while his equipment, specifically his use of bump stocks (a device that allows semiautomatic weapons to fire like fully automatic weapons), sparked fresh calls for legislation to prevent future mass shootings. Paddock killed fifty-eight people, injured more than 500 others, and sent thousands of terrified survivors fleeing for their lives before killing himself. Days after the shooting, Sen. Dianne Feinstein, D-Calif., introduced a measure to ban the sale of bump stocks. Similar measures gained bipartisan support in the House of Representatives, while the National Rifle Association (NRA), a stalwart opponent of policies that limit the sale of firearms, signaled its support to regulate the devices. Despite calls to limit bump stocks, legislation stalled in Congress. Regulation from the U.S. Bureau of Alcohol, Tobacco, Firearms and Explosives (ATF) suffered a similar fate. Months after the Las Vegas shooting, policies to address the growing gun violence epidemic in the United States continued to prove elusive.

DEADLIEST MASS SHOOTING IN U.S. HISTORY

On October 1, 2017, concertgoers flooded into an open-air venue to see country western stars including Eric Church, Sam Hunt, and Jason Aldean. Located off the Las Vegas strip across the street from the Luxor Hotel and diagonally from the Mandalay Bay Resort and Casino, the Las Vegas Village and Festival Grounds sprawls more than fifteen acres and has a capacity of 40,000 people. The final night was sold out. While people listened to their favorite artists and danced with friends and family, across the street inside of the Mandalay Bay, sixty-four-year-old Paddock of Mesquite, Nevada, prepared for what would end up being the deadliest mass shooting in the history of the United States.

Paddock, a retiree, came from a modest background. People who knew him described him as a freewheeling gambler who lived in a quiet retirement community and played golf. Officials said he had no significant criminal history and drew little attention to himself. "He was a wealthy guy, playing video poker, who went cruising all the time and lived in a hotel room," his brother, Eric Paddock, said. Even after months of investigations, officials had few insights into what drove him to rain down bullets on the concert.

Paddock set up on the 32nd floor of the Mandalay Bay, where he had unobstructed view of the concert nearly 500 yards away. He had assembled an arsenal for his attack. Law enforcement officials found at least twenty-three firearms, including a handgun and rifles equipped with scopes, in his hotel suite. Hundreds of rounds of ammunition, weapon modifications including two tripods, explosives, and electronic equipment were found as well. Twelve rifles were found modified with a bump stock. Paddock's preparations and arsenal allowed him to inflict maximum damage on the crowd and showed a level of forethought that took officials by surprise. He had shattered windows to get a clear vantage point, used tripods to stabilize his shots, and chosen a high enough position that stray shots could still have a chance to hit another target.

At 10:08 p.m., Paddock opened fire. A continuous hail of bullets struck those attending the concert for the first nine seconds. Cellphone video of the shooting captured the seemingly continuous rapid fire, which was followed by thirty-seven seconds of silence from the Mandalay Bay and panicked screaming from the crowd. Gunfire then erupted again in at least two more bursts. Law enforcement, including a SWAT team, began clearing out the top floors of the Mandalay Bay, starting on the 29th floor and working their way up. As the police closed in on the room on the 32nd floor, gunshots erupted through the hotel room door, hitting an officer in the leg, followed by a lone, final shot. When the police finally entered the room, Paddock lay dead from a self-inflicted gunshot wound.

Lawmakers Condemn the Attack

Reaction from politicians across the country was swift. Speaking at the White House the following morning, President Donald Trump condemned the shooting as an "act of pure evil," adding, "Hundreds of our fellow citizens are now mourning the sudden loss of a loved one: a parent, a child, a brother or sister." The president spoke directly to the families of the victims, saying, "We are praying for you, and we are here for you, and we ask God to help see you through this very dark period." The president quoted scripture, ordered flags to be flown at half-mast, and called for unity. "In moments of tragedy and horror, America comes together as one, and it always has. We call upon the bonds that unite us: our faith, our family, and our shared values. We call upon the bonds of citizenship, the ties of community, and the comfort of our common humanity. Our unity cannot be shattered by evil," the president said.

His remarks, however, fell short of calling for further restrictions on gun purchases or any public policy announcement to address future shootings. The president had said after previous mass shootings that they could be lessened if the victims were armed or had more liberty to buy guns, a call he did not renew in his comments at the White House. Asked at a news conference later that day about whether the president would now call for changes to gun laws, his press secretary, Sarah Huckabee Sanders, demurred. "There will be, certainly, time for that policy discussion to take place, but that's not the place that we're in at this moment," Sanders said. She also warned against overreach, saying, "I think one of the things that we don't want to do is try to create laws that won't stop these types of things from happening."

On Capitol Hill, Republican leaders offered similar calls for unity and prayer, while Democrats paired their sympathy with demands for new legislation. Senate Majority Leader Mitch McConnell, R-Ky., said the country was in a state of "national mourning" in a speech on the Senate floor. "The news we awoke to this morning was heartbreaking. What happened in Las Vegas is shocking, it's tragic and for those affected and their families it's devastating. It's hard to even imagine their pain." Rep. Nancy Pelosi, D-Calif., the House Democratic leader, sent a letter to House Speaker Paul Ryan, R-Wisc., calling for him to create a select committee on gun violence to "study and report back common sense legislation to help end this crisis." The request was a nonstarter for Republicans, who frequently indicated that any move toward additional gun legislation was not on the table.

RENEWED GUN CONTROL DEBATE GAINS A NEW FOCUS

Over the weeks following the Las Vegas attack, Republican and Democratic politicians narrowed their focus on regulating a specific device, the bump stock. The device, which replaces a gun's standard stock, frees the weapon to slide back and forth rapidly, harnessing a gun's recoil to cause the rifle to fire rapidly. The effect is fully automatic fire from a semiautomatic firearm; fully automatic weapons are banned in the United States. The Las Vegas gunman had outfitted twelve rifles, including several AR-15 assault rifles, with these devices, allowing him to fire between 400 to 800 rounds per minute.

Several Republican senators, including Nevada Sen. Dean Heller, urged the ATF to review the permitted sale of bump stock devices and issue an updated interpretation. "We recognize that it is impossible to prevent tragedy and acts of 'pure evil,' in the words of our President. We believe, however, the tragic events in Las Vegas brought to light an issue from this past Administration that we respectfully request that your Bureau swiftly review," the senators wrote. "Given the function and capability of a semi-automatic rifle that is modified by a bump stock, we respectfully request that you review the Obama Administration's interpretation and issue your own interpretation," they added. "Unfortunately, we are all now keenly aware of how this device operates and believe that this renewed review and determination will keep our citizens safe and ensure that federal law is enforced."

Two days before Republican senators wrote the ATF, Sen. Feinstein proposed a ban on the device. A longtime advocate of stricter gun control measures, Sen. Feinstein previously tried—and failed—to limit the sale of bump stocks and other similar devices. The bill introduced after the Las Vegas shooting would make it "unlawful for any person to import, sell, manufacture, transfer or possess, in or affecting interstate or foreign commerce, a trigger crank, a bump-fire device or any part, combination of parts, component, device, attachment or accessory that is designed or functions to accelerate the rate of fire of a semiautomatic rifle but not convert the semiautomatic rifle into a machine gun." Sen. Feinstein unveiled the bill with more than thirty cosponsors, all Democrats.

A handful of Republican senators signaled at least some interest in regulating the devices. "I think it's something we ought to look into," Sen. John Thune, R-S.D., said. "I don't know a lot about them and I'm somebody who, I'd like to think, is fairly familiar with a lot of firearms and you know, the use of those. And that incident out there is something that I think we need to take a look at," he added. Even the NRA, the nation's largest gun lobby and a stalwart critic of laws that curtail access to guns, signaled an openness to regulating the device, so long as it happened through regulation from the ATF and not new legislation. "The NRA believes that devices designed to allow semi-automatic rifles to function like fully-automatic rifles should be subject to additional regulations," NRA CEO Wayne LaPierre and Executive Director of the NRA Institute for Legislative Action Chris Cox said in a joint statement. That statement, Feinstein said, was "a step forward and it's appreciated," but she added her belief that it would not address the problem. Others, including Sen. McConnell, expressed caution of reacting too quickly. "I think it's particularly inappropriate to politicize an event like this," McConnell said. "The investigation's not even been completed. And I think it's premature to be discussing legislative solutions if there are any."

STALLED POLICIES LEAVE AN UNCERTAIN FUTURE FOR GUN SAFETY MEASURES

Despite seemingly bipartisan support to regulate bump stocks, legislation stalled in Congress. A bill introduced by Reps. Carlos Curbelo, R-Fla., and Seth Moulton, D-Mass., had twenty cosponsors, including ten Republican members. The House Judiciary Committee, however, refused to consider the bill or a similar one signed by 173 Democrats. Meanwhile, the Senate Judiciary Committee did not consider Sen. Feinstein's bill banning bump stocks. The NRA's support for regulating bump stocks, which many initially believed cleared the way for Republican members to support the measure, may have actually undermined the effort through its caveat calling for regulations over legislation.

A month after the Las Vegas shooting, the ATF announced a decision to initiate a six-month rule-making process to revisit its prior decisions that the agency did not have the legal authority to ban bump stocks. The move drew swift condemnation from Democrats. Sen. Feinstein argued the announcement "kicks the can down the road, and fails to take any meaningful steps to respond to the deadliest mass shooting in U.S. history." She continued, "Legislation is the only answer and Congress should not attempt to pass the buck by waiting for the ATF." By the end of 2017, and despite bipartisan support in the wake of the deadliest mass shooting in U.S. history, lawmakers and regulators failed to pass any meaningful response to the growing gun violence problem in America. Inability to act underscored the difficulty in finding consensus on policies that curb future gun-related tragedies.

—Robert Howard

Following is the text of a statement by President Donald Trump on October 2, 2017, regarding the shooting in Las Vegas; the text of a bill proposed by Sen. Dianne Feinstein to ban bump stocks, submitted for consideration on October 4, 2017; and an October 6, 2017, press release from Sen. Dean Heller's office calling for a review of bump stock regulations.

President Trump Responds to Las Vegas Shooting

October 2, 2017

My fellow Americans, we are joined together today in sadness, shock, and grief. Last night a gunman opened fire on a large crowd at a country music concert in Las Vegas, Nevada. He brutally murdered more than 50 people and wounded hundreds more. It was an act of pure evil.

The FBI and the Department of Homeland Security are working closely with local authorities to assist with the investigation, and they will provide updates as to the investigation and how it develops.

I want to thank the Las Vegas Metropolitan Police Department and all of the first responders for their courageous efforts and for helping to save the lives of so many. The speed with which they acted is miraculous and prevented further loss of life. To have found the shooter so quickly after the first shots were fired is something for which we will always be thankful and grateful. It shows what true professionalism is all about.

Hundreds of our fellow citizens are now mourning the sudden loss of a loved one: a parent, a child, a brother or sister. We cannot fathom their pain. We cannot imagine their loss. To the families of the victims: We are praying for you, and we are here for you, and we ask God to help see you through this very dark period.

Scripture teaches us, "The Lord is close to the brokenhearted and saves those who are crushed in spirit." We seek comfort in those words, for we know that God lives in the hearts of those who grieve. To the wounded who are now recovering in hospitals: We are praying for your full and speedy recovery, and pledge to you our support from this day forward.

In memory of the fallen, I have directed that our great flag be flown at half staff. I will be visiting Las Vegas on Wednesday to meet with law enforcement, first responders, and the families of the victims.

In moments of tragedy and horror, America comes together as one, and it always has. We call upon the bonds that unite us: our faith, our family, and our shared values. We call upon the bonds of citizenship, the ties of community, and the comfort of our common humanity. Our unity cannot be shattered by evil. Our bonds cannot be broken by violence. And though we feel such great anger at the senseless murder of our fellow citizens, it is our love that defines us today and always will, forever.

In times such as these, I know we are searching for some kind of meaning in the chaos, some kind of light in the darkness. The answers do not come easy. But we can take solace knowing that even the darkest space can be brightened by a single light, and even the most terrible despair can be illuminated by a single ray of hope.

Melania and I are praying for every American who has been hurt, wounded, or lost the ones they love so dearly in this terrible, terrible attack. We pray for the entire nation to find unity and peace. And we pray for the day when evil is banished and the innocent are safe from hatred and from fear.

May God bless the souls of the lives that are lost, may God give us the grace of healing, and may God provide the grieving families with strength to carry on.

Thank you. God bless America. Thank you.

SOURCE: Executive Office of the President. "Remarks on the Shootings in Las Vegas, Nevada." October 2, 2017. *Compilation of Presidential Documents* 2017, no. 00710 (October 2, 2017). https://www.gpo.gov/fdsys/pkg/DCPD-201700710/pdf/DCPD-201700710.pdf.

Sen. Feinstein Introduces Bump Stock Ban Legislation

October 4, 2017

S. 1916

To prohibit the possession or transfer of certain firearm accessories, and for other purposes.

IN THE SENATE OF THE UNITED STATES
October 4, 2017

Mrs. Feinstein (for herself, Mr. Van Hollen, Mrs. Gillibrand, Ms. Klobuchar, Mr. Markey, Mr. Murphy, Mr. Blumenthal, Mr. Durbin, Mr. Casey, Mr. Reed, Ms. Hassan, Mr. Merkley, Mr. Carper, Mr. Cardin, Mr. Coons, Mr. Franken, Mr. Booker, Ms. Harris, Mr. Whitehouse, Ms. Hirono, Mr. Sanders, Mr. Leahy, Ms. Warren, Mr. Schumer, Ms. Cantwell, Mrs. McCaskill, Mr. Nelson, Mrs. Murray, Mr. Udall, and Mr. Kaine) introduced the following bill; which was read twice and referred to the Committee on the Judiciary

A BILL

To prohibit the possession or transfer of certain firearm accessories, and for other purposes.

Be it enacted by the Senate and House of Representatives of the United States of America in Congress assembled,

SECTION 1. SHORT TITLE.

This Act may be cited as the "Automatic Gunfire Prevention Act".

SEC. 2. PROHIBITION ON POSSESSION OF CERTAIN FIREARM ACCESSORIES.

Chapter 44 of title 18, United States Code, is amended—

(1) in section 922, by inserting after subsection (u) the following:

"(v) (1) Except as provided in paragraph (2), on and after the date that is 180 days after the date of enactment of this subsection, it shall be unlawful for any person to import, sell, manufacture, transfer, or possess, in or affecting interstate or foreign commerce, a trigger crank, a bump-fire device, or any part, combination of parts, component, device, attachment, or accessory that is designed or functions to accelerate the rate of fire of a semiautomatic rifle but not convert the semiautomatic rifle into a machine gun.

"(2) This subsection does not apply with respect to the importation for, manufacture for, sale to, transfer to, or possession by or under the authority of, the United States or any department or agency thereof or a State, or a department, agency, or political subdivision thereof."; and

(2) in section 924(a)(2), by striking ", or (o)" and inserting "(o), or (v)".

SOURCE: Library of Congress. "S. 1916 – Automatic Gunfire Prevention Act." October 4, 2017. https://www.congress.gov/bill/115th-congress/senate-bill/1916/text.

Sen. Heller Calls for Bump Stock Regulation Review

October 6, 2017

U.S. Senators Dean Heller (R-NV), John Cornyn (R-TX), Joni Ernst (R-IA), Johnny Isakson (R-GA), James Lankford (R-OK), Lisa Murkowski (R-AK), Tim Scott (R-SC), John Thune (R-SD), and James Inhofe (R-OK) today urged the Trump Administration's U.S. Bureau of Alcohol, Tobacco, Firearms and Explosives (ATF) to swiftly review an Obama Administration decision that permitted the sale of bump stock devices and issue its own interpretation.

The Senators' request for review comes after a gunman opened fire on 22,000 innocent concertgoers in Las Vegas, Nevada, killing 58 people and wounding nearly 500 more. Federal authorities found 12 bump stock devices outfitted on firearms in the assailant's Mandalay Bay hotel room.

"We recognize that it is impossible to prevent tragedy and acts of "pure evil," in the words of our President. We believe, however, the tragic events in Las Vegas brought to light an issue from this past Administration that we respectfully request that your Bureau swiftly review," the Senators wrote. "Press reports of the crime scene in Las Vegas, Nevada, indicate that certain devices were used to modify the firearms involved. Specifically, these devices are designed to allow semi-automatic rifles to function like fully-automatic rifles. The sale of these devices, and bump stocks specifically, is permitted under an interpretation of the Gun Control Act (18 U.S.C. § 921(a)(23)) and National Firearms Act (26 U.S.C. § 5845(b)) made by the Obama Administration's Bureau of Alcohol, Tobacco, Firearms and Explosives (ATF)."

The Senators continued, "Given the function and capability of a semi-automatic rifle that is modified by a bump stock, we respectfully request that you review the Obama Administration's interpretation and issue your own interpretation. Unfortunately, we are all now keenly aware of how this device operates and believe that this renewed review and determination will keep our citizens safe and ensure that federal law is enforced."

The letter, available here, reads in full:

October 6, 2017

Mr. Thomas E. Brandon
Acting Director
Bureau of Alcohol, Tobacco, Firearms and Explosives
99 New York Avenue, NE
Washington, DC 20226

Dear Acting Director Brandon:

The citizens of Nevada, and of our country as a whole, continue to mourn the brutal and senseless attack on innocent concertgoers in Las Vegas the night of October 1, 2017.

We remember and pray for those lost in this tragedy, their family and friends. We honor and applaud the bravery of the first responders, both law enforcement and civilian heroes, medical professionals, and all who came to the aid of those in need.

We recognize that it is impossible to prevent tragedy and acts of "pure evil," in the words of our President. We believe, however, the tragic events in Las Vegas brought to light an issue from this past Administration that we respectfully request that your Bureau swiftly review.

Press reports of the crime scene in Las Vegas, Nevada, indicate that certain devices were used to modify the firearms involved. Specifically, these devices are designed to allow semi-automatic rifles to function like fully-automatic rifles. The sale of these devices, and bump stocks specifically, is permitted under an interpretation of the Gun Control Act (18 U.S.C. § 921(a)(23)) and National Firearms Act (26 U.S.C. § 5845(b)) made by the Obama Administration's Bureau of Alcohol, Tobacco, Firearms and Explosives (ATF).

Given the function and capability of a semi-automatic rifle that is modified by a bump stock, we respectfully request that you review the Obama Administration's interpretation and issue your own interpretation. Unfortunately, we are all now keenly aware of how this device operates and believe that this renewed review and determination will keep our citizens safe and ensure that federal law is enforced.

We appreciate your swift response and action on this important issue.

Sincerely,

Dean Heller
U.S. Senator

John Cornyn
U.S. Senator

Joni Ernst
U.S. Senator

James Inhofe
U.S. Senator

Johnny Isakson
U.S. Senator

James Lankford
U.S. Senator

Lisa Murkowski
U.S. Senator

Tim Scott
U.S. Senator

John Thune
U.S. Senator

SOURCE: Office of Senator Dean Heller. "Heller Urges Review of Obama-era Bump Stock Ruling." October 6, 2017. https://www.heller.senate.gov/public/index.cfm/pressreleases?ID=5938F763-173F-42D9-97F8-6BB6C985E039.

OTHER HISTORIC DOCUMENTS OF INTEREST

FROM PREVIOUS *HISTORIC DOCUMENTS*

British Prime Minister, European Union Leaders Remark on Continuation of Brexit Negotiations

OCTOBER 9, AND DECEMBER 8 AND 18, 2017

The United Kingdom's (UK) path out of the European Union (EU), known as Brexit, became a little smoother and clearer in the closing months of 2017. EU and UK negotiators reached an agreement on a first set of issues: a "divorce" bill, how to manage the border between Northern Ireland (part of UK) and the Republic of Ireland (an independent EU member), and the rights of EU citizens in the UK and UK citizens in the EU. That agreement, forged by December, enabled negotiators to move forward to a second phase that was more focused on sketching out their future trade relationship. It also made it increasingly likely that the UK would cease to be an EU member state on March 30, 2019, precisely two years after it applied to leave. A transition period of about two years following Brexit, where the UK would continue to apply EU laws and regulations pending finalization of a long-term agreement, also seemed more likely than not.

PRIME MINISTER MAY OUTLINES A POST-BREXIT VISION

The spring and summer of 2017 was a tumultuous period for talks as the two sides struggled to settle into the new reality of being at opposite sides of the negotiating table. When the United Kingdom joined the European Union—then the European Economic Community—in 1973, it had joined both a single market and customs union. Single market meant that there were no tariffs on goods and services traded between EU members. Customs union meant that the European Commission (the EU's executive arm) negotiated all trade deals with non-EU countries. Thus, when the Brexit talks began in summer 2017, the Commission was a far more seasoned trade negotiator than the United Kingdom. Early on, the Commission succeeded in structuring the talks in two phases, with the future EU–UK trade relationship to be discussed only after the short-term "divorce" issues were settled. There was some grumbling from the UK government about this two-phase approach but it ultimately went along with it.

After the summer break, the sides started to focus on the nuts and bolts of what would be an extremely complicated agreement given how intertwined their economies were. British Prime Minister Theresa May provided clarification on what her overarching negotiating goals were in comments she made to the UK parliament on October 9. "[W]hen we leave the European Union, we will no longer be members of its single market or its customs union. The British people voted for control of their borders, their laws, and their money," she said.

The EU single market—the area of free movement of goods, services, and capital between the member countries—is given effect by 100,000+ pages of regulations enacted by the EU lawmakers in Brussels and enforced by the EU Court of Justice in Luxembourg. However, three European countries—Iceland, Liechtenstein, and Norway—have full access to the single market, despite not being EU members, because they have agreed to apply this large corpus of EU legislation. In principle, such an option would be possible for the United Kingdom post-Brexit. But Prime Minister May rejected it as politically unpalatable because it would require the UK to enforce rules it had no role in formulating and to accept the EU Court of Justice's authority in interpreting those rules. The EU customs union is the arrangement where goods and services imported into the European Union have the same tariffs applied to them regardless of which EU country they enter. Turkey, despite not being an EU member state, is part of the EU customs union, meaning that Turkey has tariff-free access to the EU's single market of 510 million people. Again, Prime Minister May declined to advocate for this option for the United Kingdom because it would hinder its ability to conclude free trade agreements with non-EU countries.

May was calculated in determining how close an economic relationship she wanted with the European Union post-Brexit. "We will need a framework to manage where we continue to align and where we choose to differ," she said. While she excluded aligning laws as deeply and comprehensively as Norway or Iceland's single market access entails, May indicated that she did want something deeper than the free trade agreement the European Union concluded with Canada in 2014 in which trade tariffs were mostly, but not entirely, abolished.

Looking beyond the economic sphere, May said, "The United Kingdom is unconditionally committed to maintaining Europe's security" and added that she favored concluding a new treaty with the European Union on police and judicial cooperation. May restated her idea to a global audience in February 2018 when she spoke at the Munich Security Conference. As an EU member state, the United Kingdom has been a willing participant in intra-EU efforts to strengthen police and judicial cooperation. For instance, the United Kingdom signed on to the EU Arrest Warrant, a sweeping change to legal systems that replaced cumbersome, sometimes-politicized extradition procedures with a speedy transfer of accused criminals between jurisdictions. May's idea for a new security treaty was a sign the United Kingdom wished to continue to be part of such arrangements in a post-Brexit era.

Article 50 of the EU Treaty provides for a relatively short timeframe of two years for a country to exit the European Union once it notifies the body of its intent to leave. With the United Kingdom having triggered Article 50 on March 29, 2017, there were fears among the business community that a Brexit treaty, with all its complexities, would not be finalized within such a tight timeframe, a scenario that would create great legal uncertainty after the UK's exit. To assuage these fears, May pledged to negotiate a "time-limited" transition period, explaining, "We want our departure from the EU to be as smooth as possible."

DIVORCE DEAL PAVES WAY FOR PHASE II OF BREXIT TALKS

The period from mid-October to mid-December 2017 was a difficult but ultimately productive one for the negotiators. The talks on Northern Ireland were especially tense because the stakes were so high. In 1998, the Good Friday Agreement had ended thirty years of conflict in Northern Ireland between warring Catholic (pro-Irish) and Protestant (pro-UK) groups. The Good Friday Agreement also led to the removal of border checkpoints on the Northern Ireland border. Irish nationalists, led by Sinn Fein, viewed the 1998 peace treaty as paving the way for an eventual political reunification of north and south. Now the

Irish nationalists were concerned about the prospect of Brexit unravelling that progress. Northern Ireland's Unionists, by contrast, while supporting free trade between north and south, were keen to avoid any "special status" being bestowed on Northern Ireland under a Brexit deal as this would further differentiate Northern Ireland from the rest of the United Kingdom. May was more beholden to the Unionists because, having lost her Conservative party's overall majority in the June 2017 United Kingdom elections, her government had since been propped up by parliamentarians from the Democratic Unionist Party (DUP).

In Brussels in early December, May was about to finalize an agreement on the Northern Ireland border with the European Union when the DUP dramatically withdrew its support out of fear the deal would effectively keep Northern Ireland in the single market and customs union. After intense further consultations with DUP leader Arlene Foster, May tweaked the deal and finalized it to the DUP's satisfaction. It was agreed that no physical infrastructure would be erected at the Northern Ireland border and that regulatory "alignment or coherence" would exist between the north and south. However, the agreement's wording was fraught with constructive ambiguity, with neither side knowing for sure how it would be implemented.

By comparison, negotiations on the financial package, or "exit bill," that the United Kingdom would pay the European Union, although equally politically contentious, was less ambiguous because a concrete figure needed to be agreed. The United Kingdom position shifted a lot from earlier in the year when questioned whether it was willing to pay such a bill. The agreement, announced in December, provided for a £35 to £39 billion financial settlement, amounting to four years of the UK's contributions to the EU budget.

The two parties agreed that two years was an appropriate transition period post-Brexit. Elaborating on this in remarks to the UK parliament on December 18, May said, "[W]e would propose that our access to one another's markets would continue as now" despite the United Kingdom no longer being a member from March 30, 2019. She added that the United Kingdom would, during this time, be able to negotiate "and, where possible, sign" trade agreements with non-EU countries. The United Kingdom would start to register arrivals from the European Union during the transition period, she added. As an EU member state, the United Kingdom is required to grant the citizens of other EU countries full residence rights. But May was now looking to the post-Brexit era when her nation would regain its right to bar EU citizens from working and living there. As for EU citizens who arrived in the UK pre-Brexit, May said, "We want them to stay," and she pledged that UK courts would uphold their rights in areas like access to healthcare and pensions.

EU ANXIETIES EASE

At a joint press conference with Prime Minister May in Brussels on December 8, EU Commission President Jean-Claude Juncker said, "The Commission has just formally decided to recommend to the European Council that sufficient progress has now been made on the strict terms of the divorce." He continued, "I will always be sad about this development. But now we must start looking to the future. A future in which the United Kingdom will be and will remain a close friend and ally." The European Council accepted his recommendation as expected, allowing the talks to proceed to the next phase.

By early 2018, EU anxieties over Brexit had eased somewhat. While anti-EU parties had made gains in elections in 2017 in France, Germany, and the Netherlands, they had failed to win outright, leaving pro-EU voices in power in these three founding EU countries. Fears of so-called Brexit contagion were diminishing. In France, a new, young

President, Emmanuel Macron, was shifting his attention to pushing for deeper integration among the remaining EU members, especially the nineteen eurozone countries. In Germany, much of Chancellor Angela Merkel's time was taken up with forming a new "grand coalition" between her center-right Christian Democrats and the center-left Social Democrats. Merkel's first choice for coalition partners was two smaller parties, the Greens and Free Democrats, but they failed to agree to a policy platform, forcing her to team up with the Social Democrats again. The coalition talks distracted Germany somewhat from Brexit. When the issue was raised, Germany tended to voice regret over an impending Brexit and vented some frustration that the United Kingdom was not being more specific about what precise post-Brexit relationship it wanted with the European Union.

The European Union had another reason to relax over Brexit too. Having long been dubbed a sick man of the global economy due to years of low growth, the EU economy picked up speed through 2017 and unemployment steadily declined. Economic growth in the United Kingdom, meanwhile, faltered, slipping below many of its EU members. Exports of UK goods, however, did better, largely due to the British pound dropping in value in currency markets, which made UK exports more competitively priced. Approximately 43 percent of UK exports of goods and services went to the European Union in 2016. There is great uncertainty about what will happen to these trade flows post-Brexit where there may be goods inspections at borders and import tariffs. While the UK government stresses its intent to strike new trade deals with rising economic powers such as China, given its proximity and shared history, the European Union will remain one of the United Kingdom's most important trade partners for the foreseeable future.

—Brian Beary

Following is the text of a statement by British Prime Minister Theresa May, on October 9, regarding ongoing Brexit negotiations; remarks by EU Commission President Jean-Claude Junker on progress made in Brexit negotiations, on December 8, 2017; and an address by Prime Minister May to Parliament on December 18, 2017, regarding agreements made during Brexit negotiations.

Prime Minister May Addresses Parliament on Brexit Negotiations

October 9, 2017

With permission, Mr Speaker, I would like to update the House on our plans for leaving the European Union.

Today the fifth round of negotiations begins in Brussels and this government is getting on with the job of delivering the democratic will of the British people.

As I set out in my speech in Florence we want to take a creative and pragmatic approach to securing a new, deep and special partnership with the European Union which spans both a new economic relationship and a new security relationship.

So let me set out what each of these relationships could look like—before turning to how we get there.

ECONOMIC PARTNERSHIP

Mr Speaker, I have been clear that when we leave the European Union we will no longer be members of its single market or its customs union.

The British people voted for control of their borders, their laws and their money. And that is what this government is going to deliver.

At the same time we want to find a creative solution to a new economic relationship that can support prosperity for all our peoples.

We do not want to settle for adopting a model enjoyed by other countries.

So we have rejected the idea of something based on European Economic Area membership. For this would mean having to adopt—automatically and in their entirety—new EU rules over which, in future, we will have little influence and no vote.

Neither are we seeking a Canadian-style free trade agreement. For compared with what exists today, this would represent such a restriction on our mutual market access that it would benefit none of our economies.

Instead I am proposing a unique and ambitious economic partnership. It will reflect our unprecedented position of starting with the same rules and regulations. We will maintain our unequivocal commitment to free trade and high standards. And we will need a framework to manage where we continue to align and where we choose to differ.

There will be areas of policy and regulation which are outside the scope of our trade and economic relations where this should be straightforward.

There will be areas which do affect our economic relations where we and our European friends may have different goals; or where we share the same goals but want to achieve them through different means.

And there will be areas where we want to achieve the same goals in the same ways, because it makes sense for our economies.

And because rights and obligations must be held in balance, the decisions we both take will have consequences for the UK's access to the EU market—and EU access to our market.

But this dynamic, creative and unique economic partnership will enable the UK and the EU to work side by side in bringing shared prosperity to our peoples.

SECURITY RELATIONSHIP

Let me turn to the new security relationship.

As I said when I visited our troops serving on the NATO mission in Estonia last month, the United Kingdom is unconditionally committed to maintaining Europe's security.

And we will continue to offer aid and assistance to EU member states that are the victims of armed aggression, terrorism and natural or manmade disasters.

So we are proposing a bold new strategic agreement that provides a comprehensive framework for future security, law enforcement and criminal justice co-operation: a treaty between the UK and the EU.

We are also proposing a far reaching partnership on how together we protect Europe from the threats we face in the world today.

So this partnership will be unprecedented in its breadth and depth, taking in cooperation on diplomacy, defence and security, and development.

IMPLEMENTATION

Let me turn to how we build a bridge from where we are now to the new relationship that we want to see.

When we leave the European Union on 29th March 2019 neither the UK, nor the EU and its Members States, will be in a position to implement smoothly many of the detailed arrangements that will underpin this new relationship we seek.

Businesses will need time to adjust and governments will need to put new systems in place. And businesses want certainty about the position in the interim.

That is why I suggested in my speech at Lancaster House there should be a period of implementation—and why I proposed such a period in my speech in Florence last month.

During this strictly time-limited period, we will have left the EU and its institutions, but we are proposing that for this period access to one another's markets should continue on current terms and Britain also should continue to take part in existing security measures.

The framework for this period, which can be agreed under Article 50, would be the existing structure of EU rules and regulations.

Now I know some people may have some concerns about this. But there are two reasons why it makes sense.

First, we want our departure from the EU to be as smooth as possible—it wouldn't make sense to make people and businesses plan for two sets of changes in the relationship between the UK and the EU.

Second, we should concentrate our negotiating time and capital on what really matters—the future long-term relationship we will have with the EU after this temporary period ends.

During the implementation period, people will continue to be able to come and live and work in the UK; but there will be a registration system—an essential preparation for the new immigration system required to re-take control of our borders.

And our intention is that new arrivals would be subject to new rules for EU citizens on long term settlement.

We will also push forward on our future independent trade policy, talking to trading partners across the globe and preparing to introduce those deals once this period is over.

How long the period is should be determined simply by how long it will take to prepare and implement the new systems we need.

As of today, these considerations point to an implementation period of around two years.

And as I said in Florence—because I don't believe that either the EU or the British people will want us to stay longer in the existing structures than necessary, we could also agree to bring forward aspects of that future framework, such as new dispute resolution mechanisms, more quickly if this can be done smoothly.

At the heart of these arrangements, there should be a clear double lock: guaranteeing a period of implementation giving businesses and people the certainty they will be able to prepare for the change; and guaranteeing this implementation period will be time-limited, giving everyone the certainty this will not go on forever.

NEGOTIATIONS

Mr Speaker, the purpose of the Florence speech was to move the negotiations forward and that is exactly what has happened.

As Michel Barnier said after the last round, there is a "new dynamic" in the negotiations. And I want to pay tribute to my Rt Hon Friend the Secretary of State for Exiting the European Union for all he has done to drive through real and tangible progress on a number of vital areas.

On citizens' rights, as I have said many times this government greatly values the contributions of all EU citizens who have made their lives in our country. We want them to stay.

In Florence, I gave further commitments that the rights of EU citizens in the UK—and UK citizens in the EU—will not diverge over time, committing to incorporate our agreement on citizens' rights fully into UK law and making sure the UK courts can refer directly to it.

Since Florence there has been more progress including reaching agreement on reciprocal healthcare and pensions, and encouraging further alignment on a range of important social security rights.

So I hope our negotiating teams can now reach full agreement quickly.

On Northern Ireland, we have now begun drafting joint principles on preserving the Common Travel Area and associated rights. And we have both stated explicitly we will not accept any physical infrastructure at the border.

We owe it to the people of Northern Ireland—and indeed to everyone on the island of Ireland—to get this right.

Then there is the question of the EU budget.

As I have said, this can only be resolved as part of the settlement of all the issues that we are working through.

Still I do not want our partners to fear that they will need to pay more or receive less over the remainder of the current budget plan as a result of our decision to leave. The UK will honour commitments we have made during the period of our membership.

And as we move forwards, we will also want to continue working together in ways that promote the long-term economic development of our continent.

This includes continuing to take part in those specific policies and programmes which are greatly to our joint advantage, such as those that promote science, education and culture—and those that promote our mutual security.

And as I set out in my speech at Lancaster House, in doing so, we would want to make a contribution to cover our fair share of the costs involved.

Mr Speaker, I continued discussions on many of these issues when I met with European leaders in Tallinn at the end of last month.

And in the bi-lateral discussions I have had with Chancellor Merkel, Prime Minister Szydlo, President Tusk and the Taoiseach Leo Varadkar, they welcomed the tone set in Florence and the impact this was having on moving the negotiations forwards.

LEGISLATION

Mr Speaker, preparing for life outside the EU is also about the legislative steps we take.

Our EU Withdrawal Bill will shortly enter Committee Stage, carrying over EU rules and regulations into our domestic law from the moment we leave the EU.

And today we are publishing two White Papers on trade and customs. These pave the way for legislation to allow the UK to operate as an independent trading nation and to create an innovative customs system that will help us achieve the greatest possible tariff and barrier-free trade as we leave the EU.

And while I believe it is profoundly in all our interests for the negotiations to succeed, it is also our responsibility as a government to prepare for every eventuality. So that is exactly what we are doing.

These White Papers also support that work, including setting out steps to minimise disruption for businesses and travellers.

Conclusion

Mr Speaker, a new, deep and special partnership between a sovereign United Kingdom and a strong and successful European Union is our ambition and our offer to our European friends.

Achieving that partnership will require leadership and flexibility, not just from us but from our friends, the 27 nations of the EU.

And as we look forward to the next stage, the ball is in their court. But I am optimistic it will receive a positive response.

Because what we are seeking is not just the best possible deal for us—but I believe that will also be the best possible deal for our European friends too.

So while, of course, progress will not always be smooth; by approaching these negotiations in a constructive way—in a spirit of friendship and co-operation and with our sights firmly set on the future—I believe we can prove the doomsayers wrong.

And I believe we can seize the opportunities of this defining moment in the history of our nation.

Mr Speaker, a lot of the day to day coverage is about process. But this, on the other hand, is vitally important.

I am determined to deliver what the British people voted for and to get it right.

That is my duty as Prime Minister.

It is our duty as a Government.

And it is what we will do.

And I commend this Statement to the House.

SOURCE: United Kingdom Prime Minister's Office. 10 Downing Street. "PM Statement on Leaving the EU." October 9, 2017. https://www.gov.uk/government/speeches/pm-statement-on-leaving-the-eu-9-oct-2017.

EU President Junker on Brexit Negotiations Breakthrough

December 8, 2017

Prime Minister,

Ladies and Gentlemen,

This morning, Prime Minister May and I had a meeting to take stock of progress since we met on Monday. I will not hide that in between Monday and this morning we had a lot of talks—the Prime Minister and myself; the Taoiseach and myself; the Taoiseach and the Prime Minister.

And that is the reason why I would like to thank the Prime Minister for her determination. I would also like to thank Michel Barnier and David Davis, as well as their teams, for the extremely hard and skilful work over the last weeks and months.

We discussed the Joint Report agreed by the two negotiators. Prime Minister May has assured me that it has the backing of the UK Government. On that basis, I believe we have now made the breakthrough we needed.

Today's result is of course a compromise. It is the result of a long and intense discussion between the Commission's negotiators and those of the UK.

As in any negotiation, both sides had to listen to each other, adjust their position, and show a willingness to compromise. This was a difficult negotiation for the European Union as well as for the United Kingdom.

On Wednesday, the College of Commissioners gave me a mandate to conclude the negotiation of the Joint Report. And it had to be concluded today—not next week—today because next week we will have the European Council and in order to allow our partners to prepare in the best way possible the meeting of the European Council we had to make the deal today.

On the basis of that mandate, the Commission has just formally decided to recommend to the European Council that sufficient progress has now been made on the strict terms of the divorce. Es wurden genügend Fortschritte erzielt, damit wir jetzt in die zweite Phase der Verhandlungen eintreten können. Nous avons pu faire les progrès suffisants pour que désormais nous puissions entrer en deuxième phase de la négociation entre le Royaume-Uni et l'Union européenne à 27.

The decision on sufficient progress will be in the hands of the 27 Heads of State or Government. I am hopeful, sure, confident—sure—that they will share our appraisal and allow us to move on to the next phase of the negotiations.

Last Monday I also met with the European Parliament representatives. From the start of this process, cooperation between the European Parliament and the Commission has been close and our positions closely aligned. These negotiations can only be successful if we take an inclusive approach; that is exactly what we did.

Without going into all of the detail, allow me to touch on what today's agreements mean in practice. Later on today, at 09:30, my friend Michel Barnier will be available to explain all the details of the agreement we reached today.

A few remarks on citizens' rights first. In this negotiation, citizens have always come first. It has been of great importance for the Commission to make sure that EU citizens in the UK will be protected after the UK leaves the European Union.

EU citizens have made important life choices on the assumption that the United Kingdom was a member of the European Union. Brexit created great uncertainty for those citizens and for their families.

Today, we bring back the certainty. The Commission's negotiators have made sure that the choices made by EU citizens living in the UK will be protected. We have made sure that their rights will remain the same after the UK has left the European Union. This is in particular the case for: EU citizens' right to live, work and study; EU citizens' right to family reunification; the protection of the rights of EU citizens' children; and the right to healthcare, pensions and other social security benefits.

We have made sure that the administrative procedures will be cheap and will be simple. This is an issue to which the Commission will pay particular attention when drafting the withdrawal agreement.

The same goes for UK citizens living in the EU27.

On the settling of accounts, the Prime Minister said in her remarkable Florence speech that the United Kingdom would honour its commitments, including beyond 2020. This was a detailed, line-by-line process but she has been as good as her word. She was negotiating in a gentlemanly manner, and I am very grateful, Prime Minister, for that.

On Ireland, the EU has consistently supported the goal of peace and reconciliation enshrined in the Good Friday Agreement. The European Union has made it a priority to protect the peace process on the island. I have been in regular contact with the Taoiseach over the last days, including last night and including the last negotiations we had in the course of yesterday with our Irish friends. The UK has made significant commitments on the avoidance of a hard border after its withdrawal from the European Union.

All of the EU27 stand firmly behind Ireland and behind the peace process.

Let me be clear: we still have a lot of work to do.

The Joint Report is not the withdrawal agreement. That agreement still needs to be drafted by the negotiators on the basis we have agreed yesterday and today, and then approved by the Council and ratified by the UK Parliament and the European Parliament.

534 days ago, the British people voted to leave the European Union. 249 days ago the United Kingdom notified its intention to leave the European Union. And in 477 days the United Kingdom will do just that.

I will always be sad about this development. But now we must start looking to the future. A future in which the United Kingdom will be and will remain a close friend and ally. The Prime Minister and I discussed the need for a transitional period. And we dedicated much of our meeting to our joint vision of a deep and close partnership. It is crucial for us all that we continue working closely together on issues such as trade, research, security and others.

We will take things one step at a time—starting with next week's European Council. But today, I am hopeful that we are now all moving towards the second phase of these challenging negotiations. And we can do this jointly on the basis of trust, renewed trust, determination and with the perspective of a renewed friendship.

Thank you.

SOURCE: European Commission. "Remarks by President Juncker at the Joint Press Conference with Theresa May, Prime Minister of the United Kingdom." December 8, 2017. © European Union. http://europa.eu/rapid/press-release_SPEECH-17-5181_en.pdf.

Prime Minister May Remarks on Brexit Negotiations Agreements

December 18, 2017

[The portions of the prime minister's speech not related to Brexit have been omitted.]

BREXIT NEGOTIATIONS

Turning to Brexit, the European Council formally agreed on Friday that sufficient progress has been made to move on to the second stage of the negotiations.

This is an important step on the road to delivering the smooth and orderly Brexit that people voted for in June last year.

And I want to thank Jean-Claude Juncker for his personal efforts, and Donald Tusk and my fellow leaders for the constructive way they have approached this process.

With Friday's Council, we have now achieved my first priority of a reciprocal agreement on citizens' rights.

EU Citizens living in the UK will have their rights enshrined in UK law and enforced by British courts. And UK citizens living in the EU will also have their rights protected.

Mr Speaker, we needed both and that is what we have got—providing vital reassurance to all these citizens and their families in the run-up to Christmas.

On the financial settlement, I set out the principles for the House last week and the negotiations that have brought this settlement down by a substantial amount.

Based on reasonable assumptions, the settlement is estimated to stand at between £35 billion and £39 billion in current terms.

This is the equivalent of around four years of our current budget contribution, around two of which we expect will be covered by the implementation period.

And it is far removed from some of the figures that had been bandied around.

On Northern Ireland, as I set out in detail for the House last week, we have committed to maintain the Common Travel Area with Ireland; to uphold the Belfast Agreement in full; and to avoid a hard border between Northern Ireland and Ireland while upholding the constitutional and economic integrity of the whole United Kingdom.

And we will work closer than ever with all Northern Irish parties and the Irish government as we now enter the second phase of the negotiations.

Mr Speaker, the guidelines published by President Tusk on Friday point to the shared desire of the EU and the UK to make rapid progress on an implementation period, with formal talks beginning very soon.

This will help give certainty to employers and families that we are going to deliver a smooth Brexit.

As I proposed in Florence, during this strictly time-limited implementation period which we will now begin to negotiate, we would not be in the Single Market or the Customs Union, as we will have left the European Union. But we would propose that our access to one another's markets would continue as now, while we prepare and implement the new processes and new systems that will underpin our future partnership.

During this period we intend to register new arrivals from the EU as preparation for our future immigration system. And we will prepare for our future independent trade policy by negotiating—and where possible signing—trade deals with third countries, which could come into force after the conclusion of the implementation period.

Finally, the Council also confirmed on Friday that discussions will now begin on trade and the future security partnership.

I set out the framework for our approach to these discussions in my speeches at Lancaster House and in Florence.

We will now work with our European partners with ambition and creativity to develop the details of a partnership that I firmly believe will be in the best interests of both the UK and the EU.

Conclusion

Mr Speaker, since my Lancaster House speech in January we have triggered Article 50 and begun and closed negotiations on the first phase.

We have done what many said could not be done—demonstrating what can be achieved with commitment and perseverance on both sides.

And I will not be derailed from delivering the democratic will of the British people.

We are well on our way to delivering a smooth and orderly Brexit.

That is good news for those who voted to leave, who were worried the negotiations were so complicated it was never going to happen.

And it is good news for those who voted remain, who were worried that we might leave without being able to reach an agreement.

We will now move on with building a bold new economic relationship—which together with the new trade deals we strike across the world—can support generations of new jobs for our people, open up new markets for our exporters and drive new growth for our economy.

We will build a new security relationship that promotes our values in the world and keeps our families safe from threats that increasingly do not recognise geographical boundaries.

And we will bring our country together—stronger, fairer, and once again back in control of our borders, our money and our laws.

Finally, Mr Speaker, let me say this.

We are dealing with questions of great significance to our country's future, so it is natural that there are many strongly held views on all sides of this Chamber.

And it is right and proper that we should debate them—and do so with all the passion and conviction that makes our democracy what it is.

But there can never be a place for the threats of violence and intimidation against some Members that we have seen in recent days.

Our politics must be better than that.

And on that note, I commend this Statement to the House.

SOURCE: United Kingdom Prime Minister's Office. 10 Downing Street. "PM Commons Statement on European Council." December 18, 2017. https://www.gov.uk/government/speeches/pm-commons-state ment-on-european-council-18-december-2017.

OTHER HISTORIC DOCUMENTS OF INTEREST

FROM THIS VOLUME

- British Prime Minister Triggers Exit from European Union, p. 198
- Leaders of France, Germany, and the UK Respond to National Elections, p. 260

FROM PREVIOUS *HISTORIC DOCUMENTS*

- Britons Vote to Exit the European Union, *2016*, p. 280

Decertification of Iranian Nuclear Deal

OCTOBER 13, 2017

In the fall of 2017, President Donald Trump announced that he would not recertify the Iranian nuclear agreement that he had repeatedly denounced as an embarrassment and "one of the worst and most one-sided" deals the United States has ever entered into, drawing a sharp rebuke from Iran and calls from European allies to preserve the agreement. Despite the decertification, neither Trump nor Congress imposed nuclear-related sanctions on Iran or took other legislative action, effectively leaving the agreement in place.

The Joint Comprehensive Plan of Action

The Joint Comprehensive Plan of Action (JCPOA) was signed by representatives from the United States, China, France, Germany, Russia, the United Kingdom, and Iran in July 2015. The result of nearly two years of negotiations, the JCPOA required Iran to significantly scale back its nuclear activities and capabilities. For example, Iran retained the ability to enrich uranium, but can only maintain a 300kg stockpile of low-enriched uranium for the next fifteen years, as opposed to the 10,000kg it had at the time the agreement was signed. The JCPOA also limits the number of centrifuges Iran can operate and either prohibits their use for uranium enrichment or allows only for low-enriched uranium production. Other key provisions include Iran's commitment to allow the International Atomic Energy Agency (IAEA) to have a long-term presence in Iran and monitor its implementation of these measures.

In return, the United States, European Union, and United Nations agreed to remove or relax the economic sanctions that had been used as the primary tool for restricting Iran's nuclear program for approximately twenty years. The agreement took full effect, and sanctions were lifted, in January 2016 after the IAEA confirmed that Iran had met its obligations under the JCPOA.

Though hailed by many as a major international diplomatic victory, the deal was not without its opponents and skeptics. In the United States, concerns among lawmakers—particularly Republicans—prompted passage of the Iran Nuclear Agreement Review Act of 2015 (INARA), which required President Barack Obama to submit the terms of the final agreement to Congress for review. Going forward, the bill also required the president to certify every ninety days that Iran was in compliance with the deal, and that the suspension of sanctions is both "appropriate and proportionate" to the actions taken by Iran to end its nuclear program and vital to the United States' national security interests.

Trump Decertifies Agreement

Trump was among the JCPOA's vocal critics, pledging repeatedly during his presidential campaign to "rip up" the agreement as soon as he was elected. Despite these claims, Trump certified the agreement in April and July 2017, though he continued to criticize it and argue that Iran was violating the "spirit" of the agreement.

However, on October 13, Trump announced that he would not certify the agreement. He claimed that Iran had "committed multiple violations of the agreement." (The IAEA has confirmed on nine separate occasions that Iran is complying with the JCPOA.) Although Trump refused to recertify the deal, he did not withdraw from it, but he promised that the United States would abandon the deal if it was not amended so that it permanently prevented Iran from building nuclear weapons. "In just a few years, as key restrictions disappear, Iran can sprint towards a rapid nuclear weapons breakout," he said. He added, "In other words, we got weak inspections in exchange for no more than a purely short-term and temporary delay in Iran's path to nuclear weapons." Notably, Trump did not say he would reinstate nuclear-related sanctions on Iran, nor did he call on Congress to do so—acts that would have violated the United States' obligations under the deal and therefore effectively ended the agreement. Instead, Trump said he was directing his administration to "work closely with Congress and our allies to address the deal's many serious flaws so that the Iranian regime can never threaten the world with nuclear weapons." He also asked Congress to define the conditions under which sanctions would be imposed again.

JCPOA Signatories React

Trump's announcement prompted quick responses from other parties to the JCPOA. British Prime Minister Theresa May, German Chancellor Angela Merkel, and French President Emmanuel Macron issued a joint statement the same day affirming their commitment to the JCPOA and "its full implementation by all sides," and stating that the deal's preservation was "in our shared national security interest." They acknowledged some shared concerns about Iran's ballistic missile program and said they were "ready to take further appropriate measures to address these issues in close cooperation with the U.S.," noting they had asked their respective foreign ministers to reach out to the U.S. to determine how to move forward. They added, "We encourage the U.S. Administration and Congress to consider the implications to the security of the U.S. and its allies before taking any steps that might undermine the JCPOA."

Iranian President Hassan Rouhani denounced Trump's remarks in a televised address, saying they consisted of "nothing except insults and a pile of false accusations" against Iran. "For the first time, the United States took a stand against a multilateral international commitment, and immediately, major countries of the world and the European Union took a stand against the United States," he said. "The U.S. today is lonelier than ever on the JCPOA and its conspiracies against the Iranian nation."

Congress Fails to Act, Trump Extends Deal

Per INARA, Congress had sixty days from the date of Trump's decertification to reimpose nuclear sanctions on Iran using special legislative rules that allowed for expedited procedures. Sens. Bob Corker, R-Tenn., and Tom Cotton, R-Ark., circulated draft legislation in October that would have instantly restored sanctions if Iran was found to have the capability to build a nuclear weapon within a year. It also required broader assessment of Iranian compliance with the JCPOA, to include factors such as intercontinental ballistic missile tests, and changed the certification requirement to every six months instead of ninety days. However, tax reform legislation consumed the congressional agenda in the fall, and no JCPOA bill was passed.

At the next certification deadline, January 11, 2018, Trump once again declined to certify the deal; however, the following day he announced the renewal of sanctions waivers, which must be renewed every 120 days to prevent certain sanctions from being reinstated. Trump stated that he was only renewing the waivers "to secure our European allies' agreement" to fix the deal's flaws. "This is a last chance," he said. "In the absence of such an agreement, the United States will not again waive sanctions in order to stay in the Iran nuclear deal." He added, "If other nations fail to act during this time, I will terminate our deal with Iran." Trump said he was open to working with Congress on bipartisan legislation to address his concerns with the JCPOA, but that any bill must demand that Iran allow immediate inspections at all sites requested by international inspectors and ensure Iran "never even comes close to possessing a nuclear weapon." He also maintained that legislation should have no expiration date and allow for automatic resumption of U.S. sanctions if Iran violated any provision of the agreement and explicitly state that "Iran's development and testing of missiles should be subject to severe sanctions."

The sanctions waivers are set to be renewed again in May 2018.

—Linda Grimm

Following are remarks delivered by President Donald Trump on October 13, 2017, decertifying the JCPOA and outlining a new strategy toward Iran; a joint statement by British Prime Minister Theresa May, German Chancellor Angela Merkel, and French President Emmanuel Macron from October 13, 2017, responding to Trump's announcement; and a statement by Iranian President Hassan Rouhani from October 13, 2017, also responding to Trump's remarks.

DOCUMENT

President Trump Remarks on U.S.'s Strategy in Iran

October 13, 2017

Thank you very much. My fellow Americans, as President of the United States, my highest obligation is to ensure the safety and security of the American people. History has shown that the longer we ignore a threat, the more dangerous that threat becomes. For this reason, upon taking office, I've ordered a complete strategic review of our policy toward the rogue regime in Iran. That review is now complete.

Today I am announcing our strategy, along with several major steps we are taking to confront the Iranian regime's hostile actions and to ensure that Iran never—and I mean never—acquires a nuclear weapon. Our policy is based on a clear-eyed assessment of the Iranian dictatorship, its sponsorship of terrorism, and its continuing aggression in the Middle East and all around the world . . .

[The following page, discussing Iranian attacks on Americans and the country's role in unrest across the Middle East, has been omitted.]

Given the regime's murderous past and present, we should not take lightly its sinister vision for the future. The regime's two favorite chants are "Death to America" and "Death to Israel." Realizing the gravity of the situation, the United States and the United Nations

Security Council sought, over many years, to stop Iran's pursuit of nuclear weapons with a wide array of strong economic sanctions.

But the previous administration lifted these sanctions, just before what would have been the total collapse of the Iranian regime, through the deeply controversial 2015 nuclear deal with Iran. This deal is known as the Joint Comprehensive Plan of Action, or JCPOA. As I have said many times, the Iran deal was one of the worst and most one-sided transactions the United States has ever entered into . . .

The nuclear deal threw Iran's dictatorship a political and economic lifeline, providing urgently needed relief from the intense domestic pressure the sanctions had created. It also gave the regime an immediate financial boost and over $100 billion dollars its Government could use to fund terrorism.

The regime also received a massive cash settlement of $1.7 billion from the United States, a large portion of which was physically loaded onto an airplane and flown into Iran. Just imagine the sight of those huge piles of money being hauled off by the Iranians waiting at the airport for the cash. I wonder where all that money went.

Worst of all, the deal allows Iran to continue developing certain elements of its nuclear program. And importantly, in just a few years, as key restrictions disappear, Iran can sprint towards a rapid nuclear weapons breakout. In other words, we got weak inspections in exchange for no more than a purely short-term and temporary delay in Iran's path to nuclear weapons . . .

The saddest part of the deal for the United States is that all of the money was paid up front, which is unheard of, rather than at the end of the deal when they have shown they've played by the rules. But what's done is done, and that's why we are where we are.

The Iranian regime has committed multiple violations of the agreement. For example, on two separate occasions, they have exceeded the limit of 130 metric tons of heavy water. Until recently, the Iranian regime has also failed to meet our expectations in its operation of advanced centrifuges.

The Iranian regime has also intimidated international inspectors into not using the full inspection authorities that the agreement calls for. Iranian officials and military leaders have repeatedly claimed they will not allow inspectors onto military sites, even though the international community suspects some of those sites were part of Iran's clandestine nuclear weapons program.

There are also many people who believe that Iran is dealing with North Korea. I am going to instruct our intelligence agencies to do a thorough analysis and report back their findings beyond what they have already reviewed.

By its own terms, the Iran deal was supposed to contribute to "regional and international peace and security." And yet, while the United States adheres to our commitment under the deal, the Iranian regime continues to fuel conflict, terror, and turmoil throughout the Middle East and beyond. Importantly, Iran is not living up to the spirit of the deal.

So today, in recognition of the increasing menace posed by Iran, and after extensive consultations with our allies, I am announcing a new strategy to address the full range of Iran's destructive actions. First, we will work with our allies to counter the regime's destabilizing activity and support for terrorist proxies in the region. Second, we will place additional sanctions on the regime to block their financing of terror. Third, we will address the regime's proliferation of missiles and weapons that threaten its neighbors, global trade, and freedom of navigation. And finally, we will deny the regime all paths to a nuclear weapon.

Today I am also announcing several major steps my administration is taking in pursuit of this strategy. The execution of our strategy begins with the long-overdue step of imposing tough sanctions on Iran's Islamic Revolutionary Guard Corps. The Revolutionary Guard is the Iranian Supreme Leader's corrupt personal terror force and militia. It has hijacked large portions of Iran's economy and seized massive religious endowments to fund war and terror abroad. This includes arming the Syrian dictator, supplying proxies and partners with missiles and weapons to attack civilians in the region, and even plotting to bomb a popular restaurant right here in Washington, DC.

I am authorizing the Treasury Department to further sanction the entire Islamic Revolutionary Guard Corps for its support for terrorism and to apply sanctions to its officials, agents, and affiliates. I urge our allies to join us in taking strong actions to curb Iran's continued dangerous and destabilizing behavior, including thorough sanctions outside the Iran deal that target the regime's ballistic missile program, in support for terrorism, and all of its destructive activities, of which there are many.

Finally, on the grave matter of Iran's nuclear program: Since the signing of the nuclear agreement, the regime's dangerous aggression has only escalated. At the same time, it has received massive sanctions relief while continuing to develop its missiles program. Iran has also entered into lucrative business contracts with other parties to the agreement.

When the agreement was finalized in 2015, Congress passed the Iran Nuclear Agreement Review Act to ensure that Congress's voice would be heard on the deal. Among other conditions, this law requires the President, or his designee, to certify that the suspension of sanctions under the deal is "appropriate and proportionate" to measure—and other measures taken by Iran to terminate its illicit nuclear program. Based on the factual record I have put forward, I am announcing today that we cannot and will not make this certification. We will not continue down a path whose predictable conclusion is more violence, more terror, and the very real threat of Iran's nuclear breakout.

That is why I am directing my administration to work closely with Congress and our allies to address the deal's many serious flaws so that the Iranian regime can never threaten the world with nuclear weapons. These include the deal's sunset clauses that, in just a few years, will eliminate key restrictions on Iran's nuclear program.

The flaws in the deal also include insufficient enforcement and near-total silence on Iran's missile programs. Congress has already begun the work to address these problems. Key House and Senate leaders are drafting legislation that would amend the Iran Nuclear Agreement Review

Act to strengthen enforcement, prevent Iran from developing an—this is so totally important—an intercontinental ballistic missile, and make all restrictions on Iran's nuclear activity permanent under U.S. law. So important. I support these initiatives.

However, in the event we are not able to reach a solution working with Congress and our allies, then the agreement will be terminated. It is under continuous review, and our participation can be canceled by me, as President, at any time . . .

We hope that these new measures directed at the Iranian dictatorship will compel the government to reevaluate its pursuit of terror at the expense of its people. We hope that our actions today will help bring about a future of peace, stability, and prosperity in the Middle East, a future where sovereign nations respect each other and their own citizens . . .

Thank you.

SOURCE: Executive Office of the President. "Remarks on the United States Strategy toward Iran." October 13, 2017. *Compilation of Presidential Documents* 2017, no. 00749 (October 13, 2017). https://www.gpo .gov/fdsys/pkg/DCPD-201700749/pdf/DCPD-201700749.pdf.

Joint Statement from the UK, France, and Germany in Response to the U.S. Iran Strategy

October 13, 2017

We, the Leaders of France, Germany and the United Kingdom take note of President Trump's decision not to recertify Iran's compliance with the Joint Comprehensive Plan of Action to Congress and are concerned by the possible implications.

We stand committed to the JCPoA and its full implementation by all sides. Preserving the JCPoA is in our shared national security interest. The nuclear deal was the culmination of 13 years of diplomacy and was a major step towards ensuring that Iran's nuclear programme is not diverted for military purposes. The JCPoA was unanimously endorsed by the UN Security Council in Resolution 2231. The International Atomic Energy Agency has repeatedly confirmed Iran's compliance with the JCPoA through its long-term verification and monitoring programme. Therefore, we encourage the US Administration and Congress to consider the implications to the security of the US and its allies before taking any steps that might undermine the JCPoA, such as re-imposing sanctions on Iran lifted under the agreement.

At the same time as we work to preserve the JCPoA, we share concerns about Iran's ballistic missile programme and regional activities that also affect our European security interests. We stand ready to take further appropriate measures to address these issues in close cooperation with the US and all relevant partners. We look to Iran to engage in constructive dialogue to stop de-stabilising actions and work towards negotiated solutions.

Our governments are committed to ensuring the JCPoA is maintained. Independent of the JCPOA, we need to make sure that our collective wider concerns are being addressed.

We have asked our Foreign Ministers to consider with the US how to take these issues forward.

Source: Government of the United Kingdom. "Declaration by the Heads of State and Government of France, Germany and the United Kingdom." October 13, 2017. https://www.gov.uk/government/news/declaration-by-the-heads-of-state-and-government-of-france-germany-and-the-united-kingdom.

President Rouhani Responds to President Trump's Remarks on Iran, Nuclear Agreement

October 13, 2017

In the Name of Allah, the Most Beneficent, the Most Merciful

Hello and good night to the great, understanding Iranian nation. I would like to inform the great people of Iran, after the words of the current president of the United

States was heard, that firstly, in the words of Mr Trump on Iran's policy, there was nothing except insults and a pile of false accusations against the Iranian nation.

I invite the US president to read more about history, geography, international commitments, politeness and ethics, and international conventions.

Apparently, he does not know that the US government set up a coup sixty-some years ago, and it was a power that overthrew the rule of law by making money and leveraging its mercenaries.

Apparently, he has forgotten that during the integrated campaign of the Iranian people against the dictatorship to gain freedom, independence and the Islamic Republic in this land, it was the United States that greatly supported the dictator of the time in Iran.

Apparently, he has forgotten that after the glorious victory of the Islamic Revolution and at the very earliest days, the US plot in Iran was a coup which, of course, was repeated once again in 1980.

Apparently, he has forgotten that in the eight-year defence of the Iranian nation against aggression, the United States backed the aggressor; he has forgotten the bombings of the cities of Iran, as well as the chemical bombardment of Sardasht and Halabcheh, when it was supposed to issue a statement against the aggressors, it acted exactly the opposite way. We should read the history better and more precise, to find out what they have done to the Iranian people in the past sixty-some years few years; how they treated the Iranian people during the 40 years after the revolution. . . .

He has not apparently read international law. How can a president alone cancel a treaty that is a multilateral and in one sense, international document, as it has been approved in the United Nations? He apparently does not know that this is not a bilateral document between Iran and the United States, on which he can act in any way he likes.

Politeness and ethics are also important; false, defamatory lies and accusations against the great nation of Iran [is not accepted]—a great nation that, as tonight's speaker came to the Persian Gulf region, attended the great elections in historic numbers. Is a nation and government, which is respectful of democracy and its culture and faith and has consistently respected all its international treaties and obligations, rogue? Or a government that has always been pursuing aggression and coups in this region and in the world, and has killed hundreds of thousands of people in different parts of the world from Vietnam to Latin America and in other countries with bombs? The country that claims to have stood against nuclear weapons, is the only country in the history of the world that has used nuclear weapons against a nation, not once, but twice. And today, it is threatening another country in the same region with nuclear weapons. Does a nuclear-armed country that has used nuclear weapons and also contributes to the development of nuclear weapons in countries that have close relations with it, such as the usurper Zionist Regime, want to take global actions against the proliferation of nuclear weapons?

In my opinion, once again it became clear to our people that the US government is a government that continues to its previous policies against the people of the region, against the Iranian people and against the oppressed peoples. The Iranian nation is not a nation that surrenders to a dictator by false statements and hate speech and the great nation of Iran has never surrendered to any power.

The Iranian nation will not give up and yield to any power. There were many countries that supported Saddam and failed to break our nation. There were many countries that joined the sanctions against Iran and it was proved to them that they could not make the Iranian people surrender. Today, it became clearer for the Iranian nation that we should be together more than ever before.

The great people of Iran saw that for the first time, the United States took a stand against a multilateral international commitment, and immediately, major countries of the world and the European Union took a stand against the United States. The US today is lonelier than ever on the JCPOA and its conspiracies against the Iranian nation . . .

Are you worried about Iranian missiles? How come you do not protest against those weapons you give to the aggressors every day and they target the innocent people of Yemen with your own planes and bombs? You acted against Iranian oil platforms and you have always conducted acts of aggression in the region. Our weapons and missiles are for our defence. We have always been determined to defend our country and we became more determined today. We have always tried to make the weapons that we needed, and we will continue to do more efforts later on. Our weapons are for defence, and we will continue to defend and strengthen our defences.

And our last word about the JCPOA as a multilateral and international treaty, in a sense, is that as long as our rights are guaranteed, and as long as our interests require and, as long as we enjoy its benefits, we will respect the JCPOA within the framework of the interests of our nation.

We cooperated with the International Atomic Energy Agency and within the framework of international treaties and the JCPOA and we will continue to do so, but if one day our interests are not guaranteed and the other parties want to violate their commitments, they must know that Iran will not hesitate a second and will respond to them.

What was heard today from US officials was nothing but the repetition of incorrect words, false accusations and insults that have been repeatedly said during the past 40 years. We were not surprised, since we are accustomed to these words of yours for 40 years. Our nation was not surprised, because it was expected of you, but you know that with your untrue words, you yourself made our nation more united. You cannot divide the people and the government, you are not able to divide the Iranian people and the great, popular Leader.

The basis of our revolution was based on the fact that religion is not separate from politics and the link between religion and politics is the Guardianship of the Islamic Jurist and the Supreme Leader, and the Iranian people respect and will respect its leader in accordance with the law and the constitution. The commands of the Leader are the commandments for the Iranian nation and the nation is united. All factions, groups, parties, tribes and religions will stand against the enemies of the Iranian nation and against you.

Are you sad about the slogan of the Iranian nation? Abandon your hostile policy. The people of Iran respect the American people, but they do not accept your aggressive policies. The slogan of the Iranian people is not against the country and people of the United States, but against the false and aggressive policies of the government of the United States. It is up to you to correct your policies and it is up to you to learn the right way of respecting nations.

If you do so, then the people of Iran will know well how to behave with you at that time.

Our nation, as always, stands against the conspirators. Their main goal is to keep us from economic growth, the goal of the US is to shy the world away from Iran and the JCPOA, and ultimately, to prevent investment and economic growth and economic prosperity. Despite the words of Trump and despite the ominous goals of American politicians, our nation will continue to work harder for economic growth, and will make the commands the Leader of Resistive Economy realised and operational.

Peace be upon you and the mercy of Allah and His blessings.

SOURCE: Office of the President of Iran. "President in a Live Televised Speech." October 13, 2017. http://president.ir/en/101131.

OTHER HISTORIC DOCUMENTS OF INTEREST

FROM THIS VOLUME

FROM PREVIOUS *HISTORIC DOCUMENTS*

19th National Congress of the Communist Party of China Held

The 19th National Congress of the Communist Party of China was held in Beijing from October 18 to 24, 2017. Nearly 2,300 delegates attended the National Congress to set policy priorities and select new leaders for the Communist Party, which has controlled China's government for nearly seventy years. The party conducts a National Congress every five years, with a complete change in leadership occurring every ten years. The 19th National Congress was marked by a further consolidation of President Xi Jinping's power, because he was formally granted a second term and those chosen for leadership positions are expected to support his agenda. Additionally, the National Congress unanimously agreed to adopt the political doctrine known as Xi Jinping Thought on Socialism with Chinese Characteristics for a New Era into the Communist Party Constitution, placing Xi alongside such foundational party leaders as Mao Zedong.

19TH NATIONAL CONGRESS BEGINS

Observers within and outside China viewed the 19th National Congress as a referendum on President Xi Jinping, who had been selected to lead the party's Politburo Standing Committee (the highest group in the government and controller of domestic and foreign policy), chair the Central Military Commission, become General Secretary of the Central Committee, and serve as president at the last National Congress in 2012. Many anticipated that the National Congress would conclude with Xi's political power and standing as the party leader strengthened. "Under Xi Jinping, the Chinese Communist Party is headed in the direction of strongman rule," said David M. Lampton, director of China studies at the Johns Hopkins School of Advanced International Studies. "The 19th Party Congress is more likely to look like a coronation than an institutionalized transition to a leader's second term."

Xi had pursued strong anti-corruption measures during his five years in office, replacing party leaders and governors in most of China's thirty-one provinces, as well as much of the military leadership and roughly half the government's ministers. He had also taken a more global approach to defense policy than his predecessors, including by committing thousands of Chinese troops to United Nations peacekeeping missions and establishing the country's first overseas military base in Djibouti. China's "One Belt, One Road" economic plan, which encompasses a variety of planned trade deals, infrastructure projects, port developments, and new shipping lanes involving more than eight countries was a vision of Xi's. The president is also known for his efforts to impose greater discipline within the party, which had experienced political infighting ahead of prior National Congress' and subsequent transfers of power, and for cracking down on critics and activists, including by tightening censorship of the Internet and other media.

These policies and achievements were among those highlighted by Xi in his marathon three-and-a-half-hour-long speech opening the 19th National Congress. The opening speech of the National Congress is traditionally delivered as a report on behalf of the Central Committee selected at the prior National Congress. Xi told the assembled delegates that China was facing a "new era" and a "historic juncture," saying that China had "stood up, grown rich, and become strong—and it now embraces the brilliant prospects of rejuvenation." Xi acknowledged that China's development had been "unbalanced and inadequate," citing issues of economic inequality, the need to improve schools and health care, increase access to housing, and also provide fairer access to the justice system. He also talked about strengthening the country's economy by limiting financial risks, promoting innovation, and encouraging increased consumer spending, as well as tightening regulations on banks, breaking up monopolies, and making state-owned companies stronger and more efficient. Xi declared that corruption remained the greatest threat to the Communist Party's survival, stating that it must rid itself "of any virus that erodes the party's health" and that the "overwhelming force of the anti-corruption struggle has coalesced and is being consolidated and developed." He identified reducing pollution as a major policy goal, noted that China was taking more of a leadership role in addressing climate change, and said, "Any harm we inflict on nature will eventually return to haunt us." The president also discussed the need to strengthen the military, including through weaponry innovations, and promised greater censorship to help quell social discontent. Additionally, Xi affirmed China's "one country, two systems" model, a reference to territories such as Hong Kong and Taiwan, and said China would "never allow anyone, any organization, or any political party, at any time or in any form, to separate any part of Chinese territory from China."

NATIONAL CONGRESS APPROVES XI'S REPORT, ESTABLISHES POLICY BLUEPRINT

On October 24, the National Congress issued a resolution approving Xi's report on behalf of the 18th Central Committee, stating that it "sketches out an impressive blueprint for securing a decisive victory in building a moderately prosperous society in all respects and striving for the great success of socialism with Chinese characteristics for a new era, thus charting the course for continued progress in the cause of the Party and the country." The resolution acknowledged that China was at a "new historic juncture" in its development and that as it has entered a new era, "the principal contradiction facing Chinese society has evolved into one between unbalanced and inadequate development and the people's ever-growing needs for a better life."

To address these challenges, the National Congress endorsed the Central Committee's plans for "promoting socialist economic, political, cultural, social, and ecological advancement in China" and presented a "two-stage development plan" spanning 2020 to 2050. From 2020 to 2035, the National Congress said the party would focus on realizing "socialist modernization"; from 2035 to 2050, the party would "develop China into a great modern socialist country that is prosperous, strong, democratic, culturally advanced, harmonious, and beautiful." The plan called for China to focus on supply-side economic reform; accelerated industrial development, driven by technological advancement and modern finance and human resources; rural development; and the development of more effective market mechanisms to increase the country's economic competitiveness. The plan also called for improving the quality of employment in China, developing education, raising incomes and reducing poverty, strengthening the social security system, and implementing the Healthy China initiative, which seeks to promote greater health for the Chinese people through measures including enhanced access to universal health care and health insurance reforms. The National Congress' plan also identified the need for environmental and national security priorities, such as promoting green development, reforming China's environmental regulatory system, and modernizing the military.

Xi Jinping Thought Added to Party Constitution

Further cementing Xi's leadership of the party, the National Congress unanimously agreed to add Xi Jinping Thought on Socialism with Chinese Characteristics for a New Era to the Communist Party Constitution. Xi Jinping Thought is a political doctrine comprised of fourteen principles, including the supremacy of the Communist Party, the importance of governing according to the rule of law, and the need to take a people-centric approach to governance, guiding policy development. It now appears alongside Marxism-Leninism, Mao Zedong Thought, and other foundational theories as one of the "guides to action of the Party" in the Constitution. "The Congress urges all Party members to use the Thought to achieve unity in thinking and action, be more purposeful and determined in studying and applying it, and put the Thought into action throughout the drive toward China's socialist modernization and in every dimension of Party building," read the National Congress' full resolution on the matter. Xi is one of only three party leaders—including Mao Zedong, who founded the People's Republic of China in 1949, and Deng Xiaoping, who led the opening of China's economy—to have their official thought added to the party Constitution, and neither of his predecessors—Hu Jintao and Jiang Zemin—had their ideas incorporated into the document. Analysts speculate that this development will enable Xi to continue influencing the party beyond his time as president.

Party Leadership Announced

In addition to formally granting Xi a second five-year term as president, the National Congress selected a new Central Committee. The 204 individuals chosen as full members with voting rights included several younger members who some observers think may help carry Xi's influence forward to future National Congresses. One of Xi's closest economic advisors, Liu He, was reappointed to the Central Committee, suggesting a continuation of Xi's approach to economic policy.

The new members of China's Politburo—comprised of top officials, regional chiefs, party leaders, and military leaders—and Politburo Standing Committee were also announced on the last day of the National Congress. In addition to Xi and Premier Li Keqiang, the Standing Committee included Li Zhanshu, director of the Central Committee's General Office; Wang Yang, vice premier of the State Council; Wang Huning, director of the Central Committee's Central Policy Research Center; Zhao Leji, director of the Central Committee's Central Organization Department; and Han Zheng, the party secretary of Shanghai. All members except Xi and Li were new. Observers noted that four of the Standing Committee members were loyal to Hu Jintao or Jiang Zemin, though they are expected to support Xi's agenda, and suggested that their inclusion signaled the party's interest in addressing potential concerns that Xi was consolidating too much power.

Notably, Xi did not identify a potential successor among those appointed to the Standing Committee, as is customary for Chinese presidents to do after their first five-year term. All seven members are more than sixty years old; the party has an unspoken rule that officials should step down once they reach the age of sixty-eight, meaning that everyone on the Standing Committee will be too old to serve a two-term presidency by the next National Congress in 2022. This prompted speculation among some observers that Xi may try to continue serving as president beyond the standard two terms.

These changes in party leadership, when combined with the addition of Xi Jinping Thought to the Constitution and granting of a second term as president, represent a further consolidation of Xi's control over the Communist Party and thus China's government. As a result, no major changes in Chinese policy or governance are expected within the next five years.

—Linda Grimm

Following is the 19th National Congress of the Communist Party of China's resolution approving the report delivered by President Xi Jinping on behalf of the 18th Central Committee, and the Congress' resolution adding Xi Jinping Thought on Socialism with Chinese Characteristics for a New Era to the Communist Party Constitution, both from October 24, 2017.

National Congress Resolution on CPC Central Committee Report

October 24, 2017

The 19th National Congress of the Communist Party of China approves the report delivered by Comrade Xi Jinping on behalf of the Party's 18th Central Committee. The Congress holds high the banner of socialism with Chinese characteristics and is guided by Marxism-Leninism, Mao Zedong Thought, Deng Xiaoping Theory, the Theory of Three Represents, the Scientific Outlook on Development, and Xi Jinping Thought on Socialism with Chinese Characteristics for a New Era. On the basis of an analysis of the developments in the international and domestic environments and a review of the Party's work and the historic change over the past five years, the Congress forms the major political judgments that socialism with Chinese characteristics has entered a new era and the principal contradiction in Chinese society has evolved into one between unbalanced and inadequate development and the people's ever-growing needs for a better life. The Congress elaborates on the Party's historic mission in the new era and establishes the historical position of Xi Jinping Thought on Socialism with Chinese Characteristics for a New Era. It sets forth the basic policy for upholding and developing socialism with Chinese characteristics in the new era, and establishes the goal of securing a decisive victory in building a moderately prosperous society in all respects and then embarking on a journey to fully build a modern socialist China. The Congress also sets out an overall plan for advancing the great cause of socialism with Chinese characteristics and the great new project of Party building in the new era.

The report of the 18th Central Committee approved by the Congress sketches out an impressive blueprint for securing a decisive victory in building a moderately prosperous society in all respects and striving for the great success of socialism with Chinese characteristics for a new era, thus charting the course for continued progress in the cause of the Party and the country. The report is a crystallization of the wisdom of the whole Party and the Chinese people of all ethnic groups. It is a political declaration and a program of action for the Party to unite the Chinese people and lead them in upholding and developing socialism with Chinese characteristics in the new era. It is a guiding Marxist document.

The Congress believes that the theme expounded on in the report is of enormous importance to the Party leading the people toward a stronger China through tireless and groundbreaking efforts. Every one of us in the Party must remain true to our original aspiration and keep our mission firmly in mind, hold high the banner of socialism with Chinese characteristics, secure a decisive victory in building a moderately prosperous society in all respects, strive for the great success of socialism with Chinese characteristics for a new era, and work tirelessly to realize the Chinese Dream of national rejuvenation.

The Congress applauds the work of the 18th Central Committee. The five years since the 18th National Congress have been a truly remarkable five years in the course of the development of the Party and the country, with historic achievements made in reform, opening up, and socialist modernization. Over these five years, the Central Committee with Comrade Xi Jinping at its core has demonstrated tremendous political courage and a powerful sense of mission as it has developed new ideas, new thinking, and new strategies, adopted a raft of major principles and policies, launched a host of major initiatives, and pushed ahead with many major tasks. It has thus solved many tough problems that were long on the agenda but never resolved, accomplished many things that were wanted but never got done, and prompted historic shifts in the cause of the Party and the country.

The Central Committee with Comrade Xi Jinping at its core has acted with courage to confront major risks and tests facing the Party and to address prominent problems within the Party itself. With firm resolve, it has tightened discipline and improved Party conduct, fought corruption, and punished wrongdoing, and removed serious potential dangers in the Party and the country. As a result, both the intraparty political atmosphere and the political ecosystem of the Party have improved markedly. The Party's ability to create, power to unite, and energy to fight have all been significantly strengthened; Party solidarity and unity have been reinforced, and our engagement with the people has been greatly improved. Revolutionary tempering has made our Party stronger and it now radiates with great vitality. With this, efforts to develop the cause of the Party and the country have gained a strong political underpinning.

The achievements of the past five years have touched every area and broken new ground; the changes in China over the past five years have been profound and fundamental.

The Congress stresses that, with decades of hard work, socialism with Chinese characteristics has crossed the threshold into a new era. This is a new historic juncture in China's development. As socialism with Chinese characteristics has entered a new era, the principal contradiction facing Chinese society has evolved into one between unbalanced and inadequate development and the people's ever-growing needs for a better life. This represents a historic shift that affects the whole landscape and that creates many new demands for the work of the Party and the country. Building on continued efforts to sustain development, we must devote great energy to addressing development's imbalances and inadequacies, and push hard to improve the quality and effect of development. With this, we can be better placed to meet the ever-growing economic, political, cultural, social, and ecological needs of our people, and to promote well-rounded human development and all-round social progress.

The Congress stresses that the Party has been presented with the profound question of what kind of socialism with Chinese characteristics the new era requires it to uphold and develop, and how it should go about doing it. In answering this question of an era, our Party has adopted an entirely new perspective to deepen its understanding of the laws that underlie governance by the Communist party, the development of socialism, and the evolution of human society. It has worked hard to undertake theoretical explorations, and has achieved major theoretical innovations, ultimately giving shape to Xi Jinping Thought on Socialism with Chinese Characteristics for a New Era.

Xi Jinping Thought on Socialism with Chinese Characteristics for a New Era builds on and further enriches Marxism-Leninism, Mao Zedong Thought, Deng Xiaoping Theory, the Theory of Three Represents, and the Scientific Outlook on Development. It represents the latest achievement in adapting Marxism to the Chinese context, and encapsulates the practical experience and collective wisdom of our Party and the people. It is an important component of the theory of socialism with Chinese characteristics, and a guide to action for all our members and all the Chinese people as we strive to achieve national rejuvenation. This Thought must be adhered to and steadily developed on a long-term basis.

The Congress highlights the 14 points that form the basic policy underpinning our endeavors to uphold and develop socialism with Chinese characteristics in the new era. They are: Ensure Party leadership over all work; commit to a people-centered approach; continue to comprehensively deepen reform; adopt a new vision for development; see that the people run the country; ensure every dimension of governance is law-based; uphold core socialist values; ensure and improve living standards through development; ensure harmony between human and nature; pursue a holistic approach to national security; uphold absolute Party leadership over the people's forces; uphold the principle of "one country, two systems" and promote national reunification; promote the building of a community with a shared future for mankind; and exercise full and rigorous governance over the Party. All our members must fully implement the Party's basic theory, line, and policy so as to better steer the development of the Party and people's cause.

The Congress points out that the period between now and 2020 will be decisive in finishing the building of a moderately prosperous society in all respects. We must follow the requirements on building this society set out at our 16th, 17th, and 18th National Congresses; focus on priorities, address inadequacies, and shore up points of weakness. We must take tough steps to forestall and defuse major risks, carry out targeted poverty alleviation, and prevent and control pollution, so that the moderately prosperous society we build earns the people's approval and stands the test of time.

The Congress believes that the period between the 19th and the 20th National Congress is the period in which the timeframes of the two centenary goals converge. In this period, not only must we finish building a moderately prosperous society in all respects and achieve the first centenary goal; we must also build on this achievement to embark on a new journey toward the second centenary goal of fully building a modern socialist country.

Based on a comprehensive analysis of the international and domestic environments and the conditions for China's development, we have drawn up a two-stage development plan for the period from 2020 to the middle of this century. In the first stage from 2020 to 2035, we will build on the foundation created by the moderately prosperous society with a further 15 years of hard work to see that socialist modernization is basically realized. In the second stage from 2035 to the middle of the 21st century, we will, building on having basically achieved modernization, work hard for a further 15 years and develop China into a great modern socialist country that is prosperous, strong, democratic, culturally advanced, harmonious, and beautiful.

The Congress endorses the report's plans for promoting socialist economic, political, cultural, social, and ecological advancement in China. It stresses that we must apply a new vision of development and develop a modernized economy. We should put quality first and give priority to performance, pursue supply-side structural reform as our main task, and work hard for better quality, higher efficiency, and more robust drivers of economic growth through reform. We should accelerate the building of an industrial system that promotes coordinated development of the real economy with technological innovation, modern finance, and human resources, and endeavor to develop an economy with more effective market mechanisms, dynamic micro-entities, and sound macro-regulation. With this we can steadily strengthen the innovation capacity and competitiveness of China's economy. We should further supply-side structural reform, move faster to make China a country of innovators, pursue a rural vitalization strategy and the strategy for coordinated regional development, accelerate efforts to improve the socialist market economy, make new ground in pursuing opening up on all fronts, and strive to achieve better quality, more efficient, fairer, and more sustainable development.

We should improve the system of institutions through which the people run the country and develop socialist democracy. We should uphold the unity of Party leadership, the people running the country, and law-based governance. This requires us to strengthen institutional guarantees to ensure the people run the country, give play to the important role of socialist consultative democracy, and advance law-based governance. We should deepen reform of Party and government institutions and the system of government administration, consolidate and develop the patriotic united front, and consolidate and enhance political stability, unity, and vitality.

We should build stronger cultural confidence and help socialist culture to flourish. We must hold firmly the leading position in ideological work, cultivate and observe core socialist values, and raise intellectual and moral standards. We should work to see socialist literature and art thrive, promote the development of cultural programs and industries, and inspire the cultural creativity of our whole nation.

We should grow better at ensuring and improving people's wellbeing and strengthen and develop new approaches to social governance. We must focus on the most pressing, most immediate issues that concern the people the most. We should give priority to developing education, improve the quality of employment and raise incomes, strengthen the social security system, win the battle against poverty, carry out the Healthy China initiative, establish a social governance model based on collaboration, participation, and common interests, and effectively safeguard national security. With this we should see that our people always have a strong sense of fulfillment, happiness, and security.

We should speed up reform to develop sound systems for building an ecological civilization, and build a Beautiful China. We should promote green development, solve prominent environmental problems, intensify the protection of ecosystems, reform the environmental regulation system, and work to develop a new model of modernization with humans developing in harmony with nature.

The Congress stresses that, confronted with profound changes in our national security environment and responding to the demands of the day for a strong country with a strong military, we must stay committed to the Chinese path of building strong armed forces, fully implement Xi Jinping's thinking on strengthening the military, adapt military strategy to new conditions, build a powerful and modernized army, navy, air force, rocket force, and strategic support force, develop strong and efficient joint operations commanding institutions for theater commands, and create a modern combat system with distinctive Chinese characteristics. With this we can fully advance the modernization of national defense and the military and transform our people's armed forces into world-class forces.

The Congress stresses that, to maintain long-term prosperity and stability in Hong Kong and Macao, it is imperative to fully and faithfully implement the policies of "one country, two systems," "the people of Hong Kong governing Hong Kong," "the people of Macao governing Macao," and a high degree of autonomy for both regions, and to act in strict compliance with China's Constitution and the basic laws of the two special administrative regions. We shall see that our compatriots in Hong Kong and Macao share both the historic responsibility of national rejuvenation and the pride of a strong and prosperous China. We must uphold the principles of "peaceful reunification" and "one country, two systems," expand economic and cultural exchanges and cooperation between the two sides of the Taiwan Straits, encourage people from both sides to work together to promote Chinese culture, work for the peaceful development of cross-Straits relations, and advance the process toward the peaceful reunification of China. We will never allow anyone, any organization, or any political party, at any time or in any form, to separate any part of Chinese territory from China.

The Congress endorses the report's analysis of the international situation and the guiding principles it sets out for China's foreign affairs. The Congress stresses that China will keep to the path of peaceful development, hold high the banner of peace, development, cooperation, and mutual benefit, and uphold its fundamental foreign policy goal of preserving world peace and promoting common development. China remains firm in its commitment to strengthening friendship and cooperation with other countries on the basis of the Five Principles of Peaceful Coexistence. It will actively promote international cooperation through the Belt and Road Initiative, and continue to take an active part in reforming and developing the global governance system. It will work toward a new form of international relations featuring mutual respect, fairness, justice, and win-win cooperation and a community with a shared future for mankind, and work together with the people of all countries to build an open, inclusive, clean, and beautiful world that enjoys lasting peace, universal security, and common prosperity.

The Congress stresses that it takes a good blacksmith to make good steel. For the Party to unite the people and lead them in carrying out our great struggle, advancing our great cause, and realizing our great dream, we must unwaveringly uphold and improve Party leadership and make the Party still stronger. The general requirements for Party building for the new era are: Uphold and strengthen overall Party leadership and ensure that the Party exercises effective self-supervision and practices strict self-governance in every respect; take strengthening the Party's long-term governance capacity and its advanced nature and purity as the main thrust, take enhancing the Party's political building as the overarching principle, take holding dear the Party's ideals, convictions, and purpose as the underpinning, and take harnessing the whole Party's enthusiasm, initiative, and creativity as the focus of efforts; make all-round efforts to see the Party's political building enhanced, its theory strengthened, its organizations consolidated, its conduct improved, and its discipline enforced, with institution building incorporated into every aspect of Party building; step up efforts to combat corruption and continue to improve the efficacy of Party building; and build the Party into a vibrant Marxist governing party that is always at the forefront of the times, enjoys the wholehearted support of the people, has the courage to reform itself, and is able to withstand all tests.

The Congress stresses that we must put the Party's political building first. All of us in the Party must strengthen our consciousness of the need to maintain political integrity, think in big-picture terms, follow the leadership core, and keep in alignment. We must uphold the authority and centralized, unified leadership of the Party Central Committee, closely follow the Party's political line, strictly observe its political discipline and rules, and closely align ourselves with the Central Committee in terms of political stance, direction, principle, and path.

The Congress calls on the entire Party and the Chinese people of all ethnic groups to rally closely around the Party Central Committee with Comrade Xi Jinping at its core, hold high the banner of socialism with Chinese characteristics, and earnestly study and put into practice Xi Jinping Thought on Socialism with Chinese Characteristics for a New Era. We will keep on working with great determination to accomplish the three historic tasks of advancing modernization, realizing China's reunification, and preserving world peace and promoting common development, and make continued efforts to secure a decisive victory in finishing the building of a moderately prosperous society in all respects, strive for the great success of socialism with Chinese characteristics for a new era, realize the Chinese Dream of national rejuvenation, and see that our people realize their aspirations for a better life.

SOURCE: 19th CPC National Congress Press Center. "Full Text of Resolution on CPC Central Committee Report." October 24, 2017. http://19th.cpcnews.cn/english/n100/2017/1024/c154-966.html.

National Congress Resolution on Amendment to CPC Constitution

October 24, 2017

The 19th National Congress of the Communist Party of China deliberated on and unanimously adopted the revised Constitution of the Communist Party of China proposed by the 18th Party Central Committee and decided that it shall come into effect as of the date of adoption.

The Congress notes that since the Party's 18th National Congress, Chinese Communists, with Comrade Xi Jinping as their chief representative, in response to contemporary developments and by integrating theory with practice, have systematically addressed the major question of our times-what kind of socialism with Chinese characteristics the new era requires us to uphold and develop and how we should uphold and develop it, thus giving shape to Xi Jinping Thought on Socialism with Chinese Characteristics for a New Era. The Thought is a continuation and development of Marxism-Leninism, Mao Zedong Thought, Deng Xiaoping Theory, the Theory of Three Represents, and the Scientific Outlook on Development. It is the latest achievement in adapting Marxism to the Chinese context, a crystallization of the practical experience and collective wisdom of the Party and the people, an important component of the theoretical system of socialism with Chinese characteristics, and a guide to action for the entire Party and all the Chinese people to strive for the great rejuvenation of the Chinese nation, and must be upheld long term and constantly developed. Under the guidance of Xi Jinping

Thought on Socialism with Chinese Characteristics for a New Era, the Communist Party of China has led the Chinese people of all ethnic groups in a concerted effort to carry out a great struggle, develop a great project, advance a great cause, and realize a great dream, ushering in a new era of socialism with Chinese characteristics.

The Congress unanimously agrees that, Xi Jinping Thought on Socialism with Chinese Characteristics for a New Era, in addition to Marxism-Leninism, Mao Zedong Thought, Deng Xiaoping Theory, the Theory of Three Represents, and the Scientific Outlook on Development, shall constitute the guides to action of the Party in the Party Constitution. The Congress urges all Party members to use the Thought to achieve unity in thinking and action, be more purposeful and determined in studying and applying it, and put the Thought into action throughout the drive toward China's socialist modernization and in every dimension of Party building.

The Congress affirms that the culture of socialism with Chinese characteristics is a key part of socialism with Chinese characteristics and a powerful source of strength that inspires the entire Party and the Chinese people of all ethnic groups to forge ahead courageously. The Congress approves the incorporation of the culture of socialism with Chinese characteristics into the Party Constitution, along with the path of socialism with Chinese characteristics, the theoretical system of socialism with Chinese characteristics, and the system of socialism with Chinese characteristics. This addition will help all Party members deepen their understanding of socialism with Chinese characteristics and fully grasp its implications. The Congress stresses that all Party members must cherish deeply, uphold long term, and continue to develop this path, this theoretical system, this socialist system, and this culture, which the Party has developed through great hardship; hold high the great banner of socialism with Chinese characteristics; have firm confidence in the path, theory, system, and culture of socialism with Chinese characteristics; and implement the Party's basic theory, basic line, and basic policy.

The Congress holds that national rejuvenation has been the greatest dream of the Chinese people since modern times began, and that it is a solemn commitment our Party has made to our people and to history. The Congress endorses the inclusion of the two centenary goals and the Chinese Dream of national rejuvenation into the Party Constitution.

The Congress holds that a major political conclusion is drawn in the political report to the 19th Party Congress that the principal contradiction facing Chinese society has evolved and is now that between the people's ever-growing needs for a better life and unbalanced and inadequate development; it reflects the realities of the development of Chinese society, and serves as an important basis on which we formulate major policies and long-term strategies for the Party and the country. The Party Constitution is revised accordingly to provide important guidance for us to better understand the new historic juncture in China's development and its particular features in the current stage and to further advance the cause of the Party and the country.

The Congress holds that statements on our people-centered philosophy of development; on innovative, coordinated, green, and open development that is for everyone; on coordinated efforts to finish building a moderately prosperous society in all respects, comprehensively deepen reform, fully advance law-based governance, and strengthen Party self-governance in every respect; and on all-out efforts to build a great modern socialist country, represent the ultimate purpose, vision, overall strategy, and overarching goal of the Party in upholding and developing socialism with Chinese characteristics.

Also incorporated into the Party Constitution are statements on the need to achieve better quality and more efficient, equitable, and sustainable development, to improve and develop the system of socialism with Chinese characteristics, to modernize China's system and capacity for governance, and to pursue reform in a more systematic, holistic, and coordinated way. This will help all Party members closely follow, in both thinking and action, the well-conceived assessment and strategic plans of the Central Committee, uphold and put into practice the new development philosophy, and continue to break new ground in reform and development.

The Congress holds that since our 18th National Congress, the Party Central Committee with Comrade Xi Jinping at the core has developed new ideas, new thinking, and new strategies for promoting economic, political, cultural, social, and ecological advancement. The Congress agrees to add to the Party Constitution the following statements: we shall give play to the decisive role of market forces in resource allocation and ensure the government plays its role better; advance supply-side structural reform; establish a system of socialist rule of law with Chinese characteristics; advance extensive, multi-level, and institutionalized development of consultative democracy; nurture and practice core socialist values; promote the creative evolution and development of fine traditional Chinese culture; carry forward our revolutionary culture; develop an advanced socialist culture; enhance our country's cultural soft power; hold firmly the leading position in ideological work; help our people gain an increasingly stronger sense of fulfillment; strengthen and develop new approaches to social governance; pursue a holistic approach to national security; and fully understand that lucid waters and lush mountains are invaluable assets.

These statements are of great importance in helping all Party members more consciously and determinedly implement the Party's basic theory, basic line, and basic policy, and coordinate the implementation of the five-sphere integrated plan.

The Congress notes that since the Party's 18th National Congress, Comrade Xi Jinping has set forth a series of important ideas and viewpoints on strengthening national defense and the armed forces, ethnic unity, "one country, two systems" and national reunification, the united front, and foreign affairs, charting the course for staying committed to the path of building strong armed forces with Chinese characteristics; for safeguarding and developing socialist ethnic relations featuring equality, unity, mutual assistance, and harmony; for promoting national reunification; and for building a community with a shared future for mankind.

The Congress agrees to include into the Party Constitution the following statements: The Communist Party of China shall uphold its absolute leadership over the People's Liberation Army and other people's armed forces; implement Xi Jinping's thinking on strengthening the military; strengthen the development of the People's Liberation Army by enhancing its political loyalty, strengthening it through reform and technology, and running it in accordance with the law; build people's forces that obey the Party's command, can fight and win, and maintain excellent conduct; ensure that the People's Liberation Army accomplishes its missions and tasks in the new era; foster a strong sense of community for the Chinese nation; uphold justice while pursuing shared interests; work to build a community with a shared future for mankind; follow the principle of achieving shared growth through discussion and collaboration; and pursue the Belt and Road Initiative.

The inclusion of these statements will help ensure the Party's absolute leadership over the people's armed forces, modernize national defense and the military, promote ethnic unity, and develop an open economy of higher standards.

The Congress holds that since its 18th National Congress, the Party has made steady progress in exercising full and rigorous governance over the Party, taken all-around measures to explore the strengthening of Party building, and gained abundant successful experience and achieved major outcomes, which must be included into the Party Constitution in a timely manner and therefore become the common will and rule of the whole Party.

It is affirmed at the Party's 19th National Congress that the Party must firmly exercise self-supervision and practice strict self-governance in every respect; strengthen the Party's long-term governance capacity and its advanced nature and purity; and take enhancing its political building as the overarching principle and make comprehensive efforts to ensure that the Party's political work is stressed, ideology is strengthened, organizations are consolidated, conduct is improved, discipline is maintained, institutional development is always emphasized, and the fight against corruption keeps going. The Congress agrees to add the above statements to the Party Constitution.

Also included into the Party Constitution are: The Party must constantly strengthen its ability to purify, improve, reform, and excel itself; use Xi Jinping Thought on Socialism with Chinese Characteristics for a New Era to achieve unity in thinking and action; keep firmly in mind the need to maintain political integrity, think in big-picture terms, uphold the leadership core, and keep in alignment, and firmly uphold the authority and centralized, unified leadership of the Central Committee with Comrade Xi Jinping at the core; strengthen and regulate political activities within the Party; make intraparty political activities more politically oriented, up-to-date, principled, and effective; cultivate a positive and healthy intraparty political culture; and foster a sound political ecosystem featuring honesty and integrity within the Party. Firmness in exercising strict self-supervision and self-governance is included into the Party Constitution as a fundamental requirement the Party must work with firm resolve to meet in building itself.

The incorporation of these statements will ensure the Party has a clearer goal and a more complete plan for building itself. They will help the whole Party advance Party building with more well-conceived ways of thinking and more effective measures, so as to continuously improve the quality of Party building and ensure the Party is always full of vigor and vitality.

The Congress holds that the leadership of the Communist Party of China is the most essential attribute of socialism with Chinese characteristics, and the greatest strength of this system; the Party exercises overall leadership over all areas of endeavor in every part of the country. The Congress agrees to add this major political principle to the Party Constitution, which will help heighten the Party consciousness of every Party member, and ensure unity of thinking, political solidarity and concerted action of the whole Party. It will also help enhance the Party's ability to innovate, power to unite, and energy to fight; ensure the Party always provides overall leadership and coordinates the efforts of all involved; and offer the fundamental political guarantee for all areas of work of the Party and the country.

The Congress notes that in view of the successful experience gained in Party work and Party building since the 18th Party Congress and in compliance with the revisions to the General Program, appropriate revisions to some articles of the Party Constitution are necessary.

To conscientiously study Xi Jinping Thought on Socialism with Chinese Characteristics for a New Era, to consciously observe the Party's political discipline and rules, to have the courage to reveal and correct any statements and actions violating the Party's principles, to lead the way in practicing core socialist values, and to advocate traditional virtues of the Chinese nation, are obligations of Party members. Upholding political integrity as the primary criterion is the major principle that must be adhered to in admitting new Party members.

To ensure the full coverage of discipline inspection and carry out inspections at central, city (prefecture), and county levels is practical experience gained in the Party's discipline inspection work; it must be upheld and developed.

To clarify that Chairperson of the Central Military Commission assumes overall responsibility over the work of the Commission and that the Central Military Commission is responsible for Party work and political work in the armed forces, complies with the realistic requirement to ensure the Central Military Commission fulfills its responsibility for Party self-supervision and self-governance after the military reform.

To fully reflect the achievements of Party work and Party building since the 18th Party Congress, revisions are made to: adjust the term of office of general Party branch committees and Party branch committees; regularize and institutionalize the requirement for all Party members to study the Party Constitution, Party regulations, and General Secretary Xi Jinping's major policy addresses and to meet Party standards; define the status and role of Party organizations in state-owned enterprises; elaborate on the functions and responsibilities of primary-level Party organizations in social organizations; explicate the responsibilities of primary-level Party organizations in offices of the Party or the state at every level; demonstrate the position and functions of Party branches; set out new criteria and requirements for selecting officials; and adjust and elaborate on provisions related to the Party discipline and Party organs for discipline inspection.

These revisions will help all Party members grasp the guiding ideology of the Party and keep up with the times, align themselves with Xi Jinping Thought on Socialism with Chinese Characteristics for a New Era and use it to guide practice and advance work, see primary-level Party organizations become politically stronger, and move further forward with the full and rigorous governance over the Party.

The Congress urges Party organizations at all levels and all Party members to, under the firm leadership of the Party Central Committee with Comrade Xi Jinping at the core, hold high the great banner of socialism with Chinese characteristics, follow the guidance of Marxism-Leninism, Mao Zedong Thought, Deng Xiaoping Theory, the Theory of Three Represents, the Scientific Outlook on Development, and Xi Jinping Thought on Socialism with Chinese Characteristics for a New Era, and more purposefully study, observe, apply, and uphold the Party Constitution. The Congress urges the entire Party to uphold and strengthen the overall leadership of the Party, ensure the Party's strict self-supervision and strict self-governance in every respect, and keep working to secure a decisive victory in finishing building a moderately prosperous society in all respects, to strive for the great success of socialism with Chinese characteristics for a new era, to realize the Chinese Dream of national rejuvenation, and to see our people fulfill their aspirations for a better life.

SOURCE: 19th CPC National Congress Press Center. "Full Text of Resolution on Amendment to CPC Constitution." October 24, 2017. http://19th.cpcnews.cn/english/n100/2017/1024/c154-968.html.

OTHER HISTORIC DOCUMENTS OF INTEREST

FROM PREVIOUS *HISTORIC DOCUMENTS*

President Trump Declares Public Health Crisis; Drug Commission Releases Findings

OCTOBER 26 AND NOVEMBER 1, 2017

President Donald Trump made clear as a candidate his intent to focus on combatting drug addiction, and more specifically the opioid crisis that was sweeping the United States. After taking office, Trump appointed a presidential commission to investigate solutions to the problem and even declared a national public health emergency. However, by the close of 2017, neither the White House nor Congress had acted on any of the commission's recommendations, and there was no increase in federal funding to help states combat addiction. These two factors drew strong criticism from the medical community, advocacy organizations, and state officials.

TRUMP ASSEMBLES COMMISSION ON DRUG ADDICTION

In 2016, 64,000 Americans died from drug overdoses, most of which were linked to opioids, making drug overdoses the deadliest injury-related cause of death, outranking both car accidents and gun deaths. Half the opioid-related overdoses were the result of legally obtained prescription drugs, the overprescribing of which began in the mid-1990s when pharmaceutical companies aggressively campaigned to encourage doctors to ease their patient's pain through their use. Despite some abatement in the rate of drug overdose deaths in the late 1990s and early 2000s, they began skyrocketing as more powerful and dangerous drugs like fentanyl flooded the market. According to the Centers for Disease Control and Prevention (CDC), opioid overdose deaths rose 200 percent between 2000 and 2014. The growing crisis made combatting drug addiction a hot topic on the presidential campaign trail.

As a candidate, Trump promised to fight the opioid crisis, primarily through better border control that would stop the flow of drugs into the country. Specifically, Trump linked opioid deaths to drugs coming in along the U.S.–Mexico border where he proposed to build a wall. "Heroin overdoses are taking over our children and others in the MIDWEST. Coming in from our southern border. We need strong border & WALL," then-candidate Trump tweeted in 2016. The president's promises to help those who "are so seriously addicted" resonated with voters and Trump won eighteen of the twenty-five states with the highest number of drug overdose deaths in 2015.

As president, however, advocates and health organizations were disappointed at the slow pace of any action from the Trump White House. It was not until March 2017 when Trump established the President's Commission on Combating Drug Addiction and the Opioid Crisis "to study the scope and effectiveness of the Federal response to drug addiction and the opioid crisis and to make recommendations to the President for improving that response." The commission was tasked specifically with identifying potential federal funding to direct toward substance abuse treatment, the portions of the United States where treatment is lacking, possible changes to prescribing practices, and to identify how former convicts could be targeted for improved treatment. New Jersey governor Chris Christie was named the chair of the group that also included Bertha Madras of Harvard Medical School, Massachusetts governor Charlie Barker, North Carolina governor Roy Cooper, former Rhode Island congressman Patrick Kennedy, and Florida attorney general Pam Bondi.

The commission held public meetings throughout 2017 to speak with doctors, health advocates, drug manufacturers, insurance company representatives, and lawmakers about the opioid crisis and best practices and lessons learned from the various attempts that have been made at ending addiction. The commission released its preliminary findings in July. "Our citizens are dying. We must act boldly to stop it," the report opened. "The first and most urgent recommendation of this Commission is direct and completely within your control. Declare a national emergency." While primarily used for natural disasters, declaring a national emergency could open up additional federal funds to be utilized to combat the crisis. After the preliminary report's release, and while noting that all options were on the table, Trump shared his belief, "The resources that we need for the focus that we need to bring to bear to the opioid crisis, at this point can be addressed without the declaration of an emergency." Health and Human Services (HHS) Secretary Tom Price echoed the president's remarks but said, "The president certainly believes that we will treat it as an emergency."

President Declares a National Public Health Emergency

Just days before the commission was due to release its final report, President Trump did declare a national public health emergency to combat the opioid crisis. "Ending the epidemic will require mobilization of government, local communities, and private organizations. It will require the resolve of our entire country," the president said, announcing his decision. "It is time to liberate our communities from this scourge of drug addiction. . . . We can be the generation that ends the opioid epidemic," he added. Although the declaration would allow a number of steps to be taken to expand medical services in states to help address the crisis, it did not receive designation under the Stafford Act, and therefore did not provide for additional federal funding. The declaration did allow an acceleration of temporary staff appointments to address the emergency, would help the Drug Enforcement Agency (DEA) expand access to telemedicine to treat addiction, allowed the Department of Labor (DOL) to issue dislocated worker grants to those displaced due to the opioid crisis, and would allow the shifting of resources within HIV/AIDS programs to help those eligible receive substance abuse treatment. Most of these provisions, however, were subject to funding availability, and it was unclear who would oversee the work to take place under the declaration, given the many high-profile vacancies in agencies that would be involved in any such action.

As an addition to the declaration, Trump promised to "announce a new policy to overcome a restrictive 1970s-era rule that prevents states from providing care at certain treatment facilities with more than 16 beds for those suffering from drug addiction." The president was referring to the Medicaid Institutions for Mental Disease exclusion under the Medicaid program, enacted in 1965, that states, with some exceptions, that Medicaid funds cannot be used in larger facilities to treat drug addiction. The president said that a number of states had contacted his administration for assistance in treating people in need, regardless of the size of the facility, and the president promised approval to begin treatment at these facilities "very, very fast."

The overall public response was that of disappointment over the lack of federal funding provided in conjunction with the declaration. At the time of the declaration, the HHS public health emergency fund had approximately $57,000 available and would require an appropriation from Congress to replenish. Rep. David McKinley, R-W.Va., whose state has the highest opioid death rate in the nation, questioned "why more resources aren't flowing to help out a rural state like West Virginia," while Andrew Kolodny, the executive director of Physicians for Responsible Opioid Prescribing said there were "people dying of overdoses on waiting lists for an effective treatment," indicating that rhetoric and policies would not be enough without funds for enactment. Health advocates also expressed concern about shifting funds from HIV/AIDS programs, which they said would simply shortchange those suffering solely from the disease without a related substance abuse problem.

PRESIDENTIAL COMMISSION RELEASES FINAL REPORT

On November 1, the president's opioid commission released its final report. The extensive, 128-page document contained more than fifty proposals including launching an antidrug media campaign, expanding drug education programs, expanding treatment services, increasing access to the overdose reversing drug Naloxone, increasing the use of electronic prescribing of opioids, and enhancing federal sentencing for fentanyl traffickers.

Perhaps the commission's biggest recommendation was a call for the Department of Justice (DOJ) to set up drug courts across the country, which it called "a proven avenue for treatment for individuals who commit non-violent crimes because of the substance abuse disorder." These courts divert low-level drug offenders into treatment programs rather than sending them to jail. Although use of the courts has grown in popularity since they first appeared in the 1980s, only twenty-seven of the ninety-three federal district courts in the country had such programs in place at the time of the report's release. Federal funding for the programs increased under the Obama administration. Christie said the commission felt these courts "would be a twofold benefit to the justice system: One, to get help to people who need it in order to slow down recidivism, and secondly, it will lower the federal prison population."

At the event unveiling the report, Christie said that the recommendations were just a first step toward the important work that needed to be done. "We are killing ourselves and it's unacceptable from my perspective not to step up," Christie said. The governor was supportive of additional funding from Congress to benefit efforts to fight the crisis but noted that "just spending money won't be enough if we aren't spending it in a way that's evidence based." Harvard University's Madras spoke specifically to the importance of education and outreach campaigns, coupled with responsible prescribing on the part of doctors, noting, "If we don't stop the pipeline into substance use, if we don't promote prevention, we are going to have an open-ended catastrophe that goes on for generations."

By the close of 2017, the White House had not yet acted on any of the recommendations made by the commission, nor had any funds been directed to help federal agencies begin implementing the suggestions. "The overall problem here is, we've got a commission making recommendations when we need an administration putting out a plan and seeking out appropriations," said Kolodny. In his letter to the president that accompanied the report, Christie expressed a similar sentiment, writing, "We urge Congress to do their constitutionally delegated duty and appropriate sufficient funds (as soon as possible) to implement the Commission's recommendations." In December, the White House did release a response to the November 1 commission recommendations, which noted agreement with the necessity to "direct funding to areas of need with minimal bureaucratic delay and administrative burden." This funding, it said, could come through block grants. Beyond that, however, Congress would be responsible for appropriating additional funds.

—Heather Kerrigan

Following is the text of the October 26, 2017, memorandum declaring a national public health emergency in relation to the opioid crisis; excerpts from President Donald Trump's October 26, 2017, statement on the declaration of a national public health emergency; and the November 1, 2017, Summary of Recommendations from the president's commission on the drug crisis.

President Trump Declares National Public Health Emergency

October 26, 2017

Memorandum for the Heads of Executive Departments and Agencies

Subject: Combatting the National Drug Demand and Opioid Crisis

By the authority vested in me as President by the Constitution and the laws of the United States of America, it is hereby directed as follows:

Section 1. Policy. It shall be the policy of the United States to use all lawful means to combat the drug demand and opioid crisis currently afflicting our country. Individuals, families, and communities across the United States continue to be devastated by an unprecedented epidemic of drug abuse and overdose, including of prescription opioids, heroin, and illicit synthetic opioids. Last year, we lost at least 64,000 of our fellow Americans to drug overdose, primarily from opioids. This is an increase of approximately 12,000 people over the year before and more than ever recorded in United States history. Drug overdoses now kill more Americans than motor vehicle crashes or gun-related incidents, and more than 300,000 Americans have died of an opioid overdose since 2000. Further, more than 2.1 million of our fellow citizens are addicted to opioids, and in 2014 more than 1,500 people were treated each day in emergency departments for opioid-related emergencies.

This crisis has devastated our communities. It has been particularly harmful for children affected by their parents' drug abuse. The number of infants born drug-dependent increased by nearly 500 percent from 2000 to 2012. The number of children being placed into foster care due, at least in part, to parental drug abuse is increasing, and accounted for almost a third of all child removals in Fiscal Year 2015. Serious drug users are also more likely to be arrested for crimes such as burglary, robbery, and handling stolen goods. Moreover, the drug trafficking that supplies illegal drugs to our country is associated with other illegal activities, including murder and other violent crimes. All of this devastates lives and harms communities in both the United States and foreign countries involved in the illegal drug supply chain. Federal, State, and local governments; law enforcement; first responders; the medical, public health, and substance abuse treatment community; and faith-based and community organizations are working tirelessly and have even expanded their efforts to combat the drug demand and opioid crisis.

Three factors are driving the opioid aspect of this crisis in particular. First, since the 1990s, there has been a dramatic rise in opioid pain medication prescriptions. Second, heroin from Mexico has flooded the country. Third, the illicit manufacture and illegal importation of fentanyl—an extremely deadly synthetic opioid—and its analogues and related compounds have proliferated. Fentanyl is currently manufactured almost exclusively in China, and it is either shipped into the United States or smuggled across the southern border by drug traffickers. Between 2013 and 2016, the amount of fentanyl seized by Customs and Border Protection at the border increased more than 200 times over. Dealers are increasingly lacing fentanyl into other drugs and pressing it into counterfeit opioid pills. Because fentanyl is lethal in even miniscule doses, this is an extremely deadly tactic, as it too often causes users to ingest a fatal amount unknowingly.

Sec. 2. Agency Action. The Secretary of Health and Human Services shall, consistent with section 319 of the Public Health Service Act, 42 U.S.C. 247d, consider declaring that the drug demand and opioid crisis described in section 1 of this memorandum constitutes a Public Health Emergency. Additionally, the heads of executive departments and agencies, as appropriate and consistent with law, shall exercise all appropriate emergency authorities, as well as other relevant authorities, to reduce the number of deaths and minimize the devastation the drug demand and opioid crisis inflicts upon American communities.

Sec. 3. General Provisions. (a) Nothing in this memorandum shall be construed to impair or otherwise affect:

> (i)   the authority granted by law to an executive department or agency, or the head thereof; or

> (ii) the functions of the Director of the Office of Management and Budget relating to budgetary, administrative, or legislative proposals.

(b) This memorandum shall be implemented consistent with applicable law and subject to the availability of appropriations.

(c) This memorandum is not intended to, and does not, create any right or benefit, substantive or procedural, enforceable at law or in equity by any party against the United States, its departments, agencies, or entities, its officers, employees, or agents, or any other person.

(d) The Secretary of Health and Human Services is hereby authorized and directed to publish this memorandum in the *Federal Register.*

DONALD J. TRUMP

SOURCE: Executive Office of the President. "Memorandum on Combatting the National Drug Demand and Opioid Crisis." October 26, 2017. *Compilation of Presidential Documents* 2017, no. 00788 (October 26, 2017). https://www.gpo.gov/fdsys/pkg/DCPD-201700788/pdf/DCPD-201700788.pdf.

President Trump Remarks on the Opioid Crisis

October 26, 2017

Thank you, Melania, for your moving words and for your devotion—I mean, it's a very deep devotion, I can tell you that—to our Nation and its children.

Thank you also to Members of Congress, my Cabinet, Governors, Members of Congress, State, local leaders, first responders, and health care professionals gathered here today. We have some truly incredible people in this room—that I can tell you.

Most importantly, we acknowledge the families present who have lost a cherished loved one. As you all know from personal experience, families, communities, and citizens across our country are currently dealing with the worst drug crisis in American history and even, if you really think about it, world history. This is all throughout the world. The fact is, this is a worldwide problem.

This crisis of drug use, addiction, and overdose deaths in many years, it's just been so long in the making. Addressing it will require all of our effort, and it will require us to confront the crisis in all of its very real complexity.

Last year, we lost at least 64,000 Americans to overdoses. That's 175 lost American lives per day. That's seven lost lives per hour in our country. Drug overdoses are now the leading cause of unintentional death in the United States by far. More people are dying from drug overdoses today than from gun homicides and motor vehicles combined. Think of it: motor vehicle crashes, gun homicides, more people by far from drug overdoses.

These overdoses are driven by a massive increase in addiction to prescription pain-killers, heroin, and other opioids. Last year, almost 1 million Americans used heroin, and more than 11 million abused prescription opioids. The United States is by far the largest consumer of these drugs, using more opioid pills per person than any other country by far in the world. Opioid overdose deaths have quadrupled since 1999 and now account for the majority of fatal drug overdoses. Who would have thought?

No part of our society—not young or old, rich or poor, urban or rural—has been spared this plague of drug addiction and this horrible, horrible situation that's taken place with opioids. In West Virginia—a truly great State, great people—there is a hospital nursery where one in every five babies spends its first days in agony. Because these precious babies were exposed to opioids or other drugs in the womb, they endure nausea, pain, anxiety, sleeplessness, and trouble in eating, just the same as adults undergoing detox. Some of these children will likely lose one or both of their parents to drug addiction and overdose. They will join the growing ranks of America's opioid orphans. Such beautiful, beautiful babies.

Beyond the shocking death toll, the terrible measure of the opioid crisis includes the families ripped apart and, for many communities, a generation of lost potential and opportunity. This epidemic is a national health emergency, unlike many of us—we've seen, and—what we've seen in our lifetimes. Nobody has seen anything like what's going on now. As Americans, we cannot allow this to continue. It is time to liberate our communities from this scourge of drug addiction. Never been this way. We can be the generation that ends the opioid epidemic. We can do it. We can do it.

That is why, effective today, my administration is officially declaring the opioid crisis a national public health emergency under Federal law, and why I am directing all executive agencies to use every appropriate emergency authority to fight the opioid crisis. This marks a critical step in confronting the extraordinary challenge that we face.

As part of this emergency response, we will announce a new policy to overcome a restrictive 1970s-era rule that prevents States from providing care at certain treatment facilities with more than 16 beds for those suffering from drug addiction.

A number of States have reached out to us asking for relief, and you should expect to see approvals that will unlock treatment for people in need. And those approvals will come very, very fast. Not like in the past—very, very quickly.

Ending the epidemic will require mobilization of government, local communities, and private organizations. It will require the resolve of our entire country. The scale of this crisis of addiction is why, soon after coming into office, I convened a Presidential Commission, headed by Governor Chris Christie, that has consulted with experts across America to listen, to learn, and report back on potential solutions.

We await the final report, which will come in next week. And I know some of the report has already been seen, because I want to see it as quickly as possible. And some of the things that they are recommending are commonsense, but very, very important. And they're going to have a tremendous impact, believe me, tremendous impact.

Today I will detail many of these aggressive steps with my administration, which we've already taken. After we review and evaluate the Commission's findings, I will quickly move to implement approximate and appropriate recommendations.

But I want the American people to know: The Federal Government is aggressively fighting the opioid epidemic on all fronts. We're working with doctors and medical professionals to implement best practices for safe opioid prescribing, and we will do something very, very special. We are requiring federally employed prescribers to receive, finally, special training.

The Centers for Disease Control and Prevention has launched a prescription awareness campaign to put faces on the danger of opioid abuse.

I want to acknowledge CVS Caremark for announcing last month that it will limit certain first-time opioid prescriptions to 7-day supplies, among other important reforms. And I encourage other companies to do their part to help to stop this epidemic.

The FDA is now requiring drug companies that manufacture prescription opioids to provide more training to prescribers and to help prevent abuse and addiction, and has requested that one especially high-risk opioid be withdrawn from the market immediately. We are requiring that a specific opioid, which is truly evil, be taken off the market immediately.

The U.S. Postal Service and the Department of Homeland Security are strengthening the inspection of packages coming into our country to hold back the flood of cheap and deadly fentanyl, a synthetic opioid manufactured in China and 50 times stronger than heroin.

And in 2 weeks, I will be in China with President Xi, and I will mention this as a top priority. And he will do something about it. I am also pleased to report that for the first time, the Department of Justice has indicated [indicted]* major Chinese drug traffickers for distributing, and they have really put very, very strong clamps on them. They've indicted them, the drug traffickers, for distributing fentanyl into the United States. So, Jeff, thank you very much. Good job. Good job.

And they've been indicted, and we're not going to forget about them, believe me. They are doing tremendous harm to our country. The Justice Department is aggressively and, really, valiantly pursuing those who illegally prescribe and traffic in opioids, both in our communities and on the internet.

And I will be looking at the potential of the Federal Government bringing major lawsuits against bad actors. What they have and what they're doing to our people is unheard of. We will be bringing some very major lawsuits against people and against companies that are hurting our people. And that will start taking place pretty soon.

We're also supporting first responders' and medical professionals' access to the tools they need to prevent deaths through lifesaving overdose medications.

At my direction, the National Institute of Health, headed up by Francis Collins, has taken the first steps of an ambitious public-private partnership with pharmaceutical companies to develop nonaddictive painkillers and new treatments for addiction and overdose. So important.

I will be pushing the concept of nonaddictive painkillers very, very hard. We have to come up with that solution. We give away billions and billions of dollars a year, and we're going to be spending lots of money on coming up with a nonaddictive solution.

We will be asking Dr. Collins and the NIH for substantial resources in the fight against drug addiction. One of the things our administration will be doing is a massive advertising campaign to get people, especially children, not to want to take drugs in the first place, because they will see the devastation and the ruination it causes to people and people's lives.

Watch what happens, if we do our jobs, how the number of drug users and the addicted will start to tumble downward over a period of years. It will be a beautiful thing to see.

I learned, myself—I had a brother, Fred—great guy, best looking guy, best personality— much better than mine. [*Laughter*] But he had a problem. He had a problem with alcohol, and he would tell me: "Don't drink. Don't drink." He was substantially older, and I listened to him, and I respected, but he would constantly tell me, don't drink. He'd also add, don't smoke. But he would say it over and over and over again.

And to this day, I've never had a drink. And I have no longing for it. I have no interest in it. To this day, I've never had a cigarette. Don't worry, those are only two of my good things. I don't want to tell you about the bad things. [*Laughter*] There's plenty of bad things too.

But he really helped me. I had somebody that guided me, and he had a very, very, very tough life because of alcohol—believe me, very, very tough, tough life. He was a strong guy, but it was a tough, tough thing that he was going through. But I learned because of Fred. I learned. And that's what I think is so important. This was an idea that I had, where if we can teach young people not to take drugs—just not to take them. When I see friends of mine that are having difficulty with not having that drink at dinner, where it's literally almost impossible for them to stop, I say to myself—I can't even understand it—why would that be difficult? But we understand why it is difficult.

The fact is, if we can teach young people—and people, generally—not to start, it's really, really easy not to take them. And I think that's going to end up being our most important thing. Really tough, really big, really great advertising, so we get to people before they start, so they don't have to go through the problems of what people are going through. [*Applause*] Thank you.

We are already distributing nearly $1 billion in grants for addiction prevention and treatment, and over $50 million dollars to support law enforcement programs that assist those facing prison and facing addiction.

We have also launched an $81 million partnership to research better pain management techniques for our incredible veterans. And soon—[*applause*]—and, by the way, Secretary Shulkin is here. You have done an incredible job for our veterans in a very short period of time. And soon, HHS will launch a Task Force to develop and update best practices for pain management across the Federal Government.

I am urging all Americans to help fight this opioid epidemic and the broader issue of drug addiction by participating in the National Prescription Drug Take-Back Day this Saturday. When you can safely turn in these dangerous and horrible drugs for disposal, that will be a wonderful, wonderful period of time for you.

All of these actions are important parts of my administration's larger effort to confront the drug addiction crisis in America and confront it head on, straight on—strong. We're going to do it. We're going to do it.

For too long, we have allowed drugs to ravage American homes, cities, and towns. We owe it to our children and to our country to do everything in our power to address this national shame and this human tragedy.

We must stop the flow of all types of illegal drugs into our communities. For too long, dangerous criminal cartels have been allowed to infiltrate and spread throughout our Nation. An astonishing 90 percent of the heroin in America comes from south of the border, where we will be building a wall which will greatly help in this problem. It will have a great impact. My administration is dedicated to enforcing our immigration laws, defending our maritime security, and securing our borders.

We also have to work with other countries to stop these drugs where they originate. We have no choice. We have to work with others, we have to get together, because they have similar problems to what we have. Some countries have bigger problems than we have. Whether that country is China, whether it's a country in Latin America, it makes no difference. We're going to be working with all of them. We're taking the fight directly to the criminals in places that they're producing this poison.

Here in America, we are once again enforcing the law, breaking up gangs and distribution networks, and arresting criminals who peddle dangerous drugs to our youth.

In addition, we understand the need to confront reality, right smack in the face, that millions of our fellow citizens are already addicted. That's the reality. We want them to get help they need. We have no choice but to help these people that are hooked and are suffering, so they can recover and rebuild their lives with their families.

We're committed to pursuing innovative approaches that have been proven to work, like drug courts. Our efforts will be based on sound metrics and guided by evidence and guided by results. This includes making addiction treatment available to those in prison and to help them eventually reenter society as productive and law-abiding citizens.

Finally, we must adopt the most commonsense solution of all: to prevent our citizens from becoming addicted to drugs in the first place. We must and are focusing so much of our effort on drug demand reduction. We must confront the culture of drug abuse head-on to reduce demand for dangerous narcotics. Every person who buys illicit drugs here in America should know that they are risking their futures, their families, and even their lives. And every American should know that if they purchase illegal drugs, they are helping to finance some of the most violent, cruel, and ruthless organizations anywhere in the world. Illegal drug use is not a victimless crime. There is nothing admirable, positive, or socially desirable about it. There is nothing desirable about drugs. They're bad.

We want the next generation of young Americans to know the blessings of a drug-free life. In this enormous struggle against drug addiction, an opioid epidemic—it really is that; it is an epidemic—our greatest hope is the same as it has always been. Through every trial, America has encountered throughout our history, the spirit of our people and the strength of our character, we win. Each of us has a responsibility to this effort. We have a total responsibility to ourselves, to our family, to our country, including those who are struggling with this addiction.

Each of us is responsible to look out for our loved ones, our communities, our children, our neighbors, and our own health. Almost every American has witnessed the horrors of addiction, whether it's through their own struggle or through the struggle of a friend, a coworker, a neighbor or, frankly, a family member. Our current addiction crisis, and especially the epidemic of opioid deaths, will get worse before it gets better. But get better it will. It will take many years and even decades to address this scourge in our society, but we must start in earnest now to combat national health emergency.

We are inspired by the stories of everyday heroes who pull their communities from the depths of despair through leadership and through love.

Fire Chief Dan Goonan of New Hampshire—great State—runs a program, Safe Station, which allows drug-dependent residents to seek help at fire stations at any time.

Jesse and Cyndi Swafford of Dayton, Ohio, have provided a loving, stable home to children affected by the opioid crisis.

I am calling on every American to join the ranks of guardian angels like Chief Goonan and the Swaffords, who help lift up the people of our great Nation.

Together, we will care for our citizens, our children, and our orphans, and our—and you know what I'm going to say—our foster youth. So many. So many. But we're going to lift them up, and we're going to take care of them. We will work to strengthen vulnerable families and communities, and we will help to build and grow a stronger, healthier, and drug-free society.

Together, we will face this challenge as a national family with conviction, with unity, and with a commitment to love and support our neighbors in times of dire need. Working together, we will defeat this opioid epidemic. It will be defeated. We will free our Nation from the terrible affliction of drug abuse. And yes, we will overcome addiction in America. We are going to overcome addiction in America. We have fought and won many battles and many wars before, and we will win again.

Thank you. God bless you. And God bless America. Thank you. . . .

*White House correction.

SOURCE: Executive Office of the President. "Remarks on Signing a Memorandum on Combatting the National Drug Demand and Opioid Crisis." October 26, 2017. *Compilation of Presidential Documents* 2017, no. 00787 (October 26, 2017). https://www.gpo.gov/fdsys/pkg/DCPD-201700787/pdf/DCPD-201700787.pdf.

President's Commission on Combatting Drug Addiction and the Opioid Crisis Releases Recommendations

November 1, 2017

[The Chair's letter has been omitted.]

Summary of Recommendations

Federal Funding and Programs

1. The Commission urges Congress and the Administration to block grant federal funding for opioid-related and SUD-related activities to the states, where the battle is happening every day. There are multiple federal agencies and multiple grants within those agencies that cause states a significant administrative burden from an application and reporting perspective. Creating uniform block grants would allow more resources to be spent on administering life-saving programs. This was a request to the Commission by nearly every Governor, regardless of party, across the country.

2. The Commission believes that ONDCP must establish a coordinated system for tracking all federally-funded initiatives, through support from HHS and DOJ. If we are to invest in combating this epidemic, we must invest in only those programs that achieve quantifiable goals and metrics. We are operating blindly today; ONDCP must establish a system of tracking and accountability.

3. To achieve accountability in federal programs, the Commission recommends that ONDCP review is a component of every federal program and that necessary funding is provided for implementation. Cooperation by federal agencies and the states must be mandated.

Opioid Addiction Prevention

4. The Commission recommends that Department of Education (DOE) collaborate with states on student assessment programs such as Screening, Brief Intervention and Referral to Treatment (SBIRT). SBIRT is a program that uses a screening tool by trained staff to identify at-risk youth who may need treatment. This should be deployed for adolescents in middle school, high school and college levels. This is a significant prevention tool.

5. The Commission recommends the Administration fund and collaborate with private sector and non-profit partners to design and implement a wide-reaching, national multi-platform media campaign addressing the hazards of substance use, the danger of opioids, and stigma. A similar mass media/educational campaign was launched during the AIDs public health crisis.

Prescribing Guidelines, Regulations, Education

6. The Commission recommends HHS, the Department of Labor (DOL), VA/ DOD, FDA, and ONDCP work with stakeholders to develop model statutes, regulations, and policies that ensure informed patient consent prior to an opioid prescription for chronic pain. Patients need to understand the risks, benefits and alternatives to taking opioids. This is not the standard today.

7. The Commission recommends that HHS coordinate the development of a national curriculum and standard of care for opioid prescribers. An updated set of guidelines for prescription pain medications should be established by an expert committee composed of various specialty practices to supplement the CDC guideline that are specifically targeted to primary care physicians.

8. The Commission recommends that federal agencies work to collect participation data. Data on prescribing patterns should be matched with participation in continuing medical education data to determine program effectiveness and such analytics shared with clinicians and stakeholders such as state licensing boards.

9. The Commission recommends that the Administration develop a model training program to be disseminated to all levels of medical education (including all prescribers) on screening for substance use and mental health status to identify at risk patients.

10. The Commission recommends the Administration work with Congress to amend the Controlled Substances Act to allow the DEA to require that all prescribers desiring to be relicensed to prescribe opioids show participation in an approved continuing medical education program on opioid prescribing.

11. The Commission recommends that HHS, DOJ/DEA, ONDCP, and pharmacy associations train pharmacists on best practices to evaluate legitimacy of opioid prescriptions, and not penalize pharmacists for denying inappropriate prescriptions.

PDMP Enhancements

12. The Commission recommends the Administration's support of the Prescription Drug Monitoring (PDMP) Act to mandate states that receive grant funds to comply with PDMP requirements, including data sharing. This Act directs DOJ to fund the establishment and maintenance of a data-sharing hub.

13. The Commission recommends federal agencies mandate PDMP checks, and consider amending requirements under the Emergency Medical Treatment and Labor Act (EMTALA), which requires hospitals to screen and stabilize patients in an emergency department, regardless of insurance status or ability to pay.

14. The Commission recommends that PDMP data integration with electronic health records, overdose episodes, and SUD-related decision support tools for providers is necessary to increase effectiveness.

15. The Commission recommends ONDCP and DEA increase electronic prescribing to prevent diversion and forgery. The DEA should revise regulations regarding electronic prescribing for controlled substances.

16. The Commission recommends that the Federal Government work with states to remove legal barriers and ensure PDMPs incorporate available overdose/naloxone deployment data, including the Department of Transportation's (DOT) Emergency Medical Technician (EMT) overdose database. It is necessary to have overdose data/naloxone deployment data in the PDMP to allow users of the PDMP to assist patients.

Supply Reduction and Enforcement Strategies

17. The Commission recommends community-based stakeholders utilize Take Back Day to inform the public about drug screening and treatment services. The Commission encourages more hospitals/clinics and retail pharmacies to become year-round authorized collectors and explore the use of drug deactivation bags.

18. The Commission recommends that CMS remove pain survey questions entirely on patient satisfaction surveys, so that providers are never incentivized for offering opioids to raise their survey score. ONDCP and HHS should establish a policy to prevent hospital administrators from using patient ratings from CMS surveys improperly.

19. The Commission recommends CMS review and modify rate-setting policies that discourage the use of non-opioid treatments for pain, such as certain bundled payments that make alternative treatment options cost prohibitive for hospitals and doctors, particularly those options for treating immediate post-surgical pain.

20. The Commission recommends a federal effort to strengthen data collection activities enabling real-time surveillance of the opioid crisis at the national, state, local, and tribal levels.

21. The Commission recommends the Federal Government work with the states to develop and implement standardized rigorous drug testing procedures, forensic methods, and use of appropriate toxicology instrumentation in the investigation of drug-related deaths. We do not have sufficiently accurate and systematic data from medical examiners around the country to determine overdose deaths, both in their cause and the actual number of deaths.

22. The Commission recommends reinstituting the *Arrestee Drug Abuse Monitoring* (ADAM) program and the *Drug Abuse Warning Network* (DAWN) to improve data collection and provide resources for other promising surveillance systems.

23. The Commission recommends the enhancement of federal sentencing penalties for the trafficking of fentanyl and fentanyl analogues.

24. The Commission recommends that federal law enforcement agencies expressly target Drug Trafficking Organizations and other individuals who produce and sell counterfeit pills, including through the internet.

25. The Commission recommends that the Administration work with Congress to amend the law to give the DEA the authority to regulate the use of pill presses/tableting machines with requirements for the maintenance of records, inspections for verifying location and stated use, and security provisions.

26. The Commission recommends U.S. Customs and Border Protection (CBP) and the U.S. Postal Inspection Service (USPIS) use additional technologies and drug detection canines to expand efforts to intercept fentanyl (and other synthetic opioids) in envelopes and packages at international mail processing distribution centers.

27. The Commission recommends Congress and the Federal Government use advanced electronic data on international shipments from high-risk areas to identify international suppliers and their U.S.-based distributors.

28. The Commission recommends support of the Synthetics Trafficking and Overdose Prevention (STOP) Act and recommends the Federal Government work with the international community to implement the STOP Act in accordance with international laws and treaties.

29. The Commission recommends a coordinated federal/DEA effort to prevent, monitor and detect the diversion of prescription opioids, including licit fentanyl, for illicit distribution or use.

30. The Commission recommends the White House develop a national outreach plan for the *Fentanyl Safety Recommendations for First Responders*. Federal departments and agencies should partner with Governors and state fusion centers to develop and standardize data collection, analytics, and information-sharing related to first responder opioid-intoxication incidents.

Opioid Addiction Treatment, Overdose Reversal, and Recovery

31. The Commission recommends HHS, CMS, Substance Abuse and Mental Health Services Administration, the VA, and other federal agencies incorporate quality measures that address addiction screenings and treatment referrals. There is a great need to ensure that health care providers are screening for SUDs and know how to appropriately counsel, or refer a patient. HHS should review the scientific evidence on the latest OUD and SUD treatment options and collaborate with the U.S. Preventive Services Task Force (USPSTF) on provider recommendations.

32. The Commission recommends the adoption of process, outcome, and prognostic measures of treatment services as presented by the National Outcome Measurement and the American Society of Addiction Medicine (ASAM). Addiction is a chronic relapsing disease of the brain which affects multiple aspects of a person's life. Providers, practitioners, and funders often face challenges in helping individuals achieve positive long-term outcomes without relapse.

33. The Commission recommends HHS/CMS, the Indian Health Service (IHS), Tricare, the DEA, and the VA remove reimbursement and policy barriers to SUD treatment, including those, such as patient limits, that limit access to any forms of FDA-approved medication-assisted treatment (MAT), counseling, inpatient/residential treatment, and other treatment modalities, particularly fail-first protocols and frequent prior authorizations. All primary care providers employed by the above-mentioned health systems should screen for alcohol and drug use and, directly or through referral, provide treatment within 24 to 48 hours.

34. The Commission recommends HHS review and modify rate-setting (including policies that indirectly impact reimbursement) to better cover the true costs of

providing SUD treatment, including inpatient psychiatric facility rates and out-patient provider rates.

35. Because the Department of Labor (DOL) regulates health care coverage provided by many large employers, the Commission recommends that Congress provide DOL increased authority to levy monetary penalties on insurers and funders, and permit DOL to launch investigations of health insurers independently for parity violations.

36. The Commission recommends that federal and state regulators should use a standardized tool that requires health plans to document and disclose their compliance strategies for non-quantitative treatment limitations (NQTL) parity. NQTLs include stringent prior authorization and medical necessity requirements. HHS, in consultation with DOL and Treasury, should review clinical guidelines and standards to support NQTL parity requirements. Private sector insurers, including employers, should review rate-setting strategies and revise rates when necessary to increase their network of addiction treatment professionals.

37. The Commission recommends the National Institute on Corrections (NIC), the Bureau of Justice Assistance (BJA), the Substance Abuse and Mental Health Services Administration (SAMHSA), and other national, state, local, and tribal stakeholders use medication-assisted treatment (MAT) with pre-trial detainees and continuing treatment upon release.

38. The Commission recommends DOJ broadly establish federal drug courts within the federal district court system in all 93 federal judicial districts. States, local units of government, and Indian tribal governments should apply for drug court grants established by 34 U.S.C. § 10611. Individuals with an SUD who violate probation terms with substance use should be diverted into drug court, rather than prison.

39. The Commission recommends the Federal Government partner with appropriate hospital and recovery organizations to expand the use of recovery coaches, especially in hard-hit areas. Insurance companies, federal health systems, and state payers should expand programs for hospital and primary case-based SUD treatment and referral services. Recovery coach programs have been extraordinarily effective in states that have them to help direct patients in crisis to appropriate treatment. Addiction and recovery specialists can also work with patients through technology and telemedicine, to expand their reach to underserved areas.

40. The Commission recommends the Health Resources and Services Administration (HRSA) prioritize addiction treatment knowledge across all health disciplines. Adequate resources are needed to recruit and increase the number of addiction-trained psychiatrists and other physicians, nurses, psychologists, social workers, physician assistants, and community health workers and facilitate deployment in needed regions and facilities.

41. The Commission recommends that federal agencies revise regulations and reimbursement policies to allow for SUD treatment via telemedicine.

42. The Commission recommends further use of the National Health Service Corp to supply needed health care workers to states and localities with higher than average opioid use and abuse.

43. The Commission recommends the National Highway Traffic Safety Administration (NHTSA) review its National Emergency Medical Services (EMS) Scope of

Practice Model with respect to naloxone, and disseminate best practices for states that may need statutory or regulatory changes to allow Emergency Medical Technicians (EMT) to administer naloxone, including higher doses to account for the rising number of fentanyl overdoses.

44. The Commission recommends HHS implement naloxone co-prescribing pilot programs to confirm initial research and identify best practices. ONDCP should, in coordination with HHS, disseminate a summary of existing research on co-prescribing to stakeholders.

45. The Commission recommends HHS develop new guidance for Emergency Medical Treatment and Labor Act (EMTALA) compliance with regard to treating and stabilizing SUD patients and provide resources to incentivize hospitals to hire appropriate staff for their emergency rooms.

46. The Commission recommends that HHS implement guidelines and reimbursement policies for Recovery Support Services, including peer-to-peer programs, jobs and life skills training, supportive housing, and recovery housing.

47. The Commission recommends that HHS, the Substance Abuse and Mental Health Services Administration (SAMHSA), and the Administration on Children, Youth and Families (ACYF) should disseminate best practices for states regarding interventions and strategies to keep families together, when it can be done safely (e.g., using a relative for kinship care). These practices should include utilizing comprehensive family centered approaches and should ensure families have access to drug screening, substance use treatment, and parental support. Further, federal agencies should research promising models for pregnant and post-partum women with SUDs and their newborns, including screenings, treatment interventions, supportive housing, non-pharmacologic interventions for children born with neonatal abstinence syndrome, medication-assisted treatment (MAT) and other recovery supports.

48. The Commission recommends ONDCP, the Substance Abuse and Mental Health Services Administration (SAMHSA), and the Department of Education (DOE) identify successful college recovery programs, including "sober housing" on college campuses, and provide support and technical assistance to increase the number and capacity of high-quality programs to help students in recovery.

49. The Commission recommends that ONDCP, federal partners, including DOL, large employers, employee assistance programs, and recovery support organizations develop best practices on SUDs and the workplace. Employers need information for addressing employee alcohol and drug use, ensure that employees are able to seek help for SUDs through employee assistance programs or other means, supporting health and wellness, including SUD recovery, for employees, and hiring those in recovery.

50. The Commission recommends that ONDCP work with the DOJ, DOL, the National Alliance for Model State Drug Laws, the National Conference of State Legislatures, and other stakeholders to develop model state legislation/regulation for states to decouple felony convictions and eligibility for business/occupational licenses, where appropriate.

51. The Commission recommends that ONDCP, federal agencies, the National Alliance for Recovery Residents (NARR), the National Association of State

Alcohol and Drug Abuse Directors (NASADAD), and housing stakeholders should work collaboratively to develop quality standards and best practices for recovery residences, including model state and local policies. These partners should identify barriers (such as zoning restrictions and discrimination against MAT patients) and develop strategies to address these issues.

Research and Development

52. The Commission recommends federal agencies, including HHS (National Institutes of Health, CDC, CMS, FDA, and the Substance Abuse and Mental Health Services Administration), DOJ, the Department of Defense (DOD), the VA, and ONDCP, should engage in a comprehensive review of existing research programs and establish goals for pain management and addiction research (both prevention and treatment).

53. The Commission recommends Congress and the Federal Government provide additional resources to the National Institute on Drug Abuse (NIDA), the National Institute of Mental Health (NIMH), and National Institute on Alcohol Abuse and Alcoholism (NIAAA) to fund the research areas cited above. NIDA should continue research in concert with the pharmaceutical industry to develop and test innovative medications for SUDs and OUDs, including long-acting injectables, more potent opioid antagonists to reverse overdose, drugs used for detoxification, and opioid vaccines.

54. The Commission recommends further research of Technology-Assisted Monitoring and Treatment for high-risk patients and SUD patients. CMS, FDA, and the United States Preventative Services Task Force (USPSTF) should implement a fast-track review process for any new evidence-based technology supporting SUD prevention and treatments.

55. The Commission recommends that commercial insurers and CMS fast-track creation of Healthcare Common Procedure Coding System (HCPCS) codes for FDA-approved technology-based treatments, digital interventions, and biomarker-based interventions. NIH should develop a means to evaluate behavior modification apps for effectiveness.

56. The Commission recommends that the FDA establish guidelines for post-market surveillance related to diversion, addiction, and other adverse consequences of controlled substances.

[The rest of the report detailing the research has been omitted.]

SOURCE: "The White House. The President's Commission on Combatting Drug Addiction and the Opioid Crisis." November 1, 2017. https://www.whitehouse.gov/sites/whitehouse.gov/files/images/Final_Report_Draft_11-1-2017.pdf.

OTHER HISTORIC DOCUMENTS OF INTEREST

FROM PREVIOUS *HISTORIC DOCUMENTS*

Liberian President, President-elect Remark on First Democratic Transfer of Power

OCTOBER 30, NOVEMBER 7, AND DECEMBER 28, 2017

In 2017, Liberia experienced its first democratic transfer of power in more than seventy years as former soccer star George Weah succeeded Nobel Peace Prize winner and first female African leader, Ellen Johnson Sirleaf. The transition was celebrated internationally for being carried out without violence or any indication of widespread voting irregularities. The new president took office facing a host of ongoing challenges, including a struggling economy and rampant corruption within the public sector, two issues Weah promised to tackle in his first months.

JOHNSON SIRLEAF CHOOSES NOT TO SEEK REELECTION

Throughout its history, Liberia has experienced little political stability, and the situation worsened in 1980, when a series of coups began. Charles Taylor seized power in 1990, just one year after the nation's civil war began, after overthrowing the government in power. Taylor was reelected in 1997, and the ruthless dictator managed to keep himself in control by supporting rebels in neighboring Sierra Leone's civil war, for which he received illegally mined diamonds that he sold to buy weapons to support his own government. However, an increasing number of armed rebel groups began operating within the country, and the militias slowly ebbed away at Taylor's control. In 2003, Taylor was driven from the country by armed rebels and the civil war came to an end. That same year, Taylor was charged with war crimes by the International Criminal Court and was sentenced in 2012 to fifty years in prison. A succession of interim governments followed Taylor's ouster until Johnson Sirleaf's election in 2005.

Johnson Sirleaf had served in past Liberian governments and was an economist for the World Bank. She was widely known in the country as the "Iron Lady of Liberia" for her tough policies and no nonsense leadership style. After supporting Taylor's 1990 rebellion, Johnson Sirleaf ran unsuccessfully for president in 1997 and was charged with treason by Taylor. In her 2005 victory, Johnson Sirleaf defeated Weah, a famous soccer star and member of parliament, 59 percent to 41 percent. Weah challenged the outcome with the National Electoral Commission (NEC), which dismissed the case citing little evidence of voting irregularities.

Johnson Sirleaf was the first female head of state in modern African history, and was celebrated around the world for her work to rebuild Liberia after a decade of civil war. Despite earning the Nobel Peace Prize in 2011, Johnson Sirleaf was largely unpopular in Liberia by the end of her time in office. When she decided to leave office voluntarily after two terms, many Liberians were still in deep poverty, infrastructure was poor at best, and the health care and education systems were failing. Johnson Sirleaf's administration was also mired in corruption scandals, with the president herself protecting many of those accused of corruption from prosecution by arguing that the judiciary was too week to adequately prosecute the alleged crimes.

Among the field of twenty candidates vying to replace Johnson Sirleaf were a variety of politicians, the nation's wealthiest man, the founder of an African children's charity, and a former rebel leader turned senator. The two front-runners were Weah, representing the Coalition for Democratic Change, and Vice President Joseph Boakai of the Unity Party (UP). It was well known throughout Liberia that Johnson Sirleaf was not fond of her vice president and she did not officially endorse any candidate in the initial vote or runoff. Boakai had a long history in the public and private sectors, serving as Liberia's Minister of Agriculture, a consultant to the World Bank, and as managing director of the Liberia Petroleum Refinery Company. He was commonly referred to across the nation as "Sleepy Joe" for his tendency to fall asleep during official meetings and other functions. The vice president worked to distance himself from Johnson Sirleaf, calling himself "a race car in the garage" to explain how his talent and ideas had been squandered by the president and that he would turn around Liberia if given the chance. Boakai chose James Emmanuel Nuquay, the UP's vice standard bearer, as his running mate, a move that came as a surprise as Nuquay was largely unpopular, even within his own electorate.

Weah chose as his running mate Taylor's ex-wife, Jewel Howard Taylor, with whom he had served in the Liberian senate. Of his choice, Weah said he believes in "gender and equality, so I think having a woman as my vice president is a good thing" and also noted that she was hugely popular among Liberians. No candidate in the race laid out specific policy proposals or plans to move the country forward after the end of the Johnson Sirleaf administration, leaving the candidates to run primarily on past records and personality. Weah's opponents were critical of his lack of experience in politics, but his supporters appreciated that he understood the plight of the average citizen, having grown up in one of Liberia's slums, and was not beholden to the political elite. The latter made him particularly appealing to young voters.

Two Top Candidates Move to Runoff

Liberia held its first round of voting on October 10, with high turnout at 73 percent. In Liberia's electoral system, one candidate must receive at least 50 percent plus one vote to be declared victorious, otherwise, the top two vote getters from the first round move to a runoff. No candidate secured 50 percent on October 10, but instead Weah, with 38.4 percent of the vote, and Boakai, with 28.8 percent of the vote, moved on to the second round, scheduled for November 7. The October poll marked the first run entirely by the Government of Liberia since the end of the civil war, and the European Union observer mission determined that it had been carried out relatively peacefully and was effectively managed.

Charles Brumskine, who came in third in the first round, filed a legal challenge with the nation's Supreme Court, alleging that the poll was "characterized by massive systematic irregularities and fraud" including the delayed opening of polling stations that prevented some Liberians from voting. The UP appeared to support the challenge, alleging that their own president had interfered with the vote. In a statement from the president's office, Johnson Sirleaf denied the allegations, which she called "hate speech" and "inciting language which should be condemned and disavowed by all peace-loving Liberians." Johnson Sirleaf further asked of her fellow citizens that they refrain from making any similar allegations, because these undermine the political process and stability of the nation. Weah's party called the situation "sad for a ruling party that has been in power for 12 years to be crying." Johnson Sirleaf would appeal for calm multiple times in the intervening days before the Supreme Court ruled, at one point saying, "Historians will look back at this time and judge us by how we conduct ourselves at this critical moment in time. We cannot fail them. We cannot damage our future." On December 7, the Supreme Court ruled that there was little evidence to support the claim brought by Brumskine and that a runoff could proceed. A new runoff date of December 26 was set.

Turnout for the runoff was low at 56 percent, but, similar to the first vote, there were no widespread reports of violence or irregularity that would bring the result into question. On December 28, Weah was declared the winner with 61.5 percent of the vote to Boakai's 38.5 percent. After learning the results, Weah wrote on Twitter, "I measure the importance and the responsibility of the immense task which I embrace today. Change is on." In his first speech to the nation as president-elect on December 29, Weah said that "the best way to celebrate all Liberians is to improve their lives through the instruments of pro-poor public governance. I declare publicly today that transforming the lives of all Liberians is a singular mission and focus of my presidency." In a nod to his predecessor's reign that had been marred by multiple allegations of corruption, Weah promised to take on the issue, saying, "I will not encourage a corrupt government, when you are corrupt you will have a problem" adding "Those looking to cheat the Liberian people through corruption will have no place."

LIBERIA'S ONGOING CHALLENGES

Before an estimated 35,000 Liberians, Weah was inaugurated on January 22, 2018, in Liberia's capital of Monrovia. "I have spent many years of my life in stadiums," the former footballer said, "but today is a feeling like no other." Weah's inauguration marked the first peaceful transition between democratically elected leaders since 1944. Of this milestone, the new president said, "With the help of our regional partners and of the United Nations, we chose democracy as our best choice." The international organization was instrumental in brokering a peace deal in August 2003 to end the civil war that was followed by the deployment of a peacekeeping mission that has remained in the country ever since. With the successful transition of power, in early 2018 the peacekeeping team is expected to be replaced by a UN Country Team, a group that helps ensure agencies operating in the country can effectively work together to support the government's development agenda.

Weah said his biggest priorities would be to fight corruption and improve the economy by encouraging private business and increasing the wages of public sector workers. To do the former, Weah will need to answer outstanding questions regarding his ties to former president Taylor, whom Weah admitted to talking with during the election. Weah's biggest challenge, however, will be how to shore up a flagging economy that has been plagued by low foreign investment and falling commodity prices for its chief exports, rubber and iron ore. At the time of his election, upwards of a quarter of the country's gross domestic product was made up of remittance from Liberians abroad, many of whom fled the country during the civil war of 1989 to 2003. "Our economy is broken; our government is broke. Our currency is in free fall; inflation is rising," Weah said. "Unemployment is at an unprecedented high and our foreign reserves are at an all-time low." Shortly after his inauguration in late January 2018, Weah made his first display of commitment to both improving the economy and fighting corruption by announcing that he would lower his salary and benefits by 25 percent.

—Heather Kerrigan

Following are two statements from Liberian President Ellen Johnson Sirleaf, the first, on October 30, 2017, denying allegations that she had interfered with the results of the presidential election, and the second, on November 7, 2017, calling for patience and perseverance among the public during the election runoff and eventual transition of power; and a December 28, 2017, tweet from president-elect George Weah after his runoff election victory.

Johnson Sirleaf Defends UP against Allegations of Corruption

October 30, 2017

The office of the President has learned with deep regret and disappointment, grave allegations levied by the Representatives of the Unity Party, Liberty Party and the All Liberian Party against the President of the Republic of Liberia.

The Office of the President wishes to state unequivocally that these allegations are completely baseless, and are an unfortunate attempt by agent provocateurs to undermine Liberia's democratic process.

These allegations fall in the category of "hate speech" and "inciting language" which should be condemned and disavowed by all peace-loving Liberians.

We like to be specifically clear that at no time has President Sirleaf interfered in the process, outcome or results of the 2017 General and Presidential Elections.

All meetings, interactions or exchanges between the Office of the President and the National Elections Commission were consistent with her constitutional role to ensure that the process was supported and such interactions were initiated at the request of the Commission and never held secretly but in the presence of others even on occasion with the presence of international representatives, who remain concern about Liberia's progress.

President Sirleaf has met with the numerous domestic and international observation missions, as well as the various technical advisors working to support the National Elections Commission.

Furthermore, the President reminds all parties of their signature to the Farmington River Declaration, which obliges all parties to pursue a peaceful judicial resolution to electoral disputes.

The President calls on all parties to refrain from utterances and actions that have the propensity to incite people and undermine the peace and stability of the country before, during and after the conclusion of the 2017 electoral process.

We encourage any and all political parties with evidence of any issues relating to the elections to present said evidence through the appropriate legal channels so that the issues may be adjudicated and, where necessary, our elections process can be improved.

The President remains confident about the ability of the National Elections Commission (NEC) to carry out professional, credible and transparent elections that accurately reflect the will of the Liberian people and Liberia's Judicial Branch to adequately, transparently, fairly and impartially adjudicate any dispute arising thereof.

The facts must speak for themselves, and not be obscured by rumor, innuendo, fake news and false narratives.

The office of the President takes this opportunity to remind all Liberians of the appeal made to them by President Sirleaf on the eve of the October 10 Elections and ask that you take it to heart as the presidential run-off approaches:

1. Go to the polls peacefully, respecting every Liberian's right to vote with dignity and pride. Embrace your neighbor, regardless of their political choice. The peace is for you to protect and preserve.

2. Remember that you are an empowered people, the future of the country is in your hands. No one is entitled to your vote—not because of party, ethnicity, religion or tribal affiliation.

3. All must respect the outcome of the election.

Let's continue to embrace democracy and make our country proud.

I THANK YOU FOR YOUR KIND ATTENTION.

SOURCE: Executive Mansion of the President of Liberia. "Special Statement by the Office of the President Her Excellency, Ellen Johnson Sirleaf." October 30, 2017. http://www.emansion.gov.lr/doc/EM%20 Response%20To%20The%20Three%20Parties_%20Statement%20final%20final.pdf.

DOCUMENT *Johnson Sirleaf Appeals for Calm*

November 7, 2017

My dear Liberians,

As we go through this time of uncertainty in our electoral process, awaiting the country's historical presidential transition, I commend you for your patience, and your peaceful demeanor.

Liberia's laws and democratic institutions are strong. They will withstand this challenge, and they will stand the test of time.

We can strengthen them by demonstrating maturity, and not abuse our positions or misuse the platforms that have been made available to the Country through news media and new technology. We must continue to respect each other, the rule of law, human kindness and decency. Allegations, hate speech, inciting language has been defining what should be a proud moment in our history.

I am glad that all Political Parties have agreed consistently and publicly to adhere to the provisions provided under our laws. These provisions include the right to challenge, through an established and orderly process, the voting and electoral arrangements that have been put in place.

Democracy is only as strong as its weakest link and at these moments, our democracy is under assault. Our country's reputation is under assault, our economy is under stress.

We politicians must do better. Our people went the distance. We achieved 73 percent voters' turnout demonstrating confidence in our electoral process and the future of our country.

Historians will look back at this time and judge us by how we conduct ourselves at this critical moment in time.

We cannot fail them. We cannot damage our future. May God save and protect our State.

SOURCE: Executive Mansion of the President of Liberia. "Letter from President Johnson Sirleaf." November 7, 2017. http://www.emansion.gov.lr/doc/My%20fellow%20citizens.pdf.

DOCUMENT *George Weah Celebrates Victory*

December 28, 2017

My fellow Liberians, I deeply feel the emotion of all the nation. I measure the importance and the responsibility of the immense task which I embrace today. Change is on.

SOURCE: George Weah (@GeorgeWeahOff). Twitter post, December 28, 2017. https://twitter.com/GeorgeWeahOff/status/946464511485202432.

OTHER HISTORIC DOCUMENTS OF INTEREST

FROM PREVIOUS *HISTORIC DOCUMENTS*

November

Saudi Government Announces Anti-corruption Committee, Arrests Public and Private Leaders

NOVEMBER 5 AND 9, AND DECEMBER 5, 2017

The naming of Mohammed bin Salman as the crown prince of Saudi Arabia in June 2017 led to a new push for social and economic change within the kingdom, as well as a stronger Saudi presence abroad. The crown prince also played a central role in a sweeping anti-corruption campaign, announced by royal order in November 2017, that resulted in the arrest of hundreds of influential Saudis, including other princes, government ministers, and wealthy business leaders. Characterized by many as a power grab by the prince, the campaign also had an economic component, generating significant funds from settlements paid by the accused that helped replenish Saudi resources that had been depleted by falling oil prices.

A ROYAL SHAKE-UP

When King Salman of Saudi Arabia named his third son, Mohammed bin Salman, crown prince in June 2017, he circumvented royal convention, which had upheld rule by consensus within the House of Saud since the death of its first king. King Salman is a member of the Sudairi Seven, the set of full-brothers born to his father's favorite wife. Although this group has had preeminence within the royal family, the crown has customarily rotated between princely lines to prevent conflict. Mohammed bin Nayef, the king's fifty-seven-year-old nephew, had been next in line for the throne, but was removed as the crown prince—and from his position as interior minister—in the same royal order that declared Mohammed bin Salman the new crown prince. Mohammed bin Salman has steadily accumulated informal power and portfolio responsibilities following his father's accession in 2015. Media reports indicate that King Salman, who views Mohammed as his most tenacious son, also suffers from mild dementia at age eighty-two and has effectively delegated many of his responsibilities to the thirty-one-year-old.

MOHAMMED AT THE HELM: DIPLOMACY AND DISRUPTION

Since becoming the crown prince, Mohammed bin Salman has emphasized economic reform and a loosening of gender segregation at home and the projection of Saudi power abroad. In both the foreign and domestic spheres, his policies were characterized by an adventurous sensibility that undercut the preferences of older stakeholders used to deference in a kingdom famous for its aged rulers.

Mohammed bin Salman has demanded obedience from the Saudi elite, but has endorsed moderation in the kingdom's messaging. He has also been keen to demonstrate his commitment to a more liberal society, including by giving women the right to drive, restricting the authority of the country's religious police, detaining dozens of hardline clerics, and mandating pronouncements supporting religious moderation from others. In addition, the crown prince is leading implementation of Vision 2030, the kingdom's blueprint for diversifying the Saudi economy and reducing its reliance on oil revenues amid a global drop in oil prices. A major element of the plan calls for an initial public offering of 5 percent of state oil company Saudi Aramco, planned for 2019, which analysts project could generate up to $150 billion. The plan also calls for investment in emerging technologies, greater integration of women into the workforce, development of new tourism and entertainment venues, privatization of select government services and parts of the economy, improving the effectiveness and efficiency of the welfare system, and development of global economic ties and increased direct foreign investment, among other measures.

In contrast to headline domestic social policies, Saudi foreign policy under Mohammed bin Salman is characterized by hardline positions, as in the country's denial of humanitarian aid to Yemen, where Shia Houthis are challenging Saudi-backed forces in the neighboring country's civil war. The conflict is seen as a proxy war with Shia Iran, the Sunni kingdom's main competitor for regional influence, which is viewed as an existential threat by the crown prince. Mohammed bin Salman is also seen as leading Saudi Arabia's dispute with Qatar, which resulted in the kingdom joining with several other countries to sever diplomatic ties with Qatar and impose a trade embargo. Additionally, the crown prince has eagerly pursued a warm relationship with U.S. President Donald Trump and his son-in-law Jared Kushner, resulting in the signing of a series of economic and security agreements between the two countries and high praise from the president, as well as a seeming willingness to ignore the kingdom's human rights concerns or involvement in Yemen. Emboldened by U.S. acquiescence, Mohammed bin Salman is likely to advance what he perceives as Saudi regional interests more aggressively than his predecessors, with important implications for stability in the Gulf.

GOVERNMENT LAUNCHES CROWN PRINCE-LED ANTI-CORRUPTION INITIATIVE

Citing "exploitation by some of the weak souls who have put their own interests above the public interest" to "illicitly accrue money," the Saudi government on November 5 issued royal orders creating an anti-corruption committee led by the crown prince and comprised of the chairman of the monitoring and investigation commission, chairman of the national anti-corruption authority, chief of the general audit bureau, attorney general, and head of state security. The committee was charged with identifying "offenses, crimes, persons and entities involved in cases of public corruption" as well as investigating these individuals, issuing arrest warrants as needed, freezing the accused's financial accounts, and instituting individual travel bans. The royal orders also called for a major cabinet shakeup: The ministers of Economy and Planning and the National Guard were relieved of their positions, and the commander of Saudi Arabia's Navy was ordered to retire. The replacement of Prince Miteb bin Abdullah as the National Guard minister was particularly noteworthy because he was the last remaining office holder from the Shammar princely line of the Saud family and, as the favorite son of King Abdullah (Salman's predecessor), was viewed as the strongest potential challenger to the crown prince's power.

Shortly after the orders were issued, the crown prince initiated a sweeping series of arrests—characterized as a crackdown on corruption—that resulted in the detention of eleven princes (including Prince Miteb), four ministers (including the newly deposed minister of Economy and Planning), and dozens of influential businessmen, including Prince Alwaleed bin Talal, a well-known Saudi billionaire who is a major investor in Western companies. Saudi Arabia has long struggled with endemic malfeasance, and fraud charges could plausibly be leveled at most members of the royal family, given their deep involvement with state-owned companies and interests. Notwithstanding the royal orders' characterization of corruption as an offense to God and the body politic, many observers posited that the anti-corruption drive was a push by the crown prince to consolidate his power before his father dies or abdicates the thrown. In the case of Prince Alwaleed, analysts surmised that his wealth and status were viewed as a potential threat by the crown prince, who used the anti-corruption drive to publicly demote his relative and siphon off a portion of his net worth. Additionally, President Trump's support for the kingdom's internal consolidation and regional interventions were believed to embolden the crown prince to pursue punitive measures against formerly untouchable potential rivals. Others speculated that the timing was influenced by the planned Saudi Aramco public offering: The crown prince, they said, may have thought the upcoming sale would help quell disquiet among interested external investors who were otherwise allied with those arrested.

On November 9, Saudi Arabia's attorney general released an update on the anti-corruption committee's actions to date, stating that 208 people had been called in for questioning. Of those, only seven had been released without charge; the rest remained under arrest. Arrested defendants were initially held in comfort at the Ritz-Carlton in Riyadh. The attorney general estimated that at least $100 billion "has been misused through systematic corruption and embezzlement over several decades" and said the Saudi Arabian Monetary Authority had granted his request to suspend the personal bank accounts of those being investigated. The proceedings remained opaque to outsiders: The attorney general explained that "in order to ensure that the individuals continue to enjoy the full legal rights afforded to them under Saudi law, we will not be revealing any more personal details at this time. We ask that their privacy is respected while they continue to be subject to our judicial process." He did offer reassurance to Saudi businesses that "normal commercial activity in the Kingdom is not affected by these investigations."

The attorney general provided another report on the committee's work at the beginning of December, stating that a total of 320 people had been subpoenaed. He outlined the two phases of the committee's work, the first involving "negotiating with the detainees and offering them a settlement that will facilitate recouping the State's funds and assets, and eliminate the need for a prolonged litigation." In the second phase, detainees' cases were transferred to the Public Prosecution office for a determination of whether there was sufficient evidence to continue holding them—in which case they could remain under arrest for up to six months, unless extended by a court. According to the attorney general, most of those who faced corruption charges chose to settle. Some individuals, such as Prince Miteb, reportedly repaid allegedly ill-gotten gains in excess of $1 billion to the government. Prince Alwaleed was reportedly asked to pay $6 billion of his $17 billion net worth; the amount of his settlement was not disclosed.

Such settlements appeared designed in part to provide a funding stream for the kingdom, which has seen its resources depleted by dropping oil prices. Media reports indicated that the country was spending an equivalent of one third of the sovereign wealth fund every year, and foreign reserves fell from $737 billion in 2014 to $487 billion in 2017. The anti-corruption drive ultimately generated $106 billion in settlement payments.

Although most detainees were released by January 30, 2018, nearly sixty individuals were still being held due to pending charges. Saudi Arabia has not publicly specified the allegations against these individuals, citing privacy concerns.

—Anastazia Clouting

Following is a November 5, 2017, announcement of anti-graft orders; the November 9, 2017, statement by Saudi Arabia's attorney general on anti-corruption investigations; and the text of a December 5, 2017, statement from the attorney general regarding the ongoing work of the anti-corruption committee.

DOCUMENT

Saudi Government Announces Royal Anti-graft Orders

November 5, 2017

The Custodian of the Two Holy Mosques King Salman bin Abdulaziz Al Saud issued a series of royal orders.

In a statement announced here tonight, the King said the following:

In view of what we have noticed of exploitation by some of the weak souls who have put their own interests above the public interest, in order to, illicitly, accrue money and as we have taken care, in this regard, since we assumed the responsibility to follow these matters out of our pledges towards the homeland and the citizen, we decided:

First: To form a supreme committee chaired by the Crown Prince and the membership of: Chairman of the Monitoring and Investigation Commission, Chairman of the National Anti-Corruption Authority, Chief of the General Audit Bureau, Attorney General and Head of State Security.

Second: Exemption from laws, regulations, instructions, orders and decisions, while the Committee shall perform the following tasks:

1. To identify offenses, crimes, persons and entities involved in cases of public corruption.

2. The investigation, issuance of arrest warrants, travel ban, disclosure and freezing of accounts and portfolios, tracking of funds, assets and preventing their remittance or transfer by persons and entities, whatever they might be. The committee has the right to take any precautionary measures it sees, until they are referred to the investigating authorities or judicial bodies. It may takes whatever measures deemed necessary to deal with those involved in public corruption cases and take what it considers to be the right of persons, entities, funds, fixed and movable assets, at home and abroad, return funds to the state treasury and register property and assets in the name of state property.

Thirdly: The Committee may seek the assistance of those it deems necessary and may set up teams for investigation, prosecution, etc., and may delegate some or all of its powers to these teams.

Fourthly: Upon completion of its duties, the committee shall submit to us a detailed report on its findings and what it has taken, in this regard.

Fifth: Competent authorities shall be informed of this order and all parties concerned shall similarly cooperate fully to enforce the provisions of this order.

The Custodian of the Two Holy Mosques King Salman bin Abdulaziz Al Saud ordered tonight the following:

1. Prince Miteb bin Abdullah bin Abdulaziz, the Minister of National Guard, to be sacked of his office.

2. Prince Khalid bin Abdulaziz bin Mohammed bin Ayyaf Al Muqren to be appointed as Minister of the National Guard.

Competent authorities shall be informed of this order to apply it.

The Custodian of the Two Holy Mosques King Salman bin Abdulaziz Al Saud issued an order here tonight as follows:

First: Minister of Economy and Planning Eng. Adel bin Mohammed Faqih to be relieved of his post.

Second: Mohammed bin Mazyad Al-Tuwaijri to be appointed as Minister of Economy and Planning.

Competent authorities shall be informed of this order to apply it.

The Custodian of the Two Holy Mosques King Salman bin Abdulaziz Al Saud, in his capacity as the Supreme Commander-in-Chief of all Armed Forces (Military Units), issued sacking and replacement orders:

First: Tenure of Admiral Abdullah bin Sultan bin Mohammed Al-Sultan, the Commander of the Naval Forces, is to be terminated and be retired.

Second: Vice Admiral Fahd bin Abdullah Al-Ghifaili is to be promoted to the rank of admiral and be appointed as Commander of the Naval Forces.

The Minister of Defense shall carry this order, out.

SOURCE: Saudi Ministry of Communications and Information Technology. "A Series of Anti-graft Royal Orders Announced." November 5, 2017. https://www.saudi.gov.sa/wps/portal/sdg/sdgnews/cont-news-05112017%201/!ut/p/z1/rZJPc4IwEMW_Sj14zOyGQEiOjE5FB7nUKZKLkyIgnRKwzdg_n76h5yo 6456ysy-_fZM8ULAFZfSpqbVtOqPfXJ8rvktoEMWzBSaCz-cYPbJ0yRapTDYePIMCVRjb2wP kbdHYXWmmaMrPjykWnbFkOBIMKPWQhg90kPdFs4e8ktzneh8QKXhIfI2USKmRiEoIyqVk sqKQXdgfp7EP6rK93N0PzwoYwtONhkaA_N5AdmfgKrgZuBp7ZBcS7309W9cOq-2BNKbqYPvv7zt p83o8qsiFxs3LLwvba1KTDZ5HkvAnwDMVIfRtK9g30S8CWdCffjZVmwkrl3U0mfwCO5wprg!!/dz/ d5/L0lDUmlTUSEhL3dHa0FKRnNBLzROV3FpQSEhL2Vu.

Saudi Attorney General Statement on Investigations by the Supreme Anti-corruption Committee

November 9, 2017

Sheikh Saud Al Mojeb, Attorney General of the Kingdom of Saudi Arabia and member of the supreme anti-corruption committee formed by Royal Order on Saturday November 4, issued the following statement on Thursday November 9th:

"The investigations of the supreme anti-corruption committee are proceeding quickly, and we can provide the following updates:

1. A total of 208 individuals have been called in for questioning so far.

2. Of those 208 individuals, seven have been released without charge.

3. The potential scale of corrupt practices which have been uncovered is very large. Based on our investigations over the past three years, we estimate that at least $100 billion USD has been misused through systematic corruption and embezzlement over several decades.

The evidence for this wrongdoing is very strong, and confirms the original suspicions which led the Saudi Arabian authorities to begin the investigation into these suspects in the first place. Given the scale of the allegations, the Saudi Arabian authorities, under the direction of the Royal Order issued on November 4th, has a clear legal mandate to move to the next phase of our investigations, and to take action to suspend personal bank accounts.

On Tuesday, the Governor of the Saudi Arabian Monetary Authority (SAMA), agreed to my request to suspend the personal bank accounts of persons of interests in the investigation.There has been a great deal of speculation around the world regarding the identities of the individuals concerned and the details of the charges against them. In order to ensure that the individuals continue to enjoy the full legal rights afforded to them under Saudi law, we will not be revealing any more personal details at this time. We ask that their privacy is respected while they continue to be subject to our judicial process.

It is important to repeat, as all Saudi authorities have done over the past few days, that normal commercial activity in the Kingdom is not affected by these investigations. Only personal bank accounts have been suspended. Companies and banks are free to continue with transactions as usual.

The Government of Saudi Arabia, under the leadership of the Custodian of the Two Holy Mosques King Salman bin Abdulaziz Al Saud, and Crown Prince Mohammed bin Salman, is working within a clear legal and institutional framework to maintain transparency and integrity in the market.

SOURCE: Saudi Press Agency. "Statement by the Attorney General of the Kingdom of Saudi Arabia on Investigations by the Supreme Anti-corruption Committee." November 9, 2017. http://www.spa.gov.sa/viewfullstory.php?lang=en&newsid=1686225.

Saudi Attorney General Provides Update on Supreme Anti-corruption Committee Proceedings

DOCUMENT

December 5, 2017

The Attorney General Sheikh Saud Al-Mujib, a member of the Supreme Anti-Corruption Committee that was formed by Royal Order No. (A/38) on the 4th of

November 2017, issued the following statement concerning the proceedings of the Committee to date.

1. The number of individuals subpoenaed by the Committee stands at 320 individuals. Since the last update issued on the 9th of November 2017, and as a result of information revealed, additional individuals have been subpoenaed to provide any relevant information;

2. The Committee transferred a number of individuals to the Public Prosecution office. As a result, the current number of detainees is 159 individuals.

3. Most detainees faced with corruption allegations by the Committee agreed to a settlement. The necessary arrangements are being finalized to conclude such agreements;

4. The Public Prosecution office, pursuant to relevant laws, and based on evidence decided to continue detaining a limited number of individuals and release the remaining individuals; and

5. As a precautionary measure, the bank accounts of 376 individuals are frozen, all of whom are either detainees or linked to their corruption allegations.

In this context, the Attorney General confirms that all assets or corporate entities of those detained, and any rights of any other parties related to such assets or corporate entities shall not be affected or disrupted, and all measures to ensure the same have been taken.

The Attorney General indicated that the procedures in dealing with these cases is carried out in two phases:

First Phase: Negotiation and Settlement

This phase is based on what the aforementioned Royal Order stipulated. In relevant part, the Royal Order stipulates that the Committee "has the right to decide what it deems as achieving public interest especially with those who responded positively to the Committee." Therefore, in dealing with such cases, the Committee has followed internationally applied procedures by negotiating with the detainees and offering them a settlement that will facilitate recouping the State's funds and assets, and eliminate the need for a prolonged litigation. This phase is expected to be concluded within a few weeks. During this period all detainees are allowed to contact whomever they wish to contact. No detainee will be pressured in any shape or form, and each detainee has the right to refuse to settle at anytime before the settlement agreement is signed. The following steps are carried out during this phase:

1. Face each detainee with the allegations against him. If he admits to the allegation, freely and without coercion, an agreement is reached with him for a settlement in exchange for a recommendation by the Committee to issue a pardon, and end the criminal litigation. A settlement agreement to this effect is drafted and executed.

2. In case the detainee denies the allegations against him or a settlement is not reached, he will be transferred to Public Prosecution office.

Second Phase: Transfer to Public Prosecution

Upon transferring the case to the Public Prosecution office, it reviews the case of each individual transferred to it by the Committee, and implements the following procedures:

A. Continue to investigate the relevant crime and face the suspect with evidence and available information concerning his corruption crimes. This is done in accordance with investigation procedures set forth in the Law of Criminal Procedures.

B. Decide appropriate detention period as the case is investigated. If the evidence justifies detention, then it will be decided according to the relevant laws. Detention of up to six months can be decided by the Attorney General. If warranted, an extension of detention can be ordered by the relevant court.

C. If the investigation concludes that the evidence against the detainee is insufficient for the case to proceed, the Public Prosecution office will release the individual, otherwise the individual will be prosecuted according to the relevant procedures.

The Attorney General reiterates that the Law of Criminal Procedures guarantees defendant's rights, such as the right to an attorney during the processes of investigation and prosecution, the right to contact any person to inform of his detention and the right not to be detained for more than six months except by court order issued by the relevant court. The Law of Criminal Procedures also prohibits subjecting the detainee to any harm.

SOURCE: Saudi Press Agency. "Statement by the Attorney General, Kingdom of Saudi Arabia, on the Proceedings of Supreme Anti-corruption Committee." December 5, 2017. http://www.spa.gov.sa/view fullstory.php?lang=en&newsid=1695090#1695090.

OTHER HISTORIC DOCUMENTS OF INTEREST

FROM THIS VOLUME

- Qatari Diplomatic Crisis, p. 377

FROM PREVIOUS *HISTORIC DOCUMENTS*

- OPEC Takes Action to Stabilize Oil Prices, *2016,* p. 484
- G10 Ambassadors, United Nations, and Houthi Leadership Respond to Overthrow of Yemen's Government, *2015*, p. 17
- OPEC Fails to Respond to Falling Oil Prices, *2014*, p. 571

Democratic Governors Association, Candidates, and Election Officials Remark on Special Election Outcomes

NOVEMBER 8, AND DECEMBER 26 AND 28, 2017

In late 2017, three statewide elections captured the attention of the nation as they catapulted Democrats to victory despite the party suffering serious setbacks in the 2016 presidential election year. In Virginia, not only did Democrats hold on to the governor's mansion, they picked up other key statewide positions and nearly took back control of the House of Delegates. In strongly Democratic New Jersey, the race was more about which party might be able to appoint a new senator than which candidate was victorious. And in Alabama, a heavily red state, allegations of sexual assault against the Republican candidate ultimately led to his downfall. Democrats were hopeful that they could ride this wave of support into the 2018 midterm elections and potentially use their momentum to take back control of the U.S. House or Senate.

DEMOCRATS WIN BIG IN VIRGINIA

In Virginia, where governors are limited to one term, Ralph Northam, the Democratic lieutenant governor, faced former Republican National Committee (RNC) chair Ed Gillespie in a bid to replace Governor Terry McAuliffe. The candidates differed in their rhetoric and style on the campaign trail. Gillespie had a Trump-ian focus on law and order, while still trying to distance himself from President Donald Trump who had mixed popularity in the state. Northam, however, was at times criticized for the low-key nature of his campaign that relied more on his folksy demeanor to win votes than charged partisan showboating. Northam, it seemed, intended to rely on Democratic Party turnout efforts and waning support for Republicans in the state, especially those who steeped their rhetoric in bombastic, divisive undertones.

Across Virginia, Democrats did well turning out their base and working on a united front while Republicans struggled. Gillespie's primary opponent, Corey Stewart, nearly defeated the former RNC chair in the primary, and then refused to endorse Gillespie as the party nominee. This hurt Gillespie with the Republican base, specifically in the state's more rural areas where the Trump message, which Stewart had more fully embraced, still resonated. Gillespie rarely uttered the president's name during campaign appearances, and only in the lead up to Election Day did he begin turning toward some of the president's tactics, including defending Confederate monuments and linking illegal immigrants to crime.

On November 8, turnout was 47 percent, the highest it had been for a gubernatorial contest in twenty years. Based on exit poll data, turnout was extremely high among Democrats and liberals, more so than in past election cycles, while Republican turnout was at a record low. Northam defeated Gillespie 53.7 percent to 45.1 percent and earned more votes than any gubernatorial candidate in the history of Virginia. President Trump, who backed Gillespie, and who hours before the polls closed tweeted that Northam would "allow crime to be rampant in Virginia," wrote on Twitter after the race was called for Northam, "Ed Gillespie worked hard but did not embrace me or what I stand for." At his victory party, Northam said, "Virginia has told us to end the divisiveness, that we will not condone hatred and bigotry, and to end the politics that have torn this country apart." Connecticut Governor Dan Malloy, chair of the Democratic Governors Association (DGA) said the race "sends a clear message to every Republican running in 2018 that the Trump playbook of race-baiting does not work."

The race in Virginia was closely watched around the country, and Northam's victory was seen as an indication that public sentiment was shifting away from Trump and Republicans. The DGA summed up the factors contributing to the wins as "Democratic enthusiasm, a divided Republican party, and independents moving towards Democrats," something the DGA—and many other Democrats—felt would serve the party well nationwide moving into the 2018 midterm elections.

Democrats celebrated wins across the state, including the positions of lieutenant governor and attorney general. They were also victorious in a number of House of Delegates races, where all 100 seats were up for reelection, and where Democrats needed to pick up seventeen seats to take control of the body. One of their pickups came in Prince William County, where long-time incumbent Robert Marshall was defeated by Danica Roem, who would become the first openly transgender person to serve in Virginia's legislature. Ultimately, however, the party fell one seat short of a majority. In the state's 94th House District in Newport News, incumbent David Yancey defeated Democrat Shelly Simonds by a narrow margin. An automatic recount gave the victory to Simonds by one vote, which led Yancey to file suit. A three-judge panel reviewed the ballot in question and determined that it should have been counted toward Yancey, despite having markings for both candidates' names. Simonds asked the court to reconsider, but her request was denied. Because the race was declared a tie, it fell to the Virginia State Board of Elections to choose a winner. On January 4, 2018, the candidates' names were placed inside film canisters and into a bowl. James Alcorn, chair of the State Board of Elections, drew Yancey's name and noted that the race "has certainly shown the importance of every vote and the power of one single vote." After the drawing, Simonds said she was "not conceding" at the moment and would consider her options moving forward. She would eventually concede on January 10, 2018, giving Virginia Republicans a 51–49 majority in the House of Delegates.

New Jersey Democrats Retake Control of the Governor's Mansion

In New Jersey, the gubernatorial race pitted the current lieutenant governor, Kim Guadagno, a Republican, against the former U.S. ambassador to Germany and Democratic National Committee finance chair, Phil Murphy. The two were competing to win the seat held by Republican Governor Chris Christie, who was term limited after eight years in office. The contest did not draw the nationwide attention of the Virginia race because the Democrat was expected to win handily, but it took on a secondary level of importance because at the time Republican Sen. Robert Menendez was facing federal corruption and bribery charges. Should he decide to step down, the governor would be responsible for appointing a replacement. If a Democrat was in the governor's mansion, it would almost ensure the party would pick up a seat in the U.S. Senate, shifting the balance from 52–48 to 51–49.

Although New Jersey is a solidly blue state, Christie enjoyed many years of success for his bipartisan approach to governing and his knack for finding ways to push his priorities through a Democrat-controlled legislature. However, in the years leading up to the election Christie's popularity waned following the "Bridgegate" scandal and his decision to embrace then-candidate Trump. In the summer of 2017, polls showed the governor's popularity in the mid-teens. Despite his early popularity, the state became increasingly Democratic during Christie's tenure. In 2007, when Christie won his first election for governor, registered Democrats outnumbered registered Republicans by 200,000. By 2017, that number had ballooned to 800,000.

Guadagno struggled to keep up with her opponent, who outraised her three-to-one. Not only did Guadagno fail to separate herself from the unpopular Christie administration, she also embraced some of President Trump's rhetoric, which included a campaign advertisement on immigration that alleged Murphy would have the "backs of deranged murders." Trump, however, never officially endorsed Guadagno. Ultimately, Murphy defeated Guadagno 56 percent to 41.9 percent. Though unsuccessful, Guadagno said she would "continue that fight for lower taxes and a safer New Jersey. . . . We may have lost the battle but we will win this war."

Democrats Pick Up a Senate Seat in Alabama

Alabama held a special election on December 12 to fill the Senate seat of Jeff Sessions, who resigned on February 8 to assume the position of U.S. Attorney General. Luther Strange, a Republican, was named to fill the seat in the interim by then-Alabama Governor Bob Bentley. Strange would go on to be defeated by former Alabama Supreme Court chief justice Roy Moore in the Republican primary. Moore's victory came as a surprise, given the strong backing Strange had received from Trump and other leading Republicans, including Senate Majority Leader Mitch McConnell, R-Ky.

In the December special election, Moore faced off against former U.S. attorney Doug Jones. The race was characterized by questionable commentary from Moore on topics including women's health, Russia, religion, and whether Muslims can hold office in the United States. The race received nationwide media attention in the lead up to Election Day when a number of women came forward to allege that they had been sexually assaulted or received unwanted sexual advances from Moore when they were teenagers and Moore was in his thirties. The RNC withdrew financial support from Moore and a number of Republicans called on the candidate to withdraw from the race. The allegations even forced McConnell to hold meetings in the Senate over what would be done if Moore were elected. A Quinnipiac poll released on November 21 found that 60 percent of American voters thought Moore should be expelled from the Senate if victorious.

On Election Day, President Trump tweeted, "The people of Alabama will do the right thing. Doug Jones is Pro-Abortion, weak on Crime, Military and Illegal Immigration, Bad for Gun Owners and Veterans and against the WALL. Jones is a Pelosi/Schumer Puppet. Roy Moore will always vote with us. VOTE ROY MOORE!" As was customary, Moore and his wife arrived on horseback at their polling location to cast their ballots. This show of force proved futile, and at 10:23 p.m. local time, the Associated Press called the race for Jones. Trump immediately tweeted his congratulations to Jones "on a hard fought victory," but noted "the Republicans will have another shot at this seat in a very short period of time." At 11:34 p.m., Moore appeared at his election night event, refusing to concede. "Realize when the vote is this close—that it's not over," Moore said. On December 13, Moore said he believed "the heart and soul of our country is at stake," adding "[w]e are indeed in a struggle to preserve our republic, our civilization, and our religion and to set free a suffering humanity."

Moore was hoping to win based on a recount, but because one was not automatically triggered by a smaller margin of victory, Moore would be required by state law to cover the cost up front and did not have enough remaining in his campaign coffers to do so. In turn, Moore filed a lawsuit attempting to block certification of the results by claiming voter fraud impacted the outcome. The suit was rejected on December 28, and Jones was certified as the winner with 50 percent of the vote to Moore's 48.3 percent, a difference of nearly 22,000 votes. Notably, 22,852 voters opted for write-in candidates, which included Luther Strange, "Neither," and "Anyone Else." Jones won with 96 percent of the black vote and 61 percent of the votes from those under age forty-five, while Moore was more popular in the state's rural areas, but still underperformed Trump in typically Republican strongholds. Jones issued a tweet following the certification, saying his "victory marks a new chapter for our state and the nation" and promising to "work to find common ground with my colleagues on both sides of the aisle . . . to make our country a better place for all."

—Heather Kerrigan

Following is the text of two statements issued by the Democratic Governors Association on their special election victories on November 8, 2017, in Virginia and New Jersey; a December 26, 2017, press release from the Virginia Department of Elections announcing the postponement of the drawing to select a victor in House District 94; and a December 28, 2017, tweet from Doug Jones after his victory in the Alabama Senate race.

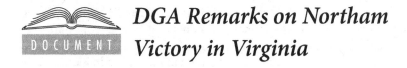

DGA Remarks on Northam Victory in Virginia

November 8, 2017

DGA Chair Governor Dan Malloy (D-CT) issued the following statement on Ralph Northam's victory in Virginia's gubernatorial race:

"Congratulations to Governor-elect Ralph Northam on his victory tonight in Virginia," said Gov. Malloy. "Ralph ran a strong campaign and will continue the economic progress the Commonwealth has made over the last four years under Governor Terry McAuliffe. This was the top race of the year for the DGA and we are excited that Virginia will remain blue for four more years.

"This election sends a clear message to every Republican running in 2018 that the Trump playbook of race-baiting does not work. Ralph Northam had a message of bringing economic opportunity to all Virginians, while Ed Gillespie tried to divide Virginia communities. If Republicans choose to run on the divisive Trump playbook in 2018, they will be rejected by voters."

"This is a major victory for the Democratic Governors Association. The DGA invested $7 million into this campaign and worked hand-in-hand with the Northam campaign on a record-setting GOTV effort. Tonight's gubernatorial sweep of Virginia and New Jersey shows Democrats will be on offense heading into the 2018 races. President Trump's deeply unpopular agenda combined with Republican candidates who refuse stand up to him, have Democrats poised for big gains next year."

SOURCE: Democratic Governors Association. "DGA Statement on Ralph Northam's Victory in VA." November 8, 2017. https://democraticgovernors.org/news/dga-statement-on-ralph-northams-victory-in-va.

DGA on Gubernatorial Victory in New Jersey

November 8, 2017

DGA Chair Governor Dan Malloy (D-CT) issued the following statement on Phil Murphy's victory in New Jersey's gubernatorial race:

"Congratulations to Governor-Elect Phil Murphy. Phil ran an incredible campaign focused on his vision for an economy that works for all Garden State families, and I look forward to working with him.

"The DGA was proud to invest nearly $4 million and play a key role in picking up this critical seat. New Jersey voters made clear that they are ready to turn the page from 8 years of failed policies and failed leadership in New Jersey. This result points to larger problems for Republicans as they play defense in many open-seat races coming up next year.

"Today's election was not just a victory for Governor-Elect Murphy. It was a victory for the nearly 9 million New Jersey residents who will now have a Governor looking out for them: for their education, for their health care, and for their jobs."

Republicans raised and spent significant money in New Jersey despite Phil Murphy's strong performance and polling throughout the campaign. In November 2016, RGA Chairman Scott Walker laid a marker that Republicans expected to compete and win in New Jersey, saying "We think we can do well in both Virginia—where we have a chance for a pickup—and New Jersey in 2017." This September, RGA Chairman Scott Walker and Governor Christie teamed up to host a fundraiser for Kim Guadagno that netted $2.1 million. On top of that, they've spent over $2 million on Guadagno's behalf.

SOURCE: Democratic Governors Association. "DGA Statement on Phil Murphy's Victory in New Jersey." November 8, 2017. https://democraticgovernors.org/news/dga-statement-on-phil-murphys-victory-in-new-jersey.

Virginia Board of Elections Postpones Winner Selection

December 26, 2017

Virginia State Board of Elections Chairman James Alcorn released the following statement:

"After receiving notice of the pending litigation concerning the HD94 election, we have decided to postpone tomorrow's planned drawing. While our planned drawing for tomorrow as in full compliance with the Code of Virginia, neutral election administrators should not be choosing election winners—or influencing the next Speaker of the House. Drawing names is an action of last resort. Any substantive concerns regarding the election or recount should be resolved before a random drawing is conducted. This will best serve the voters of HD94 and the rest of the Commonwealth."

SOURCE: Virginia State Board of Elections. "State Board of Elections Meeting Postponed." December 26, 2017. https://www.elections.virginia.gov/Files/Media/SBENewsAdvisory12-26-17.pdf.

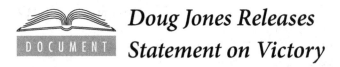

Doug Jones Releases
Statement on Victory

December 28, 2017

Today marks a new day for Alabama and our nation.

"Senate-Elect Doug Jones Statement on the Certification of His Election Victory

Washington D.C.—Today Senator-elect Doug Jones released the following statement in response to the certification of his election victory:

'I am looking forward to going to work for the people of Alabama in the new year,' said Senator-elect Doug Jones. 'As I said on election night, our victory marks a new chapter for our state and the nation. I will be an independent voice and work to find common ground with my colleagues on both sides of the aisle to get Washington back on track and fight to make our country a better place for all.'"

SOURCE: Doug Jones (@DougJones). Twitter post, December 28, 2017. https://twitter.com/DougJones/status/946458464305537024.

OTHER HISTORIC DOCUMENTS OF INTEREST

FROM THIS VOLUME

FROM PREVIOUS *HISTORIC DOCUMENTS*

Zimbabwean Military Announces Bloodless Takeover; Mugabe Resigns; African Union Responds

NOVEMBER 14, 21, AND 24, 2017

Robert Mugabe, the long-time leader of Zimbabwe, stepped down from his position on November 21, 2017, following a bloodless takeover by the nation's military. The president, who was known for both liberating the country from British colonial rule and for violent oppression to secure his power, was replaced by his former vice president, Emmerson Mnangagwa. The interim government was set to rule until mid-2018, at which time it promised to hold democratic elections. In the meantime, the new government began working toward rebuilding the nation's economy, which had suffered significantly under Mugabe.

MUGABE'S STRANGLEHOLD ON POWER

Mugabe was the first head of state in Zimbabwe after the nation gained independence from Great Britain. Although the new president was celebrated for replacing the white minority government and promising greater power for all citizens of Zimbabwe, his reign grew increasingly dictatorial. Mugabe's government quickly became known for corruption, vote rigging, and a brutal crackdown on political opposition. Mugabe also oversaw the near collapse of what was once known as Africa's "breadbasket." The mineral-rich nation that exported large amounts of food and tobacco faced chronic food shortages, staggering inflation, and widespread unemployment. Rather than his own mismanagement, Mugabe frequently blamed international organizations and western governments that had imposed sanctions against the country for Zimbabwe's economic decline. Analysts, however, linked the country's rapid downfall to both corruption at all levels of government and a program of land distribution, which involved taking farmland away from whites to end their dominance in the agricultural sector but which resulted in a further weakening of the food supply.

The 2008 election marked the first time Mugabe faced a serious challenge to his power. The election was marred by violence and controversy surrounding possible vote rigging, but it resulted in a power-sharing agreement between Mugabe's government and the leading opposition party, Movement for Democratic Change. The new government promised to focus first on rebuilding the country's economy and finding a way to provide stable supplies of food, fuel, water, and medicine to the nation's citizens. However, it was unable to agree on the seating of cabinet members as well as a framework for moving forward, and the agreement soon collapsed. Additional attempts at providing the opposition at least some power faltered, and although opposition leader Morgan Tsvangirai remained prime minister until 2013, he had little influence over the direction of the country.

Zimbabwe's Military Seizes Control

The African continent is no stranger to military takeovers and has experienced some 200 coups since the 1960s, few of which took place in the southern portion of the continent and even fewer resulting in a peaceful transfer of power. Despite having been governed for nearly four decades by a dictator who oversaw the crumbling of one of Africa's wealthiest economies, Zimbabwe had experienced few significant moments of unrest. Tensions began brewing, however, in November 2017 when President Mugabe fired Vice President Mnangagwa. Many in the nation viewed this as an attempt by the president to ensure that his wife, Grace, would become the next head of state. At the time of the announcement, Mugabe was the world's oldest leader at age ninety-three and speculation had been rampant about who his successor might be. A statement from Mugabe's office explained that the vice president was fired because he had "consistently and persistently exhibited traits of disloyalty, disrespect, deceitfulness and unreliability."

In response to the vice president's firing, on the evening of November 14, a portion of the Zimbabwe Defence Forces (ZDF) surrounded the presidential palace and took control of the nation's broadcast network. The military denied that its actions amounted to a coup and claimed that the president was safe but that he would not be released, nor would normality be restored, until those in the president's orbit who "are committing crimes that are causing social and economic suffering in the country" were brought "to justice." In a statement, ZDF Major General Sibusiso Busi Moyo explained the military needed "to pacify a degenerating political, social and economic situation in our country which if not addressed may result in a violent conflict." Moyo expressed a desire to "return our country to a dispensation that allows for investment, development and prosperity that we all fought for and for which many of our citizens paid the supreme sacrifice."

Immediately following the announcement, there was relative calm around the country. Protests were slow to break out, businesses and roads were not shuttered, and Zimbabweans generally went about their day-to-day lives. True to their word that the president was unharmed, Mugabe was even temporarily released from house arrest by the military to preside over a graduation ceremony on November 17. However, a few days into the standoff, many citizens began taking to the streets, demanding that their president resign. In the capital, protesters chanted, "He must go," and held signs reading "Mugabe Must Rest Now" and "No to Mugabe Dynasty," a hint to dissatisfaction with the elevation of Grace Mugabe's status. Governments around the world lent their support to the peaceful movement. "Zimbabwe has an opportunity to set itself on a new path, one that must include democratic elections and respect for human rights," said U.S. Secretary of State Rex Tillerson. Britain's foreign secretary, Boris Johnson, called the actions of the military "potentially a moment of hope" for Zimbabwe, while Moussa Faki Mahamat, chair of the African Union Commission, stressed "that it is crucial that the crisis is resolved in a manner that promotes democracy and human rights, as well as the socio-economic development of Zimbabwe."

Mugabe Ousted as Party Leader, Resigns

On November 19, Mugabe's Zimbabwe African National Union-Patriotic Front (ZANU-PF) ousted him as party leader and replaced him with his former vice president. The party set a deadline of November 20 for the president to resign. If he chose not to do so, parliament would convene to begin the cumbersome process of impeachment. Privately, Mugabe was said to be working with allies in the region to negotiate a dignified exit from power rather than being overthrown or impeached. The November 20 deadline came and went with Mugabe still holding on to the last remnants of his presidency, and on November 21, parliament convened to begin impeachment proceedings. The allegations brought before the body in support of impeachment included serious misconduct in office, failure to obey and uphold the constitution, willful violation of the constitution, and an inability to perform the duties required of the office due to physical or mental incapacity.

Eight days into the standoff, on November 21, the speaker of parliament read a letter from Mugabe announcing the president's intent to resign. "My decision to resign is voluntary on my part and arises from my concern for the welfare of the people of Zimbabwe and my desire to ensure a smooth, peaceful and non-violent transfer of power that underpins national security, peace and stability," Mugabe wrote. Zimbabweans quickly took to the streets to celebrate. Mnangagwa, who as the ZANU-PF party leader was Mugabe's assumed successor, said it was his "desire . . . to join all Zimbabweans in a new era . . . so that we rebuild this nation to its full glory. This is not a job for ZANU-PF alone but for all people of Zimbabwe."

International observers and Zimbabwean politicians explained that the relative ease with which Mugabe stepped down was likely carefully calculated to both remain above board with the international community—and specifically regional bodies like the African Union—while also giving credence to those who still view Mugabe as the individual responsible for liberating the nation from British colonial rule. This sentiment was echoed by African Union Commission chair Mahamat, who in a statement released by his office said, "President Mugabe will be remembered as a fearless pan-Africanist liberation fighter, and the father of the independent Zimbabwean nation. Today's decision will go down in history as an act of statesmanship that can only bolster President Mugabe's political legacy."

New Government Takes Shape

On November 23, it was announced that Mugabe and his wife would be granted immunity from prosecution and would be provided safety in Zimbabwe, a further step to ensure the new government could take power peacefully. After nearly four decades under Mugabe, on November 24, Mnangagwa was sworn in as president. In his first address to the nation, the interim president, who would serve the one year remaining in Mugabe's term, promised to pay international debts, help citizens find greater access to cash, revise import restrictions, and compensate farmers who lost their land under Mugabe's rule. "Today we are witnessing the beginning of a new and unfolding democracy," said Mnangagwa, who also offered deference to Mugabe as "a father, mentor, comrade in arms and my leader." Public response to Mnangagwa's assent to the presidency was mixed, with some celebrating him as a liberator while others questioned how much he might diverge from the policies of a man he had dutifully served.

The new government's first order of business, in early December, was to begin reviving the flagging economy. "We want to grow our economy, we want peace, we want jobs, jobs, jobs," Mnangagwa said. Despite vast mineral resources, Zimbabwe had experienced rampant inflation under Mugabe and citizens were, on average, 15 percent poorer in 2017 than they were when he first took power in 1980. The new government proposed tax breaks for local businesses to help them grow in addition to measures intended to re-attract foreign investment that had waned, partly through the revision of the indigenization law that requires Zimbabweans to hold a majority stake in any business operating in the country.

In January 2018, Mnangagwa and his government promised that democratic elections would be held within five months, with the interim president noting they would be "free, credible, fair, and indisputable elections to ensure Zimbabwe engages the world as a qualified democratic state."

—Heather Kerrigan

Following is a statement from November 14, 2017, by the Zimbabwe Defence Forces, announcing their bloodless takeover; the November 21, 2017, text of President Robert Mugabe's resignation letter; a statement by the chairperson of the African Union Commission, on November 21, 2017, welcoming the decision of President Mugabe to step down as president; and Emmerson Mnangagwa's inaugural address given on November 24, 2017.

DOCUMENT   **ZDF Announces Takeover in Zimbabwe**

November 14, 2017

Following the address we made on November 13, 2017, which we believe our main broadcaster, the Zimbabwe Broadcasting Corporation and The Herald were directed not to publicize, the situation in our country has moved to another level. Firstly, we wish to assure the nation that His Excellency the President of the Republic of Zimbabwe, and commander-in-chief of Zimbabwe Defence Forces, Comrade RG Mugabe, and his family are safe and sound and their security is guaranteed.

We are only targeting criminals around him who are committing crimes that are causing social and economic suffering in the country in order to bring them to justice.

As soon as we have accomplished our mission, we expect that the situation will return to normalcy. To the civil servants, as you are aware, there is a plan by the same individuals to influence the current purging that is taking place in the political sphere to the civil service. We are against that act of injustice and we intend to protect every one of you against that.

To the judiciary, the measures underway are intended to assure that as an independent arm of the state you are able to exercise your independent authority without fear of being obstructed as has been the case with this group of individuals.

To our members of parliament, your legislative role is of paramount importance for peace and stability in this country and it is our desire that a dispensation is created that allows you to serve your respective political constituencies according to democratic tenets.

To the generality of the people of Zimbabwe we urge you to remain calm and limit unnecessary movement. However, we encourage those who are employed and those with essential business in the city to continue their normal activities as usual. Our wish is that you enjoy your rights and freedoms and that we return our country to a dispensation that allows for investment, development and prosperity that we all fought for and for which many of our citizens paid the supreme sacrifice.

To political parties we urge you to discourage your members from engaging in violent behavior.

To the youth we call upon you to realize that the future of this country is yours. Do not be enticed with dirty coins of silver. Be disciplined and remain committed to the ethos and values of this great nation.

To all churches and religious organizations in Zimbabwe we call upon you and your congregations to pray for our country and preach the gospel of love, peace, unity and development.

To both our people and the world beyond our borders, we wish to make it abundantly clear that this is not a military takeover of government. What the Zimbabwe Defence Forces is actually doing is to pacify a degenerating political, social and economic situation in our country, which if not addressed may result in a violent conflict.

We call upon all the war veterans to play positive in ensuring peace, stability and unity in the country.

To members of the defense forces, all leave is canceled and you are all to return to your barracks with immediate effect.

To our respected traditional leaders, you are our custodians of our culture, customs, traditions and heritage and we request you to provide leadership and direction to your communities for the sake of unity and development in our country.

To the other Security Services: We urge you to cooperate for the good of our country. Let it be clear that we intend to address the human security threats in our country. Therefore any provocation will be met with an appropriate response.

To the media, we urge you report fairly and responsibly.

Thank you.

SOURCE: Zimbabwe Defence Forces. Military Statement. November 14, 2017.

Mugabe Resigns as President of Zimbabwe

November 21, 2017

NOTICE OF RESIGNATION AS PRESIDENT OF THE REPUBLIC OF ZIMBABWE

In terms of the provisions of Section 96, Sub-Section 1, of the Constitution of Zimbabwe, amendment number 20, 2013.

Following my verbal communication with the Speaker of the National Assembly, Advocate Jacob Mudenda at 13:53 hours, 21st November, 2017 intimating my intention to resign as the President of the Republic of Zimbabwe, I, Robert Gabriel Mugabe, in terms of Section 96, Sub-Section 1 of the Constitution of Zimbabwe, hereby formally tender my resignation as the President of the Republic of Zimbabwe with immediate effect.

My decision to resign is voluntary on my part and arises from my concern for the welfare of the people of Zimbabwe and my desire to ensure a smooth, peaceful and non-violent transfer of power that underpins national security, peace and stability.

Kindly give public notice of my resignation as soon as possible as required by Section 96, Sub-Section 1 of the Constitution of Zimbabwe.

Yours faithfully,
Robert Gabriel Mugabe, President of the Republic of Zimbabwe.

SOURCE: Parliament of Zimbabwe. "Notice of Resignation as President of the Republic of Zimbabwe." November 21, 2017.

DOCUMENT
African Union Chairperson Welcomes Peaceful Resolution in Zimbabwe

November 21, 2017

The Chairperson of the African Union Commission, Moussa Faki Mahamat, welcomes the decision by President Robert Mugabe to step down from his position as Head of State following a lifetime of service to the Zimbabwean nation.

President Mugabe will be remembered as a fearless pan-Africanist liberation fighter, and the father of the independent Zimbabwean nation. Today's decision will go down in history as an act of statesmanship that can only bolster President Mugabe's political legacy.

The African Union recognizes that the Zimbabwean people have expressed their will that there should be a peaceful transfer of power in a manner that secures the democratic future of their country. President Mugabe's decision to resign paves the way for a transition process, owned and led by the sovereign people of Zimbabwe.

Throughout the years, the people of Zimbabwe have demonstrated remarkable resilience and resourcefulness, and commitment to their country. The Chairperson of the Commission is confident that they, together with all their leaders, will remain steadfast in their commitment to fulfill their legitimate aspirations.

The African Union looks forward to Zimbabwe continuing to play a leading role in the affairs of the African continent, as a democratic and prosperous state meeting the aspirations of its people.

The Chairperson of the Commission, recalling the relevant African Union instruments, including the African Charter on Democracy, Elections and Governance, pledges the Union's full support to the Zimbabwean people and leaders in the period ahead. In this respect, the African Union will continue to work closely with the Southern African Development Community, the efforts and commitment of which it hails.

SOURCE: African Union. "Statement of the Chairperson of the Commission of the African Union on the Situation in Zimbabwe." November 21, 2017. https://au.int/sites/default/files/pressreleases/33382-pr-statement_of_the_chairperson_of_the_commission_of_the_african_union_on_the_situation_in_zimbabwe_.pdf.

Mnangagwa Delivers
Inaugural Address

November 24, 2017

Fellow countrymen, I feel deeply humbled by the decision of my Party, Zanu-PF, inviting me to serve our great Nation, the Republic of Zimbabwe, in the capacity of President and Commander-in-Chief of the Zimbabwe Defence Forces, with effect from today.

I admit that I hold no particularly unique qualifications that sets apart from the deep pool of able citizens of our Party and Land, who otherwise could have been chosen to occupy this onerous office. But even as I make constant reference to my Party, Zanu-PF, I am not oblivious of the many Zimbabweans from across the political, ethnic and racial divide who have helped make this day and who thus have legitimate expectations from the office I now occupy. The decision of my Party is merely for purposes of political identification, as I intend, nay am required to serve our country as the President of all citizens regardless of colour, creed, religion, tribe, totem or political affiliation.

Let me at this stage pay special tribute to one of, and the only surviving father of our Nation, Cde Robert Gabriel Mugabe. He led us in our struggle for National Independence, and assumed responsibilities of leadership at the formative and very challenging time in the birth of our Nation. That is to be lauded and celebrated for all times.

Whatever errors of commission or omission that might have occurred during that critical phase in the life of our Nation, let us all accept and acknowledge his immense contribution towards the building of our Nation.

To me personally, he remains a father, mentor, comrade-in-arms and my leader. We thus say thank you to him and trust that our history will grant him his proper place and accord him his deserved stature as one of the founders and leaders of our nation.

Let me also recognise in a very special way the presence in our midst of senior statesmen of our region and continent, led by His Excellency former President Kenneth Kaunda of Zambia.

He remains the only living member of the foundational Frontline States grouping which is synonymous with the decolonisation processes in our Southern African region.

We honour him, as indeed we remember all his colleagues now departed. The statesmen who are with us today show a story of succession which speaks well of our continent. It is a narrative that must get bolder and bolder as generations hand over to succeeding ones, all in amity.

In acknowledging the honour you have bestowed upon me, I recognise that the urgent tasks that beckon will not be accomplished through speeches, necessary as these may be.

I have to hit the ground running to make sure that I lead in stupendous efforts we all need to summon and unleash in concert, towards taking this Great Nation beyond where our immediate past President left it.

For close to two decades now, this country went through many developments. While we cannot change the past, there is a lot we can do in the present and future to give our Nation a different, positive direction.

As we do so, we should never remain hostages to our past. I thus humbly appeal to all of us that we let bygones be bygones, readily embracing each other in defining a new destiny. The task at hand is that of rebuilding our great country. It principally lies with none but ourselves.

I implore you all to declare that NEVER AGAIN should the circumstances that have put Zimbabwe in an unfavourable position be allowed to recur or overshadow its prospects. We must work together, you, me, all of us who make up this Nation.

Ours is a great country, endowed with rich resources and abounding in many opportunities for everyone who considers it home. Whilst I am aware that emotions and expectations might be high and mixed, I have no doubt that over time, we will appreciate the solid foundation laid by my predecessor, against all manner of vicissitudes, towards building an educated, enlightened, skilled and forgiving society.

This is a formidable head-start we draw from our past, a plinth upon which to build developments in the present and to erect hopes for the future.

Fellow Zimbabweans, as we chart our way forward, we must accept that our challenges as a nation emanate in part from the manner in which we have managed our politics, both nationally and internationally, leading to circumstances in which our country has undeservedly been perceived or classified as a pariah State.

However, given our historical realities, we wish the rest of the world to understand and appreciate that policies and programmes related to land reform were inevitable.

Whilst there is a lot we may need to do by way of outcomes, the principle of repossessing our land cannot be challenged or reversed. Dispossession of our ancestral land was the fundamental reason for waging the liberation struggle. It would be a betrayal of the brave men and women who sacrificed their lives in our liberation struggle if we were to reverse the gains we have made in reclaiming our land.

Therefore, I exhort beneficiaries of the Land Reform Programme to show their deservedness by demonstrating commitment to the utilisation of the land now available to them for National Food Security and for the recovery of our economy.

They must take advantage of programmes that my Government shall continue to avail to ensure that all land is utilized optimally. To that end, my Government will capacitate the Land Commission so that the Commission is seized with all outstanding issues related to land redistribution.

My Government is committed to compensating those farmers from whom land was taken, in terms of the laws of the land. As we go into the future, complex issues of land tenure will have to be addressed both urgently and definitely, in order to ensure finality and closure to the ownership and management of this key resource which is central to national stability and to sustained economic recovery. We dare not prevaricate on this key issue.

Events leading to this historic day attest to the fact that we are a unique Nation, one which is clear about what it wants as well as what it does not want.

Ordinarily, many nations, including those in the developed world, would not have ended with the sort of outcome we celebrate today. Credit goes to every Zimbabwean and my predecessor who invested a lot towards a peaceful resolution of the challenges of the situation that had risen.

From events preceding this occasion, we stand apart as a unique nation driven by impulses of mutual tolerance, peace and unity which we have displayed in the past few weeks not withstanding our diverse political persuasions. This is a wonder to the world, indeed a proud page we have added to the science of conflict resolution and settlement. That peace and harmony should be characteristic of how we relate to one another before, during and after the 2018 harmonised elections which will be held as scheduled.

Today the Republic of Zimbabwe renews itself. My Government will work towards ensuring that the pillars of the State assuring democracy in our land are strengthened and respected. We fully reaffirm our membership to the family of nations, and express our commitment to playing our part in all regional, continental and international organisations and arrangements in order to make our modest contribution towards a prosperous and peaceful world order. We subscribe and affirm the principle where all nations of the world are equal and sovereign partners working towards the maintenance of world peace as collectively cherished under the United Nations Charter.

Here at home, we must, however, appreciate the fact that over the years, our domestic politics had become poisoned, rancorous and polarizing. My goal is to preside over a polity and run an administration that recognise strength in our diversity as a people, hoping that this position and well-meant stance will be reciprocated and radiated to cover all our groups, organisation and communities. We dare not squander the moment. At the end of the day, whatever we do or chose not to do must be intended to benefit all our people.

Above all, we must always remember and realize that we hold and run this country in trust. It belongs to future generations whose possibilities must never be foreclosed or mortgaged as a result of decisions of expediency we might selfishly make today out of fear of difficult choice and decision that have to be made.

The values of Unity and Peace cherished by all Zimbabweans are the enduring foundations for the desired goal of development, itself the third pillar of the trinity of Unity, Peace and Development espoused by my Party, ZANU PF.

Our Economic Policy will be predicated on our Agriculture which is the mainstay, and on creating conditions for an Investment-led economic recovery that puts a premium on job-creation. Key choices will have to be made to attract Foreign Direct Investment to tackle high levels of unemployment while transforming our Economy towards the tertiary.

The many skilled Zimbabweans who have left the country over the years for a variety of reasons must now come into the broad economic calculus designed for our recovery and take off. Of course, the physical and social infrastructure must be repaired and expanded to position our country in readiness for economic growth, employment creation, equity, freedom and democracy, and for the provision of vital social goods, principally health, shelter, clean water, education and other key social services.

Our quest for economic development must be premised on our timeless goal to establish and sustain a just and equitable society firmly based on our historical, cultural and social experience, as well as on our aspirations for better lives for all our people.

Our system of economic organisation and management will incorporate elements of market economy in which enterprise is encouraged, protected and allowed just and merited rewards, while gainfully interacting with strategic public enterprises run professionally and profitably, all to yield a properly run national economy in which there is room and scope for everyone.

The fabulous natural resources we have as a country must now be exploited for national good through mutually gainful partnerships with international investors whose presence in our midst must be valued and secured. The bottom line is an economy which is back on its feet, and in which a variety of players make choices and fulfil roles without doubts and in an environment shorn of fickle policy shifts and unpredictability.

Only that way can we recover this economy, create jobs for our youths and reduce poverty for all our people who must witness real, positive changes in their lives.

In the immediate, the liquidity challenges which have bedevilled the economy must be tackled head on, with real solutions being generated as a matter of urgency. People must be able to access their earnings and savings as and when they need them.

As we focus on recovering our economy, we must shed misbehaviours and acts of indiscipline which have characterised the past. Acts of corruption must stop forthwith. Where these occur swift justice must be served to show each and all that crime and other acts of economic sabotage can only guarantee ruin to perpetrators. We have to aspire to be a clean nation, one sworn to high moral standards and deserved rewards.

On these ideals, my administration declares full commitment, warning that grief awaits those who depart from the path of virtue and clean business. To our civil servants, it cannot be business as usual. You now have to roll up your sleeves in readiness to deliver.

We have an economy to recover, a people to serve. Each and every one of us must now earn their hour, day, week and month at work. Gone are the days of absenteeism and desultory application, days of unduly delaying and forestalling decisions and services in the hope of extorting dirty rewards. That will have to stop.

A new culture must now inform and animate our daily conduct. Our offices must speedily answer questions and generate solutions awaited by our customers, be they our citizens or well-meaning outsiders who want to join in the recovery of our economy. Flexibility must be built into our operations so the machine of Government does not become one huge, ponderous stumbling block to decisions that must be made and communicated expeditiously. The culture in Government just has to change, unseating those little "gods" idly sitting in public offices, for a busy, empathetic civil service that Zimbabwe surely deserves.

Recognising the pivotal role that exports play in generating the much needed foreign currency, Government will ensure relaxation of export procedures, while vigorously ensuring the reduction of all costs associated with the conduct of international trade. The establishment of Special Economic Zones (SEZ) will be accelerated in the order to attract investment and generate increased exports.

The maintenance of economic stability and confidence amongst the transacting public, the local business community and foreign investors remains key to our reform agenda. To this end, Government will ensure financial sector viability and stability as well as put in place measures that encourage savings through bank deposit and other appropriate financial instruments which bring fair rewards to depositors. The current banking culture where costs are levied on depositors must come to an end. It contradicts the reasons at the heart of banking as a business.

To reduce the high country risk perception among existing and prospective investors, Government will henceforth ensure that its domestic and external debt obligations are serviced to the satisfaction of its lenders and creditors. This will apply to the whole of Government including Local Authorities and State Owned Enterprises.

In addition, my Government will also proactively curb externalisation of foreign currency and smuggling of goods. The country's border management and control systems will be strengthened.

I intend to approach security issues from a broad human, physical and social perspective. All citizens must feel secure and enjoy a sense of belonging in the Land. All activities that the national security institutions aim to achieve must be focused on overall human security from disease, hunger, unemployment, illiteracy and extreme poverty.

This shall necessarily entail that we pay equal attention to all these areas over and above enhancing the capabilities of our Security Services so that they are able to deal decisively with any and all threats, whether existing or emerging. These include threats to our vital economic interests and objectives.

Today the Republic of Zimbabwe enters the second phase of its birth. We emerge to fully affirm our belonging to the family of nations. We harbour no ill and belligerent intentions against any other nation. The Southern African Development Community, SADC, is our home; we founded it from its beginning we re-commit ourselves to furthering its vision and ideals. There can never be any doubt to our intensions to SADC, itself the fount of our foreign policy.

As we journey outward from our SADC house, we fully realise that we belong in the bigger house and family, the African Union. Whilst we were not free at the birth of OAU which championed the total liberation of the entire African continent from colonialism, we were creatures of sterling efforts of the OAU through its Liberation Committee which was based in the sister Republic of Tanzania, and of course through the Frontline States which hosted and coordinated the liberation struggles in Southern Africa, including our own in Zimbabwe.

The African Union, itself the sequel to the OAU, is our natural home and collective resource as Africans. Zimbabwe pledges its untrammelled membership, and declares here and now that it will play its role fully to make a success of the AU and all its programmes. An important subset of the AU is the COMESA economic group of nations. There we are committed to contributing meaningfully to the realisation of the AU Agenda 2063.

Zimbabwe's journey since independence, has provided us with many lessons, some bigger and others so pleasant. In particular, some bigger nations have attempted to make us bend to their dictates, working feverishly to confine us to the pariah status. We have successfully maintained good relations with the preponderant majority of the family of nations. In truth, we never deserved to be maligned and/or economically and politically mistreated. I stand here today, to say that our country is already for a sturdy re-engagement programme with all the nations of the world.

As we bear no malice towards any nation, we ask those who have punished us in the past to consider their economic and political sanctions against us. Whatever misunderstandings may have subsisted in the past, let these make way to new beginning which sees us relating to one another in multi-layered, mutually beneficial ways as equal and reciprocally dependent partners. In this global world, no nation is, can or need be an island, one unto itself. Isolation has never been splendid or viable; solidarity and partnership are and will always be the way.

We are ready to embrace each and all, on principles of mutual respect and common humanity. We will take definite steps to re-engage those Nations who have had issues with us in the past. Equally, we will take measures to ensure that we acknowledge and begin to show commitments towards settling our debts. Of course our resources remain sparse, especially at this stage when we face a myriad of pressures, but we count on the goodwill of those we owe to give us a chance. We remain committed to honouring the debts and to enter into new relationships.

Above all, all foreign investments will be safe in our country and, we will fully abide by the terms of Bilateral Investment Promotion and Protection Agreements which we have concluded with a number of nations. I ask you to join us in exploiting our potential to make a difference in the lives of our people.

The United Nations is the home of all the nations on this planet. We will contribute to the overall thinking and management of world affairs. Our plain talk arises from our deep convictions and desire to help build world peace. These should never be mistaken for ill-will.

We join the rest of the continent in calling for reforms in the UN system so the world body becomes truly representatives and thus commands universal respect. Zimbabwe will continue to contribute to the international peace and security, urging for the granting of full statehood and freedoms to the Palestinian and Saharawi people. Let us together, honestly address the sources of instabilities and terrorism in many parts of the world, all within the framework of, and under the banner of the United Nations.

I wish to thank all of you here and elsewhere, who wished us a peaceful transition, even as this nearly seemed doubtful. For the time that I shall be President of Zimbabwe, I solemnly promise that I shall to the best of my ability serve everyone who calls or considers Zimbabwe as their home. I encourage all of us to remain peaceful, even as preparations for political contestations for the next year's harmonised elections gather momentum. The task before us is much bigger than competing for political office. Let us all play our part to rebuild this great country.

May God bless our Land and our Nation.

I thank you.

SOURCE: Government of Zimbabwe. "Inaugural Address of Emmerson Mnangagwa." November 24, 2017. http://www.zim.gov.zw/live-cde-mnangagwa-sworn-zimbabwe%E2%80%99s-new-president.

OTHER HISTORIC DOCUMENTS OF INTEREST

FROM PREVIOUS *HISTORIC DOCUMENTS*

U.S. Department of Justice Sues to Block AT&T and Time Warner Merger

NOVEMBER 20, 2017

AT&T is the world's largest telecommunications company and one of the country's largest providers of mobile phones, landline telephone services, and home Internet service. Additionally, through its recent acquisition of DirecTV, it is now one of the largest pay TV companies in the United States. Time Warner, through its ownership of HBO, Warner Brothers, and Turner Broadcasting, is one of the country's largest producers of media content. On October 22, 2016, AT&T announced that it had agreed to buy Time Warner for $108 billion (including the acquisition of Time Warner debt) in one of the largest transactions in American history. More than a year later, the two companies were no closer to completing the merger and found themselves involved in a highly unusual court battle with the Department of Justice (DOJ). On November 20, 2017, the government formally moved to block the merger by filing a civil antitrust lawsuit in federal district court. AT&T in turn vowed to fight the case in court and asked for an expedited trial. The case is set to begin in March 2018.

ANTITRUST AND THE DEPARTMENT OF JUSTICE

The DOJ is responsible for enforcing the Clayton Act, Section 7 of which prohibits mergers if "the effect of such acquisition may be substantially to lessen competition." According to the DOJ's mission statement, the goal of its antitrust law enforcement "is to protect economic freedom and opportunity by promoting free and fair competition in the marketplace." Competition, the statement explains, benefits consumers by lowering prices, improving quality of products, and available consumer choices. Generally, corporate mergers fall into two broad categories: horizontal and vertical. Most of the DOJ litigation in the past forty years have concerned horizontal mergers in which one company buys out a competitor in the same industry, thus reducing competition in that industry. By contrast, a vertical merger involves two or more companies operating at different levels of production of the same product. The risk to competition is much less clear in vertical mergers, and the government must prove that the merged companies would enjoy sufficient market power to raise antitrust concerns. The federal government has not gone to trial to block a vertical merger since a case involving the trucking industry in 1979, a case the government lost.

The AT&T–Time Warner deal was a classic vertical merger. Time Warner provides media content, and AT&T provides distribution. For the past few decades, previous administrations have generally approved such vertical mergers after, if necessary, imposing numerous behavioral conditions on the approval. For example, in 2011, in the merger that in many ways most resembled the AT&T–Time Warner merger, the DOJ approved Comcast's acquisition of NBC Universal after imposing more than 150 restrictions on the resulting company, most aimed at preventing it from damaging online rivals. AT&T and Time Warner anticipated a similar path to their merger, particularly after conservative law professor, Makan Delrahim, responded to an interview question about the merger by saying, "I don't see this as a major antitrust problem."

Following the presidential election, Delrahim was appointed head of the DOJ's Antitrust Division and described a different approach to antitrust from that of previous administrations. In his view, placing behavior conditions on mergers is less effective than structural remedies such as requiring parties to a merger to sell off businesses before gaining DOJ approval. Imposing behavioral conditions on a merger, he stated, effectively impose "ongoing government oversight on what should preferably be a free market." Delrahim changed his previous stated position on the AT&T–Time Warner deal and, instead, told the companies that he would not accept the kind of commitments relied on in the Comcast–NBC Universal merger to limit the anticompetitive impact of their merger. Instead, he wanted AT&T–Time Warner to agree to sell off assets, specifically to divest of Turner Broadcasting or DirecTV. In response, AT&T CEO Randall Stephenson stated that "[a]ny agreement that results in us forfeiting control of CNN . . . is a non-starter."

DOJ Sues to Block the Merger: Parties Differ on View of Media Marketplace

On November 20, 2017, the Justice Department sued in federal district court to block AT&T's bid to acquire Time Warner. "This merger would greatly harm American consumers," said Delrahim in a released statement. "It would mean higher monthly television bills and fewer of the new, emerging innovative options that consumers are beginning to enjoy." Moreover, "absent an adequate remedy that would fully prevent the harms this merger would cause," he stated that "the only appropriate action for the Department of Justice is to seek an injunction from a federal judge blocking the entire transaction." Stephenson said the DOJ's action "defies logic, and it's unprecedented." The case was assigned to U.S. District Court Judge Richard Leon, appointed by former president George W. Bush, who was the same federal judge who approved Comcast/NBC Universal merger in 2011.

The complaint described a marketplace with "few options for traditional subscription television" and American consumers who pay "higher prices year after year." This lack of competition leads to "huge profit margins" for "traditional video distributors." If the merger of AT&T and Time Warner was allowed, the complaint alleged, it would hurt consumers in three ways. First, "the merged company would have the power to make its video distributor rivals less competitive by raising their costs, resulting in even higher monthly bills for American families." The merged company could extract higher rates for HBO, Turner's networks, and sports offerings from its competing distributors, knowing that if those competitors refuse to pay the new higher prices, any customers who leave as a result, would likely go to the merged company. Second, according to the complaint, it "would enable the merged firm to hinder the growth of online distributors that it views as a threat to the traditional pay-TV model." The complaint explains this count by describing virtual multichannel distributors such as Sling TV that employ a similar business model to traditional distributors but do so over the Internet. They too could be hurt if the merged company raised prices for Turner and HBO programming. Finally, the complaint alleges that, after the merger, "the merged company and just three other companies would control a large portion of all three levels of the industry: television studio revenue, network revenue and distribution revenue." This would increase the likelihood of oligopolistic coordination among these major players. For these reasons, the government sought to prevent the merger, whose effect, it alleged "may be substantially to lessen competition," in violation of law.

In its legal response to the government's filing of the lawsuit, AT&T described a dramatically different marketplace from the one noted in the complaint, one that is "intensely competitive and rapidly changing" and has, in just the last few years, radically and irreversibly altered the way Americans watch television. It focused on competition that is hardly even mentioned in the government's complaint. "With over 100 million global subscribers, Netflix plans to spend $17 billion on streaming content over the upcoming years. Apple, Google, and Facebook, with billions of users and a combined market capitalization of more than two trillion dollars, are likewise investing billions of dollars in their own video offerings. Hulu has 47 million unique viewers, Amazon will spend $4.5 billion on content this year alone, Snapchat has partnered with NBC for the 2018 Olympics, and even Twitter has streamed live NFL games." If AT&T and Time Warner merged, they argued, the merged company would not be able to squash this competition by raising prices for its content. By way of example, they referenced Google's YouTubeTV service, which launched as an alternative to traditional pay TV services but did not include any Time Warner networks. This fact, AT&T argued, "confirms not only that the television ecosystem is awash in content, but that Time Warner's networks are not, in any antitrust sense of the word, essential to attracting and retaining subscribers."

In a Forbes article, Larry Downes added a few other facts to support the argument that the industry was in the process of widespread transformation. For example, YouTube viewership is now at one billion hours a month, almost the same as television; Amazon Video, Hulu, and Netflix account for a third of Emmy nominations in 2017; preference for watching video on television has plunged to 23 percent in the United States; and more than two thousand self-produced YouTube channels have over one million subscribers, some have tens of millions.

AT&T argued that its vertical combination with the content of Time Warner "is necessary to allow the combined company to keep pace in an environment where cable is the incumbent market leader and viewer preferences are rapidly tilting towards the direct-to-consumer platforms of Netflix, Google, Amazon Prime, Facebook, Apple, Hulu, and others. In seeking to block this merger, then, the Government is not only departing from established antitrust precedent, but is also shielding rivals from new competition that would greatly benefit consumers."

ALLEGATIONS OF WHITE HOUSE INTERFERENCE

Many questioned whether there was any political interference from the White House that influenced the DOJ to block the merger, an assertion Stephenson called "the elephant in the room." The DOJ and the White House denied any such influence. But the theory that the suit is punishment for CNN's political coverage has sprung from President Trump's very public and ongoing derision of CNN as "fake news" and his multiple tweets criticizing their coverage of his administration. Days before the DOJ sued to block the merger, President Trump tweeted, "While in the Philippines I was forced to watch @CNN, which I have not done in months, and again realized how bad, and FAKE, it is. Loser!" These tweets could be cited during the trial as circumstantial evidence that politics motivated the government's position.

In the discovery phase of the lawsuit, AT&T's lawyers took the highly unusual steps of requesting the Trump administration's communication logs containing records of communications with top DOJ officials regarding the merger, and they added Assistant Attorney General Delrahim to their witness list. The government asked the judge to block this entire line of defense, describing it as "not true" and likely to "create a side show during the trial." On February 20, 2018, the judge ruled for the government. Judge Leon held that AT&T had not sufficiently proven its "selective enforcement" argument that it had been unfairly targeted partly because of the president's unhappiness with CNN's coverage and would not, therefore, be able to demand the White House communications logs.

REACTION TO THE DOJ LEGAL ACTION

Reaction to the government's suit among legal scholars and advocates was mixed. Gene Kimmelman, president of Public Knowledge, a consumer advocacy group, said, "It may be one of the most important antitrust battles of modern times." He had testified before Congress against the merger and issued a statement supporting the DOJ's case against the merger. "Although there is some controversy over the political environment surrounding the transaction, media consolidation in general and this transaction in particular is not in the interest of the American public," he said. "The Department of Justice has drawn a line in the sand against this violation of the Clayton Act, and we believe the courts will side with the government by preventing further media consolidation that drives up prices for consumers and undermines the competitive marketplace of ideas." Ryan Radia, a legal and regulatory expert at the Competitive Enterprise Institute, a nonprofit libertarian think-tank, supported the merger, saying, "Under established antitrust principles, the government will have a difficult time showing a court that the deal is likely to harm consumers."

—Melissa Feinberg

Following is a statement from the Department of Justice on November 20, 2017, announcing a lawsuit to block AT&T's acquisition of Time Warner; and excerpts from the DOJ's complaint, also on November 20, 2017.

DOCUMENT

DOJ Announces Attempt to Block AT&T–Time Warner Merger

November 20, 2017

The United States Department of Justice today filed a civil antitrust lawsuit to block AT&T/DirecTV's proposed acquisition of Time Warner Inc. The $108 billion acquisition would substantially lessen competition, resulting in higher prices and less innovation for millions of Americans.

The combination of AT&T/DirecTV's vast video distribution infrastructure and Time Warner's popular television programming would be one of the largest mergers in American history. Time Warner's network offerings include TBS, TNT, CNN, Cartoon Network, HBO and Cinemax, and its programming includes Game of Thrones, NCAA's March Madness, and substantial numbers of MLB and NBA regular season and playoff games.

According to the complaint, which was filed in the United States District Court for the District of Columbia, the combined company would use its control over Time Warner's valuable and highly popular networks to hinder its rivals by forcing them to pay hundreds of millions of dollars more per year for the right to distribute those networks. The combined company would also use its increased power to slow the industry's transition to new and exciting video distribution models that provide greater choice for consumers, resulting in fewer innovative offerings and higher bills for American families.

As AT&T itself has expressly acknowledged, distributors with control over popular programming "have the incentive and ability to use . . . that control as a weapon to hinder competition." And, as DirecTV itself has explained, such vertically integrated programmers "can much more credibly threaten to withhold programming from rival [distributors]" and can "use such threats to demand higher prices and more favorable terms." This merger would create just such a vertically integrated programmer and cause precisely such harms to competition.

"This merger would greatly harm American consumers. It would mean higher monthly television bills and fewer of the new, emerging innovative options that consumers are beginning to enjoy," said Assistant Attorney General Makan Delrahim of the Department's Antitrust Division. "AT&T/DirecTV's combination with Time Warner is unlawful, and absent an adequate remedy that would fully prevent the harms this merger would cause, the only appropriate action for the Department of Justice is to seek an injunction from a federal judge blocking the entire transaction."

"The merger would also enable the merged company to impede disruptive competition from online video distributors, competition that has allowed consumers greater choices at cheaper prices," Delrahim further explained. As noted in the complaint, AT&T/DirecTV describes the traditional, big bundle pay-TV model as a "cash cow" and "the golden goose." If permitted to merge, AT&T/DirecTV/Time Warner would have the incentive and ability to charge more for Time Warner's popular networks and take other actions to discourage future competitors from entering the marketplace altogether. For example, the merged firm would likely use its control of Time Warner's programming, which is important for emerging online video distributors, to hinder those innovative distributors. Indeed, a senior Time Warner executive has stated that they have leverage over an online video distributor, whose offering would be "[expletive] without Turner." That leverage would only increase if the merger were allowed to proceed.

AT&T Inc. is a Delaware corporation headquartered in Dallas, Texas. In 2016, the company posted revenues of more than $163 billion dollars, making it the largest telecommunications company in the world. AT&T is also the country's largest Multichannel Video Programming Distributor (MVPD), with more than 25 million subscribers. It has three pay-TV offerings: (1) DirecTV, a satellite-based product with almost 21 million subscribers that it acquired through a merger in 2015; (2) U-Verse, a product which uses the local AT&T fiber optic and copper network and has almost 4 million subscribers; and (3) DirecTV Now, its new online video product with almost 800,000 subscribers. It descends from the AT&T that was established in the nineteenth century and which maintained a monopoly in the provision of local telephone services until 1982, when it agreed to divest the portions of its business relating to local telephone services to settle an antitrust lawsuit filed by the Department of Justice. In 2011, AT&T attempted to purchase T-Mobile, but abandoned the transaction after the Department of Justice filed suit alleging that the merger violated the antitrust laws.

Time Warner, Inc. is a Delaware corporation headquartered in New York, New York. In 2016, its posted revenue was $29.3 billion. As of 2016, according to Time Warner, its most popular networks reach over 90 million households—of the nearly 100 million households that subscribe to traditional subscription television.

SOURCE: U.S. Justice Department. "Justice Department Challenges AT&T/DirecTV's Acquisition of Time Warner." November 20, 2017. https://www.justice.gov/opa/pr/justice-department-challenges-attdirectv-s-acquisition-time-warner.

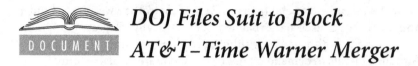

DOJ Files Suit to Block AT&T–Time Warner Merger

November 20, 2017

[All footnotes have been omitted.]

UNITED STATES DISTRICT COURT
FOR THE DISTRICT OF COLUMBIA

UNITED STATES OF AMERICA

450 Fifth Street, NW Washington, DC 20530;

Plaintiff,

v.

AT&T INC.
208 South Akard Street,
Dallas, TX 75202;

DIRECTV GROUP HOLDINGS, LLC
2260 E. Imperial Hwy,
El Segundo, CA 90245; and

TIME WARNER INC.
One Time Warner Center,
New York, NY 10019;

Defendants.

COMPLAINT

AT&T/DirecTV is the nation's largest distributor of traditional subscription television. Time Warner owns many of the country's top TV networks, including TNT, TBS, CNN, and HBO. In this proposed $108 billion transaction—one of the largest in American history—AT&T seeks to acquire control of Time Warner and its popular TV programming. As AT&T has expressly recognized, however, distributors that control popular programming "have the incentive and ability to use (and indeed have used whenever and wherever they can) that control as a weapon to hinder competition." Specifically, as DirecTV has explained, such vertically integrated programmers "can much more credibly threaten to withhold programming from rival [distributors]" and can "use such threats to demand higher prices and more favorable terms." Accordingly, were this merger allowed to proceed, the newly combined firm likely would—just as AT&T/DirecTV has already predicted—use its control of Time Warner's popular programming as a weapon to harm competition. AT&T/DirecTV would hinder its rivals by forcing them to pay hundreds of millions of dollars more per year for Time Warner's networks, and it would use its increased power to slow the industry's transition to new and exciting video distribution models that provide greater choice for consumers. The proposed merger would result in fewer innovative offerings and higher bills for American families.

For these reasons and those set forth below, the United States of America brings this civil action to prevent AT&T from acquiring Time Warner in a transaction whose effect "may be substantially to lessen competition" in violation of Section 7 of the Clayton Act, 15 U.S.C. § 18.

I. INTRODUCTION

1. American consumers have few options for traditional subscription television. For the nearly one hundred million American households that pay a monthly bill to traditional video distributors (cable, satellite, and telephone companies), this means paying higher prices year after year and waiting on hold to hear why a service technician is running late or why their monthly bill has skyrocketed. For traditional video distributors, this lack of competition means huge profit margins. Indeed, AT&T/DirecTV describes the traditional pay-TV model as a "cash cow" and "the golden goose."

2. In many industries, online distribution has enhanced consumer welfare by enabling disruptive entry. In an effort to challenge the traditional subscription television model, online video distributors are emerging and increasingly are a welcome option for consumers. Some consumers subscribe to an online video service like Netflix or Amazon Prime, often in addition to their traditional TV subscription. And a small but growing minority of consumers are replacing their traditional television subscription altogether with new choices of online services like Sling TV, which generally offer American consumers packages with fewer channels than a typical cable or satellite bundle, but at more affordable prices and without long-term commitments. As these online services improve and expand, they bring increasing competition to traditional video distributors—competition that benefits consumers, but which AT&T/DirecTV fears will disrupt the industry and deteriorate its high profit margins.

3. If allowed to proceed, this merger will harm consumers by substantially lessening competition among traditional video distributors and slowing emerging online competition. After the merger, the merged company would have the power to make its video distributor rivals less competitive by raising their costs, resulting in even higher monthly bills for American families. The merger also would enable the merged firm to hinder the growth of online distributors that it views as a threat to the traditional pay-TV model. As AT&T/DirecTV's strategic merger documents state, after the merger, disruption need not occur immediately—the

merged firm can "operate [its] pay-TV business as a 'cash cow' while slowly pivoting to new models."

4. *First*, the merger would result in higher prices for consumers of traditional subscription television because it would give the merged company the power to raise the prices that competing video distributors pay to it for Time Warner's popular TV networks for no reason other than that those networks would now be owned by AT&T/DirecTV. Time Warner's networks are some of the most valuable in the country. As Time Warner has told its shareholders, its Turner networks include three of the top five basic cable networks; Turner also has one of the top news networks. And HBO is the "[w]orld's leading premium pay TV brand." Time Warner's networks own the rights to hit shows such as *Game of Thrones*, as well as the current and future rights to "marquee sports programming," including NCAA March Madness, substantial numbers of regular season and playoff games of Major League Baseball and the NBA, as well as the PGA Championship. AT&T has concluded that Time Warner's networks have "world-class ability to attract and sustain audiences with premium content." Because these popular networks drive ratings and attract customers, video distributors consider it extremely important to carry them. As Time Warner stated in its Annual Report for 2016, its most popular Turner networks reach over 91 million households—of the nearly 100 million households with traditional video distribution subscriptions. Time Warner's own internal documents note the "high proportion of 'must carry' networks" in its Turner portfolio, which "are a critical component of the basic cable bundle."

5. Nonetheless, there is currently a limit to what video distributors will agree to pay Time Warner for its Turner networks. If, in negotiations, Time Warner seeks too high a price for the Turner TV networks, the video distributor across the table may walk away. Without a deal, Time Warner loses monthly payments from the video distributor and advertising revenue—and gains nothing in return. This merger, if allowed, would change that. After the merger, if the merged company raised prices of the Turner networks to the video distributor and no deal were reached, resulting in a blackout of such networks, the merged company would still lose monthly payments and advertising revenue from the video distributor with whom it could not reach a deal, but, importantly, it would now get an offsetting benefit. Because the video distributor walking away from a deal with the merged company would lose access to Turner's popular programming, some of the video distributor's valuable customers would be dissatisfied and switch to a competing video distributor. Some of those departing customers would sign up with AT&T/DirecTV, bringing with them significant new profits for the merged company. This improvement in Time Warner's best alternative to a deal resulting from the proposed merger—and therefore in its negotiating leverage—would give the merged firm the ability to credibly demand higher prices than it otherwise would.

6. The merger would thus substantially lessen competition by giving the merged company the additional leverage to charge its rival video distributors higher prices for its networks than Time Warner's current market power would otherwise allow, making those distributors less able to compete effectively with the merged company. This harm to competition is based on a well-accepted understanding within the industry. Indeed, tellingly, both AT&T and DirecTV have recognized in public filings and internal documents that video distributors that own popular programming have

the power and the incentive to harm competition. Congress also expressed such a concern by recognizing that "[v]ertically integrated program suppliers also have the incentive and ability to favor their affiliated cable operators over nonaffiliated cable operators and programming distributors using other technologies."

7. Because video distributors aim to cover programming cost increases by raising the prices they charge their customers, the higher prices video distributors would pay for Turner TV networks as a result of this merger would directly hit the pocket-books of American consumers. The merger would also give the merged firm the incentive and ability to use its control of HBO—which rival video distributors have used to attract customers—to lessen competition among video distributors. In sum, as DirecTV itself has explained: "[V]ertical integration of programming and distribution can, if left unchecked, give the integrated entity the incentive and ability to gain an unfair advantage over its rivals. This ultimately results in higher prices and lower quality service for consumers."

8. *Second*, the merger would enable the merged company to impede disruptive com-petition from online video distributors—competition that has allowed consumers greater choices at cheaper prices. Although it has concluded that "[t]raditional Pay-TV will be a cash cow business to AT&T for many years to come," AT&T/DirecTV fears future "disruption" from emerging competitors. Consumers are beginning to see new video distribution offerings. For example, online distributors like Sling TV offer less expensive alternatives to traditional subscription television that do not require yearly contracts or cable set top boxes, but this merger would impede that innovation. AT&T/DirecTV perceives online video distribution as an attack on its business that could, in its own words, "deteriorate[] the value of the bundle." Accordingly, AT&T/DirecTV intends to "work to make [online video services] less attractive."

   AT&T/DirecTV executives have concluded that the "runway" for the decline of traditional pay-TV "may be longer than some think given the economics of the space," and that it is "upon us to utilize our assets to extend that runway." This merger would give the merged firm key, valuable assets, empowering it to do just that.

9. Time Warner's Turner networks are extremely important for many emerging video distributors—its own analysis ranks those networks as tied for second behind only Disney in their ability to attract customers to emerging platforms. Turner benefits from the traditional pay-TV model but has also, previous to the announcement of this merger, secured a position for Case 1:17-cv-02511 Document 1 Filed 11/20/17 Page 6 of 23 7 its networks as "anchor tenants" for virtual MVPDs, which are grow-ing competitors to AT&T/DirecTV. After the merger, the merged firm would likely use Turner's important programming to hinder these online video distributors—for example, the merged firm would have the incentive and ability to charge more for Turner's popular networks and take other actions to impede entrants that might otherwise threaten the merged firm's high profit, big bundle, traditional pay-TV model. The merger would also make oligopolistic coordination more likely. For example, the merger would align the structures of the two largest traditional video distributors, who would have the incentive and ability to coordinate to impede competition from innovative online rivals and result in higher prices. In short, the merger would help the merged firm's bottom line by extending the life of the old pay-TV model, but harm consumers who are eager for new innovative options.

10. Section 7 of the Clayton Act prohibits mergers if "the effect of such acquisition may be substantially to lessen competition." This includes vertical mergers, as Congress made plain in the 1950 amendments to the Clayton Act. A vertical merger may violate the antitrust laws where the merging parties would—by means of their control of an input that their competitors need—have the incentive and ability to substantially lessen competition by withholding or raising the price for that input. The competitive conditions in this industry and specific facts of this vertical merger make it unusually problematic. It is well-recognized within the industry that popular programming is something traditional video distributors need to compete effectively. AT&T itself has previously stated that access to some of the most popular television programming is "critical to preserve and promote competition and diversity in the distribution of video programming." This merger would give the combined firm control over AT&T/DirecTV's massive video, wireless, and internet distribution network as well as Time Warner's popular and valuable TV networks and studio. It would give the merged firm the power to make its current and potential rivals less competitive. The effect of the merger would likely be substantially to lessen competition. It would violate the antitrust laws and therefore should be enjoined.

[Sections II, III, and IV, detailing the background of the industry in the case, the defendants, the merger, and markets that would be impacted, have been omitted.]

V. ANTICOMPETITIVE EFFECTS

... A. The merger would give the merged company the power to lessen competition and harm consumers in the Multichannel Video Distribution and the All Video Distribution markets by increasing the prices its rival MVPDs and virtual MVPDs pay for Turner's networks and impeding their use of HBO to attract customers.

32. Losing even a modest number of customers can have a major financial impact on an MVPD. The margins these video distributors earn from their customers are significant, and it is expensive and difficult for these distributors to obtain new customers or win back prior customers once they have cancelled their subscription or switched to a competitor.

33. Accordingly, when an MVPD considers the price it is willing to pay a programmer to carry its networks, it generally takes into account the extent of potential subscriber losses if it did not carry those networks. In fact, before negotiating with programmers for their networks, and to better understand their best alternative option if negotiations break down, MVPDs have conducted analyses to determine the percentage of likely subscriber loss that would occur if they did not carry the particular networks for which they are bargaining (a "blackout"). These analyses have concluded that, for certain popular networks, the subscriber loss rate would be significant and the subscriber losses would continue over time if the video distributor continued not to carry the networks at issue.

34. In the event an MVPD or virtual MVPD does not carry a group of popular networks, most customers who leave that distributor in response to that blackout will look elsewhere for a comparable video distributor that still offers

those networks. Because AT&T/DirecTV has an MVPD that it offers through-out the United States, it stands to gain a significant number of new custom-ers in the event a rival MVPD or virtual MVPD is foreclosed from carrying certain popular networks that the merged company continues to carry—i.e., a blackout.

35. Accordingly, were this merger to go forward, the merged company could "more credibly threaten to withhold" Turner's popular programming—including the hit shows and live sporting events carried by TNT, TBS, and Cartoon Network—as leverage in its negotiations with MVPDs and virtual MVPDs. In a given nego-tiation, both the merged company and a rival MVPD—for example, a cable company—know that if the merged company were to walk away from the bar-gaining table and the Turner networks were to go dark on that cable company's offerings, a significant number of the cable company's customers would cancel their subscriptions, and the cable company would gain fewer new subscribers during the blackout. In fact, MVPDs have done studies to determine the sub-scriber loss that would occur if they did not have the popular networks Time Warner owns. Unsurprisingly, given the popularity of Turner's networks—which carry hit shows and important live sports events—these studies confirm that the anticipated subscriber loss rate is likely to be significant. In addition, because the merged company would know beforehand that the rival MVPD would soon lack Turner programming, the merged company would be in a particularly strong position, as a result of the merger, to target the rival MVPD's customers with advertisements and telephone calls urging them to subscribe to AT&T/DirecTV's television offerings.

36. The merged company's bargaining leverage as a seller of programming would thus increase, and not through the offering of lower prices or a superior product or service offering, but directly because of this proposed merger. . . .

B. The merger would give the merged company the ability to impede and slow innova-tion by hindering emerging online competitors and would increase the likelihood of oli-gopolistic coordination.

40. The entry and growth of online video services promise to bring substantial ben-efits to consumers. But as the nation's largest provider of traditional pay-TV, AT&T/DirecTV views these services as a threat. As a result of this merger, the merged firm would have the increased market power to counter that threat and slow the emerging competition AT&T/DirecTV would otherwise face in the All Video Distribution and Multichannel Video Distribution markets. For example, after the merger, AT&T/DirecTV would have an increased ability to charge vir-tual MVPDs higher prices for Turner's and HBO's important and popular pro-gramming and could very well withhold that programming entirely from some virtual MVPDs, leading to even more severe effects on competition. Without the Turner networks, even virtual MVPDs such as Sling TV, which to date has been the most successful virtual MVPD competing with traditional MVPDs, may not continue to be the competitive force they are today. Turner knows this. Its CEO has stated that it has "leverage" over Dish, whose online Sling TV service "is shit without Turner."

41. In addition, the merger would increase the likelihood and effect of oligopolistic coordination, particularly among certain vertically integrated MVPDs. AT&T itself has noted the high levels of concentration within the pay-TV industry and their stabilizing effect. In a presentation prepared for a meeting with Time Warner executives related to this merger, AT&T noted that, after the merger, the merged company and just three other companies would control a large portion of all three levels of the industry: television studio revenue, network revenue, and distribution revenue. AT&T went on to explain that—given these high levels of concentration—its "Core Belief #1" is that, notwithstanding the emergence of online video distributors, "[t]he economic incentives of major pay-TV players will encourage stability as the ecosystem evolves." (Emphasis added.) This "stability" comes at the cost of competition that benefits consumers in the All Video Distribution and Multichannel Video Distribution markets. In addition, the nature of the subscription television industry, including the widespread use of most favored nations (MFN) clauses between video distributors and programmers, facilitates coordination. Moreover, after the merger, AT&T/DirecTV and Comcast/NBCU, which together have almost half of the country's MVPD customers, would have an increased incentive and ability to harm competition by impeding emerging online competitors that they consider a threat, and increasing the prices for the networks they own.

[Sections V and VI, on the violations alleged in the complaint and absence of countervailing factors, have been omitted.]

SOURCE: U.S. Justice Department. Case 1:170cv-02511. Complaint in *United States v. AT&T Inc. et al.* November 20, 2017. https://www.justice.gov/opa/press-release/file/1012896/download.

OTHER HISTORIC DOCUMENTS OF INTEREST

FROM THIS VOLUME

FROM PREVIOUS *HISTORIC DOCUMENTS*

December

U.S. Lawmakers Resign amid Sexual Misconduct Allegations

DECEMBER 5 AND 7, 2017

In the fall of 2017, Hollywood was rocked by a major scandal involving allegations of sexual harassment and assault against powerful film producer Harvey Weinstein. As the scope of the scandal—and the media attention focused on it—grew, hundreds of women came forward to accuse dozens of high-profile men across industries of sexual misconduct. Many of the accused were fired or resigned their positions, including at least seven U.S. lawmakers, and the flood of allegations prompted a national conversation about the prevalence of sexual harassment and abuse and how such incidents are handled.

WEINSTEIN ACCUSED OF SEXUAL ASSAULT

On October 5, *The New York Times* published a report on its investigation into previously undisclosed sexual assault allegations against Harvey Weinstein, a powerful Hollywood executive and successful film producer who cofounded both Miramax Films and The Weinstein Company. The allegations spanned nearly thirty years and involved women ranging from staff assistants at Weinstein's companies to models and well-known actresses such as Ashley Judd and Rose McGowan. The report stated that many of the women's accounts were similar: Weinstein invited them to a hotel room for a work meeting and then tried to engage them sexually, either by appearing without clothes, trying to give them a massage or pressuring them to give him a massage while he was unclothed, or asking them to watch him shower. Many of the women also said they felt tremendous pressure to acquiesce to Weinstein's requests and did not report the incidents when they first happened because they were afraid to alienate someone who was so powerful in Hollywood and could have a major impact on their careers—good or bad. *The New York Times* reported that Weinstein had settled with at least eight women who had come forward with accusations of sexual misconduct.

In response to the report, Weinstein issued a statement saying, "I appreciate the way I've behaved with colleagues in the past has caused a lot of pain, and I sincerely apologize for it. Though I'm trying to do better, I know I have a long way to go." Weinstein added that he was seeing therapists and would take a leave of absence from his companies to "deal with this issue head on." His lawyer said Weinstein "denies many of the accusations as patently false" and defended him as "an old dinosaur learning new ways." Hours after issuing his statement, Weinstein threatened to sue *The New York Times* for defamation.

Fallout from the report was swift. On October 6, a third of The Weinstein Company's board of directors resigned. The board members who remained said Weinstein would take a leave of absence. Two days later, they announced that Weinstein had been fired. However, the scandal did not end with Weinstein's firing. On October 10, *The New Yorker* reported additional allegations against Weinstein from thirteen other women, three of whom said that Weinstein had raped them. Allegations continued to pour in, including from high-profile accusers such as Gwyneth Paltrow, Angelina Jolie, and Mira Sorvino. By the end of October, eighty-four women had accused Weinstein of sexual harassment or assault, including additional rape charges. The New York, Los Angeles, and Beverly Hills Police Departments, and the London Metropolitan Police have all opened investigations into possible criminal charges in at least ten cases involving Weinstein.

DOZENS OF HIGH-PROFILE MEN NAMED IN WAVE OF SEXUAL ASSAULT ALLEGATIONS

Soon after the allegations against Weinstein surfaced, countless other women, and some men, came forward to share their stories of having been sexually harassed or assaulted. Dozens of high-profile men in Hollywood and across industries including sports, technology, media, and politics were accused of misconduct. A running tally compiled by The New York Times listed seventy-one high-profile men who had been fired or forced to resign as of February 8, 2018, due to sexual misconduct allegations. These included Stephen Wynn, casino magnate and Republican National Committee (RNC) finance chairman; Jerry Richardson, the owner of the National Football League team Carolina Panthers; Matt Lauer, co-host of NBC's "Today"; Ryan Lizza, writer for The New Yorker and CNN political analyst; Mario Batali, chef, restaurant owner, and co-host of ABC's "The Chew"; actor Kevin Spacey; Russell Simmons, co-founder of Def Jam Records; and Garrison Keillor, creator and former host of "A Prairie Home Companion." The New York Times listed another twenty-eight men who had been suspended or faced some other form of punitive action, short of being fired. Similar lists compiled by other publications, and not limited to those who had been penalized in some way, topped more than 120 accused individuals.

SEXUAL MISCONDUCT ALLEGATIONS COLOR ALABAMA SENATE RACE

Politicians were not unscathed by the wave of sexual misconduct allegations. Among the first to be accused following the Weinstein scandal was Roy Moore, the former chief justice of the Supreme Court of Alabama and the Republican candidate in the special election to fill the Senate seat of Attorney General Jeff Sessions. On November 9, The Washington Post published a report that four women interviewed by the paper said Moore had initiated a sexual encounter with them when they were between the ages of fourteen and eighteen and Moore was in his thirties. None of the women said Moore forced them into sexual acts, and only one of the encounters reportedly progressed beyond kissing. However, the legal age of consent in Alabama was and is sixteen years old.

Moore denied the reports, declaring the allegations were "completely false" and "a desperate political attack by the National Democrat Party and the Washington Post on this campaign." A campaign spokesperson noted that if the allegations were true, they would have raised during Moore's previous campaigns. At least initially, some Republican leaders seemed hesitant to call on Moore to forgo his campaign. White House Press Secretary Sarah Huckabee Sanders told reporters "the president does not believe we can allow a mere allegation . . . to destroy a person's life. However, the president also believes that if these allegations are true, Judge Moore will do the right thing and step aside." Senate Majority Leader Mitch McConnell, R-Ky., also said Moore should step aside if the allegations were found to be true. Some Republican Senators, including Jeff Flake,

R-Ariz., David Perdue, R-Ga., and Lisa Murkowski, R-Alaska, called on Moore to step aside, regardless of whether the allegations were true. "The allegations against Roy Moore are deeply disturbing and disqualifying," said Sen. John McCain, R-Ariz. "He should immediately step aside and allow the people of Alabama to elect a candidate they can be proud of."

A few days later, a fifth accuser came forward and said that Moore had sexually assaulted her when she was sixteen. This account was different from the others because the contact was not consensual; the woman said Moore tried to force himself on her. Three more women came forward to accuse Moore of sexual misconduct before the special election on December 12. *The New Yorker* also reported that Moore had been barred from a local mall for bothering girls who worked there. One of Moore's accusers said she worked at the mall and had reported Moore to her supervisor after he repeatedly made advances that made her uncomfortable. The RNC and the National Republican Senate Committee (NRSC) both withdrew financing from Moore's campaign following these reports. NRSC Chair Cory Gardner, R-Colo., said that Moore should be expelled from the Senate if he won the special election "because he does not meet the ethical and moral requirements of the United States Senate." However, the RNC resumed its support after Moore was endorsed by President Donald Trump on December 4. Trump continued to encourage support for Moore through Election Day.

Moore repeatedly denied the allegations and questioned why the women were just now coming forward with their stories after so many years. "Ritual defamation has been around for a long time, and that's what this is," he said. Moore said he had never encountered the accusers—despite previously telling Fox News that he remembered knowing two of them and calling one of them a friend—and said he had "never molested anyone." Moore ultimately lost the election to former federal prosecutor and Democratic candidate Doug Jones.

LAWMAKERS RESIGN AMID SEXUAL MISCONDUCT ALLEGATIONS

Sitting lawmakers were also named as perpetrators of sexual harassment and assault. On November 20, BuzzFeed News reported that Rep. John Conyers, D-Mich.—Congress' longest-serving member—settled a wrongful dismissal complaint in 2015 with an employee who claimed she was fired because she refused Conyers' "sexual advances." The claim was reportedly settled for $27,000 and paid out of Conyers' office budget; House of Representatives payroll documents listed the payment as severance. BuzzFeed also said it had obtained legal documents from several Conyers staff members who said the congressman repeatedly made sexual advances on female staff, with claims including that he asked for sexual favors, invited female staffers to stay in his hotel rooms, and touched women in a sexual manner. The staff members also said Conyers had used congressional resources to bring women with whom he was having an affair to Washington, D.C., and that sometimes Conyers asked the staff to bring women to his apartment or hotel rooms.

Conyers said he "expressly and vehemently" denied the allegations and that the settlement referenced in BuzzFeed's report was "to save all involved from the rigors of protracted litigation." Despite his denials, the House Ethics Committee launched an investigation into the allegations, stating Conyers "may have engaged in sexual harassment of members of his staff, discriminated against certain staff on the basis of age, and used official resources for impermissible personal purposes." Democrats, including House Minority Leader Nancy Pelosi, D-Calif., began calling for Conyers' resignation and for legislative measures to reform the system Congress uses to file and settle workplace complaints on Capitol Hill. This system has been in place for more than twenty years and gives employees 180 days to report sexual harassment to Congress' Office of Compliance. It requires victims of sexual harassment to receive counseling and participate in mediation before either taking the matter to court or pursuing an administrative hearing, which could lead to a settlement. Victims must also sign a confidentiality agreement.

Facing mounting pressure, Conyers announced his resignation in early December, calling in to a Detroit radio station from the hospital where he was receiving treatment for what his family said were stress-related illnesses. On December 5, Rep. Sheila Jackson Lee, D-Texas, read a statement from Conyers on the House floor. "Given the totality of the circumstance of not being afforded the right of due process in conjunction with my current health condition, and to preserve my legacy and good name, I am retiring," it said. "I cannot allow the great work of this body to be distracted from the important work, or the goals of the Democratic Party to be distracted."

Sen. Al Franken, D-Minn., was also accused of sexual misconduct. A total of eight women came forward, including a female radio host who claimed Franken groped her while she slept on a military plane on a return flight from a USO tour in 2006—two years before Franken was elected—and that he forcibly kissed her during a rehearsal. A photo of Franken seemingly about to grab the woman's breasts was widely published by news media. Franken apologized for the incident. Other allegations included a constituent's claim that Franken groped her during a photo opportunity at the Minnesota State Fair in 2010, and several anonymous accusers' claims that Franken groped them at other public events or tried forcibly to kiss them. Franken did not respond to all the allegations, though he did note in some cases that he was "a warm person" who hugs and is affectionate with people and that he had recently learned that for some women he had crossed a line.

At least thirty Senate Democrats called for Franken's resignation. On December 7, Franken read a statement on the Senate floor indicating that he would soon step down. "Some of the allegations against me are simply not true, others I remember very differently," Franken said, adding that he was "shocked" and "upset" by the accusations but that he felt "all women deserve to be heard and their experiences taken seriously." Franken said it was ironic that he was leaving Congress as a result of the allegations "while a man who has bragged on tape about his history of sexual assault sits in the Oval Office, and a man who has repeatedly preyed on young girls campaigns for the Senate with the full support of his party," references to Trump and Moore, respectively. (A tape recording of Trump speaking to "Access Hollywood" host Billy Bush about kissing women and grabbing them by their genitals without consent was released during the 2016 campaign.) Franken officially resigned on January 2, 2018. Minnesota Gov. Mark Dayton appointed Lt. Gov. Tina Smith to serve the remainder of Franken's term, and she was sworn in on January 3.

Franken and Conyers were not the only lawmakers to step down following sexual misconduct allegations. Others included Rep. Joe Barton, R-Texas, who announced at the end of November that he would resign after a constituent reported receiving sexually suggestive messages from the congressman. The former finance director for Rep. Ruben Kihuen, D-Nev., accused him of making unwanted sexual advances during his campaign. Kihuen denied the allegations but later said he would not seek reelection. Rep. Blake Farenthold, R-Texas, settled a sexual harassment claim by his former communications director for $84,000 but denied any wrongdoing. However, he announced his retirement in mid-December amid mounting pressure to step down. Rep. Patrick Meehan, R-Penn., was first removed from the House Ethics Committee and then announced he would not seek reelection after a former aid accused him of sexual harassment. Additionally, Rep Trent Franks, R-Ariz., resigned after it was revealed that he had repeatedly asked two female staff members to be surrogates for he and his wife and bear his children.

THE #METOO AND TIME'S UP MOVEMENTS

As sexual misconduct allegations continued to swirl, victims of harassment and assault came together to demand change. One movement that gained significant attention in the fall was MeToo, which was founded in 2006 with the mission of helping sexual violence survivors "find pathways to healing" in addition to "bringing vital conversations about sexual violence into the mainstream" and working to "de-stigmatize survivors by highlighting the breadth and impact" of sexual violence on women. On October 15, actress Alyssa Milano posted a tweet encouraging women who had experienced sexual abuse or harassment to post their own tweet using #MeToo to show how prevalent such incidents are. According to a Twitter spokesperson, the hashtag was used nearly half a million times in the first twenty-four hours following Milano's tweet. Use of the hashtag was also widespread on Facebook. Some simply posted the hashtag while others also shared details of their personal experiences. The outpouring on social media helped MeToo and its "silence breakers" earn *TIME* magazine's person of the year designation for 2017. MeToo founder Tarana Burke acknowledged the honor and that "men who have been lionized in Hollywood are having to answer for their actions" but asked what would become of the "most vulnerable" communities dealing with sexual misconduct. "Today's announcement should be an opportunity to ask ourselves: are we really committed to the hard work of ending sexual violence?" she said.

In January, more than 300 women in Hollywood formed an anti-harassment coalition called Time's Up. Described as "a unified call for change from women in entertainment for women everywhere," the coalition seeks to address "systemic inequality and injustice in the workplace" by partnering with advocacy groups to improve laws, employment agreements, and corporate policies to increase workplace equality and safety; placing more women on boards of directors and in C-suite positions; and helping women and men get the legal assistance they need to hold their abusers accountable. The group's work includes the Time's Up Legal Defense Fund, which is administered by the National Women's Law Center and subsidizes legal support for those who have been sexually harassed or have experienced related retaliation in the workplace. Initially supported by $13 million in donations, the fund connects victims with its national network of lawyers and public relations professionals to provide legal and communications assistance. Celebrities helped call attention to the movement by wearing Time's Up pins and dressing in all black at the Golden Globes awards ceremony on January 8.

—Linda Grimm

Following is Rep. John Conyers' statement of retirement, as read on the floor of the House of Representatives by Rep. Sheila Jackson Lee on December 5, 2017; and a statement made by Sen. Al Franken on the Senate floor on December 7, 2017, announcing his intent to resign.

Rep. Conyers Statement of Retirement as Read on the House Floor

December 5, 2017

Ms. JACKSON LEE. Mr. Speaker, a few minutes ago, in Detroit, the dean of the United States Congress offered his retirement immediately. He has asked me, a member of the Judiciary Committee, to offer his words to his colleagues and to put his statement in the RECORD that indicates that he has notified Speaker RYAN, Leader PELOSI, and Governor Snyder of his retirement from the United States House of Representatives.

It is important to note, as I begin, that there is no difference or no undermining of the rights of women and the abhorrence of sexual harassment and sexual assault. But this is a statement that I believe should be read on behalf of the dean of the United States Congress, Mr. JOHN CONYERS.

As a Member of Congress, I have known Mr. CONYERS to not shy away from a legislative challenge. In addition to being the first Member to introduce the Martin Luther King holiday bill, he was the first to hold hearings on police misconduct, the first to examine the problem of solitary confinement, the first to offer racial profiling legislation, the first to introduce legislation protecting against disenfranchisement of ex-felons, and the first to pursue legislation protecting Black farmers from discrimination, among many other civil rights measures.

In 2007, Representative CONYERS stood up for the prerogatives of the House of Representatives and successfully brought a suit against the former President Bush White House for failing to comply with subpoenas relating to a U.S. attorney's investigation. He has been the chairman of the Judiciary Committee; and he will continue to, in his life, as he has indicated, stand for what is right. It is now my privilege to read this statement from Mr. JOHN CONYERS. I reiterate that he says that he notified Speaker RYAN, Leader PELOSI, and Governor Snyder of his retirement from the United States House of Representatives.

It was his honor—these are his words—and his privilege to serve the constituents of Detroit, Michigan, as their United States Congressman in the 13th and 14th Congressional District for 53 years.

This is his statement again:

I came to Congress in 1964. Since then, I have devoted my entire career to improving the lives of my constituents in Detroit and on the behalf of justice everywhere. These years witnessed a profound evolution in civil rights, led by millions in the streets who marched for justice and people of conscience in the Congress—both Democrats and Republicans— who heard them and enacted the Civil Rights Act, the Voting Rights Act, and other landmark reforms. I have been in the forefront of the civil rights movement. I have been a champion of justice for the oppressed and the disenfranchised. I never wavered in my commitment to justice and democracy.

I am proud to have been part of that rich history. I have been privileged to be a founder of the Congressional Black Caucus and to represent the United States Congress by being dean. I passed, as indicated, the law dealing with the Martin Luther King, Jr., Holiday Act, the Violence Against Women Act, the Hate Crimes Act, the

USA Freedom Act, and the extension of the Voting Rights Act. I have led the fight against mandatory minimum sentences, hoping to reverse the devastating incarceration rates for African Americans and poor people. I have tried to pass a universal healthcare law, H.R. 676. Every Congress since 1989, I have introduced H.R. 40 to study reparations for slavery, and I deeply appreciate those handful of courageous colleagues who have joined me.

For Detroiters, I am proud of what we have been able to accomplish to bring hundreds of millions of dollars in critical grants and Federal funding for southeast Michigan to revitalize our great city, attract rich talent, and return to us prosperity.

I recognize that in this present environment, due process will not be afforded to me. I was taught by a great woman, my mother, to honor women. The first employee I ever hired was Mrs. Rosa Parks, who worked in my office for 22 years. It has been my great honor to work alongside some of the most talented and honorable staff on Capitol Hill and in Detroit.

I have stated my position on these allegations. I have worked with both women and men.

Given the totality of the circumstance of not being afforded the right of due process in conjunction with my current health condition, and to preserve my legacy and good name, I am retiring.

I hope that my retirement will be viewed in the larger perspective of my record of service, and as I enter a new chapter, I pledge to continue my commitment to a progressive vision and a better future for this country that I love. I owe that to the legacy of my father, John Conyers, Sr., who integrated labor unions in this country; to my brother Nathan, who integrated business, and he is my "main man;" and to my loving wife, Monica; and to my son, John III, who I believe offers hope to this generation of leadership, and who is committed to being an advocate of fairness and justice for all; and to Carl Edward, who never leaves my side.

I cannot allow the great work of this body to be distracted from the important work, or the goals of the Democratic Party to be distracted. It has been an honor and a privilege of my life to represent the people of Michigan in the House of Representatives, but that responsibility will now fall to my colleagues and my successor. They have my deepest support and prayers. Jobs, justice, and peace.

SOURCE: U.S. Congress. House. Retirement of Dean of the United States Congress. 115th Congress, 2nd Session. *Congressional Record*. vol. 163, no. 198, daily ed. (December 5, 2017): H9630. https://www.gpo.gov/fdsys/pkg/CREC-2017-12-05/pdf/CREC-2017-12-05-pt1-PgH9630.pdf.

Sen. Franken Announces Intent to Resign

December 7, 2017

Mr. FRANKEN. Mr. President, a couple of months ago, I felt we had entered an important moment in the history of this country. We were finally beginning to listen to women about the ways in which men's actions affect them. The moment was long overdue. I was excited for that conversation and hopeful it would result in real change that made life better for women all across the country and in every part of our society.

Then the conversation turned to me. Over the last few weeks, a number of women have come forward to talk about how they felt my actions had affected them. I was shocked. I was upset, but in responding to their claims, I also wanted to be respectful of that broader conversation because all women deserve to be heard and their experiences taken seriously. I think that was the right thing to do. I also think it gave some people the false impression that I was admitting to doing things that, in fact, I haven't done. Some of the allegations against me are simply not true, others I remember very differently.

I said at the outset, the Ethics Committee was the right venue for these allegations to be heard and investigated and evaluated on their merits; that I was prepared to cooperate fully and that I was confident in the outcome.

An important part of the conversation we have been having the last few months has been about how men abuse their power and privilege to hurt women. I am proud that during my time in the Senate, I have used my power to be a champion of women and that I have earned the reputation as someone who respects the women I work alongside every day. I know there has been a very different picture of me painted over the last few weeks, but I know who I really am.

Serving in the U.S. Senate has been the great honor of my life. I know in my heart that nothing I have done as a Senator—nothing—has brought dishonor on this institution, and I am confident the Ethics Committee would agree.

Nevertheless, today I am announcing that in the coming weeks, I will be resigning as a Member of the U.S. Senate. I, of all people, am aware that there is some irony in the fact that I am leaving, while a man who has bragged on tape about his history of sexual assault sits in the Oval Office, and a man who has repeatedly preyed on young girls campaigns for the Senate with the full support of his party, but this decision is not about me; it is about the people of Minnesota. It has become clear that I can't both pursue the Ethics Committee process and, at the same time, remain an effective Senator for them.

Let me be clear. I may be resigning my seat, but I am not giving up my voice. I will continue to stand up for the things I believe in as a citizen and as an activist, but Minnesotans deserve a Senator who can focus with all her energy on addressing the challenges they face every day.

There is a big part of me that will always regret having to walk away from this job with so much work left to be done, but I have faith the work will continue because I have faith in the people who have helped me do it. I have faith in the dedicated, funny, selfless, brilliant young men and women on my staff. They have so much more to contribute to our country, and I hope that as disappointed as they may feel today, everyone who has worked for me knows how much I admire and respect them.

I have faith in my colleagues, especially my senior Senator, AMY KLOBUCHAR. I would not have been able to do this job without her guidance and wisdom. I have faith—or at least hope—that Members of the Senate will find the political courage necessary to keep asking the tough questions, hold this administration accountable, and stand up for the truth.

I have faith in the activists who organized to help me win my first campaign and who have kept on organizing to help fight for the people who needed us—kids facing bullying, seniors worried about the price of prescription drugs, Native Americans who have been overlooked for far too long, working people who have been taking it on the chin for a generation, everyone in the middle class, and everyone aspiring to join it.

I have faith in the proud legacy of progressive advocacy that I have had the privilege to be a part of. I think I probably repeated these words 10,000 times over the years, Paul Wellstone's famous quote: "The future belongs to those who are passionate and work hard." It is still true. It will always be true.

Most of all, I have faith in Minnesota. A big part of this job is going around the State and listening to what people need from Washington, but more often than not, when I am home, I am blown away by how much Minnesota has to offer the entire country and the entire world. The people I have had the honor of representing are brilliant and creative and hard-working. Whoever holds this seat next will inherit the challenge I have enjoyed for the last 8½ years, being as good as the people you serve.

This has been a tough few weeks for me, but I am a very, very lucky man. I have a beautiful, healthy family whom I love and who loves me very much. I am going to be just fine.

I would just like to end with one last thing. I did not grow up wanting to be a politician. I came to this relatively late in life. I had to learn a lot on the fly. It wasn't easy, and it wasn't always fun. I am not just talking about today. This is a hard thing to do with your life. There are a lot of long hours and late nights and hard lessons, and there is no guarantee that all your work and sacrifice will ever pay off. I won my first election by 312 votes. It could have easily gone the other way. Even when you win, progress is far from inevitable. Paul Wellstone spent his whole life working for mental health parity, and it didn't pass until 6 years after Paul died.

This year, a lot of people who didn't grow up imagining they would ever get involved in politics have done just that. They have gone to their first protest march or made their first call to a Member of Congress or maybe even taken the leap and put their names on a ballot for the first time.

It can be such a rush, to look around at a room full of people ready to fight alongside you, to feel that energy, to imagine that better things are possible. But you, too, will experience setbacks and defeats and disappointments. There will be days when you will wonder whether it is worth it.

What I want you to know is that even today, even on the worst day of my political life, I feel like it has all been worth it. "Politics," Paul Wellstone told us, "is about the improvement of people's lives." I know that the work I have been able to do has improved people's lives. I would do it all over again in a heartbeat.

For a decade now, every time I would get tired, discouraged, or frustrated, I would think about the people I was doing this for, and it would get me back up on my feet. I know the same will be true for everyone who decides to pursue a politics that is about improving people's lives, and I hope you know that I will be fighting alongside you every step of the way.

With that, I yield the floor.

SOURCE: U.S. Congress. Senate. Executive Calendar, Farewell to the Senate. 115th Congress, 2nd Session. *Congressional Record.* vol. 163, no. 200, daily ed. (December 7, 2017): S7905–S7906. https://www.gpo .gov/fdsys/pkg/CREC-2017-12-07/pdf/CREC-2017-12-07-pt1-PgS7905-3.pdf.

OTHER HISTORIC DOCUMENTS OF INTEREST

United States Recognizes Jerusalem as Israel's Capital

DECEMBER 6 AND 18, 2017

At the end of 2017, President Donald Trump stunned the international community by announcing a major break with decades of U.S. foreign policy: The United States would recognize Jerusalem as Israel's capital and move its embassy to the city. While welcomed by Israeli officials, the announcement infuriated Palestinian officials, sparked protests in the Palestinian territories and around the globe, and was widely criticized by the international community. However, the United States was able to use its veto power to prevent the United Nations Security Council from approving a resolution calling for the U.S. to rescind the decision.

JERUSALEM'S PLACE IN THE ISRAELI–PALESTINIAN CONFLICT

Jerusalem's status is a central issue in the long-running Israeli–Palestinian conflict. The city is divided into West Jerusalem, controlled by Israel since 1949 and the seat of the Israeli government, and East Jerusalem, which has a primarily Palestinian population. Israel seized East Jerusalem during the Six-Day War of 1967, prior to which the area was controlled by the Arab state of Jordan. Israel declared Jerusalem its capital in 1980, but the Palestinians wanted the city to be the capital of a future Palestinian state.

The location of some of the holiest Islamic and Jewish religious sites within Jerusalem further complicates the two sides' claims to the city. Jerusalem is home to the Temple Mount, where two ancient Jewish temples once stood and where Jews believe Abraham took his son Isaac to be sacrificed as a sign of his devotion to God, as well as the Western Wall, which is a remnant of one of the temples. The Temple Mount is known to Muslims as the Noble Sanctuary and also contains the Dome of the Rock, home to the foundation stone from which the Prophet Mohammed is believed to have ascended to heaven. The al-Aqsa Mosque, to which Mohammed traveled from Mecca to pray, is also located on the mount and is considered the third holiest Islamic site. Notably, while the sites are open to Israelis and Palestinians, Israeli security forces control the entry points to the Temple Mount and have on occasion restricted access to the area during times of high tension.

The international community generally maintains that Jerusalem is an occupied territory and that the city's final status should be decided through negotiations between the Israelis and Palestinians. The UN Security Council has declared Israel's annexation of East Jerusalem a violation of international law, discouraging members from recognizing Jerusalem as the Israeli capital and prompting countries that once maintained embassies in the city to move them to Tel Aviv.

TRUMP BREAKS WITH U.S. FOREIGN POLICY PRECEDENT

On December 6, Trump issued a presidential proclamation recognizing Jerusalem as Israel's capital and announcing the relocation of the U.S. Embassy to Israel from Tel Aviv to Jerusalem. Stating that U.S. foreign policy is "grounded in principled realism" and "an honest acknowledgment of plain facts," Trump declared the proclamation a "long overdue recognition of reality" that was "in the best interests of both the United States and the pursuit of peace between Israel and the Palestinians." The president said the recognition was appropriate because Jerusalem was Israel's capital in ancient times and had been considered its capital since President Harry Truman recognized Israel as a state in 1948. He added that Jerusalem is the seat of Israel's government and where U.S. officials go to meet their Israeli counterparts. In related remarks, the president positioned the announcement as delivering on a campaign promise, noting that previous presidents had failed to follow through on similar promises.

Trump followed the announcement by issuing a memo to the State Department instructing the agency to begin the process of moving the embassy but he also signed a national security waiver allowing the administration to maintain the embassy in Tel Aviv for six months. (Presidents have signed this waiver every six months since Congress passed the Jerusalem Embassy Act of 1995, calling for the embassy to be moved to Jerusalem, to defer the law and keep the embassy in Tel Aviv.)

The proclamation represented a major break with decades of precedent in U.S. foreign relations. In keeping with the international community, the United States had declined to recognize Jerusalem as Israel's capital for nearly sixty years. Trump said this policy had brought the United States "no closer to a lasting peace agreement between Israel and the Palestinians" and that "it would be folly to assume that repeating the exact same formula would now produce a different or better result."

Analysts noted that Trump did not use the word "undivided" when describing Jerusalem, suggesting that the White House would still support partitioning the city during peace negotiations. Had Trump used this term, it would have signaled a clear U.S. position on Jerusalem's future and marked an even more significant break with precedent. Trump said that the announcement did not "reflect a departure from the strong commitment of the United States to facilitating a lasting peace agreement" and that the United States "continues to take no position on any final status issues" or on boundary or border designations. He further stated that the United States supported the "status quo at Jerusalem's holy sites."

International Community Reacts

Israeli Prime Minister Benjamin Netanyahu celebrated the announcement. "We are profoundly grateful for the president, for his courageous and just decision to recognize Jerusalem as the capital of Israel," he said. "This decision reflects the president's commitment to an ancient but enduring truth."

Palestinian officials were outraged. "These deplorable and unacceptable measures deliberately undermine all peace efforts," said President Mahmoud Abbas, who also called Jerusalem the "eternal capital of the state of Palestine." Abbas declined an invitation by Trump to come to the White House later in the year and refused to meet with Vice President Mike Pence when he visited in January. Ismail Haniya, leader of Hamas, characterized the announcement as a "war declaration against Palestinians," declaring, "We should call for and we should work on launching an intifada in the face of the Zionist enemy." Hamas was also among the Palestinian groups that called for three days of "popular anger," beginning on December 7, across Palestinian territories and in front of U.S. embassies and consulates around the world to protest the decision. The U.S. Consulate in

Jerusalem and U.S. Embassy in Jordan issued security warnings to U.S. citizens and government employees in the region.

The clear majority of world leaders were also critical of the announcement, particularly in the Middle East. "Moving the U.S. embassy is a dangerous step that provokes the feelings of Muslims around the world," warned King Salman of Saudi Arabia. Jordanian King Abdullah said the proclamation would have "dangerous repercussions on the stability and security of the region." Turkish Deputy Prime Minister Bekir Bozdag claimed the United States was "plunging the region and the world into a fire with no end in sight." In addition, Egyptian President Abdul Fattah al-Sisi said the United States was "complicating the situation in the region by introducing measures that would undermine the chances for peace in the Middle East."

In Europe, French President Emmanuel Macron described the decision as "regrettable," and a spokesperson for German Chancellor Angela Merkel said Germany "does not support this position because the status of Jerusalem can only be negotiated within the framework of a two-state solution." Federica Mogherini, High Representative of the European Union for Foreign Affairs and Security Policy, said, "We believe that any action that would undermine [peace] efforts must be absolutely avoided. A way must be found through negotiations to resolve the status of Jerusalem as a future capital of both states."

An emergency meeting of the United Nations (UN) Security Council was called for December 8, at which the U.S. decision was widely condemned. Two days later, the Arab League held an emergency meeting, with members calling Trump's action "a dangerous development that places the United States at a position of bias in favor of the occupation and the violation of international law and resolutions," adding that the move stripped the United States of its role as "sponsor and broker" in the peace process. The group called for recognition of Palestine as a sovereign state with Jerusalem as its capital and called on the UN Security Council to adopt a resolution condemning the proclamation. On December 13, President Erdoğan called a meeting of the Organisation of Islamic Coordination to discuss the U.S. action, which the group declared "null and void." They also called on the UN to "end the Israeli occupation" of Palestine.

The news also spurred internal unrest. The day after the announcement, protests broke out in the West Bank and Gaza Strip, with demonstrators burning U.S. and Israeli flags along with pictures of Trump and Netanyahu, and Israeli security forces reportedly using tear gas and stun grenades to break up protests. The Palestine Red Crescent reported that more than 100 people were injured. The same day, the Israeli military said three missiles had been fired from the Gaza Strip and that retaliatory action had been taken against two Hamas military sites. Protests continued throughout the month, and more took place in Lebanon, Morocco, Turkey, Yemen, Indonesia, Turkey, and Japan.

UNITED STATES BLOCKS UN SECURITY COUNCIL ACTION

Despite calls by member states for action, the UN Security Council failed to adopt a resolution expressing members' regret about "recent decisions regarding the status of Jerusalem" following a veto by the United States. The other fourteen Security Council members voted in favor of the resolution, which also declared that "any decisions and actions which purport to have altered, the character, status or demographic composition" of Jerusalem are "null and void" and must be rescinded.

Before the vote, UN Special Coordinator for the Middle East Peace Process Nickolay Mladenov briefed members, stating that the situation on the ground in Israel and the Palestinian territories had become more tense following Trump's announcement and linking violence in the region to the decision. "None of the developments on the ground can be divorced from the broader context in which they are happening: uncertainties about the future of the peace process; unilateral actions that undermine the two-state solution; occupation; and violence," he said.

U.S. Ambassador Nikki Haley defended her vote, saying it was in defense of the United States' role in the peace process and arguing that Trump had "taken care not to prejudge final status negotiations" in line with prior Security Council resolutions. She added that "a peace process that could be damaged simply by recognizing Jerusalem as Israel's capital was not a peace process."

Move Timeline

At the time of Trump's announcement, U.S. officials speculated it could take several years to move the embassy from Tel Aviv to Jerusalem. However, during a visit to Israel in January 2018, Vice President Pence said the embassy would open before the end of 2019.

—Linda Grimm

Following is a proclamation by President Donald Trump on December 6, 2017, recognizing Jerusalem as Israel's capital; a memo to the U.S. State Department from December 6, 2017, waiving the requirement that the U.S. Embassy to Israel be located in Jerusalem for six months; and a press release and meeting report from the United Nations Security Council from December 18, 2017, announcing the United States' veto of a resolution on Jerusalem's status.

U.S. Proclamation Recognizing Jerusalem as Israel's Capital

DOCUMENT

December 6, 2017

By the President of the United States of America

A Proclamation

The foreign policy of the United States is grounded in principled realism, which begins with an honest acknowledgment of plain facts. With respect to the State of Israel, that requires officially recognizing Jerusalem as its capital and relocating the United States Embassy to Israel to Jerusalem as soon as practicable.

The Congress, since the Jerusalem Embassy Act of 1995 (Public Law 104-45) (the "Act"), has urged the United States to recognize Jerusalem as Israel's capital and to relocate our Embassy to Israel to that city. The United States Senate reaffirmed the Act in a unanimous vote on June 5, 2017.

Now, 22 years after the Act's passage, I have determined that it is time for the United States to officially recognize Jerusalem as the capital of Israel. This long overdue recognition of reality is in the best interests of both the United States and the pursuit of peace between Israel and the Palestinians.

Seventy years ago, the United States, under President Truman, recognized the State of Israel. Since then, the State of Israel has made its capital in Jerusalem—the capital the Jewish people established in ancient times. Today, Jerusalem is the seat of Israel's government—the home of Israel's parliament, the Knesset; its Supreme Court; the residences of its Prime Minister and President; and the headquarters of many of its government ministries. Jerusalem is where officials of the United States, including the President, meet their Israeli counterparts. It is therefore appropriate for the United States to recognize Jerusalem as Israel's capital.

I have also determined that the United States will relocate our Embassy to Israel from Tel Aviv to Jerusalem. This action is consistent with the will of the Congress, as expressed in the Act.

Today's actions—recognizing Jerusalem as Israel's capital and announcing the relocation of our embassy—do not reflect a departure from the strong commitment of the United States to facilitating a lasting peace agreement. The United States continues to take no position on any final status issues. The specific boundaries of Israeli sovereignty in Jerusalem are subject to final status negotiations between the parties. The United States is not taking a position on boundaries or borders.

Above all, our greatest hope is for peace, including through a two-state solution, if agreed to by both sides. Peace is never beyond the grasp of those who are willing to reach for it. In the meantime, the United States continues to support the status quo at Jerusalem's holy sites, including at the Temple Mount, also known as Haram al Sharif. Jerusalem is today—and must remain—a place where Jews pray at the Western Wall, where Christians walk the Stations of the Cross, and where Muslims worship at Al-Aqsa Mosque.

With today's decision, my Administration reaffirms its longstanding commitment to building a future of peace and security in the Middle East. It is time for all civilized nations and people to respond to disagreement with reasoned debate—not senseless violence—and for young and moderate voices across the Middle East to claim for themselves a bright and beautiful future. Today, let us rededicate ourselves to a path of mutual understanding and respect, rethinking old assumptions and opening our hearts and minds to new possibilities. I ask the leaders of the Middle East—political and religious; Israeli and Palestinian; and Jewish, Christian, and Muslim—to join us in this noble quest for lasting peace.

Now, Therefore, I, Donald J. Trump, President of the United States of America, by virtue of the authority vested in me by the Constitution and the laws of the United States, do hereby proclaim that the United States recognizes Jerusalem as the capital of the State of Israel and that the United States Embassy to Israel will be relocated to Jerusalem as soon as practicable.

IN WITNESS WHEREOF, I have hereunto set my hand this sixth day of December, in the year of our Lord two thousand seventeen, and of the Independence of the United States of America the two hundred and forty-second.

DONALD J. TRUMP

SOURCE: Executive Office of the President. "Presidential Proclamation 9683—Recognizing Jerusalem as the Capital of the State of Israel and Relocating the United States Embassy to Israel to Jerusalem." December 6, 2017. *Compilation of Presidential Documents* 2017, no. 00887 (December 6, 2017). https://www.gpo.gov/fdsys/pkg/DCPD-201700887/pdf/DCPD-201700887.pdf.

Presidential Memorandum for the Secretary of State

December 6, 2017

Presidential Determination No. 2018-02

Memorandum for the Secretary of State

Subject: Suspension of Limitations under the Jerusalem Embassy Act

By the authority vested in me as President by the Constitution and the laws of the United States, including section 7(a) of the Jerusalem Embassy Act of 1995 (Public Law 104-45) (the "Act"), I hereby determine that it is necessary, in order to protect the national security interests of the United States, to suspend for a period of 6 months the limitations set forth in sections 3(b) and 7(b) of the Act.

You are authorized and directed to transmit this determination, accompanied by a report in accordance with section 7(a) of the Act, to the Congress and to publish this determination in the *Federal Register*.

The suspension set forth in this determination shall take effect after you transmit this determination and the accompanying report to the Congress.

DONALD J. TRUMP

Source: Executive Office of the President. "Memorandum on Suspension of Limitations under the Jerusalem Embassy Act." December 6, 2017. *Compilation of Presidential Documents* 2017, no. 00888 (December 6, 2017). https://www.gpo.gov/fdsys/pkg/DCPD-201700888/pdf/DCPD-201700888.pdf.

UN Security Council Fails to Adopt Resolution on Jerusalem

December 18, 2017

The United Nations Security Council on Monday failed to adopt the draft resolution that reflects regret among the body's members about "recent decisions regarding the status of Jerusalem," with a negative vote by the United States.

The text, tabled by Egypt, reiterated the United Nations' position on Jerusalem and would have affirmed "that any decisions and actions which purport to have altered, the character, status or demographic composition of the Holy City of Jerusalem have no legal effect, are null and void and must be rescinded in compliance with relevant resolutions of the Security Council."

The text would also have called on all States "to refrain from the establishment of diplomatic missions in the Holy City of Jerusalem."

A negative vote—or veto—from one of the Council's five permanent members—China, France, Russia, United Kingdom and the United States—blocks passage of a resolution.

Therefore, the draft was rejected despite support from the other four permanent members and from the 10 non-permanent members.

The vote followed a briefing by Nickolay Mladenov, Special Coordinator for the Middle East Peace process, who said that the Israel-Palestinian conflict has not seen significant positive moves towards peace during the reporting period from 20 September to 18 December.

He said that the security situation in Israel and the occupied Palestinian territory has become more tense in the wake of US President Donald Trump's decision on 6 December to recognize Jerusalem as the capital of Israel, citing an increase in incidents, notably rockets fired from Gaza and clashes between Palestinians and Israeli security forces.

"None of the developments on the ground can be divorced from the broader context in which they are happening: uncertainties about the future of the peace process; unilateral actions that undermine the two-state solution; occupation; and violence," Mr. Mladenov told the Council.

The Special Coordinator's briefing mainly focused on the status of implementation of Security Council resolution 2334, which was adopted in December 2016 by 14 votes, with the US abstaining.

In that text, the Council reaffirmed that Israel's establishment of settlements in Palestinian territory occupied since 1967, including East Jerusalem, had no legal validity, constituting a flagrant violation under international law and a major obstacle to the vision of two States living side-by-side in peace and security, within internationally recognized borders.

It underlined that it would not recognize any changes to the 4 June 1967 lines, including the status of Jerusalem, other than those agreed by the two sides through negotiations.

"The United Nations maintains the view that Jerusalem is a final status issue that must be resolved through direct negotiations between the two parties on the basis of the relevant Security Council and General Assembly resolutions taking into account the legitimate concerns of both the Palestinian and the Israeli sides," Mr. Mladenov stressed, warning that there is a growing risk that the parties may revert to more unilateral actions.

He said that since the US decision, the Palestinian leadership canceled meetings with visiting Vice-President Mike Pence, and called for the establishment of a new mechanism to achieve peace.

Palestinian President Mahmoud Abbas has also vowed to seek unilateral recognition of Palestine and to seek full membership in international organizations in the absence of a meaningful peace process, Mr. Mladenov added.

Regarding Israel's settlement activities, housing construction in occupied Palestinian territory has continued, with significantly more units advanced and approved in 2017, he said.

For instance, in East Jerusalem, the increase has been from 1,600 units in 2016 to some 3,100 in 2017.

In addition, 2017 has seen worrying legislative, judicial and administrative initiatives that aim to change the long-standing Israeli policy concerning the legal status of the West Bank and the use of private Palestinian land, Mr. Mladenov warned.

SOURCE: United Nations. "Middle East: Security Council Fails to Adopt Resolution on Jerusalem." December 18, 2017. https://news.un.org/en/story/2017/12/639772-middle-east-security-council-fails-adopt-resolution-jerusalem#.WjrJHbbMwRE.

U.S. Vetoes Security Council Resolution on Diplomatic Missions in Jerusalem

December 18, 2017

Due to a veto cast by the United States today, the Security Council failed to adopt a draft resolution that would have called upon all States to refrain from establishing diplomatic missions in Jerusalem.

Rejected by a vote of 14 in favour to 1 against (United States), the draft would have stressed that Jerusalem was a final status issue to be resolved through negotiations in accordance with relevant United Nations resolutions. It would also have demanded that all States comply with Council decisions on the issue, and express deep regret over recent decisions in that regard.

In addition, the draft resolution would have reiterated calls to reverse "negative trends on the ground that are imperilling the two-State solution", and for intensified and accelerated efforts to realize a just and lasting peace in the Middle East.

The meeting began at 12:24 p.m. and ended at 1:56 p.m.

Action on Draft Resolution

AMR ABDELLATIF ABOULATTA (Egypt), speaking before the vote, said his delegation had submitted the draft as a matter of urgency after the 6 December decision by the United States. It was critical to establish that such decisions had no legal standing and were null and void, he said, emphasizing that international law must be respected lest chaos ensue. Any attempts to change facts on the ground, and other such unilateral actions pre-empting the resolution of final status issues, should be opposed as being in violation of many Council resolutions as well as the United Nations Charter, which did not allow the annexation of territory, he stressed.

ELBIO OSCAR ROSSELLI FRIERI (Uruguay) reaffirmed the special status of Jerusalem under Council resolution 181 (1947), emphasizing that its final status must be resolved through bilateral negotiations. Any decision on Jerusalem by a third State would affect the peace process, he cautioned, explaining that that was the reason his delegation would vote in favour of the draft.

The Council then took action on the draft resolution, but did not adopt it, as the representative of the United States cast a negative vote.

NIKKI R. HALEY (United States), speaking after the vote, explained that she had cast the veto in defence of her country's role in the peace process. The President of the United States had taken care not to prejudge final status negotiations, including boundaries in Jerusalem, a position that was in line with previous Council resolutions, she said. He also supported the status quo on holy sites and the two-State solution. Emphasizing that the United States had not harmed the peace process, she said it had the courage to recognize a fundamental reality, and the sovereign right to decide where to put its embassy. Describing the accusation that her country was setting the peace process back as scandalous, she said that a peace process that could be damaged simply by recognizing Jerusalem as Israel's capital was not a peace process. Today, the Council had witnessed an insult that would not be forgotten, she said, adding that the United Nations was doing more harm than good for the cause of peace. For those reasons, and in the best interests of both peoples firmly in mind, the United States had voted "no", she said.

MATTHEW JOHN RYCROFT (United Kingdom) said the status of Jerusalem should be solved through negotiations between the two sides, and the city should be the capital of both Israel and Palestine. The United Kingdom disagreed with the decision to recognize Jerusalem as Israel's capital, he said, adding that the decision had no legal affect. President Trump had acknowledged that the status of Jerusalem should be the subject of negotiations between the parties, and he encouraged the United States to provide detailed proposals for a settlement, emphasizing that any peace effort must take the people into account.

FRANÇOIS DELATTRE (France) said the draft confirmed the international consensus on Jerusalem and translated it into international law. The decision by the President of the United States did not modify the foundation of any peace agreement, and in the absence of such agreement, France did not recognize any sovereignty over Jerusalem, he emphasized. All decisions aimed at altering the city's status were considered null and void, and today's vote expressed the will of 14 Council members to reaffirm the validity of international law. Expressing hope that the United States would return to the international consensus, he warned that there was a risk of converting a political conflict into a religious one, from which only the radicals would gain. Jerusalem was key for peace, he stressed.

FODÉ SECK (Senegal) said he had voted in favour of the draft because the Holy City was a symbol for the three Abrahamic religions, and the international consensus on its status must be preserved. He called for strict respect for the status quo in accordance with Security Council resolutions dating back to resolution 181 (1947). He also appealed to the parties to exercise restraint, avoid raising tensions, and progress to negotiations on the basis of previous agreements, praising previous efforts by the United States to encourage them.

TEKEDA ALEMU (Ethiopia) said that, as much as his delegation supported Israel's right to exist in peace and security, it also supported the right of Palestinians to self-determination. Jerusalem was a final status issue to be determined in negotiations towards just and lasting peace in the form of the two-State solution, he said, emphasizing that the recent decision underscored the urgent need to ease tensions, remove obstacles and progress towards direct negotiations.

VLADIMIR K. SAFRONKOV (Russian Federation) said he had voted in favour of the draft because unilateral actions in the current environment risked raising tensions and setting back the possibilities for negotiations towards the two-State solution that the Russian Federation supported. The status of Jerusalem and a lasting solution could only be established on the basis of strict international law, he emphasized. Pledging that his country would continue its efforts for peace, he reiterated its proposal to host a summit on the matter, maintaining that the Russian Federation could be an effective broker for peace since it had not interfered in regional affairs as other actors had done. The Russian Federation's proposal for a comprehensive review of the situation in the entire Middle East should also be heeded, he added.

OLOF SKOOG (Sweden) said he had voted in favour of the text because Jerusalem was a final status issue and, as a city holy to three religions, its special character, recognized in Council resolutions, must be respected. The European Union also had a firm position on those issues, he added. Today's action did not alter Jerusalem's status in international agreements, and it was critical that all international actors now work to accelerate efforts to restart negotiations towards a just and lasting two-State solution, he stressed.

SEBASTIANO CARDI (Italy) said the draft reaffirmed principles enshrined in previous Council resolutions. Jerusalem's status as the future capital of two States was subject to negotiations between Israel and Palestine. The United States could play a crucial role in that regard, and Italy looked forward to proposals for a settlement. Expressing deep concern about increased tensions, he condemned rocket attacks against Israel and called upon all actors to exercise restraint.

VOLODYMYR YELCHENKO (Ukraine) said Jerusalem was a final status issue to be resolved through negotiations. Encouraged by the draft's reaffirmation that forcible acquisition of territory was inadmissible, he said Ukraine knew only too well the consequences arising from violation of that principle. Given the highly sensitive nature of Jerusalem for all involved, Ukraine hoped the current escalation could be contained.

WU HAITAO (China) said the Palestinian issue was at the core of conflict in the Middle East, and the question of Jerusalem was particularly complicated and sensitive. Recalling the many stipulations contained in Council resolutions on Jerusalem, he said today's draft was a continuation of past texts. China supported a sovereign State of Palestine within the 1967 borders and with East Jerusalem as its capital, he said, urging the United Nations to strengthen efforts to restart negotiations in order to realize a just and lasting settlement.

PEDRO LUIS INCHAUSTE JORDÁN (Bolivia) reaffirmed that Jerusalem's final status should be resolved through negotiations, emphasizing that any action seeking to alter its status was null and void, without effect. Calling upon the Government of the United States to reconsider, he said its decision would undermine efforts to reach a long-term solution and was in flagrant violation of previous Council resolutions.

BARLYBAY SADYKOV (Kazakhstan) said his country's position remained unchanged, and urged the parties to respect Jerusalem's status. It was necessary to identify mutually acceptable principles for the resumption of peace negotiations, he said, urging Israel and the Palestinians to take concrete steps towards the two-State solution.

KORO BESSHO (Japan), Council President for December, spoke in his national capacity, emphasizing that Jerusalem's final status was among issues to be resolved through negotiations. While noting the importance of the United States President's clear acknowledgement that the final status of Jerusalem must be subject to negotiations between the parties, he expressed concern about the possibility of a worsening situation surrounding the Middle East peace process, and stressed the importance of the parties committing to meaningful progress in that regard.

RIYAD H. MANSOUR, Permanent Observer for the State of Palestine, thanked all Council members who had recognized the urgency of the matter. They had clearly reaffirmed the international consensus on Jerusalem by determining that recent decisions contravening relevant resolutions had no legal effect, he said. Describing the city as his people's political, religious and cultural capital, he said Palestinian heritage was intimately woven into Jerusalem. Appealing to all States not to establish diplomatic missions in the city, he rejected arguments by Israel and the one State standing in opposition to the rest of the world on the matter.

It was reprehensible that the United States had chosen to disregard international law and undermine its own role in any future peace process, he continued. Affirming that East Jerusalem was the capital of the State of Palestine, as recognized by the majority of States, he called upon all peace-loving nations to stand firm for the rule of law on that issue and to reject Israel's settlement policies. Palestinians would never accept occupation as a permanent reality, he stressed. "Those who want peace do not recognize illegal actions and measures but rather recognize the rights of the Palestinian people as enshrined in international law."

DANNY DANON (Israel) said the United Nations had taken another step backwards today, following resolution 2334 (2016), which had tried to designate Israel's presence at Judaism's holiest sites as violations of international law. That text had "pierced the hearts of Jews everywhere," he said, noting that those who had voted in favour of today's draft had only reaffirmed the decades-long double standard of the United Nations. Every country but Israel had the right to designate its own capital city, he noted, describing the current crisis as merely another one manufactured by the Palestinians in order to sabotage negotiations, as they had done every time there was a possibility for a settlement, starting with resolution 181 in 1947.

He went on to state that President Trump had merely stated a fact by recognizing that Jerusalem was the capital of Israel, something that Jews had maintained since 3,000 years ago, when King David established it as their capital. Many adversaries had sought to delegitimize the Jewish presence in Jerusalem, but the connection with the people had never been broken, and would never be broken, he vowed. Recalling that Jews were denied access to the Western Wall as recently as 50 years ago, he said Jerusalem under a sovereign Israel was now freer and more open to people of all religions than it had ever been at any time in history, pledging that it would remain so.

SOURCE: United Nations. "Permanent Member Vetoes Security Council Draft Calling upon States Not to Establish Diplomatic Missions in Jerusalem." December 18, 2017. http://www.un.org/press/en/2017/sc13125.doc.htm.

OTHER HISTORIC DOCUMENTS OF INTEREST

FROM PREVIOUS *HISTORIC DOCUMENTS*

UN Peacekeepers Killed in the Democratic Republic of the Congo

DECEMBER 8, 2017

On December 7, 2017, the Democratic Republic of the Congo (DRC) was the site of the deadliest attack against United Nations (UN) peacekeepers in more than two decades when rebel fighters killed fourteen. The DRC has had few periods of stability in its history, even since the end of its civil war in 2003, with multiple rebel groups vying for control of the nation's profitable natural resources. Further driving the violence in the country was the decision by its leader, Joseph Kabila, the country's first democratically elected president in a half century, not to leave office at the end of his term. Kabila failed to hold elections in 2016 and again in 2017, sparking deadly protests and sanctions from around the globe. Although the president promised to hold elections in 2018, opposition leaders were skeptical that Kabila would follow through.

UN Response to Ongoing Violence in the DRC

The DRC has experienced decades of dictatorship and back-to-back civil wars that were fought primarily over control of the nation's mineral resources. The population is extremely poor, with more than 80 percent living off $1.25 per day. As many as seventy rebel groups are estimated to be operating in the region, of which the Allied Democratic Forces (ADF) are now the biggest threat. ADF seeks to impose a strict interpretation of sharia law on the areas it controls and is known as an extremely brutal terrorist organization. ADF is estimated to have 1,500 fighters, and although its roots are in Uganda, it now operates primarily within the DRC along its eastern border. The group is thought to be responsible for an estimated 1,000 civilian deaths in the past three years. According to the United Nations, in 2017 alone, 1.7 million were forced from their homes due to the ongoing violence. The United Nations has been a leading force in working to slow or stop the ongoing rebel threat.

The United Nation's mission in the Congo, known as the UN Organization Stabilization Mission in the Democratic Republic of Congo (MONUSCO), is the largest and most expensive peacekeeping operation the international organization runs. It has an annual budget of more than $1 billion and employed nearly 19,000 peacekeepers. The mission began in 1999, and its mandate includes "the protection of civilians, humanitarian personnel and human rights defenders . . . and to support the government of the DRC in its stabilization and peace consolidation efforts." The Security Council has also granted it rare authority to go on the offensive against armed rebel groups. This has made it increasingly prone to attacks, and since 2001, 300 peacekeepers have been killed. But the mission has also experienced some successes. In 2006, it helped the nation run its first election in nearly fifty years. And in 2013, it helped weaken what was then the largest armed group in eastern Congo, M23. However, with the number of rebel groups still operating in the region, it is difficult for the mission to keep pace, and there has been a desire among several UN members to decrease the involvement and funding in the area. In March, the United Nations voted to maintain its mission in the DRC, while cutting back troops to slightly more than 16,000. The resolution also requested that conversations begin with Kabila's government to outline an exit strategy for the peacekeeping operation. The move was in line with an overall push among Security Council members, led by the United States, to review the UN peacekeeping operation around the globe that deploys upwards of 100,000 troops at a cost of more than $7.8 billion annually. As evidenced in the DRC, during the past five years, these peacekeepers have increasingly become the target of violent attacks.

UN PEACEKEEPERS TARGETED

On December 7, 2017, the ADF carried out the single deadliest attack against UN peacekeepers—known as blue helmets for their signature headwear—in more than two decades. The last major attack against the peacekeeping force occurred in June 1993 in Mogadishu, Somalia, when around two dozen were killed. Using mortars, rocket propelled grenades, and other heavy artillery, ADF engaged the military arm of the peacekeeping operation for three hours. The peacekeeping operation was hampered in its ability to quickly respond to the attack because UN helicopters have limited night vision, rendering them useless. Fourteen peacekeepers and five members of the DRC military were killed, and more than fifty were wounded. A majority of those on the UN team who were killed were from Tanzania, a country that provides an estimated 1,000 soldiers to the DRC mission. Tanzanian President John Pombe Magufuli said he was "shocked and saddened to hear of the deaths of our young, brave soldiers and heroes who lost their lives carrying out their peace mission in our neighbor the DRC."

UN Secretary General António Guterres called the attack a "war crime" and asked "the DRC authorities to investigate this incident and swiftly bring the perpetrators to justice. There must be no impunity for such assaults, here or anywhere else." MUNUSCO head Maman Sidikou echoed those remarks, condemning the attack and promising to "take all actions to ensure that the perpetrators are held accountable and brought to justice." The UN Security Council called it "a reminder of the extraordinary sacrifices made by these brave women and men every day."

In January 2018, the United Nations announced that it would open an investigation into the attack, to be led by Dmitry Titov, a former UN assistant secretary general. The team of investigators, made up of both UN officials and military officers from Tanzania, would travel to the DRC and neighboring states in an effort to determine how the attack unfolded, whether peacekeepers in the region are adequately prepared to respond to such events, and how these attacks can be avoided in the future.

KABILA CONTINUES TO HOLD POWER

The DRC constitution allows presidents to serve two terms in office. For Kabila, his second term came to an end in 2016, and presidential elections were scheduled to be held in November of that year. However, citing safety and financial concerns, the Independent National Electoral Commission and Kabila allies in parliament chose to postpone the vote and leave Kabila in office. Protests erupted, and Kabila's government violently cracked down. Dozens were killed, and the effort by Kabila's government to suppress the protests resulted in sanctions from the United States and European Union. Despite this, Kabila refused to step aside.

Out of fear that the nation could fall back into another civil war, the government and opposition attempted to find a peaceful solution to the situation. In December 2016, the National Episcopal Conference of Congo (CENCO) mediated a series of talks aimed at reaching an agreement that would result in Kabila's removal from office. The final deal, which was signed by members of the opposition and Kabila's government, although notably not the president himself, would allow Kabila to keep his seat until elections could be held in 2017. The terms of the agreement were such that a member of the opposition, chosen by the opposition, would serve as prime minister in an attempt to check Kabila's power. This presented Kabila's primary disagreement with the plan, because he believed he should be able to choose the opposition prime minister. The agreement would also require a transitional government to be put in place by March 2017 and prevented Kabila from making any changes to the nation's constitution that would allow him to seek a third term in office.

Shortly after the agreement was signed, Kabila reneged and formed his own transitional government, naming Bruno Tshibala, a member of the opposition party, as prime minister. This transitional government again failed to hold elections in 2017, resulting in additional pro-democracy protests across the country. The protesters were reportedly targeted by Kabila's government and his security forces, an assertion the president vehemently denied. Kabila's ongoing refusal to leave office, and the ensuing unrest, has further emboldened rebels operating in the region and increased tension between the country and the United Nations. The body—along with many international observers—expressed concern that a lack of progress on the part of the government to hold an election to replace Kabila could reverse the democratic progress it has made and leave it on much less stable footing. "Congo is going to go pretty badly next year. The humanitarian crisis is up there with Yemen and Syria and the situation is degrading, the region is getting nervous and the overall situation will become more fractured and more violent," said Stephanie Wolters, a researcher at the Institute for Security Studies in Pretoria, South Africa.

In January 2018, Kabila announced that he did not intend to seek a third term and would step aside after elections in December 2018. This would mark the country's first ever democratic transition of power, but there was no indication that the president would follow through. "Kabila does not have any intention to leave power . . . his strategy is to spread chaos across the country and then delay elections because he'll claim there is too much violence," according to Félix Tshisekedi, a prominent DRC leader who led the opposition in negotiations with the government in 2016.

—Heather Kerrigan

Following is the text of the UN Secretary General's remarks on December 8, 2017, after the deadly attack on UN peacekeepers in the Democratic Republic of the Congo.

DOCUMENT

Secretary-General Expresses Outrage over Deadly Attack in the DRC

December 8, 2017

I want to express my outrage and utter heartbreak at last night's attack on United Nations peacekeepers in the Democratic Republic of the Congo.

Early indications from the site of the attack in North Kivu indicate that at least 12 Tanzanian peacekeepers were killed, and at least 40 injured, 4 of them critically. We also understand that at least five members of the Armed Forces of the Democratic Republic of the Congo were killed.

I offer my deepest condolences to the families and loved ones of the victims, and to the Government and people of Tanzania. I wish a speedy recovery to all those injured.

I condemn this attack unequivocally. These deliberate attacks against UN peacekeepers are unacceptable and constitute a war crime. I call on the DRC authorities to investigate this incident and swiftly bring the perpetrators to justice. There must be no impunity for such assaults, here or anywhere else.

Military reinforcements have arrived on the scene. The Force Commander is there as well, coordinating the Mission's response. The medical evacuation of casualties is ongoing.

This is the worst attack on UN peacekeepers in the Organization's recent history. It is another indication of the enormous sacrifices made by troop contributing countries in the service of global peace. These brave women and men are putting their lives on the line every day across the world to serve peace and to protect civilians.

The situation in the DRC is one of the emergencies we are highlighting in today's appeal for the Central Emergency Response Fund. This latest attack highlights the urgency of helping people in need and addressing the volatile situation.

SOURCE: United Nations Secretary-General. "Secretary-General's Remarks on the Attack on Peacekeepers in the Democratic Republic of the Congo [as delivered]." December 8, 2017. https://www.un.org/sg/en/content/sg/statement/2017-12-08/secretary-general's-remarks-attack-peacekeepers-democratic-republic.

OTHER HISTORIC DOCUMENTS OF INTEREST

FROM PREVIOUS *HISTORIC DOCUMENTS*

International Campaign to Abolish Nuclear Weapons Awarded 2017 Nobel Peace Prize

DECEMBER 10, 2017

Since 1901, the Nobel Peace Prize has been awarded 98 times to 131 laureates, both individuals and organizations. In his will establishing the prize, Alfred Nobel outlined three types of peace work that could qualify for the award: contributions to fraternity between nations, to the abolition or reduction of standing armies, or to the holding and promotion of peace congresses. On December 10, 2017, the Nobel Committee presented the annual award, and associated $1.1 million prize, would be given to the International Campaign to Abolish Nuclear Weapons (ICAN), a conglomeration of organizations committed to the end of nuclear weapons capabilities.

ICAN RECEIVES AWARD FOR WORK TO ABOLISH NUCLEAR WEAPONS

Approximately 318 individuals and organizations were nominated for the 2017 peace prize. Although the names of the nominees are not officially made public until fifty years after the award is presented, nominating organizations sometimes reveal the names of those they have put up for the award and bookmakers around the globe frequently publicize the odds of potential victors. Thought to be on the shortlist for the 2017 award were Russian president Vladimir Putin, U.S. president Donald Trump, United Nations High Commission for Human Rights Zeid Ra'ad al Hussein, the White Helmets, Iranian foreign minister Mohammad Javad Zarif, EU foreign policy chief Federica Mogherini, the American Civil Liberties Union (ACLU), Pope Francis, and the Economic Community of West African States.

On October 6, 2017, the Norwegian Nobel Committee announced that the 2017 Nobel Peace Prize would be awarded to ICAN "for its work to draw attention to the catastrophic humanitarian consequences of any use of nuclear weapons and for its groundbreaking efforts to achieve a treaty-based prohibition of such weapons." ICAN is a coalition of more than 450 nongovernmental organizations from upwards of 100 nations that work to abolish nuclear weapons. The group was largely unknown ahead of winning the 2017 Nobel Peace Prize and was rarely included in media speculation as a possible nominee or winner.

ICAN has its roots in a 2007 nuclear disarmament conference in Austria and is today headquartered in Geneva, Switzerland. From there, ICAN lobbies the United Nations and national governments on behalf of its members and also runs nuclear awareness campaigns. The organization was instrumental in the development of the United Nations Treaty on the Prohibition of Nuclear Weapons, adopted on July 7, 2017. A total of 122 UN members supported the treaty's passage, which prohibits developing, testing, producing, manufacturing, acquiring, possessing, and stockpiling nuclear weapons. The agreement was not signed by any of the world's nuclear powers—China, France, India, Israel, North Korea, Pakistan, Russia, the United Kingdom, or the United States. To take effect, the treaty would require fifty countries to ratify it, and by the end of 2017, although fifty-three countries had signed on, only three had ratified (Guyana, Thailand, and the Vatican).

The United States did not participate in the negotiation of the treaty, stating that it would have little impact on the situation because no nuclear-armed state would join and that it would limit the influence of the nuclear Non-Proliferation Treaty (NPT). That agreement, signed in 1968, defined five nuclear-weapons states—China, France, Russia, the United Kingdom, and the United States—as the only countries in the world with a legal right to possess nuclear weapons. Any other nations that chose to ratify the NPT agreed not to acquire or possess nuclear weapons, and the five nuclear-armed states promised to negotiate toward global nuclear disarmament.

ICAN responded to the honor in a statement on its website, calling the award "a tribute to the tireless efforts of many millions of campaigners and concerned citizens worldwide who, ever since the dawn of the atomic age, have loudly protested nuclear weapons, insisting that they can serve no legitimate purpose and must be forever banished from the face of our earth." The prize "sends a message to all nuclear-armed states and all states that continue to rely on nuclear weapons for security that it is unacceptable behavior. We will not support it, we will not make excuses for it, we can't threaten to indiscriminately slaughter hundreds of thousands of civilians in the name of security. That's not how you build security," said the group's executive director Beatrice Fihn. Although many organizations work to promote the prohibition of nuclear weapons, the Norwegian Nobel Committee chose ICAN because, according to Berit Reiss-Anderson, chair of the Norwegian Nobel Committee, "they have taken the leading role in revitalizing" the pursuit of nuclear disarmament.

Nobel Committee Draws Criticism for "Symbolic" Award

This was not the first time the committee had chosen to focus on nuclear disarmament for the annual peace award. Both the 1985 and 2005 prizes, awarded to the International Physicians for the Prevention of Nuclear War and International Atomic Energy Agency, respectively, focused on organizations that promote the peaceful use of nuclear power. However, following the announcement of ICAN as the 2017 award recipient, commentary began swirling about whether the prize was simply "symbolic" given ICAN's support for the Treaty on the Prohibition on Nuclear Weapons that was unlikely to enter into force. The award also came at a time when the leaders of the United States and North Korea, two nuclear-armed nations, were ramping up their rhetoric about nuclear attacks and possible retaliation. Under Trump's leadership, the United States, which has an estimated 6,800 nuclear weapons, is looking to spend more than $1 trillion over the next thirty years to overhaul its nuclear arsenal, with the president stating it should be "at the top of the pack" worldwide. Neither Trump nor Korean Leader Kim Jong Un responded to the award.

The Norwegian Nobel Committee rejected any such assertion that their award was symbolic, noting that recognizing ICAN was meant as an "encouragement" to non-signatory nations to continue their negotiations over the abolition of nuclear weapons. "We are not kicking anybody's leg with the prize," said Reiss-Andersen. "An international legal prohibition will not in itself eliminate a single nuclear weapon, and that so far neither the states that already have nuclear weapons nor their closest allies support the nuclear weapon ban treaty," the Committee added. Fihn noted that the group does not "have unrealistic expectations that tomorrow nuclear weapons will be gone," adding "this is really a moment to be really inspired that it is possible to do something."

AWARDEE WARNS OF NUCLEAR DANGERS

Outside the Norwegian Parliament, where the award was presented on December 10, 1,000 red paper cranes were placed by ICAN. The cranes were made by children from Hiroshima, the site of the first nuclear weapon attack in 1945. In presenting the award, Reiss-Anderson spoke of the destruction caused by the U.S. atomic bombs dropped on Nagasaki and Hiroshima in 1945, and noted that "[t]oday's nuclear weapons are tremendously more destructive than the bombs that were dropped on Japan in 1945. A nuclear war could kill millions of people, dramatically alter the climate and the environment for much of the planet, and destabilise societies in a way never seen by humanity." Therefore, Reiss-Anderson said, "[t]he use of nuclear weapons—or even the threat of using them—is . . . unacceptable on any grounds, whether humanitarian, moral, or legal." Reiss-Anderson celebrated ICAN for engaging the citizens of the world, not just powerful governments and their leaders, in the discussion surrounding the abolition of nuclear weapons. While the body's existence may not have been necessary if the NPT nuclear states had followed through on their promise to negotiate the end of nuclear weapons, Reiss-Anderson said it was the committee's "firm conviction that ICAN, more than anyone else, has in the past year given the efforts to achieve a world without nuclear weapons a new direction and new vigour."

Fihn was onsite to receive the award along with ICAN campaigner Setsuko Thurlow, and the two jointly delivered the Nobel lecture. "At dozens of locations around the world—in missile silos buried in our earth, on submarines navigating through our oceans, and aboard planes flying high in our sky—lie 15,000 objects of humankind's destruction," Fihn said. "Perhaps it is the enormity of this fact, perhaps it is the unimaginable scale of the consequences, that leads many to simply accept this grim reality. To go about our daily lives with no thought to the instruments of insanity all around us," she continued, calling it "insanity to allow ourselves to be ruled by these weapons." Fihn also used her speech to call on the nuclear armed states to ratify the Treaty on the Prohibition of Nuclear Weapons. "To the nations who believe they are sheltered under the umbrella of nuclear weapons, will you be complicit in your own destruction and the destruction of others in your name? To all nations: choose the end of nuclear weapons over the end of us! This is the choice that the Treaty on the Prohibition of Nuclear Weapons represents. Join this Treaty," Fihn said.

Thurlow, a survivor of the 1945 Hiroshima bombing, spoke of her experience. "With one bomb, my beloved city was obliterated. Most of its residents were civilians who were incinerated, vaporized, carbonized—among them, members of my own family and 351 of my schoolmates," Thurlow said. It was this moment, she said, that the survivors "became convinced that we must warn the world about these apocalyptic weapons." Like Fihn, Thurlow spoke directly to the nuclear-armed countries. "Nine nations still threaten to incinerate entire cities, to destroy life on earth, to make our beautiful world uninhabitable for future generations," Thurlow said. "Heed our warning and know that your actions are consequential. You are each an integral part of the system of violence that threatens humankind."

ADDITIONAL NOBEL AWARDEES

The Nobel Prize is also given out in the categories of Physiology or Medicine, Physics, Chemistry, Literature, and Economic Sciences. In the Physics category, the award was given jointly to Rainer Weiss, Barry C. Barish, and Kip S. Thorne for their work in the observation of gravitational waves and contributions to the Laser Interferometer Gravitational-Wave Observatory (LIGO) detector. The Chemistry prize went to a group that included Jacques Dubochet, Joachim Frank, and Richard Henderson, who developed cryo-electron microscopy for "high-resolution structure determination of biomolecules in solution." The prize for Physiology or Medicine went to Jeffrey C. Hall, Michael Rosbash, and Michael W. Young for their discovery of the body's molecular mechanisms that control the circadian rhythm. The Nobel Prize in Literature went to Kazuo Ishiguro, an award-winning novelist and screenwriter whose works such as *The Remains of the Day* and *Never Let Me Go* "uncovered the abyss beneath our illusory sense of connection with the world," the committee said. The Economic Sciences prize, established in 1968, went to Richard H. Thaler for his work in behavioral economics.

—Heather Kerrigan

Following are the texts of the Nobel Peace Prize award ceremony speech and lecture, delivered on December 10, 2017, by Norwegian Nobel Committee Chair Berit Reiss-Anderson and ICAN representatives, Beatrice Fihn and Setsuko Thurlow, respectively.

DOCUMENT

Nobel Committee Awards
Nobel Peace Prize

December 10, 2017

Your Majesties, Your Royal Highnesses, Distinguished Representatives of the Nobel Peace Prize Laureate, Your Excellencies, Distinguished Guests, Ladies and Gentlemen,

The International Campaign to Abolish Nuclear Weapons (ICAN) has been awarded the Nobel Peace Prize for 2017. On behalf of the Norwegian Nobel Committee, I take great pleasure in congratulating ICAN on this award.

ICAN is receiving the award for its work to draw attention to the catastrophic humanitarian consequences of any use of nuclear weapons and for its ground-breaking efforts to achieve a treaty-based prohibition of such weapons. ICAN's efforts have given new momentum to the process of abolishing nuclear weapons.

This year's Peace Prize follows in a tradition of awards that have honoured efforts against the proliferation of nuclear weapons and for nuclear disarmament. Twelve Peace Prizes have been awarded, in whole or in part, for this type of peace work. The first went to Philip Noel-Baker in 1959, and the most recent was awarded to Barack Obama in 2009. And now, this year, to the International Campaign to Abolish Nuclear Weapons (ICAN).

On two days in August 1945, the world experienced the terrible destructive force of nuclear weapons for the first time. The bombings of Hiroshima and Nagasaki instantly killed at least 140,000 people, the vast majority of whom were civilians. Hiroshima was utterly destroyed and large sections of Nagasaki were laid in ruins. But death was not finished with Hiroshima and Nagasaki in August 1945. The death toll continued to rise significantly in the years that followed, and survivors are still suffering from the effects of radiation today.

The devastation of Hiroshima and Nagasaki has taught us that nuclear weapons are so dangerous, and inflict so much agony and death on civilian populations, that they must never, ever, be used again.

Today's nuclear weapons are tremendously more destructive than the bombs that were dropped on Japan in 1945. A nuclear war could kill millions of people, dramatically alter the climate and the environment for much of the planet, and destabilise societies in a way never before seen by humanity. The notion of a limited nuclear war is an illusion.

Nuclear weapons do not distinguish between military and civilian targets. Used in war, they would impact disproportionately on the civilian population, inflicting vast, unnecessary suffering. It is virtually impossible for civilians to protect themselves against the catastrophic effects of a nuclear attack. The use of nuclear weapons—or even the threat of using them—is therefore unacceptable on any grounds, whether humanitarian, moral or legal.

Despite all this, it remains the case that the global balance of military power is maintained by nuclear weapons. The logic of this balance of terror rests on the proposition that nuclear weapons are such a deterrent that no one would dare attack a nuclear-armed state. The deterrent effect is said to be so strong that it alone has prevented war between the nuclear powers for the last 70 years. The empirical basis for this assumption is highly debatable. It cannot be claimed with any certainty that deterrence has worked as intended. It is also worth keeping in mind that nuclear deterrence requires a credible threat to actually use nuclear weapons. The weapons exist so that they can, if necessary, be deployed.

A number of international agreements and treaties have been entered into which limit the possession and development of nuclear weapons. The most important of these is the Treaty on the Non-Proliferation of Nuclear Weapons, or NPT. It takes considerable military and political insight to fully understand all the treaties, agreements and international legal instruments that regulate disarmament and arms control. The views that dominate the political debate are those of the great powers and powerful alliances.

ICAN arose as a protest against the established order. Nuclear weapon issues are not solely a question to be addressed by governments, nor a matter for experts or high-level politicians. Nuclear weapons concern everyone, and everyone is entitled to an opinion. ICAN has succeeded in generating fresh engagement among ordinary people in the campaign against nuclear weapons. The organisation's acronym is perhaps not a coincidence: I CAN.

ICAN's main message is that the world can never be safe as long as we have nuclear weapons. This message resonates with millions of people who perceive that the threat of nuclear war is greater than it has been for a long time, not least due to the situation in North Korea.

Another major concern of ICAN is that the current international legal order is inadequate to deal with the nuclear weapons problem.

The entry into force of the Non-Proliferation Treaty in 1970 was a historic breakthrough. It gave formal status to the nuclear powers of the day—the United States, the Soviet Union, the UK, France and China—as states with the legal right to possess nuclear weapons. All other countries that acceded to the treaty pledged, in so doing, not to acquire such weapons. In return, the legally recognized nuclear-weapon states undertook to begin negotiations in good faith to seek nuclear disarmament. This dual pledge is the very core of the Non-Proliferation Treaty, and both sides of it must be honoured to maintain the treaty's legitimacy.

Ladies and gentlemen, it is no exaggeration to say that the nuclear-weapon states have only to a limited degree honoured the disarmament commitment they made in the NPT. Let me remind you that in 2000 the NPT's Review Conference stated that the treaty calls for "an unequivocal undertaking by the nuclear-weapon states to accomplish the total elimination of their arsenals leading to nuclear disarmament". From an international law perspective, the five legally recognized nuclear-weapon states and their allies have thus assumed a responsibility to help achieve disarmament and a world free of nuclear weapons. If the disarmament process had been carried out as intended, ICAN's struggle for a treaty-based ban on nuclear weapons would have been unneeded. It is the lack of progress towards nuclear disarmament that has made it necessary to supplement the Non-Proliferation Treaty with other international legal initiatives and commitments.

The Non-Proliferation Treaty applies only to the countries that have acceded to it. India, Pakistan and Israel, which all have nuclear weapons, are not NPT members. Moreover, North Korea, which has carried out six nuclear test explosions, has withdrawn from the treaty. Global nuclear disarmament cannot take place without these countries, too, participating. Yet they reserve for themselves the same right to nuclear weapons as the five states that had acquired such weapons prior to 1970. The five legally recognized nuclear-weapon states, for their part, cite the nuclear arsenals of these other countries as one of several arguments for not yet being able to comply with the NPT's nuclear disarmament requirements.

It is in part to break this vicious cycle that ICAN has advocated a universal, treaty-based ban on nuclear weapons.

ICAN does not accept that the lack of progress towards nuclear disarmament is a real-politik necessity. ICAN's premise is humanitarian, maintaining that any use of nuclear weapons will cause unacceptable human suffering. Binding international prohibitions have already been established for chemical weapons, biological weapons, land mines and cluster weapons, precisely because of the unacceptable harm and suffering that these weapons inflict on civilian populations. It defies common sense that nuclear weapons, which are far more dangerous, are not subject to a comparable ban under international law.

Pointing out this legal gap was a crucial first step on the road to a prohibition treaty. Another important step was the Humanitarian Pledge initiated by the Austrian Government in December 2014. The Pledge is a voluntary national commitment to seek to stigmatise, prohibit and eliminate nuclear weapons. ICAN has worked resolutely to muster broad international support for the Humanitarian Pledge. To date, 127 states have signed on to this commitment.

ICAN has also been a driving force in efforts to secure a binding international ban of nuclear weapons. On 7 July 2017, a final draft treaty was endorsed by 129 UN member states. The Treaty on the Prohibition of Nuclear Weapons was opened for signature this autumn, and has been signed so far by 56 states. When 50 or more states have also ratified the treaty, it will become binding under international law for the signatory states.

ICAN is a young organisation, founded in 2007 on the initiative of the International Physicians for the Prevention of Nuclear War, which won the Nobel Peace Prize in 1985. ICAN is a loose coalition of 468 NGOs from more than 100 countries. It is impressive that ICAN is able to unite so many different groups in support of a common goal and give a voice to millions of people who are convinced that nuclear weapons do not provide security, but insecurity.

In awarding this year's Peace Prize to ICAN, the Norwegian Nobel Committee seeks to honour this remarkable endeavour to serve the interests of mankind.

The Nobel Committee believes that an international ban on nuclear weapons will be an important, possibly decisive, step on the road to a world without nuclear weapons. Such a goal is fully consistent with the essence of Alfred Nobel's will.

Ladies and gentlemen, ICAN's support for a global ban on nuclear weapons is not uncontroversial. We must acknowledge that the treaty has powerful opponents, but the idea of prohibiting and abolishing nuclear weapons is neither naïve nor new. As early as 1946, in the UN General Assembly's very first resolution, the United Nations called for nuclear disarmament and an international nuclear weapons control regime.

At the Reykjavik Summit in 1986, Mikhail Gorbachev and Ronald Reagan tried to halt the spiralling nuclear arms race between the two superpowers, and came close to concluding an agreement to abolish all long-range nuclear missiles. A year and a half earlier, President Reagan had addressed the people of the United States and the Soviet Union directly, saying:

"A nuclear war cannot be won and must never be fought. The only value in our two nations possessing nuclear weapons is to make sure they never will be used. But then, would it not be better to do away with them entirely?"

Today it is more important than ever to support this vision. While the global community may trust that no responsible head of state would ever order another nuclear attack, we have no guarantees that it will not happen. Despite international legal commitments, irresponsible leaders can come to power in any nuclear-armed state and become embroiled in serious military conflicts that veer out of control.

Ultimately, nuclear weapons are controlled by human beings. In spite of advanced security mechanisms and control systems, technical and human errors can occur, with potentially catastrophic consequences. Can we be sure that the control systems of the nuclear powers will not someday be sabotaged by hackers acting on behalf of hostile states, terrorists or extremists?

In short, nuclear weapons are so dangerous that the only responsible course of action is to work for their removal and destruction.

Many people think that the vision of a nuclear weapon-free world, a Global Zero, is utopic, or even irresponsible.

Similar arguments were once used to oppose the treaties banning biological and chemical weapons, cluster weapons and land mines. Nonetheless, the prohibitions became reality and most of these weapons are far less prevalent today as a result. Using them is taboo.

Ladies and gentlemen, the Norwegian Nobel Committee is aware that nuclear weapons disarmament presents far greater challenges than disarmament of the types of weapons I just mentioned. But there is no getting around the fact that the nuclear weapon states have committed, through the Non-Proliferation Treaty, to work towards disarmament. This is the ultimate objective of the treaty. Through its efforts, ICAN has reminded the nuclear weapon states that their commitment entails a genuine obligation, and the time to honour it is now!

In his Nobel lecture in 1959, Philip Noel-Baker took issue with the widely held opinion that complete nuclear disarmament is impossible to achieve in the real world. He quoted another Peace Prize laureate, Fridtjof Nansen:

"The difficult is what takes a little while; the impossible is what takes a little longer."

The people of ICAN are impatient and visionary, but they are not naïve. ICAN recognizes that the nuclear-armed states cannot eliminate their nuclear weapons overnight. This must be achieved through a mutual, gradual and verifiable disarmament process. But it is the hope of ICAN and the Norwegian Nobel Committee that an international legal ban, and broad popular engagement, will put pressure on all nuclear-armed states and expedite the process.

Ladies and gentlemen, there are two persons on the podium today who, each in their way, are outstanding representatives of the ICAN movement.

Madam Setsuko Thurlow, you were 13 years old when you experienced the bombing of Hiroshima. You have devoted your life to bearing witness to the events of 6 August

1945. You see it as your mission to describe the suffering, fear and death inflicted on your city. No one was spared. Little children, their parents, brothers and sisters, schoolmates and grandparents were killed. You say that war cannot be waged in this way, and that it must never happen again. You do not allow us to forget.

Beatrice Fihn, you are the Executive Director of ICAN and have the challenging task of uniting different organisations and interest groups in pursuit of a common goal. You are a splendid representative of the multitude of idealists who forgo an ordinary career and instead devote all of their time and skills to the work of achieving a peaceful world.

It is an honour to have you here as our guests, and we wish to express our deep and heartfelt gratitude for the work that you do. Our tribute also goes to all the individuals and organisations that you represent.

The decision to award the Nobel Peace Prize for 2017 to the International Campaign to Abolish Nuclear Weapons has a solid grounding in Alfred Nobel's will. The will specifies three different criteria for awarding the Peace Prize: the promotion of fraternity between nations, the advancement of disarmament and arms control and the holding and promotion of peace congresses. ICAN works vigorously to achieve nuclear disarmament. ICAN and a majority of UN member states have contributed to fraternity between nations by supporting the Humanitarian Pledge. And through its inspiring and innovative support for the UN negotiations on a Nuclear Weapon Ban Treaty, ICAN has played an important role in bringing about what in our day and age is equivalent to an international peace congress.

In closing, I would like to quote His Holiness Pope Francis, who recently declared: "Weapons of mass destruction, particularly nuclear weapons, create nothing but a false sense of security. They cannot constitute the basis for peaceful coexistence between members of the human family, which must rather be inspired by an ethics of solidarity."

The Norwegian Nobel Committee shares this view. Moreover, it is our firm conviction that ICAN, more than anyone else, has in the past year given the efforts to achieve a world without nuclear weapons a new direction and new vigour.
Thank you.

SOURCE: The Nobel Foundation. "Award Ceremony Speech." December 10, 2017. © The Nobel Foundation 2017. https://www.nobelprize.org/nobel_prizes/peace/laureates/2017/presentation-speech.html.

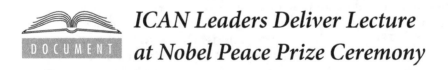

ICAN Leaders Deliver Lecture at Nobel Peace Prize Ceremony

December 10, 2017

Beatrice Fihn:

Your Majesties,
Members of the Norwegian Nobel Committee,
Esteemed guests,

Today, it is a great honour to accept the 2017 Nobel Peace Prize on behalf of thousands of inspirational people who make up the International Campaign to Abolish Nuclear

Weapons. Together we have brought democracy to disarmament and are reshaping international law.

We most humbly thank the Norwegian Nobel Committee for recognizing our work and giving momentum to our crucial cause. We want to recognize those who have so generously donated their time and energy to this campaign.

We thank the courageous foreign ministers, diplomats, Red Cross and Red Crescent staff, UN officials, academics and experts with whom we have worked in partnership to advance our common goal. And we thank all who are committed to ridding the world of this terrible threat.

At dozens of locations around the world—in missile silos buried in our earth, on submarines navigating through our oceans, and aboard planes flying high in our sky—lie 15,000 objects of humankind's destruction. Perhaps it is the enormity of this fact, perhaps it is the unimaginable scale of the consequences, that leads many to simply accept this grim reality. To go about our daily lives with no thought to the instruments of insanity all around us.

For it is insanity to allow ourselves to be ruled by these weapons. Many critics of this movement suggest that we are the irrational ones, the idealists with no grounding in reality. That nuclear-armed states will never give up their weapons. But we represent the only rational choice. We represent those who refuse to accept nuclear weapons as a fixture in our world, those who refuse to have their fates bound up in a few lines of launch code.

Ours is the only reality that is possible. The alternative is unthinkable. The story of nuclear weapons will have an ending, and it is up to us what that ending will be. Will it be the end of nuclear weapons, or will it be the end of us? One of these things will happen. The only rational course of action is to cease living under the conditions where our mutual destruction is only one impulsive tantrum away.

Today I want to talk of three things: fear, freedom, and the future. By the very admission of those who possess them, the real utility of nuclear weapons is in their ability to provoke fear. When they refer to their "deterrent" effect, proponents of nuclear weapons are celebrating fear as a weapon of war. They are puffing their chests by declaring their preparedness to exterminate, in a flash, countless thousands of human lives.

Nobel Laureate William Faulkner said when accepting his prize in 1950, that "There is only the question of 'when will I be blown up?'" But since then, this universal fear has given way to something even more dangerous: denial. Gone is the fear of Armageddon in an instant, gone is the equilibrium between two blocs that was used as the justification for deterrence, gone are the fallout shelters.

But one thing remains: the thousands upon thousands of nuclear warheads that filled us up with that fear. The risk for nuclear weapons use is even greater today than at the end of the Cold War. But unlike the Cold War, today we face many more nuclear armed states, terrorists, and cyber warfare. All of this makes us less safe. Learning to live with these weapons in blind acceptance has been our next great mistake.

Fear is rational. The threat is real. We have avoided nuclear war not through prudent leadership but good fortune. Sooner or later, if we fail to act, our luck will run out. A moment of panic or carelessness, a misconstrued comment or bruised ego, could easily lead us unavoidably to the destruction of entire cities. A calculated military escalation could lead to the indiscriminate mass murder of civilians.

If only a small fraction of today's nuclear weapons were used, soot and smoke from the firestorms would loft high into the atmosphere—cooling, darkening and drying the Earth's surface for more than a decade. It would obliterate food crops, putting billions at risk of starvation. Yet we continue to live in denial of this existential threat.

But Faulkner in his Nobel speech also issued a challenge to those who came after him. Only by being the voice of humanity, he said, can we defeat fear; can we help humanity endure. ICAN's duty is to be that voice. The voice of humanity and humanitarian law; to speak up on behalf of civilians. Giving voice to that humanitarian perspective is how we will create the end of fear, the end of denial. And ultimately, the end of nuclear weapons.

That brings me to my second point: freedom. As the International Physicians for the Prevention of Nuclear War, the first ever anti-nuclear weapons organisation to win this prize, said on this stage in 1985: "We physicians protest the outrage of holding the entire world hostage. We protest the moral obscenity that each of us is being continuously targeted for extinction."

Those words still ring true in 2017. We must reclaim the freedom to not live our lives as hostages to imminent annihilation. Man—not woman!—made nuclear weapons to control others, but instead we are controlled by them. They made us false promises. That by making the consequences of using these weapons so unthinkable it would make any conflict unpalatable. That it would keep us free from war.

But far from preventing war, these weapons brought us to the brink multiple times throughout the Cold War. And in this century, these weapons continue to escalate us towards war and conflict. In Iraq, in Iran, in Kashmir, in North Korea. Their existence propels others to join the nuclear race. They don't keep us safe, they cause conflict.

As fellow Nobel Peace Laureate, Martin Luther King Jr, called them from this very stage in 1964, these weapons are "both genocidal and suicidal". They are the madman's gun held permanently to our temple. These weapons were supposed to keep us free, but they deny us our freedoms.

It's an affront to democracy to be ruled by these weapons. But they are just weapons. They are just tools. And just as they were created by geopolitical context, they can just as easily be destroyed by placing them in a humanitarian context.

That is the task ICAN has set itself—and my third point I wish to talk about, the future. I have the honour of sharing this stage today with Setsuko Thurlow, who has made it her life's purpose to bear witness to the horror of nuclear war. She and the hibakusha were at the beginning of the story, and it is our collective challenge to ensure they will also witness the end of it.

They relive the painful past, over and over again, so that we may create a better future. There are hundreds of organisations that together as ICAN are making great strides towards that future.

There are thousands of tireless campaigners around the world who work each day to rise to that challenge. There are millions of people across the globe who have stood shoulder to shoulder with those campaigners to show hundreds of millions more that a different future is truly possible. Those who say that future is not possible need to get out of the way of those making it a reality.

As the culmination of this grassroots effort, through the action of ordinary people, this year the hypothetical marched forward towards the actual as 122 nations negotiated and concluded a UN treaty to outlaw these weapons of mass destruction.

The Treaty on the Prohibition of Nuclear Weapons provides the pathway forward at a moment of great global crisis. It is a light in a dark time. And more than that, it provides a choice. A choice between the two endings: the end of nuclear weapons or the end of us.

It is not naive to believe in the first choice. It is not irrational to think nuclear states can disarm. It is not idealistic to believe in life over fear and destruction; it is a necessity.

All of us face that choice. And I call on every nation to join the Treaty on the Prohibition of Nuclear Weapons. The United States, choose freedom over fear. Russia, choose disarmament over destruction. Britain, choose the rule of law over oppression. France, choose human rights over terror. China, choose reason over irrationality. India, choose sense over senselessness. Pakistan, choose logic over Armageddon. Israel, choose common sense over obliteration. North Korea, choose wisdom over ruin.

To the nations who believe they are sheltered under the umbrella of nuclear weapons, will you be complicit in your own destruction and the destruction of others in your name? To all nations: choose the end of nuclear weapons over the end of us! This is the choice that the Treaty on the Prohibition of Nuclear Weapons represents. Join this Treaty.

We citizens are living under the umbrella of falsehoods. These weapons are not keeping us safe, they are contaminating our land and water, poisoning our bodies and holding hostage our right to life. To all citizens of the world: Stand with us and demand your government side with humanity and sign this treaty. We will not rest until all States have joined, on the side of reason.

No nation today boasts of being a chemical weapon state. No nation argues that it is acceptable, in extreme circumstances, to use sarin nerve agent. No nation proclaims the right to unleash on its enemy the plague or polio. That is because international norms have been set, perceptions have been changed.

And now, at last, we have an unequivocal norm against nuclear weapons. Monumental strides forward never begin with universal agreement. With every new signatory and every passing year, this new reality will take hold. This is the way forward. There is only one way to prevent the use of nuclear weapons: prohibit and eliminate them.

Nuclear weapons, like chemical weapons, biological weapons, cluster munitions and land mines before them, are now illegal. Their existence is immoral. Their abolishment is in our hands. The end is inevitable. But will that end be the end of nuclear weapons or the end of us? We must choose one.

We are a movement for rationality. For democracy. For freedom from fear. We are campaigners from 468 organisations who are working to safeguard the future, and we are representative of the moral majority: the billions of people who choose life over death, who together will see the end of nuclear weapons.

Thank you.

Setsuko Thurlow:

Your Majesties,
Distinguished members of the Norwegian Nobel Committee,
My fellow campaigners, here and throughout the world,
Ladies and gentlemen,

It is a great privilege to accept this award, together with Beatrice, on behalf of all the remarkable human beings who form the ICAN movement. You each give me such tremendous hope that we can—and will—bring the era of nuclear weapons to an end.

I speak as a member of the family of hibakusha—those of us who, by some miraculous chance, survived the atomic bombings of Hiroshima and Nagasaki. For more than seven decades, we have worked for the total abolition of nuclear weapons.

We have stood in solidarity with those harmed by the production and testing of these horrific weapons around the world. People from places with long-forgotten names, like

Moruroa, Ekker, Semipalatinsk, Maralinga, Bikini. People whose lands and seas were irradiated, whose bodies were experimented upon, whose cultures were forever disrupted.

We were not content to be victims. We refused to wait for an immediate fiery end or the slow poisoning of our world. We refused to sit idly in terror as the so-called great powers took us past nuclear dusk and brought us recklessly close to nuclear midnight. We rose up. We shared our stories of survival. We said: humanity and nuclear weapons cannot coexist.

Today, I want you to feel in this hall the presence of all those who perished in Hiroshima and Nagasaki. I want you to feel, above and around us, a great cloud of a quarter million souls. Each person had a name. Each person was loved by someone. Let us ensure that their deaths were not in vain.

I was just 13 years old when the United States dropped the first atomic bomb, on my city Hiroshima. I still vividly remember that morning. At 8:15, I saw a blinding bluish-white flash from the window. I remember having the sensation of floating in the air.

As I regained consciousness in the silence and darkness, I found myself pinned by the collapsed building. I began to hear my classmates' faint cries: "Mother, help me. God, help me."

Then, suddenly, I felt hands touching my left shoulder, and heard a man saying: "Don't give up! Keep pushing! I am trying to free you. See the light coming through that opening? Crawl towards it as quickly as you can." As I crawled out, the ruins were on fire. Most of my classmates in that building were burned to death alive. I saw all around me utter, unimaginable devastation.

Processions of ghostly figures shuffled by. Grotesquely wounded people, they were bleeding, burnt, blackened and swollen. Parts of their bodies were missing. Flesh and skin hung from their bones. Some with their eyeballs hanging in their hands. Some with their bellies burst open, their intestines hanging out. The foul stench of burnt human flesh filled the air.

Thus, with one bomb my beloved city was obliterated. Most of its residents were civilians who were incinerated, vaporized, carbonized—among them, members of my own family and 351 of my schoolmates.

In the weeks, months and years that followed, many thousands more would die, often in random and mysterious ways, from the delayed effects of radiation. Still to this day, radiation is killing survivors.

Whenever I remember Hiroshima, the first image that comes to mind is of my four-year-old nephew, Eiji—his little body transformed into an unrecognizable melted chunk of flesh. He kept begging for water in a faint voice until his death released him from agony.

To me, he came to represent all the innocent children of the world, threatened as they are at this very moment by nuclear weapons. Every second of every day, nuclear weapons endanger everyone we love and everything we hold dear. We must not tolerate this insanity any longer.

Through our agony and the sheer struggle to survive—and to rebuild our lives from the ashes—we hibakusha became convinced that we must warn the world about these apocalyptic weapons. Time and again, we shared our testimonies.

But still some refused to see Hiroshima and Nagasaki as atrocities—as war crimes. They accepted the propaganda that these were "good bombs" that had ended a "just war". It was this myth that led to the disastrous nuclear arms race—a race that continues to this day.

Nine nations still threaten to incinerate entire cities, to destroy life on earth, to make our beautiful world uninhabitable for future generations. The development of nuclear weapons signifies not a country's elevation to greatness, but its descent to the darkest depths of depravity. These weapons are not a necessary evil; they are the ultimate evil.

On the seventh of July this year, I was overwhelmed with joy when a great majority of the world's nations voted to adopt the Treaty on the Prohibition of Nuclear Weapons. Having witnessed humanity at its worst, I witnessed, that day, humanity at its best. We hibakusha had been waiting for the ban for seventy-two years. Let this be the beginning of the end of nuclear weapons.

All responsible leaders will sign this treaty. And history will judge harshly those who reject it. No longer shall their abstract theories mask the genocidal reality of their practices. No longer shall "deterrence" be viewed as anything but a deterrent to disarmament. No longer shall we live under a mushroom cloud of fear.

To the officials of nuclear-armed nations—and to their accomplices under the so-called "nuclear umbrella" —I say this: Listen to our testimony. Heed our warning. And know that your actions are consequential. You are each an integral part of a system of violence that is endangering humankind. Let us all be alert to the banality of evil.

To every president and prime minister of every nation of the world, I beseech you: Join this treaty; forever eradicate the threat of nuclear annihilation.

When I was a 13-year-old girl, trapped in the smouldering rubble, I kept pushing. I kept moving toward the light. And I survived. Our light now is the ban treaty. To all in this hall and all listening around the world, I repeat those words that I heard called to me in the ruins of Hiroshima: "Don't give up! Keep pushing! See the light? Crawl towards it."

Tonight, as we march through the streets of Oslo with torches aflame, let us follow each other out of the dark night of nuclear terror. No matter what obstacles we face, we will keep moving and keep pushing and keep sharing this light with others. This is our passion and commitment for our one precious world to survive.

SOURCE: International Campaign to Abolish Nuclear Weapons. "International Campaign to Abolish Nuclear Weapons Awarded 2017 Nobel Peace Prize." December 22, 2017. © The Nobel Foundation 2017. http://www.icanw.org/campaign-news/ican-receives-2017-nobel-peace-prize.

OTHER HISTORIC DOCUMENTS OF INTEREST

FROM THIS VOLUME

FROM PREVIOUS *HISTORIC DOCUMENTS*

Federal Communications Commission Overturns Net Neutrality

DECEMBER 14, 2017

Efforts by President Donald Trump's administration to roll back regulations implemented by President Barack Obama included the Federal Communications Commission's (FCC) vote in December 2017 to reverse its 2015 Open Internet Order, which enshrined the concept of net neutrality in rules governing broadband Internet providers. Led by FCC Commissioner Ajit Pai, the push to reverse the order prompted in-person and virtual protests by net neutrality supporters, and millions of comments were submitted during the agency's public comment period. Broadband providers have promised that the rule reversal will not affect consumers' Internet access, but various officials, companies, and organizations have filed lawsuits challenging the FCC's decision.

THE 2015 OPEN INTERNET ORDER

Adopted in February 2015, the FCC's Open Internet Order reclassified broadband Internet as a telecommunications service under Title II of the Communications Act, meaning that, as an essential public utility, the FCC has more power to regulate it. The rule also sought to prohibit broadband providers from favoring some Internet traffic over others, either by blocking or slowing access to certain websites or content or imposing fees for faster services—a concept known as net neutrality. Consumer groups, free speech advocates, and open Internet supporters welcomed the order, saying it provided consumer protections and would preserve access to the Internet. However, broadband providers and telecom industry groups claimed the rules were unnecessary and burdensome, with several providers and trade associations filing lawsuits to challenge the FCC's authority to reclassify broadband.

FCC CHAIRMAN PROPOSES NET NEUTRALITY REPEAL

Following his appointment as the new FCC chair in January 2017, Pai quickly signaled his disagreement with the 2015 order and intention to revisit the net neutrality rules. Pai shared Trump's belief that the rules had stifled innovation and investment in technology. The chair's initial proposal to roll back the Obama-era regulations was adopted by the FCC on May 18 and released for public comment on May 23.

Dubbed "Restoring Internet Freedom," the proposal prompted a massive public response. By mid-July, approximately 7.4 million comments had been received by the FCC. By late September, this number had grown to more than 22 million comments. Almost immediately, the comment period became a source of controversy. Shortly after the comment period opened, news outlets reported that Internet activist organization Fight for the Future coordinated the submission of a letter to the FCC from fourteen people whose names were used to submit comments supporting Pai's proposal without their permission. The signatories asked for the comments to be removed from the FCC's docket and for the FCC to notify any others whose names may have been wrongly used. The letter prompted Rep. Frank Pallone, D-N.J., the ranking member of the House Committee on Energy and Commerce, to ask the U.S. Department of Justice to investigate the fake comments as criminal acts. Pallone was also one of nine lawmakers to request an investigation by the Government Accountability Office.

The controversy only grew following an investigation by *The Wall Street Journal* that found hundreds of thousands of comments posted to the FCC site had been submitted under stolen identities or the names of people who were deceased. For example, *The Wall Street Journal* found 818,000 identical postings of one comment supporting Pai's proposal. When the paper sent e-mail surveys to 531,000 of the e-mail addresses used to post those comments, more than 7,000 bounced back, indicating the e-mails were defunct. Roughly 2,700 people responded to the survey, of whom 72 percent said they had nothing to do with the comments. FCC spokesperson Brian Hart told *The Wall Street Journal* that the agency had received more than 7.5 million comments consisting of the same letter expressing support for the 2015 order, comments that had been submitted by about 45,000 unique e-mail addresses "generated by a single fake e-mail generator website." Hart also said more than 400,000 comments had been submitted from "the same address in Russia."

These revelations prompted New York Attorney General Eric Schneiderman to launch an investigation into the public comments process and twenty-eight Senators to write to the FCC calling for the agency's vote on Pai's proposal to be postponed due to concerns over the validity of the comments. FCC Commissioner Jessica Rosenworcel called for public hearings so that the agency could hear directly from consumers before voting on Pai's proposal, but hearings were not held, and the vote was not postponed.

Pai's proposal also led to in-person and virtual protests by supporters of the 2015 order. On July 12, more than 180 companies and organizations including Amazon, Etsy, Facebook, Google, the American Civil Liberties Union, and MoveOn.org participated in the Day of Action to Save Net Neutrality. Participants put up website blockers, images simulating website slowness, and requests for money for faster site access to illustrate the anticipated impact of net neutrality rollback. On December 7, net neutrality supporters staged in-person protests at Verizon stores across the United States. (Pai was formerly a lawyer for Verizon, and the company has been a critic of net neutrality.) December 12 was dubbed Break the Internet Day, with sites including Reddit, Kickstarter, and Mozilla posting special landing pages that urged users to contact their members of Congress to ask them to protect net neutrality rules.

The Commission Votes

On December 14, the FCC voted along party lines to reverse the 2015 Open Internet Order and adopt Pai's Restoring Internet Freedom proposal. In a press release announcing the decision, the FCC said that the 2015 order's "heavy-handed utility-style regulation" had "imposed substantial costs on the entire Internet ecosystem" and that "returning to the traditional light-touch framework" in place prior to 2015 would "protect consumers at far less cost to investment than the prior rigid and wide-ranging utility rules." Specifically, the new order restored the classification of broadband as an "information service" under Title I of the Communications Act and reinstated the classification of mobile broadband Internet access services as a private mobile service. It also restored the Federal Trade Commission's jurisdiction over consumer protection issues related to broadband. Additionally, the order included new transparency rules for Internet service providers that require them to disclose information about practices including "any blocking, throttling, paid prioritization, or affiliated prioritization."

In a statement following the vote, Pai sought to reassure consumers, saying, "Americans will still be able to access the websites they want to visit. They will still be able to enjoy the services they want to enjoy." Pai also claimed the new order would help consumers by promoting competition. "Broadband providers will have stronger incentives to build networks, especially in unserved areas, and to upgrade networks to gigabit speeds and 5G," he said. "This means there will be more competition among broadband providers." Offering a strongly worded statement of dissent, Commissioner Mignon Clyburn characterized the "Destroying Internet Freedom Order" as "fiercely-spun, legally-lightweight, consumer-harming, [and] corporate enabling" and said the FCC was abdicating its responsibility to protect consumers. She also accused Pai and Republican Commissioners Michael O'Rielly and Brendan Carr of "ignoring the will of the people" and refusing to put the thousands of net neutrality complaints filed by consumers in the record while claiming there had not been any real violations of the 2015 order.

In the wake of the FCC's vote, major telecommunications companies promised that consumers' online experience would not change. "The Internet will continue to work tomorrow just as it always has," said AT&T in a statement. Supporters of net neutrality argued that companies would not be compelled to offer consumers the best services without the 2015 order. "Let's remember why we have these rules in the first place," said Michael Beckerman, president of the Internet Association, which represents companies including Google and Facebook. "There is little competition in the broadband service market."

On January 16, 2018, the attorneys general for twenty-one states and the District of Columbia, led by Schneiderman, filed a lawsuit in the U.S. Court of Appeals for the D.C. Circuit to block the FCC's net neutrality repeal, calling it "arbitrary, capricious and an abuse of discretion." Free Press, Open Technology Institute, and Mozilla Corp. are among the other groups and companies who have filed similar lawsuits to challenge the FCC's new order. Also on January 16, Senate Democrats announced that they had fifty of the fifty-one votes needed to introduce and pass a resolution to reverse the FCC vote and restore the 2015 order. (The Congressional Review Act gives lawmakers sixty days after an independent agency decision to reverse the action.) However, any bill would also need to pass the Republican-controlled House of Representatives and would be subject to a possible presidential veto.

—Linda Grimm

Following is a press release issued by the Federal Communications Commission (FCC) on December 14, 2017, announcing the reversal of the 2015 Open Internet Order; and statements by FCC Chairman Ajit Pai and Commissioner Mignon Clyburn from December 14, 2017, in response to the decision.

FCC Reverses 2015 Net Neutrality Decision

December 14, 2017

The Federal Communications Commission today voted to restore the longstanding, bipartisan light-touch regulatory framework that has fostered rapid Internet growth, openness, and freedom for nearly 20 years.

Following detailed legal and economic analysis, as well as extensive examination of comments from consumers and stakeholders, the Commission reversed the FCC's 2015 heavy-handed utility-style regulation of broadband Internet access service, which imposed substantial costs on the entire Internet ecosystem.

In place of that heavy-handed framework, the FCC is returning to the traditional light-touch framework that was in place until 2015. Moreover, the FCC today also adopted robust transparency requirements that will empower consumers as well as facilitate effective government oversight of broadband providers' conduct. In particular, the FCC's action today has restored the jurisdiction of the Federal Trade Commission to act when broadband providers engage in anticompetitive, unfair, or deceptive acts or practices.

The framework adopted by the Commission today will protect consumers at far less cost to investment than the prior rigid and wide-ranging utility rules. And restoring a favorable climate for network investment is key to closing the digital divide, spurring competition and innovation that benefits consumers. The Declaratory Ruling, Report and Order, and Order adopted by the Commission takes the following steps to achieve these goals:

Declaratory Ruling

- Restores the classification of broadband Internet access service as an "information service" under Title I of the Communications Act—the classification affirmed by the Supreme Court in the 2005 Brand X case.

- Reinstates the classification of mobile broadband Internet access service as a private mobile service.

- Finds that the regulatory uncertainty created by utility-style Title II regulation has reduced Internet service provider (ISP) investment in networks, as well as hampered innovation, particularly among small ISPs serving rural consumers.

- Finds that public policy, in addition to legal analysis, supports the information service classification, because it is more likely to encourage broadband investment and innovation, thereby furthering the goal of closing the digital divide and benefitting the entire Internet ecosystem.

- Restores broadband consumer protection authority to the Federal Trade Commission (FTC), enabling it to apply its extensive expertise to provide uniform online protections against unfair, deceptive, and anticompetitive practices.

Report and Order

- Requires that ISPs disclose information about their practices to consumers, entrepreneurs, and the Commission, including any blocking, throttling, paid prioritization, or affiliated prioritization.

- Finds that transparency, combined with market forces as well as antitrust and consumer protection laws, achieve benefits comparable to those of the 2015 "bright line" rules at lower cost.

- Eliminates the vague and expansive Internet Conduct Standard, under which the FCC could micromanage innovative business models.

Order

- Finds that the public interest is not served by adding to the already-voluminous record in this proceeding additional materials, including confidential materials submitted in other proceedings.

The item takes effect upon approval by the Office of Management and Budget of the new transparency rule that requires the collection of additional information from industry.

Action by the Commission December 14, 2017 by Declaratory Ruling, Report and Order, and Order (FCC 17-166). Chairman Pai, Commissioners O'Rielly and Carr approving. Commissioners Clyburn and Rosenworcel dissenting. Chairman Pai, Commissioners Clyburn, O'Rielly, Carr and Rosenworcel issuing separate statements.

SOURCE: Federal Communications Commission. "FCC Acts to Restore Internet Freedom." December 14, 2017. http://transition.fcc.gov/Daily_Releases/Daily_Business/2017/db1214/DOC-348261A1.pdf.

DOCUMENT

FCC Chair Ajit Pai Statement on Net Neutrality Decision

December 14, 2017

The Internet is the greatest free-market innovation in history. It has changed the way we live, play, work, learn, and speak. During my time at the FCC, I've met with entrepreneurs who have started businesses, doctors who have helped care for patients, teachers who have educated their students, and farmers who increased their crop yields, all because of the Internet . . .

What is responsible for the phenomenal development of the Internet? It certainly wasn't heavy-handed government regulation. Quite to the contrary: At the dawn of the commercial Internet, President Clinton and a Republican Congress agreed that it would be the policy of the United States "to preserve the vibrant and competitive free market that presently exists for the Internet . . . unfettered by Federal or State regulation."

This bipartisan policy worked. Encouraged by light-touch regulation, the private sector invested over $1.5 trillion to build out fixed and mobile networks throughout the United States. 28.8k modems gave way to gigabit fiber connections. Innovators and entrepreneurs grew startups into global giants. America's Internet economy became the envy of the world.

And this light-touch approach was good for consumers, too. In a free market full of permission-less innovation, online services blossomed. Within a generation, we've gone from email as the killer app to high-definition video streaming. Entrepreneurs and innovators guided the Internet far better than the clumsy hand of government ever could have.

But then, in early 2015, the FCC jettisoned this successful, bipartisan approach to the Internet.

On express orders from the previous White House, the FCC scrapped the tried-and-true, light touch regulation of the Internet and replaced it with heavy-handed micromanagement. It decided to subject the Internet to utility-style regulation designed in the 1930s to govern Ma Bell.

This decision was a mistake. For one thing, there was no problem to solve. The Internet wasn't broken in 2015. We weren't living in a digital dystopia. To the contrary, the Internet is perhaps the one thing in American society we can all agree has been a stunning success.

Not only was there no problem, this "solution" hasn't worked. The main complaint consumers have about the Internet is not and has never been that their Internet service provider is blocking access to content. It's that they don't have access at all or enough competition. These regulations have taken us in the opposite direction from these consumer preferences. Under Title II, investment in high-speed networks has declined by billions of dollars. Notably, this is the first time that such investment has declined outside of a recession in the Internet era. When there's less investment, that means fewer next-generation networks are built. That means less competition. That means fewer jobs for Americans building those networks. And that means more Americans are left on the wrong side of the digital divide . . .

These rules have also impeded innovation. One major company, for instance, reported that it put on hold a project to build out its out-of-home Wi-Fi network due to uncertainty about the FCC's regulatory stance. And a coalition of 19 municipal Internet service providers—that is, city-owned nonprofits—have told the FCC that they "often delay or hold off from rolling out a new feature or service because [they] cannot afford to deal with a potential complaint and enforcement action."

None of this is good for consumers. We need to empower all Americans with digital opportunity, not deny them the benefits of greater access and competition.

And consider too that these are just the effects these rules have had on the Internet of today.

Think about how they'll affect the Internet we need ten, twenty years from now. . . . With the dawn of the Internet of Things, with the development of high bit-rate applications like virtual reality, with new activities like high-volume bitcoin mining that we can't yet fully grasp, we are imposing ever more demands on the network. Over time, that means our networks themselves will need to scale, too.

But they don't have to. If our rules deter the massive infrastructure investment that we need, eventually we'll pay the price in terms of less innovation . . .

So what is the FCC doing today? Quite simply, we are restoring the light-touch framework that has governed the Internet for most of its existence. We're moving from Title II to Title I. Wonkier it cannot be.

It's difficult to match that mundane reality to the apocalyptic rhetoric that we've heard from Title II supporters. And as the debate has gone on, their claims have gotten more and more outlandish. So let's be clear. Returning to the legal framework that governed the Internet from President Clinton's pronouncement in 1996 until 2015 is not going to destroy the Internet. It is not going to end the Internet as we know it. It is not going to kill democracy. It is not going to stifle free expression online. If stating these propositions alone doesn't demonstrate their absurdity, our Internet experience before 2015, and our experience tomorrow, once this order passes, will prove them so.

Simply put, by returning to the light-touch Title I framework, we are helping consumers and promoting competition. Broadband providers will have stronger incentives to build networks, especially in unserved areas, and to upgrade networks to gigabit speeds and 5G. This means there will be more competition among broadband providers. It also means more ways that startups and tech giants alike can deliver applications and content to more users. In short, it's a freer and more open Internet.

We also promote much more robust transparency among ISPs than existed three years ago. We require ISPs to disclose a variety of business practices, and the failure to do so subjects them to enforcement action. This transparency rule will ensure that consumers know what they're buying and startups get information they need as they develop new products and services.

Moreover, we empower the Federal Trade Commission to ensure that consumers and competition are protected. Two years ago, the *Title II Order* stripped the FTC of its jurisdiction over broadband providers. But today, we are putting our nation's premier consumer protection cop back on the beat. The FTC will once again have the authority to take action against Internet service providers that engage in anticompetitive, unfair, or deceptive acts . . .

So let's be absolutely clear. Following today's vote, Americans will still be able to access the websites they want to visit. They will still be able to enjoy the services they want to enjoy. There will still be cops on the beat guarding a free and open Internet. This is the way things were prior to 2015, and this is the way they will be once again.

Our decision today will also return regulatory parity to the Internet economy. . . . Look—perhaps certain companies support saddling broadband providers with heavy-handed regulations because those rules work to their economic advantage. I don't blame them for taking that position. And I'm not saying that these same rules should be slapped on them too. What I *am* saying is that the government shouldn't be in the business of picking winners and losers in the Internet economy. We should have a level playing field and let consumers decide who prevails.

Many words have been spoken during this debate but the time has come for action. It is time for the Internet once again to be driven by engineers and entrepreneurs and consumers, rather than lawyers and accountants and bureaucrats. It is time for us to act to bring faster, better, and cheaper Internet access to all Americans. It is time for us to return to the bipartisan regulatory framework under which the Internet flourished prior to 2015. It is time for us to restore Internet freedom . . .

SOURCE: Federal Communications Commission. "Oral Statement of Chairman Ajit Pai." December 14, 2017. http://transition.fcc.gov/Daily_Releases/Daily_Business/2017/db1214/DOC-348261A2.pdf.

FCC Commissioner Clyburn Dissenting Statement on Net Neutrality Decision

December 14, 2017

I dissent. I dissent from this fiercely-spun, legally-lightweight, consumer-harming, corporate-enabling *Destroying Internet Freedom Order*.

I dissent, because I am among the millions outraged. Outraged, because the FCC pulls its own teeth, abdicating responsibility to protect the nation's broadband consumers. Some may ask why are we witnessing such an unprecedented groundswell of public support, for keeping the 2015 net neutrality protections in place? Because the public can plainly see, that a soon-to-be-toothless FCC, is handing the keys to the Internet—the Internet, one of the most remarkable, empowering, enabling inventions of our lifetime—over to a handful of multi-billion dollar corporations. And if past is prologue, those very same broadband internet service providers, that the majority says you should trust to do right by you, will put profits and shareholder returns above, what is best for you . . .

I do not believe that there are any FCC or Congressional offices immune to the deluge of consumer outcry. We are even hearing about state and local offices fielding calls and what is newsworthy is that at last count, five Republican Members of Congress went on the record in calling for a halt of today's vote. Why such a bipartisan outcry? Because the large majority of Americans are in favor of keeping strong net neutrality rules in place. The sad thing about this commentary, it pains me to say, is what I can only describe as the new norm at the FCC: A majority that is ignoring the will of the people. A majority that will stand idly by while the people they are committed to serve lose . . .

Many have asked, what happens next? How will all of this—Net Neutrality, my internet experience, look after today? My answer is simple. When the current protections are abandoned, and the rules that have been officially in place since 2015 are repealed, we will have a Cheshire cat version of net neutrality. We will be in a world where regulatory substance fades to black, and all that is left is a broadband provider's toothy grin and those oh so comforting words: we have every incentive to do the right thing. What they will soon have, is every incentive to do their own thing . . .

Particularly damning is what today's repeal will mean for marginalized groups, like communities of color, that rely on platforms like the internet to communicate, because traditional outlets do not consider their issues or concerns, worthy of coverage. It was through social media that the world first heard about Ferguson, Missouri, because legacy news outlets did not consider it important until the hashtag started trending. It has been through online video services, that targeted entertainment ecosystem has thrived, where stories are finally being told because those same programs were repeatedly rejected by mainstream distribution and media outlets. And it has been through secure messaging platforms, where activists have communicated and organized for justice without gatekeepers with differing opinions blocking them.

Where will the next significant attack on internet freedom come from? Maybe from a broadband provider allowing its network to congest, making a high-traffic video provider ask what more can it pay to make the pain stop. That will never happen you say? Well it already has. The difference now, is the open question of what is stopping them? The difference after today's vote, is that no one will be able to stop them.

Maybe several providers will quietly roll out paid prioritization packages that enable deep-pocketed players to cut the queue. Maybe a vertically-integrated broadband provider decides that it will favor its own apps and services. Or some high-value internet-of-things traffic will be subject to an additional fee. Maybe some of these actions will be cloaked under nondisclosure agreements and wrapped up in mandatory arbitration clauses so that it will be a breach of contract to disclose these publicly or take the provider to court over any wrongdoing. Some may say "of course this will never happen." But after today's vote, what will be in place to stop them? . . .

And just who will be impacted the most? Consumers and small businesses, that's who. The internet continues to evolve and has become ever more critical for every participant in our 21st century ecosystem: government services have migrated online, as have educational opportunities and job notices and applications, but at the same time, broadband providers have continued to consolidate, becoming bigger. They own their own content, they own media companies, and they own or have an interest in other types of services . . .

It is abundantly clear why we see so much bad process with this item: because the fix was already in. There is no real mention of the thousands of net neutrality complaints filed by consumers. Why? The majority has refused to put them in the record while maintaining the rhetoric that there have been no real violations. Record evidence of the massive incentives and abilities of broadband providers to act in anticompetitive ways are missing from the docket? Why? Because those in charge have refused to use the data and knowledge the agency does have, and has relied upon in the past to inform our merger reviews. As the majority has shown again and again, the views of individuals do not matter, including the views of those who care deeply about the substance, but are not Washington insiders.

There is a basic fallacy underlying the majority's actions and rhetoric today: the assumption of what is best for broadband providers, is best for America. Breathless claims about unshackling broadband services from unnecessary regulation, are only about ensuring that broadband providers, have the keys to the internet. Assertions that this is merely a return to some imaginary status quo ante, cannot hide the fact, that this is the very first time, that the FCC, has disavowed substantive protections for consumers online . . .

Reclassification of broadband will do more than wreak havoc on net neutrality. It will also undermine our universal service construct for years to come, something which the Order implicitly acknowledges. It will undermine the Lifeline program. It will weaken our ability to support robust broadband infrastructure deployment. And what we will soon find out, is what a broadband market unencumbered by robust consumer protections will look like. I suspect the result will not be pretty . . .

What saddens me is that the agency that is supposed to protect you is abandoning you, but what I am pleased to be able to say is the fight to save net neutrality does not end today. This agency does not have, the final word. Thank goodness.

As I close my eulogy of our 2015 net neutrality rules, carefully crafted rules that struck an appropriate balance in providing consumer protections and enabling opportunities and investment, I take ironic comfort in the words of then Commissioner Pai from 2015, because I believe this will ring true about this *Destroying Internet Freedom Order*:

> I am optimistic, that we will look back on today's vote as an aberration, a temporary deviation from the bipartisan path, that has served us so well. I don't know whether this plan will be vacated by a court, reversed by Congress, or overturned by a future Commission. But I do believe that its days are numbered.

Amen to that, Mr. Chairman. Amen to that.

SOURCE: Federal Communications Commission. "Oral Dissenting Statement of Commissioner Mignon Clyburn." December 14, 2017. http://transition.fcc.gov/Daily_Releases/Daily_Business/2017/db1214/DOC-348261A3.pdf.

OTHER HISTORIC DOCUMENTS OF INTEREST

FROM THIS VOLUME

FROM PREVIOUS *HISTORIC DOCUMENTS*

Members of Congress, President Trump Remark on Tax Code Overhaul

DECEMBER 19 AND 20, 2017

After spending a majority of 2017 debating, and ultimately failing, to repeal the Affordable Care Act (ACA), otherwise known as Obamacare, Congressional Republicans and President Donald Trump celebrated their first major legislative victory in mid-December when they passed a massive overhaul of the U.S. tax code. The provisions of the legislation were expected to give a majority of Americans a tax break, at least in the short term. However, the biggest gains would be experienced by corporations and the highest income earners. Republicans hoped that economic growth stemming from the plan would be enough to help them maintain control of the House and Senate heading into the 2018 midterm elections, while Democrats intended to use the measure as a means to paint Republicans as beholden to corporate interests and the wealthy.

PROVISIONS OF THE LAW

Public Law 115-97, referred to in the House as the Tax Cuts and Jobs Act (that name was rejected in the Senate for procedural reasons), was the first overhaul of the U.S. tax code in more than three decades. It was pushed through both houses quickly, with a Republican self-imposed deadline of passage by the end of 2017 before newly elected Senator Doug Jones of Alabama could be seated, which would shrink the margin of control for Republicans and potentially weaken their chances of passage.

For individuals and families, major provisions of the $1.5 trillion law included expanding the child tax credit, reducing the estate tax, and nearly doubling the standard deduction. However, the legislation also cut back the mortgage deduction for new home buyers and the deduction for taxes paid to state and local governments, the latter of which could mean that some middle-class families actually see their taxes increase slightly. The law maintained the seven personal income tax brackets, but lowered many of them, including the top tax rate from 39.6 percent to 37 percent. For businesses, the law added a new deduction for pass-through business owners, repealed the corporate alternative minimum tax, and permanently reduced the corporate tax rate from 35 percent to 21 percent.

Notably, changes in personal income taxes and deductions were not made permanent and without a replacement or continuation by Congress would begin to sunset after 2025, meaning many Americans could see their taxes rise to above the 2017 rate by 2027. According to the Joint Committee on Taxation, in 2019 most taxpayers would see an average reduction in tax payments of 8 percent. But by 2027, those earning up to $75,000 would experience a tax increase. This was a frequent talking point among Democrats against the bill, who called it a tax break for the wealthy. Senate Minority Leader Chuck Schumer, D-N.Y., called the bill "crumbs and tax hikes for middle-class families in this country, and a Christmas gift to major corporations and billionaire investors." Republicans, however, promised that the middle class would benefit from higher wages and job growth, not only tax cuts. The possibility also existed for a future Congress to extend the tax cuts, which could, in effect, negate the increase on low- and middle-income earners, at least for a few more years.

Although they were unable to fully repeal the ACA through separate legislation, Republicans did include in the law a massive change to the ACA by repealing one of its key components, the individual mandate that imposes a $695 penalty on adults without health insurance. Republicans had long argued that portion of the ACA impacts primarily low- and middle-income Americans, but health economists believe the move could increase premiums across the board and price some Americans out of the health insurance market. The independent Congressional Budget Office (CBO) estimated that, within the next ten years, 13 million fewer Americans would have health insurance coverage as a result of the repeal of the individual mandate. McConnell called the decision to repeal the individual mandate taking "the heart out of Obamacare," while President Trump said, "When the individual mandate is being repealed, that means Obamacare is being repealed."

TAX REFORM PASSES BOTH HOUSES, DESPITE PROCEDURAL HICCUP

Debate in the House and Senate on December 19 and in the early morning of December 20 revolved primarily around whether the bill would actually help middle class families and whether it would provide a much-needed boost to the U.S. economy. Sen. John Cornyn, R-Texas, claimed the bill would "dramatically reduce taxes on American families and incentivize the creation of new jobs" adding that for a typical family of four with a median income of $73,000, they would see a tax cut of $2,058, a reduction of more than 50 percent from current tax levels. "That may not seem like a big deal inside the beltway, but to those families who are living paycheck to paycheck and who cannot deal with unexpected financial expenses, this will help them in a real and meaningful way." In the House, Speaker Paul Ryan, R-Wis., agreed. "Today . . . we are giving the people of this country their money back . . . we need to make sure that these people in our communities and our country, who are struggling, see their own personal economy getting better, and that is what this is all about," Ryan said.

Democrats, however, disputed these claims. Schumer said the bill "helps the wealthy and the powerful corporations, and it does so little and even hurts many in the middle class." The senator spoke to public opinion polls showing a majority of Americans opposed to the tax plan at hand. "When did you ever hear that Americans are against a tax cut bill?" Schumer asked, adding that "Republicans will rue the day that they passed this tax bill." House Speaker Nancy Pelosi, D-Calif., took a similarly negative view of the bill, saying Republicans put "donors, lobbyists, and the wealthy and well connected" ahead of average Americans. Pelosi shared, "When the Washington Post asked Edward Kleinbard, former chief of staff for the Joint Committee on Taxation, if the tax package in aggregate would mean a middle class tax cut, he said 'That is delusional or dishonest to say. It is factually untrue. The only group you can point to that wins year after year and wins in very large magnitude is the very highest incomes.'" The argument among Democrats that the bill benefited the wealthy, and more specifically corporations, drew the ire of Republicans. According to Cornyn, both Democrats and Republicans have agreed in the past of the need to cut the corporate income tax rate to encourage greater spending and investment in the American economy. "When our Democratic friends criticize us for corporate giveaways, we are embracing the very same reforms they have advocated in the past," Cornyn said.

The House was the first to pass the tax reform package on December 19, sending it to the Senate for final approval before it would be passed on to the president. The Senate passed the bill 51–48 along party lines; Vice President Mike Pence was present in the Senate chamber in the early hours of December 20 for the vote in case the body deadlocked 50–50 and he needed to break the tie. Because the final bill violated some Senate procedural rules, it had to go back to the House again for re-passage, an embarrassment that Democrats attacked as a clear indication that the legislation had been rushed and poorly vetted. The House passed the legislation a second time on December 20, 224–201, with no Democrats voting in favor and twelve Republicans joining the Democrats to vote "no." Most of those Republicans who chose to vote against their party told news outlets that they did so over concern that the elimination of the state and local tax deduction would raise taxes and place too high a burden on their constituents.

Immediately after passage in the House, Trump tweeted, "The Tax Cuts are so large and so meaningful, and yet the Fake News is working overtime to follow the lead of their friends, the defeated Dems, and only demean. This is truly a case where the results will speak for themselves, starting very soon. Jobs, Jobs, Jobs!" Republicans held a celebratory press conference with President Trump on the White House lawn. The president thanked Majority Leader McConnell and House Speaker Ryan for their work in passing the legislation. "We are making America great again," Trump said, adding, "We're going to see something that's going to be very special. We're bringing the entrepreneur back into this country." There was a question about whether the president would wait until January to sign the legislation so that Congress could avoid the PAYGO law, which requires spending cuts to other programs, such as Medicare, to cover the cost of any legislation that is expected to increase the federal deficit. Waiting until 2018 to sign the bill gave Congress until 2019 to find a solution to cover the cost of the tax code overhaul. The CBO had estimated that the law would add more than $1 trillion to the deficit over the next decade, even after taking into account any economic growth expected as a result of the legislation. Republicans disputed this figure and repeatedly claimed that economic growth would help the law pay for itself. Trump ended up signing the legislation on December 22 in conjunction with a short-term government funding bill that contained a PAYGO waiver.

EARLY VICTORIES FOR TRUMP AND REPUBLICANS

Republicans were hoping for quick economic gains from the tax plan that they could use to their advantage heading into the 2018 midterm elections. "From a Republican point of view, this is as good as it gets and we're more than happy to take our argument to the American people in an election contest," said McConnell. They would have their work cut out for them. A CNN poll found 33 percent of Americans supported the bill at the time of passage, while a POLITICO/Morning Consult poll was slightly more generous, with 42 percent in favor of the changes.

The Republicans did receive a few quick victories, when AT&T, Bank of America, Comcast, and Fifth Third Bancorp announced that they would provide employee bonuses because of the money they would save from the tax plan. Apple unveiled its plan to make a large investment in the United States by bringing back to the country a majority of its $252 billion in cash held abroad. When the money is repatriated, it will result in an immediate, one-time tax payment of $38 billion. Trump called this a "huge win for American workers and the USA!" Other companies, however, such as Cisco Systems, Pfizer, and Coca-Cola, PepsiCo, announced that the savings would be reinvested into increasing stock dividends or buying back shares. Cisco, notably, also planned to repatriate some of its foreign profits, but according to CNN its investors would be the biggest beneficiaries of its financial moves since the tax plan was unveiled, to the tune of around $44 billion.

—Heather Kerrigan

Following is the text of House and Senate floor statements delivered on December 19, 2017, by Sen. John Cornyn, R-Texas, Sen. Chuck Schumer, D-N.Y., Rep. Paul Ryan, R-Wis., and Rep. Nancy Pelosi, D-Calif.; and the text of a statement by President Donald Trump on December 20, 2017, after passage of tax reform legislation.

DOCUMENT

Sen. Cornyn Speaks in Support of Tax Reform

December 19, 2017

Mr. CORNYN. Mr. President, the second matter I would like to address is the historic vote that the House will take today and that we will take later on this evening on the Tax Cuts and Jobs Act.

This bill will dramatically reduce taxes on American families and incentivize the creation of new jobs. It is a major victory for all Americans who want to know that Washington has their best interests at heart. It does exactly what we told the voters we would do in 2016, and it is important to keep our word. We are delivering tax reform in a way that is real, comprehensive, and substantial, and we are doing it through what we usually refer to as regular order in the Senate.

I know that ever since the Affordable Care Act was written in then-Democratic Leader Harry Reid's conference room and was brought to the floor, there has been a lot of concern about the way the Senate conducts its activities. Senator McCain, who unfortunately will not be able to be with us today, has been a stickler for returning to regular order—by that, meaning introducing a bill, having it marked up and debated in the relevant committee—in this case, in the Finance Committee—then having it brought to the floor, where it is amended, and then debating it until we finally pass it. Then we go to a conference committee with the House and reconcile the differences between the Senate version and the House version. That is exactly what we did with this piece of legislation.

I have spoken at length about certain provisions in the bill before, but I want to make one point abundantly clear. For the American people, this represents the very best kind of Christmas gift we can offer them—one that will actually make their lives better and one from which they will benefit right away. This tax reform may not bear the ribbons and bows of a Christmas present, but the men and women who are trying to make ends meet will benefit from having lower taxes, bigger paychecks, and a resurgent economy that will produce more jobs and better opportunities.

I will refer to an article that came out in January of this year which cited a shocking statistic, really. The statistic is, most Americans remain one misstep away from having a financial crisis. Fifty-seven percent of Americans don't have enough cash on hand to cover an unexpected $500 expense. These findings from this CBS News report shed light on how many households continue to struggle with their basic finances more than 7 years after the official end of the great recession of 2007. A typical American household still earns 2.4 percent below what it brought home in 1999. When people talk about less purchasing power and flat wages, that is what they are talking about.

At the same time, we know costs for essentials, such as housing and childcare, have surged faster than the rate of inflation, which puts even more stress on these household budgets. That is one of the reasons we will pass this conference report later on this evening—because we believe these families deserve to keep more of what they earn so as to make sure they don't go into debt when they suffer an unexpected financial expense of $500, like the 57 percent of the respondents to the poll said they would, which was reported by CBS News. That is why it is a big deal.

For example, a typical family of four who earns the median family income of $73,000 a year will receive a tax cut of $2,058, which is a reduction of nearly 58 percent. Now, that may not seem like a big deal inside the beltway, but to those families who are living paycheck to paycheck and who cannot deal with unexpected financial expenses, this will help them in a real and meaningful way.

Consider the single mother—or father, for that matter—with one child and an annual income of $41,000. That parent, that family, will receive a tax cut of $1,304.50, which is a reduction of nearly 73 percent. This may be shocking news to most people who are listening because all they have heard about is what is bad in this bill.

There are a lot of very good things in this bill, but it could have been made better if our Democratic colleagues had worked with us rather than resisted us at every step along the way. I guess they are satisfied with the status quo—the fact that purchasing power for the average family is actually 2.4 percent below what it was in 1999. The message I would like to convey is, we are not satisfied with the status quo. We think life can be better, and one way it will be better is to start with letting people keep more of what they earn.

For a married small business owner with an income of $100,000, he will receive a tax cut of $2,603.50, which is a reduction of nearly 24 percent. So you can see, across all incomes and among people in very different circumstances, each of them will benefit from the bill we will pass tonight and send to the President.

This bill also does something for which Barack Obama had argued in 2011, that of having a bipartisan consensus formed to cut the corporate income tax rate. I know people aren't necessarily immediately attracted to the idea of cutting corporations' taxes, but the fact is, America has the highest corporate tax rate in the industrialized world. What that means is, it is cheaper for businesses to move to other countries, to invest in jobs there, and to keep the money overseas that they earn abroad. By reducing it to 21 percent, as we do in this bill, we will basically have achieved the average tax rate in the industrialized world, and we will move from a worldwide tax system to a territorial one. This really is a bipartisan consensus move.

When our Democratic friends criticize us for corporate giveaways, we are embracing the very same reforms they have advocated in the past, whether it is President Obama, Democratic leader Senator Schumer, or the ranking member of the Senate Finance Committee, Senator Wyden. All of them have advocated reducing the corporate tax rate and making our corporate business tax more competitive because they recognize, as we all recognize, the fact that the status quo kills jobs and encourages businesses to move overseas. We want to grow jobs in America, along with investment, and encourage those businesses to come back home.

I daresay that all Americans from every walk of life will benefit from this stimulus to our economy. Janet Yellin, who was last appointed Chairman of the Federal Reserve by Barack Obama, said that in part as a result of this tax package, the Federal Reserve has raised its projection on growth of the U.S. economy from 2.1 percent next year to 2.5 percent—four-tenths of 1 percent. That is a big deal.

Every American will feel the benefit of that economic growth in terms of the wages they earn, the opportunities they have, and their ability to protect themselves against unexpected financial expenses, as I mentioned earlier.

What could someone do with $2,600 more in their paycheck? Well, you could install concrete countertops or laminate flooring in your house. When it comes to a cell phone—everybody seems to have a cell phone—you can pay your cell phone expense for 2½ years. You can go online at a Texas college and pay for your education for a full year. You can breathe a little bit easier in Dallas by having enough money to pay for 2 months of average apartment rent. You can drive down Interstate Highway 35 in Texas, knowing that almost 5½ months of an average car payment is taken care of. If you need a little dental work done, you can go to your dentist for a little tune-up and pay for that out of the savings you will achieve as a result of this bill.

Stories like these, stories of how busy, hard-working and multitasking Americans will benefit from our plan, simply leave me with confusion as to why our Democratic colleagues have simply refused to participate in this process and have blocked and dragged their feet every step along the way, trying to stop us from providing this relief, from keeping our promise to the American people. It seems in the process they have given up on the American dream, they have settled for the status quo, and they are even rooting for failure.

This bill's final passage won't wait for our Democratic colleagues to wake up. We are simply determined to get this win even without them because American families need more take-home pay, they need higher wages, they need greater job opportunities, and they need a competitive economy and the benefits it brings. American families should not have to settle for anything less, and we will make sure they don't.

There is one more aspect of the bill I want to bring up. Our tax reform plan strengthens our long-term energy security by opening up an area in Alaska to responsible energy development. At the invitation of Senator Murkowski, I traveled to the North Slope of Alaska about a year or so ago, and I am amazed at the technology they were able to deploy in extracting oil from the North Slope. They literally have ice roads that don't exist except during the coldest part of the year in order to protect the environment and allow equipment to travel overland. Thanks to directional drilling, they are able to occupy basically a very small footprint and literally drill hundreds of wells in a multitude of different directions and pump the energy from that location. It creates jobs, it creates wealth, and it helps create energy security for the people of Alaska and for the United States.

I come from a State with a huge energy presence, and I understand the importance of developing our natural resources responsibly. Limited development with modern technologies will not ruin this area, as some of the critics have charged, because a very small portion of the acreage is allowed. It will provide jobs.

Let's not forget why we are doing this. One reason we are increasing our domestic energy production is because we want to make ourselves less dependent on foreign energy sources. It also helps lower the price at the pump for millions of hard-working Americans.

So I can't wait to vote on this bill later today, and I can't wait to hand-deliver to the President's desk this important bill this week and for him to sign it into law. We will all benefit from passage of this Tax Cuts and Jobs Act.

I yield the floor.

SOURCE: U.S. Congress. Senate. Tax Cuts and Jobs Bill. H.R. 1. 115th Congress, 2nd Session. *Congressional Record.* vol. 163, no. 207, daily ed. (December 19, 2017): S8074. https://www.gpo.gov/fdsys/pkg/CREC-2017-12-19/pdf/CREC-2017-12-19-pt1-PgS8074-3.pdf.

Sen. Schumer Speaks on the Senate Floor in Opposition to the Tax Reform Legislation

December 19, 2017

Mr. SCHUMER. Mr. President, I will have further comments on the tax bill that I will deliver on the Senate floor late tonight after the conference report, but I just want to say that this bill will be an anchor around the ankles of every Republican. It so helps the wealthy and the powerful corporations, and it does so little and even hurts many in the middle class. It is a loser.

In a CNN new poll, a majority of Americans oppose the tax bill. When did you ever hear that Americans are against a tax cut bill? Well, you are hearing it now.

It is because our Republican friends are listening to the thousands of really greedy multibillionaires who want their taxes cut, even though they are doing great, and don't want to share those benefits with the middle class even if they make millions of middle-class people pay more.

The Republicans will rue the day that they passed this tax bill—will rue the day—because it is so unfair to the middle class. It so blows a hole in our deficit. It so threatens Social Security, Medicare, and Medicaid. They will rue the day.

SOURCE: U.S. Congress. Senate. Tax Cuts and Jobs Bill. H.R. 1. 115th Congress, 2nd Session. *Congressional Record.* vol. 163, no. 207, daily ed. (December 19, 2017): S8082. https://www.gpo.gov/fdsys/pkg/CREC-2017-12-19/pdf/CREC-2017-12-19-pt1-PgS8082.pdf.

Rep. Pelosi Opposes the Tax Legislation

December 19, 2017

Ms. PELOSI. Mr. Speaker, I thank the gentleman for yielding and I salute him for his extraordinary leadership and being a champion for America's working families. I commend him and the Democratic members of the House Ways and Means Committee for putting forth the facts on what is in this bill.

Mr. Speaker, today we choose what kind of country America will be: one that champions the ladders of opportunity for all or one that reinforces the power of the wealthiest and well connected.

Outside the Congress, the American people have already made their decision. Polling shows that Americans oppose the GOP tax scam by a margin of 2 to 1. Hardworking families see right through the brazen con job Republicans are trying to sell them.

So why aren't our Republican colleagues standing with their constituents? Why aren't they joining us on insisting on A Better Deal for American families? Why aren't they joining us in demanding that we write real bipartisan tax reform that puts the middle class first?

Because helping the middle class has never been their goal.

From day one, the donors, lobbyists, and the wealthy and well connected came first. The Frankenstein monster of giveaways and special interest loopholes we are voting on today proves it, and this monster will come back to haunt them, as Frankenstein did.

Republicans claim that their bill is a middle class tax cut. The fact is, according to the Tax Policy Center, their bill raises taxes on 86 million middle class households.

When The Washington Post asked Edward Kleinbard, former chief of staff for the Joint Committee on Taxation, if the tax package in aggregate would mean a middle class tax cut, he said: "That is delusional or dishonest to say. It is factually untrue. The only group you can point to that wins year after year and wins in very large magnitude is the very highest incomes."

That is from the Joint Committee on Taxation former chief of staff.

The only greater delusion in this bill is the ludicrous Republican insistence, their claim that these giveaways to the wealthiest will pay for themselves.

Bruce Bartlett is the architect of Jack Kemp's supply-side economics. As Bruce Bartlett has testified in our hearing and in public, when it comes to tax breaks for the wealthy paying for themselves, he said: It is not true. It is nonsense. It is BS.

He said the whole words.

In a few minutes, Republicans will vote to explode catastrophically our national debt at minimum of $1.5 trillion, likely $2.2 trillion or more.

Where are the vaunted Republican deficit hawks? Are they endangered? Are they extinct? Do they care about the deficit when we pass giveaways for the rich and big corporations?

They don't care about deficits, then. Tax breaks for the rich, corporate tax breaks: they don't care about the deficit.

Do Republicans only care about the deficit when the issue is helping children, seniors, our veterans, who are a large part of hardworking Americans?

My colleagues, my fellow Americans, remember this vote. Remember the vote, when they will cheer at the end of this vote, they will stand up and cheer, adding trillions to the national debt in order to give tax breaks to the wealthiest 1 percent and to big corporations. They will cheer that.

They will cheer when they say we can't afford to protect the health of our innocent children. They will cheer that.

Remember, they will cheer when they tell you we can't afford the next step, we can't afford Medicaid, Medicare, and a dignified retirement our seniors spent a lifetime earning. That is an applause line for them.

Remember this day when Republicans cheer for a bill that hands a $4,000 child tax credit to families of four earning $400,000 a year. If you earn $400,000 a year, you get $4,000 in a child tax credit.

But if you are poor, a single mom, a mother of two earning only $14,500, guess how much you get?

Seventy-five dollars. Seventy-five dollars.

Today we gather on this floor in the midst of a holy season. In this season, we celebrate the miraculous blessings of God. We reflect on the wondrous joy of children and our responsibility to them.

We remember our duty to live justly. For those of us blessed to serve in this Congress, we must remember our special responsibility to govern fairly, to meet the needs of all of God's children.

In this holy time, the moral obscenity and unrepentant greed of the GOP tax scam stands out even more clearly.

As the U.S. Conference of Catholic Bishops said early on, "... this proposal appears to be the first Federal income tax modification in American history that will raise income taxes on the working poor while simultaneously providing a large tax cut to the wealthy. This is simply unconscionable."

They will be cheering it. Unconscionable. Remember what the Bishops said.

Now, here, get back to the Republicans. This is in sharp contrast to the words of Senator Hatch. Now, he is the chairman of the Finance Committee in the United States Senate and an author of this bill. He said: "I have a rough time wanting to spend billions and billions and trillions of dollars to help people who won't help themselves, won't lift a finger, and expect the Federal Government to do everything."

How about that?

Tell that to the moms we just saw speaking out with their children, children with disabilities, who wonder how this could be so cruel.

This is an act of misery, but not according to Senator Hatch. And that is in terms of getting back to our Bishops. In his encyclical, God is Love. And I have said this to my colleagues before, but with, obviously, no effect on the Republican side.

Pope Benedict quoted the urgent moral wisdom of St. Augustine 17 centuries ago, my colleagues. Seventeen centuries ago, St. Augustine said: "A State which is not governed according to justice is just a bunch of thieves."

Pope Benedict went on to say: "The State must inevitably face the question of how justice can be achieved here and now."

In his words, he cautioned against "the danger of certain ethical blindness caused by the dazzling effect of power and special interests."

Mr. Speaker, is there justice in a bill that rewards corporations shipping jobs overseas? Jobs of hardworking American men and women and veterans, shipping those jobs overseas? Is there justice in that?

No, I don't think so.

Is there justice in a bill that spikes healthcare premiums and may add 13 million Americans to the ranks of the uninsured?

No justice there.

Is there justice in a bill that raises taxes on 86 million middle class families?

Here we are. Raises taxes on 86 million middle class families, and they try to present the delusion that it is a middle class tax cut.

Is there justice in a bill that hands a breathtaking 83 percent of its benefits to the wealthiest 1 percent of Americans? Eighty-three percent of its benefits to the top 1 percent?

Is there justice in a bill that explodes the national debt to give the wealthy and the well connected a break and sticks the debt with our children? Is that justice?

I didn't think you thought so. I wish our Republican colleagues would join us.

This GOP tax scam is simply theft, monumental, brazen theft from the American middle class and from every person who aspires to reach it. The GOP tax scam is not a voice for an investment in growth or jobs. It is a vote to install a permanent plutocracy in our Nation. They will be cheering that later.

It does violence to the vision of our Founders. It disrespects the sacrifice of our men and women in uniform, who are a large part of our middle class, and to whom we owe a future worthy of their sacrifice. It betrays the future and betrays the aspirations of our children.

It morally demands a "no" vote from every Member of this House of the people.

SOURCE: U.S. Congress. House. Conference Report on H.R. 1, Tax Cuts and Jobs Act. 115th Congress, 2nd Session. *Congressional Record*. vol. 163, no. 207, daily ed. (December 19, 2017): H10209-10210. https://www.gpo.gov/fdsys/pkg/CREC-2017-12-19/pdf/CREC-2017-12-19-pt1-PgH10201-2.pdf.

Speaker Ryan Provides His Support to Tax Reform Legislation

December 19, 2017

Mr. RYAN of Wisconsin. Mr. Speaker, I appreciate the gentleman yielding time to me.

First, I want to start off by thanking all of the members and the staff of the Ways and Means Committee for all of their hard work in putting this bill together. I want to thank them for this.

I want to personally thank one of my predecessors from the Ways and Means Committee, who helped lay the foundation to get us where we are today, and that is Dave Camp. Dave Camp did a lot to help us get to where we are.

I want to, most of all, commend and express my profound admiration to the architect of this measure, Chairman Kevin Brady.

His endless patience and his persistence and his great demeanor have seen this through and gotten us to where we are today.

My colleagues, this is a day I have been looking forward to for a long time. We are about to achieve some really big things, things that the cynics have scoffed at for years, decades even; ideas that have been worked on for so long to help hardworking Americans who have been left behind for too long.

Today—today—we are giving the people of this country their money back. This is their money, after all. . . .

Mr. Speaker, I would simply like to remind my colleagues and the Speaker that my minute can last for as long as I want it to last.

Mr. Speaker, as I was saying, today we are giving the people their money back. The bottom line here is the typical family making the median income in America will get a $2,059 tax cut next year alone. What this is is real relief for families who are living paycheck to paycheck, struggling to make ends meet.

They hear about the economy getting better. They turn on the TV, and they see the stock market going up, but now we need to make sure that these people in our communities and our country, who are struggling, see their own personal economy getting better, and that is what this is all about.

We have got to understand that times are tough for a lot of people in this country right now. Today, this is about how much better things can be. This is about more jobs, fair taxes. It is about bigger paychecks. It is about faster growth and upward mobility. It is about a strong economy that makes all of us stronger and healthier. Those are the effects, those are the benefits, of tax reform.

Here is the heart of it, and here is why this is so vital that we do this. Here is what it speaks to and what I truly believe is a generational defining moment for this Nation.

Our Tax Code is so broken that it undermines the very thing that makes our Nation exceptional in the first place. It punishes hard work. It discourages our entrepreneurial spirit. It dims freedom and free enterprise. It limits the potential of our own people.

When Americans see good jobs going away, when Americans wake up and they see the companies that they grew up with in their communities going away, they wonder if we have lost something bigger.

The mission that drives us here today is to restore this beautiful American idea. What is that idea? That the condition of your birth does not determine the outcome of your life. You can work hard, play by the rules, get ahead, and make a better life for yourselves and an even better one for your kids.

It is that sense of possibility. We want people to be free to strive to make the most of their lives. We want a country with the resilience to endure and tackle all of its challenges.

Mr. Speaker, economic growth and job creation will not solve all of our problems, but it will help make all of our problems much easier to solve. This is the direction that we are choosing here today because we know exactly where the status quo leads us.

For years, the powers that be have blocked and stonewalled reform under the umbrella of an arrogant, condescending, and paternalistic ideology—an ideology that seeks to limit mobility, to limit aspirations, to accept less in our lives. It is a view of the world that sees life and the economy as a zero-sum game. Your gain comes at my loss; therefore, we can't do it.

Look at where this got us: the worst recovery since World War II, flat wages, and an economy just limping along. Stagnation is a breeding ground for a class-based society where elites predetermine the outcome of our lives. That is not the American idea.

They will tell you this: Just hand over more freedom to the unelected bureaucrats, and they will figure it out, they know more, we will all just be okay. Hand over more of your hard-earned dollars to the IRS, and it will all be okay.

There is your scam right there. We know, given the opportunity, there are no limits to what our people, our fellow citizens, our brothers and sisters can do. Yet for years now, this Tax Code has been skewed to the well connected, full of special interest carve-outs and loopholes.

Meanwhile, the hardworking family in America has got to jump through all the hoops that the IRS can muster. Reform means we bring rates down at every level. We clear out these loopholes so that people can just keep more of what they earn in the first place, because it is their money in the first place. No special favors, just basic fairness.

Reform means simplification, too. Nearly 9 out of 10 Americans will still be able to do their taxes on the form the size of a postcard. That is amazing.

And given the opportunity, there are no limits to what our workers and our entrepreneurs can do.

Yet while the world has changed, while the world has become more competitive, closer, smaller, our Tax Code has not. Instead of leading, we have been falling behind to the point where we now are the worst in the industrialized world at how we tax our businesses.

We tax our businesses a whole lot more than our foreign competitors tax theirs. They win; we lose. That is not fair.

It is basically open season for our competitors to come in and take our jobs overseas under the current Tax Code. Reform means we go from the back of the pack to the front of the pack.

Instead of the slow growth that we have been slogging through for years, we want to get back to real sustained economic growth. We want to build an opportunity economy where there is more demand for higher paying jobs. That is the whole purpose of all of this. Make sure that people can grow up and reach their potential. Make sure that the jobs are there to give people the careers they want so they can reach their potential, so their families can reach their potential. That is why we are doing this.

This is, without question, the single most important thing we can do to, once again, make America the best place to do business.

There is more than that in this bill. With this bill, were are finally restoring the freedom to make our own healthcare choices. By repealing the individual mandate at the heart of ObamaCare, we are giving back the freedom and the flexibility to buy the healthcare that is right for you and your family.

Finally, we are doing something truly to put America in the lead. We are doing something historic to develop our own energy resources. Some people have been working here since I was in the second grade on this project. After decades and decades in this Chamber, we are opening up a small, nonwilderness area of the Alaska National Wildlife Refuge for responsible development. It is the most ambitious step we have taken in years to secure our own energy future.

This is one of those times to just take a step back. Let's just take a minute, collect ourselves, and step away from the noise.

We talk a lot in this job about turning points. There is no doubt that we are at one of those turning points right now. This one will determine the kind of country we are going to have this century.

But too often, we have seen before how doubt creeps in, how the tyranny of short-term thinking takes over, and history—history—fails to turn.

There is, after all, a reason that this has not been done in 31 years. This really is a generational defining moment. And let's let this generational defining moment be defined by optimism, not by fear; by the rising aspirations of our people and not the doom and gloom of managed decline that we have become too familiar with.

This is our chance. This is our moment. Let's turn at this turning point. Let's reclaim the principles that have guided us for generations. Let's recapture our destiny for generations to come so this beautiful story of the American idea is repeated and repeated and passed on to the next generation, a nation more united, more confident, more prosperous, and, Mr. Speaker, more free. Pass this bill.

SOURCE: U.S. Congress. House. Conference Report on H.R. 1, Tax Cuts and Jobs Act. 115th Congress, 2nd Session. *Congressional Record*. vol. 163, no. 207, daily ed. (December 19, 2017): H10211–10212. https://www.gpo.gov/fdsys/pkg/CREC-2017-12-19/pdf/CREC-2017-12-19-pt1-PgH10201-2.pdf.

President Trump, Republicans Hold Press Conference on Tax Reform Passage

DOCUMENT

December 20, 2017

The President. Thank you, everybody, very much. And these are the people right behind me. They've worked so long, so hard. It's been an amazing experience, I have to tell you. Hasn't been done in 34 years, but actually, really hasn't been done, because we broke every record. It's the largest—I always say, the most massive—[*laughter*]—but it's the largest tax cut in the history of our country—and reform—but tax cut. Really something special.

And I know this just came out. Two minutes ago, they handed it to me. AT&T plans to increase U.S. capital spending $1 billion and provide $1,000 special bonus to more than

200,000 U.S. employees, and that's because of what we did. So that's pretty good. That's pretty good.

And I have a whole list of accomplishments that the group behind me have done, in terms of this administration and this Congress, but you've heard it before. Records all over the place, and that will continue and then some because of what we did. But $3.2 trillion— just think of it—in tax cuts for American families, including doubling the standard deduction and doubling the child tax credit.

The typical family of four earning $75,000 will see an income tax cut of more than $2,000. They're going to have $2,000, and that's, in my opinion, going to be less than the average. You're going to have a lot more than that.

One thing, very important, for the farmers—the great farmers, and the great small-business owners, that were forced to sell their businesses at bargain, basement numbers— we have provided, for the most part, estate tax is wiped out. So they can keep their farms in the family, and that to me is a very big factor—very big.

This is—this is going to mean companies are going to be coming back. I campaigned on the fact that we're not going to lose our companies anymore. They're going to stay in our country. And they're going to stay in our country. And you've been seeing what's been happening, even at this prospect. But they have tremendous enthusiasm right now in this country. And we have companies pouring back into our country. And that means jobs, and it means really, the formation of new young, beautiful, strong companies. So that's going to be very, very important.

The passthroughs, you know all about, and the small businesses are going to be big beneficiaries. We are going to be bring at least $4 trillion back into this country, money that was frozen overseas and in parts and worlds. And some of them don't even like us, and they had the money. Well, they're not going to have the money long. And so it's really—I guess it's very simple, when you think you haven't heard this expression, but we are making America great again. You haven't heard that, have you?

I want to have them get up and get the glamor and the glory, and I just want to have a few of them come up, and they'll speak for a little while—and short, the shorter the better. [*Laughter*] That way we can get all of you—we'll get everybody up, right?

But I want to thank Mitch McConnell. I want to thank—[*applause*]—what a job, what a job. And I want to thank Paul. They're going to speak; they're going to say a few words. But Paul Ryan and Mitch, it was a little team. We just got together, and we would work very hard. Didn't we? Huh? It seems like—it was a lot of fun. It's always a lot of fun when you win. [*Laughter*] If you work hard and lose, that's not acceptable.

But I'm just going to name a few names, and then some of them will come up. But people that I saw so much over the last month—and really over the last, almost year—because when you think of it, we haven't even been a year, and we did the largest tax cut in our history. We—I hate to say this—but we essentially repealed Obamacare, because we got rid of the individual mandate, which was terrible. And that was a primary source of funding of Obamacare....

We're going to see something that's going to be very special. We're bringing the entrepreneur back into this country. We're getting rid of all the knots and all the ties, and we're going to—you're going to see. You're going to see what happens. And ultimately, what does it mean? It means jobs, jobs, jobs, jobs.

So it's going to be, really, a special period of time. We're in a very special period of time, and it's going to be even more so. I want to thank everybody behind me. Maybe I could start with Mitch, and then we'll go to Paul, and then we're going to have a few of the folks come up and say a few words, and we'll have a little fun. Okay? Thank you. Mitch, how about you start it?

Senate Majority Leader A. Mitchell McConnell. Yes. Well, let me just say, Mr. President, you made the case for the tax bill. But this has been a year of extraordinary accomplishment for the Trump administration. We've cemented the Supreme Court right-of-center for a generation. Mr. President, thanks to your nominees, we put 12 circuit court judges in place, the most since the circuit court system was established in 1891. You hold the record.

You've ended the overregulation of the American economy. And that, coupled with what we did last night and what the House finished this morning, means America is going to start growing again. Thank you, Mr. President, for all you're doing.

Speaker Ryan. First of all, what this represents is a promise that each and every one of us made to the American people last year is a promise that is kept today. Something this big, something this generational, something this profound could not have been done without exquisite Presidential leadership. Mr. President, thank you for getting us over the finish line. Thank you for getting us where we are. Really. I appreciate it.

I just want to quickly just say a thanks because this has been such a team effort from everybody. I want to thank Gary Cohn and Steve Mnuchin from the President's economic team for what they did to get us here.

I want to thank my partner, Mitch McConnell, over in the Senate for getting us to where we are. And I want to thank these two chairmen, Orrin Hatch and Kevin Brady. Thank you so much for your leadership on this.

It is really simple. The message to the hard-working taxpayers of America is: Your tax relief is on its way. That is what's happening here. The message to the families in America who've been struggling, paycheck and paycheck, your tax rates are going down, and your paychecks are going up.

This is the kind of relief that Americans deserve. This is the kind of tax reform and tax cuts that get our economy growing to reach its potential. This gets us better wages, bigger paychecks, a simpler tax system. This gets the American economy competitive in the global economy. This is one of the most important things we could do for all of the people we represent.

This is generational. And we're so excited that we are going to launch, next year, this fantastic tax reform so that the American people can see how we can truly reach our economic growth and our economic potential. And if it weren't for all the leadership of the men and women up here, this would not have been made possible. But lastly, I just want to thank the American people. I want to thank the American people for putting their trust in us, for giving us this chance and this ability to make this moment possible. Thank you very much. Thank you, Mr. President.

The President. A man who's been working very hard. Thank you, Paul. Very, very hard for a long period of time, and last night was very much a culmination. But I don't know if we'll have bigger moments, but we hope to. We're going to try.

A very special guy and great friend of mine, Vice President Mike Pence.

Vice President Michael R. Pence. Well, thank you, Mr. President. Thank you for those kind words. But more importantly, thank you for your leadership. Thank you for your boundless faith in the American people, and thank you for keeping your promise to see this Congress deliver the largest tax cut in American history before Christmas of this year. Merry Christmas, America.

To members of our Cabinet, to Leader McConnell, to Speaker Ryan, to all these Members of Congress: Thank you. Thank you not only for being here today for this special moment, but thank you for your leadership and support throughout this year.

I truly do believe, Mr. President, that this will be remembered as a pivotal moment in the life of our Nation, a day when the Congress answered your call and made history.

But honestly, I would say to the American people: President Trump has been making history since the first day of this administration. We've been rebuilding our military, standing with our veterans; and just last week, President Trump signed one of the largest investments in our national defense since the days of Ronald Reagan. We've been defending our borders, upholding the rule of law. Illegal crossings on our southern border are down by more than 50 percent.

And President Trump has been restoring American credibility on the world stage, standing with our allies and standing up to our enemies. As the President reflected earlier today, our NATO allies are paying more toward their common defense. North Korea is more isolated than ever before. This President has put Iran on notice and put the war on Afghanistan on a path to victory. And thanks to the leadership of this Commander in Chief and the courage of our Armed Forces, ISIS is on the run, their capital has fallen, and their so-called caliphate has crumbled across Syria and Iraq.

But what brings us here today is that President Trump also knows that American strength starts with a growing American economy. And from the first day of this administration, this President championed free and fair trade; he rolled back Federal redtape at record levels; we've unleashed American energy; and today, Mr. President, you've fulfilled the promise you made to millions of Americans struggling in this economy to cut taxes across the board for working families and businesses, large and small.

In August of this year, the President laid out his vision for a tax cut that would be a middle class miracle, and that's exactly what the Congress passed today. This tax cut will put more money in the pockets of the American people; it will make our Tax Code more simple, more fair, more easy to understand. It will make businesses across America more competitive to create good-paying jobs and raise wages for working Americans.

I can tell you—I serve with him every day—President Donald Trump is a man of his word. He's a man of action. And with the strong support of these Members of Congress, President Donald Trump delivered a great victory for the American people. We made history today.

But as the President said when we gathered this morning—and a few of us, with a few less hours sleep than usual—we're just getting started. And I can assure you, this President and this entire administration will not rest and relent until the forgotten men and women of America are forgotten no more.

So thank you, Mr. President. Thank you for your leadership. Thank you for your love for this country and the people of this country. And I know in my heart, with the strong, continued support of the Members of Congress who are gathered on these steps, and with God's help, you will make America great again.

The President. Thank you, Mike, very much. A friend of mine—a very, very special man—Tim Scott. Tim, I'd like you to say a few words. He came in, and he would solve some problems that—we weren't looking too good a couple of times—[*laughter*]—and Tim was really, really a tremendous help. Thank you, Tim.

Senator Scott. Well, Mr. President, during one of those conversations that we had, we talked about ways to improve distressed communities throughout this country. Fifty-two million Americans living in distressed communities, and we talked about legislation that could move those communities forward. And you said, "Yes."

And as a part of this tax reform passage, the Investing and Opportunity Act has been included, which will bring trillions of dollars into poor communities because of your willingness to listen. . . .

Sen. Scott. . . . Let me just say to those Americans who are watching this process, this is not about Washington. It's not about the left. It's not about the right. It's about single-parent moms who are looking for a reason to be hopeful in 2018. This tax reform plan delivers for the average single mother a 70 percent tax cut.

For the average family who is working paycheck to paycheck, looking for ways to be hopeful about their future, to have an extra night for dinner out at a restaurant, this tax reform package cuts their taxes by nearly 60 percent.

And because of folks like Marco Rubio and Ivanka—when you think about the folks with kids in the household—this plan doubles the child tax credit and makes about 70 percent of it refundable. This is a plan that we can be proud of because it speaks to the hearts of everyday Americans.

The President. Diane, come on up. Diane Black. Thank you, Diane.

Representative Diane L. Black. Thank you, Mr. President. And I want to thank all of the folks that are standing behind me, because it has been a team effort. When we talk about doing tax reform and the Tax Reform and Jobs Cuts Act [Tax Cuts and Jobs Act]*, that is what the American people are going to benefit by.

And as Tim has just said, it is the average American—that's the reason why we did this tax reform. We looked at those right in the middle, those families that need the assistance and the help and the relief to be able to live their lives the way we have promised with the American Dream.

It is such an honor to stand here with the President of the United States, the Vice President of the United States, who have been an integral part in making sure that this happened. I want to thank Kevin Brady, who I know—hours and hours and hours—worked hard to make this happen in what was, really, a short period of time.

And some of the folks that are being left out right now, and I know we've thanked them before, but I want to thank them publicly, and that is all of the staff that has worked so hard, in both the House and the Senate to make this happen.

Now, we can say "Merry Christmas" to the American people, because we are giving them a huge gift for Christmas, a break in these taxes and an opportunity for our jobs to grow and to give them a bigger paycheck. And so I want to say thank you to Mr. President. Thank you, President Trump, for allowing us to have you as our President and to make America great again.

The President. Thank you, Diane, very much. And we can say "Merry Christmas" again. People are saying "Merry Christmas" again, and we like the sound.

I want to ask Lisa Murkowski and Dan Sullivan to come up from Alaska. They've been really working. And if Don Young is here—and I think he's around here. The three of them. Come here. Come here. . . .

Senator Lisa A. Murkowski. Mr. President, I don't know if you recognize—this is a very historic day, of course—but it's also the beginning of winter solstice. Now it doesn't feel like it right now, but the winter solstice is the shortest day—the darkest day.

And for in—for us, in Alaska, we've had some pretty dark days recently. But with passage of this tax bill, with passage finally, almost 40 years later, to allow us to open up the 1002 area, this is a bright day for Alaska. This is bright day for America.

So we thank you for that. We thank you for that. Think about it, 31 years——

Rep. Young. Thirty-seven, thirty-seven.

Sen. Murkowksi.—we've been working on tax reform; 38 years, now, to open up ANWR. This has been a multigenerational fight, and I look to some of our friends from Alaska who have come 5,000 miles to be here for the vote last night and today. [*Laughter*] To those who live there, to those who raise their families there, and to those who are looking to live for generations, know that our promise to you today is a bright future, one where we care for our environment, where we care for our people, and we also care for our country in providing a resource that is needed not only by the United States, by Alaskans, but by our friends and allies. This, Mr. President, is what energy dominance is all about. So let's go.

The President. Thank you, Lisa.

Senator Daniel S. Sullivan. Well, Mr. President, I want to thank you and your administration. I want to thank Secretary Zinke, who's doing a great job. But Senator Murkowski said it very well, this administration has come in and recognized this incredible, incredible resource that we have in our Nation. Developing our energy is good for jobs, it's good for energy security, it's good for manufacturing, it's good for the environment, because we have the highest standards in the world, and it's very, very good for our foreign policy and national security.

Mr. President, sir, you released your national security strategy just a couple days ago. And in there, you talk about the economy—which is what this tax bill is all about—but you also talk about energy dominance. And I want to thank you. I want to thank you on behalf of all Alaskans and the American people, because it's the right policy. And we're finally, finally doing it. . . .

The President. . . . I want to ask Orrin Hatch, a special friend of mine, I can tell you that. Somebody that spoke really well of me when it wasn't exactly the easiest thing to do. He was just always in there, always fighting for all of us, and did a fantastic job as chairman. Orrin, say a few words, please.

Senator Orrin G. Hatch. Well, Mr. President, I have to say that you're living up to everything I thought you would. You're one heck of a leader, and we're all benefiting from it. This bill could not have passed without you. It couldn't have passed without the Alaskan delegation. It couldn't have passed without the leadership in the House and the Senate— Paul Ryan and Mitch McConnell—and the other leaders as well.

All I can say is, is that we're making headway. This is just the beginning. If you stop and think about it, this President hasn't even been in office for a year, and look at all the things that he's been able to get done, by sheer will, in many ways. And I just hope that we all get behind him every way we can, and we'll get this country turned around in ways that will benefit the whole world, but above all, benefit our people and bring us all to a realization of how really great America really is and how the rest of the world depends on us.

I love this country. I came from very humble roots. And I have to say that this is one of the great privileges of my life to stand here on the White House lawn with the President of the United States, who I love and appreciate so much, and with these wonderful colleagues and Cabinet members who stand behind us.

And to see all of you and realize that you care too, all I can say is that God loves this country. We all know it. We wouldn't be where we are without Him. And we love all of you. And we're going to keep fighting, and we're going to make this the greatest Presidency that we've seen, not only in generations, but maybe ever.

God bless all of you. . . .

Representative Kevin P. Brady. Thank you. [*Applause*] Thank you. Okay, guys. People are getting a little applause here so—thank you, Mr. President. This is a historic day. It's an exciting day. And I knew I was going to be here with you to mark this momentous occasion, so I wore my Houston Astros tie because they're still the champion of the World Series. [*Laughter*] I figured, today, you would give me some slack on that.

Look, this is a historic day, in so many ways, and it didn't happen just by itself. People often ask, when did you know? When did you know tax reform could be achieved in America for the first time in 31 years? And my answer is always the same, November 8, when, President Trump, you were elected President of the United States. That's when I knew it was real.

And when you put together the great ideas on tax reform, from inside and outside Congress—and I see many of you here today with us—remarkable leadership and courage from the men and women behind me in the Senate and especially my colleagues in the House. When you put together remarkable leadership in the House and the Senate, the work that was done in the White House—Gary and Steve, Vice President Pence—and Mr. President, your willingness to make this your commitment to go across the country to sell the need for tax reform and then stay at the table with us and on the phone with us, to get this done. But for your leadership, we would not be here today. So thank you so much.

And let me finish by speaking directly to the American people. There are three dates you need to put on your calendar. The first is New Year's Day. Because on New Year's, our country will have a new Tax Code for a new era of American prosperity—New Year's Day. In February, look to your paychecks. Hard-working Americans will see the result of the hard work of this President and this Congress to make this tax reform possible. It will show in your paycheck. And then, April 15, that hated day. [*Laughter*] This April 15 will be the last time you ever file your taxes under this horrible, broken Tax Code, because you'll have a new one for the future of your family and your small business. This—[*applause*].

So this is a great day for our country. A great day for our economy and a great day for America. . . .

Leader McCarthy. To the President and Vice President: During that campaign, you listened to voices no one else was listening to. You listened to those that were trying to get a pay raise or that parent that was fighting for their children or to that person who always dreamed of being an entrepreneur or creating a small business, like you did, Mr. President. And you know what? For all those people, you heard them.

We would not be standing here today if it wasn't for you. It doesn't matter if you were overseas fighting for America, so many people back here got your phone call, fighting for tax reform. [*Laughter*] This is a big day for America. This is America's comeback. Come February, check your check—[*laughter*]—because that will be the pay raise of the vote for Donald Trump. That will be the beginning of the next century—America's century.

Thank you, and God bless.

The President. So I just want to conclude by saying this will indeed be a very big day when people look back at our country. It's a whole different attitude, a whole different way. And I really want to end by looking back and thanking all of those people standing behind me that worked for years. This was the culmination of a few months' work, but they've been working on getting this done—whether it's Mitch or Paul or Kevin or Kevin or Orrin—they have been working on this for years—years and years. And I just want to turn around, and I want to thank them all. They are very, very special people.

Thank you very much, everybody. Thank you.

*White House correction.

SOURCE: Executive Office of the President. "Remarks on Congressional Passage of Tax Reform Legislation." December 20, 2017. *Compilation of Presidential Documents* 2017, no. 00920 (December 20, 2017). https://www.gpo.gov/fdsys/pkg/DCPD-201700920/pdf/DCPD-201700920.pdf.

OTHER HISTORIC DOCUMENTS OF INTEREST

FROM THIS VOLUME

FROM PREVIOUS *HISTORIC DOCUMENTS*

Index